Forward

Our purpose for publishing the documents issued by the National Institute of Standards and Technology (NIST) is twofold. First of all, each NIST title in and of itself is very informative, however I am of the opinion that they should be looked at from the standpoint that each title is an integral part of a holistic cybersecurity strategy. Rather than look at each title just by itself, we need to look at them in groups based on how they are interrelated and designed to work together to improve cybersecurity.

For example, this particular group on PRIVACY SECURITY includes the following titles:

NIST SP 800-53 R 4   Security and Privacy Controls for Federal Information Systems and Organizations

NIST SP 800-53A R 4   Assessing Security and Privacy Controls

NIST SP 800-122   Guide to Protecting the Confidentiality of Personally Identifiable Information (PII)

NIST SP 800-188   De-Identifying Government Datasets - (2nd DRAFT)

NISTIR 8053   De-Identification of Personal Information

NISTIR 8062   Introduction to Privacy Engineering and Risk Management in Federal Systems

In order to assemble the entire picture of privacy security – from what it is, how it works, what the vulnerabilities are, and how to mitigate them, one must assemble all of these documents. Only by going through all of them can a person understand the complete picture. Leave one of them out and you would be missing a valuable piece of the privacy security puzzle.

Why buy a book you can download for free?

That brings me to the second reason to publish the NIST standards and that is the logistics of it all. These 7 publications consist of 771 pages. That's enough paper to fill two large three-ring binders. Nobody has a secretary anymore, so an engineer that is paid $75 an hour has to do this. The amount of time it would take an engineer to print all 7 publications (using a network printer shared with 100 other people – and it's out of paper, and the toner is low), punch holes in 771 pages and assemble the binders would easily take half a day.

Our ability to deliver any NIST document quickly and efficiently is unmatched because we are printing books on demand and we are backed up by Amazon, so the titles are easy to find and simple to order. Just search Amazon.com by NIST number and you can have a copy shipped to you in a matter of days. We print all books a full 8 ½ inches by 11 inches, with large text. If there are color images in the publication, the book is probably in color, unless the color is merely decorative, in which case we print in black and white to keep the cost to you as low as possible.

Luis Ayala,
My email is cybah@webplus.net Our website is: cybah.webplus.net
4th Watch Books is a Service Disabled Veteran Owned Small Business (SDVOSB).

CyberSecurity Standards Library™

Get a Complete Library of Over 300 Cybersecurity Standards on 1 Convenient DVD!

The **4th Watch CyberSecurity Standards Library** is a DVD disc that puts over 300 current and archived cybersecurity standards from NIST, DOD, DHS, CNSS and NERC at your fingertips! Many of these cybersecurity standards are hard to find and we included the current version and a previous version for many of them. The DVD includes four books written by Luis Ayala: **The Cyber Dictionary, Cybersecurity Standards, Cyber-Security Glossary of Building Hacks and Cyber-Attacks**, and **Cyber-Physical Attack Defenses: Preventing Damage to Buildings and Utilities**.

- ✓ DVD includes many Hard-to-find Cybersecurity Standards - some still in Draft.
- ✓ Docs are organized by source and listed numerically so each standard is easy to locate.
- ✓ The listing of standards on the DVD includes an abstract of the subject, and date issued.
- ✓ PDF format for use on PC, Mac, eReaders, or tablets.
- ✓ No need for WiFi / Internet.
- ✓ Save countless hours of searching and downloading.
- ✓ Carry in a briefcase - terrific for travel.

4th Watch Publishing is releasing the CyberSecurity Standards Library DVD to make it easier for you to access the tools you need to ensure the security of your computer networks and SCADA systems. We also publish many of these standards on demand so you don't need to waste valuable time searching for the latest version of a standard, printing hundreds of pages and punching holes so they can go in a three-ring binder. **Order on Amazon.com**

The DVD works on PC and Mac with the standards in PDF format. To view the CyberSecurity Standards Library on the DVD, a computer with a DVD drive is required. The most current version of your internet browser, at least 2GB of RAM, and current version of Adobe Reader is recommended. (Compatible browsers include Internet Explorer 8+, Mozilla Firefox 4+, Apple Safari 5+, Google Chrome 15+)

Assessing Security and Privacy Controls in Federal Information Systems and Organizations

Building Effective Assessment Plans

JOINT TASK FORCE
TRANSFORMATION INITIATIVE

This publication is available free of charge from:
http://dx.doi.org/10.6028/NIST.SP.800-53Ar4

National Institute of
Standards and Technology
U.S. Department of Commerce

NIST Special Publication 800-53A
Revision 4

Assessing Security and Privacy Controls in Federal Information Systems and Organizations

Building Effective Assessment Plans

JOINT TASK FORCE
TRANSFORMATION INITIATIVE

This publication is available free of charge from:
http://dx.doi.org/10.6028/NIST.SP.800-53Ar4

December 2014
INCLUDES UPDATES AS OF 12-18-2014

U.S. Department of Commerce
Penny Pritzker, Secretary

National Institute of Standards and Technology
Willie May, Acting Under Secretary of Commerce for Standards and Technology and Acting Director

Authority

This publication has been developed by NIST to further its statutory responsibilities under the Federal Information Security Management Act (FISMA), Public Law (P.L.) 107-347. NIST is responsible for developing information security standards and guidelines, including minimum requirements for federal information systems, but such standards and guidelines shall not apply to national security systems without the express approval of appropriate federal officials exercising policy authority over such systems. This guideline is consistent with the requirements of the Office of Management and Budget (OMB) Circular A-130, Section 8b(3), *Securing Agency Information Systems*, as analyzed in Circular A-130, Appendix IV: *Analysis of Key Sections*. Supplemental information is provided in Circular A-130, Appendix III, *Security of Federal Automated Information Resources*.

Nothing in this publication should be taken to contradict the standards and guidelines made mandatory and binding on federal agencies by the Secretary of Commerce under statutory authority. Nor should these guidelines be interpreted as altering or superseding the existing authorities of the Secretary of Commerce, Director of the OMB, or any other federal official. This publication may be used by nongovernmental organizations on a voluntary basis and is not subject to copyright in the United States. Attribution would, however, be appreciated by NIST.

National Institute of Standards and Technology Special Publication 800-53A, Revision 4
487 pages (December 2014)
CODEN: NSPUE2

This publication is available free of charge from: http://dx.doi.org/10.6028/NIST.SP.800-53Ar4

Certain commercial entities, equipment, or materials may be identified in this document in order to describe an experimental procedure or concept adequately. Such identification is not intended to imply recommendation or endorsement by NIST, nor is it intended to imply that the entities, materials, or equipment are necessarily the best available for the purpose.

There may be references in this publication to other publications currently under development by NIST in accordance with its assigned statutory responsibilities. The information in this publication, including concepts, practices, and methodologies, may be used by federal agencies even before the completion of such companion publications. Thus, until each publication is completed, current requirements, guidelines, and procedures, where they exist, remain operative. For planning and transition purposes, federal agencies may wish to closely follow the development of these new publications by NIST.

Organizations are encouraged to review draft publications during the designated public comment periods and provide feedback to NIST. Computer Security Division publications are available at http://csrc.nist.gov/publications.

Comments on this publication may be submitted to:

National Institute of Standards and Technology
Attn: Computer Security Division, Information Technology Laboratory
100 Bureau Drive (Mail Stop 8930) Gaithersburg, MD 20899-8930
Electronic Mail: sec-cert@nist.gov

Special Publication 800-53A
Revision 4

Assessing Security and Privacy Controls in Federal Information Systems
and Organizations — *Building Effective Assessment Plans*

Reports on Computer Systems Technology

The Information Technology Laboratory (ITL) at the National Institute of Standards and Technology (NIST) promotes the U.S. economy and public welfare by providing technical leadership for the nation's measurement and standards infrastructure. ITL develops tests, test methods, reference data, proof of concept implementations, and technical analyses to advance the development and productive use of information technology. ITL's responsibilities include the development of management, administrative, technical, and physical standards and guidelines for the cost-effective security and privacy of other than national security-related information in federal information systems. The Special Publication 800-series reports on ITL's research, guidelines, and outreach efforts in information system security, and its collaborative activities with industry, government, and academic organizations.

Abstract

This publication provides a set of procedures for conducting assessments of security controls and privacy controls employed within federal information systems and organizations. The assessment procedures, executed at various phases of the system development life cycle, are consistent with the security and privacy controls in NIST Special Publication 800-53, Revision 4. The procedures are customizable and can be easily tailored to provide organizations with the needed flexibility to conduct security control assessments and privacy control assessments that support organizational risk management processes and that are aligned with the stated risk tolerance of the organization. Information on building effective security assessment plans and privacy assessment plans is also provided along with guidance on analyzing assessment results.

Keywords

Assessment; assurance; E-Government Act; FISMA; Privacy Act; privacy controls; privacy requirements; Risk Management Framework; security controls; security requirements.

Special Publication 800-53A
Revision 4

Assessing Security and Privacy Controls in Federal Information Systems
and Organizations — *Building Effective Assessment Plans*

Acknowledgements

This publication was developed by the *Joint Task Force Transformation Initiative* Working Group with representatives from the Civilian, Defense, and Intelligence Communities to produce a *unified information security framework* for the federal government. We wish to acknowledge and thank the senior leaders from the Departments of Commerce and Defense, the Office of the Director of National Intelligence, the Committee on National Security Systems, and the members of the interagency technical working group whose dedicated efforts contributed significantly to the publication. The senior leaders, interagency working group members, and their organizational affiliations include:

U.S. Department of Defense

Terry Halvorsen
DOD Chief Information Officer (Acting)

David De Vries
Principal Deputy DOD Chief Information Officer (Acting)

Richard Hale
Deputy Chief Information Officer for Cybersecurity

Dominic Cussatt
Director, Cybersecurity Strategy and Policy

Office of the Director of National Intelligence

Adolpho Tarasiuk Jr.
Intelligence Community Chief Information Officer

Alan Royal
IC Deputy Chief Information Officer

Susan Dorr
Director, Information Assurance and IC Chief Information Security Officer

Robert Drake
Acting Chief, Risk Management and Compliance Services

National Institute of Standards and Technology

Charles H. Romine
Director, Information Technology Laboratory

Donna Dodson
Cyber Security Advisor, Information Technology Laboratory

Matthew Scholl
Chief, Computer Security Division

Ron Ross
FISMA Implementation Project and Joint Task Force Leader

Committee on National Security Systems

Terry Halvorsen
Chair, CNSS

Sherrill Nicely
CNSS Co-Chair

Dominic Cussatt, Jeffrey Wilk, Daniel Dister
CNSS Subcommittee Tri-Chairs

Joint Task Force Transformation Initiative Interagency Working Group

Ron Ross *NIST*	Karen Quigg *The MITRE Corporation*	Kelley Dempsey *NIST*	Patricia Toth *NIST*
Esten Porter *The MITRE Corporation*	Christian Enloe *NIST*	Bennett Hodge *Booz Allen Hamilton*	Kevin Stine *NIST*

We wish to express our sincere appreciation to Elizabeth Lennon and Peggy Himes for their superb technical editing and administrative support as well to Harold Booth for developing the XML schema and for his help in correcting many difficult-to-find formatting errors. The authors also wish to recognize the following individuals for their significant contributions in helping to develop the initial content of this publication and refine its content during subsequent revisions: Claire Barrett; Lindy Burkhart; Jonathan Cantor; Mitali Chatterjee; Jonathan Chiu; Sharon Ehlers; Jennifer Fabius; Peter Gouldmann; James Govekar; Terrance Hazelwood; Austin Hershey; Laurie Hestor; Arnold Johnson; Mary Kitson; Martha Landesberg; Naomi Lefkovitz; Jason Mackanick; Timothy Potter; Jennifer Puma; Roanne Shaddox; Terry Sherald; Gary Stoneburner; Julie Trei; Gail Tryon; Ricki Vanetesse; Cynthia Whitmer; and Peter Williams. Finally, the authors gratefully acknowledge and appreciate the significant contributions from individuals and organizations in the public and private sectors, whose thoughtful and constructive comments improved the overall quality and usefulness of this publication.

Special Publication 800-53A
Revision 4

Assessing Security and Privacy Controls in Federal Information Systems
and Organizations — *Building Effective Assessment Plans*

ASSESSMENT PROCEDURES FOR PRIVACY CONTROLS

Appendix J, *Privacy Assessment Procedures*, is a new addition to NIST Special Publication 800-53A. The appendix, when completed, will provide a complete set of assessment procedures for the privacy controls in NIST Special Publication 800-53, Appendix J. The new privacy control assessment procedures are under development and will be added to the appendix after a thorough public review and vetting process. The terminology throughout this publication has been updated to include references to privacy in all aspects of the assessment process to include mirroring the artifacts that are essential inputs to the current security authorization process. Each organization employing these guidelines has the flexibility to address the privacy assessment process and the integration of privacy-related artifacts into the organization's risk management processes in the manner that best supports the organizational missions and business objectives consist with Office of Management and Budget policies.

Standardized assessment procedures for privacy controls provide a more disciplined and structured approach for determining compliance to federal privacy requirements and also promote more cost-effective methods to determine such compliance. There will be a strong similarity in the structure of the assessment procedures for privacy controls in Appendix J and the assessment procedures for security controls in Appendix F. This similarity will promote closer cooperation between privacy and security officials within the federal government to help achieve the objectives of senior leaders/executives in enforcing the requirements in federal privacy legislation, directives, policies, regulations, standards, and guidance.

Finally, it should be noted that as the assessment procedures for privacy controls are added to Appendix J, certain terminology traditionally associated with security controls and security control assessments contained in earlier versions of this publication is being modified where appropriate, to include references to privacy. However, there are some security-related terms (e.g., security categorization, security control baseline, tailored security control baseline) that are unique to security controls and do not have direct analogs in the privacy arena. In such cases, the equivalent privacy-related terminology has not been added to the publication. Privacy officials, at their discretion, may choose to adopt any or all of the security-related terms in this publication in support of privacy control assessments.

Special Publication 800-53A
Revision 4

Assessing Security and Privacy Controls in Federal Information Systems
and Organizations — *Building Effective Assessment Plans*

ASSESSMENT PROCEDURE FORMATTING

A new format for assessment procedures is introduced in this revision to Special Publication 800-53A. The format reflects the decomposition of assessment objectives into more *granular* determination statements wherever possible—thus providing the capability to identify and assess specific parts of security and privacy controls. The changes have been initiated to: (i) help improve the readability of assessment procedures; (ii) provide a better format and structure for automated tools when assessment information is imported into such tools; (iii) provide greater flexibility in conducting assessments by giving organizations the capability to target certain aspects of security controls and privacy controls (highlighting the particular weaknesses and/or deficiencies in controls); (iv) improve the efficiency of security and privacy assessments; and (v) support continuous monitoring and ongoing authorization programs by providing a greater number of component parts of security and privacy controls that can be assessed at organization-defined frequencies and degrees of rigor. Having the ability to apply assessment and monitoring resources in a targeted and precise manner and simultaneously maximize the use of automation technologies, can result in more timely and cost-effective assessment processes for organizations.

Note: Special Publication 800-53 will be updated accordingly to ensure that the numbering scheme for all security and privacy controls is consistent with the new format introduced in this publication.

Special Publication 800-53A
Revision 4

Assessing Security and Privacy Controls in Federal Information Systems
and Organizations — *Building Effective Assessment Plans*

ALIGNING REVISION NUMBERS

WHAT HAPPENED TO SPECIAL PUBLICATION 800-53A REVISIONS 2 AND 3?

Revision numbers between NIST Special Publications 800-53 and 800-53A were misaligned from the start because the initial publication of SP 800-53A did not occur until after the publication of SP 800-53, Revision 2. When SP 800-53, Revision 3 was published, SP 800-53A was updated to Revision 1 for consistency with the updates to SP 800-53. This revision number mismatch created ongoing uncertainty and confusion regarding which revision of SP 800-53 was consistent with which revision of SP 800-53A. To reduce this uncertainty going forward, revision numbers 2 and 3 have been skipped for SP 800-53A, and this version of SP 800-53A has been given revision number 4 since this version is consistent with the updates to SP 800-53, Revision 4. Future revisions of SPs 800-53 and 800-53A will maintain the revision number consistency.

Special Publication 800-53A
Revision 4

Assessing Security and Privacy Controls in Federal Information Systems
and Organizations — *Building Effective Assessment Plans*

DEVELOPING COMMON INFORMATION SECURITY FOUNDATIONS

COLLABORATION AMONG PUBLIC AND PRIVATE SECTOR ENTITIES

In developing standards and guidelines required by FISMA, NIST consults with other federal agencies and offices as well as the private sector entities to improve information security, avoid unnecessary and costly duplication of effort, and ensure that NIST publications are complementary with the standards and guidelines employed for the protection of national security systems. In addition to its comprehensive public review and vetting process, NIST is collaborating with the Office of the Director of National Intelligence (ODNI), the Department of Defense (DoD), and the Committee on National Security Systems (CNSS) to establish a unified framework and common foundation for information security across the federal government. A common foundation and framework for information security will provide the Intelligence, Defense, and Civilian sectors of the federal government and their contractors, more uniform and consistent ways to manage the risk to organizational operations and assets, individuals, other organizations, and the Nation that results from the operation and use of information systems. A common foundation and framework will also provide a strong basis for reciprocal acceptance of security authorization decisions and facilitate information sharing. NIST is also working with public and private sector entities to establish specific mappings and relationships between the security standards and guidelines developed by NIST and the International Organization for Standardization (ISO) and the International Electrotechnical Commission (IEC).

Special Publication 800-53A
Revision 4

Assessing Security and Privacy Controls in Federal Information Systems
and Organizations — *Building Effective Assessment Plans*

Table of Contents

Special Publication 800-53A
Revision 4

Assessing Security and Privacy Controls in Federal Information Systems
and Organizations — *Building Effective Assessment Plans*

Prologue

"...Through the process of risk management, leaders must consider risk to U.S. interests from adversaries using cyberspace to their advantage and from our own efforts to employ the global nature of cyberspace to achieve objectives in military, intelligence, and business operations... "

"...For operational plans development, the combination of threats, vulnerabilities, and impacts must be evaluated in order to identify important trends and decide where effort should be applied to eliminate or reduce threat capabilities; eliminate or reduce vulnerabilities; and assess, coordinate, and deconflict all cyberspace operations..."

"...Leaders at all levels are accountable for ensuring readiness and security to the same degree as in any other domain..."

-- THE NATIONAL STRATEGY FOR CYBERSPACE OPERATIONS
    OFFICE OF THE CHAIRMAN, JOINT CHIEFS OF STAFF, U.S. DEPARTMENT OF DEFENSE

Special Publication 800-53A
Revision 4

Assessing Security and Privacy Controls in Federal Information Systems
and Organizations — *Building Effective Assessment Plans*

Foreword

Security control assessments and privacy control assessments are not about checklists, simple pass-fail results, or generating paperwork to pass inspections or audits—rather, such assessments are the principal vehicle used to verify that implemented security controls and privacy controls are meeting their stated goals and objectives. Special Publication 800-53A, *Assessing Security and Privacy Controls in Federal Information Systems and Organizations*, is written to facilitate security control assessments and privacy control assessments conducted within an effective risk management framework. The control assessment results provide organizational officials with:

- Evidence about the effectiveness of implemented controls;

- An indication of the quality of the risk management processes employed within the organization; and

- Information about the strengths and weaknesses of information systems which are supporting organizational missions and business functions in a global environment of sophisticated and changing threats.

The findings produced by assessors are used to determine the overall effectiveness of security and privacy controls associated with information systems (including system-specific, common, and hybrid controls) and their environments of operation and to provide credible and meaningful inputs to the organization's risk management process. A well-executed assessment helps to: (i) determine the validity of the controls contained in the organization's security plans and privacy plans and subsequently employed in organizational information systems and environments of operation; and (ii) facilitate a cost-effective approach to correcting weaknesses or deficiencies in systems in an orderly and disciplined manner consistent with organizational mission/business needs.

Special Publication 800-53A is a companion guideline to Special Publication 800-53, *Security and Privacy Controls for Federal Information Systems and Organizations*. Each publication provides guidance for implementing specific steps in the Risk Management Framework (RMF).[1] Special Publication 800-53 covers Step 2 in the RMF, security and privacy control selection (i.e., determining what controls are needed to manage risks to organizational operations and assets, individuals, other organizations, and the Nation). Special Publication 800-53A covers RMF Step 4, Assess, and RMF Step 6, Monitor, and provides guidance on the security assessment and privacy assessment processes. This guidance includes how to build effective assessment plans and how to analyze and manage assessment results.

Special Publication 800-53A allows organizations to tailor the basic assessment procedures provided. The concepts of tailoring used in this document are similar to the concepts described in Special Publication 800-53. Tailoring involves customizing the assessment procedures to more closely match the characteristics of the information system and its environment of operation. The tailoring process gives organizations the flexibility needed to avoid assessment approaches that are unnecessarily complex or costly while simultaneously meeting the assessment requirements established by applying the fundamental concepts in the RMF. Tailoring can also include adding assessment procedures or assessment details to adequately meet the risk management needs of the organization (e.g., adding system/platform-specific information for selected controls). Tailoring decisions are left to the discretion of the organization in order to maximize the flexibility in

---

[1] Special Publication 800-37 provides guidance on applying the RMF to federal information systems.

Special Publication 800-53A
Revision 4

Assessing Security and Privacy Controls in Federal Information Systems
and Organizations — *Building Effective Assessment Plans*

developing assessment plans—applying the results of risk assessments to determine the extent, rigor, and level of intensity of the assessments. While flexibility continues to be an important factor in developing security assessment plans and privacy assessment plans, consistency of assessments is also an important consideration. A major design objective for Special Publication 800-53A is to provide an assessment framework and initial starting point for assessment procedures that are essential for achieving such consistency.

NIST initiated the Security Content Automation Protocol (SCAP)[2] project that supports the approach for achieving consistent, cost-effective security control assessments. The primary purpose of SCAP is to standardize the format and nomenclature used for communicating information about configurations and security flaws. This standardization enables automated system configuration assessment, vulnerability assessment, patch checking, as well as report aggregation and interoperability between SCAP-enabled security products. As a result, SCAP enables organizations to identify and reduce vulnerabilities associated with products that are not patched or insecurely configured. SCAP also includes the Open Checklist Interactive Language (OCIL)[3] specification that provides the capability to express the determination statements in the assessment procedures in Appendix F in a framework that will establish interoperability with the SCAP-enabled tools. Privacy control assessments are discussed separately in Appendix J to this publication.

---

[2] Special Publication 800-126 provides guidance on the technical specification of SCAP. Additional details on the SCAP initiative, as well as freely available SCAP reference data, can be found at http://nvd.nist.gov.

[3] OCIL is a framework for expressing security checks that cannot be evaluated without some human interaction or feedback. It is used to determine the state of a system by presenting one or more questionnaires to its intended users. The language includes constructs for questions, instructions for guiding users towards an answer, responses to questions, artifacts, and evaluation results.

Special Publication 800-53A
Revision 4

Assessing Security and Privacy Controls in Federal Information Systems
and Organizations — *Building Effective Assessment Plans*

Errata

The following changes have been incorporated into Special Publication 800-53A, Revision 4. Errata updates include corrections, clarifications, or other minor changes in the publication that are either *editorial* or *substantive* in nature.

DATE	TYPE	CHANGE	PAGE
12-18-2014	Editorial	Changed "AT-4(b)[2][a]" to "AT-4(a)[2][a]."	F-60
12-18-2014	Editorial	Changed "AT-4(b)[2][b]" to "AT-4(a)[2][b]."	F-60
12-18-2014	Editorial	Changed "PL-8(c)[2]" to "PL-8(c)[3]."	F-241
12-18-2014	Editorial	Changed "SA-1(a)(2)[1]" to "SA-1(b)(2)[1]."	F-269
12-18-2014	Editorial	Changed "SI-1(b)(2)[1]" to "SI-1(b)(2)[2]."	F-369

Special Publication 800-53A
Revision 4

Assessing Security and Privacy Controls in Federal Information Systems
and Organizations — *Building Effective Assessment Plans*

CHAPTER ONE

INTRODUCTION

THE NEED TO ASSESS SECURITY AND PRIVACY CONTROL EFFECTIVENESS

Today's information systems[4] are complex assemblages of technology (i.e., hardware, software, and firmware), processes, and people, working together to provide organizations with the capability to process, store, and transmit information in a timely manner to support various missions and business functions. The degree to which organizations have come to depend upon these information systems to conduct routine, important, and critical missions and business functions means that the protection of the underlying systems and environments of operation is paramount to the success of the organization. The selection of appropriate security and privacy controls for an information system is an important task that can have significant implications on the operations and assets of an organization as well as the welfare of individuals.[5] Security and privacy controls are the safeguards or countermeasures prescribed for an information system or an organization designed to protect the confidentiality, integrity, and availability of its information.

Once employed within an information system, security and privacy controls are assessed to provide the information necessary to determine their overall effectiveness, that is, the extent to which the controls are implemented correctly, operating as intended, and producing the desired outcome with respect to meeting the security and privacy requirements for the system and the organization. Understanding the overall effectiveness of implemented security and privacy controls is essential in determining the risk to the organization's operations and assets, to individuals, to other organizations, and to the Nation resulting from the use of the system.

1.1 PURPOSE AND APPLICABILITY

The purpose of this publication is to provide: (i) guidelines for building effective security assessment plans and privacy assessment plans; and (ii) a comprehensive set of procedures for assessing the effectiveness of security controls and privacy controls employed in information systems and organizations supporting the executive agencies of the federal government. The guidelines apply to the security and privacy controls defined in Special Publication 800-53 (as amended), *Security and Privacy Controls for Federal Information Systems and Organizations*. The guidelines have been developed to help achieve more secure information systems within the federal government by:

- Enabling more consistent, comparable, and repeatable assessments of security controls and privacy controls with reproducible results;

- Promoting a better understanding of the risks to organizational operations, organizational assets, individuals, other organizations, and the Nation resulting from the operation and use of federal information systems;

---

[4] An information system is a discrete set of information resources organized expressly for the collection, processing, maintenance, use, sharing, dissemination, or disposition of information.

[5] When selecting security controls and privacy controls for an information system, the organization also considers potential impacts to other organizations and, in accordance with the USA PATRIOT Act of 2001 and Homeland Security Presidential Directives, potential national-level impacts.

Special Publication 800-53A
Revision 4

Assessing Security and Privacy Controls in Federal Information Systems
and Organizations — *Building Effective Assessment Plans*

- Facilitating more cost-effective assessments of security controls and privacy controls contributing to the determination of overall control effectiveness; and

- Creating more complete, reliable, and trustworthy information for organizational officials to support risk management decisions, reciprocity of assessment results, information sharing, and compliance to federal laws, Executive Orders, directives, regulations, and policies.

This publication satisfies the requirements of the Federal Information Security Management Act (FISMA) and meets or exceeds the information security and privacy requirements established for executive agencies[6] by the Office of Management and Budget (OMB) in Circular A-130, Appendix I, *Federal Agency Responsibilities for Maintaining Records About Individuals*, and Appendix III, *Security of Federal Automated Information Resources.* The security guidelines in this publication are applicable to federal information systems other than those systems designated as national security systems as defined in 44 U.S.C., Section 3542. The guidelines have been broadly developed from a technical perspective to complement similar guidelines for national security systems and may be used for such systems with the approval of appropriate federal officials exercising policy authority over such systems. The guidelines in Appendix J may have broader applicability, depending upon organizational authorities and missions. State, local, and tribal governments, as well as private sector organizations are encouraged to consider using these guidelines, as appropriate.[7]

Organizations use this publication in conjunction with approved security plans and privacy plans in developing viable assessment plans for producing and compiling the information necessary to determine the effectiveness of the security and privacy controls employed in the information system and organization. This publication has been developed with the intention of enabling organizations to tailor the basic assessment procedures provided. The assessment procedures are used as a starting point for and as input to the assessment plan. In developing effective security assessment plans and privacy assessment plans, organizations take into consideration existing information about the controls to be assessed (e.g., results from organizational assessments of risk, platform-specific dependencies in the hardware, software, or firmware, and any assessment procedures needed as a result of organization-specific controls not included in Special Publication 800-53).[8]

The selection of appropriate assessment procedures and the rigor, intensity, and scope of the assessment depend on three factors:

---

[6] An *executive agency* is: (i) an executive department specified in 5 U.S.C., Section 101; (ii) a military department specified in 5 U.S.C., Section 102; (iii) an independent establishment as defined in 5 U.S.C., Section 104(1); and (iv) a wholly owned government corporation fully subject to the provisions of 31 U.S.C., Chapter 91. In this publication, the term executive agency is synonymous with the term *federal agency*.

[7] In accordance with the provisions of FISMA and OMB policy, whenever the interconnection of federal information systems to information systems operated by state/local/tribal governments, contractors, or grantees involves the processing, storage, or transmission of federal information, the information security standards and guidelines described in this publication apply. Specific information security requirements and the terms and conditions of the system interconnections, are expressed in the Memoranda of Understanding and Interconnection Security Agreements established by participating organizations.

[8] For example, detailed test scripts may need to be developed for the specific operating system, network component, middleware, or application employed within the information system to adequately assess certain characteristics of a particular security or privacy control. Such test scripts are at a lower level of detail than provided by the assessment procedures contained in Appendices F and J and are therefore beyond the scope of this publication. Additional details for assessments are provided in the supporting assessment cases described in Appendix H.

Special Publication 800-53A
Revision 4

Assessing Security and Privacy Controls in Federal Information Systems
and Organizations — *Building Effective Assessment Plans*

- The security categorization of the information system;[9]

- The assurance requirements that the organization intends to meet in determining the overall effectiveness of the security and privacy controls; and

- The security and privacy controls from Special Publication 800-53 as identified in the approved security plans and privacy plans.[10]

The assessment process is an information-gathering activity, not a security- or privacy-producing activity. Organizations determine the most cost-effective implementation of this key element in the organization's information security and privacy programs by applying the results of risk assessments, considering the maturity and quality level of the organization's risk management processes, and taking advantage of the flexibility in the concepts described in this publication. The use of Special Publication 800-53A as a starting point in the process of defining procedures for assessing the security and privacy controls in information systems and organizations, promotes a consistent level of security and privacy and offers the needed flexibility to customize the assessment based on organizational policies and requirements, known threat and vulnerability information, operational considerations, information system and platform dependencies, and tolerance for risk.[11] The information produced during control assessments can be used by an organization to:

- Identify potential problems or shortfalls in the organization's implementation of the Risk Management Framework;

- Identify security- and privacy-related weaknesses and deficiencies in the information system and in the environment in which the system operates;

- Prioritize risk mitigation decisions and associated risk mitigation activities;

- Confirm that identified security- and privacy-related weaknesses and deficiencies in the information system and in the environment of operation have been addressed;

- Support monitoring activities and information security and privacy situational awareness;

- Facilitate security authorization decisions, privacy authorization decisions, and ongoing authorization decisions; and

- Inform budgetary decisions and the capital investment process.

Organizations are not expected to employ *all* of the assessment methods and assessment objects contained within the assessment procedures identified in this publication for the associated security and privacy controls deployed within or inherited by organizational information systems. Rather, organizations have the inherent flexibility to determine the level of effort needed and the assurance required for a particular assessment (e.g., which assessment methods and assessment objects are deemed to be the most useful in obtaining the desired results). This determination is

---

[9] For national security systems, security categorization is accomplished in accordance with CNSS Instruction 1253. For other than national security systems, security categorization is accomplished in accordance with Federal Information Processing Standard (FIPS) 199 and NIST Special Publication 800-60.

[10] The security and privacy controls for the information system and organization are documented in the security plans and privacy plans after the initial selection and tailoring of the controls as described in NIST Special Publication 800-53 and CNSS Instruction 1253.

[11] In this publication, the term *risk* is used to mean risk to organizational operations (i.e., mission, functions, image, and reputation), organizational assets, individuals, other organizations, and the Nation.

Special Publication 800-53A
Revision 4

Assessing Security and Privacy Controls in Federal Information Systems
and Organizations — *Building Effective Assessment Plans*

made on the basis of what will accomplish the assessment objectives in the most cost-effective manner and with sufficient confidence to support the subsequent determination of the resulting mission or business risk. Organizations should balance the resources expended on the deployment of security and privacy controls (i.e., safeguards and countermeasures implemented for security and privacy protection) versus the resources expended to determine overall control effectiveness, both initially and on an ongoing basis through continuous monitoring programs.

1.2 TARGET AUDIENCE

This publication is intended to serve a diverse group of information system, information security, and privacy professionals including:

- Individuals with information system development responsibilities (e.g., program managers, system designers and developers, systems integrators, information security engineers);

- Individuals with information security assessment and monitoring responsibilities (e.g., Inspectors General, system evaluators, assessors, independent verifiers/validators, auditors, analysts, information system owners, common control providers);

- Individuals with information system, security, privacy, and risk management and oversight responsibilities (e.g., authorizing officials, chief information officers, senior information security officers,[12] senior agency officials for privacy/chief privacy officers, information system managers, information security managers); and

- Individuals with information security implementation and operational responsibilities (e.g., information system owners, common control providers, information owners/stewards, mission/business owners, systems administrators, information system security officers).

1.3 RELATED PUBLICATIONS AND ASSESSMENT PROCESSES

Special Publication 800-53A is designed to support Special Publication 800-37, *Guide for Applying the Risk Management Framework to Federal Information Systems: A Security Life Cycle Approach*. In particular, the assessment procedures contained in this publication and the guidelines provided for developing security and privacy assessment plans for organizational information systems directly support the assessment and monitoring activities that are integral to the risk management process. This includes providing near real-time security- and privacy-related information to organizational officials regarding the ongoing security and privacy state of their systems and organizations.

Organizations are encouraged, whenever possible, to take advantage of the assessment results and associated assessment documentation and evidence available on information system components from previous assessments including independent third-party testing, evaluation, and validation.[13] Product testing, evaluation, and validation may be conducted on cryptographic modules and general-purpose information technology products such as operating systems, database systems, firewalls, intrusion detection devices, Web browsers, Web applications, smart cards, biometrics

---

[12] At the *agency* level, this position is known as the Senior Agency Information Security Officer. Organizations may also refer to this position as the *Senior Information Security Officer* or the *Chief Information Security Officer*.

[13] Assessment results can be obtained from many activities that occur routinely during the system development life cycle. For example, assessment results are produced during the testing and evaluation of new information system components during system upgrades or system integration activities. Organizations can take advantage of previous assessment results whenever possible, to reduce the overall cost of assessments and to make the assessment process more efficient.

Special Publication 800-53A
Revision 4

Assessing Security and Privacy Controls in Federal Information Systems
and Organizations — *Building Effective Assessment Plans*

devices, personal identity verification devices, network devices, and hardware platforms using national and international standards. If an information system component product is identified as providing support for the implementation of a particular security or privacy control in Special Publication 800-53, then evidence produced during the product testing, evaluation, and validation processes (e.g., security specifications, analyses and test results, validation reports, and validation certificates)[14] is used to the extent that it is applicable. This evidence can be combined with the assessment-related evidence obtained from the application of the assessment procedures in this publication, to cost-effectively produce the information necessary to determine whether the security and privacy controls are effective in their application.

1.4 ORGANIZATION OF THIS SPECIAL PUBLICATION

The remainder of this special publication is organized as follows:

- **Chapter Two** describes the fundamental concepts associated with security and privacy control assessments including: (i) the integration of assessments into the system development life cycle; (ii) the importance of an organization-wide strategy for conducting security and privacy control assessments; (iii) the development of effective assurance cases to help increase the grounds for confidence in the effectiveness of the security and privacy controls being assessed; and (iv) the format and content of assessment procedures.

- **Chapter Three** describes the process of assessing the security and privacy controls in organizational information systems and their environments of operation including: (i) the activities carried out by organizations and assessors to prepare for security and privacy control assessments; (ii) the development of security assessment plans; (iii) the conduct of security and privacy control assessments and the analysis, documentation, and reporting of assessment results; and (iv) the post-assessment report analysis and follow-on activities carried out by organizations.

- **Supporting appendices** provide detailed assessment-related information including: (i) general references; (ii) definitions and terms; (iii) acronyms; (iv) a description of assessment methods; (v) penetration testing guidelines; (vi) a catalog of assessment procedures that can be used to develop plans for assessing security controls; (vii) content of security assessment reports; (viii) the definition, format, and use of assessment cases; (ix) automation support for ongoing assessments; and (x) a catalog of assessment procedures that can be used to develop plans for assessing privacy controls.

---

[14] Organizations review the available information from component information technology products to determine: (i) what security and privacy controls are implemented by the product; (ii) if those security and privacy controls meet the intended control requirements of the information system under assessment; (iii) if the configuration of the product and the environment in which the product operates are consistent with the environmental and product configuration stated by the vendor and/or developer; and (iv) if the assurance requirements stated in the developer/vendor specification satisfy the assurance requirements for assessing those controls. Meeting the above criteria provides a sound rationale that the product is suitable and meets the intended security and privacy control requirements of the information system under assessment.

Special Publication 800-53A
Revision 4

Assessing Security and Privacy Controls in Federal Information Systems
and Organizations — *Building Effective Assessment Plans*

CHAPTER TWO

THE FUNDAMENTALS
BASIC CONCEPTS ASSOCIATED WITH SECURITY AND PRIVACY CONTROL ASSESSMENTS

This chapter describes the basic concepts associated with assessing the security and privacy controls in organizational information systems and the environments in which those systems operate including: (i) the integration of assessments into the system development life cycle; (ii) the importance of an organization-wide strategy for conducting assessments; (iii) the development of effective assurance cases to help increase the grounds for confidence in the effectiveness of security and privacy controls; and (iv) the format and content of assessment procedures. While flexibility continues to be an important factor in developing assessment plans, consistency of assessments is also an important consideration. A fundamental design objective for Special Publication 800-53A is to provide an assessment framework and a starting point for assessment procedures that are essential for achieving such consistency.

2.1 ASSESSMENTS WITHIN THE SYSTEM DEVELOPMENT LIFE CYCLE

Security and privacy assessments can be effectively carried out at various stages in the system development life cycle[15] to increase the grounds for confidence that the security and privacy controls employed within or inherited by an information system are effective in their application. This publication provides a comprehensive set of assessment procedures to support security and privacy assessment activities throughout the system development life cycle. For example, security assessments are routinely conducted by system developers and system integrators during the development/acquisition and implementation phases of the life cycle. Privacy assessments are conducted by senior agency officials for privacy/privacy officers and privacy staff in these early life cycle phases as well. This helps to ensure that the required security and privacy controls for the system are properly designed and developed, correctly implemented, and consistent with the established organizational information security architecture *before* the system enters the operations and maintenance phase. Security assessments in the initial system development life cycle phases include, for example, design and code reviews, application scanning, and regression testing. Privacy assessments include reviews to ensure that applicable privacy laws and policies are adhered to and that privacy protections are embedded in system design. Security-related and privacy-related weaknesses and deficiencies identified early in the system development life cycle can be resolved more quickly and in a much more cost-effective manner before proceeding to subsequent phases in the life cycle. The objective is to identify the security and privacy controls early in the life cycle to ensure that the system design and testing validate the implementation of these controls. The assessment procedures described in Appendices F and J support assessments carried out during the initial stages of the system development life cycle.

Security and privacy assessments are also conducted during the operations and maintenance phase of the life cycle to ensure that security and privacy controls continue to be effective in the operational environment and can protect against constantly evolving threats. Security assessments are typically conducted by information system owners, common control providers, information system security officers, independent assessors, auditors, and Inspectors General. Privacy assessments are typically conducted by senior agency officials for privacy/privacy officers and

---

[15] There are typically five phases in a generic system development life cycle: (i) initiation; (ii) development/acquisition; (iii) implementation; (iv) operations and maintenance; and (v) disposition (disposal). Special Publication 800-64 provides guidance on security considerations in the system development life cycle.

Special Publication 800-53A
Revision 4

Assessing Security and Privacy Controls in Federal Information Systems
and Organizations — *Building Effective Assessment Plans*

privacy staff. For example, organizations assess all security controls and privacy controls employed within and inherited by the information system during the initial security authorization. Subsequent to the initial authorization, the organization assesses all implemented security controls on an ongoing basis in accordance with its Information Security Continuous Monitoring strategy.[16] Privacy controls are also assessed on an ongoing basis to ensure compliance with applicable privacy laws and policies. The ongoing assessment and monitoring of security controls and privacy controls use the assessment procedures defined in this publication. The frequency of such assessments and monitoring is determined by the organization and/or information system owner or common control provider and approved by the authorizing official. Finally, at the end of the life cycle, security assessments are conducted to ensure that important organizational information is purged from the information system prior to disposal. Privacy assessments are also conducted to ensure adherence to organizational retention schedules.

2.2 STRATEGY FOR CONDUCTING CONTROL ASSESSMENTS

Organizations are encouraged to develop a broad-based, organization-wide strategy for conducting security and privacy assessments, facilitating more cost-effective and consistent assessments across the inventory of information systems. An organization-wide strategy begins by applying the initial steps of the Risk Management Framework to all information systems within the organization, with an organizational view of the security categorization process and the security and privacy control selection process (including the identification of common controls). Categorizing information systems as an organization-wide activity taking into consideration not only the criticality and sensitivity of information but also the enterprise architecture and the information security architecture helps to ensure that the individual systems are categorized based on the mission and business objectives of the organization.[17] Maximizing the number of common controls employed within an organization: (i) significantly reduces the cost of development, implementation, and assessment of security and privacy controls; (ii) allows organizations to centralize and automate control assessments and to amortize the cost of those assessments across all information systems organization-wide; and (iii) increases the consistency of security and privacy controls. An organization-wide approach to identifying common controls early in the application of the RMF facilitates a more global strategy for assessing those controls and sharing essential assessment results with information system owners and authorizing officials. The sharing of assessment results among key organizational officials across information system boundaries has many important benefits including:

- Providing the capability to review assessment results for all information systems and to make mission/business-related decisions on risk mitigation activities according to organizational priorities, the security categorization of the information systems, and risk assessments;

- Providing a more global view of systemic weaknesses and deficiencies occurring in information systems across the organization and an opportunity to develop organization-wide solutions to information security and privacy problems; and

- Increasing the organization's knowledge base regarding threats, vulnerabilities, and strategies for more cost-effective solutions to common information security and privacy problems.

Organizations can also promote a more focused and cost-effective assessment process by: (i) developing more specific assessment procedures that are tailored for their specific environments

---

[16] Special Publications 800-37 and 800-137 provide guidance on the continuous monitoring of security controls.

[17] Privacy controls are selected and implemented irrespective of the security categorization of the information system.

Special Publication 800-53A
Revision 4

Assessing Security and Privacy Controls in Federal Information Systems
and Organizations — *Building Effective Assessment Plans*

of operation and requirements (instead of relegating these tasks to each control assessor or assessment team); and (ii) providing organization-wide tools, templates, and techniques to support more consistent assessments throughout the organization.[18]

The conduct of security control assessments is the primary responsibility of information system owners and common control providers with oversight by their respective authorizing officials. The conduct of privacy control assessments is the primary responsibility of senior agency officials for privacy/chief privacy officers and privacy staff. There is also significant involvement in the assessment process by other parties within the organization who have a vested interest in the outcome of assessments. Other interested parties include, for example, mission/business owners, information owners/stewards (when those roles are filled by someone other than the information system owner), information security personnel, and designated privacy staff. It is imperative that information system owners and common control providers coordinate with the other parties in the organization having an interest in control assessments to help ensure that the organization's core missions and business functions are adequately addressed in the selection of security and privacy controls to be assessed.

CAUTIONARY NOTE

Organizations should carefully consider the potential impacts of employing the assessment procedures defined in this Special Publication when assessing the security and privacy controls in *operational* systems. Certain assessment procedures, particularly those procedures that directly impact the operation or function of the hardware, software, or firmware components of an information system, may inadvertently affect the routine processing, transmission, or storage of information supporting organizational missions or business functions. For example, a critical information system component may be taken offline for assessment purposes or a component may suffer a fault or failure during the assessment process. Organizations should also take the necessary precautions to ensure that organizational missions and business functions continue to be supported by information systems and that any potential impacts to operational effectiveness resulting from assessment activities are considered in advance.

2.3 BUILDING AN EFFECTIVE ASSURANCE CASE

Building an effective assurance case[19] for security and privacy control effectiveness is a process that involves: (i) compiling evidence from a variety of activities conducted during the system development life cycle that the controls employed in the information system are implemented correctly, operating as intended, and producing the desired outcome with respect to meeting the security and privacy requirements of the system and the organization; and (ii) presenting this

---

[18] Organizations may also provide security assessment plans including tailored assessment procedures to external service providers that are operating information systems on behalf of those organizations. In addition, these plans can recommend supporting templates, tools, and techniques and also be further tailored specific to the contract with the service provider, helping to make assessments more consistent and to maximize reuse of assessment-related artifacts. This reuse can improve security through uniformity and reduce/eliminate contracting ambiguity, resulting in reduced costs and risk to the organization.

[19] An assurance case is a body of evidence organized into an argument demonstrating that some claim about an information system holds (i.e., is assured). An assurance case is needed when it is important to show that a system exhibits some complex property such as safety, security, or reliability.

Special Publication 800-53A
Revision 4

Assessing Security and Privacy Controls in Federal Information Systems
and Organizations — *Building Effective Assessment Plans*

evidence in a manner that decision makers are able to use effectively in making risk-based decisions about the operation or use of the system. The evidence described above comes from the implementation of the security and privacy controls in the information system and inherited by the system (i.e., common controls) and from the assessments of that implementation. Ideally, the assessor is building on previously developed materials that started with the specification of the organization's information security and privacy needs and was further developed during the design, development, and implementation of the information system. These materials, developed while implementing security and privacy throughout the life cycle of the information system, provide the initial evidence for an assurance case.

Assessors obtain the required evidence during the assessment process to allow the appropriate organizational officials to make objective determinations about the effectiveness of the security and privacy controls and the overall security and privacy state of the information system. The assessment evidence needed to make such determinations can be obtained from a variety of sources including, for example, information technology product and system assessments and, in the case of privacy assessments, privacy compliance documentation such as Privacy Impact Assessments and Privacy Act System of Record Notices. Product assessments (also known as product testing, evaluation, and validation) are typically conducted by independent, third-party testing organizations. These assessments examine the security and privacy functions of products and established configuration settings. Assessments can be conducted to demonstrate compliance to industry, national, or international information security standards, privacy standards embodied in applicable laws and policies, and developer/vendor claims. Since many information technology products are assessed by commercial testing organizations and then subsequently deployed in millions of information systems, these types of assessments can be carried out at a greater level of depth and provide deeper insights into the security and privacy capabilities of the particular products.

System assessments are typically conducted by information systems developers, systems integrators, information system owners, common control providers, assessors, auditors, Inspectors General, and the information security and privacy staffs of organizations. The assessors or assessment teams bring together available information about the information system such as the results from individual component product assessments, if available, and conduct additional system-level assessments using a variety of methods and techniques. System assessments are used to compile and evaluate the evidence needed by organizational officials to determine how effective the security and privacy controls employed in the information system are likely to be in mitigating risks to organizational operations and assets, to individuals, to other organizations, and to the Nation. The results of assessments conducted using information system-specific and organization-specific assessment procedures derived from the guidelines in this publication contribute to compiling the necessary evidence to determine security and privacy control effectiveness in accordance with the assurance requirements documented in the security and privacy plans.

2.4 ASSESSMENT PROCEDURES

An assessment procedure consists of a set of assessment *objectives*, each with an associated set of potential assessment *methods* and assessment *objects*. An assessment objective includes a set of *determination statements* related to the particular security or privacy control under assessment. The determination statements are linked to the content of the security or privacy control (i.e., the security/privacy control functionality) to ensure traceability of assessment results back to the fundamental control requirements. The application of an assessment procedure to a security or

Special Publication 800-53A
Revision 4

Assessing Security and Privacy Controls in Federal Information Systems
and Organizations — *Building Effective Assessment Plans*

privacy control produces assessment *findings*. These findings reflect, or are subsequently used, to help determine the overall effectiveness of the security or privacy control.

Assessment objects identify the specific items being assessed and include *specifications*, *mechanisms*, *activities*, and *individuals*. Specifications are the document-based artifacts (e.g., policies, procedures, plans, system security and privacy requirements, functional specifications, architectural designs) associated with an information system. Mechanisms are the specific hardware, software, or firmware safeguards and countermeasures employed within an information system.[20] Activities are the specific protection-related actions supporting an information system that involve people (e.g., conducting system backup operations, monitoring network traffic, exercising a contingency plan). Individuals, or groups of individuals, are people applying the specifications, mechanisms, or activities described above.

Assessment methods define the nature of the assessor actions and include *examine*, *interview*, and *test*. The *examine* method is the process of reviewing, inspecting, observing, studying, or analyzing one or more assessment objects (i.e., specifications, mechanisms, or activities). The purpose of the examine method is to facilitate assessor understanding, achieve clarification, or obtain evidence. The *interview* method is the process of holding discussions with individuals or groups of individuals within an organization to once again, facilitate assessor understanding, achieve clarification, or obtain evidence. The *test* method is the process of exercising one or more assessment objects (i.e., activities or mechanisms) under specified conditions to compare actual with expected behavior. In all three assessment methods, the results are used in making specific determinations called for in the determination statements and thereby achieving the objectives for the assessment procedure. A complete description of assessment methods and assessment objects is provided in Appendix D.

Assessment methods have a set of associated attributes, *depth* and *coverage*, which help define the level of effort for the assessment. These attributes are hierarchical in nature, providing the means to define the rigor and scope of the assessment for the increased assurances that may be needed for some information systems. The depth attribute addresses the rigor of and level of detail in the examination, interview, and testing processes. Values for the depth attribute include *basic*, *focused*, and *comprehensive*. The coverage attribute addresses the scope or breadth of the examination, interview, and testing processes including the number and type of specifications, mechanisms, and activities to be examined or tested, and the number and types of individuals to be interviewed. Similar to the depth attribute, values for the coverage attribute include *basic*, *focused*, and *comprehensive*. The appropriate depth and coverage attribute values for a particular assessment method are based on the assurance requirements specified by the organization.[21] As assurance requirements increase with regard to the development, implementation, and operation of security and privacy controls within or inherited by the information system, the rigor and scope of the assessment activities (as reflected in the selection of assessment methods and objects and the assignment of depth and coverage attribute values) tend to increase as well. Appendix D provides a detailed description of assessment method attributes and attribute values.

---

[20] Mechanisms also include physical protection devices associated with an information system (e.g., locks, keypads, security cameras, fire protection devices, fireproof safes, etc.).

[21] For other than national security systems, organizations meet minimum assurance requirements specified in Special Publication 800-53, Appendix E.

Special Publication 800-53A
Revision 4

Assessing Security and Privacy Controls in Federal Information Systems
and Organizations — *Building Effective Assessment Plans*

Figure 1 illustrates an example of an assessment procedure developed to assess the effectiveness of security control CP-9. The assessment objective for CP-9 is derived from the base control statement described in NIST Special Publication 800-53, Appendix F. Potential assessment methods and objects are added to the assessment procedure.

CP-9	INFORMATION SYSTEM BACKUP		
	ASSESSMENT OBJECTIVE: *Determine if the organization:*		
	CP-9(a)	CP-9(a)[1]	*defines a frequency, consistent with recovery time objectives and recovery point objectives as specified in the information system contingency plan, to conduct backups of user-level information contained in the information system;*
		CP-9(a)[2]	*conducts backups of user-level information contained in the information system with the organization-defined frequency;*
	CP-9(b)	CP-9(b)[1]	*defines a frequency, consistent with recovery time objectives and recovery point objectives as specified in the information system contingency plan, to conduct backups of system-level information contained in the information system;*
		CP-9(b)[2]	*conducts backups of system-level information contained in the information system with the organization-defined frequency;*
	CP-9(c)	CP-9(c)[1]	*defines a frequency, consistent with recovery time objectives and recovery point objectives as specified in the information system contingency plan, to conduct backups of information system documentation including security-related documentation;*
		CP-9(c)[2]	*conducts backups of information system documentation, including security-related documentation, with the organization-defined frequency; and*
	CP-9(d)	*protects the confidentiality, integrity, and availability of backup information at storage locations.*	
	POTENTIAL ASSESSMENT METHODS AND OBJECTS: **Examine**: [*SELECT FROM:* Contingency planning policy; procedures addressing information system backup; contingency plan; backup storage location(s); information system backup logs or records; other relevant documents or records]. **Interview**: [*SELECT FROM:* Organizational personnel with information system backup responsibilities; organizational personnel with information security responsibilities]. **Test**: [*SELECT FROM:* Organizational processes for conducting information system backups; automated mechanisms supporting and/or implementing information system backups].		

FIGURE 1: ASSESSMENT PROCEDURE FOR SECURITY CONTROL

The assessment objectives are numbered sequentially, first in accordance with the numbering scheme in Special Publication 800-53, and subsequently, where necessary to further apportion the security or privacy control requirements to facilitate assessment, **bracketed** sequential numbers or letters, as opposed to parentheses, are used to make that distinction (e.g., CP-9(a), CP-9(a)[1], CP-9(a)[2], CP-9(b)[1], CP-9(b)[2], CP-9(c)[1], CP-9(c)[2], CP-9(d), etc.). The initial bracketed character is always a number. For some controls, the column with the initial control designation (e.g., CP-9, CP-9(a), CP-9(b), and CP-9(c) in Figure 1) is simply a placeholder to help facilitate apportioning the control while maintaining the formatting scheme. Although not explicitly noted with each identified assessment method in the assessment procedure, the attribute values of depth

Special Publication 800-53A
Revision 4

Assessing Security and Privacy Controls in Federal Information Systems
and Organizations — *Building Effective Assessment Plans*

and coverage described in Appendix D are assigned by the organization and applied by the assessor/assessment team in the execution of the assessment method against an assessment object.

If the control has any enhancements (as designated by sequential parenthetical numbers, for example, CP-9 (3) for the third enhancement for CP-9), assessment objectives are developed for each enhancement using the same process as for the base control. The resulting assessment objectives are numbered sequentially in the same way as the assessment procedure for the base control, first in accordance with the numbering scheme in Special Publication 800-53, and subsequently, using bracketed sequential numbers or letters to further apportion control enhancement requirements to facilitate assessments (e.g., CP-9(3)[1], CP-9(3)[2]). Figure 2 illustrates an example of an assessment procedure developed to assess the effectiveness of the third enhancement to security control CP-9.

CP-9(3)	INFORMATION SYSTEM BACKUP | *SEPARATE STORAGE FOR CRITICAL INFORMATION*		
	ASSESSMENT OBJECTIVE: *Determine if the organization:*		
	CP-9(3)[1]	**CP-9(3)[1][a]**	*defines critical information system software and other security-related information requiring backup copies to be stored in a separate facility; or*
		CP-9(3)[1][b]	*defines critical information system software and other security-related information requiring backup copies to be stored in a fire-rated container that is not collocated with the operational system; and*
	CP-9(3)[2]	*stores backup copies of organization-defined critical information system software and other security-related information in a separate facility or in a fire-rated container that is not collocated with the operational system.*	
	POTENTIAL ASSESSMENT METHODS AND OBJECTS: **Examine**: [*SELECT FROM:* Contingency planning policy; procedures addressing information system backup; contingency plan; backup storage location(s); information system backup configurations and associated documentation; information system backup logs or records; other relevant documents or records]. **Interview**: [*SELECT FROM:* Organizational personnel with contingency planning and plan implementation responsibilities; organizational personnel with information system backup responsibilities; organizational personnel with information security responsibilities].		

FIGURE 2:   ASSESSMENT PROCEDURE FOR SECURITY CONTROL ENHANCEMENT

Recall that *numbers* in parentheses immediately after the base control designation (as in Figure 2) indicate the number of the control enhancement while *letters* in parentheses immediately after the base control designation (as in Figure 1) indicate division of the base control into separate control requirements. When further division of a control is necessary to support assessment, bracketed characters that alternate between numbers and letters (e.g., CP-9(3)[1][a], CP-9(3)[1][b]) are used with the initial bracketed character always being a number whether it follows a parenthetical letter (base control) or number (control enhancement).

The Security Content Automation Protocol (SCAP) supports the assessment process for security controls and facilitates more efficient and cost-effective assessments. SCAP is a collection of related specifications for automating the collection and representation of evidence in a standards-based format that enables interoperability between SCAP-enabled tools. The SCAP specifications define the formats by which assessment criteria, also called *SCAP content*, can be exchanged and

Special Publication 800-53A
Revision 4

Assessing Security and Privacy Controls in Federal Information Systems
and Organizations — *Building Effective Assessment Plans*

provided to assessment tools. This content can be used to automate the collection and evaluation of evidence sourced from both machine- and human-oriented artifacts. SCAP also defines formats that capture and enable the exchange of results of collecting and evaluating artifacts. Typically, machine-oriented artifacts that can be collected and evaluated using SCAP pertain to mechanisms (e.g., configuration settings, installed hardware/software, operational state of countermeasures). Additionally, human-oriented artifacts, such as those that pertain to specifications and activities, can be collected using the Open Checklist Interactive Language (OCIL). OCIL is an SCAP component specification that enables the collection and representation of interview data in a standards-based format. The content-driven nature of SCAP-enabled automation solutions can support flexible and consistent assessment of security and privacy controls.

Special Publication 800-53A
Revision 4

Assessing Security and Privacy Controls in Federal Information Systems
and Organizations — *Building Effective Assessment Plans*

CHAPTER THREE

THE PROCESS
CONDUCTING EFFECTIVE SECURITY AND PRIVACY CONTROL ASSESSMENTS

This chapter describes the process of assessing the security and privacy controls in organizational information systems and environments of operation including: (i) the activities carried out by organizations and assessors to prepare for security and privacy control assessments; (ii) the development of security and privacy assessment plans; (iii) the conduct of control assessments and the analysis, documentation, and reporting of assessment results; and (iv) post-assessment report analysis and follow-on activities.

3.1 PREPARING FOR SECURITY AND PRIVACY CONTROL ASSESSMENTS

Conducting security control assessments and privacy control assessments in today's complex environment of sophisticated information technology infrastructures and high-visibility, mission-critical applications can be difficult, challenging, and resource-intensive. Security and privacy control assessments may be conducted by different organizational entities with distinct oversight responsibilities. However, success requires the cooperation and collaboration among all parties having a vested interest in the organization's information security or privacy posture, including information system owners, common control providers, authorizing officials, chief information officers, senior information security officers, senior agency officials for privacy/chief privacy officers, chief executive officers/heads of agencies, security and privacy staffs, Inspectors General, and OMB. Establishing an appropriate set of expectations before, during, and after an assessment is paramount to achieving an acceptable outcome—that is, producing information necessary to help the authorizing official make a credible, risk-based decision on whether to place the information system into operation or continue its operation.

Thorough preparation by the organization and the assessors is an important aspect of conducting effective security control assessments and privacy control assessments. Preparatory activities address a range of issues relating to the cost, schedule, and performance of the assessment. From the organizational perspective, preparing for a security or privacy control assessment includes the following key activities:

- Ensuring that appropriate policies covering security and privacy control assessments, respectively, are in place and understood by all affected organizational elements;

- Ensuring that all steps in the RMF[22] prior to the security or privacy control assessment step, have been successfully completed and received appropriate management oversight;[23]

- Establishing the objective and scope of assessments (i.e., the purpose of the assessments and what is being assessed);

---

[22] While the RMF can be employed for privacy controls (see Special Publication 800-53, Appendix J), privacy control *selection* is conducted irrespective of the security categories of organizational information systems.

[23] Conducting security control assessments in parallel with the development/acquisition and implementation phases of the life cycle permits the identification of weaknesses and deficiencies early and provides the most cost-effective method for initiating corrective actions. Issues found during these assessments can be referred to authorizing officials for early resolution, as appropriate. The results of security control assessments carried out during system development and implementation can also be used (consistent with reuse criteria) during the security authorization process to avoid system fielding delays or costly repetition of assessments.

Special Publication 800-53A
Revision 4

Assessing Security and Privacy Controls in Federal Information Systems
and Organizations — *Building Effective Assessment Plans*

- Ensuring that security and privacy controls identified as common controls (and the common portion of hybrid controls) have been assigned to appropriate organizational entities (i.e., common control providers) for development and implementation;[24]

- Notifying key organizational officials of impending assessments and allocating necessary resources to carry out the assessments;

- Establishing appropriate communication channels among organizational officials having an interest in the assessments;[25]

- Establishing time frames for completing the assessments and key milestone decision points required by the organization to effectively manage the assessments;

- Identifying and selecting competent assessors/assessment teams that will be responsible for conducting the assessments, considering issues of assessor independence;

- Collecting artifacts to provide to the assessors/assessment teams (e.g., policies, procedures, plans, specifications, designs, records, administrator/operator manuals, information system documentation, interconnection agreements, previous assessment results, legal requirements); and

- Establishing a mechanism between the organization and the assessors and/or assessment teams to minimize ambiguities or misunderstandings about the implementation of security or privacy controls and security/privacy control weaknesses/deficiencies identified during the assessments.

Security and privacy control assessors/assessment teams begin preparing for their respective assessments by:

- Obtaining a general understanding of the organization's operations (including mission, functions, and business processes) and how the information system that is the subject of the particular assessment supports those organizational operations;

- Obtaining an understanding of the structure of the information system (i.e., system architecture) and the security or privacy controls being assessed (including system-specific, hybrid, and common controls);

- Identifying the organizational entities responsible for the development and implementation of the common controls (or the common portion of hybrid controls) supporting the information system;

- Meeting with appropriate organizational officials to ensure common understanding for assessment objectives and the proposed rigor and scope of the assessment;

- Obtaining artifacts needed for the assessment (e.g., policies, procedures, plans, specifications, designs, records, administrator and operator manuals, information system documentation, interconnection agreements, previous assessment results);

---

[24] Security control assessments and privacy control assessments include common controls that are the responsibility of organizational entities other than the information system owner inheriting the controls or hybrid controls where there is shared responsibility among the system (or program) owner and designated organizational entities.

[25] Depending upon whether security controls or privacy controls are being assessed, these individuals typically include authorizing officials, information system (or program) owners, common control providers, mission/business owners, information owners/stewards, chief information officers, senior information security officers, senior agency officials for privacy/chief privacy officers, privacy staff, Inspectors General, information system security officers, users from organizations that the information system supports, and assessors.

Special Publication 800-53A
Revision 4

Assessing Security and Privacy Controls in Federal Information Systems
and Organizations — *Building Effective Assessment Plans*

- Establishing appropriate organizational points of contact needed to carry out the assessments;

- Obtaining previous assessment results that may be appropriately reused for the current assessment (e.g., Inspector General reports, audits, vulnerability scans, physical security inspections, prior security or privacy assessments, developmental testing and evaluation, vendor flaw remediation activities, ISO/IEC 15408 [Common Criteria] evaluations); and

- Developing security and privacy assessment plans which may be integrated into one plan or developed separately.

In preparation for the assessment of security or privacy controls, the necessary background information is assembled and made available to the assessors or assessment team.[26] To the extent necessary to support the specific assessment, and depending upon whether security controls or privacy controls are being assessed, the organization identifies and arranges access to: (i) elements of the organization responsible for developing, documenting, disseminating, reviewing, and updating all security or privacy policies and associated procedures for implementing policy-compliant controls; (ii) the security or privacy policies for the information system and any associated implementing procedures; (iii) individuals or groups responsible for the development, implementation, operation, and maintenance of security or privacy controls; (iv) any materials (e.g., security or privacy plans, records, schedules, assessment reports, after-action reports, agreements, authorization packages) associated with the implementation and operation of the security or privacy controls to be assessed; and (v) the specific objects to be assessed.[27] The availability of essential documentation as well as access to key organizational personnel and the information system being assessed are paramount to a successful assessment.

Organizations consider both the *technical expertise* and level of *independence* required in selecting security or privacy control assessors. Organizations ensure that assessors possess the required skills and technical expertise to successfully carry out assessments of system-specific, hybrid, and common controls.[28] This includes knowledge of and experience with the specific hardware, software, and firmware components employed by the organization. An independent assessor is any individual capable of conducting an impartial assessment of security and privacy controls employed within or inherited by an information system. Impartiality implies that security control assessors and privacy control assessors are free from any perceived or actual conflicts of interest with respect to the development, operation, and/or management of the information system or the determination of security or privacy control effectiveness.[29] The authorizing official or designated representative determines the required level of independence for assessors based on the results of the security categorization process for the information system (in the case of security control assessments) and the risk to organizational operations and assets, individuals, other organizations, and the Nation. The authorizing official determines if the level of assessor independence is sufficient to provide confidence that the assessment results produced are sound

---

[26] Information system (or program) owners and organizational entities developing, implementing, and/or administering common controls (i.e., common control providers) are responsible for providing needed information to assessors.

[27] In situations where there are multiple security or privacy assessments ongoing or planned within an organization, access to organizational elements, individuals, and artifacts supporting the assessments is centrally managed by the organization to ensure a cost-effective use of time and resources.

[28] The National Cybersecurity Workforce Framework provides information about skill sets and technical expertise needed by security or privacy control assessors. See www.niccs.us-cert.gov/training/tc/framework.

[29] Contracted assessment services are considered independent if the information system (or program) owner is not directly involved in the contracting process or cannot unduly influence the independence of the assessor(s) conducting the assessment of the security or privacy controls.

Special Publication 800-53A
Revision 4

Assessing Security and Privacy Controls in Federal Information Systems
and Organizations — *Building Effective Assessment Plans*

and can be used to make a risk-based decision on whether to place the information system into operation or continue its operation.

Independent security and privacy control assessment services can be obtained from other elements within the organization or can be contracted to a public or private sector entity outside of the organization. In special situations, for example when the organization that owns the information system is small or the organizational structure requires that the security or privacy control assessment be accomplished by individuals that are in the developmental, operational, and/or management chain of the system owner, independence in the assessment process can be achieved by ensuring that the assessment results are carefully reviewed and analyzed by an independent team of experts to validate the completeness, consistency, and veracity of the results.[30]

3.2 DEVELOPING SECURITY AND PRIVACY ASSESSMENT PLANS

The *security assessment plan* and *privacy assessment plan* provide the objectives for the security and privacy control assessments, respectively, and a detailed roadmap of how to conduct such assessments. These plans may be developed as one integrated plan or as distinct plans, depending upon organizational needs. The following steps are considered by assessors in developing plans to assess the security or privacy controls in organizational information systems or inherited by those systems:

- Determine which security and privacy controls/control enhancements are to be included in assessments based upon the contents of the security plan and privacy plan and the purpose and scope of the assessments;

- Select the appropriate assessment procedures to be used during assessments based on the security or privacy controls and control enhancements to be included in the assessments;

- Tailor the selected assessment procedures (e.g., select appropriate assessment methods and objects, assign depth and coverage attribute values);

- Develop additional assessment procedures to address any security requirements or privacy requirements or controls that are not sufficiently covered by Special Publication 800-53;

- Optimize the assessment procedures to reduce duplication of effort (e.g., sequencing and consolidating assessment procedures) and provide cost-effective assessment solutions; and

- Finalize assessment plans and obtain the necessary approvals to execute the plans.

3.2.1 *Determine which security or privacy controls are to be assessed.*

The security plan and privacy plan provide an overview of the security and privacy requirements, respectively, for the information system and organization and describe the security controls and privacy controls in place or planned for meeting those requirements. The assessor starts with the security or privacy controls described in the security or privacy plan and considers the purpose of the assessment. A security or privacy control assessment can be a *complete* assessment of all controls in the information system or inherited by the system (e.g., during an initial security or privacy authorization process) or a *partial* assessment of the controls in the information system or inherited by the system (e.g., during system development as part of a targeted assessment

---

[30] The authorizing official consults with the Office of the Inspector General, the senior information security officer, senior agency officials for privacy/chief privacy officers, and the chief information officer, as appropriate, to discuss the implications of any decisions on assessor independence in the types of special circumstances described above.

Special Publication 800-53A
Revision 4

Assessing Security and Privacy Controls in Federal Information Systems
and Organizations — *Building Effective Assessment Plans*

resulting from changes affecting specific controls, or where controls were previously assessed and the results accepted in the reciprocity process).

For partial assessments, information system owners and common control providers collaborate with organizational officials having an interest in the assessment (e.g., senior information security officers, senior agency officials for privacy/chief privacy officers, mission/information owners, Inspectors General, and authorizing officials) to determine which security or privacy controls are to be assessed. The determination of the controls to be assessed depends on the purpose of the assessment. For example, during the initial phases of the system development life cycle, specific controls may be selected for assessment to promote early detection of weakness and deficiencies and a more cost-effective approach to risk mitigation. After the initial authorization to operate has been granted, targeted assessments may need to be conducted when changes are made to the system, specific security or privacy controls, or to the environment of operation. In such cases, the focus for the assessment is on the security or privacy controls that may have been affected by the change.

3.2.2 *Select procedures to assess the security or privacy controls.*

Special Publication 800-53A provides assessment procedures for each security and privacy control and control enhancement in Special Publication 800-53. For each security or privacy control in the security plan and privacy plan to be included in the assessment, assessors select the corresponding assessment procedure from Appendix F (security assessment procedures) or Appendix J (privacy assessment procedures). The selected assessment procedures can vary from assessment to assessment based on the current content of the security plans and privacy plans and the purpose of the assessment (e.g., complete assessment, partial assessment).

3.2.3 *Tailor assessment procedures.*

In a similar manner to how the security controls and privacy controls from Special Publication 800-53 are tailored for the organization's mission, business functions, characteristics of the information system, and operating environment, organizations tailor the assessment procedures listed in Appendices F and J to meet specific organizational needs. Organizations have the flexibility to perform the tailoring process at the organization level for all information systems, at the individual information-system level, or using a combination of organization-level and system-specific approaches. Security control assessors and privacy control assessors determine if the organization provides additional tailoring guidance prior to initiating the tailoring process. Assessment procedures are tailored by:

- Selecting the appropriate assessment methods and objects needed to satisfy the stated assessment objectives;

- Selecting the appropriate depth and coverage attribute values to define the rigor and scope of the assessment;

- Identifying common controls that have been assessed by a separately documented security assessment plan or privacy assessment plan, and do not require the repeated execution of the assessment procedures;

- Developing information system/platform-specific and organization-specific assessment procedures (which may be adaptations to those procedures in Appendices F and J);

- Incorporating assessment results from previous assessments where the results are deemed applicable; and

Special Publication 800-53A
Revision 4

Assessing Security and Privacy Controls in Federal Information Systems
and Organizations — *Building Effective Assessment Plans*

- Making appropriate adjustments in assessment procedures to be able to obtain the requisite assessment evidence from external providers.

Assessment method and object-related considerations—

It is recognized that organizations can specify, document, and configure their information systems in a variety of ways, and that the content and applicability of existing assessment evidence will vary. This may result in the need to apply a variety of assessment methods to various assessment objects to generate the assessment evidence needed to determine whether the security or privacy controls are effective in their application. Therefore, the assessment methods and objects provided with each assessment procedure are termed *potential* to reflect the need to be able to choose the methods and objects most appropriate for a specific assessment. The assessment methods and objects chosen are those deemed as necessary to produce the evidence needed to make the determinations described in the determination statements. The potential methods and objects in the assessment procedure are provided as a resource to assist in the selection of appropriate methods and objects, and not with the intent to limit the selection. Organizations use their judgment in selecting from the potential assessment methods and the list of assessment objects associated with each selected method. Organizations select those methods and objects that most cost-effectively contribute to making the determinations associated with the assessment objective.[31] The measure of the quality of assessment results is based on the soundness of the rationale provided, not the specific set of methods and objects applied. It will not be necessary, in most cases, to apply every assessment method to every assessment object to obtain the desired assessment results. And for certain assessments, it may be appropriate to employ a method not currently listed in the set of potential methods.

Depth and coverage-related considerations—

In addition to selecting appropriate assessment methods and objects, each assessment method (i.e., examine, interview, and test) is associated with depth and coverage attributes that are described in Appendix D. The attribute values identify the rigor and scope of the assessment procedures executed by the assessor. The values selected by the organization are based on the characteristics of the information system being assessed (including assurance requirements) and the specific determinations to be made. The depth and coverage attribute values are associated with the assurance requirements specified by the organization (i.e., the rigor and scope of the assessment increases in direct relationship to the assurance requirements). For security controls, SCAP checklists provide a profile-based mechanism that enables tailoring of attribute values and selection of specific control requirements based on the desired level of assurance required for an information system. These checklists enable customizable, automated assessment using SCAP-validated products.

Common control-related considerations—

Assessors note which security or privacy controls (or parts of such controls) in security plans or privacy plans are designated as *common controls*.[32] Since the assessment of common controls is

---

[31] The selection of assessment methods and objects (including the number and type of assessment objects) can be a significant factor in cost-effectively meeting the assessment objectives.

[32] Common controls support multiple information systems within the organization, and the protection measures provided by those controls are inherited by the individual systems. Therefore, the organization determines the appropriate set of common controls to ensure that both the strength of the controls (i.e., security capability) and level of rigor and intensity of the control assessments are commensurate with the criticality and/or sensitivity of the individual information systems inheriting those controls. Weaknesses or deficiencies in common controls have the potential to adversely affect large portions of the organization and thus require significant attention.

Special Publication 800-53A
Revision 4

Assessing Security and Privacy Controls in Federal Information Systems
and Organizations — *Building Effective Assessment Plans*

the responsibility of the organizational entity that developed and implemented the controls (i.e., common control provider), the assessment procedures in Appendices F and J used to assess these controls incorporate assessment results from that organizational entity. Common controls may have been previously assessed as part of the organization's information security program or privacy program or as part of an information system providing common controls inherited by other organizational systems. There may also be separate plans to assess common controls. In either situation, information system owners coordinate the assessment of common controls with appropriate organizational officials (e.g., chief information officer, senior information security officer, senior agency official for privacy/chief privacy officer, mission/information owners, authorizing officials) obtaining the results of common control assessments or, if the common controls have not been assessed or are due to be reassessed, making the necessary arrangements to include or reference the common control assessment results in the current assessment.[33]

Another consideration in assessing common controls is that there are occasionally system-specific aspects of a common control that are not covered by the organizational entities responsible for the common aspects of the control. These types of controls are referred to as *hybrid controls*. For example, CP-2, the contingency planning security control, may be considered a hybrid control by the organization if there is a contingency plan developed by the organization for all organizational information systems. Following up on the initial contingency plan, information system owners are expected to adjust or tailor the contingency plan as necessary, when there are specific aspects of the plan that need to be defined for the particular system where the control is employed. For each hybrid control, assessors include in security assessment plans or privacy assessment plans, the portions of the assessment procedures from Appendices F or J related to the parts of the control that are system-specific to ensure that, along with the results from common control assessments, all aspects of the control are assessed.

System/platform and organization-related considerations—

The assessment procedures in Special Publication 800-53A may be adapted to address system- and platform-specific or organization-specific dependencies. For example, the assessment of a UNIX implementation of the IA-2 control for identification and authentication of users might include an explicit examination of the *.rhosts* file for UNIX systems since improper entries in that file can result in bypassing user authentication. Recent test results may also be applicable to the current assessment if those test methods provide a high degree of transparency (e.g., what was tested, when was it tested, how was it tested). Standards-based testing protocols such as SCAP provide an example of how organizations can help achieve this level of transparency. SCAP provides transparency through the use of standardized content that defines testing methods, and through standardized results that indicate what content was used, what system state was tested, what state was found, what tool was used to perform the testing, and when the testing was performed.

Reuse of assessment evidence-related considerations—

Reuse of assessment results from previously accepted or approved assessments is considered in the body of evidence for determining overall security or privacy control effectiveness. Previously accepted or approved assessments include: (i) those assessments of common controls that are managed by the organization and support multiple information systems; (ii) assessments of

---

[33] If assessment results are not currently available for the common controls, the assessment plans for the information systems under assessment that depend on those controls are duly noted. The assessments cannot be considered complete until the assessment results for the common controls are made available to information system owners.

Special Publication 800-53A
Revision 4

Assessing Security and Privacy Controls in Federal Information Systems
and Organizations — *Building Effective Assessment Plans*

security or privacy controls that are reviewed as part of the control implementation (e.g., CP-2 requires a review of the contingency plan); or (iii) security-related information generated by the organization's Information Security Continuous Monitoring program. The acceptability of using previous assessment results in a security control assessment or privacy control assessment is coordinated with and approved by the users of the assessment results. It is essential that information system owners and common control providers collaborate with authorizing officials and other appropriate organizational officials in determining the acceptability of using previous assessment results. When considering the reuse of previous assessment results and the value of those results to the current assessment, assessors determine: (i) the credibility of the assessment evidence; (ii) the appropriateness of previous analysis; and (iii) the applicability of the assessment evidence to current information system operating conditions. If previous assessment results are reused, the date of the original assessment and type of assessment are documented in the security assessment plan or privacy assessment plan and security assessment report or privacy assessment report. When applicable, the standardized security assessment results provided by SCAP tools may be reused by multiple parties.

It may be necessary, in certain situations, to supplement previous assessment results under consideration for reuse with additional assessment activities to fully address the assessment objectives. For example, if an independent evaluation of an information technology product did not test a particular configuration setting that is employed by the organization in an information system, then the assessor may need to supplement the original test results with additional testing to cover that configuration setting for the current information system environment. The decision to reuse assessment results is documented in the security assessment plan or privacy assessment plan and the final security assessment report or privacy assessment report, and is consistent with federal legislation, policies, directives, standards, and guidelines.

The following items are considered in validating previous assessment results for reuse:

- **Changing conditions associated with security controls and privacy controls over time.**

Security and privacy controls that were deemed effective during previous assessments may have become ineffective due to changing conditions within the information system or its environment of operation, including emergent threat information. Assessment results that were found to be previously acceptable may no longer provide credible evidence for the determination of security or privacy control effectiveness, and therefore, a reassessment would be required. Applying previous assessment results to a current assessment necessitates the identification of any changes that have occurred since the previous assessment and the impact of these changes on the previous results. For example, reusing previous assessment results from examining an organization's security or privacy policies and procedures may be acceptable if it is determined that there have not been any significant changes to the identified policies and procedures. Reusing assessment results produced during the previous authorization of an information system is a cost-effective method for supporting continuous monitoring activities and annual FISMA reporting requirements when the related controls have not changed, and there are adequate reasons for confidence in their continued application.

- **Amount of time that has transpired since previous assessments.**

In general, as the time period between current and previous assessments increases, the credibility and utility of the previous assessment results decrease. This is primarily due to the fact that the information system or the environment in which the information system operates is more likely to change with the passage of time, possibly invalidating the original conditions or assumptions on which the previous assessment was based.

Special Publication 800-53A
Revision 4

Assessing Security and Privacy Controls in Federal Information Systems
and Organizations — *Building Effective Assessment Plans*

- **Degree of independence of previous assessments.**

Assessor independence can be a critical factor in certain types of assessments. The degree of independence required from assessment to assessment should be consistent. For example, it is not appropriate to reuse results from a previous self-assessment where no assessor independence was required, in a current assessment requiring a greater degree of independence.

External information system-related considerations—

The assessment procedures in Appendices F and J need to be adjusted, as appropriate, to accommodate the assessment of external information systems.[34] Because the organization does not always have direct control over the security or privacy controls used in external information systems, or sufficient visibility into the development, implementation, and assessment of those controls, alternative assessment approaches may need to be applied, resulting in the need to tailor the assessment procedures described in Appendices F and J. Where required assurances of agreed-upon security or privacy controls within an information system or inherited by the system are documented in contracts or service-level agreements, assessors review these contracts or agreements, and where appropriate, tailor the assessment procedures to assess either the security or privacy controls or the security control assessment or privacy control assessment results provided through these agreements. In addition, assessors take into account any other assessments that have been conducted or are in the process of being conducted, for external information systems that are relied upon with regard to protecting the information system under assessment. Applicable information from these assessments, if deemed reliable, is incorporated into the security assessment report or privacy assessment report, as appropriate.

3.2.4 Develop assessment procedures for organization-specific controls.

Based on organizational policies, mission or business function requirements, and an assessment of risk, organizations may choose to develop and implement additional (organization-specific) security or privacy controls or control enhancements for their information systems that are beyond the scope of Special Publication 800-53. Such controls are documented in the security plan or privacy plan as controls not found in Special Publication 800-53. To assess the security or privacy controls in this situation, assessors use the guidelines in Chapter Two to develop assessment procedures for those controls and control enhancements. The assessment procedures developed are subsequently integrated into the security assessment plan or privacy assessment plan, as appropriate.

3.2.5 Optimize selected assessment procedures to ensure maximum efficiency.

Assessors have a great deal of flexibility in organizing assessment plans that meet the needs of the organization and that provide the best opportunity for obtaining the necessary evidence to determine security or privacy control effectiveness, while reducing overall assessment costs. Combining and consolidating assessment procedures is one area where this flexibility can be applied. During the assessment of an information system, assessment methods are applied numerous times to a variety of assessment objects within a particular family of security or privacy controls. To save time, reduce assessment costs, and maximize the usefulness of assessment results, assessors review the selected assessment procedures for the security or privacy control

---

[34] An *external information system* is an information system or component of an information system that is outside of the authorization boundary established by the organization and for which the organization typically has no direct control over the application of required security and privacy controls or the assessment of security and privacy control effectiveness. Special Publications 800-37 and 800-53 provide additional guidance on external information systems and the effect of employing security controls in those types of environments.

Special Publication 800-53A
Revision 4

Assessing Security and Privacy Controls in Federal Information Systems
and Organizations — *Building Effective Assessment Plans*

families and combine or consolidate the procedures (or parts of procedures) whenever possible or practicable. For example, assessors may wish to consolidate interviews with key organizational officials dealing with a variety of security- or privacy-related topics. Assessors may have other opportunities for significant consolidations and cost savings by examining all policies and procedures from the families of security controls and privacy controls at the same time or by organizing groups of related policies and procedures that could be examined as a unified entity. Obtaining and examining configuration settings from similar hardware and software components within the information system is another example that can provide significant assessment efficiencies.

An additional area for consideration in optimizing the assessment process is the sequence in which security or privacy controls are assessed. The assessment of some security controls and privacy controls before others may provide useful information that facilitates understanding and more efficient assessments of other controls. For example, security controls such as CM-2 (Baseline Configuration), CM-8 (Information System Component Inventory), PL-2 (System Security Plan), RA-2 (Security Categorization), and RA-3 (Risk Assessment) produce general descriptions of the information system. Assessing these security controls early in the assessment process may provide a basic understanding of the information system that can aid in assessing other security controls. The supplemental guidance for many security controls and privacy controls also identifies related controls that can provide useful information in organizing the assessment procedures. For example, AC-19 (Access Control for Portable and Mobile Devices) lists security controls MP-4 (Media Storage) and MP-5 (Media Transport) as being related to AC-19. Since AC-19 is related to MP-4 and MP-5, the sequence in which assessments are conducted for AC-19, MP-4, and MP-5 may facilitate the reuse of assessment information from one control in assessing other related controls.

3.2.6 *Finalize assessment plan and obtain approval to execute plan.*

After selecting the assessment procedures (including developing necessary procedures not contained in the Special Publication 800-53A catalog of procedures), tailoring the procedures for information system/platform-specific and organization-specific conditions, optimizing the procedures for efficiency, and addressing the potential for unexpected events impacting the assessment, the assessment plan is finalized, and the schedule is established including key milestones for the assessment process. Once the security assessment plan or privacy assessment plan is completed, the plan is reviewed and approved by appropriate organizational officials[35] to ensure that the plan is: (i) complete; (ii) consistent with the security or privacy objectives of the organization, as appropriate, and the organization's assessment of risk; and (iii) cost-effective with regard to the resources allocated for the assessment.

3.3 CONDUCTING SECURITY AND PRIVACY CONTROL ASSESSMENTS

After the security assessment plan or privacy assessment plan is approved by the organization, the assessor(s) or assessment team executes the plan in accordance with the agreed-upon schedule. Determining the size and organizational makeup of the assessment team (i.e., skill sets, technical expertise, and assessment experience of the individuals composing the team) is part of the risk management decisions made by the organization requesting and initiating the assessment. The

---

[35] Organizations establish a security and privacy assessment plan approval process with the specific organizational officials (e.g., information systems owners, common control providers, information system security officers, senior information security officers, senior agency officials for privacy/chief privacy officers, authorizing officials) designated as approving authorities.

Special Publication 800-53A
Revision 4

Assessing Security and Privacy Controls in Federal Information Systems
and Organizations — *Building Effective Assessment Plans*

results of security control assessments and privacy control assessments are documented in *security assessment reports* and *privacy assessment reports*, respectively, which are key inputs to the authorization package developed by information system owners and common control providers for authorizing officials.[36] Security assessment reports and privacy assessment reports include information from assessors (in the form of assessment findings) necessary to determine the effectiveness of the security or privacy controls employed within or inherited by the information system. These assessment reports are an important factor in an authorizing official's determination of risk. Organizations may choose to develop an assessment *summary* from the detailed findings that are generated by assessors during the security control assessments and privacy control assessments. An assessment summary can provide an authorizing official with an abbreviated version of an assessment report focusing on the highlights of the assessment, synopsis of key findings, and recommendations for addressing weaknesses and deficiencies in the security or privacy controls assessed. Appendix G provides information on the recommended content of assessment reports.

Assessment objectives are achieved by applying the designated assessment methods to selected assessment objects and compiling/producing the evidence necessary to make the determination associated with each assessment objective. Each determination statement contained within an assessment procedure executed by an assessor produces one of the following findings: (i) *satisfied (S)*; or (ii) *other than satisfied (O)*. A finding of satisfied indicates that for the portion of the security or privacy control addressed by the determination statement, the assessment information obtained (i.e., evidence collected) indicates that the assessment objective for the control has been met producing a fully acceptable result. A finding of other than satisfied indicates that for the portion of the security or privacy control addressed by the determination statement, the assessment information obtained indicates potential anomalies in the operation or implementation of the control that may need to be addressed by the organization. A finding of other than satisfied may also indicate that for reasons specified in the assessment report, the assessor was unable to obtain sufficient information to make the particular determination called for in the determination statement. For assessment findings that are *other than satisfied*, organizations may choose to define *subcategories* of findings indicating the severity and/or criticality of the weaknesses or deficiencies discovered and the potential adverse effects on organizational operations (i.e., mission, functions, image, or reputation), organizational assets, individuals, other organizations, and the Nation. Defining such subcategories can help to establish priorities for needed risk mitigation actions.

Assessor findings are an unbiased, factual reporting of what was found concerning the security or privacy control assessed. For each finding of other than satisfied, assessors indicate which parts of the security or privacy control are affected by the finding (i.e., aspects of the control that were deemed not satisfied or were not able to be assessed) and describe how the control differs from the planned or expected state. The potential for compromises to confidentiality, integrity, and availability due to *other than satisfied* findings are also noted by the assessor in the security or privacy assessment report. This notation reflects the lack of a specified protection and the exploitation that could occur as a result (i.e., workstation, dataset, root level access). Risk determination and acceptance activities are conducted by the organization post-assessment as part of the risk management strategy established by the organization. These risk management activities involve the senior leadership of the organization including, for example, heads of agencies, mission/business owners, information owners/stewards, risk executive (function), and

---

[36] In accordance with Special Publication 800-37, the security authorization package consists of the security plan, the security assessment report, and the plan of action and milestones (POAM).

Special Publication 800-53A
Revision 4

Assessing Security and Privacy Controls in Federal Information Systems
and Organizations — *Building Effective Assessment Plans*

authorizing officials, in consultation with appropriate organizational support staff (e.g., senior information security officers, senior agency officials for privacy/chief privacy officers, chief information officers, information system owners, common control providers, and assessors). Security control assessment and privacy control assessment results are documented at the level of detail appropriate for the assessment in accordance with the reporting format prescribed by organizational policy, NIST guidelines, and OMB policy. The reporting format is appropriate for the type of assessment conducted (e.g., self-assessments by information system owners and common control providers, independent verification and validation, independent assessments supporting the authorization process, automated assessments, or independent audits or inspections).

Information system owners and common control providers rely on the expertise and the technical judgment of assessors to: (i) assess the security and privacy controls in the information system and inherited by the system; and (ii) provide recommendations on how to correct weaknesses or deficiencies in the controls and reduce or eliminate identified vulnerabilities. The assessment results produced by the assessor (i.e., findings of *satisfied* or *other than satisfied*, identification of the parts of the security or privacy control that did not produce a satisfactory result, and a description of resulting potential for compromises to the information system or its environment of operation) are provided to information system owners and common control providers in the initial security assessment reports and privacy assessment reports. System owners and common control providers may choose to act on selected recommendations of the assessor before the assessment reports are finalized if there are specific opportunities to correct weaknesses or deficiencies in the security or privacy controls or to correct and/or clarify misunderstandings or interpretations of assessment results.[37] Security or privacy controls that are modified, enhanced, or added during this process are reassessed by the assessor prior to the production of the final assessment reports.

3.4 ANALYZING ASSESSMENT REPORT RESULTS

The results of security control assessments and privacy control assessments ultimately influence control implementations, the content of security plans and privacy plans, and the respective plans of action and milestones. Accordingly, information system owners and common control providers review the security assessment reports and privacy assessment reports and the updated risk assessment and with the concurrence of designated organizational officials (e.g., authorizing officials, chief information officer, senior information security officer, senior agency officials for privacy/chief privacy officers, mission/information owners), determine the appropriate steps required to respond to those weaknesses and deficiencies identified during the assessment. By using the labels of *satisfied* and *other than satisfied*, the reporting format for the assessment findings provides visibility for organizational officials into specific weaknesses and deficiencies in security or privacy controls within the information system or inherited by the system and facilitates a disciplined and structured approach to responding to risks in accordance with organizational priorities. For example, information system owners or common control providers in consultation with designated organizational officials, may decide that certain assessment

---

[37] The correction of weaknesses or deficiencies in security or privacy controls or carrying out recommendations during the review of the initial security assessment reports or privacy assessment reports by information system owners or common control providers is not intended to replace the formal risk response process by the organization which occurs after the delivery of the final reports. Rather, it provides the information system owner or common control provider with an opportunity to address weaknesses or deficiencies that may be quickly corrected. However, in situations where limited resources exist for remediating weaknesses and deficiencies discovered during the security control assessments or privacy control assessments, organizations may decide without prejudice that waiting for the risk assessment to prioritize remediation efforts is the better course of action.

Special Publication 800-53A
Revision 4

Assessing Security and Privacy Controls in Federal Information Systems
and Organizations — *Building Effective Assessment Plans*

findings marked as other than satisfied are of an inconsequential nature and present no significant risk to the organization. Conversely, system owners or common control providers may decide that certain findings marked as other than satisfied are significant, requiring immediate remediation actions. In all cases, the organization reviews each assessor finding of other than satisfied and applies its judgment with regard to the severity or seriousness of the finding and whether the finding is significant enough to be worthy of further investigation or remedial action.[38]

Senior leadership involvement in the mitigation process may be necessary in order to ensure that the organization's resources are effectively allocated in accordance with organizational priorities, providing resources first to the information systems that are supporting the most critical and sensitive missions for the organization or correcting the deficiencies that pose the greatest degree of risk. Ultimately, the assessment findings and any subsequent mitigation actions (informed by the updated risk assessment) initiated by information system owners or common control providers in collaboration with designated organizational officials, trigger updates to the key documents used by authorizing officials to determine the security or privacy status of the information system and its suitability for authorization to operate. These documents include security plans and privacy plans, security assessment reports and privacy assessment reports, and the respective plans of action and milestones.

3.5 ASSESSING SECURITY AND PRIVACY CAPABILITIES

In accordance with NIST Special Publication 800-53, organizations may define a set of security capabilities or privacy capabilities as a precursor to the security control or privacy control selection process. The concept of *capability*[39] recognizes that the protection of information being processed, stored, or transmitted by information systems, seldom derives from a single security safeguard or countermeasure. In most cases, such protection results from the selection and implementation of a set of mutually reinforcing security controls and privacy controls. Each control contributes to the overall organization-defined capability—with some controls potentially contributing to a greater degree and other controls contributing to a lesser degree. For example, organizations may wish to define a capability for *secure remote authentication*. This capability can be achieved by the implementation of a set of security controls from Special Publication 800-53, Appendix F (i.e., IA-2[1], IA-2[2], IA-2[8], IA-2[9], and SC-8[1]).

Security and privacy capabilities can address a variety of areas that can include technical means, physical means, procedural means, or any combination thereof. By employing the capability concept, organizations can obtain greater visibility into and a better understanding of: (i) the relationships (i.e., dependencies) among controls; (ii) the effects of specific control failures on organization-defined capabilities; and (iii) the potential severity of control weaknesses or deficiencies. However, this approach may add complexity to assessments and necessitate root cause failure analysis when specific capabilities are affected by the failure of particular security or privacy controls in order to determine which control or controls are contributing to the failure. The greater the number of controls included in an organization-defined capability, the more difficult it may be to ascertain the root cause of failures. There may also be interactions among defined capabilities which may contribute to the complexity of assessments. If it is found that a

---

[38] Potential risk response actions include risk acceptance, risk mitigation, risk rejection, and risk transfer/sharing. NIST Special Publication 800-39 provides guidance on risk response actions from a risk management perspective.

[39] A *security capability* or *privacy capability* is a combination of mutually reinforcing security controls or privacy controls (i.e., safeguards and countermeasures) implemented by technical means (i.e., functionality in hardware, software, and firmware), physical means (i.e., physical devices and protective measures), and procedural means (i.e., procedures performed by individuals).

Special Publication 800-53A
Revision 4

Assessing Security and Privacy Controls in Federal Information Systems
and Organizations — *Building Effective Assessment Plans*

control is neither contributing to a defined capability nor to the overall security of the system, the organization revisits RMF Step 2, tailoring the control set and documenting the rationale in the security plan.

Traditionally, assessments have been conducted on a control-by-control basis producing results that are characterized as pass (i.e., control satisfied) or fail (i.e., control not satisfied). However, the failure of a single control or in some cases, the failure of multiple controls, may *not* affect the overall security capability or privacy capability required by an organization. This is not to say that such controls are not *contributing* to the security or privacy of the system and/or organization (as defined by the security requirements and privacy requirements during the initiation phase of the system development life cycle), but rather that such controls may not be supporting the particular security capability or privacy capability. Furthermore, every implemented security control or privacy control may not necessarily support or need to support an organization-defined capability.

When organizations employ the concept of capabilities, both automated and manual assessments take into account all security controls and privacy controls that comprise the security or privacy capabilities. Assessors are aware of how the controls work together to provide such capabilities. In this way, when assessments identify a failure in a capability, a root cause analysis can be conducted to determine the specific control or controls that are responsible for the failure based on the established relationships among controls. Moreover, employing the broader capability construct allows organizations to assess the *severity* of vulnerabilities discovered in their systems and organizations and determine if the failure of a particular security control or privacy control (associated with a vulnerability) or the decision not to deploy a certain control during the initial tailoring process (RMF Select step), affects the overall capability needed for mission/business protection. For example, the failure of a security control deemed critical for a particular security capability may be assigned a higher severity rating than a failed control of lesser importance to the capability.

Ultimately, authorization decisions (i.e., risk acceptance decisions) are made based on the degree to which the desired security capabilities and privacy capabilities have been effectively achieved and are meeting the security requirements and privacy requirements defined by an organization. These risk-based decisions are directly related to organizational risk tolerance that is defined as part of an organization's risk management strategy.

CAPABILITY-BASED ASSESSMENTS

The grouping of controls into security capabilities and privacy capabilities necessitates the conduct of *root cause* analyses to determine if the failure of a particular security or privacy capability can be traced to the failure of one or more security or privacy controls based on the established relationships among controls. The structure of the assessment procedures in this publication with the token-level decomposition and labelling of assessment objectives linked to the specific content of security and privacy controls, supports such root cause analysis. Thus, assessments of security and privacy controls (defined as part of capabilities) can be tailored based on the guidance in Section 3.2.3 and Special Publication 800-137, to define the resource expenditures (e.g., frequency and level of effort) associated with such assessments. This additional precision in assessments is essential in supporting the continuous monitoring strategies developed by organizations and the ongoing authorization decisions by senior leaders.

Special Publication 800-53A
Revision 4

Assessing Security and Privacy Controls in Federal Information Systems
and Organizations — *Building Effective Assessment Plans*

Figure 3 summarizes the security control and privacy control assessment process including the activities carried out during pre-assessment, assessment, and post-assessment.

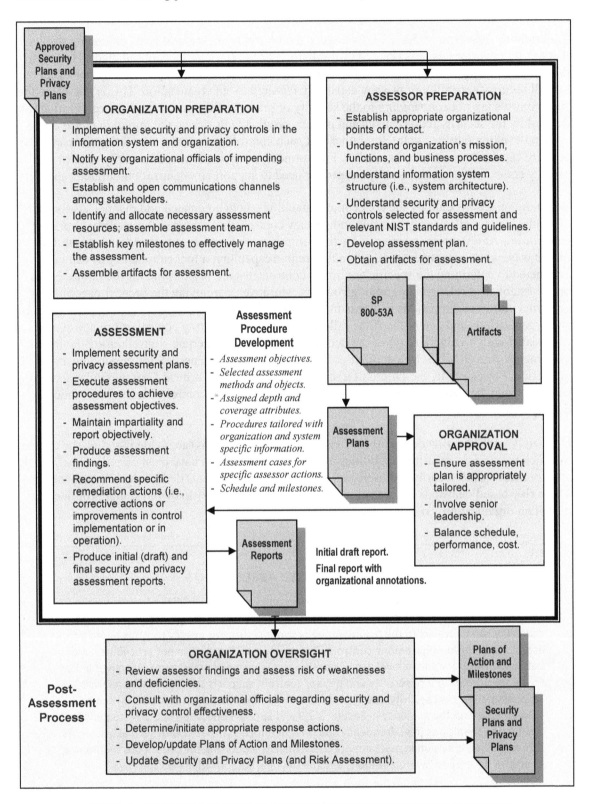

FIGURE 3: SECURITY AND PRIVACY CONTROL ASSESSMENT PROCESS OVERVIEW

Special Publication 800-53A
Revision 4

Assessing Security and Privacy Controls in Federal Information Systems
and Organizations — *Building Effective Assessment Plans*

APPENDIX A

REFERENCES

LAWS, POLICIES, DIRECTIVES, INSTRUCTIONS, STANDARDS, AND GUIDELINES

LEGISLATION

1. E-Government Act [includes FISMA] (P.L. 107-347), December
   2002. http://www.gpo.gov/fdsys/pkg/PLAW-107publ347/pdf/PLAW-107publ347.pdf
   (accessed 12/4/14).

2. Federal Information Security Management Act (P.L. 107-347, Title III), December
   2002. http://www.gpo.gov/fdsys/pkg/PLAW-107publ347/pdf/PLAW-107publ347.pdf
   (accessed 12/4/14).

3. Privacy Act of 1974 (P.L. 93-579), December 1974.
   http://www.justice.gov/opcl/privacy-act-1974 (accessed 12/4/14).

POLICIES, DIRECTIVES, INSTRUCTIONS

1. Committee on National Security Systems (CNSS) Instruction 4009, *National Information
   Assurance Glossary*, April 2010.
   https://www.cnss.gov/CNSS/issuances/Instructions.cfm (accessed 12/4/14).

2. Committee on National Security Systems (CNSS) Instruction 1253, *Security
   Categorization and Control Selection for National Security Systems*, March 2014.
   https://www.cnss.gov/CNSS/issuances/Instructions.cfm (accessed 12/4/14).

3. Office of Management and Budget, Circular A-130, Appendix I, Transmittal
   Memorandum #4, *Federal Agency Responsibilities for Maintaining Records About
   Individual*, November 2000.
   http://www.whitehouse.gov/omb/circulars_a130_a130appendix_i (accessed 12/4/14).

4. Office of Management and Budget, Circular A-130, Appendix III, Transmittal
   Memorandum #4, *Management of Federal Information Resources*, November 2000.
   http://www.whitehouse.gov/omb/circulars_a130_a130appendix_iii (accessed 12/4/14).

5. Office of Management and Budget Memorandum M-02-01, *Guidance for Preparing and
   Submitting Security Plans of Action and Milestones*, October 2001.
   http://www.whitehouse.gov/omb/memoranda_m02-01 (accessed 12/4/14).

STANDARDS

1. National Institute of Standards and Technology Federal Information Processing
   Standards Publication 199, *Standards for Security Categorization of Federal Information
   and Information Systems*, February 2004.
   http://csrc.nist.gov/publications/fips/fips199/FIPS-PUB-199-final.pdf (accessed 12/4/14).

2. National Institute of Standards and Technology Federal Information Processing
   Standards Publication 200, *Minimum Security Requirements for Federal Information and
   Information Systems*, March 2006.
   http://csrc.nist.gov/publications/fips/fips200/FIPS-200-final-march.pdf (accessed
   12/4/14).

3. ISO/IEC 15408, *Common Criteria for Information Technology Security Evaluation*, (as
   amended).

Special Publication 800-53A
Revision 4

Assessing Security and Privacy Controls in Federal Information Systems
and Organizations — *Building Effective Assessment Plans*

GUIDELINES

1. National Institute of Standards and Technology Special Publication 800-18, Revision 1, *Guide for Developing Security Plans for Federal Information Systems*, February 2006. http://csrc.nist.gov/publications/nistpubs/800-18-Rev1/sp800-18-Rev1-final.pdf (accessed 12/4/14).

2. National Institute of Standards and Technology Special Publication 800-30, Revision 1, *Guide for Conducting Risk Assessments*, September 2012. http://csrc.nist.gov/publications/nistpubs/800-30-rev1/sp800_30_r1.pdf (accessed 12/4/14).

3. National Institute of Standards and Technology Special Publication 800-37, Revision 1, *Guide for Applying the Risk Management Framework to Federal Information Systems: A Security Life Cycle Approach*, February 2010. http://dx.doi.org/10.6028/NIST.SP.800-37r1.

4. National Institute of Standards and Technology Special Publication 800-39, *Managing Information Security Risk: Organization, Mission, and Information System View*, March 2011. http://csrc.nist.gov/publications/nistpubs/800-39/SP800-39-final.pdf (accessed 12/4/14).

5. National Institute of Standards and Technology Special Publication 800-40, Revision 3, *Guide to Enterprise Patch Management Technologies*, July 2013. http://dx.doi.org/10.6028/NIST.SP.800-40r3.

6. National Institute of Standards and Technology Special Publication 800-53, Revision 4, *Security and Privacy Controls for Federal Information Systems and Organizations*, April 2013. http://dx.doi.org/10.6028/NIST.SP.800-53r4.

7. National Institute of Standards and Technology Special Publication 800-59, *Guideline for Identifying an Information System as a National Security System*, August 2003. http://csrc.nist.gov/publications/nistpubs/800-59/SP800-59.pdf (accessed 12/4/14).

8. National Institute of Standards and Technology Special Publication 800-60, Revision 1, *Guide for Mapping Types of Information and Information Systems to Security Categories*, August 2008. http://csrc.nist.gov/publications/PubsSPs.html#800-60 (accessed 12/4/14).

9. National Institute of Standards and Technology Special Publication 800-64, Revision 2, *Security Considerations in the System Development Life Cycle*, October 2008. http://csrc.nist.gov/publications/nistpubs/800-64-Rev2/SP800-64-Revision2.pdf (accessed 12/4/14).

10. National Institute of Standards and Technology Special Publication 800-115, *Technical Guide to Information Security Testing and Assessment*, September 2008. http://csrc.nist.gov/publications/nistpubs/800-115/SP800-115.pdf (accessed 12/4/14).

11. National Institute of Standards and Technology Special Publication 800-126, Revision 2, *The Technical Specification for the Security Content Automation Protocol (SCAP): SCAP Version 1.2*, September 2011. http://csrc.nist.gov/publications/nistpubs/800-126-rev2/SP800-126r2.pdf

Special Publication 800-53A
Revision 4

Assessing Security and Privacy Controls in Federal Information Systems
and Organizations — *Building Effective Assessment Plans*

12. National Institute of Standards and Technology Special Publication 800-137, *Information Security Continuous Monitoring for Federal Information Systems and Organizations*, September 2011.
http://csrc.nist.gov/publications/nistpubs/800-137/SP800-137-Final.pdf (accessed 12/4/14).

Special Publication 800-53A
Revision 4

Assessing Security and Privacy Controls in Federal Information Systems
and Organizations — *Building Effective Assessment Plans*

APPENDIX B

GLOSSARY

COMMON TERMS AND DEFINITIONS

This appendix provides definitions for security terminology used within Special Publication 800-53A. The terms in the glossary are consistent with the terms used in the suite of FISMA-related security standards and guidelines developed by NIST. Unless otherwise stated, all terms used in this publication are also consistent with the definitions contained in the CNSS Instruction 4009, *National Information Assurance Glossary*.

Activities	An assessment object that includes specific protection-related pursuits or actions supporting an information system that involve people (e.g., conducting system backup operations, monitoring network traffic).
Adequate Security [OMB Circular A-130, Appendix III]	Security commensurate with the risk and the magnitude of harm resulting from the loss, misuse, or unauthorized access to or modification of information.
Agency	See *Executive Agency*.
Assessment	See *Security Control Assessment* or *Privacy Control Assessment*.
Assessment Findings	Assessment results produced by the application of an assessment procedure to a security control, privacy control, or control enhancement to achieve an assessment objective; the execution of a determination statement within an assessment procedure by an assessor that results in either a *satisfied* or *other than satisfied* condition.
Assessment Method	One of three types of actions (i.e., examine, interview, test) taken by assessors in obtaining evidence during an assessment.
Assessment Object	The item (i.e., specifications, mechanisms, activities, individuals) upon which an assessment method is applied during an assessment.
Assessment Objective	A set of determination statements that expresses the desired outcome for the assessment of a security control, privacy control, or control enhancement.
Assessment Procedure	A set of assessment *objectives* and an associated set of assessment *methods* and assessment *objects*.
Assessor	See *Security Control Assessor* or *Privacy Control Assessor*.
Assurance	The grounds for confidence that the set of intended security controls or privacy controls in an information system or organization are effective in their application.

Special Publication 800-53A
Revision 4

Assessing Security and Privacy Controls in Federal Information Systems
and Organizations — *Building Effective Assessment Plans*

Assurance Case [Software Engineering Institute, Carnegie Mellon University]	A structured set of arguments and a body of evidence showing that an information system satisfies specific claims with respect to a given quality attribute.
Authentication [FIPS 200]	Verifying the identity of a user, process, or device, often as a prerequisite to allowing access to resources in an information system.
Authenticity	The property of being genuine and being able to be verified and trusted; confidence in the validity of a transmission, a message, or message originator. See Authentication.
Authorization (to operate) [NIST SP 800-37, Adapted]	The official management decision given by a senior organizational official to authorize operation of an information system and to explicitly accept the risk to organizational operations (including mission, functions, image, or reputation), organizational assets, individuals, other organizations, and the Nation based on the implementation of an agreed-upon set of security controls and privacy controls.
Authorization Boundary [NIST SP 800-37]	All components of an information system to be authorized for operation by an authorizing official and excludes separately authorized systems, to which the information system is connected.
Authorizing Official [NIST SP 800-37]	A senior (federal) official or executive with the authority to formally assume responsibility for operating an information system at an acceptable level of risk to organizational operations (including mission, functions, image, or reputation), organizational assets, individuals, other organizations, and the Nation.
Authorizing Official Designated Representative [NIST SP 800-37, Adapted]	An organizational official acting on behalf of an authorizing official in carrying out and coordinating the required activities associated with security authorization or privacy authorization.
Availability [44 U.S.C., Sec. 3542]	Ensuring timely and reliable access to and use of information.
Basic Testing	A test methodology that assumes no knowledge of the internal structure and implementation detail of the assessment object. Also known as black box testing.
Black Box Testing	See *Basic Testing*.

Special Publication 800-53A
Revision 4

Assessing Security and Privacy Controls in Federal Information Systems
and Organizations — *Building Effective Assessment Plans*

Chief Information Officer [PL 104-106, Sec. 5125(b)]	Agency official responsible for: (i) Providing advice and other assistance to the head of the executive agency and other senior management personnel of the agency to ensure that information technology is acquired and information resources are managed in a manner that is consistent with laws, Executive Orders, directives, policies, regulations, and priorities established by the head of the agency; (ii) Developing, maintaining, and facilitating the implementation of a sound and integrated information technology architecture for the agency; and (iii) Promoting the effective and efficient design and operation of all major information resources management processes for the agency, including improvements to work processes of the agency.
Chief Information Security Officer	See *Senior Agency Information Security Officer.*
Chief Privacy Officer	See *Senior Agency Official for Privacy.*
Common Control [NIST SP 800-37, Adapted]	A security control or privacy control that is inherited by one or more organizational information systems. See *Security Control Inheritance* or *Privacy Control Inheritance.*
Common Control Provider [NIST SP 800-37, Adapted]	An organizational official responsible for the development, implementation, assessment, and monitoring of common controls (i.e., security controls and privacy controls inherited by information systems).
Compensating Security Controls [NIST SP 800-53]	The security controls employed in lieu of the recommended controls in the security control baselines described in NIST Special Publication 800-53 and CNSS Instruction 1253 that provide equivalent or comparable protection for an information system or organization.
Comprehensive Testing	A test methodology that assumes explicit and substantial knowledge of the internal structure and implementation detail of the assessment object. Also known as white box testing.
Confidentiality [44 U.S.C., Sec. 3542]	Preserving authorized restrictions on information access and disclosure, including means for protecting personal privacy and proprietary information.

Special Publication 800-53A
Revision 4

Assessing Security and Privacy Controls in Federal Information Systems
and Organizations — *Building Effective Assessment Plans*

Controlled Unclassified Information	A categorical designation that refers to unclassified information that does not meet the standards for National Security Classification under Executive Order 12958, as amended, but is (i) pertinent to the national interests of the United States or to the important interests of entities outside the federal government, and (ii) under law or policy requires protection from unauthorized disclosure, special handling safeguards, or prescribed limits on exchange or dissemination. Henceforth, the designation CUI replaces *Sensitive But Unclassified (SBU)*.
Coverage	An attribute associated with an assessment method that addresses the scope or breadth of the assessment objects included in the assessment (e.g., types of objects to be assessed and the number of objects to be assessed by type). The values for the coverage attribute, hierarchically from less coverage to more coverage, are basic, focused, and comprehensive.
Depth	An attribute associated with an assessment method that addresses the rigor and level of detail associated with the application of the method. The values for the depth attribute, hierarchically from less depth to more depth, are basic, focused, and comprehensive.
Environment of Operation [NIST SP 800-37]	The physical surroundings in which an information system processes, stores, and transmits information.
Examine	A type of assessment method that is characterized by the process of checking, inspecting, reviewing, observing, studying, or analyzing one or more assessment objects to facilitate understanding, achieve clarification, or obtain evidence, the results of which are used to support the determination of security control or privacy control effectiveness over time.
Executive Agency [41 U.S.C., Sec. 403]	An executive department specified in 5 U.S.C., Sec. 101; a military department specified in 5 U.S.C., Sec. 102; an independent establishment as defined in 5 U.S.C., Sec. 104(1); and a wholly owned Government corporation fully subject to the provisions of 31 U.S.C., Chapter 91.
Federal Agency	See *Executive Agency*.
Federal Information System [40 U.S.C., Sec. 11331]	An information system used or operated by an executive agency, by a contractor of an executive agency, or by another organization on behalf of an executive agency.
Focused Testing	A test methodology that assumes some knowledge of the internal structure and implementation detail of the assessment object. Also known as gray box testing.
Gray Box Testing	See *Focused Testing*.

Special Publication 800-53A
Revision 4

Assessing Security and Privacy Controls in Federal Information Systems
and Organizations — *Building Effective Assessment Plans*

Hybrid Control [NIST SP 800-53, Adapted]	A security control or privacy control that is implemented in an information system in part as a common control and in part as a system-specific control. See *Common Control* and *System-Specific Security Control*.
Individuals	An assessment object that includes people applying specifications, mechanisms, or activities.
Industrial Control System	An information system used to control industrial processes such as manufacturing, product handling, production, and distribution. Industrial control systems include supervisory control and data acquisition systems used to control geographically dispersed assets, as well as distributed control systems and smaller control systems using programmable logic controllers to control localized processes.
Information [FIPS 199]	An instance of an information type.
Information Owner [CNSSI 4009]	Official with statutory or operational authority for specified information and responsibility for establishing the controls for its generation, collection, processing, dissemination, and disposal.
Information Resources [44 U.S.C., Sec. 3502]	Information and related resources, such as personnel, equipment, funds, and information technology.
Information Security [44 U.S.C., Sec. 3542]	The protection of information and information systems from unauthorized access, use, disclosure, disruption, modification, or destruction in order to provide confidentiality, integrity, and availability.
Information Security Program Plan [NIST SP 800-53]	Formal document that provides an overview of the security requirements for an organization-wide information security program and describes the program management controls and common controls in place or planned for meeting those requirements.
Information System [44 U.S.C., Sec. 3502]	A discrete set of information resources organized for the collection, processing, maintenance, use, sharing, dissemination, or disposition of information.
Information System Boundary	See *Authorization Boundary*.
Information System Owner (or Program Manager)	Official responsible for the overall procurement, development, integration, modification, or operation and maintenance of an information system.
Information System Security Officer	Individual assigned responsibility by the senior agency information security officer, authorizing official, management official, or information system owner for maintaining the appropriate operational security posture for an information system or program.

Special Publication 800-53A
Revision 4

Assessing Security and Privacy Controls in Federal Information Systems
and Organizations — *Building Effective Assessment Plans*

Information System-related Security Risks	Information system-related security risks are those risks that arise through the loss of confidentiality, integrity, or availability of information or information systems and consider impacts to the organization (including assets, mission, functions, image, or reputation), individuals, other organizations, and the Nation. See *Risk*.
Information Technology [40 U.S.C., Sec. 1401]	Any equipment or interconnected system or subsystem of equipment that is used in the automatic acquisition, storage, manipulation, management, movement, control, display, switching, interchange, transmission, or reception of data or information by the executive agency. For purposes of the preceding sentence, equipment is used by an executive agency if the equipment is used by the executive agency directly or is used by a contractor under a contract with the executive agency which: (i) requires the use of such equipment; or (ii) requires the use, to a significant extent, of such equipment in the performance of a service or the furnishing of a product. The term information technology includes computers, ancillary equipment, software, firmware, and similar procedures, services (including support services), and related resources.
Information Type [FIPS 199]	A specific category of information (e.g., privacy, medical, proprietary, financial, investigative, contractor sensitive, security management) defined by an organization or in some instances, by a specific law, Executive Order, directive, policy, or regulation.
Integrity [44 U.S.C., Sec. 3542]	Guarding against improper information modification or destruction, and includes ensuring information non-repudiation and authenticity.
Interview	A type of assessment method that is characterized by the process of conducting discussions with individuals or groups within an organization to facilitate understanding, achieve clarification, or lead to the location of evidence, the results of which are used to support the determination of security control and privacy control effectiveness over time.
Mechanisms	An assessment object that includes specific protection-related items (e.g., hardware, software, or firmware) employed within or at the boundary of an information system.
Ongoing Assessment	The continuous evaluation of the effectiveness of security control or privacy control implementation; with respect to security controls, a subset of Information Security Continuous Monitoring (ISCM) activities.

Special Publication 800-53A
Revision 4

Assessing Security and Privacy Controls in Federal Information Systems
and Organizations — *Building Effective Assessment Plans*

National Security Information	Information that has been determined pursuant to Executive Order 12958 as amended by Executive Order 13292, or any predecessor order, or by the Atomic Energy Act of 1954, as amended, to require protection against unauthorized disclosure and is marked to indicate its classified status.
National Security System [44 U.S.C., Sec. 3542]	Any information system (including any telecommunications system) used or operated by an agency or by a contractor of an agency, or other organization on behalf of an agency—(i) the function, operation, or use of which involves intelligence activities; involves cryptologic activities related to national security; involves command and control of military forces; involves equipment that is an integral part of a weapon or weapons system; or is critical to the direct fulfillment of military or intelligence missions (excluding a system that is to be used for routine administrative and business applications, for example, payroll, finance, logistics, and personnel management applications); or (ii) is protected at all times by procedures established for information that have been specifically authorized under criteria established by an Executive Order or an Act of Congress to be kept classified in the interest of national defense or foreign policy.
Organization [FIPS 200, Adapted]	An entity of any size, complexity, or positioning within an organizational structure (e.g., a federal agency or, as appropriate, any of its operational elements).
Penetration Testing	A test methodology in which assessors, using all available documentation (e.g., system design, source code, manuals) and working under specific constraints, attempt to circumvent the security features of an information system.
Plan of Action and Milestones [OMB Memorandum 02-01]	A document that identifies tasks needing to be accomplished. It details resources required to accomplish the elements of the plan, any milestones in meeting the tasks, and scheduled completion dates for the milestones.
Privacy Capability	A combination of mutually-reinforcing privacy controls (i.e., safeguards and countermeasures) implemented by technical means (i.e., functionality in hardware, software, and firmware), physical means (i.e., physical devices and protective measures), and procedural means (i.e., procedures performed by individuals).
Privacy Control Assessment	The testing or evaluation of privacy controls to determine the extent to which the controls are implemented correctly, operating as intended, and producing the desired outcome with respect to meeting the privacy requirements for an information system or organization.

Special Publication 800-53A
Revision 4

Assessing Security and Privacy Controls in Federal Information Systems
and Organizations — *Building Effective Assessment Plans*

Privacy Control Assessor	The individual, group, or organization responsible for conducting a privacy control assessment.
Privacy Control Enhancements	Statements of privacy capability to: (i) build in additional, but related, functionality to a basic control; and/or (ii) increase the strength of a basic control.
Privacy Control Inheritance	A situation in which an information system or application receives protection from privacy controls (or portions of privacy controls) that are developed, implemented, assessed, authorized, and monitored by entities other than those responsible for the system or application; entities either internal or external to the organization where the system or application resides. *See Common Control.*
Privacy Plan	Formal document that provides an overview of the privacy requirements for an information system or program and describes the privacy controls in place or planned for meeting those requirements. The privacy plan may be integrated into the organizational security plan or developed as a separate plan.
Privacy Requirements	Requirements levied on an organization, information program, or information system that are derived from applicable laws, Executive Orders, directives, policies, standards, instructions, regulations, procedures, or organizational mission/business case needs to ensure that privacy protections are implemented in the collection, use, sharing, storage, transmittal, and disposal of information.
Reciprocity	Mutual agreement among participating organizations to accept each other's security assessments in order to reuse information system resources and/or to accept each other's assessed security posture in order to share information.
Records	The recordings (automated and/or manual) of evidence of activities performed or results achieved (e.g., forms, reports, test results), which serve as a basis for verifying that the organization and the information system are performing as intended. Also used to refer to units of related data fields (i.e., groups of data fields that can be accessed by a program and that contain the complete set of information on particular items).

Special Publication 800-53A
Revision 4

Assessing Security and Privacy Controls in Federal Information Systems
and Organizations — *Building Effective Assessment Plans*

Risk
[CNSSI 4009]

A measure of the extent to which an entity is threatened by a potential circumstance or event, and typically a function of: (i) the adverse impacts that would arise if the circumstance or event occurs; and (ii) the likelihood of occurrence.

[Note: Information system-related security risks are those risks that arise from the loss of confidentiality, integrity, or availability of information or information systems and reflect the potential adverse impacts to organizational operations (including mission, functions, image, or reputation), organizational assets, individuals, other organizations, and the Nation. Adverse impacts to the Nation include, for example, compromises to information systems that support critical infrastructure applications or are paramount to government continuity of operations as defined by the Department of Homeland Security.]

Risk Assessment

The process of identifying risks to organizational operations (including mission, functions, image, reputation), organizational assets, individuals, other organizations, and the Nation, resulting from the operation of an information system.

Part of risk management, incorporates threat and vulnerability analyses, and considers mitigations provided by security controls or privacy controls planned or in place. Synonymous with risk analysis.

Risk Executive (Function)
[NIST SP 800-37, Adapted]

An individual or group within an organization that helps to ensure that: (i) security and privacy risk-related considerations for individual information systems, to include the authorization decisions, are viewed from an organization-wide perspective with regard to the overall strategic goals and objectives of the organization in carrying out its missions and business functions; and (ii) managing information system-related security and privacy risks is consistent across the organization, reflects organizational risk tolerance, and is considered along with other organizational risks affecting mission/business success.

Risk Management
[CNSSI 4009, Adapted]

The process of managing risks to organizational operations (including mission, functions, image, reputation), organizational assets, individuals, other organizations, and the Nation, resulting from the operation of an information system, and includes: (i) the conduct of a risk assessment; (ii) the implementation of a risk mitigation strategy; and (iii) employment of techniques and procedures for the continuous monitoring of the security and privacy state of the information system.

Security Authorization

See *Authorization*.

Special Publication 800-53A
Revision 4

Assessing Security and Privacy Controls in Federal Information Systems
and Organizations — *Building Effective Assessment Plans*

Security Capability	A combination of mutually-reinforcing security controls (i.e., safeguards and countermeasures) implemented by technical means (i.e., functionality in hardware, software, and firmware), physical means (i.e., physical devices and protective measures), and procedural means (i.e., procedures performed by individuals).
Security Categorization	The process of determining the security category for information or an information system. Security categorization methodologies are described in CNSS Instruction 1253 for national security systems and in FIPS 199 for other than national security systems.
Security Control Assessment	The testing or evaluation of security controls to determine the extent to which the controls are implemented correctly, operating as intended, and producing the desired outcome with respect to meeting the security requirements for an information system or organization.
Security Control Assessor	The individual, group, or organization responsible for conducting a security control assessment.
Security Control Baseline [FIPS 200, Adapted]	One of the sets of minimum security controls defined for federal information systems in NIST Special Publication 800-53 and CNSS Instruction 1253.
Security Control Enhancements	Statements of security capability to: (i) build in additional, but related, functionality to a basic control; and/or (ii) increase the strength of a basic control.
Security Control Inheritance	A situation in which an information system or application receives protection from security controls (or portions of security controls) that are developed, implemented, assessed, authorized, and monitored by entities other than those responsible for the system or application; entities either internal or external to the organization where the system or application resides. See *Common Control*.
Security Controls [NIST SP 800-53]	A safeguard or countermeasure prescribed for an information system or an organization designed to protect the confidentiality, integrity, and availability of its information and to meet a set of defined security requirements.
Security Impact Analysis [NIST SP 800-37]	The analysis conducted by an organizational official to determine the extent to which changes to the information system have affected the security state of the system.
Security Objective [FIPS 199]	Confidentiality, integrity, or availability.

Special Publication 800-53A
Revision 4

Assessing Security and Privacy Controls in Federal Information Systems
and Organizations — *Building Effective Assessment Plans*

Security Plan [NIST SP 800-18]	Formal document that provides an overview of the security requirements for an information system or an information security program and describes the security controls in place or planned for meeting those requirements.
	See *System Security Plan* or *Information Security Program Plan*.
Security Requirements [FIPS 200]	Requirements levied on an information system that are derived from applicable laws, Executive Orders, directives, policies, standards, instructions, regulations, procedures, or organizational mission/business case needs to ensure the confidentiality, integrity, and availability of the information being processed, stored, or transmitted.
Senior Agency Information Security Officer [44 U.S.C., Sec. 3544]	Official responsible for carrying out the Chief Information Officer responsibilities under FISMA and serving as the Chief Information Officer's primary liaison to the agency's authorizing officials, information system owners, and information system security officers.
	[Note: Organizations subordinate to federal agencies may use the term *Senior Information Security Officer* or *Chief Information Security Officer* to denote individuals filling positions with similar responsibilities to Senior Agency Information Security Officers.]
Senior Agency Official for Privacy	The senior organizational official with overall organization-wide responsibility for information privacy issues.
Senior Information Security Officer	See *Senior Agency Information Security Officer*.
Specification	An assessment object that includes document-based artifacts (e.g., policies, procedures, plans, system security requirements, functional specifications, architectural designs) associated with an information system.
Subsystem	A major subdivision or component of an information system consisting of information, information technology, and personnel that performs one or more specific functions.
System	See *Information System*.
System Security Plan [NIST SP 800-18]	Formal document that provides an overview of the security requirements for an information system and describes the security controls in place or planned for meeting those requirements.
System-Specific Control [NIST SP 800-37, Adapted]	A security control or privacy control for an information system that has not been designated as a common control or the portion of a hybrid control that is to be implemented within an information system.

Special Publication 800-53A
Revision 4

Assessing Security and Privacy Controls in Federal Information Systems
and Organizations — *Building Effective Assessment Plans*

Tailoring [NIST SP 800-53]	The process by which security control baselines are modified by: (i) identifying and designating common controls; (ii) applying scoping considerations on the applicability and implementation of baseline controls; (iii) selecting compensating security controls; (iv) assigning specific values to organization-defined security control parameters; (v) supplementing baselines with additional security controls or control enhancements; and (vi) providing additional specification information for control implementation. [Note: Certain tailoring activities can also be applied to privacy controls.]
Tailoring (Assessment Procedures)	The process by which assessment procedures defined in Special Publication 800-53A are adjusted, or scoped, to match the characteristics of the information system under assessment, providing organizations with the flexibility needed to meet specific organizational requirements and to avoid overly-constrained assessment approaches.
Tailored Security Control Baseline	A set of security controls resulting from the application of tailoring guidance to the security control baseline. See *Tailoring*.
Test	A type of assessment method that is characterized by the process of exercising one or more assessment objects under specified conditions to compare actual with expected behavior, the results of which are used to support the determination of security control or privacy control effectiveness over time.
Threat [CNSSI 4009]	Any circumstance or event with the potential to adversely impact organizational operations (including mission, functions, image, or reputation), organizational assets, individuals, other organizations, or the Nation through an information system via unauthorized access, destruction, disclosure, modification of information, and/or denial of service.
Threat Assessment [CNSSI 4009]	Process of formally evaluating the degree of threat to an information system or enterprise and describing the nature of the threat.
Threat Source [FIPS 200]	The intent and method targeted at the intentional exploitation of a vulnerability or a situation and method that may accidentally trigger a vulnerability. Synonymous with threat agent.
Vulnerability [CNSSI 4009]	Weakness in an information system, system security procedures, internal controls, or implementation that could be exploited or triggered by a threat source.

Special Publication 800-53A
Revision 4

Assessing Security and Privacy Controls in Federal Information Systems
and Organizations — *Building Effective Assessment Plans*

Vulnerability Assessment [CNSSI 4009, Adapted]	Systematic examination of an information system or product to determine the adequacy of security and privacy measures, identify security and privacy deficiencies, provide data from which to predict the effectiveness of proposed security and privacy measures, and confirm the adequacy of such measures after implementation.
White Box Testing	See *Comprehensive Testing*.

Special Publication 800-53A
Revision 4

Assessing Security and Privacy Controls in Federal Information Systems
and Organizations — *Building Effective Assessment Plans*

APPENDIX C

ACRONYMS

COMMON ABBREVIATIONS

CIO	Chief Information Officer
CPO	Chief Privacy Officer
CNSS	Committee on National Security Systems
CUI	Controlled Unclassified Information
COTS	Commercial Off-The-Shelf
DoD	Department of Defense
FIPS	Federal Information Processing Standards
FISMA	Federal Information Security Management Act
ICS	Industrial Control System
IEC	International Electrotechnical Commission
ISO	International Organization for Standardization
NCP	National Checklist Program
NIST	National Institute of Standards and Technology
NSA	National Security Agency
OCIL	Open Checklist Interactive Language
ODNI	Office of the Director of National Intelligence
OMB	Office of Management and Budget
PKI	Public Key Infrastructure
POAM	Plan of Action and Milestones
RMF	Risk Management Framework
SAOP	Senior Agency Official for Privacy
SCAP	Security Content Automation Protocol
SP	Special Publication
U.S.C.	United States Code

Special Publication 800-53A
Revision 4

Assessing Security and Privacy Controls in Federal Information Systems
and Organizations — *Building Effective Assessment Plans*

ASSESSMENT METHOD DESCRIPTIONS
ASSESSMENT METHOD DEFINITIONS, APPLICABLE OBJECTS, AND ATTRIBUTES

This appendix defines the three assessment methods that can be used by assessors during security and privacy control assessments: (i) *examine*; (ii) *interview*; and (iii) *test*. Included in the definition of each assessment method are types of objects to which the method can be applied. The application of each method is described in terms of the attributes of *depth* and *coverage*, progressing from *basic* to *focused* to *comprehensive*. The attribute values correlate to the assurance requirements specified by the organization.[40]

The depth attribute addresses the rigor and level of detail of the assessment. For the depth attribute, the *focused* attribute value includes and builds upon the assessment rigor and level of detail defined for the *basic* attribute value; the *comprehensive* attribute value includes and builds upon the assessment rigor and level of detail defined for the *focused* attribute value.

The coverage attribute addresses the scope or breadth of the assessment. For the coverage attribute, the *focused* attribute value includes and builds upon the number and type of assessment objects defined for the *basic* attribute value; the *comprehensive* attribute value includes and builds upon the number and type of assessment objects defined for the *focused* attribute value.

The use of **bolded text** in the assessment method description indicates the content that was added to and appears for the first time, in the description indicating greater rigor and level of detail for the attribute value.

---

[40] For other than national security systems, organizations meet minimum assurance requirements specified in Special Publication 800-53, Appendix E.

Special Publication 800-53A
Revision 4

Assessing Security and Privacy Controls in Federal Information Systems
and Organizations — *Building Effective Assessment Plans*

ASSESSMENT METHOD: Examine

ASSESSMENT OBJECTS: Specifications (e.g., policies, plans, procedures, system requirements, designs)
Mechanisms (e.g., functionality implemented in hardware, software, firmware)
Activities (e.g., system operations, administration, management; exercises)

DEFINITION: The process of checking, inspecting, reviewing, observing, studying, or analyzing one or more assessment objects to facilitate understanding, achieve clarification, or obtain evidence, the results of which are used to support the determination of security and privacy control existence, functionality, correctness, completeness, and potential for improvement over time.

SUPPLEMENTAL GUIDANCE: Typical assessor actions may include, for example: reviewing information security policies, plans, and procedures; analyzing system design documentation and interface specifications; observing system backup operations; reviewing the results of contingency plan exercises; observing incident response activities; studying technical manuals and user/administrator guides; checking, studying, or observing the operation of an information technology mechanism in the information system hardware/software; or checking, studying, or observing physical security measures related to the operation of an information system.

SCAP-validated tools that support the OCIL component specification may be used to automate the collection of assessment objects from specific, responsible individuals within an organization. The resulting information can then be examined by assessors during the security and privacy control assessments.

ATTRIBUTES: Depth, Coverage

* The *depth* attribute addresses the rigor of and level of detail in the examination process. There are three possible values for the depth attribute: (i) *basic*; (ii) *focused*; and (iii) *comprehensive.*

  - Basic examination: Examination that consists of high-level reviews, checks, observations, or inspections of the assessment object. This type of examination is conducted using a limited body of evidence or documentation (e.g., functional-level descriptions for mechanisms; high-level process descriptions for activities; actual documents for specifications). Basic examinations provide a level of understanding of the security and privacy controls necessary for determining whether the controls are implemented and free of obvious errors.

  - Focused examination: Examination that consists of high-level reviews, checks, observations, or inspections **and more in-depth studies/analyses** of the assessment object. This type of examination is conducted using a **substantial** body of evidence or documentation (e.g., functional-level descriptions **and where appropriate and available, high-level design information** for mechanisms; high-level process descriptions **and implementation procedures** for activities; the actual documents **and related documents** for specifications). **Focused** examinations provide a level of understanding of the security and privacy controls necessary for determining whether the controls are implemented and free of obvious errors **and whether there are increased grounds for confidence that the controls are implemented correctly and operating as intended**.

  - Comprehensive examination: Examination that consists of high-level reviews, checks, observations, or inspections and more in-depth, **detailed, and thorough** studies/analyses of the assessment object. This type of examination is conducted using an **extensive** body of evidence or documentation (e.g., functional-level descriptions and where appropriate and available, high-level design information, **low-level design information, and implementation information** for mechanisms; high-level process descriptions and **detailed** implementation procedures for activities; the actual documents and related documents for specifications[41]). **Comprehensive** examinations provide a level of understanding of the security and privacy controls necessary for determining whether the controls are implemented and free of obvious errors and whether there are **further** increased grounds for confidence that the controls are implemented correctly and operating as intended **on an ongoing and consistent basis, and that there is support for continuous improvement in the effectiveness of the controls.**

---

[41] While additional documentation is likely for mechanisms when moving from basic to focused to comprehensive examinations, the documentation associated with specifications and activities may be the same or similar for focused and comprehensive examinations, with the rigor of the examinations of these documents being increased at the comprehensive level.

Special Publication 800-53A
Revision 4

Assessing Security and Privacy Controls in Federal Information Systems
and Organizations — *Building Effective Assessment Plans*

- The *coverage* attribute addresses the scope or breadth of the examination process and includes the types of assessment objects to be examined, the number of objects to be examined (by type), and specific objects to be examined.[42] There are three possible values for the coverage attribute: (i) *basic*; (ii) *focused*; and (iii) *comprehensive*.

  - Basic examination: Examination that uses a representative sample of assessment objects (by type and number within type) to provide a level of coverage necessary for determining whether the security and privacy controls are implemented and free of obvious errors.

  - Focused examination: Examination that uses a representative sample of assessment objects (by type and number within type) **and other specific assessment objects deemed particularly important to achieving the assessment objective** to provide a level of coverage necessary for determining whether the security and privacy controls are implemented and free of obvious errors **and whether there are increased grounds for confidence that the controls are implemented correctly and operating as intended**.

  - Comprehensive examination: Examination that uses a **sufficiently large** sample of assessment objects (by type and number within type) and other specific assessment objects deemed particularly important to achieving the assessment objective to provide a level of coverage necessary for determining whether the security and privacy controls are implemented and free of obvious errors and whether there are **further** increased grounds for confidence that the controls are implemented correctly and operating as intended **on an ongoing and consistent basis, and that there is support for continuous improvement in the effectiveness of the controls**.

---

[42] The organization, considering a variety of factors (e.g., available resources, importance of the assessment, the organization's overall assessment goals and objectives), confers with assessors and provides direction on the type, number, and specific objects to be examined for the particular attribute value described.

Special Publication 800-53A
Revision 4

Assessing Security and Privacy Controls in Federal Information Systems
and Organizations — *Building Effective Assessment Plans*

ASSESSMENT METHOD: Interview

ASSESSMENT OBJECTS: Individuals or groups of individuals.

DEFINITION: The process of conducting discussions with individuals or groups within an organization to facilitate understanding, achieve clarification, or lead to the location of evidence, the results of which are used to support the determination of security and privacy control existence, functionality, correctness, completeness, and potential for improvement over time.

SUPPLEMENTAL GUIDANCE: Typical assessor actions may include, for example, interviewing agency heads, chief information officers, senior agency information security officers, authorizing officials, information owners, information system and mission owners, information system security officers, information system security managers, personnel officers, human resource managers, facilities managers, training officers, information system operators, network and system administrators, site managers, physical security officers, and users.

SCAP-validated tools that support the OCIL component specification may be used to automate the interview process for specific individuals or groups of individuals. The resulting information can then be examined by assessors during the security and privacy control assessments.

ATTRIBUTES: Depth, Coverage

- The *depth* attribute addresses the rigor of and level of detail in the interview process. There are three possible values for the depth attribute: (i) *basic*; (ii) *focused*; and (iii) *comprehensive*.

    - Basic interview: Interview that consists of broad-based, high-level discussions with individuals or groups of individuals. This type of interview is conducted using a set of generalized, high-level questions. Basic interviews provide a level of understanding of the security and privacy controls necessary for determining whether the controls are implemented and free of obvious errors.

    - Focused interview: Interview that consists of broad-based, high-level discussions **and more in-depth discussions in specific areas** with individuals or groups of individuals. This type of interview is conducted using a set of generalized, high-level questions **and more in-depth questions in specific areas where responses indicate a need for more in-depth investigation**. Focused interviews provide a level of understanding of the security and privacy controls necessary for determining whether the controls are implemented and free of obvious errors **and whether there are increased grounds for confidence that the controls are implemented correctly and operating as intended**.

    - Comprehensive interview: Interview that consists of broad-based, high-level discussions and more in-depth, **probing** discussions in specific areas with individuals or groups of individuals. This type of interview is conducted using a set of generalized, high-level questions and more in-depth, **probing** questions in specific areas where responses indicate a need for more in-depth investigation. **Comprehensive** interviews provide a level of understanding of the security and privacy controls necessary for determining whether the controls are implemented and free of obvious errors and whether there are **further** increased grounds for confidence that the controls are implemented correctly and operating as intended **on an ongoing and consistent basis, and that there is support for continuous improvement in the effectiveness of the controls**.

- The *coverage* attribute addresses the scope or breadth of the interview process and includes the types of individuals to be interviewed (by organizational role and associated responsibility), the number of individuals to be interviewed (by type), and specific individuals to be interviewed.[43] There are three possible values for the coverage attribute: (i) *basic*; (ii) *focused*; and (iii) *comprehensive*.

    - Basic interview: Interview that uses a representative sample of individuals in key organizational roles to provide a level of coverage necessary for determining whether the security and privacy controls are implemented and free of obvious errors.

    - Focused interview: Interview that uses a representative sample of individuals in key organizational roles **and other specific individuals deemed particularly important to achieving the assessment objective** to provide a level of coverage necessary for determining whether the security and privacy controls are

---

[43] The organization, considering a variety of factors (e.g., available resources, importance of the assessment, the organization's overall assessment goals and objectives), confers with assessors and provides direction on the type, number, and specific individuals to be interviewed for the particular attribute value described.

Special Publication 800-53A
Revision 4

Assessing Security and Privacy Controls in Federal Information Systems
and Organizations — *Building Effective Assessment Plans*

implemented and free of obvious errors **and whether there are increased grounds for confidence that the controls are implemented correctly and operating as intended**.

- Comprehensive interview: Interview that uses a **sufficiently large** sample of individuals in key organizational roles and other specific individuals deemed particularly important to achieving the assessment objective to provide a level of coverage necessary for determining whether the security and privacy controls are implemented and free of obvious errors and whether there are **further** increased grounds for confidence that the controls are implemented correctly and operating as intended **on an ongoing and consistent basis, and that there is support for continuous improvement in the effectiveness of the controls**.

Special Publication 800-53A
Revision 4

Assessing Security and Privacy Controls in Federal Information Systems
and Organizations — *Building Effective Assessment Plans*

ASSESSMENT METHOD: Test

ASSESSMENT OBJECTS: Mechanisms (e.g., hardware, software, firmware)
Activities (e.g., system operations, administration, management; exercises)

DEFINITION: The process of exercising one or more assessment objects under specified conditions to compare actual with expected behavior, the results of which are used to support the determination of security and privacy control existence, functionality, correctness, completeness, and potential for improvement over time.[44]

SUPPLEMENTAL GUIDANCE: Typical assessor actions may include, for example: testing access control, identification and authentication, and audit mechanisms; testing security configuration settings; testing physical access control devices; conducting penetration testing of key information system components; testing information system backup operations; testing incident response capability; and exercising contingency planning capability.

SCAP-validated tools can be used to automate the collection of assessment objects and evaluate these objects against expected behavior. The use of SCAP is specifically relevant to the testing of mechanisms that involve assessment of actual machine state. The National Checklist Program catalogs a number of SCAP-enabled checklists that are suitable for assessing the configuration posture of specific operating systems and applications. SCAP-validated tools can use these checklists to determine the aggregate compliance of a system against all of the configuration settings in the checklist (e.g., CM-6) or specific configurations that are relevant to a security or privacy control that pertains to one or more configuration settings. SCAP-validated tools can also determine the absence of a patch or the presence of a vulnerable condition. The results produced by the SCAP tools can then be examined by assessors as part of the security and privacy control assessments.

ATTRIBUTES: Depth, Coverage

- The *depth* attribute addresses the types of testing to be conducted. There are three possible values for the depth attribute: (i) *basic* testing; (ii) *focused* testing; and (iii) *comprehensive* testing.

  - Basic testing: Test methodology (also known as *black box* testing) that assumes no knowledge of the internal structure and implementation detail of the assessment object. This type of testing is conducted using a functional specification for mechanisms and a high-level process description for activities. Basic testing provides a level of understanding of the security and privacy controls necessary for determining whether the controls are implemented and free of obvious errors.

  - Focused testing: Test methodology (also known as *gray box* testing) that assumes **some** knowledge of the internal structure and implementation detail of the assessment object. This type of testing is conducted using a functional specification **and limited system architectural information (e.g., high-level design)** for mechanisms and a high-level process description **and high-level description of integration into the operational environment** for activities. Focused testing provides a level of understanding of the security and privacy controls necessary for determining whether the controls are implemented and free of obvious errors **and whether there are increased grounds for confidence that the controls are implemented correctly and operating as intended**.

  - Comprehensive testing: Test methodology (also known as *white box* testing) that assumes **explicit and substantial** knowledge of the internal structure and implementation detail of the assessment object. This type of testing is conducted using a functional specification, **extensive** system architectural information (e.g., high-level design, **low-level design) and implementation representation (e.g., source code, schematics)** for mechanisms and a high-level process description and **detailed** description of integration into the operational environment for activities. Comprehensive testing provides a level of understanding of the security and privacy controls necessary for determining whether the controls are implemented and free of obvious errors and whether there are **further** increased grounds for confidence that the controls are

---

[44] Testing is typically used to determine if mechanisms or activities meet a set of predefined specifications. Testing can also be performed to determine characteristics of a security or privacy control that are not commonly associated with predefined specifications, with an example of such testing being penetration testing. Guidelines for conducting penetration testing are provided in Appendix E.

Special Publication 800-53A
Revision 4

Assessing Security and Privacy Controls in Federal Information Systems
and Organizations — *Building Effective Assessment Plans*

implemented correctly and operating as intended **on an ongoing and consistent basis, and that there is support for continuous improvement in the effectiveness of the controls**.

- The *coverage* attribute addresses the scope or breadth of the testing process and includes the types of assessment objects to be tested, the number of objects to be tested (by type), and specific objects to be tested.[45] There are three possible values for the coverage attribute: (i) *basic*; (ii) *focused*; and (iii) *comprehensive*.

    - <u>Basic testing</u>: Testing that uses a representative sample of assessment objects (by type and number within type) to provide a level of coverage necessary for determining whether the security and privacy controls are implemented and free of obvious errors.

    - <u>Focused testing</u>: Testing that uses a representative sample of assessment objects (by type and number within type) **and other specific assessment objects deemed particularly important to achieving the assessment objective** to provide a level of coverage necessary for determining whether the security and privacy controls are implemented and free of obvious errors **and whether there are increased grounds for confidence that the controls are implemented correctly and operating as intended**.

    - <u>Comprehensive testing</u>: Testing that uses a **sufficiently large** sample of assessment objects (by type and number within type) and other specific assessment objects deemed particularly important to achieving the assessment objective to provide a level of coverage necessary for determining whether the security and privacy controls are implemented and free of obvious errors and whether there are **further** increased grounds for confidence that the controls are implemented correctly and operating as intended **on an ongoing and consistent basis, and that there is support for continuous improvement in the effectiveness of the controls**.

---

[45] The organization, considering a variety of factors (e.g., available resources, importance of the assessment, the organization's overall assessment goals and objectives), confers with assessors and provides direction on the type, number, and specific objects to be tested for the particular attribute value described. For mechanism-related testing, the coverage attribute also addresses the extent of the testing conducted (e.g., for software, the number of test cases and modules tested; for hardware, the range of inputs, number of components tested, and range of environmental factors over which the testing is conducted).

Special Publication 800-53A
Revision 4

Assessing Security and Privacy Controls in Federal Information Systems
and Organizations — *Building Effective Assessment Plans*

PENETRATION TESTING

ASSESSMENT TOOLS AND TECHNIQUES TO IDENTIFY INFORMATION SYSTEM WEAKNESSES

Organizations may consider adding controlled penetration testing to their arsenal of tools and techniques used to assess the security and privacy controls in organizational information systems. Penetration testing is a specific type of assessment in which assessors simulate the actions of a given class of attacker by using a defined set of documentation (that is, the documentation representative of what that class of attacker is likely to possess) and working under other specific constraints to attempt to circumvent the security or privacy features of an information system. Penetration testing is conducted as a controlled attempt to breach the security and privacy controls employed within the information system using the attacker's techniques and appropriate hardware and software tools. Penetration testing represents the results of a specific assessor or group of assessors at a specific point in time using agreed-upon *rules of engagement*. Considering the complexity of the information technologies commonly employed by organizations today, penetration testing can be viewed not as a means to verify the security or privacy features of an information system, but rather as a means to: (i) enhance the organization's understanding of the system; (ii) uncover weaknesses or deficiencies in the system; and (iii) indicate the level of effort required on the part of adversaries to breach the system safeguards.

Penetration testing exercises can be scheduled and/or random in accordance with organizational policy and organizational assessments of risk. Consideration can be given to performing penetration tests: (i) on any newly developed information system (or legacy system undergoing a major upgrade) before the system is authorized for operation; (ii) after important changes are made to the environment in which the information system operates; and (iii) when a new type of attack is discovered that may impact the system. Organizations actively monitor the information systems environment and the threat landscape (e.g., new vulnerabilities, attack techniques, new technology deployments, user security and privacy awareness and training) to identify changes that require out-of-cycle penetration testing.

Organizations specify which components within the information system are subject to penetration testing and the attacker's profile to be adopted throughout the penetration testing exercises. Organizations train selected personnel in the use and maintenance of penetration testing tools and techniques. Effective penetration testing tools have the capability to readily update the list of attack techniques and exploitable vulnerabilities used during the exercises. Organizations update the list of attack techniques and exploitable vulnerabilities used in penetration testing based on an organizational assessment of risk or when significant new vulnerabilities or threats are identified and reported. Whenever possible, organizations employ tools and attack techniques that include the capability to perform penetration testing exercises on information systems and security and privacy controls in an automated manner.[46]

The information obtained from the penetration testing process can be shared with appropriate personnel throughout the organization to help prioritize the vulnerabilities in the information

---

[46] While automated penetration testing tools provide repeatable results and reduce the resources used, organizations carefully consider the potential detrimental effects of automated exploits on system availability when employing automated penetration testing tools. Additionally, penetration testing based solely on automated tools may not provide the level of attempted system compromise that organizations might experience from an actual attacker.

Special Publication 800-53A
Revision 4

Assessing Security and Privacy Controls in Federal Information Systems
and Organizations — *Building Effective Assessment Plans*

system that are demonstrably subject to compromise by attackers of a profile equivalent to the ones used in the penetration testing exercises. The prioritization helps to determine effective strategies for eliminating the identified vulnerabilities and mitigating associated risks to the organization's operations and assets, to individuals, to other organizations, and to the Nation resulting from the operation and use of the information system. Penetration testing can be integrated into the network security testing process and the patch and vulnerability management process. Special Publication 800-40 provides guidance on patch and vulnerability management. Special Publication 800-115 provides guidance on information and network security testing.

Penetration Testing Considerations

Organizations consider the following criteria in developing and implementing a controlled penetration testing program. An effective penetration test:

- Goes beyond vulnerability scanning, to provide an explicit and often dramatic proof of mission risks and an indicator of the level of effort an adversary would need to expend in order to cause harm to the organization's operations and assets, to individuals, to other organizations, or to the Nation;

- Approaches the information system as the adversary would, considering vulnerabilities, incorrect system configurations, trust relationships between organizations, and architectural weaknesses in the environment under test;

- Has a clearly defined scope and contains as a minimum:

  - A definition of the environment subject to test (e.g., facilities, users, organizational groups);

  - A definition of the attack surface to be tested (e.g., servers, desktop systems, wireless networks, Web applications, intrusion detection and prevention systems, firewalls, email accounts, user security awareness and training posture, incident response posture);

  - A definition of the threat sources to simulate (e.g., an enumeration of attacker's profiles to be used: internal attacker, casual attacker, single or group of external targeted attackers, criminal organization);

  - A definition of the objectives for the simulated attacker (e.g., gain domain administrator access on the organization's LDAP (Lightweight Directory Access Protocol) structure, access and modify information in the organization's financial system);

  - A definition of level of effort (time and resources) to be expended; and

  - A definition of the rules of engagement.

- Thoroughly documents all activities performed during the test, including all exploited vulnerabilities and how the vulnerabilities were combined into attacks;

- Produces results indicating a likelihood of occurrence for a given attacker by using the level of effort the team needed to expend in penetrating the information system as an indicator of the penetration resistance of the system;

- Validates existing security and privacy controls (including risk mitigation mechanisms such as firewalls, intrusion detection and prevention systems);

- Provides a verifiable and reproducible log of all the activities performed during the test; and

Special Publication 800-53A
Revision 4

Assessing Security and Privacy Controls in Federal Information Systems
and Organizations — *Building Effective Assessment Plans*

- Provides actionable results with information about possible remediation measures for the successful attacks performed.

Special Publication 800-53A
Revision 4

Assessing Security and Privacy Controls in Federal Information Systems
and Organizations — *Building Effective Assessment Plans*

APPENDIX F

SECURITY ASSESSMENT PROCEDURES
OBJECTIVES, METHODS, AND OBJECTS FOR ASSESSING SECURITY CONTROLS

This appendix provides a catalog of procedures to assess the security controls and control enhancements in Special Publication 800-53.[47] Assessors select assessment procedures from the catalog in accordance with the guidance provided in Section 3.2. Since the contents of the security plan affect the development of the security assessment plan and the assessment, there will likely be assessment procedures in the catalog that assessors will not use because: (i) the associated security controls or control enhancements are not contained in the security plan for the information system;[48] or (ii) the security controls or control enhancements are not being assessed at this particular time.

Assessment objectives are numbered sequentially, first in accordance with the numbering scheme in Special Publication 800-53, and subsequently, where necessary to further apportion the security control requirements to facilitate assessment, **bracketed** sequential numbers or letters, as opposed to parentheses, are used to make that distinction (e.g., CP-9(a), CP-9(a)[1], CP-9(a)[2], etc.). The initial bracketed character is always a number. For some security controls, the column with the initial control designation (e.g., CP-9, CP-9(a)) is simply a placeholder to help facilitate apportioning the control while maintaining the formatting scheme. Although not explicitly noted with each identified assessment method in the assessment procedure, the attribute values of *depth* and *coverage* described in Appendix D are typically assigned by the organization and applied by the assessor or assessment team in the execution of the assessment method against an assessment object.

If the security control has any enhancements (as designated by sequential parenthetical numbers, for example, CP-9(3) for the third enhancement to CP-9), assessment objectives are numbered sequentially in the same way as the assessment procedure for the base control, first in accordance with the numbering scheme in Special Publication 800-53, and subsequently, using bracketed sequential numbers or letters to further apportion control enhancement requirements to facilitate assessments (e.g., CP-9(3)[1], CP-9(3)[2]).

The same assessment object may appear in multiple object lists in a variety of assessment procedures. The same object may be used in multiple contexts to obtain needed information or evidence for a particular aspect of an assessment. Assessors use the general references as appropriate to obtain the necessary information to make the specified determinations required by the assessment objective. For example, a reference to access control policy appears in the assessment procedures for AC-2 and AC-7. For assessment procedure AC-2, assessors use the access control policy to find information about that portion of the policy that addresses account management for the information system. For assessment procedure AC-7, assessors use the

---

[47] In the event of any differences between the assessment objectives identified for assessing the security controls and the underlying intent expressed by the security control statements defined in the most recent version of Special Publication 800-53. Special Publication 800-53 remains the definitive expression of the control or enhancement.

[48] The execution of the RMF includes the selection of an initial set of security controls employed within or inherited by an organizational information system followed by a control *tailoring* process. The tailoring process will likely change the set of security controls that will be contained in the final security plan. Therefore, the selection of assessment procedures from the catalog of available procedures is based solely on the content of the security plan after the tailoring activities are completed.

Special Publication 800-53A
Revision 4

Assessing Security and Privacy Controls in Federal Information Systems
and Organizations — *Building Effective Assessment Plans*

access control policy to find information about that portion of the policy that addresses unsuccessful login attempts for the information system.

Assessors are responsible for combining and consolidating the assessment procedures whenever possible or practical. Optimizing assessment procedures can save time, reduce assessment costs, and maximize the usefulness of assessment results. Assessors optimize assessment procedures by determining the best sequencing of the procedures. The assessment of some security controls before others may provide information that facilitates understanding and assessment of other controls.

IMPLEMENTATION TIPS

TIP #1: Select only those assessment procedures from Appendix F that correspond to the security controls and control enhancements in the *approved security plan* and that are to be included in the assessment.

TIP #2: The assessment procedures selected from Appendix F are simply *example* procedures that serve as a starting point for organizations preparing for assessments. These assessment procedures are tailored as necessary, in accordance with the guidance in Section 3.2 to adapt the procedures to specific organizational requirements and operating environments.

TIP #3: With respect to the *assessment procedures* in Appendix F, assessors need apply only those procedures, methods, and objects necessary for making a final determination that a particular security control objective is satisfied or not satisfied (see Section 3.3).

TIP #4: Assessors apply to each assessment method, values for depth and coverage (described in Appendix D) that are commensurate with the characteristics of the information system (including assurance requirements) and the specific assessment activity that supports making a determination of the effectiveness of the security controls under review. The values selected for the depth and coverage attributes indicate the relative effort required in applying an assessment method to an assessment object (i.e., the rigor and scope of the activities associated with the assessment). The depth and coverage attributes, while not repeated in every assessment procedure in this appendix, can be represented as follows:

Interview: [*ASSIGN ATTRIBUTE VALUES:* <depth>, <coverage>].
[*SELECT FROM:* Organizational personnel with contingency planning and plan implementation responsibilities].

TIP #5: Assessors may find useful assessment-related information in the Supplemental Guidance section of each security control described in Special Publication 800-53. This information can be used to carry out more effective assessments with regard to the application of assessment procedures.

Note: When assessing agency compliance with NIST guidance, auditors, Inspectors General, evaluators, and/or assessors consider the intent of the security concepts and principles articulated within the particular guidance document and how the agency applied the guidance in the context of its specific mission responsibilities, operational environments, and unique organizational conditions.

Special Publication 800-53A
Revision 4

Assessing Security and Privacy Controls in Federal Information Systems
and Organizations — *Building Effective Assessment Plans*

CAUTIONARY NOTE

Whereas a set of *potential assessment methods* have been included in the following catalog of assessment procedures, these are not intended to be mandatory or exclusive. Depending on the particular circumstances of the information system or organization to be assessed, not all methods may be required or other assessment methods may also be used. In addition, the set of *potential assessment objects* listed in the catalog are not intended to be mandatory, but rather a set from which the necessary and sufficient set of objects for a given assessment can be selected to make the appropriate determinations.

Special Publication 800-53A
Revision 4

Assessing Security and Privacy Controls in Federal Information Systems
and Organizations — *Building Effective Assessment Plans*

FAMILY: ACCESS CONTROL

AC-1	ACCESS CONTROL POLICY AND PROCEDURES			
	ASSESSMENT OBJECTIVE: *Determine if the organization:*			
	AC-1(a)(1)	AC-1(a)(1)[1]	*develops and documents an access control policy that addresses:*	
			AC-1(a)(1)[1][a]	*purpose;*
			AC-1(a)(1)[1][b]	*scope;*
			AC-1(a)(1)[1][c]	*roles;*
			AC-1(a)(1)[1][d]	*responsibilities;*
			AC-1(a)(1)[1][e]	*management commitment;*
			AC-1(a)(1)[1][f]	*coordination among organizational entities;*
			AC-1(a)(1)[1][g]	*compliance;*
		AC-1(a)(1)[2]	*defines personnel or roles to whom the access control policy are to be disseminated;*	
		AC-1(a)(1)[3]	*disseminates the access control policy to organization-defined personnel or roles;*	
	AC-1(a)(2)	AC-1(a)(2)[1]	*develops and documents procedures to facilitate the implementation of the access control policy and associated access control controls;*	
		AC-1(a)(2)[2]	*defines personnel or roles to whom the procedures are to be disseminated;*	
		AC-1(a)(2)[3]	*disseminates the procedures to organization-defined personnel or roles;*	
	AC-1(b)(1)	AC-1(b)(1)[1]	*defines the frequency to review and update the current access control policy;*	
		AC-1(b)(1)[2]	*reviews and updates the current access control policy with the organization-defined frequency;*	
	AC-1(b)(2)	AC-1(b)(2)[1]	*defines the frequency to review and update the current access control procedures; and*	
		AC-1(b)(2)[2]	*reviews and updates the current access control procedures with the organization-defined frequency.*	
	POTENTIAL ASSESSMENT METHODS AND OBJECTS: **Examine:** [*SELECT FROM:* Access control policy and procedures; other relevant documents or records]. **Interview:** [*SELECT FROM:* Organizational personnel with access control responsibilities; organizational personnel with information security responsibilities].			

Special Publication 800-53A
Revision 4

Assessing Security and Privacy Controls in Federal Information Systems
and Organizations — *Building Effective Assessment Plans*

AC-2	ACCOUNT MANAGEMENT		
	ASSESSMENT OBJECTIVE: *Determine if the organization:*		
	AC-2(a)	AC-2(a)[1]	*defines information system account types to be identified and selected to support organizational missions/business functions;*
		AC-2(a)[2]	*identifies and selects organization-defined information system account types to support organizational missions/business functions;*
	AC-2(b)	*assigns account managers for information system accounts;*	
	AC-2(c)	*establishes conditions for group and role membership;*	
	AC-2(d)	*specifies for each account (as required):*	
		AC-2(d)[1]	*authorized users of the information system;*
		AC-2(d)[2]	*group and role membership;*
		AC-2(d)[3]	*access authorizations (i.e., privileges);*
		AC-2(d)[4]	*other attributes;*
	AC-2(e)	AC-2(e)[1]	*defines personnel or roles required to approve requests to create information system accounts;*
		AC-2(e)[2]	*requires approvals by organization-defined personnel or roles for requests to create information system accounts;*
	AC-2(f)	AC-2(f)[1]	*defines procedures or conditions to:*
			AC-2(f)[1][a] *create information system accounts;*
			AC-2(f)[1][b] *enable information system accounts;*
			AC-2(f)[1][c] *modify information system accounts;*
			AC-2(f)[1][d] *disable information system accounts;*
			AC-2(f)[1][e] *remove information system accounts;*
		AC-2(f)[2]	*in accordance with organization-defined procedures or conditions:*
			AC-2(f)[2][a] *creates information system accounts;*
			AC-2(f)[2][b] *enables information system accounts;*
			AC-2(f)[2][c] *modifies information system accounts;*
			AC-2(f)[2][d] *disables information system accounts;*
			AC-2(f)[2][e] *removes information system accounts;*
	AC-2(g)	*monitors the use of information system accounts;*	
	AC-2(h)	*notifies account managers:*	
		AC-2(h)(1)	*when accounts are no longer required;*
		AC-2(h)(2)	*when users are terminated or transferred;*
		AC-2(h)(3)	*when individual information system usage or need to know changes;*
	AC-2(i)	*authorizes access to the information system based on;*	

Special Publication 800-53A
Revision 4

Assessing Security and Privacy Controls in Federal Information Systems
and Organizations — *Building Effective Assessment Plans*

		AC-2(i)(1)	*a valid access authorization;*
		AC-2(i)(2)	*intended system usage;*
		AC-2(i)(3)	*other attributes as required by the organization or associated missions/business functions;*
	AC-2(j)	AC-2(j)[1]	*defines the frequency to review accounts for compliance with account management requirements;*
		AC-2(j)[2]	*reviews accounts for compliance with account management requirements with the organization-defined frequency; and*
	AC-2(k)		*establishes a process for reissuing shared/group account credentials (if deployed) when individuals are removed from the group.*

POTENTIAL ASSESSMENT METHODS AND OBJECTS:

Examine: [*SELECT FROM:* Access control policy; procedures addressing account management; security plan; information system design documentation; information system configuration settings and associated documentation; list of active system accounts along with the name of the individual associated with each account; list of conditions for group and role membership; notifications or records of recently transferred, separated, or terminated employees; list of recently disabled information system accounts along with the name of the individual associated with each account; access authorization records; account management compliance reviews; information system monitoring records; information system audit records; other relevant documents or records].

Interview: [*SELECT FROM:* Organizational personnel with account management responsibilities; system/network administrators; organizational personnel with information security responsibilities].

Test: [*SELECT FROM:* Organizational processes account management on the information system; automated mechanisms for implementing account management].

AC-2(1)	ACCOUNT MANAGEMENT | *AUTOMATED SYSTEM ACCOUNT MANAGEMENT*

ASSESSMENT OBJECTIVE:

Determine if the organization employs automated mechanisms to support the management of information system accounts.

POTENTIAL ASSESSMENT METHODS AND OBJECTS:

Examine: [*SELECT FROM:* Access control policy; procedures addressing account management; information system design documentation; information system configuration settings and associated documentation; information system audit records; other relevant documents or records].

Interview: [*SELECT FROM:* Organizational personnel with account management responsibilities; system/network administrators; organizational personnel with information security responsibilities; system developers].

Test: [*SELECT FROM:* Automated mechanisms implementing account management functions].

AC-2(2)	ACCOUNT MANAGEMENT | *REMOVAL OF TEMPORARY/EMERGENCY ACCOUNTS*

ASSESSMENT OBJECTIVE:

Determine if:

AC-2(2)[1]	*the organization defines the time period after which the information system automatically removes or disables temporary and emergency accounts; and*
AC-2(2)[2]	*the information system automatically removes or disables temporary and emergency accounts after the organization-defined time period for each type of account.*

Special Publication 800-53A
Revision 4

Assessing Security and Privacy Controls in Federal Information Systems
and Organizations — *Building Effective Assessment Plans*

POTENTIAL ASSESSMENT METHODS AND OBJECTS:

Examine: [*SELECT FROM*: Access control policy; procedures addressing account management; security plan; information system design documentation; information system configuration settings and associated documentation; information system-generated list of temporary accounts removed and/or disabled; information system-generated list of emergency accounts removed and/or disabled; information system audit records; other relevant documents or records].

Interview: [*SELECT FROM*: Organizational personnel with account management responsibilities; system/network administrators; organizational personnel with information security responsibilities; system developers].

Test: [*SELECT FROM*: Automated mechanisms implementing account management functions].

AC-2(3)	ACCOUNT MANAGEMENT | *DISABLE INACTIVE ACCOUNTS*

ASSESSMENT OBJECTIVE:

Determine if:

AC-2(3)[1]	*the organization defines the time period after which the information system automatically disables inactive accounts; and*
AC-2(3)[2]	*the information system automatically disables inactive accounts after the organization-defined time period.*

POTENTIAL ASSESSMENT METHODS AND OBJECTS:

Examine: [*SELECT FROM*: Access control policy; procedures addressing account management; security plan; information system design documentation; information system configuration settings and associated documentation; information system-generated list of temporary accounts removed and/or disabled; information system-generated list of emergency accounts removed and/or disabled; information system audit records; other relevant documents or records].

Interview: [*SELECT FROM*: Organizational personnel with account management responsibilities; system/network administrators; organizational personnel with information security responsibilities; system developers].

Test: [*SELECT FROM*: Automated mechanisms implementing account management functions].

AC-2(4)	ACCOUNT MANAGEMENT | *AUTOMATED AUDIT ACTIONS*

ASSESSMENT OBJECTIVE:

Determine if:

AC-2(4)[1]	*the information system automatically audits the following account actions:*	
	AC-2(4)[1][a]	*creation;*
	AC-2(4)[1][b]	*modification;*
	AC-2(4)[1][c]	*enabling;*
	AC-2(4)[1][d]	*disabling;*
	AC-2(4)[1][e]	*removal;*
AC-2(4)[2]	*the organization defines personnel or roles to be notified of the following account actions:*	
	AC-2(4)[2][a]	*creation;*
	AC-2(4)[2][b]	*modification;*
	AC-2(4)[2][c]	*enabling;*
	AC-2(4)[2][d]	*disabling;*
	AC-2(4)[2][e]	*removal;*

Special Publication 800-53A
Revision 4

Assessing Security and Privacy Controls in Federal Information Systems
and Organizations — *Building Effective Assessment Plans*

AC-2(4)[3]	*the information system notifies organization-defined personnel or roles of the following account actions:*	
	AC-2(4)[3][a]	*creation;*
	AC-2(4)[3][b]	*modification;*
	AC-2(4)[3][c]	*enabling;*
	AC-2(4)[3][d]	*disabling; and*
	AC-2(4)[3][e]	*removal.*

POTENTIAL ASSESSMENT METHODS AND OBJECTS:

Examine: [*SELECT FROM:* Access control policy; procedures addressing account management; information system design documentation; information system configuration settings and associated documentation; notifications/alerts of account creation, modification, enabling, disabling, and removal actions; information system audit records; other relevant documents or records].

Interview: [*SELECT FROM:* Organizational personnel with account management responsibilities; system/network administrators; organizational personnel with information security responsibilities].

Test: [*SELECT FROM:* Automated mechanisms implementing account management functions].

AC-2(5)	ACCOUNT MANAGEMENT	*INACTIVITY LOGOUT*

ASSESSMENT OBJECTIVE:

Determine if the organization:

AC-2(5)[1]	*defines either the time period of expected inactivity that requires users to log out or the description of when users are required to log out; and*
AC-2(5)[2]	*requires that users log out when the organization-defined time period of inactivity is reached or in accordance with organization-defined description of when to log out.*

POTENTIAL ASSESSMENT METHODS AND OBJECTS:

Examine: [*SELECT FROM:* Access control policy; procedures addressing account management; security plan; information system design documentation; information system configuration settings and associated documentation; security violation reports; information system audit records; other relevant documents or records].

Interview: [*SELECT FROM:* Organizational personnel with account management responsibilities; system/network administrators; organizational personnel with information security responsibilities; users that must comply with inactivity logout policy].

AC-2(6)	ACCOUNT MANAGEMENT	*DYNAMIC PRIVILEGE MANAGEMENT*

ASSESSMENT OBJECTIVE:

Determine if:

AC-2(6)[1]	*the organization defines a list of dynamic privilege management capabilities to be implemented by the information system; and*
AC-2(6)[2]	*the information system implements the organization-defined list of dynamic privilege management capabilities.*

Special Publication 800-53A
Revision 4

Assessing Security and Privacy Controls in Federal Information Systems
and Organizations — *Building Effective Assessment Plans*

POTENTIAL ASSESSMENT METHODS AND OBJECTS:

Examine: [*SELECT FROM:* Access control policy; procedures addressing account management; information system design documentation; information system configuration settings and associated documentation; system-generated list of dynamic privilege management capabilities; information system audit records; other relevant documents or records].

Interview: [*SELECT FROM:* Organizational personnel with account management responsibilities; system/network administrators; organizational personnel with information security responsibilities; system developers].

Test: [*SELECT FROM:* Information system implementing dynamic privilege management capabilities].

AC-2(7)	ACCOUNT MANAGEMENT | *ROLE-BASED SCHEMES*	
	ASSESSMENT OBJECTIVE: *Determine if the organization:*	
	AC-2(7)(a)	*establishes and administers privileged user accounts in accordance with a role-based access scheme that organizes allowed information system access and privileges into roles;*
	AC-2(7)(b)	*monitors privileged role assignments;*
	AC-2(7)(c) AC-2(7)(c)[1]	*defines actions to be taken when privileged role assignments are no longer appropriate; and*
	AC-2(7)(c)[2]	*takes organization-defined actions when privileged role assignments are no longer appropriate.*

POTENTIAL ASSESSMENT METHODS AND OBJECTS:

Examine: [*SELECT FROM:* Access control policy; procedures addressing account management; information system design documentation; information system configuration settings and associated documentation; information system-generated list of privileged user accounts and associated role; records of actions taken when privileged role assignments are no longer appropriate; information system audit records; audit tracking and monitoring reports; information system monitoring records; other relevant documents or records].

Interview: [*SELECT FROM:* Organizational personnel with account management responsibilities; system/network administrators; organizational personnel with information security responsibilities].

Test: [*SELECT FROM:* Automated mechanisms implementing account management functions; automated mechanisms monitoring privileged role assignments].

AC-2(8)	ACCOUNT MANAGEMENT | *DYNAMIC ACCOUNT CREATION*	
	ASSESSMENT OBJECTIVE: *Determine if:*	
	AC-2(8)[1]	*the organization defines information system accounts to be created by the information system dynamically; and*
	AC-2(8)[2]	*the information system creates organization-defined information system accounts dynamically.*

POTENTIAL ASSESSMENT METHODS AND OBJECTS:

Examine: [*SELECT FROM:* Access control policy; procedures addressing account management; information system design documentation; information system configuration settings and associated documentation; system-generated list of information system accounts; information system audit records; other relevant documents or records].

Interview: [*SELECT FROM:* Organizational personnel with account management responsibilities; system/network administrators; organizational personnel with information security responsibilities; system developers].

Test: [*SELECT FROM:* Automated mechanisms implementing account management functions].

Special Publication 800-53A
Revision 4

Assessing Security and Privacy Controls in Federal Information Systems
and Organizations — *Building Effective Assessment Plans*

AC-2(9)	ACCOUNT MANAGEMENT	*RESTRICTIONS ON USE OF SHARED / GROUP ACCOUNTS*

	ASSESSMENT OBJECTIVE: *Determine if the organization:*
AC-2(9)[1]	*defines conditions for establishing shared/group accounts; and*
AC-2(9)[2]	*only permits the use of shared/group accounts that meet organization-defined conditions for establishing shared/group accounts.*

POTENTIAL ASSESSMENT METHODS AND OBJECTS:
Examine: [*SELECT FROM:* Access control policy; procedures addressing account management; information system design documentation; information system configuration settings and associated documentation; system-generated list of shared/group accounts and associated role; information system audit records; other relevant documents or records].
Interview: [*SELECT FROM:* Organizational personnel with account management responsibilities; system/network administrators; organizational personnel with information security responsibilities].
Test: [*SELECT FROM:* Automated mechanisms implementing management of shared/group accounts].

AC-2(10)	ACCOUNT MANAGEMENT	*SHARED / GROUP ACCOUNT CREDENTIAL TERMINATION*

ASSESSMENT OBJECTIVE: *Determine if the information system terminates shared/group account credentials when members leave the group.*

POTENTIAL ASSESSMENT METHODS AND OBJECTS:
Examine: [*SELECT FROM:* Access control policy; procedures addressing account management; information system design documentation; information system configuration settings and associated documentation; account access termination records; information system audit records; other relevant documents or records].
Interview: [*SELECT FROM:* Organizational personnel with account management responsibilities; system/network administrators; organizational personnel with information security responsibilities; system developers].
Test: [*SELECT FROM:* Automated mechanisms implementing account management functions].

AC-2(11)	ACCOUNT MANAGEMENT	*USAGE CONDITIONS*

	ASSESSMENT OBJECTIVE: *Determine if:*
AC-2(11)[1]	*the organization defines circumstances and/or usage conditions to be enforced for information system accounts;*
AC-2(11)[2]	*the organization defines information system accounts for which organization-defined circumstances and/or usage conditions are to be enforced; and*
AC-2(11)[3]	*the information system enforces organization-defined circumstances and/or usage conditions for organization-defined information system accounts.*

Special Publication 800-53A
Revision 4

Assessing Security and Privacy Controls in Federal Information Systems
and Organizations — *Building Effective Assessment Plans*

POTENTIAL ASSESSMENT METHODS AND OBJECTS:

Examine: [*SELECT FROM:* Access control policy; procedures addressing account management; information system design documentation; information system configuration settings and associated documentation; system-generated list of information system accounts and associated assignments of usage circumstances and/or usage conditions; information system audit records; other relevant documents or records].

Interview: [*SELECT FROM:* Organizational personnel with account management responsibilities; system/network administrators; organizational personnel with information security responsibilities; system developers].

Test: [*SELECT FROM:* Automated mechanisms implementing account management functions].

AC-2(12)	ACCOUNT MANAGEMENT | *ACCOUNT MONITORING / ATYPICAL USAGE*		
	ASSESSMENT OBJECTIVE: *Determine if the organization:*		
	AC-2(12)(a)	AC-2(12)(a)[1]	*defines atypical usage to be monitored for information system accounts;*
		AC-2(12)(a)[2]	*monitors information system accounts for organization-defined atypical usage;*
	AC-2(12)(b)	AC-2(12)(b)[1]	*defines personnel or roles to whom atypical usage of information system accounts are to be reported; and*
		AC-2(12)(b)[2]	*reports atypical usage of information system accounts to organization-defined personnel or roles.*
	POTENTIAL ASSESSMENT METHODS AND OBJECTS: **Examine:** [*SELECT FROM:* Access control policy; procedures addressing account management; information system design documentation; information system configuration settings and associated documentation; information system monitoring records; information system audit records; audit tracking and monitoring reports; other relevant documents or records]. **Interview:** [*SELECT FROM:* Organizational personnel with account management responsibilities; system/network administrators; organizational personnel with information security responsibilities]. **Test:** [*SELECT FROM:* Automated mechanisms implementing account management functions].		

AC-2(13)	ACCOUNT MANAGEMENT | *DISABLE ACCOUNTS FOR HIGH-RISK INDIVIDUALS*	
	ASSESSMENT OBJECTIVE: *Determine if the organization:*	
	AC-2(13)[1]	*defines the time period within which accounts are disabled upon discovery of a significant risk posed by users of such accounts; and*
	AC-2(13)[2]	*disables accounts of users posing a significant risk within the organization-defined time period of discovery of the risk.*
	POTENTIAL ASSESSMENT METHODS AND OBJECTS: **Examine:** [*SELECT FROM:* Access control policy; procedures addressing account management; information system design documentation; information system configuration settings and associated documentation; system-generated list of disabled accounts; list of user activities posing significant organizational risk; information system audit records; other relevant documents or records]. **Interview:** [*SELECT FROM:* Organizational personnel with account management responsibilities; system/network administrators; organizational personnel with information security responsibilities]. **Test:** [*SELECT FROM:* Automated mechanisms implementing account management functions].	

Special Publication 800-53A
Revision 4

Assessing Security and Privacy Controls in Federal Information Systems
and Organizations — *Building Effective Assessment Plans*

AC-3	ACCESS ENFORCEMENT
	ASSESSMENT OBJECTIVE: *Determine if the information system enforces approved authorizations for logical access to information and system resources in accordance with applicable access control policies.*
	POTENTIAL ASSESSMENT METHODS AND OBJECTS: **Examine**: [*SELECT FROM:* Access control policy; procedures addressing access enforcement; information system design documentation; information system configuration settings and associated documentation; list of approved authorizations (user privileges); information system audit records; other relevant documents or records]. **Interview**: [*SELECT FROM:* Organizational personnel with access enforcement responsibilities; system/network administrators; organizational personnel with information security responsibilities; system developers]. **Test**: [*SELECT FROM:* Automated mechanisms implementing access control policy].

AC-3(1)	ACCESS ENFORCEMENT | *RESTRICTED ACCESS TO PRIVILEGED FUNCTIONS*
[Withdrawn: Incorporated into AC-6].	

AC-3(2)	ACCESS ENFORCEMENT | *DUAL AUTHORIZATION*
	ASSESSMENT OBJECTIVE: *Determine if:*
	AC-3(2)[1] *the organization defines privileged commands and/or other actions for which dual authorization is to be enforced; and*
	AC-3(2)[2] *the information system enforces dual authorization for organization-defined privileged commands and/or other organization-defined actions.*
	POTENTIAL ASSESSMENT METHODS AND OBJECTS: **Examine**: [*SELECT FROM:* Access control policy; procedures addressing access enforcement and dual authorization; security plan; information system design documentation; information system configuration settings and associated documentation; list of privileged commands requiring dual authorization; list of actions requiring dual authorization; list of approved authorizations (user privileges); other relevant documents or records]. **Interview**: [*SELECT FROM:* Organizational personnel with access enforcement responsibilities; system/network administrators; organizational personnel with information security responsibilities; system developers]. **Test**: [*SELECT FROM:* Dual authorization mechanisms implementing access control policy].

AC-3(3)	ACCESS ENFORCEMENT | *MANDATORY ACCESS CONTROL*
	ASSESSMENT OBJECTIVE: *Determine if:*
	AC-3(3)[1] *the organization defines mandatory access control policies to be enforced over all subjects and objects;*
	AC-3(3)[2] *the organization defines subjects over which organization-defined mandatory access control policies are to be enforced;*
	AC-3(3)[3] *the organization defines objects over which organization-defined mandatory access control policies are to be enforced;*

Special Publication 800-53A
Revision 4

Assessing Security and Privacy Controls in Federal Information Systems
and Organizations — *Building Effective Assessment Plans*

	AC-3(3)[4]	*the organization defines subjects that may explicitly be granted privileges such that they are not limited by the constraints specified elsewhere within this control;*			
	AC-3(3)[5]	*the organization defines privileges that may be granted to organization-defined subjects;*			
	AC-3(3)[6]	*the information system enforces organization-defined mandatory access control policies over all subjects and objects where the policy specifies that:*			
		AC-3(3)[6](a)	*the policy is uniformly enforced across all subjects and objects within the boundary of the information system;*		
		AC-3(3)[6](b)	*a subject that has been granted access to information is constrained from doing any of the following:*		
			AC-3(3)[6](b)(1)	*passing the information to unauthorized subjects or objects;*	
			AC-3(3)[6](b)(2)	*granting its privileges to other subjects;*	
			AC-3(3)[6](b)(3)	*changing one or more security attributes on:*	
				AC-3(3)[6](b)(3)[a]	*subjects;*
				AC-3(3)[6](b)(3)[b]	*objects;*
				AC-3(3)[6](b)(3)[c]	*the information system; or*
				AC-3(3)[6](b)(3)[d]	*system components;*
			AC-3(3)[6](b)(4)	*choosing the security attributes and attribute values to be associated with newly created or modified objects; or*	
			AC-3(3)[6](b)(5)	*changing the rules governing access control; and*	
		AC-3(3)[6](c)	*organization-defined subjects may explicitly be granted organization-defined privileges such that they are not limited by some or all of the above constraints.*		

POTENTIAL ASSESSMENT METHODS AND OBJECTS:

Examine: [*SELECT FROM:* Access control policy; mandatory access control policies; procedures addressing access enforcement; security plan; information system design documentation; information system configuration settings and associated documentation; list of subjects and objects (i.e., users and resources) requiring enforcement of mandatory access control policies; information system audit records; other relevant documents or records].

Interview: [*SELECT FROM:* Organizational personnel with access enforcement responsibilities; system/network administrators; organizational personnel with information security responsibilities; system developers].

Test: [*SELECT FROM:* Automated mechanisms implementing mandatory access control].

AC-3(4)	ACCESS ENFORCEMENT	*DISCRETIONARY ACCESS CONTROL*	
	ASSESSMENT OBJECTIVE: *Determine if:*		
	AC-3(4)[1]	*the organization defines discretionary access control policies to be enforced over defined subjects and objects;*	

Special Publication 800-53A
Revision 4

Assessing Security and Privacy Controls in Federal Information Systems
and Organizations — *Building Effective Assessment Plans*

AC-3(4)[2]	the information system enforces organization-defined discretionary access control policies over defined subjects and objects where the policy specifies that a subject has been granted access to information and can do one or more of the following:		
	AC-3(4)[2](a)	pass the information to any other subjects or objects;	
	AC-3(4)[2](b)	grant its privileges to other subjects;	
	AC-3(4)[2](c)	change security attributes on:	
		AC-3(4)[2](c)[a]	subjects,
		AC-3(4)[2](c)[b]	objects,
		AC-3(4)[2](c)[c]	the information system, or
		AC-3(4)[2](c)[d]	the information system's components;
	AC-3(4)[2](d)	choose the security attributes to be associated with newly created or revised objects; or	
	AC-3(4)[2](e)	change the rules governing access control.	

POTENTIAL ASSESSMENT METHODS AND OBJECTS:

Examine: [*SELECT FROM:* Access control policy; discretionary access control policies; procedures addressing access enforcement; security plan; information system design documentation; information system configuration settings and associated documentation; list of subjects and objects (i.e., users and resources) requiring enforcement of discretionary access control policies; information system audit records; other relevant documents or records].

Interview: [*SELECT FROM:* Organizational personnel with access enforcement responsibilities; system/network administrators; organizational personnel with information security responsibilities; system developers].

Test: [*SELECT FROM:* Automated mechanisms implementing discretionary access control policy].

AC-3(5)	**ACCESS ENFORCEMENT**	*SECURITY-RELEVANT INFORMATION*

ASSESSMENT OBJECTIVE:

Determine if:

AC-3(5)[1]	the organization defines security-relevant information to which the information system prevents access except during secure, non-operable system states; and
AC-3(5)[2]	the information system prevents access to organization-defined security-relevant information except during secure, non-operable system states.

POTENTIAL ASSESSMENT METHODS AND OBJECTS:

Examine: [*SELECT FROM:* Access control policy; procedures addressing access enforcement; security plan; information system design documentation; information system configuration settings and associated documentation; information system audit records; other relevant documents or records].

Interview: [*SELECT FROM:* Organizational personnel with access enforcement responsibilities; system/network administrators; organizational personnel with information security responsibilities; system developers].

Test: [*SELECT FROM:* Automated mechanisms preventing access to security-relevant information within the information system].

AC-3(6)	**ACCESS ENFORCEMENT**	*PROTECTION OF USER AND SYSTEM INFORMATION*

[Withdrawn: Incorporated into MP-4 and SC-28].

Special Publication 800-53A
Revision 4

Assessing Security and Privacy Controls in Federal Information Systems
and Organizations — *Building Effective Assessment Plans*

AC-3(7)	ACCESS ENFORCEMENT | *ROLE-BASED ACCESS CONTROL*	
	ASSESSMENT OBJECTIVE: *Determine if:*	
	AC-3(7)[1]	*the organization defines roles to control information system access;*
	AC-3(7)[2]	*the organization defines users authorized to assume the organization-defined roles;*
	AC-3(7)[3]	*the information system controls access based on organization-defined roles and users authorized to assume such roles;*
	AC-3(7)[4]	*the information system enforces a role-based access control policy over defined:*
	AC-3(7)[4][a]	*subjects, and*
	AC-3(7)[4][b]	*objects.*
	POTENTIAL ASSESSMENT METHODS AND OBJECTS: **Examine**: [*SELECT FROM:* Access control policy; role-based access control policies; procedures addressing access enforcement; security plan, information system design documentation; information system configuration settings and associated documentation; list of roles, users, and associated privileges required to control information system access; information system audit records; other relevant documents or records]. **Interview**: [*SELECT FROM:* Organizational personnel with access enforcement responsibilities; system/network administrators; organizational personnel with information security responsibilities; system developers]. **Test**: [*SELECT FROM:* Automated mechanisms implementing role-based access control policy].	

AC-3(8)	ACCESS ENFORCEMENT | *REVOCATION OF ACCESS AUTHORIZATIONS*	
	ASSESSMENT OBJECTIVE: *Determine if:*	
	AC-3(8)[1]	*the organization defines rules governing the timing of revocations of access authorizations; and*
	AC-3(8)[2]	*the information system enforces the revocation of access authorizations resulting from changes to the security attributes of subjects and objects based on organization-defined rules governing the timing of revocations of access authorizations.*
	POTENTIAL ASSESSMENT METHODS AND OBJECTS: **Examine**: [*SELECT FROM:* Access control policy; procedures addressing access enforcement; information system design documentation; information system configuration settings and associated documentation; rules governing revocation of access authorizations, information system audit records; other relevant documents or records]. **Interview**: [*SELECT FROM:* Organizational personnel with access enforcement responsibilities; system/network administrators; organizational personnel with information security responsibilities; system developers]. **Test**: [*SELECT FROM:* Automated mechanisms implementing access enforcement functions].	

AC-3(9)	ACCESS ENFORCEMENT | *CONTROLLED RELEASE*
	ASSESSMENT OBJECTIVE: *Determine if:*

Special Publication 800-53A
Revision 4

Assessing Security and Privacy Controls in Federal Information Systems
and Organizations — *Building Effective Assessment Plans*

AC-3(9)[1]	*the organization defines the information system or system component authorized to receive information released outside of the established system boundary of the information system releasing such information;*	
AC-3(9)[2]	*the organization defines security safeguards to be provided by organization-defined information system or system component receiving information released from an information system outside of the established system boundary;*	
AC-3(9)[3]	*the organization defines security safeguards to be used to validate the appropriateness of the information designated for release;*	
AC-3(9)[4]	*the information system does not release information outside of the established system boundary unless:*	
	AC-3(9)[4](a)	*the receiving organization-defined information system or system component provides organization-defined security safeguards; and*
	AC-3(9)[4](b)	*the organization-defined security safeguards are used to validate the appropriateness of the information designated for release.*

POTENTIAL ASSESSMENT METHODS AND OBJECTS:

Examine: [*SELECT FROM:* Access control policy; procedures addressing access enforcement; information system design documentation; information system configuration settings and associated documentation; list of security safeguards provided by receiving information system or system components; list of security safeguards validating appropriateness of information designated for release; information system audit records; other relevant documents or records].

Interview: [*SELECT FROM:* Organizational personnel with access enforcement responsibilities; system/network administrators; organizational personnel with information security responsibilities; system developers].

Test: [*SELECT FROM:* Automated mechanisms implementing access enforcement functions].

AC-3(10)	**ACCESS ENFORCEMENT	*AUDITED OVERRIDE OF ACCESS CONTROL MECHANISMS***
	ASSESSMENT OBJECTIVE: *Determine if the organization:*

AC-3(10)[1]	*defines conditions under which to employ an audited override of automated access control mechanisms; and*
AC-3(10)[2]	*employs an audited override of automated access control mechanisms under organization-defined conditions.*

POTENTIAL ASSESSMENT METHODS AND OBJECTS:

Examine: [*SELECT FROM:* Access control policy; procedures addressing access enforcement; information system design documentation; information system configuration settings and associated documentation; conditions for employing audited override of automated access control mechanisms; information system audit records; other relevant documents or records].

Interview: [*SELECT FROM:* Organizational personnel with access enforcement responsibilities; system/network administrators; organizational personnel with information security responsibilities].

Test: [*SELECT FROM:* Automated mechanisms implementing access enforcement functions].

AC-4	**INFORMATION FLOW ENFORCEMENT**
	ASSESSMENT OBJECTIVE: *Determine if:*

Special Publication 800-53A
Revision 4

Assessing Security and Privacy Controls in Federal Information Systems
and Organizations — *Building Effective Assessment Plans*

AC-4[1]	*the organization defines information flow control policies to control the flow of information within the system and between interconnected systems; and*
AC-4[2]	*the information system enforces approved authorizations for controlling the flow of information within the system and between interconnected systems based on organization-defined information flow control policies.*

POTENTIAL ASSESSMENT METHODS AND OBJECTS:

Examine: [*SELECT FROM:* Access control policy; information flow control policies; procedures addressing information flow enforcement; information system design documentation; information system configuration settings and associated documentation; information system baseline configuration; list of information flow authorizations; information system audit records; other relevant documents or records].

Interview: [*SELECT FROM:* System/network administrators; organizational personnel with information security responsibilities; system developers].

Test: [*SELECT FROM:* Automated mechanisms implementing information flow enforcement policy].

AC-4(1)	**INFORMATION FLOW ENFORCEMENT** | *OBJECT SECURITY ATTRIBUTES*

ASSESSMENT OBJECTIVE:

Determine if:

AC-4(1)[1]	*the organization defines information flow control policies as a basis for flow control decisions;*
AC-4(1)[2]	*the organization defines security attributes to be associated with information, source, and destination objects;*
AC-4(1)[3]	*the organization defines the following objects to be associated with organization-defined security attributes:*

	AC-4(1)[3][a]	*information;*
	AC-4(1)[3][b]	*source;*
	AC-4(1)[3][c]	*destination; and*

AC-4(1)[4]	*the information system uses organization-defined security attributes associated with organization-defined information, source, and destination objects to enforce organization-defined information flow control policies as a basis for flow control decisions.*

POTENTIAL ASSESSMENT METHODS AND OBJECTS:

Examine: [*SELECT FROM:* Access control policy; information flow control policies; procedures addressing information flow enforcement; information system design documentation; information system configuration settings and associated documentation; list of security attributes and associated information, source, and destination objects enforcing information flow control policies; information system audit records; other relevant documents or records].

Interview: [*SELECT FROM:* System/network administrators; organizational personnel with information security responsibilities; system developers].

Test: [*SELECT FROM:* Automated mechanisms implementing information flow enforcement policy].

AC-4(2)	**INFORMATION FLOW ENFORCEMENT** | *PROCESSING DOMAINS*

ASSESSMENT OBJECTIVE:

Determine if:

AC-4(2)[1]	*the organization defines information flow control policies as a basis for flow control decisions; and*

Special Publication 800-53A
Revision 4

Assessing Security and Privacy Controls in Federal Information Systems
and Organizations — *Building Effective Assessment Plans*

AC-4(2)[2]	*the information system uses protected processing domains to enforce organization-defined information flow control policies as a basis for flow control decisions.*

POTENTIAL ASSESSMENT METHODS AND OBJECTS:

Examine: [*SELECT FROM:* Access control policy; information flow control policies; procedures addressing information flow enforcement; information system design documentation; information system security architecture and associated documentation; information system configuration settings and associated documentation; information system audit records; other relevant documents or records].

Interview: [*SELECT FROM:* System/network administrators; organizational personnel with information security responsibilities].

Test: [*SELECT FROM:* Automated mechanisms implementing information flow enforcement policy].

AC-4(3)	**INFORMATION FLOW ENFORCEMENT** | *DYNAMIC INFORMATION FLOW CONTROL*

ASSESSMENT OBJECTIVE:

Determine if:

AC-4(3)[1]	*the organization defines policies to enforce dynamic information flow control; and*
AC-4(3)[2]	*the information system enforces dynamic information flow control based on organization-defined policies.*

POTENTIAL ASSESSMENT METHODS AND OBJECTS:

Examine: [*SELECT FROM:* Access control policy; information flow control policies; procedures addressing information flow enforcement; information system design documentation; information system security architecture and associated documentation; information system configuration settings and associated documentation; information system audit records; other relevant documents or records].

Interview: [*SELECT FROM:* System/network administrators; organizational personnel with information security responsibilities; system developers].

Test: [*SELECT FROM:* Automated mechanisms implementing information flow enforcement policy].

AC-4(4)	**INFORMATION FLOW ENFORCEMENT** | *CONTENT CHECK ENCRYPTED INFORMATION*

ASSESSMENT OBJECTIVE:

Determine if:

AC-4(4)[1]	*the organization defines a procedure or method to be employed to prevent encrypted information from bypassing content-checking mechanisms;*
AC-4(4)[2]	*the information system prevents encrypted information from bypassing content-checking mechanisms by doing one or more of the following:*

	AC-4(4)[2][a]	*decrypting the information;*
	AC-4(4)[2][b]	*blocking the flow of the encrypted information;*
	AC-4(4)[2][c]	*terminating communications sessions attempting to pass encrypted information; and/or*
	AC-4(4)[2][d]	*employing the organization-defined procedure or method.*

Special Publication 800-53A
Revision 4

Assessing Security and Privacy Controls in Federal Information Systems
and Organizations — *Building Effective Assessment Plans*

POTENTIAL ASSESSMENT METHODS AND OBJECTS:

Examine: [*SELECT FROM*: Access control policy; information flow control policies; procedures addressing information flow enforcement; information system design documentation; information system configuration settings and associated documentation; information system audit records; other relevant documents or records].

Interview: [*SELECT FROM*: System/network administrators; organizational personnel with information security responsibilities; system developers].

Test: [*SELECT FROM*: Automated mechanisms implementing information flow enforcement policy].

AC-4(5)	INFORMATION FLOW ENFORCEMENT	*EMBEDDED DATA TYPES*

ASSESSMENT OBJECTIVE:

Determine if:

AC-4(5)[1]	*the organization defines limitations to be enforced on embedding data types within other data types; and*
AC-4(5)[2]	*the information system enforces organization-defined limitations on embedding data types within other data types.*

POTENTIAL ASSESSMENT METHODS AND OBJECTS:

Examine: [*SELECT FROM*: Access control policy; procedures addressing information flow enforcement; information system design documentation; information system configuration settings and associated documentation; list of limitations to be enforced on embedding data types within other data types; information system audit records; other relevant documents or records].

Interview: [*SELECT FROM*: System/network administrators; organizational personnel with information security responsibilities; system developers].

Test: [*SELECT FROM*: Automated mechanisms implementing information flow enforcement policy].

AC-4(6)	INFORMATION FLOW ENFORCEMENT	*METADATA*

ASSESSMENT OBJECTIVE:

Determine if:

AC-4(6)[1]	*the organization defines metadata to be used as a means of enforcing information flow control; and*
AC-4(6)[2]	*the information system enforces information flow control based on organization-defined metadata.*

POTENTIAL ASSESSMENT METHODS AND OBJECTS:

Examine: [*SELECT FROM*: Access control policy; information flow control policies; procedures addressing information flow enforcement; information system design documentation; information system configuration settings and associated documentation; types of metadata used to enforce information flow control decisions; information system audit records; other relevant documents or records].

Interview: [*SELECT FROM*: System/network administrators; organizational personnel with information security responsibilities; system developers].

Test: [*SELECT FROM*: Automated mechanisms implementing information flow enforcement policy].

AC-4(7)	INFORMATION FLOW ENFORCEMENT	*ONE-WAY FLOW MECHANISMS*

ASSESSMENT OBJECTIVE:

Determine if:

AC-4(7)[1]	*the organization defines one-way information flows to be enforced by the information system; and*

Special Publication 800-53A
Revision 4

Assessing Security and Privacy Controls in Federal Information Systems
and Organizations — *Building Effective Assessment Plans*

AC-4(7)[2]	*the information system enforces organization-defined one-way information flows using hardware mechanisms.*

POTENTIAL ASSESSMENT METHODS AND OBJECTS:

Examine: [*SELECT FROM:* Access control policy; information flow control policies; procedures addressing information flow enforcement; information system design documentation; information system configuration settings and associated documentation; information system hardware mechanisms and associated configurations; information system audit records; other relevant documents or records].

Interview: [*SELECT FROM:* System/network administrators; organizational personnel with information security responsibilities; system developers].

Test: [*SELECT FROM:* Hardware mechanisms implementing information flow enforcement policy].

AC-4(8)	**INFORMATION FLOW ENFORCEMENT**	*SECURITY POLICY FILTERS*

ASSESSMENT OBJECTIVE:

Determine if:

AC-4(8)[1]	*the organization defines security policy filters to be used as a basis for enforcing flow control decisions;*
AC-4(8)[2]	*the organization defines information flows for which flow control decisions are to be applied and enforced; and*
AC-4(8)[3]	*the information system enforces information flow control using organization-defined security policy filters as a basis for flow control decisions for organization-defined information flows.*

POTENTIAL ASSESSMENT METHODS AND OBJECTS:

Examine: [*SELECT FROM:* Access control policy; information flow control policies; procedures addressing information flow enforcement; information system design documentation; information system configuration settings and associated documentation; list of security policy filters regulating flow control decisions; information system audit records; other relevant documents or records].

Interview: [*SELECT FROM:* System/network administrators; organizational personnel with information security responsibilities; system developers].

Test: [*SELECT FROM:* Automated mechanisms implementing information flow enforcement policy].

AC-4(9)	**INFORMATION FLOW ENFORCEMENT**	*HUMAN REVIEWS*

ASSESSMENT OBJECTIVE:
Determine if:

AC-4(9)[1]	*the organization defines information flows requiring the use of human reviews;*
AC-4(9)[2]	*the organization defines conditions under which the use of human reviews for organization-defined information flows is to be enforced; and*
AC-4(9)[3]	*the information system enforces the use of human reviews for organization-defined information flows under organization-defined conditions.*

Special Publication 800-53A
Revision 4

Assessing Security and Privacy Controls in Federal Information Systems
and Organizations — *Building Effective Assessment Plans*

POTENTIAL ASSESSMENT METHODS AND OBJECTS:

Examine: [*SELECT FROM:* Access control policy; information flow control policies; procedures addressing information flow enforcement; information system design documentation; information system configuration settings and associated documentation; records of human reviews regarding information flows; list of conditions requiring human reviews for information flows; information system audit records; other relevant documents or records].

Interview: [*SELECT FROM:* System/network administrators; organizational personnel with information security responsibilities; organizational personnel with information flow enforcement responsibilities; system developers].

Test: [*SELECT FROM:* Automated mechanisms enforcing the use of human reviews].

AC-4(10)	INFORMATION FLOW ENFORCEMENT | *ENABLE / DISABLE SECURITY POLICY FILTERS*
	ASSESSMENT OBJECTIVE: *Determine if:*
	AC-4(10)[1] · *the organization defines security policy filters that privileged administrators have the capability to enable/disable;*
	AC-4(10)[2] · *the organization-defined conditions under which privileged administrators have the capability to enable/disable organization-defined security policy filters; and*
	AC-4(10)[3] · *the information system provides the capability for privileged administrators to enable/disable organization-defined security policy filters under organization-defined conditions.*
	POTENTIAL ASSESSMENT METHODS AND OBJECTS: **Examine**: [*SELECT FROM:* Access control policy; information flow information policies; procedures addressing information flow enforcement; information system design documentation; information system configuration settings and associated documentation; list of security policy filters enabled/disabled by privileged administrators; information system audit records; other relevant documents or records]. **Interview**: [*SELECT FROM:* Organizational personnel with responsibilities for enabling/disabling security policy filters; system/network administrators; organizational personnel with information security responsibilities; system developers]. **Test**: [*SELECT FROM:* Automated mechanisms implementing information flow enforcement policy].

AC-4(11)	INFORMATION FLOW ENFORCEMENT | *CONFIGURATION OF SECURITY POLICY FILTERS*
	ASSESSMENT OBJECTIVE: *Determine if:*
	AC-4(11)[1] · *the organization defines security policy filters that privileged administrators have the capability to configure to support different security policies; and*
	AC-4(11)[2] · *the information system provides the capability for privileged administrators to configure organization-defined security policy filters to support different security policies.*
	POTENTIAL ASSESSMENT METHODS AND OBJECTS: **Examine**: [*SELECT FROM:* Access control policy; information flow control policies; procedures addressing information flow enforcement; information system design documentation; information system configuration settings and associated documentation; list of security policy filters; information system audit records; other relevant documents or records]. **Interview**: [*SELECT FROM:* Organizational personnel with responsibilities for configuring security policy filters; system/network administrators; organizational personnel with information security responsibilities; system developers]. **Test**: [*SELECT FROM:* Automated mechanisms implementing information flow enforcement policy].

Special Publication 800-53A
Revision 4

Assessing Security and Privacy Controls in Federal Information Systems
and Organizations — *Building Effective Assessment Plans*

AC-4(12)	INFORMATION FLOW ENFORCEMENT	*DATA TYPE IDENTIFIERS*
	ASSESSMENT OBJECTIVE: *Determine if:*	
	AC-4(12)[1]	*the organization defines data type identifiers to be used, when transferring information between different security domains, to validate data essential for information flow decisions; and*
	AC-4(12)[2]	*the information system, when transferring information between different security domains, uses organization-defined data type identifiers to validate data essential for information flow decisions.*
	POTENTIAL ASSESSMENT METHODS AND OBJECTS: **Examine**: [*SELECT FROM:* Access control policy; information flow control policies; procedures addressing information flow enforcement; information system design documentation; information system configuration settings and associated documentation; list of data type identifiers; information system audit records; other relevant documents or records]. **Interview**: [*SELECT FROM:* System/network administrators; organizational personnel with information security responsibilities; system developers]. **Test**: [*SELECT FROM:* Automated mechanisms implementing information flow enforcement policy].	

AC-4(13)	INFORMATION FLOW ENFORCEMENT	*DECOMPOSITION INTO POLICY-RELEVANT SUBCOMPONENTS*
	ASSESSMENT OBJECTIVE: *Determine if:*	
	AC-4(13)[1]	*the organization defines policy-relevant subcomponents to decompose information for submission to policy enforcement mechanisms when transferring such information between different security domains; and*
	AC-4(13)[2]	*the information system, when transferring information between different security domains, decomposes information into organization-defined policy-relevant subcomponents for submission to policy enforcement mechanisms.*
	POTENTIAL ASSESSMENT METHODS AND OBJECTS: **Examine**: [*SELECT FROM:* Access control policy; information flow control policies; procedures addressing information flow enforcement; information system design documentation; information system configuration settings and associated documentation; information system audit records; other relevant documents or records]. **Interview**: [*SELECT FROM:* System/network administrators; organizational personnel with information security responsibilities; system developers]. **Test**: [*SELECT FROM:* Automated mechanisms implementing information flow enforcement policy].	

AC-4(14)	INFORMATION FLOW ENFORCEMENT	*SECURITY POLICY FILTER CONSTRAINTS*
	ASSESSMENT OBJECTIVE: *Determine if:*	
	AC-4(14)[1]	*the organization defines security policy filters to be implemented that require fully enumerated formats restricting data structure and content when transferring information between different security domains; and*
	AC-4(14)[2]	*the information system, when transferring information between different security domains, implements organization-defined security policy filters requiring fully enumerated formats that restrict data structure and content.*

Special Publication 800-53A
Revision 4

Assessing Security and Privacy Controls in Federal Information Systems
and Organizations — *Building Effective Assessment Plans*

POTENTIAL ASSESSMENT METHODS AND OBJECTS:

Examine: [*SELECT FROM:* Access control policy; information flow control policies; procedures addressing information flow enforcement; information system design documentation; information system configuration settings and associated documentation; list of security policy filters; list of data content policy filters; information system audit records; other relevant documents or records].

Interview: [*SELECT FROM:* System/network administrators; organizational personnel with information security responsibilities; system developers].

Test: [*SELECT FROM:* Automated mechanisms implementing information flow enforcement policy].

AC-4(15)	INFORMATION FLOW ENFORCEMENT | *DETECTION OF UNSANCTIONED INFORMATION*

ASSESSMENT OBJECTIVE:

Determine if:

AC-4(15)[1]	*the organization defines unsanctioned information to be detected when transferring information between different security domains;*
AC-4(15)[2]	*the organization defines the security policy that requires the transfer of organization-defined unsanctioned information between different security domains to be prohibited when the presence of such information is detected; and*
AC-4(15)[3]	*the information system, when transferring information between different security domains, examines the information for the presence of organization-defined unsanctioned information and prohibits the transfer of such information in accordance with the organization-defined security policy.*

POTENTIAL ASSESSMENT METHODS AND OBJECTS:

Examine: [*SELECT FROM:* Access control policy; information flow control policies; procedures addressing information flow enforcement; information system design documentation; information system configuration settings and associated documentation; list of unsanctioned information types and associated information; information system audit records; other relevant documents or records].

Interview: [*SELECT FROM:* Organizational personnel with information security responsibilities; system developers].

Test: [*SELECT FROM:* Automated mechanisms implementing information flow enforcement policy].

AC-4(16)	INFORMATION FLOW ENFORCEMENT | *INFORMATION TRANSFERS ON INTERCONNECTED SYSTEMS*

[Withdrawn: Incorporated into AC-4].

AC-4(17)	INFORMATION FLOW ENFORCEMENT | *DOMAIN AUTHENTICATION*

ASSESSMENT OBJECTIVE:

Determine if the information system uniquely identifies and authenticates:

AC-4(17)[1]	**AC-4(17)[1][a]**	*source points for information transfer;*
	AC-4(17)[1][b]	*destination points for information transfer;*
AC-4(17)[2]	*by one or more of the following:*	
	AC-4(17)[2][a]	*organization;*
	AC-4(17)[2][b]	*system;*
	AC-4(17)[2][c]	*application; and/or*

Special Publication 800-53A
Revision 4

Assessing Security and Privacy Controls in Federal Information Systems
and Organizations — *Building Effective Assessment Plans*

	AC-4(17)[2][d]	*individual.*
	POTENTIAL ASSESSMENT METHODS AND OBJECTS:	

Examine: [*SELECT FROM:* Access control policy; information flow control policies; procedures addressing information flow enforcement; procedures addressing source and destination domain identification and authentication; information system design documentation; information system configuration settings and associated documentation; information system audit records; other relevant documents or records].

Interview: [*SELECT FROM:* System/network administrators; organizational personnel with information security responsibilities; system developers].

Test: [*SELECT FROM:* Automated mechanisms implementing information flow enforcement policy].

AC-4(18)	INFORMATION FLOW ENFORCEMENT	*SECURITY ATTRIBUTE BINDING*

ASSESSMENT OBJECTIVE:

Determine if:

AC-4(18)[1]	*the organization defines binding techniques to be used to facilitate information flow policy enforcement; and*
AC-4(18)[2]	*the information system binds security attributes to information using organization-defined binding techniques to facilitate information flow policy enforcement.*

POTENTIAL ASSESSMENT METHODS AND OBJECTS:

Examine: [*SELECT FROM:* Information flow enforcement policy; information flow control policies; procedures addressing information flow enforcement; information system design documentation; information system configuration settings and associated documentation; list of binding techniques to bind security attributes to information; information system audit records; other relevant documents or records].

Interview: [*SELECT FROM:* Organizational personnel with information flow enforcement responsibilities; system/network administrators; organizational personnel with information security responsibilities; system developers].

Test: [*SELECT FROM:* Automated mechanisms implementing information flow enforcement functions].

AC-4(19)	INFORMATION FLOW ENFORCEMENT	*VALIDATION OF METADATA*

ASSESSMENT OBJECTIVE:

Determine if the information system, when transferring information between different security domains, applies the same security policy filtering to metadata as it applies to data payloads.

POTENTIAL ASSESSMENT METHODS AND OBJECTS:

Examine: [*SELECT FROM:* Information flow enforcement policy; information flow control policies; procedures addressing information flow enforcement; information system design documentation; information system configuration settings and associated documentation; list of security policy filtering criteria applied to metadata and data payloads; information system audit records; other relevant documents or records].

Interview: [*SELECT FROM:* Organizational personnel with information flow enforcement responsibilities; system/network administrators; organizational personnel with information security responsibilities; system developers].

Test: [*SELECT FROM:* Automated mechanisms implementing information flow enforcement functions].

AC-4(20)	INFORMATION FLOW ENFORCEMENT	*APPROVED SOLUTIONS*

ASSESSMENT OBJECTIVE:

Determine if the organization:

Special Publication 800-53A
Revision 4

Assessing Security and Privacy Controls in Federal Information Systems
and Organizations — *Building Effective Assessment Plans*

	AC-4(20)[1]	*defines solutions in approved configurations to control the flow of information across security domains;*
	AC-4(20)[2]	*defines information for which organization-defined solutions in approved configurations are to be employed to control the flow of such information across security domains; and*
	AC-4(20)[3]	*employs organization-defined solutions in approved configurations to control the flow of organization-defined information across security domains.*

POTENTIAL ASSESSMENT METHODS AND OBJECTS:

Examine: [*SELECT FROM:* Information flow enforcement policy; information flow control policies; procedures addressing information flow enforcement; information system design documentation; information system configuration settings and associated documentation; list of solutions in approved configurations; approved configuration baselines; information system audit records; other relevant documents or records].

Interview: [*SELECT FROM:* Organizational personnel with information flow enforcement responsibilities; system/network administrators; organizational personnel with information security responsibilities].

Test: [*SELECT FROM:* Automated mechanisms implementing information flow enforcement functions].

AC-4(21)	**INFORMATION FLOW ENFORCEMENT** | *PHYSICAL / LOGICAL SEPARATION OF INFORMATION FLOWS*	

ASSESSMENT OBJECTIVE:

Determine if:

	AC-4(21)[1]	*the organization defines the required separations of information flows by types of information;*
	AC-4(21)[2]	*the organization defines the mechanisms and/or techniques to be used to separate information flows logically or physically; and*
	AC-4(21)[3]	*the information system separates information flows logically or physically using organization-defined mechanisms and/or techniques to accomplish organization-defined required separations by types of information.*

POTENTIAL ASSESSMENT METHODS AND OBJECTS:

Examine: [*SELECT FROM:* Information flow enforcement policy; information flow control policies; procedures addressing information flow enforcement; information system design documentation; information system configuration settings and associated documentation; list of required separation of information flows by information types; list of mechanisms and/or techniques used to logically or physically separate information flows; information system audit records; other relevant documents or records].

Interview: [*SELECT FROM:* Organizational personnel with information flow enforcement responsibilities; system/network administrators; organizational personnel with information security responsibilities; system developers].

Test: [*SELECT FROM:* Automated mechanisms implementing information flow enforcement functions].

AC-4(22)	**INFORMATION FLOW ENFORCEMENT** | *ACCESS ONLY*

ASSESSMENT OBJECTIVE:

Determine if the information system provides access from a single device to computing platforms, applications, or data residing on multiple different security domains, while preventing any information flow between the different security domains.

Special Publication 800-53A
Revision 4

Assessing Security and Privacy Controls in Federal Information Systems
and Organizations — *Building Effective Assessment Plans*

POTENTIAL ASSESSMENT METHODS AND OBJECTS:

Examine: [*SELECT FROM:* Information flow enforcement policy; procedures addressing information flow enforcement; information system design documentation; information system configuration settings and associated documentation; information system audit records; other relevant documents or records].

Interview: [*SELECT FROM:* Organizational personnel with information flow enforcement responsibilities; system/network administrators; organizational personnel with information security responsibilities].

Test: [*SELECT FROM:* Automated mechanisms implementing information flow enforcement functions].

AC-5	SEPARATION OF DUTIES		

ASSESSMENT OBJECTIVE:

Determine if the organization:

AC-5(a)	AC-5(a)[1]	*defines duties of individuals to be separated;*
	AC-5(a)[2]	*separates organization-defined duties of individuals;*
AC-5(b)	*documents separation of duties; and*	
AC-5(c)	*defines information system access authorizations to support separation of duties.*	

POTENTIAL ASSESSMENT METHODS AND OBJECTS:

Examine: [*SELECT FROM:* Access control policy; procedures addressing divisions of responsibility and separation of duties; information system configuration settings and associated documentation; list of divisions of responsibility and separation of duties; information system access authorizations; information system audit records; other relevant documents or records].

Interview: [*SELECT FROM:* Organizational personnel with responsibilities for defining appropriate divisions of responsibility and separation of duties; organizational personnel with information security responsibilities; system/network administrators].

Test: [*SELECT FROM:* Automated mechanisms implementing separation of duties policy].

AC-6	LEAST PRIVILEGE

ASSESSMENT OBJECTIVE:

Determine if the organization employs the principle of least privilege, allowing only authorized access for users (and processes acting on behalf of users) which are necessary to accomplish assigned tasks in accordance with organizational missions and business functions.

POTENTIAL ASSESSMENT METHODS AND OBJECTS:

Examine: [*SELECT FROM:* Access control policy; procedures addressing least privilege; list of assigned access authorizations (user privileges); information system configuration settings and associated documentation; information system audit records; other relevant documents or records].

Interview: [*SELECT FROM:* Organizational personnel with responsibilities for defining least privileges necessary to accomplish specified tasks; organizational personnel with information security responsibilities; system/network administrators].

Test: [*SELECT FROM:* Automated mechanisms implementing least privilege functions].

AC-6(1)	LEAST PRIVILEGE	*AUTHORIZE ACCESS TO SECURITY FUNCTIONS*

ASSESSMENT OBJECTIVE:

Determine if the organization:

AC-6(1)[1]	*defines security-relevant information for which access must be explicitly authorized;*

Special Publication 800-53A
Revision 4

Assessing Security and Privacy Controls in Federal Information Systems
and Organizations — *Building Effective Assessment Plans*

AC-6(1)[2]	*defines security functions deployed in:*	
	AC-6(1)[2][a]	*hardware;*
	AC-6(1)[2][b]	*software;*
	AC-6(1)[2][c]	*firmware;*
AC-6(1)[3]	*explicitly authorizes access to:*	
	AC-6(1)[3][a]	*organization-defined security functions; and*
	AC-6(1)[3][b]	*security-relevant information.*

POTENTIAL ASSESSMENT METHODS AND OBJECTS:

Examine: [*SELECT FROM:* Access control policy; procedures addressing least privilege; list of security functions (deployed in hardware, software, and firmware) and security-relevant information for which access must be explicitly authorized; information system configuration settings and associated documentation; information system audit records; other relevant documents or records].

Interview: [*SELECT FROM:* Organizational personnel with responsibilities for defining least privileges necessary to accomplish specified tasks; organizational personnel with information security responsibilities; system/network administrators].

Test: [*SELECT FROM:* Automated mechanisms implementing least privilege functions].

AC-6(2)	**LEAST PRIVILEGE	*NON-PRIVILEGED ACCESS FOR NONSECURITY FUNCTIONS***	
	ASSESSMENT OBJECTIVE: *Determine if the organization:*	
	AC-6(2)[1]	*defines security functions or security-relevant information to which users of information system accounts, or roles, have access; and*
	AC-6(2)[2]	*requires that users of information system accounts, or roles, with access to organization-defined security functions or security-relevant information, use non-privileged accounts, or roles, when accessing nonsecurity functions.*

POTENTIAL ASSESSMENT METHODS AND OBJECTS:

Examine: [*SELECT FROM:* Access control policy; procedures addressing least privilege; list of system-generated security functions or security-relevant information assigned to information system accounts or roles; information system configuration settings and associated documentation; information system audit records; other relevant documents or records].

Interview: [*SELECT FROM:* Organizational personnel with responsibilities for defining least privileges necessary to accomplish specified tasks; organizational personnel with information security responsibilities; system/network administrators].

Test: [*SELECT FROM:* Automated mechanisms implementing least privilege functions].

AC-6(3)	**LEAST PRIVILEGE	*NETWORK ACCESS TO PRIVILEGED COMMANDS***	
	ASSESSMENT OBJECTIVE: *Determine if the organization:*	
	AC-6(3)[1]	*defines privileged commands to which network access is to be authorized only for compelling operational needs;*
	AC-6(3)[2]	*defines compelling operational needs for which network access to organization-defined privileged commands are to be solely authorized;*
	AC-6(3)[3]	*authorizes network access to organization-defined privileged commands only for organization-defined compelling operational needs; and*

Special Publication 800-53A
Revision 4

Assessing Security and Privacy Controls in Federal Information Systems
and Organizations — *Building Effective Assessment Plans*

	AC-6(3)[4]	*documents the rationale for authorized network access to organization-defined privileged commands in the security plan for the information system.*

POTENTIAL ASSESSMENT METHODS AND OBJECTS:

Examine: [*SELECT FROM:* Access control policy; procedures addressing least privilege; security plan; information system configuration settings and associated documentation; information system audit records; list of operational needs for authorizing network access to privileged commands; other relevant documents or records].

Interview: [*SELECT FROM:* Organizational personnel with responsibilities for defining least privileges necessary to accomplish specified tasks; organizational personnel with information security responsibilities].

Test: [*SELECT FROM:* Automated mechanisms implementing least privilege functions].

AC-6(4)	LEAST PRIVILEGE	*SEPARATE PROCESSING DOMAINS*

ASSESSMENT OBJECTIVE:

Determine if the information system provides separate processing domains to enable finer-grained allocation of user privileges.

POTENTIAL ASSESSMENT METHODS AND OBJECTS:

Examine: [*SELECT FROM:* Access control policy; procedures addressing least privilege; information system design documentation; information system configuration settings and associated documentation; information system audit records; other relevant documents or records].

Interview: [*SELECT FROM:* Organizational personnel with responsibilities for defining least privileges necessary to accomplish specified tasks; organizational personnel with information security responsibilities; system developers].

Test: [*SELECT FROM:* Automated mechanisms implementing least privilege functions].

AC-6(5)	LEAST PRIVILEGE	*PRIVILEGED ACCOUNTS*

ASSESSMENT OBJECTIVE:

Determine if the organization:

AC-6(5)[1]	*defines personnel or roles for which privileged accounts on the information system are to be restricted; and*
AC-6(5)[2]	*restricts privileged accounts on the information system to organization-defined personnel or roles.*

POTENTIAL ASSESSMENT METHODS AND OBJECTS:

Examine: [*SELECT FROM:* Access control policy; procedures addressing least privilege; list of system-generated privileged accounts; list of system administration personnel; information system configuration settings and associated documentation; information system audit records; other relevant documents or records].

Interview: [*SELECT FROM:* Organizational personnel with responsibilities for defining least privileges necessary to accomplish specified tasks; organizational personnel with information security responsibilities; system/network administrators].

Test: [*SELECT FROM:* Automated mechanisms implementing least privilege functions].

AC-6(6)	LEAST PRIVILEGE	*PRIVILEGED ACCESS BY NON-ORGANIZATIONAL USERS*

ASSESSMENT OBJECTIVE:

Determine if the organization prohibits privileged access to the information system by non-organizational users.

Special Publication 800-53A
Revision 4

Assessing Security and Privacy Controls in Federal Information Systems
and Organizations — *Building Effective Assessment Plans*

	POTENTIAL ASSESSMENT METHODS AND OBJECTS: **Examine**: [*SELECT FROM:* Access control policy; procedures addressing least privilege; list of system-generated privileged accounts; list of non-organizational users; information system configuration settings and associated documentation; information system audit records; other relevant documents or records]. **Interview**: [*SELECT FROM:* Organizational personnel with responsibilities for defining least privileges necessary to accomplish specified tasks; organizational personnel with information security responsibilities; system/network administrators]. **Test**: [*SELECT FROM:* Automated mechanisms prohibiting privileged access to the information system].

AC-6(7)	LEADST PRIVILEGE | *REVIEW OF USER PRIVILEGES*		
	ASSESSMENT OBJECTIVE: *Determine if the organization:*		
	AC-6(7)(a)	**AC-6(7)(a)[1]**	*defines roles or classes of users to which privileges are assigned;*
		AC-6(7)(a)[2]	*defines the frequency to review the privileges assigned to organization-defined roles or classes of users to validate the need for such privileges;*
		AC-6(7)(a)[3]	*reviews the privileges assigned to organization-defined roles or classes of users with the organization-defined frequency to validate the need for such privileges; and*
	AC-6(7)(b)	*reassigns or removes privileges, if necessary, to correctly reflect organizational missions/business needs.*	
	POTENTIAL ASSESSMENT METHODS AND OBJECTS: **Examine**: [*SELECT FROM:* Access control policy; procedures addressing least privilege; list of system-generated roles or classes of users and assigned privileges; information system design documentation; information system configuration settings and associated documentation; validation reviews of privileges assigned to roles or classes or users; records of privilege removals or reassignments for roles or classes of users; information system audit records; other relevant documents or records]. **Interview**: [*SELECT FROM:* Organizational personnel with responsibilities for reviewing least privileges necessary to accomplish specified tasks; organizational personnel with information security responsibilities; system/network administrators]. **Test**: [*SELECT FROM:* Automated mechanisms implementing review of user privileges].		

AC-6(8)	LEAST PRIVILEGE | *PRIVILEGE LEVELS FOR CODE EXECUTION*	
	ASSESSMENT OBJECTIVE: *Determine if:*	
	AC-6(8)[1]	*the organization defines software that should not execute at higher privilege levels than users executing the software; and*
	AC-6(8)[2]	*the information system prevents organization-defined software from executing at higher privilege levels than users executing the software.*

Special Publication 800-53A
Revision 4

Assessing Security and Privacy Controls in Federal Information Systems
and Organizations — *Building Effective Assessment Plans*

POTENTIAL ASSESSMENT METHODS AND OBJECTS:

Examine: [*SELECT FROM:* Access control policy; procedures addressing least privilege; list of software that should not execute at higher privilege levels than users executing software; information system design documentation; information system configuration settings and associated documentation; information system audit records; other relevant documents or records].

Interview: [*SELECT FROM:* Organizational personnel with responsibilities for defining least privileges necessary to accomplish specified tasks; organizational personnel with information security responsibilities; system/network administrators; system developers].

Test: [*SELECT FROM:* Automated mechanisms implementing least privilege functions for software execution].

AC-6(9)	LEAST PRIVILEGE	*AUDITING USE OF PRIVILEGED FUNCTIONS*

ASSESSMENT OBJECTIVE:

Determine if the information system audits the execution of privileged functions.

POTENTIAL ASSESSMENT METHODS AND OBJECTS:

Examine: [*SELECT FROM:* Access control policy; procedures addressing least privilege; information system design documentation; information system configuration settings and associated documentation; list of privileged functions to be audited; list of audited events; information system audit records; other relevant documents or records].

Interview: [*SELECT FROM:* Organizational personnel with responsibilities for reviewing least privileges necessary to accomplish specified tasks; organizational personnel with information security responsibilities; system/network administrators; system developers].

Test: [*SELECT FROM:* Automated mechanisms auditing the execution of least privilege functions].

AC-6(10)	LEAST PRIVILEGE	*PROHIBIT NON-PRIVILEGED USERS FROM EXECUTING PRIVILEGED FUNCTIONS*

ASSESSMENT OBJECTIVE:

Determine if the information system prevents non-privileged users from executing privileged functions to include:

AC-6(10)[1]	*disabling implemented security safeguards/countermeasures;*
AC-6(10)[2]	*circumventing security safeguards/countermeasures; or*
AC-6(10)[3]	*altering implemented security safeguards/countermeasures.*

POTENTIAL ASSESSMENT METHODS AND OBJECTS:

Examine: [*SELECT FROM:* Access control policy; procedures addressing least privilege; information system design documentation; information system configuration settings and associated documentation; list of privileged functions and associated user account assignments; information system audit records; other relevant documents or records].

Interview: [*SELECT FROM:* Organizational personnel with responsibilities for defining least privileges necessary to accomplish specified tasks; organizational personnel with information security responsibilities; system developers].

Test: [*SELECT FROM:* Automated mechanisms implementing least privilege functions for non-privileged users].

AC-7	UNSUCCESSFUL LOGIN ATTEMPTS	
	ASSESSMENT OBJECTIVE: *Determine if:*	
AC-7(a)	AC-7(a)[1]	*the organization defines the number of consecutive invalid logon attempts allowed to the information system by a user during an organization-defined time period;*

Special Publication 800-53A
Revision 4

Assessing Security and Privacy Controls in Federal Information Systems
and Organizations — *Building Effective Assessment Plans*

		AC-7(a)[2]	*the organization defines the time period allowed by a user of the information system for an organization-defined number of consecutive invalid logon attempts;*
		AC-7(a)[3]	*the information system enforces a limit of organization-defined number of consecutive invalid logon attempts by a user during an organization-defined time period;*
	AC-7(b)	AC-7(b)[1]	*the organization defines account/node lockout time period or logon delay algorithm to be automatically enforced by the information system when the maximum number of unsuccessful logon attempts is exceeded;*
		AC-7(b)[2]	*the information system, when the maximum number of unsuccessful logon attempts is exceeded, automatically:*
			AC-7(b)[2][a]	*locks the account/node for the organization-defined time period;*
			AC-7(b)[2][b]	*locks the account/node until released by an administrator; or*
			AC-7(b)[2][c]	*delays next logon prompt according to the organization-defined delay algorithm.*

POTENTIAL ASSESSMENT METHODS AND OBJECTS:

Examine: [*SELECT FROM:* Access control policy; procedures addressing unsuccessful logon attempts; security plan; information system design documentation; information system configuration settings and associated documentation; information system audit records; other relevant documents or records].

Interview: [*SELECT FROM:* Organizational personnel with information security responsibilities; system developers; system/network administrators].

Test: [*SELECT FROM:* Automated mechanisms implementing access control policy for unsuccessful logon attempts].

AC-7(1)	UNSUCCESSFUL LOGON ATTEMPTS	*AUTOMATIC ACCOUNT LOCK*

[Withdrawn: Incorporated into AC-7].

AC-7(2)	UNSUCCESSFUL LOGON ATTEMPTS	*PURGE / WIPE MOBILE DEVICE*

ASSESSMENT OBJECTIVE:
Determine if:

AC-7(2)[1]	*the organization defines mobile devices to be purged/wiped after organization-defined number of consecutive, unsuccessful device logon attempts;*
AC-7(2)[2]	*the organization defines purging/wiping requirements/techniques to be used when organization-defined mobile devices are purged/wiped after organization-defined number of consecutive, unsuccessful device logon attempts;*
AC-7(2)[3]	*the organization defines the number of consecutive, unsuccessful logon attempts allowed for accessing mobile devices before the information system purges/wipes information from such devices; and*
AC-7(2)[4]	*the information system purges/wipes information from organization-defined mobile devices based on organization-defined purging/wiping requirements/techniques after organization-defined number of consecutive, unsuccessful logon attempts.*

Special Publication 800-53A
Revision 4

Assessing Security and Privacy Controls in Federal Information Systems
and Organizations — *Building Effective Assessment Plans*

	POTENTIAL ASSESSMENT METHODS AND OBJECTS: **Examine**: [*SELECT FROM:* Access control policy; procedures addressing unsuccessful login attempts on mobile devices; information system design documentation; information system configuration settings and associated documentation; list of mobile devices to be purged/wiped after organization-defined consecutive, unsuccessful device logon attempts; list of purging/wiping requirements or techniques for mobile devices; information system audit records; other relevant documents or records]. **Interview**: [*SELECT FROM:* System/network administrators; organizational personnel with information security responsibilities]. **Test**: [*SELECT FROM:* Automated mechanisms implementing access control policy for unsuccessful device logon attempts].

AC-8	SYSTEM USE NOTIFICATION			
	ASSESSMENT OBJECTIVE: *Determine if:*			
	AC-8(a)	**AC-8(a)[1]**	*the organization defines a system use notification message or banner to be displayed by the information system to users before granting access to the system;*	
		AC-8(a)[2]	*the information system displays to users the organization-defined system use notification message or banner before granting access to the information system that provides privacy and security notices consistent with applicable federal laws, Executive Orders, directives, policies, regulations, standards, and guidance, and states that:*	
			AC-8(a)[2](1)	*users are accessing a U.S. Government information system;*
			AC-8(a)[2](2)	*information system usage may be monitored, recorded, and subject to audit;*
			AC-8(a)[2](3)	*unauthorized use of the information system is prohibited and subject to criminal and civil penalties;*
			AC-8(a)[2](4)	*use of the information system indicates consent to monitoring and recording;*
	AC-8(b)	*the information system retains the notification message or banner on the screen until users acknowledge the usage conditions and take explicit actions to log on to or further access the information system;*		
	AC-8(c)	*for publicly accessible systems:*		
		AC-8(c)(1)	**AC-8(c)(1)[1]**	*the organization defines conditions for system use to be displayed by the information system before granting further access;*
			AC-8(c)(1)[2]	*the information system displays organization-defined conditions before granting further access;*
		AC-8(c)(2)	*the information system displays references, if any, to monitoring, recording, or auditing that are consistent with privacy accommodations for such systems that generally prohibit those activities; and*	
		AC-8(c)(3)	*the information system includes a description of the authorized uses of the system.*	

Special Publication 800-53A
Revision 4

Assessing Security and Privacy Controls in Federal Information Systems
and Organizations — *Building Effective Assessment Plans*

	POTENTIAL ASSESSMENT METHODS AND OBJECTS: **Examine**: [*SELECT FROM*: Access control policy; privacy and security policies, procedures addressing system use notification; documented approval of information system use notification messages or banners; information system audit records; user acknowledgements of notification message or banner; information system design documentation; information system configuration settings and associated documentation; information system use notification messages; other relevant documents or records]. **Interview**: [*SELECT FROM*: System/network administrators; organizational personnel with information security responsibilities; organizational personnel with responsibility for providing legal advice; system developers]. **Test**: [*SELECT FROM*: Automated mechanisms implementing system use notification].

AC-9	**PREVIOUS LOGON (ACCESS) NOTIFICATION**
	ASSESSMENT OBJECTIVE: *Determine if the information system notifies the user, upon successful logon (access) to the system, of the date and time of the last logon (access).*
	POTENTIAL ASSESSMENT METHODS AND OBJECTS: **Examine**: [*SELECT FROM*: Access control policy; procedures addressing previous logon notification; information system design documentation; information system configuration settings and associated documentation; information system notification messages; other relevant documents or records]. **Interview**: [*SELECT FROM*: System/network administrators; organizational personnel with information security responsibilities; system developers]. **Test**: [*SELECT FROM*: Automated mechanisms implementing access control policy for previous logon notification].

AC-9(1)	**PREVIOUS LOGON NOTIFICATION	*UNSUCCESSFUL LOGONS***
	ASSESSMENT OBJECTIVE: *Determine if the information system notifies the user, upon successful logon/access, of the number of unsuccessful logon/access attempts since the last successful logon/access.*
	POTENTIAL ASSESSMENT METHODS AND OBJECTS: **Examine**: [*SELECT FROM*: Access control policy; procedures addressing previous logon notification; information system design documentation; information system configuration settings and associated documentation; information system audit records; other relevant documents or records]. **Interview**: [*SELECT FROM*: System/network administrators; organizational personnel with information security responsibilities; system developers]. **Test**: [*SELECT FROM*: Automated mechanisms implementing access control policy for previous logon notification].

AC-9(2)	**PREVIOUS LOGON NOTIFICATION	*SUCCESSFUL / UNSUCCESSFUL LOGONS***		
	ASSESSMENT OBJECTIVE: *Determine if:*		
	AC-9(2)[1]	*the organization defines the time period within which the information system must notify the user of the number of:*	
		AC-9(2)[1][a]	*successful logons/accesses; and/or*
		AC-9(2)[1][b]	*unsuccessful logon/access attempts;*
	AC-9(2)[2]	*the information system, during the organization-defined time period, notifies the user of the number of:*	

Special Publication 800-53A
Revision 4

Assessing Security and Privacy Controls in Federal Information Systems
and Organizations — *Building Effective Assessment Plans*

	AC-9(2)[2][a]	*successful logons/accesses; and/or*
	AC-9(2)[2][b]	*unsuccessful logon/access attempts.*

POTENTIAL ASSESSMENT METHODS AND OBJECTS:

Examine: [*SELECT FROM:* Access control policy; procedures addressing previous logon notification; information system design documentation; information system configuration settings and associated documentation; information system audit records; other relevant documents or records].

Interview: [*SELECT FROM:* System/network administrators; organizational personnel with information security responsibilities; system developers].

Test: [*SELECT FROM:* Automated mechanisms implementing access control policy for previous logon notification].

AC-9(3)	PREVIOUS LOGON NOTIFICATION	*NOTIFICATION OF ACCOUNT CHANGES*

ASSESSMENT OBJECTIVE:

Determine if:

AC-9(3)[1]	*the organization defines security-related characteristics/parameters of a user's account;*
AC-9(3)[2]	*the organization defines the time period within which changes to organization-defined security-related characteristics/parameters of a user's account must occur; and*
AC-9(3)[3]	*the information system notifies the user of changes to organization-defined security-related characteristics/parameters of the user's account during the organization-defined time period.*

POTENTIAL ASSESSMENT METHODS AND OBJECTS:

Examine: [*SELECT FROM:* Access control policy; procedures addressing previous logon notification; information system design documentation; information system configuration settings and associated documentation; information system audit records; other relevant documents or records].

Interview: [*SELECT FROM:* System/network administrators; organizational personnel with information security responsibilities; system developers].

Test: [*SELECT FROM:* Automated mechanisms implementing access control policy for previous logon notification].

AC-9(4)	PREVIOUS LOGON NOTIFICATION	*ADDITIONAL LOGON INFORMATION*

ASSESSMENT OBJECTIVE:

Determine if:

AC-9(4)[1]	*the organization defines information to be included in addition to the date and time of the last logon (access); and*
AC-9(4)[2]	*the information system notifies the user, upon successful logon (access), of the organization-defined information to be included in addition to the date and time of the last logon (access).*

Special Publication 800-53A
Revision 4

Assessing Security and Privacy Controls in Federal Information Systems
and Organizations — *Building Effective Assessment Plans*

	POTENTIAL ASSESSMENT METHODS AND OBJECTS: **Examine**: [*SELECT FROM:* Access control policy; procedures addressing previous logon notification; information system design documentation; information system configuration settings and associated documentation; information system audit records; other relevant documents or records]. **Interview**: [*SELECT FROM:* System/network administrators; organizational personnel with information security responsibilities; system developers]. **Test**: [*SELECT FROM:* Automated mechanisms implementing access control policy for previous logon notification].

AC-10	CONCURRENT SESSION CONTROL	
	ASSESSMENT OBJECTIVE: *Determine if:*	
	AC-10[1]	*the organization defines account and/or account types for the information system;*
	AC-10[2]	*the organization defines the number of concurrent sessions to be allowed for each organization-defined account and/or account type; and*
	AC-10[3]	*the information system limits the number of concurrent sessions for each organization-defined account and/or account type to the organization-defined number of concurrent sessions allowed.*
	POTENTIAL ASSESSMENT METHODS AND OBJECTS: **Examine**: [*SELECT FROM:* Access control policy; procedures addressing concurrent session control; information system design documentation; information system configuration settings and associated documentation; security plan; other relevant documents or records]. **Interview**: [*SELECT FROM:* System/network administrators; organizational personnel with information security responsibilities; system developers]. **Test**: [*SELECT FROM:* Automated mechanisms implementing access control policy for concurrent session control].	

AC-11	SESSION LOCK		
	ASSESSMENT OBJECTIVE: *Determine if:*		
	AC-11(a)	AC-11(a)[1]	*the organization defines the time period of user inactivity after which the information system initiates a session lock;*
		AC-11(a)[2]	*the information system prevents further access to the system by initiating a session lock after organization-defined time period of user inactivity or upon receiving a request from a user; and*
	AC-11(b)	*the information system retains the session lock until the user reestablishes access using established identification and authentication procedures.*	
	POTENTIAL ASSESSMENT METHODS AND OBJECTS: **Examine**: [*SELECT FROM:* Access control policy; procedures addressing session lock; procedures addressing identification and authentication; information system design documentation; information system configuration settings and associated documentation; security plan; other relevant documents or records]. **Interview**: [*SELECT FROM:* System/network administrators; organizational personnel with information security responsibilities; system developers]. **Test**: [*SELECT FROM:* Automated mechanisms implementing access control policy for session lock].		

Special Publication 800-53A
Revision 4

Assessing Security and Privacy Controls in Federal Information Systems
and Organizations — *Building Effective Assessment Plans*

AC-11(1)	SESSION LOCK | *PATTERN-HIDING DISPLAYS*
	ASSESSMENT OBJECTIVE: *Determine if the information system conceals, via the session lock, information previously visible on the display with a publicly viewable image.*
	POTENTIAL ASSESSMENT METHODS AND OBJECTS: **Examine**: [*SELECT FROM:* Access control policy; procedures addressing session lock; display screen with session lock activated; information system design documentation; information system configuration settings and associated documentation; other relevant documents or records]. **Interview**: [*SELECT FROM:* System/network administrators; organizational personnel with information security responsibilities; system developers]. **Test**: [*SELECT FROM:* Information system session lock mechanisms].

AC-12	SESSION TERMINATION	
	ASSESSMENT OBJECTIVE: *Determine if:*	
	AC-12[1]	*the organization defines conditions or trigger events requiring session disconnect; and*
	AC-12[2]	*the information system automatically terminates a user session after organization-defined conditions or trigger events requiring session disconnect occurs.*
	POTENTIAL ASSESSMENT METHODS AND OBJECTS: **Examine**: [*SELECT FROM:* Access control policy; procedures addressing session termination; information system design documentation; information system configuration settings and associated documentation; list of conditions or trigger events requiring session disconnect; information system audit records; other relevant documents or records]. **Interview**: [*SELECT FROM:* System/network administrators; organizational personnel with information security responsibilities; system developers]. **Test**: [*SELECT FROM:* Automated mechanisms implementing user session termination].	

AC-12(1)	SESSION TERMINATION | *USER-INITIATED LOGOUTS/MESSAGE DISPLAYS*		
	ASSESSMENT OBJECTIVE: *Determine if:*		
	AC-12(1)(a)	AC-12(1)(a)[1]	*the organization defines information resources for which user authentication is required to gain access to such resources;*
		AC-12(1)(a)[2]	*the information system provides a logout capability for user-initiated communications sessions whenever authentication is used to gain access to organization-defined information resources; and*
	AC-12(1)(b)	*the information system displays an explicit logout message to users indicating the reliable termination of authenticated communications sessions.*	

Special Publication 800-53A
Revision 4

Assessing Security and Privacy Controls in Federal Information Systems
and Organizations — *Building Effective Assessment Plans*

POTENTIAL ASSESSMENT METHODS AND OBJECTS:

Examine: [*SELECT FROM:* Access control policy; procedures addressing session termination; user logout messages; information system design documentation; information system configuration settings and associated documentation; information system audit records; other relevant documents or records].

Interview: [*SELECT FROM:* System/network administrators; organizational personnel with information security responsibilities; system developers].

Test: [*SELECT FROM:* Information system session lock mechanisms].

AC-13	SUPERVISION AND REVIEW – ACCESS CONTROL
[Withdrawn: Incorporated into AC-2 and AU-6].	

AC-14	PERMITTED ACTIONS WITHOUT IDENTIFICATION OR AUTHENTICATION

ASSESSMENT OBJECTIVE:

Determine if the organization:

AC-14(a)	AC-14(a)[1]	*defines user actions that can be performed on the information system without identification or authentication consistent with organizational missions/business functions;*
	AC-14(a)[2]	*identifies organization-defined user actions that can be performed on the information system without identification or authentication consistent with organizational missions/business functions; and*
AC-14(b)		*documents and provides supporting rationale in the security plan for the information system, user actions not requiring identification or authentication.*

POTENTIAL ASSESSMENT METHODS AND OBJECTS:

Examine: [*SELECT FROM:* Access control policy; procedures addressing permitted actions without identification or authentication; information system configuration settings and associated documentation; security plan; list of user actions that can be performed without identification or authentication; information system audit records; other relevant documents or records].

Interview: [*SELECT FROM:* System/network administrators; organizational personnel with information security responsibilities].

AC-14(1)	PERMITTED ACTIONS WITHOUT IDENTIFICATION OR AUTHENTICATION | *NECESSARY USES*
[Withdrawn: Incorporated into AC-14].	

AC-15	AUTOMATED MARKING
[Withdrawn: Incorporated into MP-3].	

AC-16	SECURITY ATTRIBUTES

ASSESSMENT OBJECTIVE:

Determine if the organization:

AC-16(a)	AC-16(a)[1]	*defines types of security attributes to be associated with information:*	
		AC-16(a)[1][a]	*in storage;*
		AC-16(a)[1][b]	*in process; and/or*

Special Publication 800-53A
Revision 4

Assessing Security and Privacy Controls in Federal Information Systems
and Organizations — *Building Effective Assessment Plans*

		AC-16(a)[1][c]	*in transmission;*
	AC-16(a)[2]	*defines security attribute values for organization-defined types of security attributes;*	
	AC-16(a)[3]	*provides the means to associate organization-defined types of security attributes having organization-defined security attribute values with information:*	
		AC-16(a)[3][a]	*in storage;*
		AC-16(a)[3][b]	*in process; and/or*
		AC-16(a)[3][c]	*in transmission;*
AC-16(b)	*ensures that the security attribute associations are made and retained with the information;*		
AC-16(c)	AC-16(c)[1]	*defines information systems for which the permitted organization-defined security attributes are to be established;*	
	AC-16(c)[2]	*defines security attributes that are permitted for organization-defined information systems;*	
	AC-16(c)[3]	*establishes the permitted organization-defined security attributes for organization-defined information systems;*	
AC-16(d)	AC-16(d)[1]	*defines values or ranges for each of the established security attributes; and*	
	AC-16(d)[2]	*determines the permitted organization-defined values or ranges for each of the established security attributes.*	

POTENTIAL ASSESSMENT METHODS AND OBJECTS:

Examine: [*SELECT FROM:* Access control policy; procedures addressing the association of security attributes to information in storage, in process, and in transmission; information system design documentation; information system configuration settings and associated documentation; information system audit records; other relevant documents or records].

Interview: [*SELECT FROM:* System/network administrators; organizational personnel with information security responsibilities; system developers].

Test: [*SELECT FROM:* Organizational capability supporting and maintaining the association of security attributes to information in storage, in process, and in transmission].

AC-16(1)	SECURITY ATTRIBUTES | *DYNAMIC ATTRIBUTE ASSOCIATION*
	ASSESSMENT OBJECTIVE: *Determine if:*

	AC-16(1)[1]	*the organization defines subjects and objects to which security attributes are to be dynamically associated as information is created and combined;*
	AC-16(1)[2]	*the organization defines security policies requiring the information system to dynamically associate security attributes with organization-defined subjects and objects; and*
	AC-16(1)[3]	*the information system dynamically associates security attributes with organization-defined subjects and objects in accordance with organization-defined security policies as information is created and combined.*

Special Publication 800-53A
Revision 4

Assessing Security and Privacy Controls in Federal Information Systems
and Organizations — *Building Effective Assessment Plans*

POTENTIAL ASSESSMENT METHODS AND OBJECTS:

Examine: [*SELECT FROM:* Access control policy; procedures addressing dynamic association of security attributes to information; information system design documentation; information system configuration settings and associated documentation; information system audit records; other relevant documents or records].

Interview: [*SELECT FROM:* System/network administrators; organizational personnel with information security responsibilities; system developers].

Test: [*SELECT FROM:* Automated mechanisms implementing dynamic association of security attributes to information].

AC-16(2)	SECURITY ATTRIBUTES	*ATTRIBUTE VALUE CHANGES BY AUTHORIZED INDIVIDUALS*

ASSESSMENT OBJECTIVE:

Determine if the information system provides authorized individuals (or processes acting on behalf on individuals) the capability to define or change the value of associated security attributes.

POTENTIAL ASSESSMENT METHODS AND OBJECTS:

Examine: [*SELECT FROM:* Access control policy; procedures addressing the change of security attribute values; information system design documentation; information system configuration settings and associated documentation; list of individuals authorized to change security attributes; information system audit records; other relevant documents or records].

Interview: [*SELECT FROM:* Organizational personnel with responsibilities for changing values of security attributes; organizational personnel with information security responsibilities; system developers].

Test: [*SELECT FROM:* Automated mechanisms permitting changes to values of security attributes].

AC-16(3)	SECURITY ATTRIBUTES	*MAINTENANCE OF ATTRIBUTE ASSOCIATIONS BY INFORMATION SYSTEM*

ASSESSMENT OBJECTIVE:

Determine if:

AC-16(3)[1]	*the organization defines security attributes to be associated with organization-defined subjects and objects;*
AC-16(3)[2]	*the organization defines subjects and objects requiring the association and integrity of security attributes to such subjects and objects to be maintained; and*
AC-16(3)[3]	*the information system maintains the association and integrity of organization-defined security attributes to organization-defined subjects and objects.*

POTENTIAL ASSESSMENT METHODS AND OBJECTS:

Examine: [*SELECT FROM:* Access control policy; procedures addressing the association of security attributes to information; information system design documentation; information system configuration settings and associated documentation; other relevant documents or records].

Interview: [*SELECT FROM:* Organizational personnel with information security responsibilities; system developers].

Test: [*SELECT FROM:* Automated mechanisms maintaining association and integrity of security attributes to information].

AC-16(4)	SECURITY ATTRIBUTES	*ASSOCIATION OF ATTRIBUTES BY AUTHORIZED INDIVIDUALS*

ASSESSMENT OBJECTIVE:

Determine if:

Special Publication 800-53A
Revision 4

Assessing Security and Privacy Controls in Federal Information Systems
and Organizations — *Building Effective Assessment Plans*

	AC-16(4)[1]	*the organization defines security attributes to be associated with subjects and objects by authorized individuals (or processes acting on behalf of individuals);*
	AC-16(4)[2]	*the organization defines subjects and objects requiring the association of organization-defined security attributes by authorized individuals (or processes acting on behalf of individuals); and*
	AC-16(4)[3]	*the information system supports the association of organization-defined security attributes with organization-defined subjects and objects by authorized individuals (or processes acting on behalf of individuals).*

POTENTIAL ASSESSMENT METHODS AND OBJECTS:

Examine: [*SELECT FROM:* Access control policy; procedures addressing the association of security attributes to information; information system design documentation; information system configuration settings and associated documentation; list of users authorized to associate security attributes to information; information system audit records; other relevant documents or records].

Interview: [*SELECT FROM:* Organizational personnel with responsibilities for associating security attributes to information; organizational personnel with information security responsibilities; system developers].

Test: [*SELECT FROM:* Automated mechanisms supporting user associations of security attributes to information].

AC-16(5)	SECURITY ATTRIBUTES	*ATTRIBUTE DISPLAYS FOR OUTPUT DEVICES*

ASSESSMENT OBJECTIVE:

Determine if:

	AC-16(5)[1]	*the organization identifies special dissemination, handling, or distribution instructions to be used for each object that the information system transmits to output devices;*
	AC-16(5)[2]	*the organization identifies human-readable, standard naming conventions for the security attributes to be displayed in human-readable form on each object that the information system transmits to output devices; and*
	AC-16(5)[3]	*the information system displays security attributes in human-readable form on each object that the system transmits to output devices to identify organization-identified special dissemination, handling, or distribution instructions using organization-identified human readable, standard naming conventions.*

POTENTIAL ASSESSMENT METHODS AND OBJECTS:

Examine: [*SELECT FROM:* Access control policy; procedures addressing display of security attributes in human-readable form; special dissemination, handling, or distribution instructions; types of human-readable, standard naming conventions; information system design documentation; information system configuration settings and associated documentation; information system audit records; other relevant documents or records].

Interview: [*SELECT FROM:* Organizational personnel with information security responsibilities; system developers].

Test: [*SELECT FROM:* System output devices displaying security attributes in human-readable form on each object].

AC-16(6)	SECURITY ATTRIBUTES	*MAINTENANCE OF ATTRIBUTE ASSOCIATION BY ORGANIZATION*

ASSESSMENT OBJECTIVE:

Determine if the organization:

	AC-16(6)[1]	*defines security attributes to be associated with subjects and objects;*

Special Publication 800-53A
Revision 4

Assessing Security and Privacy Controls in Federal Information Systems
and Organizations — *Building Effective Assessment Plans*

	AC-16(6)[2]	*defines subjects and objects to be associated with organization-defined security attributes;*
	AC-16(6)[3]	*defines security policies to allow personnel to associate, and maintain the association of organization-defined security attributes with organization-defined subjects and objects; and*
	AC-16(6)[4]	*allows personnel to associate, and maintain the association of organization-defined security attributes with organization-defined subjects and objects in accordance with organization-defined security policies.*

POTENTIAL ASSESSMENT METHODS AND OBJECTS:

Examine: [*SELECT FROM:* Access control policy; procedures addressing association of security attributes with subjects and objects; other relevant documents or records].

Interview: [*SELECT FROM:* Organizational personnel with responsibilities for associating and maintaining association of security attributes with subjects and objects; organizational personnel with information security responsibilities; system developers].

Test: [*SELECT FROM:* Automated mechanisms supporting associations of security attributes to subjects and objects].

AC-16(7)	**SECURITY ATTRIBUTES** | *CONSISTENT ATTRIBUTE INTERPRETATION*

ASSESSMENT OBJECTIVE:

Determine if the organization provides a consistent interpretation of security attributes transmitted between distributed information system components.

POTENTIAL ASSESSMENT METHODS AND OBJECTS:

Examine: [*SELECT FROM:* Access control policy; procedures addressing consistent interpretation of security attributes transmitted between distributed information system components; procedures addressing access enforcement; procedures addressing information flow enforcement; information system design documentation; information system configuration settings and associated documentation; information system audit records; other relevant documents or records].

Interview: [*SELECT FROM:* Organizational personnel with responsibilities for providing consistent interpretation of security attributes used in access enforcement and information flow enforcement actions; organizational personnel with information security responsibilities; system developers].

Test: [*SELECT FROM:* Automated mechanisms implementing access enforcement and information flow enforcement functions].

AC-16(8)	**SECURITY ATTRIBUTES** | *ASSOCIATION TECHNIQUES/TECHNOLOGIES*

ASSESSMENT OBJECTIVE:
Determine if:

	AC-16(8)[1]	*the organization defines techniques or technologies to be implemented in associating security attributes to information;*
	AC-16(8)[2]	*the organization defines level of assurance to be provided when the information system implements organization-defined technologies or technologies to associate security attributes to information; and*
	AC-16(8)[3]	*the information system implements organization-defined techniques or technologies with organization-defined level of assurance in associating security attributes to information.*

Special Publication 800-53A
Revision 4

Assessing Security and Privacy Controls in Federal Information Systems
and Organizations — *Building Effective Assessment Plans*

POTENTIAL ASSESSMENT METHODS AND OBJECTS:

Examine: [*SELECT FROM:* Access control policy; procedures addressing association of security attributes to information; information system design documentation; information system configuration settings and associated documentation; information system audit records; other relevant documents or records].

Interview: [*SELECT FROM:* Organizational personnel with responsibilities for associating security attributes to information; organizational personnel with information security responsibilities; system developers].

Test: [*SELECT FROM:* Automated mechanisms implementing techniques or technologies associating security attributes to information].

AC-16(9)	SECURITY ATTRIBUTES | *ATTRIBUTE REASSIGNMENT*

ASSESSMENT OBJECTIVE:

Determine if the organization:

AC-16(9)[1]	*defines techniques or procedures to validate re-grading mechanisms used to reassign association of security attributes with information; and*
AC-16(9)[2]	*ensures that security attributes associated with information are reassigned only via re-grading mechanisms validated using organization-defined techniques or procedures.*

POTENTIAL ASSESSMENT METHODS AND OBJECTS:

Examine: [*SELECT FROM:* Access control policy; procedures addressing reassignment of security attributes to information; information system design documentation; information system configuration settings and associated documentation; information system audit records; other relevant documents or records].

Interview: [*SELECT FROM:* Organizational personnel with responsibilities for reassigning association of security attributes to information; organizational personnel with information security responsibilities; system developers].

Test: [*SELECT FROM:* Automated mechanisms implementing techniques or procedures for reassigning association of security attributes to information].

AC-16(10)	SECURITY ATTRIBUTES | *ATTRIBUTE CONFIGURATION BY AUTHORIZED INDIVIDUALS*

ASSESSMENT OBJECTIVE:

Determine if the information system provides authorized individuals the capability to define or change the type and value of security attributes available for association with subjects and objects.

POTENTIAL ASSESSMENT METHODS AND OBJECTS:

Examine: [*SELECT FROM:* Access control policy; procedures addressing configuration of security attributes by authorized individuals; information system design documentation; information system configuration settings and associated documentation; information system audit records; other relevant documents or records].

Interview: [*SELECT FROM:* Organizational personnel with responsibilities for defining or changing security attributes associated with information; organizational personnel with information security responsibilities; system developers].

Test: [*SELECT FROM:* Automated mechanisms implementing capability for defining or changing security attributes].

AC-17	REMOTE ACCESS

ASSESSMENT OBJECTIVE:

Determine if the organization:

Special Publication 800-53A
Revision 4

Assessing Security and Privacy Controls in Federal Information Systems
and Organizations — *Building Effective Assessment Plans*

	AC-17(a)	AC-17(a)[1]	*identifies the types of remote access allowed to the information system;*
		AC-17(a)[2]	*establishes for each type of remote access allowed:*
		AC-17(a)[2][a]	*usage restrictions;*
		AC-17(a)[2][b]	*configuration/connection requirements;*
		AC-17(a)[2][c]	*implementation guidance;*
		AC-17(a)[3]	*documents for each type of remote access allowed:*
		AC-17(a)[3][a]	*usage restrictions;*
		AC-17(a)[3][b]	*configuration/connection requirements;*
		AC-17(a)[3][c]	*implementation guidance; and*
	AC-17(b)		*authorizes remote access to the information system prior to allowing such connections.*

POTENTIAL ASSESSMENT METHODS AND OBJECTS:

Examine: [*SELECT FROM:* Access control policy; procedures addressing remote access implementation and usage (including restrictions); configuration management plan; security plan; information system configuration settings and associated documentation; remote access authorizations; information system audit records; other relevant documents or records].

Interview: [*SELECT FROM:* Organizational personnel with responsibilities for managing remote access connections; system/network administrators; organizational personnel with information security responsibilities].

Test: [*SELECT FROM:* Remote access management capability for the information system].

AC-17(1)	REMOTE ACCESS	*AUTOMATED MONITORING/CONTROL*

ASSESSMENT OBJECTIVE:

Determine if the information system monitors and controls remote access methods.

POTENTIAL ASSESSMENT METHODS AND OBJECTS:

Examine: [*SELECT FROM:* Access control policy; procedures addressing remote access to the information system; information system design documentation; information system configuration settings and associated documentation; information system audit records; information system monitoring records; other relevant documents or records].

Interview: [*SELECT FROM:* System/network administrators; organizational personnel with information security responsibilities; system developers].

Test: [*SELECT FROM:* Automated mechanisms monitoring and controlling remote access methods].

AC-17(2)	REMOTE ACCESS	*PROTECTION OF CONFIDENTIALITY/INTEGRITY USING ENCRYPTION*

ASSESSMENT OBJECTIVE:

Determine if the information system implements cryptographic mechanisms to protect the confidentiality and integrity of remote access sessions.

POTENTIAL ASSESSMENT METHODS AND OBJECTS:

Examine: [*SELECT FROM:* Access control policy; procedures addressing remote access to the information system; information system design documentation; information system configuration settings and associated documentation; cryptographic mechanisms and associated configuration documentation; information system audit records; other relevant documents or records].

Interview: [*SELECT FROM:* System/network administrators; organizational personnel with information security responsibilities; system developers].

Test: [*SELECT FROM:* Cryptographic mechanisms protecting confidentiality and integrity of remote access sessions].

Special Publication 800-53A
Revision 4

Assessing Security and Privacy Controls in Federal Information Systems
and Organizations — *Building Effective Assessment Plans*

AC-17(3)	REMOTE ACCESS	*MANAGED ACCESS CONTROL POINTS*

ASSESSMENT OBJECTIVE:

Determine if:

AC-17(3)[1]	*the organization defines the number of managed network access control points through which all remote accesses are to be routed; and*
AC-17(3)[2]	*the information system routes all remote accesses through the organization-defined number of managed network access control points.*

POTENTIAL ASSESSMENT METHODS AND OBJECTS:

Examine: [*SELECT FROM:* Access control policy; procedures addressing remote access to the information system; information system design documentation; list of all managed network access control points; information system configuration settings and associated documentation; information system audit records; other relevant documents or records].

Interview: [*SELECT FROM:* System/network administrators; organizational personnel with information security responsibilities].

Test: [*SELECT FROM:* Automated mechanisms routing all remote accesses through managed network access control points].

AC-17(4)	REMOTE ACCESS	*PRIVILEGED COMMANDS / ACCESS*

ASSESSMENT OBJECTIVE:

Determine if the organization:

AC-17(4)(a)	AC-17(4)(a)[1]	*defines needs to authorize the execution of privileged commands and access to security-relevant information via remote access;*
	AC-17(4)(a)[2]	*authorizes the execution of privileged commands and access to security-relevant information via remote access only for organization-defined needs; and*
AC-17(4)(b)		*documents the rationale for such access in the information system security plan.*

POTENTIAL ASSESSMENT METHODS AND OBJECTS:

Examine: [*SELECT FROM:* Access control policy; procedures addressing remote access to the information system; information system configuration settings and associated documentation; security plan; information system audit records; other relevant documents or records].

Interview: [*SELECT FROM:* System/network administrators; organizational personnel with information security responsibilities].

Test: [*SELECT FROM:* Automated mechanisms implementing remote access management].

AC-17(5)	REMOTE ACCESS	*MONITORING FOR UNAUTHORIZED CONNECTIONS*

[Withdrawn: Incorporated into SI-4].

AC-17(6)	REMOTE ACCESS	*PROTECTION OF INFORMATION*

ASSESSMENT OBJECTIVE:

Determine if the organization ensures that users protect information about remote access mechanisms from unauthorized use and disclosure.

Special Publication 800-53A
Revision 4

Assessing Security and Privacy Controls in Federal Information Systems
and Organizations — *Building Effective Assessment Plans*

POTENTIAL ASSESSMENT METHODS AND OBJECTS:

Examine: [*SELECT FROM:* Access control policy; procedures addressing remote access to the information system; other relevant documents or records].

Interview: [*SELECT FROM:* Organizational personnel with responsibilities for implementing or monitoring remote access to the information system; information system users with knowledge of information about remote access mechanisms; organizational personnel with information security responsibilities].

AC-17(7)	REMOTE ACCESS | *ADDITIONAL PROTECTION FOR SECURITY FUNCTION ACCESS*

[Withdrawn: Incorporated into AC-3 (10)].

AC-17(8)	REMOTE ACCESS | *DISABLE NONSECURE NETWORK PROTOCOLS*

[Withdrawn: Incorporated into CM-7].

AC-17(9)	REMOTE ACCESS | *DISCONNECT/DISABLE ACCESS*

ASSESSMENT OBJECTIVE:

Determine if the organization:

AC-17(9)[1]	*defines the time period within which to expeditiously disconnect or disable remote access to the information system; and*
AC-17(9)[2]	*provides the capability to expeditiously disconnect or disable remote access to the information system within the organization-defined time period.*

POTENTIAL ASSESSMENT METHODS AND OBJECTS:

Examine: [*SELECT FROM:* Access control policy; procedures addressing disconnecting or disabling remote access to the information system; information system design documentation; information system configuration settings and associated documentation; security plan, information system audit records; other relevant documents or records].

Interview: [*SELECT FROM:* System/network administrators; organizational personnel with information security responsibilities; system developers].

Test: [*SELECT FROM:* Automated mechanisms implementing capability to disconnect or disable remote access to information system].

AC-18	WIRELESS ACCESS

ASSESSMENT OBJECTIVE:

Determine if the organization:

AC-18(a)	*establishes for wireless access:*	
	AC-18(a)[1]	*usage restrictions;*
	AC-18(a)[2]	*configuration/connection requirement;*
	AC-18(a)[3]	*implementation guidance; and*
AC-18(b)	*authorizes wireless access to the information system prior to allowing such connections.*	

Special Publication 800-53A
Revision 4

Assessing Security and Privacy Controls in Federal Information Systems
and Organizations — *Building Effective Assessment Plans*

	POTENTIAL ASSESSMENT METHODS AND OBJECTS: **Examine**: [*SELECT FROM:* Access control policy; procedures addressing wireless access implementation and usage (including restrictions); configuration management plan; security plan; information system design documentation; information system configuration settings and associated documentation; wireless access authorizations; information system audit records; other relevant documents or records]. **Interview**: [*SELECT FROM:* Organizational personnel with responsibilities for managing wireless access connections; organizational personnel with information security responsibilities]. **Test**: [*SELECT FROM:* Wireless access management capability for the information system].

AC-18(1)	**WIRELESS ACCESS** | *AUTHENTICATION AND ENCRYPTION*
	ASSESSMENT OBJECTIVE: *Determine if the information system protects wireless access to the system using encryption and one or more of the following:*

AC-18(1)[1]	*authentication of users; and/or*
AC-18(1)[2]	*authentication of devices.*

POTENTIAL ASSESSMENT METHODS AND OBJECTS: **Examine**: [*SELECT FROM:* Access control policy; procedures addressing wireless implementation and usage (including restrictions); information system design documentation; information system configuration settings and associated documentation; information system audit records; other relevant documents or records]. **Interview**: [*SELECT FROM:* System/network administrators; organizational personnel with information security responsibilities; system developers]. **Test**: [*SELECT FROM:* Automated mechanisms implementing wireless access protections to the information system].

AC-18(2)	**WIRELESS ACCESS** | *MONITORING UNAUTHORIZED CONNECTIONS*
[Withdrawn: Incorporated into SI-4].	

AC-18(3)	**WIRELESS ACCESS** | *DISABLE WIRELESS NETWORKING*
	ASSESSMENT OBJECTIVE: *Determine if the organization disables, when not intended for use, wireless networking capabilities internally embedded within information system components prior to issuance and deployment.*
	POTENTIAL ASSESSMENT METHODS AND OBJECTS: **Examine**: [*SELECT FROM:* Access control policy; procedures addressing wireless implementation and usage (including restrictions); information system design documentation; information system configuration settings and associated documentation; information system audit records; other relevant documents or records]. **Interview**: [*SELECT FROM:* System/network administrators; organizational personnel with information security responsibilities]. **Test**: [*SELECT FROM:* Automated mechanisms managing the disabling of wireless networking capabilities internally embedded within information system components].

AC-18(4)	**WIRELESS ACCESS** | *RESTRICT CONFIGURATIONS BY USERS*
	ASSESSMENT OBJECTIVE: *Determine if the organization:*

Special Publication 800-53A
Revision 4

Assessing Security and Privacy Controls in Federal Information Systems
and Organizations — *Building Effective Assessment Plans*

AC-18(4)[1]	*identifies users allowed to independently configure wireless networking capabilities; and*
AC-18(4)[2]	*explicitly authorizes the identified users allowed to independently configure wireless networking capabilities.*

POTENTIAL ASSESSMENT METHODS AND OBJECTS:

Examine: [*SELECT FROM*: Access control policy; procedures addressing wireless implementation and usage (including restrictions); information system design documentation; information system configuration settings and associated documentation; information system audit records; other relevant documents or records].

Interview: [*SELECT FROM*: System/network administrators; organizational personnel with information security responsibilities].

Test: [*SELECT FROM*: Automated mechanisms authorizing independent user configuration of wireless networking capabilities].

AC-18(5)	**WIRELESS ACCESS	*ANTENNAS/TRANSMISSION POWER LEVELS***

ASSESSMENT OBJECTIVE:

Determine if the organization:

AC-18(5)[1]	*selects radio antennas to reduce the probability that usable signals can be received outside of organization-controlled boundaries; and*
AC-18(5)[2]	*calibrates transmission power levels to reduce the probability that usable signals can be received outside of organization-controlled boundaries.*

POTENTIAL ASSESSMENT METHODS AND OBJECTS:

Examine: [*SELECT FROM*: Access control policy; procedures addressing wireless implementation and usage (including restrictions); information system design documentation; information system configuration settings and associated documentation; information system audit records; other relevant documents or records].

Interview: [*SELECT FROM*: System/network administrators; organizational personnel with information security responsibilities].

Test: [*SELECT FROM*: Wireless access capability protecting usable signals from unauthorized access outside organization-controlled boundaries].

AC-19	**ACCESS CONTROL FOR MOBILE DEVICES**

ASSESSMENT OBJECTIVE:

Determine if the organization:

AC-19(a)	*establishes for organization-controlled mobile devices:*	
	AC-19(a)[1]	*usage restrictions;*
	AC-19(a)[2]	*configuration/connection requirement;*
	AC-19(a)[3]	*implementation guidance; and*
AC-19(b)	*authorizes the connection of mobile devices to organizational information systems.*	

Special Publication 800-53A
Revision 4

Assessing Security and Privacy Controls in Federal Information Systems
and Organizations — *Building Effective Assessment Plans*

POTENTIAL ASSESSMENT METHODS AND OBJECTS:

Examine: [*SELECT FROM:* Access control policy; procedures addressing access control for mobile device usage (including restrictions); configuration management plan; security plan; information system design documentation; information system configuration settings and associated documentation; authorizations for mobile device connections to organizational information systems; information system audit records; other relevant documents or records].

Interview: [*SELECT FROM:* Organizational personnel using mobile devices to access organizational information systems; system/network administrators; organizational personnel with information security responsibilities].

Test: [*SELECT FROM:* Access control capability authorizing mobile device connections to organizational information systems].

AC-19(1)	ACCESS CONTROL FOR MOBILE DEVICES | *USE OF WRITABLE/PORTABLE STORAGE DEVICES*
[Withdrawn: Incorporated into MP-7].	

AC-19(2)	ACCESS CONTROL FOR MOBILE DEVICES | *USE OF PERSONALLY OWNED PORTABLE STORAGE DEVICES*
[Withdrawn: Incorporated into MP-7].	

AC-19(3)	ACCESS CONTROL FOR MOBILE DEVICES | *USE OF PORTABLE STORAGE DEVICES WITH NO IDENTIFIABLE OWNER*
[Withdrawn: Incorporated into MP-7].	

AC-19(4)	ACCESS CONTROL FOR MOBILE DEVICES | *RESTRICTIONS FOR CLASSIFIED INFORMATION*		
	ASSESSMENT OBJECTIVE: *Determine if the organization:*		
	AC-19(4)(a)	*prohibits the use of unclassified mobile devices in facilities containing information systems processing, storing, or transmitting classified information unless specifically permitted by the authorizing official;*	
	AC-19(4)(b)	*enforces the following restrictions on individuals permitted by the authorizing official to use unclassified mobile devices in facilities containing information systems processing, storing, or transmitting classified information:*	
		AC-19(4)(b)(1)	*connection of unclassified mobile devices to classified information systems is prohibited;*
		AC-19(4)(b)(2)	*connection of unclassified mobile devices to unclassified information systems requires approval from the authorizing official;*
		AC-19(4)(b)(3)	*use of internal or external modems or wireless interfaces within the unclassified mobile devices is prohibited;*
		AC-19(4)(b)(4) · AC-19(4)(b)(4)[1]	*defines security officials responsible for reviews and inspections of unclassified mobile devices and the information stored on those devices;*

Special Publication 800-53A
Revision 4

Assessing Security and Privacy Controls in Federal Information Systems
and Organizations — *Building Effective Assessment Plans*

			AC-19(4)(b)(4)[2]	*unclassified mobile devices and the information stored on those devices are subject to random reviews/inspections by organization-defined security officials;*
			AC-19(4)(b)(4)[3]	*the incident handling policy is followed if classified information is found;*
	AC-19(4)(c)	AC-19(4)(c)[1]		*defines security policies to restrict the connection of classified mobile devices to classified information systems; and*
		AC-19(4)(c)[2]		*restricts the connection of classified mobile devices to classified information systems in accordance with organization-defined security policies.*

POTENTIAL ASSESSMENT METHODS AND OBJECTS:

Examine: [*SELECT FROM:* Access control policy; incident handling policy; procedures addressing access control for mobile devices; information system design documentation; information system configuration settings and associated documentation; evidentiary documentation for random inspections and reviews of mobile devices; information system audit records; other relevant documents or records].

Interview: [*SELECT FROM:* Organizational personnel responsible for random reviews/inspections of mobile devices; organizational personnel using mobile devices in facilities containing information systems processing, storing, or transmitting classified information; organizational personnel with incident response responsibilities; system/network administrators; organizational personnel with information security responsibilities].

Test: [*SELECT FROM:* Automated mechanisms prohibiting the use of internal or external modems or wireless interfaces with mobile devices].

AC-19(5)	ACCESS CONTROL FOR MOBILE DEVICES | *FULL DEVICE / CONTAINER-BASED ENCRYPTION*
	ASSESSMENT OBJECTIVE: *Determine if the organization:*

	AC-19(5)[1]	*defines mobile devices for which full-device encryption or container encryption is required to protect the confidentiality and integrity of information on such devices; and*
	AC-19(5)[2]	*employs full-device encryption or container encryption to protect the confidentiality and integrity of information on organization-defined mobile devices.*

POTENTIAL ASSESSMENT METHODS AND OBJECTS:

Examine: [*SELECT FROM:* Access control policy; procedures addressing access control for mobile devices; information system design documentation; information system configuration settings and associated documentation; encryption mechanism s and associated configuration documentation; information system audit records; other relevant documents or records].

Interview: [*SELECT FROM:* Organizational personnel with access control responsibilities for mobile devices; system/network administrators; organizational personnel with information security responsibilities].

Test: [*SELECT FROM:* Encryption mechanisms protecting confidentiality and integrity of information on mobile devices].

AC-20	USE OF EXTERNAL INFORMATION SYSTEMS
	ASSESSMENT OBJECTIVE: *Determine if the organization establishes terms and conditions, consistent with any trust relationships established with other organizations owning, operating, and/or maintaining external information systems, allowing authorized individuals to:*

Special Publication 800-53A
Revision 4

Assessing Security and Privacy Controls in Federal Information Systems
and Organizations — *Building Effective Assessment Plans*

AC-20(a)	*access the information system from the external information systems; and*
AC-20(b)	*process, store, or transmit organization-controlled information using external information systems.*

POTENTIAL ASSESSMENT METHODS AND OBJECTS:

Examine: [*SELECT FROM:* Access control policy; procedures addressing the use of external information systems; external information systems terms and conditions; list of types of applications accessible from external information systems; maximum security categorization for information processed, stored, or transmitted on external information systems; information system configuration settings and associated documentation; other relevant documents or records].

Interview: [*SELECT FROM:* Organizational personnel with responsibilities for defining terms and conditions for use of external information systems to access organizational systems; system/network administrators; organizational personnel with information security responsibilities].

Test: [*SELECT FROM:* Automated mechanisms implementing terms and conditions on use of external information systems].

AC-20(1)	USE OF EXTERNAL INFORMATION SYSTEMS	*LIMITS ON AUTHORIZED USE*

ASSESSMENT OBJECTIVE:

Determine if the organization permits authorized individuals to use an external information system to access the information system or to process, store, or transmit organization-controlled information only when the organization:

AC-20(1)(a)	*verifies the implementation of required security controls on the external system as specified in the organization's information security policy and security plan; or*
AC-20(1)(b)	*retains approved information system connection or processing agreements with the organizational entity hosting the external information system.*

POTENTIAL ASSESSMENT METHODS AND OBJECTS:

Examine: [*SELECT FROM:* Access control policy; procedures addressing the use of external information systems; security plan; information system connection or processing agreements; account management documents; other relevant documents or records].

Interview: [*SELECT FROM:* System/network administrators; organizational personnel with information security responsibilities].

Test: [*SELECT FROM:* Automated mechanisms implementing limits on use of external information systems].

AC-20(2)	USE OF EXTERNAL INFORMATION SYSTEMS	*PORTABLE STORAGE DEVICES*

ASSESSMENT OBJECTIVE:

Determine if the organization restricts or prohibits the use of organization-controlled portable storage devices by authorized individuals on external information systems.

POTENTIAL ASSESSMENT METHODS AND OBJECTS:

Examine: [*SELECT FROM:* Access control policy; procedures addressing the use of external information systems; security plan; information system configuration settings and associated documentation; information system connection or processing agreements; account management documents; other relevant documents or records].

Interview: [*SELECT FROM:* Organizational personnel with responsibilities for restricting or prohibiting use of organization-controlled storage devices on external information systems; system/network administrators; organizational personnel with information security responsibilities].

Test: [*SELECT FROM:* Automated mechanisms implementing restrictions on use of portable storage devices].

Special Publication 800-53A
Revision 4

Assessing Security and Privacy Controls in Federal Information Systems
and Organizations — *Building Effective Assessment Plans*

AC-20(3)	USE OF EXTERNAL INFORMATION SYSTEMS | *NON-ORGANIZATIONALLY OWNED SYSTEMS / COMPONENTS / DEVICES*
	ASSESSMENT OBJECTIVE:
	Determine if the organization restricts or prohibits the use of non-organizationally owned information systems, system components, or devices to process, store, or transmit organizational information.
	POTENTIAL ASSESSMENT METHODS AND OBJECTS:
	Examine: [*SELECT FROM:* Access control policy; procedures addressing the use of external information systems; security plan; information system design documentation; information system configuration settings and associated documentation; information system connection or processing agreements; account management documents; information system audit records, other relevant documents or records].
	Interview: [*SELECT FROM:* Organizational personnel with responsibilities for restricting or prohibiting use of non-organizationally owned information systems, system components, or devices; system/network administrators; organizational personnel with information security responsibilities].
	Test: [*SELECT FROM:* Automated mechanisms implementing restrictions on the use of non-organizationally owned systems/components/devices].

AC-20(4)	USE OF EXTERNAL INFORMATION SYSTEMS | *NETWORK ACCESSIBLE STORAGE DEVICES*	
	ASSESSMENT OBJECTIVE:	
	Determine if the organization:	
	AC-20(4)[1]	*defines network accessible storage devices to be prohibited from use in external information systems; and*
	AC-20(4)[2]	*prohibits the use of organization-defined network accessible storage devices in external information systems.*
	POTENTIAL ASSESSMENT METHODS AND OBJECTS:	
	Examine: [*SELECT FROM:* Access control policy; procedures addressing use of network accessible storage devices in external information systems; security plan, information system design documentation; information system configuration settings and associated documentation; information system connection or processing agreements; list of network accessible storage devices prohibited from use in external information systems; information system audit records; other relevant documents or records].	
	Interview: [*SELECT FROM:* Organizational personnel with responsibilities for prohibiting use of network accessible storage devices in external information systems; system/network administrators; organizational personnel with information security responsibilities].	
	Test: [*SELECT FROM:* Automated mechanisms prohibiting the use of network accessible storage devices in external information systems].	

AC-21	INFORMATION SHARING		
	ASSESSMENT OBJECTIVE:		
	Determine if the organization:		
	AC-21(a)	AC-21(a)[1]	*defines information sharing circumstances where user discretion is required;*
		AC-21(a)[2]	*facilitates information sharing by enabling authorized users to determine whether access authorizations assigned to the sharing partner match the access restrictions on the information for organization-defined information sharing circumstances;*

Special Publication 800-53A
Revision 4

Assessing Security and Privacy Controls in Federal Information Systems
and Organizations — *Building Effective Assessment Plans*

| AC-21(b) | AC-21(b)[1] | *defines automated mechanisms or manual processes to be employed to assist users in making information sharing/collaboration decisions; and* |
| | AC-21(b)[2] | *employs organization-defined automated mechanisms or manual processes to assist users in making information sharing/collaboration decisions.* |

POTENTIAL ASSESSMENT METHODS AND OBJECTS:

Examine: [*SELECT FROM:* Access control policy; procedures addressing user-based collaboration and information sharing (including restrictions); information system design documentation; information system configuration settings and associated documentation; list of users authorized to make information sharing/collaboration decisions; list of information sharing circumstances requiring user discretion; other relevant documents or records].

Interview: [*SELECT FROM:* Organizational personnel responsible for making information sharing/collaboration decisions; system/network administrators; organizational personnel with information security responsibilities].

Test: [*SELECT FROM:* Automated mechanisms or manual process implementing access authorizations supporting information sharing/user collaboration decisions].

AC-21(1)	INFORMATION SHARING | *AUTOMATED DECISION SUPPORT*

ASSESSMENT OBJECTIVE:

Determine if the information system enforces information-sharing decisions by authorized users based on:

| AC-21(1)[1] | *access authorizations of sharing partners; and* |
| AC-21(1)[2] | *access restrictions on information to be shared.* |

POTENTIAL ASSESSMENT METHODS AND OBJECTS:

Examine: [*SELECT FROM:* Access control policy; procedures addressing user-based collaboration and information sharing (including restrictions); information system design documentation; information system configuration settings and associated documentation; system-generated list of users authorized to make information sharing/collaboration decisions; system-generated list of sharing partners and access authorizations; system-generated list of access restrictions regarding information to be shared; other relevant documents or records].

Interview: [*SELECT FROM:* System/network administrators; organizational personnel with information security responsibilities; system developers].

Test: [*SELECT FROM:* Automated mechanisms implementing access authorizations supporting information sharing/user collaboration decisions].

AC-21(2)	INFORMATION SHARING | *INFORMATION SEARCH AND RETRIEVAL*

ASSESSMENT OBJECTIVE:

Determine if:

| AC-21(2)[1] | *the organization defines information sharing restrictions to be enforced through information search and retrieval services; and* |
| AC-21(2)[2] | *the information system implements information search and retrieval services that enforce organization-defined information sharing restrictions.* |

Special Publication 800-53A
Revision 4

Assessing Security and Privacy Controls in Federal Information Systems
and Organizations — *Building Effective Assessment Plans*

	POTENTIAL ASSESSMENT METHODS AND OBJECTS: **Examine**: [*SELECT FROM:* Access control policy; procedures addressing user-based collaboration and information sharing (including restrictions); information system design documentation; information system configuration settings and associated documentation; system-generated list of access restrictions regarding information to be shared; information search and retrieval records; information system audit records; other relevant documents or records]. **Interview**: [*SELECT FROM:* Organizational personnel with access enforcement responsibilities for information system search and retrieval services; system/network administrators; organizational personnel with information security responsibilities; system developers]. **Test**: [*SELECT FROM:* Information system search and retrieval services enforcing information sharing restrictions].

AC-22	**PUBLICLY ACCESSIBLE CONTENT**	
	ASSESSMENT OBJECTIVE: *Determine if the organization:*	
	AC-22(a)	*designates individuals authorized to post information onto a publicly accessible information system;*
	AC-22(b)	*trains authorized individuals to ensure that publicly accessible information does not contain nonpublic information;*
	AC-22(c)	*reviews the proposed content of information prior to posting onto the publicly accessible information system to ensure that nonpublic information is not included;*
	AC-22(d) **AC-22(d)[1]**	*defines the frequency to review the content on the publicly accessible information system for nonpublic information;*
	AC-22(d)[2]	*reviews the content on the publicly accessible information system for nonpublic information with the organization-defined frequency; and*
	AC-22(d)[3]	*removes nonpublic information from the publicly accessible information system, if discovered.*
	POTENTIAL ASSESSMENT METHODS AND OBJECTS: **Examine**: [*SELECT FROM:* Access control policy; procedures addressing publicly accessible content; list of users authorized to post publicly accessible content on organizational information systems; training materials and/or records; records of publicly accessible information reviews; records of response to nonpublic information on public websites; system audit logs; security awareness training records; other relevant documents or records]. **Interview**: [*SELECT FROM:* Organizational personnel with responsibilities for managing publicly accessible information posted on organizational information systems; organizational personnel with information security responsibilities]. **Test**: [*SELECT FROM:* Automated mechanisms implementing management of publicly accessible content].	

AC-23	**DATA MINING PROTECTION**	
	ASSESSMENT OBJECTIVE: *Determine if the organization:*	
	AC-23[1]	*defines data mining prevention and detection techniques to be employed for organization-defined storage objects to adequately detect and protect against data mining;*
	AC-23[2]	*defines data storage objects to be protected from data mining; and*

Special Publication 800-53A
Revision 4

Assessing Security and Privacy Controls in Federal Information Systems
and Organizations — *Building Effective Assessment Plans*

AC-23[3]	*employs organization-defined data mining prevention and detection techniques for organization-defined data storage objects to adequately detect and protect against data mining.*

POTENTIAL ASSESSMENT METHODS AND OBJECTS:

Examine: [*SELECT FROM:* Access control policy; procedures addressing data mining techniques; procedures addressing protection of data storage objects against data mining; information system design documentation; information system configuration settings and associated documentation; information system audit logs; information system audit records; other relevant documents or records].

Interview: [*SELECT FROM:* Organizational personnel with responsibilities for implementing data mining detection and prevention techniques for data storage objects; organizational personnel with information security responsibilities; system developers].

Test: [*SELECT FROM:* Automated mechanisms implementing data mining prevention and detection].

AC-24	**ACCESS CONTROL DECISIONS**

ASSESSMENT OBJECTIVE:

Determine if the organization:

AC-24[1]	*defines access control decisions to be applied to each access request prior to access control enforcement; and*
AC-24[2]	*establishes procedures to ensure organization-defined access control decisions are applied to each access request prior to access control enforcement.*

POTENTIAL ASSESSMENT METHODS AND OBJECTS:

Examine: [*SELECT FROM:* Access control policy; procedures addressing access control decisions; information system design documentation; information system configuration settings and associated documentation; information system audit records; other relevant documents or records].

Interview: [*SELECT FROM:* Organizational personnel with responsibilities for establishing procedures regarding access control decisions to the information system; organizational personnel with information security responsibilities].

Test: [*SELECT FROM:* Automated mechanisms applying established access control decisions and procedures].

AC-24(1)	**ACCESS CONTROL DECISIONS** | *TRANSMIT ACCESS AUTHORIZATION INFORMATION*

ASSESSMENT OBJECTIVE:

Determine if:

AC-24(1)[1]	*the organization defines access authorization information that the information system transmits to organization-defined information systems that enforce access control decisions;*
AC-24(1)[2]	*the organization defines security safeguards to be used when the information system transmits organization-defined authorization information to organization-defined information systems that enforce access control decisions;*
AC-24(1)[3]	*the organization defines the information systems that enforce access control decisions; and*
AC-24(1)[4]	*the information system transmits organization-defined access authorization information using organization-defined security safeguards to organization-defined information systems that enforce access control decisions.*

Special Publication 800-53A
Revision 4

Assessing Security and Privacy Controls in Federal Information Systems
and Organizations — *Building Effective Assessment Plans*

POTENTIAL ASSESSMENT METHODS AND OBJECTS:

Examine: [*SELECT FROM:* Access control policy; procedures addressing access enforcement; information system design documentation; information system configuration settings and associated documentation; information system audit records; other relevant documents or records].

Interview: [*SELECT FROM:* Organizational personnel with access enforcement responsibilities; system/network administrators; organizational personnel with information security responsibilities; system developers].

Test: [*SELECT FROM:* Automated mechanisms implementing access enforcement functions].

AC-24(2)	ACCESS CONTROL DECISIONS | *NO USER OR PROCESS IDENTITY*

ASSESSMENT OBJECTIVE:

Determine if:

AC-24(2)[1]	*the organization defines security attributes that support access control decisions that do not include the identity of the user or processes acting on behalf of the user; and*
AC-24(2)[2]	*the information system enforces access control decisions based on organization-defined security attributes that do not include the identity of the user or process acting on behalf of the user.*

POTENTIAL ASSESSMENT METHODS AND OBJECTS:

Examine: [*SELECT FROM:* Access control policy; procedures addressing access enforcement; information system design documentation; information system configuration settings and associated documentation; information system audit records; other relevant documents or records].

Interview: [*SELECT FROM:* Organizational personnel with access enforcement responsibilities; system/network administrators; organizational personnel with information security responsibilities; system developers].

Test: [*SELECT FROM:* Automated mechanisms implementing access enforcement functions].

AC-25	REFERENCE MONITOR

ASSESSMENT OBJECTIVE:

Determine if:

AC-25[1]	*the organization defines access control policies for which the information system implements a reference monitor to enforce such policies; and*
AC-25[2]	*the information system implements a reference monitor for organization-defined access control policies that is tamperproof, always invoked, and small enough to be subject to analysis and testing, the completeness of which can be assured.*

POTENTIAL ASSESSMENT METHODS AND OBJECTS:

Examine: [*SELECT FROM:* Access control policy; procedures addressing access enforcement; information system design documentation; information system configuration settings and associated documentation; information system audit records; other relevant documents or records].

Interview: [*SELECT FROM:* Organizational personnel with access enforcement responsibilities; system/network administrators; organizational personnel with information security responsibilities; system developers].

Test: [*SELECT FROM:* Automated mechanisms implementing access enforcement functions].

Special Publication 800-53A
Revision 4

Assessing Security and Privacy Controls in Federal Information Systems
and Organizations — *Building Effective Assessment Plans*

FAMILY: AWARENESS AND TRAINING

AT-1	SECURITY AWARENESS AND TRAINING POLICY AND PROCEDURES			
	ASSESSMENT OBJECTIVE: *Determine if the organization:*			
	AT-1(a)(1)	AT-1(a)(1)[1]	*develops and documents an security awareness and training policy that addresses:*	
			AT-1(a)(1)[1][a]	*purpose;*
			AT-1(a)(1)[1][b]	*scope;*
			AT-1(a)(1)[1][c]	*roles;*
			AT-1(a)(1)[1][d]	*responsibilities;*
			AT-1(a)(1)[1][e]	*management commitment;*
			AT-1(a)(1)[1][f]	*coordination among organizational entities;*
			AT-1(a)(1)[1][g]	*compliance;*
		AT-1(a)(1)[2]	*defines personnel or roles to whom the security awareness and training policy are to be disseminated;*	
		AT-1(a)(1)[3]	*disseminates the security awareness and training policy to organization-defined personnel or roles;*	
	AT-1(a)(2)	AT-1(a)(2)[1]	*develops and documents procedures to facilitate the implementation of the security awareness and training policy and associated awareness and training controls;*	
		AT-1(a)(2)[2]	*defines personnel or roles to whom the procedures are to be disseminated;*	
		AT-1(a)(2)[3]	*disseminates the procedures to organization-defined personnel or roles;*	
	AT-1(b)(1)	AT-1(b)(1)[1]	*defines the frequency to review and update the current security awareness and training policy;*	
		AT-1(b)(1)[2]	*reviews and updates the current security awareness and training policy with the organization-defined frequency;*	
	AT-1(b)(2)	AT-1(b)(2)[1]	*defines the frequency to review and update the current security awareness and training procedures; and*	
		AT-1(b)(2)[2]	*reviews and updates the current security awareness and training procedures with the organization-defined frequency.*	
	POTENTIAL ASSESSMENT METHODS AND OBJECTS: **Examine**: [*SELECT FROM*: Security awareness and training policy and procedures; other relevant documents or records]. **Interview**: [*SELECT FROM*: Organizational personnel with security awareness and training responsibilities; organizational personnel with information security responsibilities].			

Special Publication 800-53A
Revision 4

Assessing Security and Privacy Controls in Federal Information Systems
and Organizations — *Building Effective Assessment Plans*

AT-2	SECURITY AWARENESS TRAINING	
	ASSESSMENT OBJECTIVE: *Determine if the organization:*	
	AT-2(a)	*provides basic security awareness training to information system users (including managers, senior executives, and contractors) as part of initial training for new users;*
	AT-2(b)	*provides basic security awareness training to information system users (including managers, senior executives, and contractors) when required by information system changes; and*
	AT-2(c) **AT-2(c)[1]**	*defines the frequency to provide refresher security awareness training thereafter to information system users (including managers, senior executives, and contractors); and*
	AT-2(c)[2]	*provides refresher security awareness training to information users (including managers, senior executives, and contractors) with the organization-defined frequency.*
	POTENTIAL ASSESSMENT METHODS AND OBJECTS: **Examine**: [*SELECT FROM*: Security awareness and training policy; procedures addressing security awareness training implementation; appropriate codes of federal regulations; security awareness training curriculum; security awareness training materials; security plan; training records; other relevant documents or records]. **Interview**: [*SELECT FROM*: Organizational personnel with responsibilities for security awareness training; organizational personnel with information security responsibilities; organizational personnel comprising the general information system user community]. **Test**: [*SELECT FROM*: Automated mechanisms managing security awareness training].	

AT-2(1)	SECURITY AWARENESS TRAINING | *PRACTICAL EXERCISE*
	ASSESSMENT OBJECTIVE: *Determine if the organization includes practical exercises in security awareness training that simulate actual cyber attacks.*
	POTENTIAL ASSESSMENT METHODS AND OBJECTS: **Examine**: [*SELECT FROM*: Security awareness and training policy; procedures addressing security awareness training implementation; security awareness training curriculum; security awareness training materials; security plan; other relevant documents or records]. **Interview**: [*SELECT FROM*: Organizational personnel that participate in security awareness training; organizational personnel with responsibilities for security awareness training; organizational personnel with information security responsibilities]. **Test**: [*SELECT FROM*: Automated mechanisms implementing cyber attack simulations in practical exercises].

AT-2(2)	SECURITY AWARENESS TRAINING | *INSIDER THREAT*
	ASSESSMENT OBJECTIVE: *Determine if the organization includes security awareness training on recognizing and reporting potential indicators of insider threat.*

Special Publication 800-53A
Revision 4

Assessing Security and Privacy Controls in Federal Information Systems
and Organizations — *Building Effective Assessment Plans*

POTENTIAL ASSESSMENT METHODS AND OBJECTS:

Examine: [*SELECT FROM:* Security awareness and training policy; procedures addressing security awareness training implementation; security awareness training curriculum; security awareness training materials; security plan; other relevant documents or records].

Interview: [*SELECT FROM:* Organizational personnel that participate in security awareness training; organizational personnel with responsibilities for basic security awareness training; organizational personnel with information security responsibilities].

AT-3	ROLE-BASED SECURITY TRAINING

ASSESSMENT OBJECTIVE:

Determine if the organization:

AT-3(a)		*provides role-based security training to personnel with assigned security roles and responsibilities before authorizing access to the information system or performing assigned duties;*
AT-3(b)		*provides role-based security training to personnel with assigned security roles and responsibilities when required by information system changes; and*
AT-3(c)	AT-3(c)[1]	*defines the frequency to provide refresher role-based security training thereafter to personnel with assigned security roles and responsibilities; and*
	AT-3(c)[2]	*provides refresher role-based security training to personnel with assigned security roles and responsibilities with the organization-defined frequency.*

POTENTIAL ASSESSMENT METHODS AND OBJECTS:

Examine: [*SELECT FROM:* Security awareness and training policy; procedures addressing security training implementation; codes of federal regulations; security training curriculum; security training materials; security plan; training records; other relevant documents or records].

Interview: [*SELECT FROM:* Organizational personnel with responsibilities for role-based security training; organizational personnel with assigned information system security roles and responsibilities].

Test: [*SELECT FROM:* Automated mechanisms managing role-based security training].

AT-3(1)	ROLE-BASED SECURITY TRAINING	*ENVIRONMENTAL CONTROLS*

ASSESSMENT OBJECTIVE:

Determine if the organization:

AT-3(1)[1]	*defines personnel or roles to be provided with initial and refresher training in the employment and operation of environmental controls;*
AT-3(1)[2]	*provides organization-defined personnel or roles with initial and refresher training in the employment and operation of environmental controls;*
AT-3(1)[3]	*defines the frequency to provide refresher training in the employment and operation of environmental controls; and*
AT-3(1)[4]	*provides refresher training in the employment and operation of environmental controls with the organization-defined frequency.*

Special Publication 800-53A
Revision 4

Assessing Security and Privacy Controls in Federal Information Systems
and Organizations — *Building Effective Assessment Plans*

	POTENTIAL ASSESSMENT METHODS AND OBJECTS: **Examine**: [*SELECT FROM*: Security awareness and training policy; procedures addressing security training implementation; security training curriculum; security training materials; security plan; training records; other relevant documents or records]. **Interview**: [*SELECT FROM*: Organizational personnel with responsibilities for role-based security training; organizational personnel with responsibilities for employing and operating environmental controls].

AT-3(2)	ROLE-BASED SECURITY TRAINING | *PHYSICAL SECURITY CONTROLS*
	ASSESSMENT OBJECTIVE: *Determine if the organization:*

	AT-3(2)[1]	*defines personnel or roles to be provided with initial and refresher training in the employment and operation of physical security controls;*
	AT-3(2)[2]	*provides organization-defined personnel or roles with initial and refresher training in the employment and operation of physical security controls;*
	AT-3(2)[3]	*defines the frequency to provide refresher training in the employment and operation of physical security controls; and*
	AT-3(2)[4]	*provides refresher training in the employment and operation of physical security controls with the organization-defined frequency.*

	POTENTIAL ASSESSMENT METHODS AND OBJECTS: **Examine**: [*SELECT FROM*: Security awareness and training policy; procedures addressing security training implementation; security training curriculum; security training materials; security plan; training records; other relevant documents or records]. **Interview**: [*SELECT FROM*: Organizational personnel with responsibilities for role-based security training; organizational personnel with responsibilities for employing and operating physical security controls].

AT-3(3)	ROLE-BASED SECURITY TRAINING | *PRACTICAL EXERCISES*
	ASSESSMENT OBJECTIVE: *Determine if the organization includes practical exercises in security training that reinforce training objectives.*
	POTENTIAL ASSESSMENT METHODS AND OBJECTS: **Examine**: [*SELECT FROM*: Security awareness and training policy; procedures addressing security awareness training implementation; security awareness training curriculum; security awareness training materials; security plan; other relevant documents or records]. **Interview**: [*SELECT FROM*: Organizational personnel with responsibilities for role-based security training; organizational personnel that participate in security awareness training].

AT-3(4)	ROLE-BASED SECURITY TRAINING | *SUSPICIOUS COMMUNICATIONS AND ANOMALOUS SYSTEM BEHAVIOR*
	ASSESSMENT OBJECTIVE: *Determine if the organization:*

	AT-3(4)[1]	*defines indicators of malicious code; and*
	AT-3(4)[2]	*provides training to its personnel on organization-defined indicators of malicious code to recognize suspicious communications and anomalous behavior in organizational information systems.*

Special Publication 800-53A
Revision 4

Assessing Security and Privacy Controls in Federal Information Systems
and Organizations — *Building Effective Assessment Plans*

POTENTIAL ASSESSMENT METHODS AND OBJECTS:

Examine: [*SELECT FROM:* Security awareness and training policy; procedures addressing security training implementation; security training curriculum; security training materials; security plan; training records; other relevant documents or records].

Interview: [*SELECT FROM:* Organizational personnel with responsibilities for role-based security training; organizational personnel that participate in security awareness training].

AT-4	SECURITY TRAINING RECORDS

ASSESSMENT OBJECTIVE:

Determine if the organization:

AT-4(a)	AT-4(a)[1]	*documents individual information system security training activities including:*	
		AT-4(a)[1][a]	*basic security awareness training;*
		AT-4(a)[1][b]	*specific role-based information system security training;*
	AT-4(a)[2]	*monitors individual information system security training activities including:*	
		AT-4(a)[2][a]	*basic security awareness training;*
		AT-4(a)[2][b]	*specific role-based information system security training;*
AT-4(b)	AT-4(b)[1]	*defines a time period to retain individual training records; and*	
	AT-4(b)[2]	*retains individual training records for the organization-defined time period.*	

POTENTIAL ASSESSMENT METHODS AND OBJECTS:

Examine: [*SELECT FROM:* Security awareness and training policy; procedures addressing security training records; security awareness and training records; security plan; other relevant documents or records].

Interview: [*SELECT FROM:* Organizational personnel with security training record retention responsibilities].

Test: [*SELECT FROM:* Automated mechanisms supporting management of security training records].

AT-5	CONTACTS WITH SECURITY GROUPS AND ASSOCIATIONS
[Withdrawn: Incorporated into PM-15].	

Special Publication 800-53A
Revision 4

Assessing Security and Privacy Controls in Federal Information Systems
and Organizations — *Building Effective Assessment Plans*

FAMILY: AUDIT AND ACCOUNTABILITY

AU-1	AUDIT AND ACCOUNTABILITY POLICY AND PROCEDURES		
	ASSESSMENT OBJECTIVE: *Determine if the organization:*		
	AU-1(a)(1)	AU-1(a)(1)[1]	*develops and documents an audit and accountability policy that addresses:*
		AU-1(a)(1)[1][a]	*purpose;*
		AU-1(a)(1)[1][b]	*scope;*
		AU-1(a)(1)[1][c]	*roles;*
		AU-1(a)(1)[1][d]	*responsibilities;*
		AU-1(a)(1)[1][e]	*management commitment;*
		AU-1(a)(1)[1][f]	*coordination among organizational entities;*
		AU-1(a)(1)[1][g]	*compliance;*
		AU-1(a)(1)[2]	*defines personnel or roles to whom the audit and accountability policy are to be disseminated;*
		AU-1(a)(1)[3]	*disseminates the audit and accountability policy to organization-defined personnel or roles;*
	AU-1(a)(2)	AU-1(a)(2)[1]	*develops and documents procedures to facilitate the implementation of the audit and accountability policy and associated audit and accountability controls;*
		AU-1(a)(2)[2]	*defines personnel or roles to whom the procedures are to be disseminated;*
		AU-1(a)(2)[3]	*disseminates the procedures to organization-defined personnel or roles;*
	AU-1(b)(1)	AU-1(b)(1)[1]	*defines the frequency to review and update the current audit and accountability policy;*
		AU-1(b)(1)[2]	*reviews and updates the current audit and accountability policy with the organization-defined frequency;*
	AU-1(b)(2)	AU-1(b)(2)[1]	*defines the frequency to review and update the current audit and accountability procedures; and*
		AU-1(b)(2)[2]	*reviews and updates the current audit and accountability procedures in accordance with the organization-defined frequency.*
	POTENTIAL ASSESSMENT METHODS AND OBJECTS: **Examine:** [*SELECT FROM:* Audit and accountability policy and procedures; other relevant documents or records]. **Interview:** [*SELECT FROM:* Organizational personnel with audit and accountability responsibilities; organizational personnel with information security responsibilities].		

Special Publication 800-53A
Revision 4

Assessing Security and Privacy Controls in Federal Information Systems
and Organizations — *Building Effective Assessment Plans*

AU-2	AUDIT EVENTS		
	ASSESSMENT OBJECTIVE: *Determine if the organization:*		
	AU-2(a)	AU-2(a)[1]	*defines the auditable events that the information system must be capable of auditing;*
		AU-2(a)[2]	*determines that the information system is capable of auditing organization-defined auditable events;*
	AU-2(b)	*coordinates the security audit function with other organizational entities requiring audit-related information to enhance mutual support and to help guide the selection of auditable events;*	
	AU-2(c)	*provides a rationale for why the auditable events are deemed to be adequate to support after-the-fact investigations of security incidents;*	
	AU-2(d)	AU-2(d)[1]	*defines the subset of auditable events defined in AU-2a that are to be audited within the information system;*
		AU-2(d)[2]	*determines that the subset of auditable events defined in AU-2a are to be audited within the information system; and*
		AU-2(d)[3]	*determines the frequency of (or situation requiring) auditing for each identified event.*
	POTENTIAL ASSESSMENT METHODS AND OBJECTS: **Examine**: [*SELECT FROM:* Audit and accountability policy; procedures addressing auditable events; security plan; information system design documentation; information system configuration settings and associated documentation; information system audit records; information system auditable events; other relevant documents or records]. **Interview**: [*SELECT FROM:* Organizational personnel with audit and accountability responsibilities; organizational personnel with information security responsibilities; system/network administrators]. **Test**: [*SELECT FROM:* Automated mechanisms implementing information system auditing].		

AU-2(1)	AUDIT EVENTS | *COMPILATION OF AUDIT RECORDS FROM MULTIPLE SOURCES*
[Withdrawn: Incorporated into AU-12].	

AU-2(2)	AUDIT EVENTS | *SELECTION OF AUDIT EVENTS BY COMPONENT*
[Withdrawn: Incorporated into AU-12].	

AU-2(3)	AUDIT EVENTS | *REVIEWS AND UPDATES*	
	ASSESSMENT OBJECTIVE: *Determine if the organization:*	
	AU-2(3)[1]	*defines the frequency to review and update the audited events; and*
	AU-2(3)[2]	*reviews and updates the auditable events with organization-defined frequency.*

Special Publication 800-53A
Revision 4

Assessing Security and Privacy Controls in Federal Information Systems
and Organizations — *Building Effective Assessment Plans*

	POTENTIAL ASSESSMENT METHODS AND OBJECTS:
	Examine: [*SELECT FROM:* Audit and accountability policy; procedures addressing auditable events; security plan; list of organization-defined auditable events; auditable events review and update records; information system audit records; information system incident reports; other relevant documents or records].
	Interview: [*SELECT FROM:* Organizational personnel with audit and accountability responsibilities; organizational personnel with information security responsibilities].
	Test: [*SELECT FROM:* Automated mechanisms supporting review and update of auditable events].

AU-2(4)	**AUDIT EVENTS	*PRIVILEGED FUNCTIONS***
	[Withdrawn: Incorporated into AC-6(9)].

AU-3	**CONTENT OF AUDIT RECORDS**
	ASSESSMENT OBJECTIVE:
	Determine if the information system generates audit records containing information that establishes:

AU-3[1]	*what type of event occurred;*
AU-3[2]	*when the event occurred;*
AU-3[3]	*where the event occurred;*
AU-3[4]	*the source of the event;*
AU-3[5]	*the outcome of the event; and*
AU-3[6]	*the identity of any individuals or subjects associated with the event.*

	POTENTIAL ASSESSMENT METHODS AND OBJECTS:
	Examine: [*SELECT FROM:* Audit and accountability policy; procedures addressing content of audit records; information system design documentation; information system configuration settings and associated documentation; list of organization-defined auditable events; information system audit records; information system incident reports; other relevant documents or records].
	Interview: [*SELECT FROM:* Organizational personnel with audit and accountability responsibilities; organizational personnel with information security responsibilities; system/network administrators].
	Test: [*SELECT FROM:* Automated mechanisms implementing information system auditing of auditable events].

AU-3(1)	**CONTENT OF AUDIT RECORDS	*ADDITIONAL AUDIT INFORMATION***
	ASSESSMENT OBJECTIVE:
	Determine if:

AU-3(1)[1]	*the organization defines additional, more detailed information to be contained in audit records that the information system generates; and*
AU-3(1)[2]	*the information system generates audit records containing the organization-defined additional, more detailed information.*

Special Publication 800-53A
Revision 4

Assessing Security and Privacy Controls in Federal Information Systems
and Organizations — *Building Effective Assessment Plans*

	POTENTIAL ASSESSMENT METHODS AND OBJECTS: **Examine**: [*SELECT FROM:* Audit and accountability policy; procedures addressing content of audit records; information system design documentation; information system configuration settings and associated documentation; list of organization-defined auditable events; information system audit records; other relevant documents or records]. **Interview**: [*SELECT FROM:* Organizational personnel with audit and accountability responsibilities; organizational personnel with information security responsibilities; system/network administrators; system developers]. **Test**: [*SELECT FROM:* Information system audit capability].

AU-3(2)	**CONTENT OF AUDIT RECORDS** | *CENTRALIZED MANAGEMENT OF PLANNED AUDIT RECORD CONTENT*
	ASSESSMENT OBJECTIVE: *Determine if:*
		AU-3(2)[1]	*the organization defines information system components that generate audit records whose content is to be centrally managed and configured by the information system; and*
		AU-3(2)[2]	*the information system provides centralized management and configuration of the content to be captured in audit records generated by the organization-defined information system components.*
	POTENTIAL ASSESSMENT METHODS AND OBJECTS: **Examine**: [*SELECT FROM:* Audit and accountability policy; procedures addressing content of audit records; information system design documentation; information system configuration settings and associated documentation; list of organization-defined auditable events; information system audit records; other relevant documents or records]. **Interview**: [*SELECT FROM:* Organizational personnel with audit and accountability responsibilities; organizational personnel with information security responsibilities; system/network administrators; system developers]. **Test**: [*SELECT FROM:* Information system capability implementing centralized management and configuration of audit record content].

AU-4	**AUDIT STORAGE CAPACITY**
	ASSESSMENT OBJECTIVE: *Determine if the organization:*
		AU-4[1]	*defines audit record storage requirements; and*
		AU-4[2]	*allocates audit record storage capacity in accordance with the organization-defined audit record storage requirements.*
	POTENTIAL ASSESSMENT METHODS AND OBJECTS: **Examine**: [*SELECT FROM:* Audit and accountability policy; procedures addressing audit storage capacity; information system design documentation; information system configuration settings and associated documentation; audit record storage requirements; audit record storage capability for information system components; information system audit records; other relevant documents or records]. **Interview**: [*SELECT FROM:* Organizational personnel with audit and accountability responsibilities; organizational personnel with information security responsibilities; system/network administrators; system developers]. **Test**: [*SELECT FROM:* Audit record storage capacity and related configuration settings].

Special Publication 800-53A
Revision 4

Assessing Security and Privacy Controls in Federal Information Systems
and Organizations — *Building Effective Assessment Plans*

AU-4(1)	AUDIT STORAGE CAPACITY	*TRANSFER TO ALTERNATE STORAGE*	

ASSESSMENT OBJECTIVE:

Determine if:

AU-4(1)[1]	*the organization defines the frequency to off-load audit records onto a different system or media than the system being audited; and*
AU-4(1)[2]	*the information system off-loads audit records onto a different system or media than the system being audited with the organization-defined frequency.*

POTENTIAL ASSESSMENT METHODS AND OBJECTS:

Examine: [*SELECT FROM*: Audit and accountability policy; procedures addressing audit storage capacity; procedures addressing transfer of information system audit records to secondary or alternate systems; information system design documentation; information system configuration settings and associated documentation; logs of audit record transfers to secondary or alternate systems; information system audit records transferred to secondary or alternate systems; other relevant documents or records].

Interview: [*SELECT FROM*: Organizational personnel with audit storage capacity planning responsibilities; organizational personnel with information security responsibilities; system/network administrators].

Test: [*SELECT FROM*: Automated mechanisms supporting transfer of audit records onto a different system].

AU-5	RESPONSE TO AUDIT PROCESSING FAILURES		

ASSESSMENT OBJECTIVE:

Determine if:

AU-5(a)	AU-5(a)[1]	*the organization defines the personnel or roles to be alerted in the event of an audit processing failure;*
	AU-5(a)[2]	*the information system alerts the organization-defined personnel or roles in the event of an audit processing failure;*
AU-5(b)	AU-5(b)[1]	*the organization defines additional actions to be taken (e.g., shutdown information system, overwrite oldest audit records, stop generating audit records) in the event of an audit processing failure; and*
	AU-5(b)[2]	*the information system takes the additional organization-defined actions in the event of an audit processing failure.*

POTENTIAL ASSESSMENT METHODS AND OBJECTS:

Examine: [*SELECT FROM*: Audit and accountability policy; procedures addressing response to audit processing failures; information system design documentation; security plan; information system configuration settings and associated documentation; list of personnel to be notified in case of an audit processing failure; information system audit records; other relevant documents or records].

Interview: [*SELECT FROM*: Organizational personnel with audit and accountability responsibilities; organizational personnel with information security responsibilities; system/network administrators; system developers].

Test: [*SELECT FROM*: Automated mechanisms implementing information system response to audit processing failures].

Special Publication 800-53A
Revision 4

Assessing Security and Privacy Controls in Federal Information Systems
and Organizations — *Building Effective Assessment Plans*

AU-5(1)	RESPONSE TO AUDIT PROCESSING FAILURES | *AUDIT STORAGE CAPACITY*		
	ASSESSMENT OBJECTIVE: *Determine if:*		
	AU-5(1)[1]	*the organization defines:*	
		AU-5(1)[1][a]	*personnel to be warned when allocated audit record storage volume reaches organization-defined percentage of repository maximum audit record storage capacity;*
		AU-5(1)[1][b]	*roles to be warned when allocated audit record storage volume reaches organization-defined percentage of repository maximum audit record storage capacity; and/or*
		AU-5(1)[1][c]	*locations to be warned when allocated audit record storage volume reaches organization-defined percentage of repository maximum audit record storage capacity;*
	AU-5(1)[2]	*the organization defines the time period within which the information system is to provide a warning to the organization-defined personnel, roles, and/or locations when allocated audit record storage volume reaches the organization-defined percentage of repository maximum audit record storage capacity;*	
	AU-5(1)[3]	*the organization defines the percentage of repository maximum audit record storage capacity that, if reached, requires a warning to be provided; and*	
	AU-5(1)[4]	*the information system provides a warning to the organization-defined personnel, roles, and/or locations within the organization-defined time period when allocated audit record storage volume reaches the organization-defined percentage of repository maximum audit record storage capacity.*	
	POTENTIAL ASSESSMENT METHODS AND OBJECTS: **Examine**: [*SELECT FROM:* Audit and accountability policy; procedures addressing response to audit processing failures; information system design documentation; security plan; information system configuration settings and associated documentation; information system audit records; other relevant documents or records]. **Interview**: [*SELECT FROM:* Organizational personnel with audit and accountability responsibilities; organizational personnel with information security responsibilities; system/network administrators; system developers]. **Test**: [*SELECT FROM:* Automated mechanisms implementing audit storage limit warnings].		

AU-5(2)	RESPONSE TO AUDIT PROCESSING FAILURES | *REAL-TIME ALERTS*		
	ASSESSMENT OBJECTIVE: *Determine if:*		
	AU-5(2)[1]	*the organization defines audit failure events requiring real-time alerts;*	
	AU-5(2)[2]	*the organization defines:*	
		AU-5(2)[2][a]	*personnel to be alerted when organization-defined audit failure events requiring real-time alerts occur;*
		AU-5(2)[2][b]	*roles to be alerted when organization-defined audit failure events requiring real-time alerts occur; and/or*
		AU-5(2)[2][c]	*locations to be alerted when organization-defined audit failure events requiring real-time alerts occur;*

Special Publication 800-53A
Revision 4

Assessing Security and Privacy Controls in Federal Information Systems
and Organizations — *Building Effective Assessment Plans*

AU-5(2)[3]	*the organization defines the real-time period within which the information system is to provide an alert to the organization-defined personnel, roles, and/or locations when the organization-defined audit failure events requiring real-time alerts occur; and*	
AU-5(2)[4]	*the information system provides an alert within the organization-defined real-time period to the organization-defined personnel, roles, and/or locations when organization-defined audit failure events requiring real-time alerts occur.*	

POTENTIAL ASSESSMENT METHODS AND OBJECTS:

Examine: [*SELECT FROM:* Audit and accountability policy; procedures addressing response to audit processing failures; information system design documentation; security plan; information system configuration settings and associated documentation; records of notifications or real-time alerts when audit processing failures occur; information system audit records; other relevant documents or records].

Interview: [*SELECT FROM:* Organizational personnel with audit and accountability responsibilities; organizational personnel with information security responsibilities; system/network administrators; system developers].

Test: [*SELECT FROM:* Automated mechanisms implementing real-time audit alerts when organization-defined audit failure events occur].

AU-5(3)	**RESPONSE TO AUDIT PROCESSING FAILURES	*CONFIGURABLE TRAFFIC VOLUME THRESHOLDS***

ASSESSMENT OBJECTIVE:
Determine if:

AU-5(3)[1]	*the information system enforces configurable network communications traffic volume thresholds reflecting limits on auditing capacity;*	
AU-5(3)[2]	*the organization selects if network traffic above configurable traffic volume thresholds is to be:*	
	AU-5(3)[2][a]	*rejected; or*
	AU-5(3)[2][b]	*delayed; and*
AU-5(3)[3]	*the information system rejects or delays network communications traffic generated above configurable traffic volume thresholds.*	

POTENTIAL ASSESSMENT METHODS AND OBJECTS:

Examine: [*SELECT FROM:* Audit and accountability policy; procedures addressing response to audit processing failures; information system design documentation; security plan; information system configuration settings and associated documentation; configuration of network communications traffic volume thresholds; information system audit records; other relevant documents or records].

Interview: [*SELECT FROM:* Organizational personnel with audit and accountability responsibilities; organizational personnel with information security responsibilities; system/network administrators; system developers].

Test: [*SELECT FROM:* Information system capability implementing configurable traffic volume thresholds].

AU-5(4)	**RESPONSE TO AUDIT PROCESSING FAILURES	*SHUTDOWN ON FAILURE***

ASSESSMENT OBJECTIVE:
Determine if:

AU-5(4)[1]	*the organization selects one of the following specific actions for the information system to invoke in the event of organization-defined audit failures:*	
	AU-5(4)[1][a]	*full system shutdown;*

Special Publication 800-53A
Revision 4

Assessing Security and Privacy Controls in Federal Information Systems
and Organizations — *Building Effective Assessment Plans*

		AU-5(4)[1][b]	*partial system shutdown; or*
		AU-5(4)[1][c]	*degraded operational mode with limited mission/business functionality available;*
	AU-5(4)[2]		*the organization defines audit failures that, unless an alternate audit capability exists, are to trigger the information system to invoke a specific action; and*
	AU-5(4)[3]		*the information system invokes the selected specific action in the event of organization-defined audit failures, unless an alternate audit capability exists.*

POTENTIAL ASSESSMENT METHODS AND OBJECTS:

Examine: [*SELECT FROM:* Audit and accountability policy; procedures addressing response to audit processing failures; information system design documentation; security plan; information system configuration settings and associated documentation; information system audit records; other relevant documents or records].

Interview: [*SELECT FROM:* Organizational personnel with audit and accountability responsibilities; organizational personnel with information security responsibilities; system/network administrators; system developers].

Test: [*SELECT FROM:* Information system capability invoking system shutdown or degraded operational mode in the event of an audit processing failure].

AU-6	**AUDIT REVIEW, ANALYSIS, AND REPORTING**	

ASSESSMENT OBJECTIVE:
Determine if the organization:

	AU-6(a)	AU-6(a)[1]	*defines the types of inappropriate or unusual activity to look for when information system audit records are reviewed and analyzed;*
		AU-6(a)[2]	*defines the frequency to review and analyze information system audit records for indications of organization-defined inappropriate or unusual activity;*
		AU-6(a)[3]	*reviews and analyzes information system audit records for indications of organization-defined inappropriate or unusual activity with the organization-defined frequency;*
	AU-6(b)	AU-6(b)[1]	*defines personnel or roles to whom findings resulting from reviews and analysis of information system audit records are to be reported; and*
		AU-6(b)[2]	*reports findings to organization-defined personnel or roles.*

POTENTIAL ASSESSMENT METHODS AND OBJECTS:

Examine: [*SELECT FROM:* Audit and accountability policy; procedures addressing audit review, analysis, and reporting; reports of audit findings; records of actions taken in response to reviews/analyses of audit records; other relevant documents or records].

Interview: [*SELECT FROM:* Organizational personnel with audit review, analysis, and reporting responsibilities; organizational personnel with information security responsibilities].

AU-6(1)	**AUDIT REVIEW, ANALYSIS, AND REPORTING**	*PROCESS INTEGRATION*	

ASSESSMENT OBJECTIVE:
Determine if the organization:

	AU-6(1)[1]	*employs automated mechanisms to integrate:*	
		AU-6(1)[1][a]	*audit review;*

Special Publication 800-53A
Revision 4

Assessing Security and Privacy Controls in Federal Information Systems
and Organizations — *Building Effective Assessment Plans*

		AU-6(1)[1][b]	*analysis;*
		AU-6(1)[1][c]	*reporting processes;*
	AU-6(1)[2]		*uses integrated audit review, analysis and reporting processes to support organizational processes for:*
		AU-6(1)[2][a]	*investigation of suspicious activities; and*
		AU-6(1)[2][b]	*response to suspicious activities.*

POTENTIAL ASSESSMENT METHODS AND OBJECTS:

Examine: [*SELECT FROM:* Audit and accountability policy; procedures addressing audit review, analysis, and reporting; procedures addressing investigation and response to suspicious activities; information system design documentation; information system configuration settings and associated documentation; information system audit records; other relevant documents or records].

Interview: [*SELECT FROM:* Organizational personnel with audit review, analysis, and reporting responsibilities; organizational personnel with information security responsibilities].

Test: [*SELECT FROM:* Automated mechanisms integrating audit review, analysis, and reporting processes].

AU-6(2)	AUDIT REVIEW, ANALYSIS, AND REPORTING | *AUTOMATED SECURITY ALERTS*

[Withdrawn: Incorporated into SI-4].

AU-6(3)	AUDIT REVIEW, ANALYSIS, AND REPORTING | *CORRELATE AUDIT REPOSITORIES*

ASSESSMENT OBJECTIVE:

Determine if the organization analyzes and correlates audit records across different repositories to gain organization-wide situational awareness.

POTENTIAL ASSESSMENT METHODS AND OBJECTS:

Examine: [*SELECT FROM:* Audit and accountability policy; procedures addressing audit review, analysis, and reporting; information system design documentation; information system configuration settings and associated documentation; information system audit records across different repositories; other relevant documents or records].

Interview: [*SELECT FROM:* Organizational personnel with audit review, analysis, and reporting responsibilities; organizational personnel with information security responsibilities].

Test: [*SELECT FROM:* Automated mechanisms supporting analysis and correlation of audit records].

AU-6(4)	AUDIT REVIEW, ANALYSIS, AND REPORTING | *CENTRAL REVIEW AND ANALYSIS*

ASSESSMENT OBJECTIVE:

Determine if the information system provides the capability to centrally review and analyze audit records from multiple components within the system.

POTENTIAL ASSESSMENT METHODS AND OBJECTS:

Examine: [*SELECT FROM:* Audit and accountability policy; procedures addressing audit review, analysis, and reporting; information system design documentation; information system configuration settings and associated documentation; security plan; information system audit records; other relevant documents or records].

Interview: [*SELECT FROM:* Organizational personnel with audit review, analysis, and reporting responsibilities; organizational personnel with information security responsibilities; system developers].

Test: [*SELECT FROM:* Information system capability to centralize review and analysis of audit records].

Special Publication 800-53A
Revision 4

Assessing Security and Privacy Controls in Federal Information Systems
and Organizations — *Building Effective Assessment Plans*

AU-6(5)	AUDIT REVIEW, ANALYSIS, AND REPORTING | *INTEGRATION/SCANNING AND MONITORING CAPABILITIES*	
	ASSESSMENT OBJECTIVE: *Determine if the organization:*	
	AU-6(5)[1]	*defines data/information to be collected from other sources;*
	AU-6(5)[2]	*selects sources of data/information to be analyzed and integrated with the analysis of audit records from one or more of the following:*
		AU-6(5)[2][a] *vulnerability scanning information;*
		AU-6(5)[2][b] *performance data;*
		AU-6(5)[2][c] *information system monitoring information; and/or*
		AU-6(5)[2][d] *organization-defined data/information collected from other sources; and*
	AU-6(5)[3]	*integrates the analysis of audit records with the analysis of selected data/information to further enhance the ability to identify inappropriate or unusual activity.*
	POTENTIAL ASSESSMENT METHODS AND OBJECTS: **Examine**: [*SELECT FROM:* Audit and accountability policy; procedures addressing audit review, analysis, and reporting; information system design documentation; information system configuration settings and associated documentation; integrated analysis of audit records, vulnerability scanning information, performance data, network monitoring information and associated documentation; other relevant documents or records]. **Interview**: [*SELECT FROM:* Organizational personnel with audit review, analysis, and reporting responsibilities; organizational personnel with information security responsibilities]. **Test**: [*SELECT FROM:* Automated mechanisms implementing capability to integrate analysis of audit records with analysis of data/information sources].	

AU-6(6)	AUDIT REVIEW, ANALYSIS, AND REPORTING | *CORRELATION WITH PHYSICAL MONITORING*
	ASSESSMENT OBJECTIVE: *Determine if the organization correlates information from audit records with information obtained from monitoring physical access to enhance the ability to identify suspicious, inappropriate, unusual, or malevolent activity.*
	POTENTIAL ASSESSMENT METHODS AND OBJECTS: **Examine**: [*SELECT FROM:* Audit and accountability policy; procedures addressing audit review, analysis, and reporting; procedures addressing physical access monitoring; information system design documentation; information system configuration settings and associated documentation; documentation providing evidence of correlated information obtained from audit records and physical access monitoring records; security plan; other relevant documents or records]. **Interview**: [*SELECT FROM:* Organizational personnel with audit review, analysis, and reporting responsibilities; organizational personnel with physical access monitoring responsibilities; organizational personnel with information security responsibilities]. **Test**: [*SELECT FROM:* Automated mechanisms implementing capability to correlate information from audit records with information from monitoring physical access].

Special Publication 800-53A
Revision 4

Assessing Security and Privacy Controls in Federal Information Systems
and Organizations — *Building Effective Assessment Plans*

AU-6(7)	AUDIT REVIEW, ANALYSIS, AND REPORTING | *PERMITTED ACTIONS*
	ASSESSMENT OBJECTIVE: *Determine if the organization specifies the permitted actions for each one or more of the following associated with the review, analysis and reporting of audit information:*

AU-6(7)[1]	*information system process;*
AU-6(7)[2]	*role; and/or*
AU-6(7)[3]	*user.*

POTENTIAL ASSESSMENT METHODS AND OBJECTS:
Examine: [*SELECT FROM:* Audit and accountability policy; procedures addressing process, role and/or user permitted actions from audit review, analysis, and reporting; security plan; other relevant documents or records].
Interview: [*SELECT FROM:* Organizational personnel with audit review, analysis, and reporting responsibilities; organizational personnel with information security responsibilities].
Test: [*SELECT FROM:* Automated mechanisms supporting permitted actions for review, analysis, and reporting of audit information].

AU-6(8)	AUDIT REVIEW, ANALYSIS, AND REPORTING | *FULL TEXT ANALYSIS OF PRIVILEGED COMMANDS*
	ASSESSMENT OBJECTIVE: *Determine if the organization performs a full text analysis of audited privileged commands in:*

AU-6(8)[1]	*a physically distinct component or subsystem of the information system; or*
AU-6(8)[2]	*other information system that is dedicated to that analysis.*

POTENTIAL ASSESSMENT METHODS AND OBJECTS:
Examine: [*SELECT FROM:* Audit and accountability policy; procedures addressing audit review, analysis, and reporting; information system design documentation; information system configuration settings and associated documentation; text analysis tools and techniques; text analysis documentation of audited privileged commands; security plan; other relevant documents or records].
Interview: [*SELECT FROM:* Organizational personnel with audit review, analysis, and reporting responsibilities; organizational personnel with information security responsibilities].
Test: [*SELECT FROM:* Automated mechanisms implementing capability to perform a full text analysis of audited privilege commands].

AU-6(9)	AUDIT REVIEW, ANALYSIS, AND REPORTING | *CORRELATION WITH INFORMATION FROM NONTECHNICAL SOURCES*
	ASSESSMENT OBJECTIVE: *Determine if the organization correlates information from nontechnical sources with audit information to enhance organization-wide situational awareness.*

Special Publication 800-53A
Revision 4

Assessing Security and Privacy Controls in Federal Information Systems
and Organizations — *Building Effective Assessment Plans*

POTENTIAL ASSESSMENT METHODS AND OBJECTS:

Examine: [*SELECT FROM:* Audit and accountability policy; procedures addressing audit review, analysis, and reporting; information system design documentation; information system configuration settings and associated documentation; documentation providing evidence of correlated information obtained from audit records and organization-defined nontechnical sources; list of information types from nontechnical sources for correlation with audit information; other relevant documents or records].

Interview: [*SELECT FROM:* Organizational personnel with audit review, analysis, and reporting responsibilities; organizational personnel with information security responsibilities].

Test: [*SELECT FROM:* Automated mechanisms implementing capability to correlate information from non-technical sources].

AU-6(10)	AUDIT REVIEW, ANALYSIS, AND REPORTING | *AUDIT LEVEL ADJUSTMENT*

ASSESSMENT OBJECTIVE:

Determine if the organization adjusts the level of audit review, analysis, and reporting within the information system when there is a change in risk based on:

AU-6(10)[1]	*law enforcement information;*
AU-6(10)[2]	*intelligence information; and/or*
AU-6(10)[3]	*other credible sources of information.*

POTENTIAL ASSESSMENT METHODS AND OBJECTS:

Examine: [*SELECT FROM:* Audit and accountability policy; procedures addressing audit review, analysis, and reporting; organizational risk assessment; security control assessment; vulnerability assessment; security plan; other relevant documents or records].

Interview: [*SELECT FROM:* Organizational personnel with audit review, analysis, and reporting responsibilities; organizational personnel with information security responsibilities].

Test: [*SELECT FROM:* Automated mechanisms supporting review, analysis, and reporting of audit information].

AU-7	AUDIT REDUCTION AND REPORT GENERATION

ASSESSMENT OBJECTIVE:

Determine if the information system provides an audit reduction and report generation capability that supports:

AU-7(a)	AU-7(a)[1]	*on-demand audit review;*
	AU-7(a)[2]	*analysis;*
	AU-7(a)[3]	*reporting requirements;*
	AU-7(a)[4]	*after-the-fact investigations of security incidents; and*
AU-7(b)	*does not alter the original content or time ordering of audit records.*	

POTENTIAL ASSESSMENT METHODS AND OBJECTS:

Examine: [*SELECT FROM:* Audit and accountability policy; procedures addressing audit reduction and report generation; information system design documentation; information system configuration settings and associated documentation; audit reduction, review, analysis, and reporting tools; information system audit records; other relevant documents or records].

Interview: [*SELECT FROM:* Organizational personnel with audit reduction and report generation responsibilities; organizational personnel with information security responsibilities].

Test: [*SELECT FROM:* Audit reduction and report generation capability].

Special Publication 800-53A
Revision 4

Assessing Security and Privacy Controls in Federal Information Systems
and Organizations — *Building Effective Assessment Plans*

AU-7(1)	AUDIT REDUCTION AND REPORT GENERATION	*AUTOMATIC PROCESSING*

	ASSESSMENT OBJECTIVE:
	Determine if:
AU-7(1)[1]	*the organization defines audit fields within audit records in order to process audit records for events of interest; and*
AU-7(1)[2]	*the information system provides the capability to process audit records for events of interest based on the organization-defined audit fields within audit records.*

POTENTIAL ASSESSMENT METHODS AND OBJECTS:

Examine: [*SELECT FROM*: Audit and accountability policy; procedures addressing audit reduction and report generation; information system design documentation; information system configuration settings and associated documentation; audit reduction, review, analysis, and reporting tools; audit record criteria (fields) establishing events of interest; information system audit records; other relevant documents or records].

Interview: [*SELECT FROM*: Organizational personnel with audit reduction and report generation responsibilities; organizational personnel with information security responsibilities; system developers].

Test: [*SELECT FROM*: Audit reduction and report generation capability].

AU-7(2)	AUDIT REDUCTION AND REPORT GENERATION	*AUTOMATIC SORT AND SEARCH*

	ASSESSMENT OBJECTIVE:
	Determine if:
AU-7(2)[1]	*the organization defines audit fields within audit records in order to sort and search audit records for events of interest based on content of such audit fields; and*
AU-7(2)[2]	*the information system provides the capability to sort and search audit records for events of interest based on the content of organization-defined audit fields within audit records.*

POTENTIAL ASSESSMENT METHODS AND OBJECTS:

Examine: [*SELECT FROM*: Audit and accountability policy; procedures addressing audit reduction and report generation; information system design documentation; information system configuration settings and associated documentation; audit reduction, review, analysis, and reporting tools; audit record criteria (fields) establishing events of interest; information system audit records; other relevant documents or records].

Interview: [*SELECT FROM*: Organizational personnel with audit reduction and report generation responsibilities; organizational personnel with information security responsibilities; system developers].

Test: [*SELECT FROM*: Audit reduction and report generation capability].

AU-8	TIME STAMPS

	ASSESSMENT OBJECTIVE:	
	Determine if:	
AU-8(a)	*the information system uses internal system clocks to generate time stamps for audit records;*	
AU-8(b)	**AU-8(b)[1]**	*the information system records time stamps for audit records that can be mapped to Coordinated Universal Time (UTC) or Greenwich Mean Time (GMT);*

Special Publication 800-53A
Revision 4

Assessing Security and Privacy Controls in Federal Information Systems
and Organizations — *Building Effective Assessment Plans*

		AU-8(b)[2]	*the organization defines the granularity of time measurement to be met when recording time stamps for audit records; and*
		AU-8(b)[3]	*the organization records time stamps for audit records that meet the organization-defined granularity of time measurement.*

POTENTIAL ASSESSMENT METHODS AND OBJECTS:

Examine: [*SELECT FROM:* Audit and accountability policy; procedures addressing time stamp generation; information system design documentation; information system configuration settings and associated documentation; information system audit records; other relevant documents or records].

Interview: [*SELECT FROM:* Organizational personnel with information security responsibilities; system/network administrators; system developers].

Test: [*SELECT FROM:* Automated mechanisms implementing time stamp generation].

AU-8(1)	TIME STAMPS | *SYNCHRONIZATION WITH AUTHORITATIVE TIME SOURCE*

ASSESSMENT OBJECTIVE:

Determine if:

AU-8(1)(a)	AU-8(1)(a)[1]	*the organization defines the authoritative time source to which internal information system clocks are to be compared;*
	AU-8(1)(a)[2]	*the organization defines the frequency to compare the internal information system clocks with the organization-defined authoritative time source; and*
	AU-8(1)(a)[3]	*the information system compares the internal information system clocks with the organization-defined authoritative time source with organization-defined frequency; and*
AU-8(1)(b)	AU-8(1)(b)[1]	*the organization defines the time period that, if exceeded by the time difference between the internal system clocks and the authoritative time source, will result in the internal system clocks being synchronized to the authoritative time source; and*
	AU-8(1)(b)[2]	*the information system synchronizes the internal information system clocks to the authoritative time source when the time difference is greater than the organization-defined time period.*

POTENTIAL ASSESSMENT METHODS AND OBJECTS:

Examine: [*SELECT FROM:* Audit and accountability policy; procedures addressing time stamp generation; information system design documentation; information system configuration settings and associated documentation; information system audit records; other relevant documents or records].

Interview: [*SELECT FROM:* Organizational personnel with information security responsibilities; system/network administrators; system developers].

Test: [*SELECT FROM:* Automated mechanisms implementing internal information system clock synchronization].

AU-8(2)	TIME STAMPS | *SECONDARY AUTHORITATIVE TIME SOURCE*

ASSESSMENT OBJECTIVE:

Determine if the information system identifies a secondary authoritative time source that is located in a different geographic region than the primary authoritative time source.

Special Publication 800-53A
Revision 4

Assessing Security and Privacy Controls in Federal Information Systems
and Organizations — *Building Effective Assessment Plans*

POTENTIAL ASSESSMENT METHODS AND OBJECTS:

Examine: [*SELECT FROM:* Audit and accountability policy; procedures addressing time stamp generation; information system design documentation; information system configuration settings and associated documentation; information system audit records; other relevant documents or records].

Interview: [*SELECT FROM:* Organizational personnel with information security responsibilities; system/network administrators; system developers].

Test: [*SELECT FROM:* Automated mechanisms implementing internal information system clock authoritative time sources].

AU-9	PROTECTION OF AUDIT INFORMATION

ASSESSMENT OBJECTIVE:

Determine if:

AU-9[1]		*the information system protects audit information from unauthorized:*
	AU-9[1][a]	*access;*
	AU-9[1][b]	*modification;*
	AU-9[1][c]	*deletion;*
AU-9[2]		*the information system protects audit tools from unauthorized:*
	AU-9[2][a]	*access;*
	AU-9[2][b]	*modification; and*
	AU-9[2][c]	*deletion.*

POTENTIAL ASSESSMENT METHODS AND OBJECTS:

Examine: [*SELECT FROM:* Audit and accountability policy; access control policy and procedures; procedures addressing protection of audit information; information system design documentation; information system configuration settings and associated documentation, information system audit records; audit tools; other relevant documents or records].

Interview: [*SELECT FROM:* Organizational personnel with audit and accountability responsibilities; organizational personnel with information security responsibilities; system/network administrators; system developers].

Test: [*SELECT FROM:* Automated mechanisms implementing audit information protection].

AU-9(1)	PROTECTION OF AUDIT INFORMATION | *HARDWARE WRITE-ONCE MEDIA*

ASSESSMENT OBJECTIVE:

Determine if the information system writes audit trails to hardware-enforced, write-once media.

POTENTIAL ASSESSMENT METHODS AND OBJECTS:

Examine: [*SELECT FROM:* Audit and accountability policy; access control policy and procedures; procedures addressing protection of audit information; information system design documentation; information system hardware settings; information system configuration settings and associated documentation; information system storage media; information system audit records; other relevant documents or records].

Interview: [*SELECT FROM:* Organizational personnel with audit and accountability responsibilities; organizational personnel with information security responsibilities; system/network administrators; system developers].

Test: [*SELECT FROM:* Information system media storing audit trails].

Special Publication 800-53A
Revision 4

Assessing Security and Privacy Controls in Federal Information Systems
and Organizations — *Building Effective Assessment Plans*

AU-9(2)	PROTECTION OF AUDIT INFORMATION | *AUDIT BACKUP ON SEPARATE PHYSICAL SYSTEMS / COMPONENTS*
	ASSESSMENT OBJECTIVE: *Determine if:*
	AU-9(2)[1] — *the organization defines the frequency to back up audit records onto a physically different system or system component than the system or component being audited; and*
	AU-9(2)[2] — *the information system backs up audit records with the organization-defined frequency, onto a physically different system or system component than the system or component being audited.*
	POTENTIAL ASSESSMENT METHODS AND OBJECTS: **Examine**: [*SELECT FROM:* Audit and accountability policy; procedures addressing protection of audit information; information system design documentation; information system configuration settings and associated documentation, system or media storing backups of information system audit records; information system audit records; other relevant documents or records]. **Interview**: [*SELECT FROM:* Organizational personnel with audit and accountability responsibilities; organizational personnel with information security responsibilities; system/network administrators; system developers]. **Test**: [*SELECT FROM:* Automated mechanisms implementing the backing up of audit records].

AU-9(3)	PROTECTION OF AUDIT INFORMATION | *CRYPTOGRAPHIC PROTECTION*
	ASSESSMENT OBJECTIVE: *Determine if the information system:*
	AU-9(3)[1] — *uses cryptographic mechanisms to protect the integrity of audit information; and*
	AU-9(3)[2] — *uses cryptographic mechanisms to protect the integrity of audit tools.*
	POTENTIAL ASSESSMENT METHODS AND OBJECTS: **Examine**: [*SELECT FROM:* Audit and accountability policy; access control policy and procedures; procedures addressing protection of audit information; information system design documentation; information system hardware settings; information system configuration settings and associated documentation, information system audit records; other relevant documents or records]. **Interview**: [*SELECT FROM:* Organizational personnel with audit and accountability responsibilities; organizational personnel with information security responsibilities; system/network administrators; system developers]. **Test**: [*SELECT FROM:* Cryptographic mechanisms protecting integrity of audit information and tools].

AU-9(4)	PROTECTION OF AUDIT INFORMATION | *ACCESS BY SUBSET OF PRIVILEGED USERS*
	ASSESSMENT OBJECTIVE: *Determine if the organization:*
	AU-9(4)[1] — *defines a subset of privileged users to be authorized access to management of audit functionality; and*
	AU-9(4)[2] — *authorizes access to management of audit functionality to only the organization-defined subset of privileged users.*

Special Publication 800-53A
Revision 4

Assessing Security and Privacy Controls in Federal Information Systems
and Organizations — *Building Effective Assessment Plans*

POTENTIAL ASSESSMENT METHODS AND OBJECTS:

Examine: [*SELECT FROM:* Audit and accountability policy; access control policy and procedures; procedures addressing protection of audit information; information system design documentation; information system configuration settings and associated documentation, system-generated list of privileged users with access to management of audit functionality; access authorizations; access control list; information system audit records; other relevant documents or records].

Interview: [*SELECT FROM:* Organizational personnel with audit and accountability responsibilities; organizational personnel with information security responsibilities; system/network administrators].

Test: [*SELECT FROM:* Automated mechanisms managing access to audit functionality].

AU-9(5)	PROTECTION OF AUDIT INFORMATION | *DUAL AUTHORIZATION*

ASSESSMENT OBJECTIVE:

Determine if the organization:

AU-9(5)[1]	*defines audit information for which dual authorization is to be enforced;*
AU-9(5)[2]	*defines one or more of the following types of operations on audit information for which dual authorization is to be enforced:*

	AU-9(5)[2][a]	*movement; and/or*
	AU-9(5)[2][b]	*deletion; and*

AU-9(5)[3]	*enforces dual authorization for the movement and/or deletion of organization-defined audit information.*

POTENTIAL ASSESSMENT METHODS AND OBJECTS:

Examine: [*SELECT FROM:* Audit and accountability policy; access control policy and procedures; procedures addressing protection of audit information; information system design documentation; information system configuration settings and associated documentation, access authorizations; information system audit records; other relevant documents or records].

Interview: [*SELECT FROM:* Organizational personnel with audit and accountability responsibilities; organizational personnel with information security responsibilities; system/network administrators].

Test: [*SELECT FROM:* Automated mechanisms implementing enforcement of dual authorization].

AU-9(6)	PROTECTION OF AUDIT INFORMATION | *READ ONLY ACCESS*

ASSESSMENT OBJECTIVE:

Determine if the organization:

AU-9(6)[1]	*defines the subset of privileged users to be authorized read-only access to audit information; and*
AU-9(6)[2]	*authorizes read-only access to audit information to the organization-defined subset of privileged users.*

Special Publication 800-53A
Revision 4

Assessing Security and Privacy Controls in Federal Information Systems
and Organizations — *Building Effective Assessment Plans*

POTENTIAL ASSESSMENT METHODS AND OBJECTS:

Examine: [*SELECT FROM:* Audit and accountability policy; access control policy and procedures; procedures addressing protection of audit information; information system design documentation; information system configuration settings and associated documentation, system-generated list of privileged users with read-only access to audit information; access authorizations; access control list; information system audit records; other relevant documents or records].

Interview: [*SELECT FROM:* Organizational personnel with audit and accountability responsibilities; organizational personnel with information security responsibilities; system/network administrators].

Test: [*SELECT FROM:* Automated mechanisms managing access to audit information].

AU-10	NON-REPUDIATION

ASSESSMENT OBJECTIVE:

Determine if:

AU-10[1]	*the organization defines actions to be covered by non-repudiation; and*
AU-10[2]	*the information system protects against an individual (or process acting on behalf of an individual) falsely denying having performed organization-defined actions to be covered by non-repudiation.*

POTENTIAL ASSESSMENT METHODS AND OBJECTS:

Examine: [*SELECT FROM:* Audit and accountability policy; procedures addressing non-repudiation; information system design documentation; information system configuration settings and associated documentation; information system audit records; other relevant documents or records].

Interview: [*SELECT FROM:* Organizational personnel with information security responsibilities; system/network administrators; system developers].

Test: [*SELECT FROM:* Automated mechanisms implementing non-repudiation capability].

AU-10(1)	NON-REPUDIATION	*ASSOCIATION OF IDENTITIES*

ASSESSMENT OBJECTIVE:

Determine if:

AU-10(1)(a)	AU-10(1)(a)[1]	*the organization defines the strength of binding to be employed between the identity of the information producer and the information;*
	AU-10(1)(a)[2]	*the information system binds the identity of the information producer with the information to the organization-defined strength of binding; and*
AU-10(1)(b)	*the information system provides the means for authorized individuals to determine the identity of the producer of the information.*	

POTENTIAL ASSESSMENT METHODS AND OBJECTS:

Examine: [*SELECT FROM:* Audit and accountability policy; procedures addressing non-repudiation; information system design documentation; information system configuration settings and associated documentation; information system audit records; other relevant documents or records].

Interview: [*SELECT FROM:* Organizational personnel with information security responsibilities; system/network administrators; system developers].

Test: [*SELECT FROM:* Automated mechanisms implementing non-repudiation capability].

Special Publication 800-53A
Revision 4

Assessing Security and Privacy Controls in Federal Information Systems
and Organizations — *Building Effective Assessment Plans*

AU-10(2)	NON-REPUDIATION | *VALIDATE BINDING OF INFORMATION PRODUCER IDENTITY*		

ASSESSMENT OBJECTIVE:

Determine if:

AU-10(2)(a)	AU-10(2)(a)[1]	*the organization defines the frequency to validate the binding of the information producer identity to the information;*
	AU-10(2)(a)[2]	*the information system validates the binding of the information producer identity to the information at the organization-defined frequency; and*
AU-10(2)(b)	AU-10(2)(b)[1]	*the organization defines actions to be performed in the event of a validation error; and*
	AU-10(2)(b)[2]	*the information system performs organization-defined actions in the event of a validation error.*

POTENTIAL ASSESSMENT METHODS AND OBJECTS:

Examine: [*SELECT FROM:* Audit and accountability policy; procedures addressing non-repudiation; information system design documentation; information system configuration settings and associated documentation; validation records; information system audit records; other relevant documents or records].

Interview: [*SELECT FROM:* Organizational personnel with information security responsibilities; system/network administrators; system developers].

Test: [*SELECT FROM:* Automated mechanisms implementing non-repudiation capability].

AU-10(3)	NON-REPUDIATION | *CHAIN OF CUSTODY*

ASSESSMENT OBJECTIVE:

Determine if the information system:

AU-10(3)[1]	*maintains reviewer/releaser identity within the established chain of custody for all information reviewed;*
AU-10(3)[2]	*maintains reviewer/releaser identity within the established chain of custody for all information released;*
AU-10(3)[3]	*maintains reviewer/releaser credentials within the established chain of custody for all information reviewed; and*
AU-10(3)[4]	*maintains reviewer/releaser credentials within the established chain of custody for all information released.*

POTENTIAL ASSESSMENT METHODS AND OBJECTS:

Examine: [*SELECT FROM:* Audit and accountability policy; procedures addressing non-repudiation; information system design documentation; information system configuration settings and associated documentation; records of information reviews and releases; information system audit records; other relevant documents or records].

Interview: [*SELECT FROM:* Organizational personnel with information security responsibilities; system/network administrators; system developers].

Test: [*SELECT FROM:* Automated mechanisms implementing non-repudiation capability].

AU-10(4)	NON-REPUDIATION | *VALIDATE BINDING OF INFORMATION REVIEWER IDENTITY*

ASSESSMENT OBJECTIVE:

Determine if:

Special Publication 800-53A
Revision 4

Assessing Security and Privacy Controls in Federal Information Systems
and Organizations — *Building Effective Assessment Plans*

	AU-10(4)(a)	AU-10(4)(a)[1]	*the organization defines security domains for which the binding of the information reviewer identity to the information is to be validated at the transfer or release points prior to release/transfer between such domains;*
		AU-10(4)(a)[2]	*the information system validates the binding of the information reviewer identity to the information at the transfer or release points prior to release/transfer between organization-defined security domains;*
	AU-10(4)(b)	AU-10(4)(b)[1]	*the organization defines actions to be performed in the event of a validation error; and*
		AU-10(4)(b)[2]	*the information system performs organization-defined actions in the event of a validation error.*

POTENTIAL ASSESSMENT METHODS AND OBJECTS:

Examine: [*SELECT FROM:* Audit and accountability policy; procedures addressing non-repudiation; information system design documentation; information system configuration settings and associated documentation; validation records; information system audit records; other relevant documents or records].

Interview: [*SELECT FROM:* Organizational personnel with information security responsibilities; system/network administrators; system developers].

Test: [*SELECT FROM:* Automated mechanisms implementing non-repudiation capability].

AU-10(5)	NON-REPUDIATION | *DIGITAL SIGNATURES*
[Withdrawn: Incorporated into SI-7].	

AU-11	AUDIT RECORD RETENTION

ASSESSMENT OBJECTIVE:

Determine if the organization:

AU-11[1]	*defines a time period to retain audit records that is consistent with records retention policy;*	
AU-11[2]	*retains audit records for the organization-defined time period consistent with records retention policy to:*	
	AU-11[2][a]	*provide support for after-the-fact investigations of security incidents; and*
	AU-11[2][b]	*meet regulatory and organizational information retention requirements.*

POTENTIAL ASSESSMENT METHODS AND OBJECTS:

Examine: [*SELECT FROM:* Audit and accountability policy; audit record retention policy and procedures; security plan; organization-defined retention period for audit records; audit record archives; audit logs; audit records; other relevant documents or records].

Interview: [*SELECT FROM:* Organizational personnel with audit record retention responsibilities; organizational personnel with information security responsibilities; system/network administrators].

AU-11(1)	AUDIT RECORD RETENTION | *LONG-TERM RETRIEVAL CAPABILITY*

ASSESSMENT OBJECTIVE:

Determine if the organization:

Special Publication 800-53A
Revision 4

Assessing Security and Privacy Controls in Federal Information Systems
and Organizations — *Building Effective Assessment Plans*

AU-11(1)[1]	*defines measures to be employed to ensure that long-term audit records generated by the information system can be retrieved; and*
AU-11(1)[2]	*employs organization-defined measures to ensure that long-term audit records generated by the information system can be retrieved.*

POTENTIAL ASSESSMENT METHODS AND OBJECTS:

Examine: [*SELECT FROM:* Audit and accountability policy; audit record retention policy and procedures; information system design documentation; information system configuration settings and associated documentation; audit record archives; audit logs; audit records; other relevant documents or records].

Interview: [*SELECT FROM:* Organizational personnel with audit record retention responsibilities; organizational personnel with information security responsibilities; system/network administrators].

Test: [*SELECT FROM:* Automated mechanisms implementing audit record retention capability].

AU-12	**AUDIT GENERATION**	

ASSESSMENT OBJECTIVE:

Determine if:

AU-12(a)	AU-12(a)[1]	*the organization defines the information system components which are to provide audit record generation capability for the auditable events defined in AU-2a;*
	AU-12(a)[2]	*the information system provides audit record generation capability, for the auditable events defined in AU-2a, at organization-defined information system components;*
AU-12(b)	AU-12(b)[1]	*the organization defines the personnel or roles allowed to select which auditable events are to be audited by specific components of the information system;*
	AU-12(b)[2]	*the information system allows the organization-defined personnel or roles to select which auditable events are to be audited by specific components of the system; and*
AU-12(c)		*the information system generates audit records for the events defined in AU-2d with the content in defined in AU-3.*

POTENTIAL ASSESSMENT METHODS AND OBJECTS:

Examine: [*SELECT FROM:* Audit and accountability policy; procedures addressing audit record generation; security plan; information system design documentation; information system configuration settings and associated documentation; list of auditable events; information system audit records; other relevant documents or records].

Interview: [*SELECT FROM:* Organizational personnel with audit record generation responsibilities; organizational personnel with information security responsibilities; system/network administrators; system developers].

Test: [*SELECT FROM:* Automated mechanisms implementing audit record generation capability].

AU-12(1)	**AUDIT GENERATION** | *SYSTEM-WIDE / TIME-CORRELATED AUDIT TRAIL*	

ASSESSMENT OBJECTIVE:

Determine if:

AU-12(1)[1]	*the organization defines the information system components from which audit records are to be compiled into a system-wide (logical or physical) audit trail;*

Special Publication 800-53A
Revision 4

Assessing Security and Privacy Controls in Federal Information Systems
and Organizations — *Building Effective Assessment Plans*

AU-12(1)[2]	*the organization defines the level of tolerance for the relationship between time stamps of individual records in the audit trail; and*
AU-12(1)[3]	*the information system compiles audit records from organization-defined information system components into a system-wide (logical or physical) audit trail that is time-correlated to within the organization-defined level of tolerance for the relationship between time stamps of individual records in the audit trail.*

POTENTIAL ASSESSMENT METHODS AND OBJECTS:

Examine: [*SELECT FROM:* Audit and accountability policy; procedures addressing audit record generation; information system design documentation; information system configuration settings and associated documentation; system-wide audit trail (logical or physical); information system audit records; other relevant documents or records].

Interview: [*SELECT FROM:* Organizational personnel with audit record generation responsibilities; organizational personnel with information security responsibilities; system/network administrators; system developers].

Test: [*SELECT FROM:* Automated mechanisms implementing audit record generation capability].

AU-12(2)	**AUDIT GENERATION** | *STANDARDIZED FORMATS*

ASSESSMENT OBJECTIVE:

Determine if the information system produces a system-wide (logical or physical) audit trail composed of audit records in a standardized format.

POTENTIAL ASSESSMENT METHODS AND OBJECTS:

Examine: [*SELECT FROM:* Audit and accountability policy; procedures addressing audit record generation; information system design documentation; information system configuration settings and associated documentation; system-wide audit trail (logical or physical); information system audit records; other relevant documents or records].

Interview: [*SELECT FROM:* Organizational personnel with audit record generation responsibilities; organizational personnel with information security responsibilities; system/network administrators; system developers].

Test: [*SELECT FROM:* Automated mechanisms implementing audit record generation capability].

AU-12(3)	**AUDIT GENERATION** | *CHANGES BY AUTHORIZED INDIVIDUALS*

ASSESSMENT OBJECTIVE:

Determine if:

AU-12(3)[1]	*the organization defines information system components on which auditing is to be performed;*
AU-12(3)[2]	*the organization defines individuals or roles authorized to change the auditing to be performed on organization-defined information system components;*
AU-12(3)[3]	*the organization defines time thresholds within which organization-defined individuals or roles can change the auditing to be performed on organization-defined information system components;*
AU-12(3)[4]	*the organization defines selectable event criteria that support the capability for organization-defined individuals or roles to change the auditing to be performed on organization-defined information system components; and*

Special Publication 800-53A
Revision 4

Assessing Security and Privacy Controls in Federal Information Systems
and Organizations — *Building Effective Assessment Plans*

	AU-12(3)[5]	*the information system provides the capability for organization-defined individuals or roles to change the auditing to be performed on organization-defined information system components based on organization-defined selectable event criteria within organization-defined time thresholds.*

POTENTIAL ASSESSMENT METHODS AND OBJECTS:

Examine: [*SELECT FROM:* Audit and accountability policy; procedures addressing audit record generation; information system design documentation; information system configuration settings and associated documentation; system-generated list of individuals or roles authorized to change auditing to be performed; information system audit records; other relevant documents or records].

Interview: [*SELECT FROM:* Organizational personnel with audit record generation responsibilities; organizational personnel with information security responsibilities; system/network administrators; system developers].

Test: [*SELECT FROM:* Automated mechanisms implementing audit record generation capability].

AU-13	**MONITORING FOR INFORMATION DISCLOSURE**

ASSESSMENT OBJECTIVE:

Determine if the organization:

AU-13[1]	*defines open source information and/or information sites to be monitored for evidence of unauthorized disclosure of organizational information;*
AU-13[2]	*defines a frequency to monitor organization-defined open source information and/or information sites for evidence of unauthorized disclosure of organizational information; and*
AU-13[3]	*monitors organization-defined open source information and/or information sites for evidence of unauthorized disclosure of organizational information with the organization-defined frequency.*

POTENTIAL ASSESSMENT METHODS AND OBJECTS:

Examine: [*SELECT FROM:* Audit and accountability policy; procedures addressing information disclosure monitoring; information system design documentation; information system configuration settings and associated documentation; monitoring records; information system audit records; other relevant documents or records].

Interview: [*SELECT FROM:* Organizational personnel with responsibilities for monitoring open source information and/or information sites; organizational personnel with information security responsibilities].

Test: [*SELECT FROM:* Automated mechanisms implementing monitoring for information disclosure].

AU-13(1)	**MONITORING FOR INFORMATION DISCLOSURE	*USE OF AUTOMATED TOOLS***

ASSESSMENT OBJECTIVE:

Determine if the organization employs automated mechanisms to determine if organizational information has been disclosed in an unauthorized manner.

POTENTIAL ASSESSMENT METHODS AND OBJECTS:

Examine: [*SELECT FROM:* Audit and accountability policy; procedures addressing information disclosure monitoring; information system design documentation; information system configuration settings and associated documentation; automated monitoring tools; information system audit records; other relevant documents or records].

Interview: [*SELECT FROM:* Organizational personnel with responsibilities for monitoring information disclosures; organizational personnel with information security responsibilities].

Test: [*SELECT FROM:* Automated mechanisms implementing monitoring for information disclosure].

Special Publication 800-53A
Revision 4

Assessing Security and Privacy Controls in Federal Information Systems
and Organizations — *Building Effective Assessment Plans*

AU-13(2)	MONITORING FOR INFORMATION DISCLOSURE | *REVIEW OF MONITORED SITES*

ASSESSMENT OBJECTIVE:

Determine if the organization:

AU-13(2)[1]	*defines a frequency to review the open source information sites being monitored; and*
AU-13(2)[2]	*reviews the open source information sites being monitored with the organization-defined frequency.*

POTENTIAL ASSESSMENT METHODS AND OBJECTS:

Examine: [*SELECT FROM:* Audit and accountability policy; procedures addressing information disclosure monitoring; information system design documentation; information system configuration settings and associated documentation; reviews for open source information sites being monitored; information system audit records; other relevant documents or records].

Interview: [*SELECT FROM:* Organizational personnel with responsibilities for monitoring open source information sites; organizational personnel with information security responsibilities].

Test: [*SELECT FROM:* Automated mechanisms implementing monitoring for information disclosure].

AU-14	SESSION AUDIT

ASSESSMENT OBJECTIVE:

Determine if the information system provides the capability for authorized users to select a user session to:

AU-14[1]	*capture/record; and/or*
AU-14[2]	*view/hear.*

POTENTIAL ASSESSMENT METHODS AND OBJECTS:

Examine: [*SELECT FROM:* Audit and accountability policy; procedures addressing user session auditing; information system design documentation; information system configuration settings and associated documentation; information system audit records; other relevant documents or records].

Interview: [*SELECT FROM:* Organizational personnel with information security responsibilities; system/network administrators; system developers].

Test: [*SELECT FROM:* Automated mechanisms implementing user session auditing capability].

AU-14(1)	SESSION AUDIT | *SYSTEM START-UP*

ASSESSMENT OBJECTIVE:

Determine if the information system initiates session audits at system start-up.

POTENTIAL ASSESSMENT METHODS AND OBJECTS:

Examine: [*SELECT FROM:* Audit and accountability policy; procedures addressing user session auditing; information system design documentation; information system configuration settings and associated documentation; information system audit records; other relevant documents or records].

Interview: [*SELECT FROM:* Organizational personnel with information security responsibilities; system/network administrators; system developers].

Test: [*SELECT FROM:* Automated mechanisms implementing user session auditing capability].

Special Publication 800-53A
Revision 4

Assessing Security and Privacy Controls in Federal Information Systems
and Organizations — *Building Effective Assessment Plans*

AU-14(2)	SESSION AUDIT	*CAPTURE / RECORD AND LOG CONTENT*

ASSESSMENT OBJECTIVE:

Determine if the information system provides the capability for authorized users to:

AU-14(2)[1]	*capture/record content related to a user session; and*
AU-14(2)[2]	*log content related to a user session.*

POTENTIAL ASSESSMENT METHODS AND OBJECTS:

Examine: [*SELECT FROM:* Audit and accountability policy; procedures addressing user session auditing; information system design documentation; information system configuration settings and associated documentation; information system audit records; other relevant documents or records].

Interview: [*SELECT FROM:* Organizational personnel with information security responsibilities; system/network administrators; system developers].

Test: [*SELECT FROM:* Automated mechanisms implementing user session auditing capability].

AU-14(3)	SESSION AUDIT	*REMOTE VIEWING / LISTENING*

ASSESSMENT OBJECTIVE:

Determine if the information system provides the capability for authorized users to remotely view/hear all content related to an established user session in real time.

POTENTIAL ASSESSMENT METHODS AND OBJECTS:

Examine: [*SELECT FROM:* Audit and accountability policy; procedures addressing user session auditing; information system design documentation; information system configuration settings and associated documentation; information system audit records; other relevant documents or records].

Interview: [*SELECT FROM:* Organizational personnel with information security responsibilities; system/network administrators; system developers].

Test: [*SELECT FROM:* Automated mechanisms implementing user session auditing capability].

AU-15	ALTERNATE AUDIT CAPABILITY

ASSESSMENT OBJECTIVE:

Determine if the organization:

AU-15[1]	*defines alternative audit functionality to be provided in the event of a failure in primary audit capability; and*
AU-15[2]	*provides an alternative audit capability in the event of a failure in primary audit capability that provides organization-defined alternative audit functionality.*

POTENTIAL ASSESSMENT METHODS AND OBJECTS:

Examine: [*SELECT FROM:* Audit and accountability policy; procedures addressing alternate audit capability; information system design documentation; information system configuration settings and associated documentation; test records for alternative audit capability; information system audit records; other relevant documents or records].

Interview: [*SELECT FROM:* Organizational personnel responsible for providing alternate audit capability; organizational personnel with information security responsibilities].

Test: [*SELECT FROM:* Automated mechanisms implementing alternative audit capability].

Special Publication 800-53A
Revision 4

Assessing Security and Privacy Controls in Federal Information Systems
and Organizations — *Building Effective Assessment Plans*

AU-16	CROSS-ORGANIZATIONAL AUDITING
	ASSESSMENT OBJECTIVE: *Determine if the organization:*
	AU-16[1] — *defines audit information to be coordinated among external organizations when audit information is transmitted across organizational boundaries;*
	AU-16[2] — *defines methods for coordinating organization-defined audit information among external organizations when audit information is transmitted across organizational boundaries; and*
	AU-16[3] — *employs organization-defined methods for coordinating organization-defined audit information among external organizations when audit information is transmitted across organizational boundaries.*
	POTENTIAL ASSESSMENT METHODS AND OBJECTS: **Examine**: [*SELECT FROM:* Audit and accountability policy; procedures addressing methods for coordinating audit information among external organizations; information system design documentation; information system configuration settings and associated documentation; methods for coordinating audit information among external organizations; information system audit records; other relevant documents or records]. **Interview**: [*SELECT FROM:* Organizational personnel with responsibilities for coordinating audit information among external organizations; organizational personnel with information security responsibilities]. **Test**: [*SELECT FROM:* Automated mechanisms implementing cross-organizational auditing (if applicable)].

AU-16(1)	CROSS-ORGANIZATIONAL AUDITING | *IDENTITY PRESERVATION*
	ASSESSMENT OBJECTIVE: *Determine if the organization requires that the identity of individuals be preserved in cross-organizational audit trails.*
	POTENTIAL ASSESSMENT METHODS AND OBJECTS: **Examine**: [*SELECT FROM:* Audit and accountability policy; procedures addressing cross-organizational audit trails; information system design documentation; information system configuration settings and associated documentation; information system audit records; other relevant documents or records]. **Interview**: [*SELECT FROM:* Organizational personnel with cross-organizational audit responsibilities; organizational personnel with information security responsibilities]. **Test**: [*SELECT FROM:* Automated mechanisms implementing cross-organizational auditing (if applicable)].

AU-16(2)	CROSS-ORGANIZATIONAL AUDITING | *SHARING OF AUDIT INFORMATION*
	ASSESSMENT OBJECTIVE: *Determine if the organization:*
	AU-16(2)[1] — *defines organizations with whom cross-organizational audit information is to be shared;*
	AU-16(2)[2] — *defines cross-organizational sharing agreements to be used when providing cross-organizational audit information to organization-defined organizations; and*
	AU-16(2)[3] — *provides cross-organizational audit information to organization-defined organizations based on organization-defined cross-organizational sharing agreements.*

Special Publication 800-53A
Revision 4

Assessing Security and Privacy Controls in Federal Information Systems
and Organizations — *Building Effective Assessment Plans*

	POTENTIAL ASSESSMENT METHODS AND OBJECTS: **Examine**: [*SELECT FROM:* Audit and accountability policy; procedures addressing cross-organizational sharing of audit information; cross-organizational sharing agreements; data sharing agreements; other relevant documents or records]. **Interview**: [*SELECT FROM:* Organizational personnel with responsibilities for sharing cross-organizational audit information; organizational personnel with information security responsibilities].

Special Publication 800-53A
Revision 4

Assessing Security and Privacy Controls in Federal Information Systems
and Organizations — *Building Effective Assessment Plans*

FAMILY: SECURITY ASSESSMENT AND AUTHORIZATION

CA-1	SECURITY ASSESSMENT AND AUTHORIZATION POLICY AND PROCEDURES			
	ASSESSMENT OBJECTIVE: *Determine if the organization:*			
	CA-1(a)(1)	CA-1(a)(1)[1]	*develops and documents a security assessment and authorization policy that addresses:*	
			CA-1(a)(1)[1][a]	*purpose;*
			CA-1(a)(1)[1][b]	*scope;*
			CA-1(a)(1)[1][c]	*roles;*
			CA-1(a)(1)[1][d]	*responsibilities;*
			CA-1(a)(1)[1][e]	*management commitment;*
			CA-1(a)(1)[1][f]	*coordination among organizational entities;*
			CA-1(a)(1)[1][g]	*compliance;*
		CA-1(a)(1)[2]	*defines personnel or roles to whom the security assessment and authorization policy is to be disseminated;*	
		CA-1(a)(1)[3]	*disseminates the security assessment and authorization policy to organization-defined personnel or roles;*	
	CA-1(a)(2)	CA-1(a)(2)[1]	*develops and documents procedures to facilitate the implementation of the security assessment and authorization policy and associated assessment and authorization controls;*	
		CA-1(a)(2)[2]	*defines personnel or roles to whom the procedures are to be disseminated;*	
		CA-1(a)(2)[3]	*disseminates the procedures to organization-defined personnel or roles;*	
	CA-1(b)(1)	CA-1(b)(1)[1]	*defines the frequency to review and update the current security assessment and authorization policy;*	
		CA-1(b)(1)[2]	*reviews and updates the current security assessment and authorization policy with the organization-defined frequency;*	
	CA-1(b)(2)	CA-1(b)(2)[1]	*defines the frequency to review and update the current security assessment and authorization procedures; and*	
		CA-1(b)(2)[2]	*reviews and updates the current security assessment and authorization procedures with the organization-defined frequency.*	
	POTENTIAL ASSESSMENT METHODS AND OBJECTS: **Examine:** [*SELECT FROM:* Security assessment and authorization policy and procedures; other relevant documents or records]. **Interview:** [*SELECT FROM:* Organizational personnel with security assessment and authorization responsibilities; organizational personnel with information security responsibilities].				

Special Publication 800-53A
Revision 4

Assessing Security and Privacy Controls in Federal Information Systems
and Organizations — *Building Effective Assessment Plans*

CA-2	SECURITY ASSESSMENTS		
	ASSESSMENT OBJECTIVE: *Determine if the organization:*		
	CA-2(a)	*develops a security assessment plan that describes the scope of the assessment including:*	
		CA-2(a)(1)	*security controls and control enhancements under assessment;*
		CA-2(a)(2)	*assessment procedures to be used to determine security control effectiveness;*
		CA-2(a)(3)	**CA-2(a)(3)[1]** *assessment environment;*
			CA-2(a)(3)[2] *assessment team;*
			CA-2(a)(3)[3] *assessment roles and responsibilities;*
	CA-2(b)	**CA-2(b)[1]**	*defines the frequency to assess the security controls in the information system and its environment of operation;*
		CA-2(b)[2]	*assesses the security controls in the information system with the organization-defined frequency to determine the extent to which the controls are implemented correctly, operating as intended, and producing the desired outcome with respect to meeting established security requirements;*
	CA-2(c)	*produces a security assessment report that documents the results of the assessment;*	
	CA-2(d)	**CA-2(d)[1]**	*defines individuals or roles to whom the results of the security control assessment are to be provided; and*
		CA-2(d)[2]	*provides the results of the security control assessment to organization-defined individuals or roles.*
	POTENTIAL ASSESSMENT METHODS AND OBJECTS: **Examine**: [*SELECT FROM*: Security assessment and authorization policy; procedures addressing security assessment planning; procedures addressing security assessments; security assessment plan; other relevant documents or records]. **Interview**: [*SELECT FROM*: Organizational personnel with security assessment responsibilities; organizational personnel with information security responsibilities]. **Test**: [*SELECT FROM*: Automated mechanisms supporting security assessment, security assessment plan development, and/or security assessment reporting].		

CA-2(1)	SECURITY ASSESSMENTS	*INDEPENDENT ASSESSORS*	
	ASSESSMENT OBJECTIVE: *Determine if the organization:*		
	CA-2(1)[1]	*defines the level of independence to be employed to conduct security control assessments; and*	
	CA-2(1)[2]	*employs assessors or assessment teams with the organization-defined level of independence to conduct security control assessments.*	

Special Publication 800-53A
Revision 4

Assessing Security and Privacy Controls in Federal Information Systems
and Organizations — *Building Effective Assessment Plans*

	POTENTIAL ASSESSMENT METHODS AND OBJECTS: **Examine**: [*SELECT FROM:* Security assessment and authorization policy; procedures addressing security assessments; security authorization package (including security plan, security assessment plan, security assessment report, plan of action and milestones, authorization statement); other relevant documents or records]. **Interview**: [*SELECT FROM:* Organizational personnel with security assessment responsibilities; organizational personnel with information security responsibilities].

CA-2(2)	**SECURITY ASSESSMENTS** | *SPECIALIZED ASSESSMENTS*		
	ASSESSMENT OBJECTIVE: *Determine if the organization:*		
	CA-2(2)[1]	*selects one or more of the following forms of specialized security assessment to be included as part of security control assessments:*	
		CA-2(2)[1][a]	*in-depth monitoring;*
		CA-2(2)[1][b]	*vulnerability scanning;*
		CA-2(2)[1][c]	*malicious user testing;*
		CA-2(2)[1][d]	*insider threat assessment;*
		CA-2(2)[1][e]	*performance/load testing; and/or*
		CA-2(2)[1][f]	*other forms of organization-defined specialized security assessment;*
	CA-2(2)[2]	*defines the frequency for conducting the selected form(s) of specialized security assessment;*	
	CA-2(2)[3]	*defines whether the specialized security assessment will be announced or unannounced; and*	
	CA-2(2)[4]	*conducts announced or unannounced organization-defined forms of specialized security assessments with the organization-defined frequency as part of security control assessments.*	
	POTENTIAL ASSESSMENT METHODS AND OBJECTS: **Examine**: [*SELECT FROM:* Security assessment and authorization policy; procedures addressing security assessments; security plan; security assessment plan; security assessment report; security assessment evidence; other relevant documents or records]. **Interview**: [*SELECT FROM:* Organizational personnel with security assessment responsibilities; organizational personnel with information security responsibilities]. **Test**: [*SELECT FROM:* Automated mechanisms supporting security control assessment].		

CA-2(3)	**SECURITY ASSESSMENTS** | *EXTERNAL ORGANIZATIONS*	
	ASSESSMENT OBJECTIVE: *Determine if the organization:*	
	CA-2(3)[1]	*defines an information system for which the results of a security assessment performed by an external organization are to be accepted;*
	CA-2(3)[2]	*defines an external organization from which to accept a security assessment performed on an organization-defined information system;*

Special Publication 800-53A
Revision 4

Assessing Security and Privacy Controls in Federal Information Systems
and Organizations — *Building Effective Assessment Plans*

CA-2(3)[3]	*defines the requirements to be met by a security assessment performed by organization-defined external organization on organization-defined information system; and*
CA-2(3)[4]	*accepts the results of an assessment of an organization-defined information system performed by an organization-defined external organization when the assessment meets organization-defined requirements.*

POTENTIAL ASSESSMENT METHODS AND OBJECTS:

Examine: [*SELECT FROM:* Security assessment and authorization policy; procedures addressing security assessments; security plan; security assessment requirements; security assessment plan; security assessment report; security assessment evidence; plan of action and milestones; other relevant documents or records].

Interview: [*SELECT FROM:* Organizational personnel with security assessment responsibilities; organizational personnel with information security responsibilities; personnel performing security assessments for the specified external organization].

CA-3	**SYSTEM INTERCONNECTIONS**	
	ASSESSMENT OBJECTIVE: *Determine if the organization:*	
	CA-3(a)	*authorizes connections from the information system to other information systems through the use of Interconnection Security Agreements;*
	CA-3(b)	*documents, for each interconnection:*
	CA-3(b)[1]	*the interface characteristics;*
	CA-3(b)[2]	*the security requirements;*
	CA-3(b)[3]	*the nature of the information communicated;*
	CA-3(c) — CA-3(c)[1]	*defines the frequency to review and update Interconnection Security Agreements; and*
	CA-3(c)[2]	*reviews and updates Interconnection Security Agreements with the organization-defined frequency.*

POTENTIAL ASSESSMENT METHODS AND OBJECTS:

Examine: [*SELECT FROM:* Access control policy; procedures addressing information system connections; system and communications protection policy; information system Interconnection Security Agreements; security plan; information system design documentation; information system configuration settings and associated documentation; other relevant documents or records].

Interview: [*SELECT FROM:* Organizational personnel with responsibility for developing, implementing, or approving information system interconnection agreements; organizational personnel with information security responsibilities; personnel managing the system(s) to which the Interconnection Security Agreement applies].

CA-3(1)	**SYSTEM INTERCONNECTIONS	*UNCLASSIFIED NATIONAL SECURITY SYSTEM CONNECTIONS***	
	ASSESSMENT OBJECTIVE: *Determine if the organization:*	
	CA-3(1)[1]	*defines an unclassified, national security system whose direct connection to an external network is to be prohibited without the use of approved boundary protection device;*

Special Publication 800-53A
Revision 4

Assessing Security and Privacy Controls in Federal Information Systems
and Organizations — *Building Effective Assessment Plans*

| | CA-3(1)[2] | *defines a boundary protection device to be used to establish the direct connection of an organization-defined unclassified, national security system to an external network; and* |
| | CA-3(1)[3] | *prohibits the direct connection of an organization-defined unclassified, national security system to an external network without the use of an organization-defined boundary protection device.* |

POTENTIAL ASSESSMENT METHODS AND OBJECTS:

Examine: [*SELECT FROM:* Access control policy; procedures addressing information system connections; system and communications protection policy; information system interconnection security agreements; security plan; information system design documentation; information system configuration settings and associated documentation; security assessment report; information system audit records; other relevant documents or records].

Interview: [*SELECT FROM:* Organizational personnel with responsibility for managing direct connections to external networks; network administrators; organizational personnel with information security responsibilities; personnel managing directly connected external networks].

Test: [*SELECT FROM:* Automated mechanisms supporting the management of external network connections].

| CA-3(2) | SYSTEM INTERCONNECTIONS | *CLASSIFIED NATIONAL SECURITY SYSTEM CONNECTIONS* |

ASSESSMENT OBJECTIVE:

Determine if the organization:

| | CA-3(2)[1] | *defines a boundary protection device to be used to establish the direct connection of a classified, national security system to an external network; and* |
| | CA-3(2)[2] | *prohibits the direct connection of a classified, national security system to an external network without the use of an organization-defined boundary protection device.* |

POTENTIAL ASSESSMENT METHODS AND OBJECTS:

Examine: [*SELECT FROM:* Access control policy; procedures addressing information system connections; system and communications protection policy; information system interconnection security agreements; security plan; information system design documentation; information system configuration settings and associated documentation; security assessment report; information system audit records; other relevant documents or records].

Interview: [*SELECT FROM:* Organizational personnel with responsibility for managing direct connections to external networks; network administrators; organizational personnel with information security responsibilities; personnel managing directly connected external networks].

Test: [*SELECT FROM:* Automated mechanisms supporting the management of external network connections].

| CA-3(3) | SYSTEM INTERCONNECTIONS | *UNCLASSIFIED NON-NATIONAL SECURITY SYSTEM CONNECTIONS* |

ASSESSMENT OBJECTIVE:

Determine if the organization:

| | CA-3(3)[1] | *defines an unclassified, non-national security system whose direct connection to an external network is to be prohibited without the use of approved boundary protection device;* |
| | CA-3(3)[2] | *defines a boundary protection device to be used to establish the direct connection of an organization-defined unclassified, non-national security system to an external network; and* |

Special Publication 800-53A
Revision 4

Assessing Security and Privacy Controls in Federal Information Systems
and Organizations — *Building Effective Assessment Plans*

	CA-3(3)[3]	*prohibits the direct connection of an organization-defined unclassified, non-national security system to an external network without the use of an organization-defined boundary protection device.*

POTENTIAL ASSESSMENT METHODS AND OBJECTS:

Examine: [*SELECT FROM:* Access control policy; procedures addressing information system connections; system and communications protection policy; information system interconnection security agreements; security plan; information system design documentation; information system configuration settings and associated documentation; security assessment report; information system audit records; other relevant documents or records].

Interview: [*SELECT FROM:* Organizational personnel with responsibility for managing direct connections to external networks; network administrators; organizational personnel with information security responsibilities; personnel managing directly connected external networks].

Test: [*SELECT FROM:* Automated mechanisms supporting the management of external network connections].

CA-3(4)	SYSTEM INTERCONNECTIONS	*CONNECTIONS TO PUBLIC NETWORKS*

ASSESSMENT OBJECTIVE:

Determine if the organization:

	CA-3(4)[1]	*defines an information system whose direct connection to a public network is to be prohibited; and*
	CA-3(4)[2]	*prohibits the direct connection of an organization-defined information system to a public network.*

POTENTIAL ASSESSMENT METHODS AND OBJECTS:

Examine: [*SELECT FROM:* Access control policy; procedures addressing information system connections; system and communications protection policy; information system interconnection security agreements; security plan; information system design documentation; ; information system configuration settings and associated documentation; security assessment report; information system audit records; other relevant documents or records].

Interview: [*SELECT FROM:* Network administrators; organizational personnel with information security responsibilities].

Test: [*SELECT FROM:* Automated mechanisms supporting the management of public network connections].

CA-3(5)	SYSTEM INTERCONNECTIONS	*RESTRICTIONS ON EXTERNAL SYSTEM CONNECTIONS*

ASSESSMENT OBJECTIVE:

Determine if the organization:

	CA-3(5)[1]	*defines information systems to be allowed to connect to external information systems;*
	CA-3(5)[2]	*employs one of the following policies for allowing organization-defined information systems to connect to external information systems:*
		CA-3(5)[2][a] *allow-all policy;*
		CA-3(5)[2][b] *deny-by-exception policy;*
		CA-3(5)[2][c] *deny-all policy; or*
		CA-3(5)[2][d] *permit-by-exception policy.*

Special Publication 800-53A
Revision 4

Assessing Security and Privacy Controls in Federal Information Systems
and Organizations — *Building Effective Assessment Plans*

POTENTIAL ASSESSMENT METHODS AND OBJECTS:

Examine: [*SELECT FROM:* Access control policy; procedures addressing information system connections; system and communications protection policy; information system interconnection agreements; security plan; information system design documentation; information system configuration settings and associated documentation; security assessment report; information system audit records; other relevant documents or records].

Interview: [*SELECT FROM:* Organizational personnel with responsibility for managing connections to external information systems; network administrators; organizational personnel with information security responsibilities].

Test: [*SELECT FROM:* Automated mechanisms implementing restrictions on external system connections].

CA-4	SECURITY CERTIFICATION
[Withdrawn: Incorporated into CA-2].	

CA-5	PLAN OF ACTION AND MILESTONES			
	ASSESSMENT OBJECTIVE: *Determine if the organization:*			
	CA-5(a)	*develops a plan of action and milestones for the information system to:*		
		CA-5(a)[1]	*document the organization's planned remedial actions to correct weaknesses or deficiencies noted during the assessment of the security controls;*	
		CA-5(a)[2]	*reduce or eliminate known vulnerabilities in the system;*	
	CA-5(b)	CA-5(b)[1]	*defines the frequency to update the existing plan of action and milestones;*	
		CA-5(b)[2]	*updates the existing plan of action and milestones with the organization-defined frequency based on the findings from:*	
			CA-5(b)[2][a]	*security controls assessments;*
			CA-5(b)[2][b]	*security impact analyses; and*
			CA-5(b)[2][c]	*continuous monitoring activities.*

POTENTIAL ASSESSMENT METHODS AND OBJECTS:

Examine: [*SELECT FROM:* Security assessment and authorization policy; procedures addressing plan of action and milestones; security plan; security assessment plan; security assessment report; security assessment evidence; plan of action and milestones; other relevant documents or records].

Interview: [*SELECT FROM:* Organizational personnel with plan of action and milestones development and implementation responsibilities; organizational personnel with information security responsibilities].

Test: [*SELECT FROM:* Automated mechanisms for developing, implementing, and maintaining plan of action and milestones].

CA-5(1)	PLAN OF ACTION AND MILESTONES	*AUTOMATION SUPPORT FOR ACCURACY / CURRENCY*	
	ASSESSMENT OBJECTIVE: *Determine if the organization employs automated mechanisms to help ensure that the plan of action and milestones for the information system is:*	
	CA-5(1)[1]	*accurate;*

Special Publication 800-53A
Revision 4

Assessing Security and Privacy Controls in Federal Information Systems
and Organizations — *Building Effective Assessment Plans*

	CA-5(1)[2]	*up to date; and*
	CA-5(1)[3]	*readily available.*

POTENTIAL ASSESSMENT METHODS AND OBJECTS:

Examine: [*SELECT FROM:* Security assessment and authorization policy; procedures addressing plan of action and milestones; information system design documentation, information system configuration settings and associated documentation; information system audit records; plan of action and milestones; other relevant documents or records].

Interview: [*SELECT FROM:* Organizational personnel with plan of action and milestones development and implementation responsibilities; organizational personnel with information security responsibilities].

Test: [*SELECT FROM:* Automated mechanisms for developing, implementing and maintaining plan of action and milestones].

CA-6	SECURITY AUTHORIZATION	

ASSESSMENT OBJECTIVE:

Determine if the organization:

CA-6(a)		*assigns a senior-level executive or manager as the authorizing official for the information system;*
CA-6(b)		*ensures that the authorizing official authorizes the information system for processing before commencing operations;*
CA-6(c)	CA-6(c)[1]	*defines the frequency to update the security authorization; and*
	CA-6(c)[2]	*updates the security authorization with the organization-defined frequency.*

POTENTIAL ASSESSMENT METHODS AND OBJECTS:

Examine: [*SELECT FROM:* Security assessment and authorization policy; procedures addressing security authorization; security authorization package (including security plan; security assessment report; plan of action and milestones; authorization statement); other relevant documents or records].

Interview: [*SELECT FROM:* Organizational personnel with security authorization responsibilities; organizational personnel with information security responsibilities].

Test: [*SELECT FROM:* Automated mechanisms that facilitate security authorizations and updates].

CA-7	CONTINUOUS MONITORING	

ASSESSMENT OBJECTIVE:

Determine if the organization:

CA-7(a)	CA-7(a)[1]	*develops a continuous monitoring strategy that defines metrics to be monitored;*
	CA-7(a)[2]	*develops a continuous monitoring strategy that includes monitoring of organization-defined metrics;*
	CA-7(a)[3]	*implements a continuous monitoring program that includes monitoring of organization-defined metrics in accordance with the organizational continuous monitoring strategy;*
CA-7(b)	CA-7(b)[1]	*develops a continuous monitoring strategy that defines frequencies for monitoring;*
	CA-7(b)[2]	*defines frequencies for assessments supporting monitoring;*

Special Publication 800-53A
Revision 4

Assessing Security and Privacy Controls in Federal Information Systems
and Organizations — *Building Effective Assessment Plans*

		CA-7(b)[3]	*develops a continuous monitoring strategy that includes establishment of the organization-defined frequencies for monitoring and for assessments supporting monitoring;*
		CA-7(b)[4]	*implements a continuous monitoring program that includes establishment of organization-defined frequencies for monitoring and for assessments supporting such monitoring in accordance with the organizational continuous monitoring strategy;*
	CA-7(c)	CA-7(c)[1]	*develops a continuous monitoring strategy that includes ongoing security control assessments;*
		CA-7(c)[2]	*implements a continuous monitoring program that includes ongoing security control assessments in accordance with the organizational continuous monitoring strategy;*
	CA-7(d)	CA-7(d)[1]	*develops a continuous monitoring strategy that includes ongoing security status monitoring of organization-defined metrics;*
		CA-7(d)[2]	*implements a continuous monitoring program that includes ongoing security status monitoring of organization-defined metrics in accordance with the organizational continuous monitoring strategy;*
	CA-7(e)	CA-7(e)[1]	*develops a continuous monitoring strategy that includes correlation and analysis of security-related information generated by assessments and monitoring;*
		CA-7(e)[2]	*implements a continuous monitoring program that includes correlation and analysis of security-related information generated by assessments and monitoring in accordance with the organizational continuous monitoring strategy;*
	CA-7(f)	CA-7(f)[1]	*develops a continuous monitoring strategy that includes response actions to address results of the analysis of security-related information;*
		CA-7(f)[2]	*implements a continuous monitoring program that includes response actions to address results of the analysis of security-related information in accordance with the organizational continuous monitoring strategy;*
	CA-7(g)	CA-7(g)[1]	*develops a continuous monitoring strategy that defines the personnel or roles to whom the security status of the organization and information system are to be reported;*
		CA-7(g)[2]	*develops a continuous monitoring strategy that defines the frequency to report the security status of the organization and information system to organization-defined personnel or roles;*
		CA-7(g)[3]	*develops a continuous monitoring strategy that includes reporting the security status of the organization or information system to organizational-defined personnel or roles with the organization-defined frequency; and*
		CA-7(g)[4]	*implements a continuous monitoring program that includes reporting the security status of the organization and information system to organization-defined personnel or roles with the organization-defined frequency in accordance with the organizational continuous monitoring strategy.*

Special Publication 800-53A
Revision 4

Assessing Security and Privacy Controls in Federal Information Systems
and Organizations — *Building Effective Assessment Plans*

	POTENTIAL ASSESSMENT METHODS AND OBJECTS: **Examine**: [*SELECT FROM:* Security assessment and authorization policy; procedures addressing continuous monitoring of information system security controls; procedures addressing configuration management; security plan; security assessment report; plan of action and milestones; information system monitoring records; configuration management records, security impact analyses; status reports; other relevant documents or records]. **Interview**: [*SELECT FROM:* Organizational personnel with continuous monitoring responsibilities; organizational personnel with information security responsibilities; system/network administrators]. **Test**: [*SELECT FROM:* Mechanisms implementing continuous monitoring].

CA-7(1)	**CONTINUOUS MONITORING	*INDEPENDENT ASSESSMENT***
	ASSESSMENT OBJECTIVE: *Determine if the organization:*
		CA-7(1)[1]	*defines a level of independence to be employed to monitor the security controls in the information system on an ongoing basis; and*
		CA-7(1)[2]	*employs assessors or assessment teams with the organization-defined level of independence to monitor the security controls in the information system on an ongoing basis.*
	POTENTIAL ASSESSMENT METHODS AND OBJECTS: **Examine**: [*SELECT FROM:* Security assessment and authorization policy; procedures addressing continuous monitoring of information system security controls; security plan; security assessment report; plan of action and milestones; information system monitoring records; security impact analyses; status reports; other relevant documents or records]. **Interview**: [*SELECT FROM:* Organizational personnel with continuous monitoring responsibilities; organizational personnel with information security responsibilities].

CA-7(2)	**CONTINUOUS MONITORING	*TYPES OF ASSESSMENTS***
[Withdrawn: Incorporated into CA-2].	

CA-7(3)	**CONTINUOUS MONITORING	*TREND ANALYSIS***
	ASSESSMENT OBJECTIVE: *Determine if the organization employs trend analyses to determine if the following items need to be modified based on empirical data:*
		CA-7(3)[1]	*security control implementations;*
		CA-7(3)[2]	*the frequency of continuous monitoring activities; and/or*
		CA-7(3)[3]	*the types of activities used in the continuous monitoring process.*
	POTENTIAL ASSESSMENT METHODS AND OBJECTS: **Examine**: [*SELECT FROM:* Continuous monitoring strategy; Security assessment and authorization policy; procedures addressing continuous monitoring of information system security controls; security plan; security assessment report; plan of action and milestones; information system monitoring records; security impact analyses; status reports; other relevant documents or records]. **Interview**: [*SELECT FROM:* Organizational personnel with continuous monitoring responsibilities; organizational personnel with information security responsibilities].

Special Publication 800-53A
Revision 4

Assessing Security and Privacy Controls in Federal Information Systems
and Organizations — *Building Effective Assessment Plans*

CA-8	PENETRATION TESTING
	ASSESSMENT OBJECTIVE: *Determine if the organization:*
	CA-8[1] — *defines information systems or system components on which penetration testing is to be conducted;*
	CA-8[2] — *defines the frequency to conduct penetration testing on organization-defined information systems or system components; and*
	CA-8[3] — *conducts penetration testing on organization-defined information systems or system components with the organization-defined frequency.*
	POTENTIAL ASSESSMENT METHODS AND OBJECTS: **Examine**: [*SELECT FROM:* Security assessment and authorization policy; procedures addressing penetration testing; security plan; security assessment plan; penetration test report; security assessment report; security assessment evidence; other relevant documents or records]. **Interview**: [*SELECT FROM:* Organizational personnel with security assessment responsibilities; organizational personnel with information security responsibilities, system/network administrators]. **Test**: [*SELECT FROM:* Automated mechanisms supporting penetration testing].

CA-8(1)	PENETRATION TESTING | *INDEPENDENT PENETRATION AGENT OR TEAM*
	ASSESSMENT OBJECTIVE: *Determine if the organization employs an independent penetration agent or penetration team to perform penetration testing on the information system or system components.*
	POTENTIAL ASSESSMENT METHODS AND OBJECTS: **Examine**: [*SELECT FROM:* Security assessment and authorization policy; procedures addressing penetration testing; security plan; security assessment plan; penetration test report; security assessment report; security assessment evidence; other relevant documents or records]. **Interview**: [*SELECT FROM:* Organizational personnel with security assessment responsibilities; organizational personnel with information security responsibilities].

CA-8(2)	PENETRATION TESTING | *RED TEAM EXERCISES*
	ASSESSMENT OBJECTIVE: *Determine if the organization:*
	CA-8(2)[1] — *defines red team exercises to be employed to simulate attempts by adversaries to compromise organizational information systems;*
	CA-8(2)[2] — *defines rules of engagement for employing organization-defined red team exercises; and*
	CA-8(2)[3] — *employs organization-defined red team exercises to simulate attempts by adversaries to compromise organizational information systems in accordance with organization-defined rules of engagement.*

Special Publication 800-53A
Revision 4

Assessing Security and Privacy Controls in Federal Information Systems
and Organizations — *Building Effective Assessment Plans*

POTENTIAL ASSESSMENT METHODS AND OBJECTS:

Examine: [*SELECT FROM:* Security assessment and authorization policy; procedures addressing penetration testing; procedures addressing red team exercises; security plan; security assessment plan; results of red team exercise; penetration test report; security assessment report; rules of engagement; security assessment evidence; other relevant documents or records].

Interview: [*SELECT FROM:* Organizational personnel with security assessment responsibilities; organizational personnel with information security responsibilities; system/network administrators].

Test: [*SELECT FROM:* Automated mechanisms supporting employment of red team exercises].

CA-9	INTERNAL SYSTEM CONNECTIONS

ASSESSMENT OBJECTIVE:

Determine if the organization:

CA-9(a)	CA-9(a)[1]	*defines information system components or classes of components to be authorized as internal connections to the information system;*
	CA-9(a)[2]	*authorizes internal connections of organization-defined information system components or classes of components to the information system;*
CA-9(b)	*documents, for each internal connection:*	
	CA-9(b)[1]	*the interface characteristics;*
	CA-9(b)[2]	*the security requirements; and*
	CA-9(b)[3]	*the nature of the information communicated.*

POTENTIAL ASSESSMENT METHODS AND OBJECTS:

Examine: [*SELECT FROM:* Access control policy; procedures addressing information system connections; system and communications protection policy; security plan; information system design documentation; information system configuration settings and associated documentation; list of components or classes of components authorized as internal system connections; security assessment report; information system audit records; other relevant documents or records].

Interview: [*SELECT FROM:* Organizational personnel with responsibility for developing, implementing, or authorizing internal system connections; organizational personnel with information security responsibilities].

CA-9(1)	INTERNAL SYSTEM CONNECTIONS	*SECURITY COMPLIANCE CHECKS*

ASSESSMENT OBJECTIVE:

Determine if the information system performs security compliance checks on constituent system components prior to the establishment of the internal connection.

POTENTIAL ASSESSMENT METHODS AND OBJECTS:

Examine: [*SELECT FROM:* Access control policy; procedures addressing information system connections; system and communications protection policy; security plan; information system design documentation; information system configuration settings and associated documentation; list of components or classes of components authorized as internal system connections; security assessment report; information system audit records; other relevant documents or records].

Interview: [*SELECT FROM:* Organizational personnel with responsibility for developing, implementing, or authorizing internal system connections; organizational personnel with information security responsibilities].

Test: [*SELECT FROM:* Automated mechanisms supporting compliance checks].

Special Publication 800-53A
Revision 4

Assessing Security and Privacy Controls in Federal Information Systems
and Organizations — *Building Effective Assessment Plans*

FAMILY: CONFIGURATION MANAGEMENT

CM-1	CONFIGURATION MANAGEMENT POLICY AND PROCEDURES			
	ASSESSMENT OBJECTIVE: *Determine if the organization:*			
	CM-1(a)(1)	CM-1(a)(1)[1]	*develops and documents a configuration management policy that addresses:*	
			CM-1(a)(1)[1][a]	*purpose;*
			CM-1(a)(1)[1][b]	*scope;*
			CM-1(a)(1)[1][c]	*roles;*
			CM-1(a)(1)[1][d]	*responsibilities;*
			CM-1(a)(1)[1][e]	*management commitment;*
			CM-1(a)(1)[1][f]	*coordination among organizational entities;*
			CM-1(a)(1)[1][g]	*compliance;*
		CM-1(a)(1)[2]	*defines personnel or roles to whom the configuration management policy is to be disseminated;*	
		CM-1(a)(1)[3]	*disseminates the configuration management policy to organization-defined personnel or roles;*	
	CM-1(a)(2)	CM-1(a)(2)[1]	*develops and documents procedures to facilitate the implementation of the configuration management policy and associated configuration management controls;*	
		CM-1(a)(2)[2]	*defines personnel or roles to whom the procedures are to be disseminated;*	
		CM-1(a)(2)[3]	*disseminates the procedures to organization-defined personnel or roles;*	
	CM-1(b)(1)	CM-1(b)(1)[1]	*defines the frequency to review and update the current configuration management policy;*	
		CM-1(b)(1)[2]	*reviews and updates the current configuration management policy with the organization-defined frequency;*	
	CM-1(b)(2)	CM-1(b)(2)[1]	*defines the frequency to review and update the current configuration management procedures; and*	
		CM-1(b)(2)[2]	*reviews and updates the current configuration management procedures with the organization-defined frequency.*	
	POTENTIAL ASSESSMENT METHODS AND OBJECTS: **Examine**: [*SELECT FROM:* Configuration management policy and procedures; other relevant documents or records]. **Interview**: [*SELECT FROM:* Organizational personnel with configuration management responsibilities; organizational personnel with information security responsibilities; system/network administrators].				

Special Publication 800-53A
Revision 4

Assessing Security and Privacy Controls in Federal Information Systems
and Organizations — *Building Effective Assessment Plans*

CM-2	BASELINE CONFIGURATION
	ASSESSMENT OBJECTIVE: *Determine if the organization:*

	CM-2[1]	*develops and documents a current baseline configuration of the information system; and*
	CM-2[2]	*maintains, under configuration control, a current baseline configuration of the information system.*

	POTENTIAL ASSESSMENT METHODS AND OBJECTS: **Examine**: [*SELECT FROM:* Configuration management policy; procedures addressing the baseline configuration of the information system; configuration management plan; enterprise architecture documentation; information system design documentation; information system architecture and configuration documentation; information system configuration settings and associated documentation; change control records; other relevant documents or records]. **Interview**: [*SELECT FROM:* Organizational personnel with configuration management responsibilities; organizational personnel with information security responsibilities; system/network administrators]. **Test**: [*SELECT FROM:* Organizational processes for managing baseline configurations; automated mechanisms supporting configuration control of the baseline configuration].

CM-2(1)	BASELINE CONFIGURATION	*REVIEWS AND UPDATES*

	ASSESSMENT OBJECTIVE: *Determine if the organization:*

CM-2(1)(a)	CM-2(1)(a)[1]	*defines the frequency to review and update the baseline configuration of the information system;*
	CM-2(1)(a)[2]	*reviews and updates the baseline configuration of the information system with the organization-defined frequency;*
CM-2(1)(b)	CM-2(1)(b)[1]	*defines circumstances that require the baseline configuration of the information system to be reviewed and updated;*
	CM-2(1)(b)[2]	*reviews and updates the baseline configuration of the information system when required due to organization-defined circumstances; and*
CM-2(1)(c)	*reviews and updates the baseline configuration of the information system as an integral part of information system component installations and upgrades.*	

	POTENTIAL ASSESSMENT METHODS AND OBJECTS: **Examine**: [*SELECT FROM:* Configuration management policy; configuration management plan; procedures addressing the baseline configuration of the information system; procedures addressing information system component installations and upgrades; information system architecture and configuration documentation; information system configuration settings and associated documentation; records of information system baseline configuration reviews and updates; information system component installations/upgrades and associated records; change control records; other relevant documents or records]. **Interview**: [*SELECT FROM:* Organizational personnel with configuration management responsibilities; organizational personnel with information security responsibilities; system/network administrators]. **Test**: [*SELECT FROM:* Organizational processes for managing baseline configurations; automated mechanisms supporting review and update of the baseline configuration].

Special Publication 800-53A
Revision 4

Assessing Security and Privacy Controls in Federal Information Systems
and Organizations — *Building Effective Assessment Plans*

CM-2(2)	BASELINE CONFIGURATION	*AUTOMATION SUPPORT FOR ACCURACY / CURRENCY*
	ASSESSMENT OBJECTIVE: *Determine if the organization employs automated mechanisms to maintain:*

	CM-2(2)[1]	*an up-to-date baseline configuration of the information system;*
	CM-2(2)[2]	*a complete baseline configuration of the information system;*
	CM-2(2)[3]	*an accurate baseline configuration of the information system; and*
	CM-2(2)[4]	*a readily available baseline configuration of the information system.*

POTENTIAL ASSESSMENT METHODS AND OBJECTS:

Examine: [*SELECT FROM:* Configuration management policy; procedures addressing the baseline configuration of the information system; configuration management plan; information system design documentation; information system architecture and configuration documentation; information system configuration settings and associated documentation; configuration change control records; other relevant documents or records].

Interview: [*SELECT FROM:* Organizational personnel with configuration management responsibilities; organizational personnel with information security responsibilities; system/network administrators].

Test: [*SELECT FROM:* Organizational processes for managing baseline configurations; automated mechanisms implementing baseline configuration maintenance].

CM-2(3)	BASELINE CONFIGURATION	*RETENTION OF PREVIOUS CONFIGURATIONS*
	ASSESSMENT OBJECTIVE: *Determine if the organization:*

	CM-2(3)[1]	*defines previous versions of baseline configurations of the information system to be retained to support rollback; and*
	CM-2(3)[2]	*retains organization-defined previous versions of baseline configurations of the information system to support rollback.*

POTENTIAL ASSESSMENT METHODS AND OBJECTS:

Examine: [*SELECT FROM:* Configuration management policy; procedures addressing the baseline configuration of the information system; configuration management plan; information system architecture and configuration documentation; information system configuration settings and associated documentation; copies of previous baseline configuration versions; other relevant documents or records].

Interview: [*SELECT FROM:* Organizational personnel with configuration management responsibilities; organizational personnel with information security responsibilities; system/network administrators].

Test: [*SELECT FROM:* Organizational processes for managing baseline configurations].

CM-2(4)	BASELINE CONFIGURATION	*UNAUTHORIZED SOFTWARE*
[Withdrawn: Incorporated into CM-7].	

CM-2(5)	BASELINE CONFIGURATION	*AUTHORIZED SOFTWARE*
[Withdrawn: Incorporated into CM-7].	

Special Publication 800-53A
Revision 4

Assessing Security and Privacy Controls in Federal Information Systems
and Organizations — *Building Effective Assessment Plans*

CM-2(6)	BASELINE CONFIGURATION | *DEVELOPMENT AND TEST ENVIRONMENTS*
	ASSESSMENT OBJECTIVE: *Determine if the organization maintains a baseline configuration for information system development and test environments that is managed separately from the operational baseline configuration.*
	POTENTIAL ASSESSMENT METHODS AND OBJECTS: **Examine**: [*SELECT FROM:* Configuration management policy; procedures addressing the baseline configuration of the information system; configuration management plan; information system design documentation; information system architecture and configuration documentation; information system configuration settings and associated documentation; other relevant documents or records]. **Interview**: [*SELECT FROM:* Organizational personnel with configuration management responsibilities; organizational personnel with information security responsibilities; system/network administrators]. **Test**: [*SELECT FROM:* Organizational processes for managing baseline configurations; automated mechanisms implementing separate baseline configurations for development, test, and operational environments].

CM-2(7)	BASELINE CONFIGURATION | *CONFIGURE SYSTEMS, COMPONENTS, OR DEVICES FOR HIGH-RISK AREAS*		
	ASSESSMENT OBJECTIVE: *Determine if the organization:*		
	CM-2(7)(a)	CM-2(7)(a)[1]	*defines information systems, system components, or devices to be issued to individuals traveling to locations that the organization deems to be of significant risk;*
		CM-2(7)(a)[2]	*defines configurations to be employed on organization-defined information systems, system components, or devices issued to individuals traveling to such locations;*
		CM-2(7)(a)[3]	*issues organization-defined information systems, system components, or devices with organization-defined configurations to individuals traveling to locations that the organization deems to be of significant risk;*
	CM-2(7)(b)	CM-2(7)(b)[1]	*defines security safeguards to be applied to the devices when the individuals return; and*
		CM-2(7)(b)[2]	*applies organization-defined safeguards to the devices when the individuals return.*
	POTENTIAL ASSESSMENT METHODS AND OBJECTS: **Examine**: [*SELECT FROM:* Configuration management policy; configuration management plan; procedures addressing the baseline configuration of the information system; procedures addressing information system component installations and upgrades; information system architecture and configuration documentation; information system configuration settings and associated documentation; records of information system baseline configuration reviews and updates; information system component installations/upgrades and associated records; change control records; other relevant documents or records]. **Interview**: [*SELECT FROM:* Organizational personnel with configuration management responsibilities; organizational personnel with information security responsibilities; system/network administrators]. **Test**: [*SELECT FROM:* Organizational processes for managing baseline configurations].		

Special Publication 800-53A
Revision 4

Assessing Security and Privacy Controls in Federal Information Systems
and Organizations — *Building Effective Assessment Plans*

CM-3	CONFIGURATION CHANGE CONTROL		
	ASSESSMENT OBJECTIVE: *Determine if the organization:*		
	CM-3(a)	*determines the type of changes to the information system that must be configuration-controlled;*	
	CM-3(b)	*reviews proposed configuration-controlled changes to the information system and approves or disapproves such changes with explicit consideration for security impact analyses;*	
	CM-3(c)	*documents configuration change decisions associated with the information system;*	
	CM-3(d)	*implements approved configuration-controlled changes to the information system;*	
	CM-3(e)	CM-3(e)[1]	*defines a time period to retain records of configuration-controlled changes to the information system;*
		CM-3(e)[2]	*retains records of configuration-controlled changes to the information system for the organization-defined time period;*
	CM-3(f)	*audits and reviews activities associated with configuration-controlled changes to the information system;*	
	CM-3(g)	CM-3(g)[1]	*defines a configuration change control element (e.g., committee, board) responsible for coordinating and providing oversight for configuration change control activities;*
		CM-3(g)[2]	*defines the frequency with which the configuration change control element must convene; and/or*
		CM-3(g)[3]	*defines configuration change conditions that prompt the configuration change control element to convene; and*
		CM-3(g)[4]	*coordinates and provides oversight for configuration change control activities through organization-defined configuration change control element that convenes at organization-defined frequency and/or for any organization-defined configuration change conditions.*
	POTENTIAL ASSESSMENT METHODS AND OBJECTS: **Examine**: [*SELECT FROM:* Configuration management policy; procedures addressing information system configuration change control; configuration management plan; information system architecture and configuration documentation; security plan; change control records; information system audit records; change control audit and review reports; agenda /minutes from configuration change control oversight meetings; other relevant documents or records]. **Interview**: [*SELECT FROM:* Organizational personnel with configuration change control responsibilities; organizational personnel with information security responsibilities; system/network administrators; members of change control board or similar]. **Test**: [*SELECT FROM:* Organizational processes for configuration change control; automated mechanisms that implement configuration change control].		

CM-3(1)	CONFIGURATION CHANGE CONTROL | *AUTOMATED DOCUMENT / NOTIFICATION / PROHIBITION OF CHANGES*	
	ASSESSMENT OBJECTIVE: *Determine if the organization:*	
	CM-3(1)(a)	*employs automated mechanisms to document proposed changes to the information system;*

Special Publication 800-53A
Revision 4

Assessing Security and Privacy Controls in Federal Information Systems
and Organizations — *Building Effective Assessment Plans*

	CM-3(1)(b)	CM-3(1)(b)[1]	*defines approval authorities to be notified of proposed changes to the information system and request change approval;*
		CM-3(1)(b)[2]	*employs automated mechanisms to notify organization-defined approval authorities of proposed changes to the information system and request change approval;*
	CM-3(1)(c)	CM-3(1)(c)[1]	*defines the time period within which proposed changes to the information system that have not been approved or disapproved must be highlighted;*
		CM-3(1)(c)[2]	*employs automated mechanisms to highlight proposed changes to the information system that have not been approved or disapproved by organization-defined time period;*
	CM-3(1)(d)	*employs automated mechanisms to prohibit changes to the information system until designated approvals are received;*	
	CM-3(1)(e)	*employs automated mechanisms to document all changes to the information system;*	
	CM-3(1)(f)	CM-3(1)(f)[1]	*defines personnel to be notified when approved changes to the information system are completed; and*
		CM-3(1)(f)[2]	*employs automated mechanisms to notify organization-defined personnel when approved changes to the information system are completed.*

POTENTIAL ASSESSMENT METHODS AND OBJECTS:

Examine: [*SELECT FROM:* Configuration management policy; procedures addressing information system configuration change control; configuration management plan; information system design documentation; information system architecture and configuration documentation; automated configuration control mechanisms; information system configuration settings and associated documentation; change control records; information system audit records; change approval requests; change approvals; other relevant documents or records].

Interview: [*SELECT FROM:* Organizational personnel with configuration change control responsibilities; organizational personnel with information security responsibilities; system/network administrators; system developers].

Test: [*SELECT FROM:* Organizational processes for configuration change control; automated mechanisms implementing configuration change control activities].

CM-3(2)	**CONFIGURATION CHANGE CONTROL** | *TEST / VALIDATE / DOCUMENT CHANGES*	
	ASSESSMENT OBJECTIVE: *Determine if the organization, before implementing changes on the operational system:*	
	CM-3(2)[1]	*tests changes to the information system;*
	CM-3(2)[2]	*validates changes to the information system; and*
	CM-3(2)[3]	*documents changes to the information system.*

Special Publication 800-53A
Revision 4

Assessing Security and Privacy Controls in Federal Information Systems
and Organizations — *Building Effective Assessment Plans*

POTENTIAL ASSESSMENT METHODS AND OBJECTS:

Examine: [*SELECT FROM:* Configuration management policy; configuration management plan; procedures addressing information system configuration change control; information system design documentation; information system architecture and configuration documentation; information system configuration settings and associated documentation; test records; validation records; change control records; information system audit records; other relevant documents or records].

Interview: [*SELECT FROM:* Organizational personnel with configuration change control responsibilities; organizational personnel with information security responsibilities; system/network administrators].

Test: [*SELECT FROM:* Organizational processes for configuration change control; automated mechanisms supporting and/or implementing testing, validating, and documenting information system changes].

CM-3(3)	CONFIGURATION CHANGE CONTROL | *AUTOMATED CHANGE IMPLEMENTATION*

ASSESSMENT OBJECTIVE:

Determine if the organization:

CM-3(3)[1]	*employs automated mechanisms to implement changes to the current information system baseline; and*
CM-3(3)[2]	*deploys the updated baseline across the installed base.*

POTENTIAL ASSESSMENT METHODS AND OBJECTS:

Examine: [*SELECT FROM:* Configuration management policy; configuration management plan; procedures addressing information system configuration change control; information system design documentation; information system architecture and configuration documentation; automated configuration control mechanisms; change control records; information system audit records; other relevant documents or records].

Interview: [*SELECT FROM:* Organizational personnel with configuration change control responsibilities; organizational personnel with information security responsibilities; system/network administrators; system developers].

Test: [*SELECT FROM:* Organizational processes for configuration change control; automated mechanisms implementing changes to current information system baseline].

CM-3(4)	CONFIGURATION CHANGE CONTROL | *SECURITY REPRESENTATIVE*

ASSESSMENT OBJECTIVE:

Determine if the organization:

CM-3(4)[1]	*specifies the configuration change control elements (as defined in CM-3g) of which an information security representative is to be a member; and*
CM-3(4)[2]	*requires an information security representative to be a member of the specified configuration control element.*

POTENTIAL ASSESSMENT METHODS AND OBJECTS:

Examine: [*SELECT FROM:* Configuration management policy; procedures addressing information system configuration change control; configuration management plan; security plan; other relevant documents or records].

Interview: [*SELECT FROM:* Organizational personnel with configuration change control responsibilities; organizational personnel with information security responsibilities].

Test: [*SELECT FROM:* Organizational processes for configuration change control].

CM-3(5)	CONFIGURATION CHANGE CONTROL | *AUTOMATED SECURITY RESPONSE*

ASSESSMENT OBJECTIVE:

Determine if:

Special Publication 800-53A
Revision 4

Assessing Security and Privacy Controls in Federal Information Systems
and Organizations — *Building Effective Assessment Plans*

	CM-3(5)[1]	*the organization defines security responses to be implemented automatically if baseline configurations are changed in an unauthorized manner; and*
	CM-3(5)[2]	*the information system implements organization-defined security responses automatically if baseline configurations are changed in an unauthorized manner.*

POTENTIAL ASSESSMENT METHODS AND OBJECTS:

Examine: [*SELECT FROM:* Configuration management policy; procedures addressing information system configuration change control; configuration management plan; security plan; information system design documentation; information system architecture and configuration documentation; information system configuration settings and associated documentation; alerts/notifications of unauthorized baseline configuration changes; information system audit records; other relevant documents or records].

Interview: [*SELECT FROM:* Organizational personnel with configuration change control responsibilities; organizational personnel with information security responsibilities; system/network administrators; system developers].

Test: [*SELECT FROM:* Organizational processes for configuration change control; automated mechanisms implementing security responses to changes to the baseline configurations].

CM-3(6)	CONFIGURATION CHANGE CONTROL	*CRYPTOGRAPHY MANAGEMENT*

ASSESSMENT OBJECTIVE:

Determine if the organization:

	CM-3(6)[1]	*defines security safeguards provided by cryptographic mechanisms that are to be under configuration management; and*
	CM-3(6)[2]	*ensures that cryptographic mechanisms used to provide organization-defined security safeguards are under configuration management.*

POTENTIAL ASSESSMENT METHODS AND OBJECTS:

Examine: [*SELECT FROM:* Configuration management policy; procedures addressing information system configuration change control; configuration management plan; security plan; information system design documentation; information system architecture and configuration documentation; information system configuration settings and associated documentation; other relevant documents or records].

Interview: [*SELECT FROM:* Organizational personnel with configuration change control responsibilities; organizational personnel with information security responsibilities; system/network administrators].

Test: [*SELECT FROM:* Organizational processes for configuration change control; cryptographic mechanisms implementing organizational security safeguards].

CM-4	SECURITY IMPACT ANALYSIS

ASSESSMENT OBJECTIVE:

Determine if the organization analyzes changes to the information system to determine potential security impacts prior to change implementation.

POTENTIAL ASSESSMENT METHODS AND OBJECTS:

Examine: [*SELECT FROM:* Configuration management policy; procedures addressing security impact analysis for changes to the information system; configuration management plan; security impact analysis documentation; analysis tools and associated outputs; change control records; information system audit records; other relevant documents or records].

Interview: [*SELECT FROM:* Organizational personnel with responsibility for conducting security impact analysis; organizational personnel with information security responsibilities; system/network administrators].

Test: [*SELECT FROM:* Organizational processes for security impact analysis].

Special Publication 800-53A
Revision 4

Assessing Security and Privacy Controls in Federal Information Systems
and Organizations — *Building Effective Assessment Plans*

CM-4(1)	SECURITY IMPACT ANALYSIS | *SEPARATE TEST ENVIRONMENTS*
	ASSESSMENT OBJECTIVE: *Determine if the organization:*

	CM-4(1)[1]	*analyzes changes to the information system in a separate test environment before implementation in an operational environment;*
	CM-4(1)[2]	*when analyzing changes to the information system in a separate test environment, looks for security impacts due to:*
		CM-4(1)[2][a]	*flaws;*
		CM-4(1)[2][b]	*weaknesses;*
		CM-4(1)[2][c]	*incompatibility; and*
		CM-4(1)[2][d]	*intentional malice.*

POTENTIAL ASSESSMENT METHODS AND OBJECTS:

Examine: [*SELECT FROM:* Configuration management policy; procedures addressing security impact analysis for changes to the information system; configuration management plan; security impact analysis documentation; analysis tools and associated outputs information system design documentation; information system architecture and configuration documentation; change control records; information system audit records; documentation evidence of separate test and operational environments; other relevant documents or records].

Interview: [*SELECT FROM:* Organizational personnel with responsibility for conducting security impact analysis; organizational personnel with information security responsibilities; system/network administrators].

Test: [*SELECT FROM:* Organizational processes for security impact analysis; automated mechanisms supporting and/or implementing security impact analysis of changes].

CM-4(2)	SECURITY IMPACT ANALYSIS | *VERIFICATION OF SECURITY FUNCTIONS*
	ASSESSMENT OBJECTIVE: *Determine if the organization, after the information system is changed, checks the security functions to verify that the functions are:*

	CM-4(2)[1]	*implemented correctly;*
	CM-4(2)[2]	*operating as intended; and*
	CM-4(2)[3]	*producing the desired outcome with regard to meeting the security requirements for the system.*

POTENTIAL ASSESSMENT METHODS AND OBJECTS:

Examine: [*SELECT FROM:* Configuration management policy; procedures addressing security impact analysis for changes to the information system; configuration management plan; security impact analysis documentation; analysis tools and associated outputs; change control records; information system audit records; other relevant documents or records].

Interview: [*SELECT FROM:* Organizational personnel with responsibility for conducting security impact analysis; organizational personnel with information security responsibilities; system/network administrators].

Test: [*SELECT FROM:* Organizational processes for security impact analysis; automated mechanisms supporting and/or implementing verification of security functions].

CM-5	ACCESS RESTRICTIONS FOR CHANGE
	ASSESSMENT OBJECTIVE: *Determine if the organization:*

Special Publication 800-53A
Revision 4

Assessing Security and Privacy Controls in Federal Information Systems
and Organizations — *Building Effective Assessment Plans*

	CM-5[1]	*defines physical access restrictions associated with changes to the information system;*
	CM-5[2]	*documents physical access restrictions associated with changes to the information system;*
	CM-5[3]	*approves physical access restrictions associated with changes to the information system;*
	CM-5[4]	*enforces physical access restrictions associated with changes to the information system;*
	CM-5[5]	*defines logical access restrictions associated with changes to the information system;*
	CM-5[6]	*documents logical access restrictions associated with changes to the information system;*
	CM-5[7]	*approves logical access restrictions associated with changes to the information system; and*
	CM-5[8]	*enforces logical access restrictions associated with changes to the information system.*

POTENTIAL ASSESSMENT METHODS AND OBJECTS:

Examine: [*SELECT FROM:* Configuration management policy; procedures addressing access restrictions for changes to the information system; configuration management plan; information system design documentation; information system architecture and configuration documentation; information system configuration settings and associated documentation; logical access approvals; physical access approvals; access credentials; change control records; information system audit records; other relevant documents or records].

Interview: [*SELECT FROM:* Organizational personnel with logical access control responsibilities; organizational personnel with physical access control responsibilities; organizational personnel with information security responsibilities; system/network administrators].

Test: [*SELECT FROM:* Organizational processes for managing access restrictions to change; automated mechanisms supporting/implementing/enforcing access restrictions associated with changes to the information system].

CM-5(1)	ACCESS RESTRICTIONS FOR CHANGE | *AUTOMATED ACCESS ENFORCEMENT / AUDITING*
	ASSESSMENT OBJECTIVE: *Determine if the information system:*

	CM-5(1)[1]	*enforces access restrictions for change; and*
	CM-5(1)[2]	*supports auditing of the enforcement actions.*

POTENTIAL ASSESSMENT METHODS AND OBJECTS:

Examine: [*SELECT FROM:* Configuration management policy; procedures addressing access restrictions for changes to the information system; information system design documentation; information system architecture and configuration documentation; information system configuration settings and associated documentation; change control records; information system audit records; other relevant documents or records].

Interview: [*SELECT FROM:* Organizational personnel with information security responsibilities; system/network administrators; system developers].

Test: [*SELECT FROM:* Organizational processes for managing access restrictions to change; automated mechanisms implementing enforcement of access restrictions for changes to the information system; automated mechanisms supporting auditing of enforcement actions].

Special Publication 800-53A
Revision 4

Assessing Security and Privacy Controls in Federal Information Systems
and Organizations — *Building Effective Assessment Plans*

CM-5(2)	ACCESS RESTRICTIONS FOR CHANGE | *REVIEW SYSTEM CHANGES*
	ASSESSMENT OBJECTIVE: *Determine if the organization, in an effort to ascertain whether unauthorized changes have occurred:*

	CM-5(2)[1]	*defines the frequency to review information system changes;*
	CM-5(2)[2]	*defines circumstances that warrant review of information system changes;*
	CM-5(2)[3]	*reviews information system changes with the organization-defined frequency; and*
	CM-5(2)[4]	*reviews information system changes with the organization-defined circumstances.*

	POTENTIAL ASSESSMENT METHODS AND OBJECTS: **Examine**: [*SELECT FROM:* Configuration management policy; procedures addressing access restrictions for changes to the information system; configuration management plan; security plan; reviews of information system changes; audit and review reports; change control records; information system audit records; other relevant documents or records]. **Interview**: [*SELECT FROM:* Organizational personnel with information security responsibilities; system/network administrators]. **Test**: [*SELECT FROM:* Organizational processes for managing access restrictions to change; automated mechanisms supporting/implementing information system reviews to determine whether unauthorized changes have occurred].

CM-5(3)	ACCESS RESTRICTIONS FOR CHANGE | *SIGNED COMPONENTS*
	ASSESSMENT OBJECTIVE: *Determine if:*

	CM-5(3)[1]	*the organization defines software and firmware components that the information system will prevent from being installed without verification that such components have been digitally signed using a certificate that is recognized and approved by the organization; and*
	CM-5(3)[2]	*the information system prevents the installation of organization-defined software and firmware components without verification that such components have been digitally signed using a certificate that is recognized and approved by the organization.*

	POTENTIAL ASSESSMENT METHODS AND OBJECTS: **Examine**: [*SELECT FROM:* Configuration management policy; procedures addressing access restrictions for changes to the information system; configuration management plan; security plan; list of software and firmware components to be prohibited from installation without a recognized and approved certificate; information system design documentation; information system architecture and configuration documentation; information system configuration settings and associated documentation; change control records; information system audit records; other relevant documents or records]. **Interview**: [*SELECT FROM:* Organizational personnel with information security responsibilities; system/network administrators; system developers]. **Test**: [*SELECT FROM:* Organizational processes for managing access restrictions to change; automated mechanisms preventing installation of software and firmware components not signed with an organization-recognized and approved certificate].

Special Publication 800-53A
Revision 4

Assessing Security and Privacy Controls in Federal Information Systems
and Organizations — *Building Effective Assessment Plans*

CM-5(4)	ACCESS RESTRICTIONS FOR CHANGE	*DUAL AUTHORIZATION*	
	ASSESSMENT OBJECTIVE: *Determine if the organization:*		
	CM-5(4)[1]	*defines information system components and system-level information requiring dual authorization to be enforced when implementing changes; and*	
	CM-5(4)[2]	*enforces dual authorization for implementing changes to organization-defined information system components and system-level information.*	
	POTENTIAL ASSESSMENT METHODS AND OBJECTS: **Examine**: [*SELECT FROM:* Configuration management policy; procedures addressing access restrictions for changes to the information system; configuration management plan; security plan; information system design documentation; information system architecture and configuration documentation; information system configuration settings and associated documentation; change control records; information system audit records; other relevant documents or records]. **Interview**: [*SELECT FROM:* Organizational personnel with dual authorization enforcement responsibilities for implementing information system changes; organizational personnel with information security responsibilities; system/network administrators]. **Test**: [*SELECT FROM:* Organizational processes for managing access restrictions to change; automated mechanisms implementing dual authorization enforcement].		

CM-5(5)	ACCESS RESTRICTIONS FOR CHANGE	*LIMIT PRODUCTION / OPERATIONAL PRIVILEGES*		
	ASSESSMENT OBJECTIVE: *Determine if the organization:*			
	CM-5(5)(a)	*limits privileges to change information system components and system-related information within a production or operational environment;*		
	CM-5(5)(b)	**CM-5(5)(b)[1]**	*defines the frequency to review and reevaluate privileges; and*	
		CM-5(5)(b)[2]	*reviews and reevaluates privileges with the organization-defined frequency.*	
	POTENTIAL ASSESSMENT METHODS AND OBJECTS: **Examine**: [*SELECT FROM:* Configuration management policy; procedures addressing access restrictions for changes to the information system; configuration management plan; security plan; information system design documentation; information system architecture and configuration documentation; information system configuration settings and associated documentation; user privilege reviews; user privilege recertifications; change control records; information system audit records; other relevant documents or records]. **Interview**: [*SELECT FROM:* Organizational personnel with information security responsibilities; system/network administrators]. **Test**: [*SELECT FROM:* Organizational processes for managing access restrictions to change; automated mechanisms supporting and/or implementing access restrictions for change].			

CM-5(6)	ACCESS RESTRICTIONS FOR CHANGE	*LIMIT LIBRARY PRIVILEGES*
	ASSESSMENT OBJECTIVE: *Determine if the organization limits privileges to change software resident within software libraries.*

Special Publication 800-53A
Revision 4

Assessing Security and Privacy Controls in Federal Information Systems
and Organizations — *Building Effective Assessment Plans*

POTENTIAL ASSESSMENT METHODS AND OBJECTS:

Examine: [*SELECT FROM:* Configuration management policy; procedures addressing access restrictions for changes to the information system; configuration management plan; information system design documentation; information system architecture and configuration documentation; information system configuration settings and associated documentation; change control records; information system audit records; other relevant documents or records].

Interview: [*SELECT FROM:* Organizational personnel with information security responsibilities; system/network administrators].

Test: [*SELECT FROM:* Organizational processes for managing access restrictions to change; automated mechanisms supporting and/or implementing access restrictions for change].

CM-5(7)	ACCESS RESTRICTIONS FOR CHANGE | *AUTOMATIC IMPLEMENTATION OF SECURITY SAFEGUARDS*

[Withdrawn: Incorporated into SI-7].

CM-6	CONFIGURATION SETTINGS		
	ASSESSMENT OBJECTIVE: *Determine if the organization:*		
	CM-6(a)	CM-6(a)[1]	*defines security configuration checklists to be used to establish and document configuration settings for the information technology products employed;*
		CM-6(a)[2]	*ensures the defined security configuration checklists reflect the most restrictive mode consistent with operational requirements;*
		CM-6(a)[3]	*establishes and documents configuration settings for information technology products employed within the information system using organization-defined security configuration checklists;*
	CM-6(b)	*implements the configuration settings established/documented in CM-6(a);;*	
	CM-6(c)	CM-6(c)[1]	*defines information system components for which any deviations from established configuration settings must be:*
		CM-6(c)[1][a]	*identified;*
		CM-6(c)[1][b]	*documented;*
		CM-6(c)[1][c]	*approved;*
		CM-6(c)[2]	*defines operational requirements to support:*
		CM-6(c)[2][a]	*the identification of any deviations from established configuration settings;*
		CM-6(c)[2][b]	*the documentation of any deviations from established configuration settings;*
		CM-6(c)[2][c]	*the approval of any deviations from established configuration settings;*
		CM-6(c)[3]	*identifies any deviations from established configuration settings for organization-defined information system components based on organizational-defined operational requirements;*
		CM-6(c)[4]	*documents any deviations from established configuration settings for organization-defined information system components based on organizational-defined operational requirements;*

Special Publication 800-53A
Revision 4

Assessing Security and Privacy Controls in Federal Information Systems
and Organizations — *Building Effective Assessment Plans*

		CM-6(c)[5]	*approves any deviations from established configuration settings for organization-defined information system components based on organizational-defined operational requirements;*
	CM-6(d)	CM-6(d)[1]	*monitors changes to the configuration settings in accordance with organizational policies and procedures; and*
		CM-6(d)[2]	*controls changes to the configuration settings in accordance with organizational policies and procedures.*

POTENTIAL ASSESSMENT METHODS AND OBJECTS:

Examine: [*SELECT FROM:* Configuration management policy; procedures addressing configuration settings for the information system; configuration management plan; security plan; information system design documentation; information system configuration settings and associated documentation; security configuration checklists; evidence supporting approved deviations from established configuration settings; change control records; information system audit records; other relevant documents or records].

Interview: [*SELECT FROM:* Organizational personnel with security configuration management responsibilities; organizational personnel with information security responsibilities; system/network administrators].

Test: [*SELECT FROM:* Organizational processes for managing configuration settings; automated mechanisms that implement, monitor, and/or control information system configuration settings; automated mechanisms that identify and/or document deviations from established configuration settings].

CM-6(1)	**CONFIGURATION SETTINGS**	*AUTOMATED CENTRAL MANAGEMENT / APPLICATION / VERIFICATION*		
	ASSESSMENT OBJECTIVE: *Determine if the organization:*			
	CM-6(1)[1]	*defines information system components for which automated mechanisms are to be employed to:*		
		CM-6(1)[1][a]	*centrally manage configuration settings of such components;*	
		CM-6(1)[1][b]	*apply configuration settings of such components;*	
		CM-6(1)[1][c]	*verify configuration settings of such components;*	
	CM-6(1)[2]	*employs automated mechanisms to:*		
		CM-6(1)[2][a]	*centrally manage configuration settings for organization-defined information system components;*	
		CM-6(1)[2][b]	*apply configuration settings for organization-defined information system components; and*	
		CM-6(1)[2][c]	*verify configuration settings for organization-defined information system components.*	

Special Publication 800-53A
Revision 4

Assessing Security and Privacy Controls in Federal Information Systems
and Organizations — *Building Effective Assessment Plans*

POTENTIAL ASSESSMENT METHODS AND OBJECTS:

Examine: [*SELECT FROM:* Configuration management policy; procedures addressing configuration settings for the information system; configuration management plan; information system design documentation; information system configuration settings and associated documentation; security configuration checklists; change control records; information system audit records; other relevant documents or records].

Interview: [*SELECT FROM:* Organizational personnel with security configuration management responsibilities; organizational personnel with information security responsibilities; system/network administrators; system developers].

Test: [*SELECT FROM:* Organizational processes for managing configuration settings; automated mechanisms implemented to centrally manage, apply, and verify information system configuration settings].

CM-6(2)	CONFIGURATION SETTINGS | *RESPOND TO UNAUTHORIZED CHANGES*

ASSESSMENT OBJECTIVE:

Determine if the organization:

CM-6(2)[1]	*defines configuration settings that, if modified by unauthorized changes, result in organizational security safeguards being employed to respond to such changes;*
CM-6(2)[2]	*defines security safeguards to be employed to respond to unauthorized changes to organization-defined configuration settings; and*
CM-6(2)[3]	*employs organization-defined security safeguards to respond to unauthorized changes to organization-defined configuration settings.*

POTENTIAL ASSESSMENT METHODS AND OBJECTS:

Examine: [*SELECT FROM:* Configuration management policy; procedures addressing configuration settings for the information system; configuration management plan; security plan; information system design documentation; information system configuration settings and associated documentation; alerts/notifications of unauthorized changes to information system configuration settings; documented responses to unauthorized changes to information system configuration settings; change control records; information system audit records; other relevant documents or records].

Interview: [*SELECT FROM:* Organizational personnel with security configuration management responsibilities; organizational personnel with information security responsibilities; system/network administrators].

Test: [*SELECT FROM:* Organizational process for responding to unauthorized changes to information system configuration settings; automated mechanisms supporting and/or implementing security safeguards for response to unauthorized changes].

CM-6(3)	CONFIGURATION SETTINGS | *UNAUTHORIZED CHANGE DETECTION*

[Withdrawn: Incorporated into SI-7].

CM-6(4)	CONFIGURATION SETTINGS | *CONFORMANCE DEMONSTRATION*

[Withdrawn: Incorporated into CM-4].

CM-7	LEAST FUNCTIONALITY

ASSESSMENT OBJECTIVE:

Determine if the organization:

CM-7(a)	*configures the information system to provide only essential capabilities;*

Special Publication 800-53A
Revision 4

Assessing Security and Privacy Controls in Federal Information Systems
and Organizations — *Building Effective Assessment Plans*

	CM-7(b)	CM-7(b)[1]	*defines prohibited or restricted:*	
			CM-7(b)[1][a]	*functions;*
			CM-7(b)[1][b]	*ports;*
			CM-7(b)[1][c]	*protocols; and/or*
			CM-7(b)[1][d]	*services;*
		CM-7(b)[2]	*prohibits or restricts the use of organization-defined:*	
			CM-7(b)[2][a]	*functions;*
			CM-7(b)[2][b]	*ports;*
			CM-7(b)[2][c]	*protocols; and/or*
			CM-7(b)[2][d]	*services.*

POTENTIAL ASSESSMENT METHODS AND OBJECTS:

Examine: [*SELECT FROM:* Configuration management policy; configuration management plan; procedures addressing least functionality in the information system; security plan; information system design documentation; information system configuration settings and associated documentation; security configuration checklists; other relevant documents or records].

Interview: [*SELECT FROM:* Organizational personnel with security configuration management responsibilities; organizational personnel with information security responsibilities; system/network administrators].

Test: [*SELECT FROM:* Organizational processes prohibiting or restricting functions, ports, protocols, and/or services; automated mechanisms implementing restrictions or prohibition of functions, ports, protocols, and/or services].

CM-7(1)	**LEAST FUNCTIONALITY** | *PERIODIC REVIEW*			
	ASSESSMENT OBJECTIVE: *Determine if the organization:*			
	CM-7(1)(a)	CM-7(1)(a)[1]	*defines the frequency to review the information system to identify unnecessary and/or nonsecure:*	
			CM-7(1)(a)[1][a]	*functions;*
			CM-7(1)(a)[1][b]	*ports;*
			CM-7(1)(a)[1][c]	*protocols; and/or*
			CM-7(1)(a)[1][d]	*services;*
		CM-7(1)(a)[2]	*reviews the information system with the organization-defined frequency to identify unnecessary and/or nonsecure:*	
			CM-7(1)(a)[2][a]	*functions;*
			CM-7(1)(a)[2][b]	*ports;*
			CM-7(1)(a)[2][c]	*protocols; and/or*
			CM-7(1)(a)[2][d]	*services;*
	CM-7(1)(b)	CM-7(1)(b)[1]	*defines, within the information system, unnecessary and/or nonsecure:*	
			CM-7(1)(b)[1][a]	*functions;*
			CM-7(1)(b)[1][b]	*ports;*

Special Publication 800-53A
Revision 4

Assessing Security and Privacy Controls in Federal Information Systems
and Organizations — *Building Effective Assessment Plans*

			CM-7(1)(b)[1][c]	*protocols; and/or*
			CM-7(1)(b)[1][d]	*services;*
		CM-7(1)(b)[2]	*disables organization-defined unnecessary and/or nonsecure:*	
			CM-7(1)(b)[2][a]	*functions;*
			CM-7(1)(b)[2][b]	*ports;*
			CM-7(1)(b)[2][c]	*protocols; and/or*
			CM-7(1)(b)[2][d]	*services.*

POTENTIAL ASSESSMENT METHODS AND OBJECTS:

Examine: [*SELECT FROM:* Configuration management policy; procedures addressing least functionality in the information system; configuration management plan; security plan; information system design documentation; information system configuration settings and associated documentation; security configuration checklists; documented reviews of functions, ports, protocols, and/or services; change control records; information system audit records; other relevant documents or records].

Interview: [*SELECT FROM:* Organizational personnel with responsibilities for reviewing functions, ports, protocols, and services on the information system; organizational personnel with information security responsibilities; system/network administrators].

Test: [*SELECT FROM:* Organizational processes for reviewing/disabling nonsecure functions, ports, protocols, and/or services; automated mechanisms implementing review and disabling of nonsecure functions, ports, protocols, and/or services].

CM-7(2)	**LEAST FUNCTIONALITY** | *PREVENT PROGRAM EXECUTION*	
	ASSESSMENT OBJECTIVE: *Determine if:*	
	CM-7(2)[1]	*the organization defines policies regarding software program usage and restrictions;*
	CM-7(2)[2]	*the information system prevents program execution in accordance with one or more of the following:*
	CM-7(2)[2][a]	*organization-defined policies regarding program usage and restrictions; and/or*
	CM-7(2)[2][b]	*rules authorizing the terms and conditions of software program usage.*

POTENTIAL ASSESSMENT METHODS AND OBJECTS:

Examine: [*SELECT FROM:* Configuration management policy; procedures addressing least functionality in the information system; configuration management plan; security plan; information system design documentation; specifications for preventing software program execution; information system configuration settings and associated documentation; change control records; information system audit records; other relevant documents or records].

Interview: [*SELECT FROM:* Organizational personnel with information security responsibilities; system/network administrators; system developers].

Test: [*SELECT FROM:* Organizational processes preventing program execution on the information system; organizational processes for software program usage and restrictions; automated mechanisms preventing program execution on the information system; automated mechanisms supporting and/or implementing software program usage and restrictions].

Special Publication 800-53A
Revision 4

Assessing Security and Privacy Controls in Federal Information Systems
and Organizations — *Building Effective Assessment Plans*

CM-7(3)	LEAST FUNCTIONALITY | *REGISTRATION COMPLIANCE*		
	ASSESSMENT OBJECTIVE: *Determine if the organization:*		
	CM-7(3)[1]	*defines registration requirements for:*	
		CM-7(3)[1][a]	*functions;*
		CM-7(3)[1][b]	*ports;*
		CM-7(3)[1][c]	*protocols; and/or*
		CM-7(3)[1][d]	*services;*
	CM-7(3)[2]	*ensures compliance with organization-defined registration requirements for:*	
		CM-7(3)[2][a]	*functions;*
		CM-7(3)[2][b]	*ports;*
		CM-7(3)[2][c]	*protocols; and/or*
		CM-7(3)[2][d]	*services.*
	POTENTIAL ASSESSMENT METHODS AND OBJECTS: **Examine**: [*SELECT FROM:* Configuration management policy; procedures addressing least functionality in the information system; configuration management plan; security plan; information system configuration settings and associated documentation; audit and compliance reviews; information system audit records; other relevant documents or records]. **Interview**: [*SELECT FROM:* Organizational personnel with information security responsibilities; system/network administrators]. **Test**: [*SELECT FROM:* Organizational processes ensuring compliance with registration requirements for functions, ports, protocols, and/or services; automated mechanisms implementing compliance with registration requirements for functions, ports, protocols, and/or services].		

CM-7(4)	LEAST FUNCTIONALITY | *UNAUTHORIZED SOFTWARE (BLACKLISTING)*		
	ASSESSMENT OBJECTIVE: *Determine if the organization:*		
	CM-7(4)(a)	*Identifies/defines software programs not authorized to execute on the information system;*	
	CM-7(4)(b)	*employs an allow-all, deny-by-exception policy to prohibit the execution of unauthorized software programs on the information system;*	
	CM-7(4)(c)	CM-7(4)(c)[1]	*defines the frequency to review and update the list of unauthorized software programs on the information system; and*
		CM-7(4)(c)[2]	*reviews and updates the list of unauthorized software programs with the organization-defined frequency.*

Special Publication 800-53A
Revision 4

Assessing Security and Privacy Controls in Federal Information Systems
and Organizations — *Building Effective Assessment Plans*

POTENTIAL ASSESSMENT METHODS AND OBJECTS:

Examine: [*SELECT FROM:* Configuration management policy; procedures addressing least functionality in the information system; configuration management plan; information system design documentation; information system configuration settings and associated documentation; list of software programs not authorized to execute on the information system; security configuration checklists; review and update records associated with list of unauthorized software programs; change control records; information system audit records; other relevant documents or records].

Interview: [*SELECT FROM:* Organizational personnel with responsibilities for identifying software not authorized to execute on the information system; organizational personnel with information security responsibilities; system/network administrators].

Test: [*SELECT FROM:* Organizational process for identifying, reviewing, and updating programs not authorized to execute on the information system; organizational process for implementing blacklisting; automated mechanisms supporting and/or implementing blacklisting].

CM-7(5)	LEAST FUNCTIONALITY | *AUTHORIZED SOFTWARE (WHITELISTING)*		
	ASSESSMENT OBJECTIVE: *Determine if the organization:*		
	CM-7(5)(a)	*Identifies/defines software programs authorized to execute on the information system;*	
	CM-7(5)(b)	*employs a deny-all, permit-by-exception policy to allow the execution of authorized software programs on the information system;*	
	CM-7(5)(c)	**CM-7(5)(c)[1]**	*defines the frequency to review and update the list of authorized software programs on the information system; and*
		CM-7(5)(c)[2]	*reviews and updates the list of authorized software programs with the organization-defined frequency.*

POTENTIAL ASSESSMENT METHODS AND OBJECTS:

Examine: [*SELECT FROM:* Configuration management policy; procedures addressing least functionality in the information system; configuration management plan; information system design documentation; information system configuration settings and associated documentation; list of software programs authorized to execute on the information system; security configuration checklists; review and update records associated with list of authorized software programs; change control records; information system audit records; other relevant documents or records].

Interview: [*SELECT FROM:* Organizational personnel with responsibilities for identifying software authorized to execute on the information system; organizational personnel with information security responsibilities; system/network administrators].

Test: [*SELECT FROM:* Organizational process for identifying, reviewing, and updating programs authorized to execute on the information system; organizational process for implementing whitelisting; automated mechanisms implementing whitelisting].

CM-8	INFORMATION SYSTEM COMPONENT INVENTORY		
	ASSESSMENT OBJECTIVE: *Determine if the organization:*		
	CM-8(a)	**CM-8(a)(1)**	*develops and documents an inventory of information system components that accurately reflects the current information system;*
		CM-8(a)(2)	*develops and documents an inventory of information system components that includes all components within the authorization boundary of the information system;*

Special Publication 800-53A
Revision 4

Assessing Security and Privacy Controls in Federal Information Systems
and Organizations — *Building Effective Assessment Plans*

		CM-8(a)(3)		*develops and documents an inventory of information system components that is at the level of granularity deemed necessary for tracking and reporting;*
		CM-8(a)(4)	CM-8(a)(4)[1]	*defines the information deemed necessary to achieve effective information system component accountability;*
			CM-8(a)(4)[2]	*develops and documents an inventory of information system components that includes organization-defined information deemed necessary to achieve effective information system component accountability;*
	CM-8(b)	CM-8(b)[1]		*defines the frequency to review and update the information system component inventory; and*
		CM-8(b)[2]		*reviews and updates the information system component inventory with the organization-defined frequency.*
	POTENTIAL ASSESSMENT METHODS AND OBJECTS:			
	Examine: [*SELECT FROM:* Configuration management policy; procedures addressing information system component inventory; configuration management plan; security plan; information system inventory records; inventory reviews and update records; other relevant documents or records].			
	Interview: [*SELECT FROM:* Organizational personnel with responsibilities for information system component inventory; organizational personnel with information security responsibilities; system/network administrators].			
	Test: [*SELECT FROM:* Organizational processes for developing and documenting an inventory of information system components; automated mechanisms supporting and/or implementing the information system component inventory].			

CM-8(1)	INFORMATION SYSTEM COMPONENT INVENTORY | *UPDATES DURING INSTALLATIONS / REMOVALS*
	ASSESSMENT OBJECTIVE:
	Determine if the organization updates the inventory of information system components as an integral part of:

	CM-8(1)[1]	*component installations;*
	CM-8(1)[2]	*component removals; and*
	CM-8(1)[3]	*information system updates.*
	POTENTIAL ASSESSMENT METHODS AND OBJECTS:	
	Examine: [*SELECT FROM:* Configuration management policy; procedures addressing information system component inventory; configuration management plan; security plan; information system inventory records; inventory reviews and update records; component installation records; component removal records; other relevant documents or records].	
	Interview: [*SELECT FROM:* Organizational personnel with responsibilities for updating the information system component inventory; organizational personnel with information security responsibilities; system/network administrators].	
	Test: [*SELECT FROM:* Organizational processes for updating inventory of information system components; automated mechanisms implementing updating of the information system component inventory].	

Special Publication 800-53A
Revision 4

Assessing Security and Privacy Controls in Federal Information Systems
and Organizations — *Building Effective Assessment Plans*

CM-8(2)	INFORMATION SYSTEM COMPONENT INVENTORY	*AUTOMATED MAINTENANCE*	
	ASSESSMENT OBJECTIVE: *Determine if the organization employs automated mechanisms to maintain an inventory of information system components that is:*		
	CM-8(2)[1]	*up-to-date;*	
	CM-8(2)[2]	*complete;*	
	CM-8(2)[3]	*accurate; and*	
	CM-8(2)[4]	*readily available.*	
	POTENTIAL ASSESSMENT METHODS AND OBJECTS: **Examine:** [*SELECT FROM:* Configuration management policy; configuration management plan; procedures addressing information system component inventory; information system design documentation; information system configuration settings and associated documentation; information system inventory records; change control records; information system maintenance records; information system audit records; other relevant documents or records]. **Interview:** [*SELECT FROM:* Organizational personnel with responsibilities for managing the automated mechanisms implementing the information system component inventory; organizational personnel with information security responsibilities; system/network administrators; system developers]. **Test:** [*SELECT FROM:* Organizational processes for maintaining the inventory of information system components; automated mechanisms implementing the information system component inventory].		

CM-8(3)	INFORMATION SYSTEM COMPONENT INVENTORY	*AUTOMATED UNAUTHORIZED COMPONENT DETECTION*		
	ASSESSMENT OBJECTIVE: *Determine if the organization:*			
	CM-8(3)(a)	**CM-8(3)(a)[1]**	*defines the frequency to employ automated mechanisms to detect the presence of unauthorized:*	
			CM-8(3)(a)[1][a]	*hardware components within the information system;*
			CM-8(3)(a)[1][b]	*software components within the information system;*
			CM-8(3)(a)[1][c]	*firmware components within the information system;*
		CM-8(3)(a)[2]	*employs automated mechanisms with the organization-defined frequency to detect the presence of unauthorized:*	
			CM-8(3)(a)[2][a]	*hardware components within the information system;*
			CM-8(3)(a)[2][b]	*software components within the information system;*
			CM-8(3)(a)[2][c]	*firmware components within the information system;*
	CM-8(3)(b)	**CM-8(3)(b)[1]**	*defines personnel or roles to be notified when unauthorized components are detected;*	
		CM-8(3)(b)[2]	*takes one or more of the following actions when unauthorized components are detected:*	

Special Publication 800-53A
Revision 4

Assessing Security and Privacy Controls in Federal Information Systems
and Organizations — *Building Effective Assessment Plans*

			CM-8(3)(b)[2][a]	*disables network access by such components;*
			CM-8(3)(b)[2][b]	*isolates the components; and/or*
			CM-8(3)(b)[2][c]	*notifies organization-defined personnel or roles.*

POTENTIAL ASSESSMENT METHODS AND OBJECTS:

Examine: [*SELECT FROM:* Configuration management policy; procedures addressing information system component inventory; configuration management plan; security plan; information system design documentation; information system configuration settings and associated documentation; information system inventory records; alerts/notifications of unauthorized components within the information system; information system monitoring records; change control records; information system audit records; other relevant documents or records].

Interview: [*SELECT FROM:* Organizational personnel with responsibilities for managing the automated mechanisms implementing unauthorized information system component detection; organizational personnel with information security responsibilities; system/network administrators; system developers].

Test: [*SELECT FROM:* Organizational processes for detection of unauthorized information system components; automated mechanisms implementing the detection of unauthorized information system components].

CM-8(4)	INFORMATION SYSTEM COMPONENT INVENTORY | *ACCOUNTABILITY INFORMATION*

ASSESSMENT OBJECTIVE:

Determine if the organization includes in the information system component inventory for information system components, a means for identifying the individuals responsible and accountable for administering those components by one or more of the following:

CM-8(4)[1]	*name;*
CM-8(4)[2]	*position; and/or*
CM-8(4)[3]	*role.*

POTENTIAL ASSESSMENT METHODS AND OBJECTS:

Examine: [*SELECT FROM:* Configuration management policy; procedures addressing information system component inventory; configuration management plan; security plan; information system inventory records; other relevant documents or records].

Interview: [*SELECT FROM:* Organizational personnel with responsibilities for managing the information system component inventory; organizational personnel with information security responsibilities; system/network administrators].

Test: [*SELECT FROM:* Organizational processes for maintaining the inventory of information system components; automated mechanisms implementing the information system component inventory].

CM-8(5)	INFORMATION SYSTEM COMPONENT INVENTORY | *NO DUPLICATE ACCOUNTING OF COMPONENTS*

ASSESSMENT OBJECTIVE:

Determine if the organization verifies that all components within the authorization boundary of the information system are not duplicated in other information system inventories.

Special Publication 800-53A
Revision 4

Assessing Security and Privacy Controls in Federal Information Systems
and Organizations — *Building Effective Assessment Plans*

<table>
<tr><td></td><td>

POTENTIAL ASSESSMENT METHODS AND OBJECTS:

Examine: [*SELECT FROM:* Configuration management policy; procedures addressing information system component inventory; configuration management plan; security plan; information system inventory records; other relevant documents or records].

Interview: [*SELECT FROM:* Organizational personnel with information system inventory responsibilities; organizational personnel with responsibilities for defining information system components within the authorization boundary of the system; organizational personnel with information security responsibilities; system/network administrators].

Test: [*SELECT FROM:* Organizational processes for maintaining the inventory of information system components; automated mechanisms implementing the information system component inventory].

</td></tr>
</table>

CM-8(6)	INFORMATION SYSTEM COMPONENT INVENTORY | *ASSESSED CONFIGURATIONS / APPROVED DEVIATIONS*

ASSESSMENT OBJECTIVE:

Determine if the organization includes in the information system component inventory:

CM-8(6)[1]	*assessed component configurations; and*
CM-8(6)[2]	*any approved deviations to current deployed configurations.*

POTENTIAL ASSESSMENT METHODS AND OBJECTS:

Examine: [*SELECT FROM:* Configuration management policy; procedures addressing information system component inventory; configuration management plan; security plan; information system design documentation; information system configuration settings and associated documentation; information system inventory records; other relevant documents or records].

Interview: [*SELECT FROM:* Organizational personnel with inventory management and assessment responsibilities for information system components; organizational personnel with information security responsibilities; system/network administrators].

Test: [*SELECT FROM:* Organizational processes for maintaining the inventory of information system components; automated mechanisms implementing the information system component inventory].

CM-8(7)	INFORMATION SYSTEM COMPONENT INVENTORY | *CENTRALIZED REPOSITORY*

ASSESSMENT OBJECTIVE:

Determine if the organization provides a centralized repository for the inventory of information system components.

POTENTIAL ASSESSMENT METHODS AND OBJECTS:

Examine: [*SELECT FROM:* Configuration management policy; procedures addressing information system component inventory; configuration management plan; information system design documentation; information system inventory repository; information system inventory records; other relevant documents or records].

Interview: [*SELECT FROM:* Organizational personnel with inventory management responsibilities for information system components; organizational personnel with information security responsibilities].

Test: [*SELECT FROM:* Automated mechanisms implementing the information system component inventory in a centralized repository].

CM-8(8)	INFORMATION SYSTEM COMPONENT INVENTORY | *AUTOMATED LOCATION TRACKING*

ASSESSMENT OBJECTIVE:

Determine if the organization employs automated mechanisms to support tracking of information system components by geographic location.

Special Publication 800-53A
Revision 4

Assessing Security and Privacy Controls in Federal Information Systems
and Organizations — *Building Effective Assessment Plans*

POTENTIAL ASSESSMENT METHODS AND OBJECTS:

Examine: [*SELECT FROM:* Configuration management policy; procedures addressing information system component inventory; configuration management plan; information system design documentation; information system configuration settings and associated documentation; information system inventory records; information system audit records; other relevant documents or records].

Interview: [*SELECT FROM:* Organizational personnel with inventory management responsibilities for information system components; organizational personnel with information security responsibilities; system/network administrators; system developers].

Test: [*SELECT FROM:* Automated mechanisms implementing the information system component inventory; automated mechanisms supporting tracking of information system components by geographic location].

CM-8(9)	INFORMATION SYSTEM COMPONENT INVENTORY | *ASSIGNMENT OF COMPONENTS TO SYSTEMS*		
	ASSESSMENT OBJECTIVE: *Determine if the organization:*		
	CM-8(9)(a)	CM-8(9)(a)[1]	*defines acquired information system components to be assigned to an information system; and*
		CM-8(9)(a)[2]	*assigns organization-defined acquired information system components to an information system; and*
	CM-8(9)(b)	*receives an acknowledgement from the information system owner of the assignment.*	

POTENTIAL ASSESSMENT METHODS AND OBJECTS:

Examine: [*SELECT FROM:* Configuration management policy; procedures addressing information system component inventory; configuration management plan; security plan; information system design documentation; acknowledgements of information system component assignments; information system inventory records; other relevant documents or records].

Interview: [*SELECT FROM:* Organizational personnel with inventory management responsibilities for information system components; information system owner; organizational personnel with information security responsibilities; system/network administrators].

Test: [*SELECT FROM:* Organizational processes for assigning components to systems; organizational processes for acknowledging assignment of components to systems; automated mechanisms implementing assignment of acquired components to the information system; automated mechanisms implementing acknowledgment of assignment of acquired components to the information system].

CM-9	CONFIGURATION MANAGEMENT PLAN		
	ASSESSMENT OBJECTIVE: *Determine if the organization develops, documents, and implements a configuration management plan for the information system that:*		
	CM-9(a)	CM-9(a)[1]	*addresses roles;*
		CM-9(a)[2]	*addresses responsibilities;*
		CM-9(a)[3]	*addresses configuration management processes and procedures;*
	CM-9(b)	*establishes a process for:*	
		CM-9(b)[1]	*identifying configuration items throughout the SDLC;*
		CM-9(b)[2]	*managing the configuration of the configuration items;*
	CM-9(c)	CM-9(c)[1]	*defines the configuration items for the information system;*

Special Publication 800-53A
Revision 4

Assessing Security and Privacy Controls in Federal Information Systems
and Organizations — *Building Effective Assessment Plans*

		CM-9(c)[2]	*places the configuration items under configuration management;*
	CM-9(d)	*protects the configuration management plan from unauthorized:*	
		CM-9(d)[1]	*disclosure; and*
		CM-9(d)[2]	*modification.*

POTENTIAL ASSESSMENT METHODS AND OBJECTS:

Examine: [*SELECT FROM:* Configuration management policy; procedures addressing configuration management planning; configuration management plan; security plan; other relevant documents or records].

Interview: [*SELECT FROM:* Organizational personnel with responsibilities for developing the configuration management plan; organizational personnel with responsibilities for implementing and managing processes defined in the configuration management plan; organizational personnel with responsibilities for protecting the configuration management plan; organizational personnel with information security responsibilities; system/network administrators].

Test: [*SELECT FROM:* Organizational processes for developing and documenting the configuration management plan; organizational processes for identifying and managing configuration items; organizational processes for protecting the configuration management plan; automated mechanisms implementing the configuration management plan; automated mechanisms for managing configuration items; automated mechanisms for protecting the configuration management plan].

CM-9(1)	**CONFIGURATION MANAGEMENT PLAN	*ASSIGNMENT OF RESPONSIBILITY***
	ASSESSMENT OBJECTIVE: *Determine if the organization assigns responsibility for developing the configuration management process to organizational personnel that are not directly involved in information system development.* **POTENTIAL ASSESSMENT METHODS AND OBJECTS:** **Examine**: [*SELECT FROM:* Configuration management policy; procedures addressing responsibilities for configuration management process development; configuration management plan; security plan; other relevant documents or records]. **Interview**: [*SELECT FROM:* Organizational personnel with responsibilities for configuration management process development; organizational personnel with information security responsibilities].

CM-10	**SOFTWARE USAGE RESTRICTIONS**	
	ASSESSMENT OBJECTIVE: *Determine if the organization:*	
	CM-10(a)	*uses software and associated documentation in accordance with contract agreements and copyright laws;*
	CM-10(b)	*tracks the use of software and associated documentation protected by quantity licenses to control copying and distribution; and*
	CM-10(c)	*controls and documents the use of peer-to-peer file sharing technology to ensure that this capability is not used for the unauthorized distribution, display, performance, or reproduction of copyrighted work.*

Special Publication 800-53A
Revision 4

Assessing Security and Privacy Controls in Federal Information Systems
and Organizations — *Building Effective Assessment Plans*

POTENTIAL ASSESSMENT METHODS AND OBJECTS:

Examine: [*SELECT FROM:* Configuration management policy; procedures addressing software usage restrictions; configuration management plan; security plan; software contract agreements and copyright laws; site license documentation; list of software usage restrictions; software license tracking reports; other relevant documents or records].

Interview: [*SELECT FROM:* Organizational personnel with information security responsibilities; system/network administrators; organizational personnel operating, using, and/or maintaining the information system; organizational personnel with software license management responsibilities].

Test: [*SELECT FROM:* Organizational process for tracking the use of software protected by quantity licenses; organization process for controlling/documenting the use of peer-to-peer file sharing technology; automated mechanisms implementing software license tracking; automated mechanisms implementing and controlling the use of peer-to-peer files sharing technology].

CM-10(1)	**SOFTWARE USAGE RESTRICTIONS** | *OPEN SOURCE SOFTWARE*

ASSESSMENT OBJECTIVE:

Determine if the organization:

CM-10(1)[1]	*defines restrictions on the use of open source software; and*
CM-10(1)[2]	*establishes organization-defined restrictions on the use of open source software.*

POTENTIAL ASSESSMENT METHODS AND OBJECTS:

Examine: [*SELECT FROM:* Configuration management policy; procedures addressing restrictions on use of open source software; configuration management plan; security plan; other relevant documents or records].

Interview: [*SELECT FROM:* Organizational personnel with responsibilities for establishing and enforcing restrictions on use of open source software; organizational personnel with information security responsibilities; system/network administrators].

Test: [*SELECT FROM:* Organizational process for restricting the use of open source software; automated mechanisms implementing restrictions on the use of open source software].

CM-11	**USER-INSTALLED SOFTWARE**	

ASSESSMENT OBJECTIVE:

Determine if the organization:

CM-11(a)	CM-11(a)[1]	*defines policies to govern the installation of software by users;*
	CM-11(a)[2]	*establishes organization-defined policies governing the installation of software by users;*
CM-11(b)	CM-11(b)[1]	*defines methods to enforce software installation policies;*
	CM-11(b)[2]	*enforces software installation policies through organization-defined methods;*
CM-11(c)	CM-11(c)[1]	*defines frequency to monitor policy compliance; and*
	CM-11(c)[2]	*monitors policy compliance at organization-defined frequency.*

Special Publication 800-53A
Revision 4

Assessing Security and Privacy Controls in Federal Information Systems
and Organizations — *Building Effective Assessment Plans*

	POTENTIAL ASSESSMENT METHODS AND OBJECTS: **Examine**: [*SELECT FROM:* Configuration management policy; procedures addressing user installed software; configuration management plan; security plan; information system design documentation; information system configuration settings and associated documentation; list of rules governing user installed software; information system monitoring records; information system audit records; other relevant documents or records; continuous monitoring strategy]. **Interview**: [*SELECT FROM:* Organizational personnel with responsibilities for governing user-installed software; organizational personnel operating, using, and/or maintaining the information system; organizational personnel monitoring compliance with user-installed software policy; organizational personnel with information security responsibilities; system/network administrators]. **Test**: [*SELECT FROM:* Organizational processes governing user-installed software on the information system; automated mechanisms enforcing rules/methods for governing the installation of software by users; automated mechanisms monitoring policy compliance].

CM-11(1)	USER-INSTALLED SOFTWARE | *ALERTS FOR UNAUTHORIZED INSTALLATIONS*
	ASSESSMENT OBJECTIVE: *Determine if:*

CM-11(1)[1]	*the organization defines personnel or roles to be alerted when the unauthorized installation of software is detected; and*
CM-11(1)[2]	*the information system alerts organization-defined personnel or roles when the unauthorized installation of software is detected.*

POTENTIAL ASSESSMENT METHODS AND OBJECTS: **Examine**: [*SELECT FROM:* Configuration management policy; procedures addressing user installed software; configuration management plan; security plan; information system design documentation; information system configuration settings and associated documentation; information system audit records; other relevant documents or records]. **Interview**: [*SELECT FROM:* Organizational personnel with responsibilities for governing user-installed software; organizational personnel operating, using, and/or maintaining the information system; organizational personnel with information security responsibilities; system/network administrators; system developers]. **Test**: [*SELECT FROM:* Organizational processes governing user-installed software on the information system; automated mechanisms for alerting personnel/roles when unauthorized installation of software is detected].

CM-11(2)	USER-INSTALLED SOFTWARE | *PROHIBIT INSTALLATION WITHOUT PRIVILEGED STATUS*
	ASSESSMENT OBJECTIVE: *Determine if the information system prohibits user installation of software without explicit privileged status.*

POTENTIAL ASSESSMENT METHODS AND OBJECTS: **Examine**: [*SELECT FROM:* Configuration management policy; procedures addressing user installed software; configuration management plan; security plan; information system design documentation; information system configuration settings and associated documentation; alerts/notifications of unauthorized software installations; information system audit records; other relevant documents or records]. **Interview**: [*SELECT FROM:* Organizational personnel with responsibilities for governing user-installed software; organizational personnel operating, using, and/or maintaining the information system]. **Test**: [*SELECT FROM:* Organizational processes governing user-installed software on the information system; automated mechanisms for prohibiting installation of software without privileged status (e.g., access controls)].

Special Publication 800-53A
Revision 4

Assessing Security and Privacy Controls in Federal Information Systems
and Organizations — *Building Effective Assessment Plans*

FAMILY: CONTINGENCY PLANNING

CP-1	CONTINGENCY PLANNING POLICY AND PROCEDURES		
	ASSESSMENT OBJECTIVE: *Determine if:*		
	CP-1(a)(1)	CP-1(a)(1)[1]	*the organization develops and documents a contingency planning policy that addresses:*
			CP-1(a)(1)[1][a]	*purpose;*
			CP-1(a)(1)[1][b]	*scope;*
			CP-1(a)(1)[1][c]	*roles;*
			CP-1(a)(1)[1][d]	*responsibilities;*
			CP-1(a)(1)[1][e]	*management commitment;*
			CP-1(a)(1)[1][f]	*coordination among organizational entities;*
			CP-1(a)(1)[1][g]	*compliance;*
		CP-1(a)(1)[2]	*the organization defines personnel or roles to whom the contingency planning policy is to be disseminated;*
		CP-1(a)(1)[3]	*the organization disseminates the contingency planning policy to organization-defined personnel or roles;*
	CP-1(a)(2)	CP-1(a)(2)[1]	*the organization develops and documents procedures to facilitate the implementation of the contingency planning policy and associated contingency planning controls;*
		CP-1(a)(2)[2]	*the organization defines personnel or roles to whom the procedures are to be disseminated;*
		CP-1(a)(2)[3]	*the organization disseminates the procedures to organization-defined personnel or roles;*
	CP-1(b)(1)	CP-1(b)(1)[1]	*the organization defines the frequency to review and update the current contingency planning policy;*
		CP-1(b)(1)[2]	*the organization reviews and updates the current contingency planning with the organization-defined frequency;*
	CP-1(b)(2)	CP-1(b)(2)[1]	*the organization defines the frequency to review and update the current contingency planning procedures; and*
		CP-1(b)(2)[2]	*the organization reviews and updates the current contingency planning procedures with the organization-defined frequency.*
	POTENTIAL ASSESSMENT METHODS AND OBJECTS: **Examine:** [*SELECT FROM:* Contingency planning policy and procedures; other relevant documents or records]. **Interview:** [*SELECT FROM:* Organizational personnel with contingency planning responsibilities; organizational personnel with information security responsibilities].		

Special Publication 800-53A
Revision 4

Assessing Security and Privacy Controls in Federal Information Systems
and Organizations — *Building Effective Assessment Plans*

CP-2	CONTINGENCY PLAN		
	ASSESSMENT OBJECTIVE: *Determine if the organization:*		
	CP-2(a)	*develops and documents a contingency plan for the information system that:*	
		CP-2(a)(1)	*identifies essential missions and business functions and associated contingency requirements;*
		CP-2(a)(2)	CP-2(a)(2)[1] *provides recovery objectives;*
			CP-2(a)(2)[2] *provides restoration priorities;*
			CP-2(a)(2)[3] *provides metrics;*
		CP-2(a)(3)	CP-2(a)(3)[1] *addresses contingency roles;*
			CP-2(a)(3)[2] *addresses contingency responsibilities;*
			CP-2(a)(3)[3] *addresses assigned individuals with contact information;*
		CP-2(a)(4)	*addresses maintaining essential missions and business functions despite an information system disruption, compromise, or failure;*
		CP-2(a)(5)	*addresses eventual, full information system restoration without deterioration of the security safeguards originally planned and implemented;*
		CP-2(a)(6)	CP-2(a)(6)[1] *defines personnel or roles to review and approve the contingency plan for the information system;*
			CP-2(a)(6)[2] *is reviewed and approved by organization-defined personnel or roles;*
	CP-2(b)	CP-2(b)[1]	*defines key contingency personnel (identified by name and/or by role) and organizational elements to whom copies of the contingency plan are to be distributed;*
		CP-2(b)[2]	*distributes copies of the contingency plan to organization-defined key contingency personnel and organizational elements;*
	CP-2(c)	*coordinates contingency planning activities with incident handling activities;*	
	CP-2(d)	CP-2(d)[1]	*defines a frequency to review the contingency plan for the information system;*
		CP-2(d)[2]	*reviews the contingency plan with the organization-defined frequency;*
	CP-2(e)	*updates the contingency plan to address:*	
		CP-2(e)[1]	*changes to the organization, information system, or environment of operation;*
		CP-2(e)[2]	*problems encountered during plan implementation, execution, and testing;*
	CP-2(f)	CP-2(f)[1]	*defines key contingency personnel (identified by name and/or by role) and organizational elements to whom contingency plan changes are to be communicated;*

Special Publication 800-53A
Revision 4

Assessing Security and Privacy Controls in Federal Information Systems
and Organizations — *Building Effective Assessment Plans*

	CP-2(f)[2]	*communicates contingency plan changes to organization-defined key contingency personnel and organizational elements; and*
	CP-2(g)	*protects the contingency plan from unauthorized disclosure and modification.*

POTENTIAL ASSESSMENT METHODS AND OBJECTS:

Examine: [*SELECT FROM:* Contingency planning policy; procedures addressing contingency operations for the information system; contingency plan; security plan; evidence of contingency plan reviews and updates; other relevant documents or records].

Interview: [*SELECT FROM:* Organizational personnel with contingency planning and plan implementation responsibilities; organizational personnel with incident handling responsibilities; organizational personnel with information security responsibilities].

Test: [*SELECT FROM:* Organizational processes for contingency plan development, review, update, and protection; automated mechanisms for developing, reviewing, updating and/or protecting the contingency plan].

CP-2(1)	**CONTINGENCY PLAN** | *COORDINATE WITH RELATED PLANS*

ASSESSMENT OBJECTIVE:

Determine if the organization coordinates contingency plan development with organizational elements responsible for related plans.

POTENTIAL ASSESSMENT METHODS AND OBJECTS:

Examine: [*SELECT FROM:* Contingency planning policy; procedures addressing contingency operations for the information system; contingency plan; business contingency plans; disaster recovery plans; continuity of operations plans; crisis communications plans; critical infrastructure plans; cyber incident response plan; insider threat implementation plans; occupant emergency plans; security plan; other relevant documents or records].

Interview: [*SELECT FROM:* Organizational personnel with contingency planning and plan implementation responsibilities; organizational personnel with information security responsibilities; personnel with responsibility for related plans].

CP-2(2)	**CONTINGENCY PLAN** | *CAPACITY PLANNING*

ASSESSMENT OBJECTIVE:

Determine if the organization conducts capacity planning so that necessary capacity exists during contingency operations for:

	CP-2(2)[1]	*information processing;*
	CP-2(2)[2]	*telecommunications; and*
	CP-2(2)[3]	*environmental support.*

POTENTIAL ASSESSMENT METHODS AND OBJECTS:

Examine: [*SELECT FROM:* Contingency planning policy; procedures addressing contingency operations for the information system; contingency plan; capacity planning documents; other relevant documents or records].

Interview: [*SELECT FROM:* Organizational personnel with contingency planning and plan implementation responsibilities; organizational personnel with information security responsibilities].

CP-2(3)	**CONTINGENCY PLAN** | *RESUME ESSENTIAL MISSIONS/BUSINESS FUNCTIONS*

ASSESSMENT OBJECTIVE:

Determine if the organization:

	CP-2(3)[1]	*defines the time period to plan for the resumption of essential missions and business functions as a result of contingency plan activation; and*

Special Publication 800-53A
Revision 4

Assessing Security and Privacy Controls in Federal Information Systems
and Organizations — *Building Effective Assessment Plans*

	CP-2(3)[2]	*plans for the resumption of essential missions and business functions within organization-defined time period of contingency plan activation.*

POTENTIAL ASSESSMENT METHODS AND OBJECTS:

Examine: [*SELECT FROM:* Contingency planning policy; procedures addressing contingency operations for the information system; contingency plan; security plan; business impact assessment; other related plans; other relevant documents or records].

Interview: [*SELECT FROM:* Organizational personnel with contingency planning and plan implementation responsibilities; organizational personnel with information security responsibilities].

Test: [*SELECT FROM:* Organizational processes for resumption of missions and business functions].

CP-2(4)	CONTINGENCY PLAN	*RESUME ALL MISSIONS / BUSINESS FUNCTIONS*

ASSESSMENT OBJECTIVE:

Determine if the organization:

	CP-2(4)[1]	*defines the time period to plan for the resumption of all missions and business functions as a result of contingency plan activation; and*
	CP-2(4)[2]	*plans for the resumption of all missions and business functions within organization-defined time period of contingency plan activation.*

POTENTIAL ASSESSMENT METHODS AND OBJECTS:

Examine: [*SELECT FROM:* Contingency planning policy; procedures addressing contingency operations for the information system; contingency plan; security plan; business impact assessment; other related plans; other relevant documents or records].

Interview: [*SELECT FROM:* Organizational personnel with contingency planning and plan implementation responsibilities; organizational personnel with information security responsibilities].

Test: [*SELECT FROM:* Organizational processes for resumption of missions and business functions].

CP-2(5)	CONTINGENCY PLAN	*CONTINUE ESSENTIAL MISSIONS / BUSINESS FUNCTIONS*

ASSESSMENT OBJECTIVE:

Determine if the organization:

	CP-2(5)[1]	*plans for the continuance of essential missions and business functions with little or no loss of operational continuity; and*
	CP-2(5)[2]	*sustains that operational continuity until full information system restoration at primary processing and/or storage sites.*

POTENTIAL ASSESSMENT METHODS AND OBJECTS:

Examine: [*SELECT FROM:* Contingency planning policy; procedures addressing contingency operations for the information system; contingency plan; business impact assessment; primary processing site agreements; primary storage site agreements; alternate processing site agreements; alternate storage site agreements; contingency plan test documentation; contingency plan test results; other relevant documents or records].

Interview: [*SELECT FROM:* Organizational personnel with contingency planning and plan implementation responsibilities; organizational personnel with information security responsibilities].

Test: [*SELECT FROM:* Organizational processes for continuing missions and business functions].

CP-2(6)	CONTINGENCY PLAN	*ALTERNATE PROCESSING / STORAGE SITE*

ASSESSMENT OBJECTIVE:

Determine if the organization:

Special Publication 800-53A
Revision 4

Assessing Security and Privacy Controls in Federal Information Systems
and Organizations — *Building Effective Assessment Plans*

	CP-2(6)[1]	*plans for the transfer of essential missions and business functions to alternate processing and/or storage sites with little or no loss of operational continuity; and*
	CP-2(6)[2]	*sustains that operational continuity through information system restoration to primary processing and/or storage sites.*

POTENTIAL ASSESSMENT METHODS AND OBJECTS:

Examine: [*SELECT FROM:* Contingency planning policy; procedures addressing contingency operations for the information system; contingency plan; business impact assessment; alternate processing site agreements; alternate storage site agreements; contingency plan testing documentation; contingency plan test results; other relevant documents or records].

Interview: [*SELECT FROM:* Organizational personnel with contingency planning and plan implementation responsibilities; organizational personnel with information security responsibilities].

Test: [*SELECT FROM:* Organizational processes for transfer of essential missions and business functions to alternate processing/storage sites].

CP-2(7)	**CONTINGENCY PLAN** | *COORDINATE WITH EXTERNAL SERVICE PROVIDERS*

ASSESSMENT OBJECTIVE:

Determine if the organization coordinates its contingency plan with the contingency plans of external service provides to ensure contingency requirements can be satisfied.

POTENTIAL ASSESSMENT METHODS AND OBJECTS:

Examine: [*SELECT FROM:* Contingency planning policy; procedures addressing contingency operations for the information system; contingency plan; contingency plans of external; service providers; service level agreements; security plan; contingency plan requirements; other relevant documents or records].

Interview: [*SELECT FROM:* Organizational personnel with contingency planning and plan implementation responsibilities; external service providers; organizational personnel with information security responsibilities].

CP-2(8)	**CONTINGENCY PLAN** | *IDENTIFY CRITICAL ASSETS*

ASSESSMENT OBJECTIVE:

Determine if the organization identifies critical information system assets supporting essential missions and business functions.

POTENTIAL ASSESSMENT METHODS AND OBJECTS:

Examine: [*SELECT FROM:* Contingency planning policy; procedures addressing contingency operations for the information system; contingency plan; business impact assessment; security plan; other relevant documents or records].

Interview: [*SELECT FROM:* Organizational personnel with contingency planning and plan implementation responsibilities; organizational personnel with information security responsibilities].

CP-3	**CONTINGENCY TRAINING**	

ASSESSMENT OBJECTIVE:
Determine if the organization:

CP-3(a)	CP-3(a)[1]	*defines a time period within which contingency training is to be provided to information system users assuming a contingency role or responsibility;*
	CP-3(a)[2]	*provides contingency training to information system users consistent with assigned roles and responsibilities within the organization-defined time period of assuming a contingency role or responsibility;*

Special Publication 800-53A
Revision 4

Assessing Security and Privacy Controls in Federal Information Systems
and Organizations — *Building Effective Assessment Plans*

	CP-3(b)		*provides contingency training to information system users consistent with assigned roles and responsibilities when required by information system changes;*
	CP-3(c)	CP-3(c)[1]	*defines the frequency for contingency training thereafter; and*
		CP-3(c)[2]	*provides contingency training to information system users consistent with assigned roles and responsibilities with the organization-defined frequency thereafter.*

POTENTIAL ASSESSMENT METHODS AND OBJECTS:

Examine: [*SELECT FROM:* Contingency planning policy; procedures addressing contingency training; contingency plan; contingency training curriculum; contingency training material; security plan; contingency training records; other relevant documents or records].

Interview: [*SELECT FROM:* Organizational personnel with contingency planning, plan implementation, and training responsibilities; organizational personnel with information security responsibilities].

Test: [*SELECT FROM:* Organizational processes for contingency training].

CP-3(1)	CONTINGENCY TRAINING │ *SIMULATED EVENTS*

ASSESSMENT OBJECTIVE:

Determine if the organization incorporates simulated events into contingency training to facilitate effective response by personnel in crisis situations.

POTENTIAL ASSESSMENT METHODS AND OBJECTS:

Examine: [*SELECT FROM:* Contingency planning policy; procedures addressing contingency training; contingency plan; contingency training curriculum; contingency training material; other relevant documents or records].

Interview: [*SELECT FROM:* Organizational personnel with contingency planning, plan implementation, and training responsibilities; organizational personnel with information security responsibilities].

Test: [*SELECT FROM:* Organizational processes for contingency training; automated mechanisms for simulating contingency events].

CP-3(2)	CONTINGENCY TRAINING │ *AUTOMATED TRAINING ENVIRONMENTS*

ASSESSMENT OBJECTIVE:

Determine if the organization employs automated mechanisms to provide a more thorough and realistic contingency training environment.

POTENTIAL ASSESSMENT METHODS AND OBJECTS:

Examine: [*SELECT FROM:* Contingency planning policy; procedures addressing contingency training; contingency plan; contingency training curriculum; contingency training material; other relevant documents or records].

Interview: [*SELECT FROM:* Organizational personnel with contingency planning, plan implementation, and training responsibilities; organizational personnel with information security responsibilities].

Test: [*SELECT FROM:* Organizational processes for contingency training; automated mechanisms for providing contingency training environments].

CP-4	CONTINGENCY PLAN TESTING		
	ASSESSMENT OBJECTIVE: *Determine if the organization:*		
	CP-4(a)	CP-4(a)[1]	*defines tests to determine the effectiveness of the contingency plan and the organizational readiness to execute the plan;*
		CP-4(a)[2]	*defines a frequency to test the contingency plan for the information system;*

Special Publication 800-53A
Revision 4

Assessing Security and Privacy Controls in Federal Information Systems
and Organizations — Building Effective Assessment Plans

		CP-4(a)[3]	*tests the contingency plan for the information system with the organization-defined frequency, using organization-defined tests to determine the effectiveness of the plan and the organizational readiness to execute the plan;*
	CP-4(b)		*reviews the contingency plan test results; and*
	CP-4(c)		*initiates corrective actions, if needed.*

POTENTIAL ASSESSMENT METHODS AND OBJECTS:

Examine: [*SELECT FROM:* Contingency planning policy; procedures addressing contingency plan testing; contingency plan; security plan; contingency plan test documentation; contingency plan test results; other relevant documents or records].

Interview: [*SELECT FROM:* Organizational personnel with responsibilities for contingency plan testing, reviewing or responding to contingency plan tests; organizational personnel with information security responsibilities].

Test: [*SELECT FROM:* Organizational processes for contingency plan testing; automated mechanisms supporting the contingency plan and/or contingency plan testing].

CP-4(1)	**CONTINGENCY PLAN TESTING	*COORDINATE WITH RELATED PLANS***

ASSESSMENT OBJECTIVE:

Determine if the organization coordinates contingency plan testing with organizational elements responsible for related plans.

POTENTIAL ASSESSMENT METHODS AND OBJECTS:

Examine: [*SELECT FROM:* Contingency planning policy; incident response policy; procedures addressing contingency plan testing; contingency plan testing documentation; contingency plan; business continuity plans; disaster recovery plans; continuity of operations plans; crisis communications plans; critical infrastructure plans; cyber incident response plans; occupant emergency plans; security plan; other relevant documents or records].

Interview: [*SELECT FROM:* Organizational personnel with contingency plan testing responsibilities; organizational personnel; personnel with responsibilities for related plans; organizational personnel with information security responsibilities].

CP-4(2)	**CONTINGENCY PLAN TESTING	*ALTERNATE PROCESSING SITE***

ASSESSMENT OBJECTIVE:

Determine if the organization tests the contingency plan at the alternate processing site to:

CP-4(2)(a)	*familiarize contingency personnel with the facility and available resources; and*
CP-4(2)(b)	*evaluate the capabilities of the alternate processing site to support contingency operations.*

POTENTIAL ASSESSMENT METHODS AND OBJECTS:

Examine: [*SELECT FROM:* Contingency planning policy; procedures addressing contingency plan testing; contingency plan; contingency plan test documentation; contingency plan test results; alternate processing site agreements; service-level agreements; other relevant documents or records].

Interview: [*SELECT FROM:* Organizational personnel with contingency planning and plan implementation responsibilities; organizational personnel with information security responsibilities].

Test: [*SELECT FROM:* Organizational processes for contingency plan testing; automated mechanisms supporting the contingency plan and/or contingency plan testing].

Special Publication 800-53A
Revision 4

Assessing Security and Privacy Controls in Federal Information Systems
and Organizations — *Building Effective Assessment Plans*

CP-4(3)	CONTINGENCY PLAN TESTING | *AUTOMATED TESTING*
	ASSESSMENT OBJECTIVE: *Determine if the organization employs automated mechanisms to more thoroughly and effectively test the contingency plan.*
	POTENTIAL ASSESSMENT METHODS AND OBJECTS: **Examine**: [*SELECT FROM:* Contingency planning policy; procedures addressing contingency plan testing; contingency plan; automated mechanisms supporting contingency plan testing; contingency plan test documentation; contingency plan test results; other relevant documents or records]. **Interview**: [*SELECT FROM:* Organizational personnel with contingency plan testing responsibilities; organizational personnel with information security responsibilities]. **Test**: [*SELECT FROM:* Organizational processes for contingency plan testing; automated mechanisms supporting contingency plan testing].

CP-4(4)	CONTINGENCY PLAN TESTING | *FULL RECOVERY / RECONSTITUTION*
	ASSESSMENT OBJECTIVE: *Determine if the organization:*
	CP-4(4)[1] *includes a full recovery of the information system to a known state as part of contingency plan testing; and*
	CP-4(4)[2] *includes a full reconstitution of the information system to a known state as part of contingency plan testing.*
	POTENTIAL ASSESSMENT METHODS AND OBJECTS: **Examine**: [*SELECT FROM:* Contingency planning policy; procedures addressing information system recovery and reconstitution; contingency plan; contingency plan test documentation; contingency plan test results; other relevant documents or records]. **Interview**: [*SELECT FROM:* Organizational personnel with contingency plan testing responsibilities; organizational personnel with information system recovery and reconstitution responsibilities; organizational personnel with information security responsibilities]. **Test**: [*SELECT FROM:* Organizational processes for contingency plan testing; automated mechanisms supporting contingency plan testing; automated mechanisms supporting recovery and reconstitution of the information system].

CP-5	CONTINGENCY PLAN UPDATE
[Withdrawn: Incorporated into CP-2].	

CP-6	ALTERNATE STORAGE SITE
	ASSESSMENT OBJECTIVE: *Determine if the organization:*
	CP-6[1] *establishes an alternate storage site including necessary agreements to permit the storage and retrieval of information system backup information; and*
	CP-6[2] *ensures that the alternate storage site provides information security safeguards equivalent to that of the primary site.*

Special Publication 800-53A
Revision 4

Assessing Security and Privacy Controls in Federal Information Systems
and Organizations — *Building Effective Assessment Plans*

POTENTIAL ASSESSMENT METHODS AND OBJECTS:

Examine: [*SELECT FROM:* Contingency planning policy; procedures addressing alternate storage sites; contingency plan; alternate storage site agreements; primary storage site agreements; other relevant documents or records].

Interview: [*SELECT FROM:* Organizational personnel with contingency plan alternate storage site responsibilities; organizational personnel with information system recovery responsibilities; organizational personnel with information security responsibilities].

Test: [*SELECT FROM:* Organizational processes for storing and retrieving information system backup information at the alternate storage site; automated mechanisms supporting and/or implementing storage and retrieval of information system backup information at the alternate storage site].

CP-6(1)	ALTERNATE STORAGE SITE | *SEPARATION FROM PRIMARY SITE*

ASSESSMENT OBJECTIVE:

Determine if the organization identifies an alternate storage site that is separated from the primary storage site to reduce susceptibility to the same threats.

POTENTIAL ASSESSMENT METHODS AND OBJECTS:

Examine: [*SELECT FROM:* Contingency planning policy; procedures addressing alternate storage sites; contingency plan; alternate storage site; alternate storage site agreements; primary storage site agreements; other relevant documents or records].

Interview: [*SELECT FROM:* Organizational personnel with contingency plan alternate storage site responsibilities; organizational personnel with information system recovery responsibilities; organizational personnel with information security responsibilities].

CP-6(2)	ALTERNATE STORAGE SITE | *RECOVERY TIME / POINT OBJECTIVES*

ASSESSMENT OBJECTIVE:

Determine if the organization configures the alternate storage site to facilitate recovery operations in accordance with recovery time objectives and recovery point objectives (as specified in the information system contingency plan).

POTENTIAL ASSESSMENT METHODS AND OBJECTS:

Examine: [*SELECT FROM:* Contingency planning policy; procedures addressing alternate storage sites; contingency plan; alternate storage site; alternate storage site agreements; alternate storage site configurations; other relevant documents or records].

Interview: [*SELECT FROM:* Organizational personnel with contingency plan testing responsibilities; organizational personnel with responsibilities for testing related plans; organizational personnel with information security responsibilities].

Test: [*SELECT FROM:* Organizational processes for contingency plan testing; automated mechanisms supporting recovery time/point objectives].

CP-6(3)	ALTERNATE STORAGE SITE | *ACCESSIBILITY*

ASSESSMENT OBJECTIVE:
Determine if the organization:

CP-6(3)[1]	*identifies potential accessibility problems to the alternate storage site in the event of an area-wide disruption or disaster; and*
CP-6(3)[2]	*outlines explicit mitigation actions for such potential accessibility problems to the alternate storage site in the event of an area-wide disruption or disaster.*

Special Publication 800-53A
Revision 4

Assessing Security and Privacy Controls in Federal Information Systems
and Organizations — *Building Effective Assessment Plans*

<table>
<tr><td colspan="3">

POTENTIAL ASSESSMENT METHODS AND OBJECTS:

Examine: [*SELECT FROM:* Contingency planning policy; procedures addressing alternate storage sites; contingency plan; alternate storage site; list of potential accessibility problems to alternate storage site; mitigation actions for accessibility problems to alternate storage site; organizational risk assessments; other relevant documents or records].

Interview: [*SELECT FROM:* Organizational personnel with contingency plan alternate storage site responsibilities; organizational personnel with information system recovery responsibilities; organizational personnel with information security responsibilities].
</td></tr>
</table>

CP-7	ALTERNATE PROCESSING SITE		
	ASSESSMENT OBJECTIVE: *Determine if the organization:*		
	CP-7(a)	**CP-7(a)[1]**	*defines information system operations requiring an alternate processing site to be established to permit the transfer and resumption of such operations;*
		CP-7(a)[2]	*defines the time period consistent with recovery time objectives and recovery point objectives (as specified in the information system contingency plan) for transfer/resumption of organization-defined information system operations for essential missions/business functions;*
		CP-7(a)[3]	*establishes an alternate processing site including necessary agreements to permit the transfer and resumption of organization-defined information system operations for essential missions/business functions, within the organization-defined time period, when the primary processing capabilities are unavailable;*
	CP-7(b)	**CP-7(b)[1]**	*ensures that equipment and supplies required to transfer and resume operations are available at the alternate processing site; or*
		CP-7(b)[2]	*ensures that contracts are in place to support delivery to the site within the organization-defined time period for transfer/resumption; and*
	CP-7(c)	*ensures that the alternate processing site provides information security safeguards equivalent to those of the primary site.*	

POTENTIAL ASSESSMENT METHODS AND OBJECTS:

Examine: [*SELECT FROM:* Contingency planning policy; procedures addressing alternate processing sites; contingency plan; alternate processing site agreements; primary processing site agreements; spare equipment and supplies inventory at alternate processing site; equipment and supply contracts; service-level agreements; other relevant documents or records].

Interview: [*SELECT FROM:* Organizational personnel with responsibilities for contingency planning and/or alternate site arrangements; organizational personnel with information security responsibilities].

Test: [*SELECT FROM:* Organizational processes for recovery at the alternate site; automated mechanisms supporting and/or implementing recovery at the alternate processing site].

CP-7(1)	ALTERNATE PROCESSING SITE | *SEPARATION FROM PRIMARY SITE*
	ASSESSMENT OBJECTIVE: *Determine if the organization identifies an alternate processing site that is separated from the primary storage site to reduce susceptibility to the same threats.*

Special Publication 800-53A
Revision 4

Assessing Security and Privacy Controls in Federal Information Systems
and Organizations — *Building Effective Assessment Plans*

	POTENTIAL ASSESSMENT METHODS AND OBJECTS: **Examine**: [*SELECT FROM:* Contingency planning policy; procedures addressing alternate processing sites; contingency plan; alternate processing site; alternate processing site agreements; primary processing site agreements; other relevant documents or records]. **Interview**: [*SELECT FROM:* Organizational personnel with contingency plan alternate processing site responsibilities; organizational personnel with information system recovery responsibilities; organizational personnel with information security responsibilities].

CP-7(2)	**ALTERNATE PROCESSING SITE** | *ACCESSIBILITY*
	ASSESSMENT OBJECTIVE: *Determine if the organization:*

	CP-7(2)[1]	*identifies potential accessibility problems to the alternate processing site in the event of an area-wide disruption or disaster; and*
	CP-7(2)[2]	*outlines explicit mitigation actions for such potential accessibility problems to the alternate processing site in the event of an area-wide disruption or disaster.*

	POTENTIAL ASSESSMENT METHODS AND OBJECTS: **Examine**: [*SELECT FROM:* Contingency planning policy; procedures addressing alternate processing sites; contingency plan; alternate processing site; alternate processing site agreements; primary processing site agreements; other relevant documents or records]. **Interview**: [*SELECT FROM:* Organizational personnel with contingency plan alternate processing site responsibilities; organizational personnel with information system recovery responsibilities; organizational personnel with information security responsibilities].

CP-7(3)	**ALTERNATE PROCESSING SITE** | *PRIORITY OF SERVICE*
	ASSESSMENT OBJECTIVE: *Determine if the organization develops alternate processing site agreements that contain priority-of-service provisions in accordance with organizational availability requirements (including recovery time objectives as specified in the information system contingency plan).*
	POTENTIAL ASSESSMENT METHODS AND OBJECTS: **Examine**: [*SELECT FROM:* Contingency planning policy; procedures addressing alternate processing sites; contingency plan; alternate processing site agreements; service-level agreements; other relevant documents or records]. **Interview**: [*SELECT FROM:* Organizational personnel with contingency plan alternate processing site responsibilities; organizational personnel with information system recovery responsibilities; organizational personnel with information security responsibilities; organizational personnel with responsibility for acquisitions/contractual agreements].

CP-7(4)	**ALTERNATE PROCESSING SITE** | *PREPARATION FOR USE*
	ASSESSMENT OBJECTIVE: *Determine if the organization prepares the alternate processing site so that the site is ready to be used as the operational site supporting essential missions and business functions.*

Special Publication 800-53A
Revision 4

Assessing Security and Privacy Controls in Federal Information Systems
and Organizations — *Building Effective Assessment Plans*

	POTENTIAL ASSESSMENT METHODS AND OBJECTS: **Examine**: [*SELECT FROM:* Contingency planning policy; procedures addressing alternate processing sites; contingency plan; alternate processing site; alternate processing site agreements; alternate processing site configurations; other relevant documents or records]. **Interview**: [*SELECT FROM:* Organizational personnel with contingency plan alternate processing site responsibilities; organizational personnel with information system recovery responsibilities; organizational personnel with information security responsibilities]. **Test**: [*SELECT FROM:* Automated mechanisms supporting and/or implementing recovery at the alternate processing site].

CP-7(5)	ALTERNATE PROCESSING SITE | *EQUIVALENT INFORMATION SECURITY SAFEGUARDS*
[Withdrawn: Incorporated into CP-7].	

CP-7(6)	ALTERNATE PROCESSING SITE | *INABILITY TO RETURN TO PRIMARY SITE*
	ASSESSMENT OBJECTIVE: *Determine if the organization plans and prepares for circumstances that preclude returning to the primary processing site.*
	POTENTIAL ASSESSMENT METHODS AND OBJECTS: **Examine**: [*SELECT FROM:* Contingency planning policy; procedures addressing alternate processing sites; contingency plan; alternate processing site; alternate processing site agreements; alternate processing site configurations; other relevant documents or records]. **Interview**: [*SELECT FROM:* Organizational personnel with information system reconstitution responsibilities; organizational personnel with information security responsibilities].

CP-8	TELECOMMUNICATIONS SERVICES	
	ASSESSMENT OBJECTIVE: *Determine if the organization:*	
	CP-8[1]	*defines information system operations requiring alternate telecommunications services to be established to permit the resumption of such operations;*
	CP-8[2]	*defines the time period to permit resumption of organization-defined information system operations for essential missions and business functions; and*
	CP-8[3]	*establishes alternate telecommunications services including necessary agreements to permit the resumption of organization-defined information system operations for essential missions and business functions, within the organization-defined time period, when the primary telecommunications capabilities are unavailable at either the primary or alternate processing or storage sites.*
	POTENTIAL ASSESSMENT METHODS AND OBJECTS: **Examine**: [*SELECT FROM:* Contingency planning policy; procedures addressing alternate telecommunications services; contingency plan; primary and alternate telecommunications service agreements; other relevant documents or records]. **Interview**: [*SELECT FROM:* Organizational personnel with contingency plan telecommunications responsibilities; organizational personnel with information system recovery responsibilities; organizational personnel with information security responsibilities; organizational personnel with responsibility for acquisitions/contractual agreements]. **Test**: [*SELECT FROM:* Automated mechanisms supporting telecommunications].	

Special Publication 800-53A
Revision 4

Assessing Security and Privacy Controls in Federal Information Systems
and Organizations — *Building Effective Assessment Plans*

CP-8(1)	TELECOMMUNICATIONS SERVICES | *PRIORITY OF SERVICE PROVISIONS*	
	ASSESSMENT OBJECTIVE: *Determine if the organization:*	
	CP-8(1)[1]	*develops primary and alternate telecommunications service agreements that contain priority-of-service provisions in accordance with organizational availability requirements (including recovery time objectives as specified in the information system contingency plan); and*
	CP-8(1)[2]	*requests Telecommunications Service Priority for all telecommunications services used for national security emergency preparedness in the event that the primary and/or alternate telecommunications services are provided by a common carrier.*
	POTENTIAL ASSESSMENT METHODS AND OBJECTS: **Examine**: [*SELECT FROM:* Contingency planning policy; procedures addressing primary and alternate telecommunications services; contingency plan; primary and alternate telecommunications service agreements; Telecommunications Service Priority documentation; other relevant documents or records]. **Interview**: [*SELECT FROM:* Organizational personnel with contingency plan telecommunications responsibilities; organizational personnel with information system recovery responsibilities; organizational personnel with information security responsibilities; organizational personnel with responsibility for acquisitions/contractual agreements]. **Test**: [*SELECT FROM:* Automated mechanisms supporting telecommunications].	

CP-8(2)	TELECOMMUNICATIONS SERVICES | *SINGLE POINTS OF FAILURE*
	ASSESSMENT OBJECTIVE: *Determine if the organization obtains alternate telecommunications services to reduce the likelihood of sharing a single point of failure with primary telecommunications services.*
	POTENTIAL ASSESSMENT METHODS AND OBJECTS: **Examine**: [*SELECT FROM:* Contingency planning policy; procedures addressing primary and alternate telecommunications services; contingency plan; primary and alternate telecommunications service agreements; other relevant documents or records]. **Interview**: [*SELECT FROM:* Organizational personnel with contingency plan telecommunications responsibilities; organizational personnel with information system recovery responsibilities; primary and alternate telecommunications service providers; organizational personnel with information security responsibilities].

CP-8(3)	TELECOMMUNICATIONS SERVICES | *SEPARATION OF PRIMARY / ALTERNATE PROVIDERS*
	ASSESSMENT OBJECTIVE: *Determine if the organization obtains alternate telecommunications services from providers that are separated from primary service providers to reduce susceptibility to the same threats.*
	POTENTIAL ASSESSMENT METHODS AND OBJECTS: **Examine**: [*SELECT FROM:* Contingency planning policy; procedures addressing primary and alternate telecommunications services; contingency plan; primary and alternate telecommunications service agreements; alternate telecommunications service provider site; primary telecommunications service provider site; other relevant documents or records]. **Interview**: [*SELECT FROM:* Organizational personnel with contingency plan telecommunications responsibilities; organizational personnel with information system recovery responsibilities; primary and alternate telecommunications service providers; organizational personnel with information security responsibilities].

Special Publication 800-53A
Revision 4

Assessing Security and Privacy Controls in Federal Information Systems
and Organizations — *Building Effective Assessment Plans*

CP-8(4)	TELECOMMUNICATIONS SERVICES | *PROVIDER CONTINGENCY PLAN*		
	ASSESSMENT OBJECTIVE: *Determine if the organization:*		
	CP-8(4)(a)	CP-8(4)(a)[1]	*requires primary telecommunications service provider to have contingency plans;*
		CP-8(4)(a)[2]	*requires alternate telecommunications service provider(s) to have contingency plans;*
	CP-8(4)(b)	*reviews provider contingency plans to ensure that the plans meet organizational contingency requirements;*	
	CP-8(4)(c)	CP-8(4)(c)[1]	*defines the frequency to obtain evidence of contingency testing/training by providers; and*
		CP-8(4)(c)[2]	*obtains evidence of contingency testing/training by providers with the organization-defined frequency.*
	POTENTIAL ASSESSMENT METHODS AND OBJECTS: **Examine**: [*SELECT FROM:* Contingency planning policy; procedures addressing primary and alternate telecommunications services; contingency plan; provider contingency plans; evidence of contingency testing/training by providers; primary and alternate telecommunications service agreements; other relevant documents or records]. **Interview**: [*SELECT FROM:* Organizational personnel with contingency planning, plan implementation, and testing responsibilities; primary and alternate telecommunications service providers; organizational personnel with information security responsibilities; organizational personnel with responsibility for acquisitions/contractual agreements].		

CP-8(5)	TELECOMMUNICATIONS SERVICES | *ALTERNATE TELECOMMUNICATION SERVICE TESTING*	
	ASSESSMENT OBJECTIVE: *Determine if the organization:*	
	CP-8(5)[1]	*defines the frequency to test alternate telecommunication services; and*
	CP-8(5)[2]	*tests alternate telecommunication services with the organization-defined frequency.*
	POTENTIAL ASSESSMENT METHODS AND OBJECTS: **Examine**: [*SELECT FROM:* Contingency planning policy; procedures addressing alternate telecommunications services; contingency plan; evidence of testing alternate telecommunications services; alternate telecommunications service agreements; other relevant documents or records]. **Interview**: [*SELECT FROM:* Organizational personnel with contingency planning, plan implementation, and testing responsibilities; alternate telecommunications service providers; organizational personnel with information security responsibilities]. **Test**: [*SELECT FROM:* Automated mechanisms supporting testing alternate telecommunications services].	

CP-9	INFORMATION SYSTEM BACKUP		
	ASSESSMENT OBJECTIVE: *Determine if the organization:*		
	CP-9(a)	CP-9(a)[1]	*defines a frequency, consistent with recovery time objectives and recovery point objectives as specified in the information system contingency plan, to conduct backups of user-level information contained in the information system;*

Special Publication 800-53A
Revision 4

Assessing Security and Privacy Controls in Federal Information Systems
and Organizations — *Building Effective Assessment Plans*

		CP-9(a)[2]	*conducts backups of user-level information contained in the information system with the organization-defined frequency;*
	CP-9(b)	CP-9(b)[1]	*defines a frequency, consistent with recovery time objectives and recovery point objectives as specified in the information system contingency plan, to conduct backups of system-level information contained in the information system;*
		CP-9(b)[2]	*conducts backups of system-level information contained in the information system with the organization-defined frequency;*
	CP-9(c)	CP-9(c)[1]	*defines a frequency, consistent with recovery time objectives and recovery point objectives as specified in the information system contingency plan, to conduct backups of information system documentation including security-related documentation;*
		CP-9(c)[2]	*conducts backups of information system documentation, including security-related documentation, with the organization-defined frequency; and*
	CP-9(d)		*protects the confidentiality, integrity, and availability of backup information at storage locations.*

POTENTIAL ASSESSMENT METHODS AND OBJECTS:

Examine: [*SELECT FROM:* Contingency planning policy; procedures addressing information system backup; contingency plan; backup storage location(s); information system backup logs or records; other relevant documents or records].

Interview: [*SELECT FROM:* Organizational personnel with information system backup responsibilities; organizational personnel with information security responsibilities].

Test: [*SELECT FROM:* Organizational processes for conducting information system backups; automated mechanisms supporting and/or implementing information system backups].

CP-9(1)	INFORMATION SYSTEM BACKUP	*TESTING FOR RELIABILITY / INTEGRITY*

ASSESSMENT OBJECTIVE:

Determine if the organization:

CP-9(1)[1]	*defines the frequency to test backup information to verify media reliability and information integrity; and*
CP-9(1)[2]	*tests backup information with the organization-defined frequency to verify media reliability and information integrity.*

POTENTIAL ASSESSMENT METHODS AND OBJECTS:

Examine: [*SELECT FROM:* Contingency planning policy; procedures addressing information system backup; contingency plan; information system backup test results; contingency plan test documentation; contingency plan test results; other relevant documents or records].

Interview: [*SELECT FROM:* Organizational personnel with information system backup responsibilities; organizational personnel with information security responsibilities].

Test: [*SELECT FROM:* Organizational processes for conducting information system backups; automated mechanisms supporting and/or implementing information system backups].

CP-9(2)	INFORMATION SYSTEM BACKUP	*TEST RESTORATION USING SAMPLING*

ASSESSMENT OBJECTIVE:

Determine if the organization uses a sample of backup information in the restoration of selected information system functions as part of contingency plan testing.

Special Publication 800-53A
Revision 4

Assessing Security and Privacy Controls in Federal Information Systems
and Organizations — *Building Effective Assessment Plans*

POTENTIAL ASSESSMENT METHODS AND OBJECTS:

Examine: [*SELECT FROM:* Contingency planning policy; procedures addressing information system backup; contingency plan; information system backup test results; contingency plan test documentation; contingency plan test results; other relevant documents or records].

Interview: [*SELECT FROM:* Organizational personnel with information system backup responsibilities; organizational personnel with contingency planning/contingency plan testing responsibilities; organizational personnel with information security responsibilities].

Test: [*SELECT FROM:* Organizational processes for conducting information system backups; automated mechanisms supporting and/or implementing information system backups].

CP-9(3)	INFORMATION SYSTEM BACKUP | *SEPARATE STORAGE FOR CRITICAL INFORMATION*		
	ASSESSMENT OBJECTIVE: *Determine if the organization:*		
	CP-9(3)[1]	CP-9(3)[1][a]	*defines critical information system software and other security-related information requiring backup copies to be stored in a separate facility; or*
		CP-9(3)[1][b]	*defines critical information system software and other security-related information requiring backup copies to be stored in a fire-rated container that is not collocated with the operational system; and*
	CP-9(3)[2]	*stores backup copies of organization-defined critical information system software and other security-related information in a separate facility or in a fire-rated container that is not collocated with the operational system.*	
	POTENTIAL ASSESSMENT METHODS AND OBJECTS: **Examine**: [*SELECT FROM:* Contingency planning policy; procedures addressing information system backup; contingency plan; backup storage location(s); information system backup configurations and associated documentation; information system backup logs or records; other relevant documents or records]. **Interview**: [*SELECT FROM:* Organizational personnel with contingency planning and plan implementation responsibilities; organizational personnel with information system backup responsibilities; organizational personnel with information security responsibilities].		

CP-9(4)	INFORMATION SYSTEM BACKUP | *PROTECTION FROM UNAUTHORIZED MODIFICATION*
[Withdrawn: Incorporated into CP-9].	

CP-9(5)	INFORMATION SYSTEM BACKUP | *TRANSFER TO ALTERNATE STORAGE SITE*	
	ASSESSMENT OBJECTIVE: *Determine if the organization:*	
	CP-9(5)[1]	*defines a time period, consistent with recovery time objectives and recovery point objectives as specified in the information system contingency plan, to transfer information system backup information to the alternate storage site;*
	CP-9(5)[2]	*defines a transfer rate, consistent with recovery time objectives and recovery point objectives as specified in the information system contingency plan, to transfer information system backup information to the alternate storage site; and*
	CP-9(5)[3]	*transfers information system backup information to the alternate storage site with the organization-defined time period and transfer rate.*

Special Publication 800-53A
Revision 4

Assessing Security and Privacy Controls in Federal Information Systems
and Organizations — *Building Effective Assessment Plans*

POTENTIAL ASSESSMENT METHODS AND OBJECTS:

Examine: [*SELECT FROM:* Contingency planning policy; procedures addressing information system backup; contingency plan; information system backup logs or records; evidence of system backup information transferred to alternate storage site; alternate storage site agreements; other relevant documents or records].

Interview: [*SELECT FROM:* Organizational personnel with information system backup responsibilities; organizational personnel with information security responsibilities].

Test: [*SELECT FROM:* Organizational processes for transferring information system backups to the alternate storage site; automated mechanisms supporting and/or implementing information system backups; automated mechanisms supporting and/or implementing information transfer to the alternate storage site].

CP-9(6)	**INFORMATION SYSTEM BACKUP**	*REDUNDANT SECONDARY SYSTEM*

ASSESSMENT OBJECTIVE:

Determine if the organization accomplishes information system backup by maintaining a redundant secondary system that:

CP-9(6)[1]	*is not collocated with the primary system; and*
CP-9(6)[2]	*can be activated without loss of information or disruption to operations.*

POTENTIAL ASSESSMENT METHODS AND OBJECTS:

Examine: [*SELECT FROM:* Contingency planning policy; procedures addressing information system backup; contingency plan; information system backup test results; contingency plan test results; contingency plan test documentation; redundant secondary system for information system backups; location(s) of redundant secondary backup system(s); other relevant documents or records].

Interview: [*SELECT FROM:* Organizational personnel with information system backup responsibilities; organizational personnel with information security responsibilities; organizational personnel with responsibility for the redundant secondary system].

Test: [*SELECT FROM:* Organizational processes for maintaining redundant secondary systems; automated mechanisms supporting and/or implementing information system backups; automated mechanisms supporting and/or implementing information transfer to a redundant secondary system].

CP-9(7)	**INFORMATION SYSTEM BACKUP**	*DUAL AUTHORIZATION*

ASSESSMENT OBJECTIVE:

Determine if the organization:

CP-9(7)[1]	*defines backup information that requires dual authorization to be enforced for the deletion or destruction of such information; and*
CP-9(7)[2]	*enforces dual authorization for the deletion or destruction of organization-defined backup information.*

POTENTIAL ASSESSMENT METHODS AND OBJECTS:

Examine: [*SELECT FROM:* Contingency planning policy; procedures addressing information system backup; contingency plan; information system design documentation; information system configuration settings and associated documentation; system generated list of dual authorization credentials or rules; logs or records of deletion or destruction of backup information; other relevant documents or records].

Interview: [*SELECT FROM:* Organizational personnel with information system backup responsibilities; organizational personnel with information security responsibilities].

Test: [*SELECT FROM:* Automated mechanisms supporting and/or implementing dual authorization; automated mechanisms supporting and/or implementing deletion/destruction of backup information].

Special Publication 800-53A
Revision 4

Assessing Security and Privacy Controls in Federal Information Systems
and Organizations — *Building Effective Assessment Plans*

CP-10	INFORMATION SYSTEM RECOVERY AND RECONSTITUTION
	ASSESSMENT OBJECTIVE:
	Determine if the organization provides for:

	CP-10[1]	*the recovery of the information system to a known state after:*
		CP-10[1][a]	*a disruption;*
		CP-10[1][b]	*a compromise; or*
		CP-10[1][c]	*a failure;*
	CP-10[2]	*the reconstitution of the information system to a known state after:*
		CP-10[2][a]	*a disruption;*
		CP-10[2][b]	*a compromise; or*
		CP-10[2][c]	*a failure.*

POTENTIAL ASSESSMENT METHODS AND OBJECTS:

Examine: [*SELECT FROM:* Contingency planning policy; procedures addressing information system backup; contingency plan; information system backup test results; contingency plan test results; contingency plan test documentation; redundant secondary system for information system backups; location(s) of redundant secondary backup system(s); other relevant documents or records].

Interview: [*SELECT FROM:* Organizational personnel with contingency planning, recovery, and/or reconstitution responsibilities; organizational personnel with information security responsibilities].

Test: [*SELECT FROM:* Organizational processes implementing information system recovery and reconstitution operations; automated mechanisms supporting and/or implementing information system recovery and reconstitution operations].

CP-10(1)	INFORMATION SYSTEM RECOVERY AND RECONSTITUTION | *CONTINGENCY PLAN TESTING*
[Withdrawn: Incorporated into CP-4].	

CP-10(2)	INFORMATION SYSTEM RECOVERY AND RECONSTITUTION | *TRANSACTION RECOVERY*
	ASSESSMENT OBJECTIVE:
	Determine if the information system implements transaction recovery for systems that are transaction-based.

POTENTIAL ASSESSMENT METHODS AND OBJECTS:

Examine: [*SELECT FROM:* Contingency planning policy; procedures addressing information system recovery and reconstitution; contingency plan; information system design documentation; information system configuration settings and associated documentation; contingency plan test documentation; contingency plan test results; information system transaction recovery records; information system audit records; other relevant documents or records].

Interview: [*SELECT FROM:* Organizational personnel with responsibility for transaction recovery; organizational personnel with information security responsibilities].

Test: [*SELECT FROM:* Automated mechanisms supporting and/or implementing transaction recovery capability].

CP-10(3)	INFORMATION SYSTEM RECOVERY AND RECONSTITUTION | *COMPENSATING SECURITY CONTROLS*
[Withdrawn: Addressed through tailoring procedures].	

Special Publication 800-53A
Revision 4

Assessing Security and Privacy Controls in Federal Information Systems
and Organizations — *Building Effective Assessment Plans*

CP-10(4)	INFORMATION SYSTEM RECOVERY AND RECONSTITUTION | *RESTORE WITHIN TIME PERIOD*

ASSESSMENT OBJECTIVE:

Determine if the organization:

CP-10(4)[1]	*defines a time period to restore information system components from configuration-controlled and integrity-protected information representing a known, operational state for the components; and*
CP-10(4)[2]	*provides the capability to restore information system components within the organization-defined time period from configuration-controlled and integrity-protected information representing a known, operational state for the components.*

POTENTIAL ASSESSMENT METHODS AND OBJECTS:

Examine: [*SELECT FROM:* Contingency planning policy; procedures addressing information system recovery and reconstitution; contingency plan; information system design documentation; information system configuration settings and associated documentation; contingency plan test documentation; contingency plan test results; evidence of information system recovery and reconstitution operations; other relevant documents or records].

Interview: [*SELECT FROM:* Organizational personnel with information system recovery and reconstitution responsibilities; organizational personnel with information security responsibilities].

Test: [*SELECT FROM:* Automated mechanisms supporting and/or implementing recovery/reconstitution of information system information].

CP-10(5)	INFORMATION SYSTEM RECOVERY AND RECONSTITUTION | *FAILOVER CAPABILITY*

[Withdrawn: Incorporated into SI-13].

CP-10(6)	INFORMATION SYSTEM RECOVERY AND RECONSTITUTION | *COMPONENT PROTECTION*

ASSESSMENT OBJECTIVE:

Determine if the organization protects backup and restoration:

CP-10(6)[1]	*hardware;*
CP-10(6)[2]	*firmware; and*
CP-10(6)[3]	*software.*

POTENTIAL ASSESSMENT METHODS AND OBJECTS:

Examine: [*SELECT FROM:* Contingency planning policy; procedures addressing information system recovery and reconstitution; contingency plan; information system design documentation; information system configuration settings and associated documentation; logical access credentials; physical access credentials; logical access authorization records; physical access authorization records; other relevant documents or records].

Interview: [*SELECT FROM:* Organizational personnel with information system recovery and reconstitution responsibilities; organizational personnel with information security responsibilities].

Test: [*SELECT FROM:* Organizational processes for protecting backup and restoration hardware, firmware, and software; automated mechanisms supporting and/or implementing protection of backup and restoration hardware, firmware, and software].

CP-11	ALTERNATE COMMUNICATIONS PROTOCOLS

ASSESSMENT OBJECTIVE:

Determine if:

Special Publication 800-53A
Revision 4

Assessing Security and Privacy Controls in Federal Information Systems
and Organizations — *Building Effective Assessment Plans*

CP-11[1]	*the organization defines alternative communications protocols to be employed in support of maintaining continuity of operations; and*
CP-11[2]	*the information system provides the capability to employ organization-defined alternative communications protocols in support of maintaining continuity of operations.*

POTENTIAL ASSESSMENT METHODS AND OBJECTS:

Examine: [*SELECT FROM:* Contingency planning policy; procedures addressing alternative communications protocols; contingency plan; continuity of operations plan; information system design documentation; information system configuration settings and associated documentation; list of alternative communications protocols supporting continuity of operations; other relevant documents or records].

Interview: [*SELECT FROM:* Organizational personnel with contingency planning and plan implementation responsibilities; organizational personnel with continuity of operations planning and plan implementation responsibilities; organizational personnel with information security responsibilities; system/network administrators; system developers].

Test: [*SELECT FROM:* Automated mechanisms employing alternative communications protocols].

CP-12	**SAFE MODE**

ASSESSMENT OBJECTIVE:

Determine if:

CP-12[1]	*the organization defines conditions that, when detected, requires the information system to enter a safe mode of operation;*
CP-12[2]	*the organization defines restrictions of safe mode of operation; and*
CP-12[3]	*the information system, when organization-defined conditions are detected, enters a safe mode of operation with organization-defined restrictions of safe mode of operation.*

POTENTIAL ASSESSMENT METHODS AND OBJECTS:

Examine: [*SELECT FROM:* Contingency planning policy; procedures addressing safe mode of operation for the information system; contingency plan; information system design documentation; information system configuration settings and associated documentation; information system administration manuals; information system operation manuals; information system installation manuals; contingency plan test records; incident handling records; information system audit records; other relevant documents or records].

Interview: [*SELECT FROM:* Organizational personnel with information system operation responsibilities; organizational personnel with information security responsibilities; system/network administrators; system developers].

Test: [*SELECT FROM:* Automated mechanisms implementing safe mode of operation].

CP-13	**ALTERNATIVE SECURITY MECHANISMS**

ASSESSMENT OBJECTIVE:

Determine if the organization:

CP-13[1]	*defines alternative or supplemental security mechanisms to be employed when the primary means of implementing the security function is unavailable or compromised;*
CP-13[2]	*defines security functions to be satisfied using organization-defined alternative or supplemental security mechanisms when the primary means of implementing the security function is unavailable or compromised; and*

Special Publication 800-53A
Revision 4

Assessing Security and Privacy Controls in Federal Information Systems
and Organizations — *Building Effective Assessment Plans*

CP-13[3]	*employs organization-defined alternative or supplemental security mechanisms satisfying organization-defined security functions when the primary means of implementing the security function is unavailable or compromised.*

POTENTIAL ASSESSMENT METHODS AND OBJECTS:

Examine: [*SELECT FROM*: Contingency planning policy; procedures addressing alternate security mechanisms; contingency plan; continuity of operations plan; information system design documentation; information system configuration settings and associated documentation; contingency plan test records; contingency plan test results; other relevant documents or records].

Interview: [*SELECT FROM:* Organizational personnel with information system operation responsibilities; organizational personnel with information security responsibilities].

Test: [*SELECT FROM:* Information system capability implementing alternative security mechanisms].

Special Publication 800-53A
Revision 4

Assessing Security and Privacy Controls in Federal Information Systems
and Organizations — *Building Effective Assessment Plans*

FAMILY: IDENTIFICATION AND AUTHENTICATION

IA-1	IDENTIFICATION AND AUTHENTICATION POLICY AND PROCEDURES			
	ASSESSMENT OBJECTIVE: *Determine if the organization:*			
	IA-1(a)(1)	IA-1(a)(1)[1]	*develops and documents an identification and authentication policy that addresses:*	
			IA-1(a)(1)[1][a]	*purpose;*
			IA-1(a)(1)[1][b]	*scope;*
			IA-1(a)(1)[1][c]	*roles;*
			IA-1(a)(1)[1][d]	*responsibilities;*
			IA-1(a)(1)[1][e]	*management commitment;*
			IA-1(a)(1)[1][f]	*coordination among organizational entities;*
			IA-1(a)(1)[1][g]	*compliance;*
		IA-1(a)(1)[2]	*defines personnel or roles to whom the identification and authentication policy is to be disseminated; and*	
		IA-1(a)(1)[3]	*disseminates the identification and authentication policy to organization-defined personnel or roles;*	
	IA-1(a)(2)	IA-1(a)(2)[1]	*develops and documents procedures to facilitate the implementation of the identification and authentication policy and associated identification and authentication controls;*	
		IA-1(a)(2)[2]	*defines personnel or roles to whom the procedures are to be disseminated;*	
		IA-1(a)(2)[3]	*disseminates the procedures to organization-defined personnel or roles;*	
	IA-1(b)(1)	IA-1(b)(1)[1]	*defines the frequency to review and update the current identification and authentication policy;*	
		IA-1(b)(1)[2]	*reviews and updates the current identification and authentication policy with the organization-defined frequency; and*	
	IA-1(b)(2)	IA-1(b)(2)[1]	*defines the frequency to review and update the current identification and authentication procedures; and*	
		IA-1(b)(2)[2]	*reviews and updates the current identification and authentication procedures with the organization-defined frequency.*	
	POTENTIAL ASSESSMENT METHODS AND OBJECTS: **Examine**: [*SELECT FROM:* Identification and authentication policy and procedures; other relevant documents or records]. **Interview**: [*SELECT FROM:* Organizational personnel with identification and authentication responsibilities; organizational personnel with information security responsibilities].			

Special Publication 800-53A
Revision 4

Assessing Security and Privacy Controls in Federal Information Systems
and Organizations — *Building Effective Assessment Plans*

IA-2	IDENTIFICATION AND AUTHENTICATION (ORGANIZATIONAL USERS)
	ASSESSMENT OBJECTIVE: *Determine if the information system uniquely identifies and authenticates organizational users (or processes acting on behalf of organizational users).*
	POTENTIAL ASSESSMENT METHODS AND OBJECTS: **Examine**: [*SELECT FROM:* Identification and authentication policy; procedures addressing user identification and authentication; information system design documentation; information system configuration settings and associated documentation; information system audit records; list of information system accounts; other relevant documents or records]. **Interview**: [*SELECT FROM:* Organizational personnel with information system operations responsibilities; organizational personnel with information security responsibilities; system/network administrators; organizational personnel with account management responsibilities; system developers]. **Test**: [*SELECT FROM:* Organizational processes for uniquely identifying and authenticating users; automated mechanisms supporting and/or implementing identification and authentication capability].

IA-2(1)	IDENTIFICATION AND AUTHENTICATION | *NETWORK ACCESS TO PRIVILEGED ACCOUNTS*
	ASSESSMENT OBJECTIVE: *Determine if the information system implements multifactor authentication for network access to privileged accounts.*
	POTENTIAL ASSESSMENT METHODS AND OBJECTS: **Examine**: [*SELECT FROM:* Identification and authentication policy; procedures addressing user identification and authentication; information system design documentation; information system configuration settings and associated documentation; information system audit records; list of information system accounts; other relevant documents or records]. **Interview**: [*SELECT FROM:* Organizational personnel with information system operations responsibilities; organizational personnel with account management responsibilities; organizational personnel with information security responsibilities; system/network administrators; system developers]. **Test**: [*SELECT FROM:* Automated mechanisms supporting and/or implementing multifactor authentication capability].

IA-2(2)	IDENTIFICATION AND AUTHENTICATION | *NETWORK ACCESS TO NON-PRIVILEGED ACCOUNTS*
	ASSESSMENT OBJECTIVE: *Determine if the information system implements multifactor authentication for network access to non-privileged accounts.*
	POTENTIAL ASSESSMENT METHODS AND OBJECTS: **Examine**: [*SELECT FROM:* Identification and authentication policy; procedures addressing user identification and authentication; information system design documentation; information system configuration settings and associated documentation; information system audit records; list of information system accounts; other relevant documents or records]. **Interview**: [*SELECT FROM:* Organizational personnel with information system operations responsibilities; organizational personnel with account management responsibilities; organizational personnel with information security responsibilities; system/network administrators; system developers]. **Test**: [*SELECT FROM:* Automated mechanisms supporting and/or implementing multifactor authentication capability].

Special Publication 800-53A
Revision 4

Assessing Security and Privacy Controls in Federal Information Systems
and Organizations — *Building Effective Assessment Plans*

IA-2(3)	IDENTIFICATION AND AUTHENTICATION │ *LOCAL ACCESS TO PRIVILEGED ACCOUNTS*
	ASSESSMENT OBJECTIVE: *Determine if the information system implements multifactor authentication for local access to privileged accounts.*
	POTENTIAL ASSESSMENT METHODS AND OBJECTS: **Examine**: [*SELECT FROM:* Identification and authentication policy; procedures addressing user identification and authentication; information system design documentation; information system configuration settings and associated documentation; information system audit records; list of information system accounts; other relevant documents or records]. **Interview**: [*SELECT FROM:* Organizational personnel with information system operations responsibilities; organizational personnel with account management responsibilities; organizational personnel with information security responsibilities; system/network administrators; system developers]. **Test**: [*SELECT FROM:* Automated mechanisms supporting and/or implementing multifactor authentication capability].

IA-2(4)	IDENTIFICATION AND AUTHENTICATION │ *LOCAL ACCESS TO NON-PRIVILEGED ACCOUNTS*
	ASSESSMENT OBJECTIVE: *Determine if the information system implements multifactor authentication for local access to non-privileged accounts.*
	POTENTIAL ASSESSMENT METHODS AND OBJECTS: **Examine**: [*SELECT FROM:* Identification and authentication policy; procedures addressing user identification and authentication; information system design documentation; information system configuration settings and associated documentation; information system audit records; list of information system accounts; other relevant documents or records]. **Interview**: [*SELECT FROM:* Organizational personnel with information system operations responsibilities; organizational personnel with account management responsibilities; organizational personnel with information security responsibilities; system/network administrators; system developers]. **Test**: [*SELECT FROM:* Automated mechanisms supporting and/or implementing multifactor authentication capability].

IA-2(5)	IDENTIFICATION AND AUTHENTICATION │ *GROUP AUTHENTICATION*
	ASSESSMENT OBJECTIVE: *Determine if the organization requires individuals to be authenticated with an individual authenticator when a group authenticator is employed.*
	POTENTIAL ASSESSMENT METHODS AND OBJECTS: **Examine**: [*SELECT FROM:* Identification and authentication policy; procedures addressing user identification and authentication; information system design documentation; information system configuration settings and associated documentation; information system audit records; list of information system accounts; other relevant documents or records]. **Interview**: [*SELECT FROM:* Organizational personnel with information system operations responsibilities; organizational personnel with account management responsibilities; organizational personnel with information security responsibilities; system/network administrators; system developers]. **Test**: [*SELECT FROM:* Automated mechanisms supporting and/or implementing authentication capability for group accounts].

IA-2(6)	IDENTIFICATION AND AUTHENTICATION │ *NETWORK ACCESS TO PRIVILEGED ACCOUNTS — SEPARATE DEVICE*
	ASSESSMENT OBJECTIVE: *Determine if:*

Special Publication 800-53A
Revision 4

Assessing Security and Privacy Controls in Federal Information Systems
and Organizations — *Building Effective Assessment Plans*

IA-2(6)[1]	*the information system implements multifactor authentication for network access to privileged accounts such that one of the factors is provided by a device separate from the system gaining access;*
IA-2(6)[2]	*the organization defines strength of mechanism requirements to be enforced by a device separate from the system gaining network access to privileged accounts; and*
IA-2(6)[3]	*the information system implements multifactor authentication for network access to privileged accounts such that a device, separate from the system gaining access, meets organization-defined strength of mechanism requirements.*

POTENTIAL ASSESSMENT METHODS AND OBJECTS:

Examine: [*SELECT FROM:* Identification and authentication policy; procedures addressing user identification and authentication; information system design documentation; information system configuration settings and associated documentation; information system audit records; list of information system accounts; other relevant documents or records].

Interview: [*SELECT FROM:* Organizational personnel with information system operations responsibilities; organizational personnel with account management responsibilities; organizational personnel with information security responsibilities; system/network administrators; system developers].

Test: [*SELECT FROM:* Automated mechanisms supporting and/or implementing multifactor authentication capability].

IA-2(7)	**IDENTIFICATION AND AUTHENTICATION**	*NETWORK ACCESS TO NON-PRIVILEGED ACCOUNTS – SEPARATE DEVICE*

ASSESSMENT OBJECTIVE:

Determine if:

IA-2(7)[1]	*the information system implements multifactor authentication for network access to non-privileged accounts such that one of the factors is provided by a device separate from the system gaining access;*
IA-2(7)[2]	*the organization defines strength of mechanism requirements to be enforced by a device separate from the system gaining network access to non-privileged accounts; and*
IA-2(7)[3]	*the information system implements multifactor authentication for network access to non-privileged accounts such that a device, separate from the system gaining access, meets organization-defined strength of mechanism requirements.*

POTENTIAL ASSESSMENT METHODS AND OBJECTS:

Examine: [*SELECT FROM:* Identification and authentication policy; procedures addressing user identification and authentication; information system design documentation; information system configuration settings and associated documentation; information system audit records; list of information system accounts; other relevant documents or records].

Interview: [*SELECT FROM:* Organizational personnel with information system operations responsibilities; organizational personnel with account management responsibilities; organizational personnel with information security responsibilities; system/network administrators; system developers].

Test: [*SELECT FROM:* Automated mechanisms supporting and/or implementing multifactor authentication capability].

Special Publication 800-53A
Revision 4

Assessing Security and Privacy Controls in Federal Information Systems
and Organizations — *Building Effective Assessment Plans*

IA-2(8)	IDENTIFICATION AND AUTHENTICATION | *NETWORK ACCESS TO PRIVILEGED ACCOUNTS – REPLAY RESISTANT*
	ASSESSMENT OBJECTIVE: *Determine if the information system implements replay-resistant authentication mechanisms for network access to privileged accounts.*
	POTENTIAL ASSESSMENT METHODS AND OBJECTS: **Examine**: [*SELECT FROM:* Identification and authentication policy; procedures addressing user identification and authentication; information system design documentation; information system configuration settings and associated documentation; information system audit records; list of privileged information system accounts; other relevant documents or records]. **Interview**: [*SELECT FROM:* Organizational personnel with information system operations responsibilities; organizational personnel with account management responsibilities; organizational personnel with information security responsibilities; system/network administrators; system developers]. **Test**: [*SELECT FROM:* Automated mechanisms supporting and/or implementing identification and authentication capability; automated mechanisms supporting and/or implementing replay resistant authentication mechanisms].

IA-2(9)	IDENTIFICATION AND AUTHENTICATION | *NETWORK ACCESS TO NON-PRIVILEGED ACCOUNTS – REPLAY RESISTANT*
	ASSESSMENT OBJECTIVE: *Determine if the information system implements replay-resistant authentication mechanisms for network access to non-privileged accounts.*
	POTENTIAL ASSESSMENT METHODS AND OBJECTS: **Examine**: [*SELECT FROM:* Identification and authentication policy; procedures addressing user identification and authentication; information system design documentation; information system configuration settings and associated documentation; information system audit records; list of non-privileged information system accounts; other relevant documents or records]. **Interview**: [*SELECT FROM:* Organizational personnel with information system operations responsibilities; organizational personnel with account management responsibilities; organizational personnel with information security responsibilities; system/network administrators; system developers]. **Test**: [*SELECT FROM:* Automated mechanisms supporting and/or implementing identification and authentication capability; automated mechanisms supporting and/or implementing replay resistant authentication mechanisms].

IA-2(10)	IDENTIFICATION AND AUTHENTICATION | *SINGLE SIGN-ON*	
	ASSESSMENT OBJECTIVE: *Determine if:*	
	IA-2(10)[1]	*the organization defines a list of information system accounts and services for which a single sign-on capability must be provided; and*
	IA-2(10)[2]	*the information system provides a single sign-on capability for organization-defined information system accounts and services.*

Special Publication 800-53A
Revision 4

Assessing Security and Privacy Controls in Federal Information Systems
and Organizations — *Building Effective Assessment Plans*

POTENTIAL ASSESSMENT METHODS AND OBJECTS:

Examine: [*SELECT FROM:* Identification and authentication policy; procedures addressing single sign-on capability for information system accounts and services; procedures addressing identification and authentication; information system design documentation; information system configuration settings and associated documentation; information system audit records; list of information system accounts and services requiring single sign-on capability; other relevant documents or records].

Interview: [*SELECT FROM:* Organizational personnel with information system operations responsibilities; organizational personnel with account management responsibilities; organizational personnel with information security responsibilities; system/network administrators; system developers].

Test: [*SELECT FROM:* Automated mechanisms supporting and/or implementing identification and authentication capability; automated mechanisms supporting and/or implementing single sign-on capability for information system accounts and services].

IA-2(11)	IDENTIFICATION AND AUTHENTICATION │ *REMOTE ACCESS – SEPARATE DEVICE*
	ASSESSMENT OBJECTIVE: *Determine if:*
	IA-2(11)[1] · *the information system implements multifactor authentication for remote access to privileged accounts such that one of the factors is provided by a device separate from the system gaining access;*
	IA-2(11)[2] · *the information system implements multifactor authentication for remote access to non-privileged accounts such that one of the factors is provided by a device separate from the system gaining access;*
	IA-2(11)[3] · *the organization defines strength of mechanism requirements to be enforced by a device separate from the system gaining remote access to privileged accounts;*
	IA-2(11)[4] · *the organization defines strength of mechanism requirements to be enforced by a device separate from the system gaining remote access to non-privileged accounts;*
	IA-2(11)[5] · *the information system implements multifactor authentication for remote access to privileged accounts such that a device, separate from the system gaining access, meets organization-defined strength of mechanism requirements; and*
	IA-2(11)[6] · *the information system implements multifactor authentication for remote access to non-privileged accounts such that a device, separate from the system gaining access, meets organization-defined strength of mechanism requirements.*

POTENTIAL ASSESSMENT METHODS AND OBJECTS:

Examine: [*SELECT FROM:* Identification and authentication policy; procedures addressing user identification and authentication; information system design documentation; information system configuration settings and associated documentation; information system audit records; list of privileged and non-privileged information system accounts; other relevant documents or records].

Interview: [*SELECT FROM:* Organizational personnel with information system operations responsibilities; organizational personnel with account management responsibilities; organizational personnel with information security responsibilities; system/network administrators; system developers].

Test: [*SELECT FROM:* Automated mechanisms supporting and/or implementing identification and authentication capability].

Special Publication 800-53A
Revision 4

Assessing Security and Privacy Controls in Federal Information Systems
and Organizations — *Building Effective Assessment Plans*

IA-2(12)	IDENTIFICATION AND AUTHENTICATION | *ACCEPTANCE OF PIV CREDENTIALS*	
	ASSESSMENT OBJECTIVE: *Determine if the information system:*	
	IA-2(12)[1]	*accepts Personal Identity Verification (PIV) credentials; and*
	IA-2(12)[2]	*electronically verifies Personal Identity Verification (PIV) credentials.*
	POTENTIAL ASSESSMENT METHODS AND OBJECTS: **Examine:** [*SELECT FROM:* Identification and authentication policy; procedures addressing user identification and authentication; information system design documentation; information system configuration settings and associated documentation; information system audit records; PIV verification records; evidence of PIV credentials; PIV credential authorizations; other relevant documents or records]. **Interview:** [*SELECT FROM:* Organizational personnel with information system operations responsibilities; organizational personnel with account management responsibilities; organizational personnel with information security responsibilities; system/network administrators; system developers]. **Test:** [*SELECT FROM:* Automated mechanisms supporting and/or implementing acceptance and verification of PIV credentials].	

IA-2(13)	IDENTIFICATION AND AUTHENTICATION | *OUT-OF-BAND AUTHENTICATION*	
	ASSESSMENT OBJECTIVE: *Determine if:*	
	IA-2(13)[1]	*the organization defines out-of-band authentication to be implemented by the information system;*
	IA-2(13)[2]	*the organization defines conditions under which the information system implements organization-defined out-of-band authentication; and*
	IA-2(13)[3]	*the information system implements organization-defined out-of-band authentication under organization-defined conditions.*
	POTENTIAL ASSESSMENT METHODS AND OBJECTS: **Examine:** [*SELECT FROM:* Identification and authentication policy; procedures addressing user identification and authentication; information system design documentation; information system configuration settings and associated documentation; information system audit records; system-generated list of out-of-band authentication paths; other relevant documents or records]. **Interview:** [*SELECT FROM:* Organizational personnel with information system operations responsibilities; organizational personnel with account management responsibilities; organizational personnel with information security responsibilities; system/network administrators; system developers]. **Test:** [*SELECT FROM:* Automated mechanisms supporting and/or implementing out-of-band authentication capability].	

IA-3	DEVICE IDENTIFICATION AND AUTHENTICATION		
	ASSESSMENT OBJECTIVE: *Determine if:*		
	IA-3[1]	*the organization defines specific and/or types of devices that the information system uniquely identifies and authenticates before establishing one or more of the following:*	
		IA-3[1][a]	*a local connection;*
		IA-3[1][b]	*a remote connection; and/or*

Special Publication 800-53A
Revision 4

Assessing Security and Privacy Controls in Federal Information Systems
and Organizations — *Building Effective Assessment Plans*

	IA-3[1][c]	*a network connection; and*
IA-3[2]		*the information system uniquely identifies and authenticates organization-defined devices before establishing one or more of the following:*
	IA-3[2][a]	*a local connection;*
	IA-3[2][b]	*a remote connection; and/or*
	IA-3[2][c]	*a network connection.*

POTENTIAL ASSESSMENT METHODS AND OBJECTS:

Examine: [*SELECT FROM:* Identification and authentication policy; procedures addressing device identification and authentication; information system design documentation; list of devices requiring unique identification and authentication; device connection reports; information system configuration settings and associated documentation; other relevant documents or records].

Interview: [*SELECT FROM:* Organizational personnel with operational responsibilities for device identification and authentication; organizational personnel with information security responsibilities; system/network administrators; system developers].

Test: [*SELECT FROM:* Automated mechanisms supporting and/or implementing device identification and authentication capability].

IA-3(1)	**DEVICE IDENTIFICATION AND AUTHENTICATION**	*CRYPTOGRAPHIC BIDIRECTIONAL AUTHENTICATION*

ASSESSMENT OBJECTIVE:

Determine if:

IA-3(1)[1]		*the organization defines specific and/or types of devices requiring use of cryptographically based, bidirectional authentication to authenticate before establishing one or more of the following:*
	IA-3(1)[1][a]	*a local connection;*
	IA-3(1)[1][b]	*a remote connection; and/or*
	IA-3(1)[1][c]	*a network connection;*
IA-3(1)[2]		*the information system uses cryptographically based bidirectional authentication to authenticate organization-defined devices before establishing one or more of the following:*
	IA-3(1)[2][a]	*a local connection;*
	IA-3(1)[2][b]	*a remote connection; and/or*
	IA-3(1)[2][c]	*a network connection.*

POTENTIAL ASSESSMENT METHODS AND OBJECTS:

Examine: [*SELECT FROM:* Identification and authentication policy; procedures addressing device identification and authentication; information system design documentation; list of devices requiring unique identification and authentication; device connection reports; information system configuration settings and associated documentation; other relevant documents or records].

Interview: [*SELECT FROM:* Organizational personnel with operational responsibilities for device identification and authentication; organizational personnel with information security responsibilities; system/network administrators; system developers].

Test: [*SELECT FROM:* Automated mechanisms supporting and/or implementing device authentication capability; cryptographically based bidirectional authentication mechanisms].

Special Publication 800-53A
Revision 4

Assessing Security and Privacy Controls in Federal Information Systems
and Organizations — *Building Effective Assessment Plans*

IA-3(2)	DEVICE IDENTIFICATION AND AUTHENTICATION	*CRYPTOGRAPHIC BIDIRECTIONAL NETWORK AUTHENTICATION*
[Withdrawn: Incorporated into IA-3(1)].	

IA-3(3)	DEVICE IDENTIFICATION AND AUTHENTICATION	*DYNAMIC ADDRESS ALLOCATION*		
	ASSESSMENT OBJECTIVE: *Determine if the organization:*		
	IA-3(3)(a)	IA-3(3)(a)[1]	*defines lease information to be employed to standardize dynamic address allocation for devices;*
		IA-3(3)(a)[2]	*defines lease duration to be employed to standardize dynamic address allocation for devices;*
		IA-3(3)(a)[3]	*standardizes dynamic address allocation of lease information assigned to devices in accordance with organization-defined lease information;*
		IA-3(3)(a)[4]	*standardizes dynamic address allocation of the lease duration assigned to devices in accordance with organization-defined lease duration; and*
	IA-3(3)(b)	*audits lease information when assigned to a device.*	
	POTENTIAL ASSESSMENT METHODS AND OBJECTS: **Examine**: [*SELECT FROM:* Identification and authentication policy; procedures addressing device identification and authentication; information system design documentation; information system configuration settings and associated documentation; evidence of lease information and lease duration assigned to devices; device connection reports; information system audit records; other relevant documents or records]. **Interview**: [*SELECT FROM:* Organizational personnel with operational responsibilities for device identification and authentication; organizational personnel with information security responsibilities; system/network administrators; system developers]. **Test**: [*SELECT FROM:* Automated mechanisms supporting and/or implementing device identification and authentication capability; automated mechanisms supporting and/or implementing dynamic address allocation; automated mechanisms supporting and/or implanting auditing of lease information].		

IA-3(4)	DEVICE IDENTIFICATION AND AUTHENTICATION	*DEVICE ATTESTATION*	
	ASSESSMENT OBJECTIVE: *Determine if the organization:*	
	IA-3(4)[1]	*defines configuration management process to be employed to handle device identification and authentication based on attestation; and*
	IA-3(4)[2]	*ensures that device identification and authentication based on attestation is handled by organization-defined configuration management process.*

Special Publication 800-53A
Revision 4

Assessing Security and Privacy Controls in Federal Information Systems
and Organizations — *Building Effective Assessment Plans*

POTENTIAL ASSESSMENT METHODS AND OBJECTS:

Examine: [*SELECT FROM:* Identification and authentication policy; procedures addressing device identification and authentication; procedures addressing device configuration management; information system design documentation; information system configuration settings and associated documentation; configuration management records; change control records; information system audit records; other relevant documents or records].

Interview: [*SELECT FROM:* Organizational personnel with operational responsibilities for device identification and authentication; organizational personnel with information security responsibilities; system/network administrators].

Test: [*SELECT FROM:* Automated mechanisms supporting and/or implementing device identification and authentication capability; automated mechanisms supporting and/or implementing configuration management; cryptographic mechanisms supporting device attestation].

IA-4	**IDENTIFIER MANAGEMENT**		
	ASSESSMENT OBJECTIVE:		
	Determine if the organization manages information system identifiers by:		
	IA-4(a)	IA-4(a)[1]	*defining personnel or roles from whom authorization must be received to assign:*
		IA-4(a)[1][a]	*an individual identifier;*
		IA-4(a)[1][b]	*a group identifier;*
		IA-4(a)[1][c]	*a role identifier; and/or*
		IA-4(a)[1][d]	*a device identifier;*
		IA-4(a)[2]	*receiving authorization from organization-defined personnel or roles to assign:*
		IA-4(a)[2][a]	*an individual identifier;*
		IA-4(a)[2][b]	*a group identifier;*
		IA-4(a)[2][c]	*a role identifier; and/or*
		IA-4(a)[2][d]	*a device identifier;*
	IA-4(b)	*selecting an identifier that identifies:*	
		IA-4(b)[1]	*an individual;*
		IA-4(b)[2]	*a group;*
		IA-4(b)[3]	*a role; and/or*
		IA-4(b)[4]	*a device;*
	IA-4(c)	*assigning the identifier to the intended:*	
		IA-4(c)[1]	*individual;*
		IA-4(c)[2]	*group;*
		IA-4(c)[3]	*role; and/or*
		IA-4(c)[4]	*device;*
	IA-4(d)	IA-4(d)[1]	*defining a time period for preventing reuse of identifiers;*
		IA-4(d)[2]	*preventing reuse of identifiers for the organization-defined time period;*

Special Publication 800-53A
Revision 4

Assessing Security and Privacy Controls in Federal Information Systems
and Organizations — *Building Effective Assessment Plans*

| IA-4(e) | IA-4(e)[1] | *defining a time period of inactivity to disable the identifier; and* |
| | IA-4(e)[2] | *disabling the identifier after the organization-defined time period of inactivity.* |

POTENTIAL ASSESSMENT METHODS AND OBJECTS:

Examine: [*SELECT FROM:* Identification and authentication policy; procedures addressing identifier management; procedures addressing account management; security plan; information system design documentation; information system configuration settings and associated documentation; list of information system accounts; list of identifiers generated from physical access control devices; other relevant documents or records].

Interview: [*SELECT FROM:* Organizational personnel with identifier management responsibilities; organizational personnel with information security responsibilities; system/network administrators; system developers].

Test: [*SELECT FROM:* Automated mechanisms supporting and/or implementing identifier management].

| IA-4(1) | **IDENTIFIER MANAGEMENT** | *PROHIBIT ACCOUNT IDENTIFIERS AS PUBLIC IDENTIFIERS* |

ASSESSMENT OBJECTIVE:

Determine if the organization prohibits the use of information system account identifiers that are the same as public identifiers for individual electronic mail accounts.

POTENTIAL ASSESSMENT METHODS AND OBJECTS:

Examine: [*SELECT FROM:* Identification and authentication policy; procedures addressing identifier management; procedures addressing account management; information system design documentation; information system configuration settings and associated documentation; information system audit records; other relevant documents or records].

Interview: [*SELECT FROM:* Organizational personnel with identifier management responsibilities; organizational personnel with information security responsibilities; system/network administrators].

Test: [*SELECT FROM:* Automated mechanisms supporting and/or implementing identifier management].

| IA-4(2) | **IDENTIFIER MANAGEMENT** | *SUPERVISOR AUTHORIZATION* |

ASSESSMENT OBJECTIVE:

Determine if the organization requires that the registration process to receive an individual identifier includes supervisor authorization.

POTENTIAL ASSESSMENT METHODS AND OBJECTS:

Examine: [*SELECT FROM:* Identification and authentication policy; procedures addressing identifier management; procedures addressing account management; information system design documentation; information system configuration settings and associated documentation; information system audit records; other relevant documents or records].

Interview: [*SELECT FROM:* Organizational personnel with identifier management responsibilities; supervisors responsible for authorizing identifier registration; organizational personnel with information security responsibilities; system/network administrators].

Test: [*SELECT FROM:* Automated mechanisms supporting and/or implementing identifier management].

| IA-4(3) | **IDENTIFIER MANAGEMENT** | *MULTIPLE FORMS OF CERTIFICATION* |

ASSESSMENT OBJECTIVE:

Determine if the organization requires multiple forms of certification of individual identification such as documentary evidence or a combination of documents and biometrics be presented to the registration authority.

Special Publication 800-53A
Revision 4

Assessing Security and Privacy Controls in Federal Information Systems
and Organizations — *Building Effective Assessment Plans*

POTENTIAL ASSESSMENT METHODS AND OBJECTS:

Examine: [*SELECT FROM*: Identification and authentication policy; procedures addressing identifier management; procedures addressing account management; information system design documentation; information system configuration settings and associated documentation; information system audit records; other relevant documents or records].

Interview: [*SELECT FROM*: Organizational personnel with identifier management responsibilities; organizational personnel with information security responsibilities].

Test: [*SELECT FROM*: Automated mechanisms supporting and/or implementing identifier management].

IA-4(4)	IDENTIFIER MANAGEMENT	*IDENTIFY USER STATUS*

ASSESSMENT OBJECTIVE:

Determine if the organization:

IA-4(4)[1]	*defines a characteristic to be used to identify individual status; and*
IA-4(4)[2]	*manages individual identifiers by uniquely identifying each individual as the organization-defined characteristic identifying individual status.*

POTENTIAL ASSESSMENT METHODS AND OBJECTS:

Examine: [*SELECT FROM*: Identification and authentication policy; procedures addressing identifier management; procedures addressing account management; list of characteristics identifying individual status; other relevant documents or records].

Interview: [*SELECT FROM*: Organizational personnel with identifier management responsibilities; organizational personnel with information security responsibilities; system/network administrators].

Test: [*SELECT FROM*: Automated mechanisms supporting and/or implementing identifier management].

IA-4(5)	IDENTIFIER MANAGEMENT	*DYNAMIC MANAGEMENT*

ASSESSMENT OBJECTIVE:

Determine if the information system dynamically manages identifiers.

POTENTIAL ASSESSMENT METHODS AND OBJECTS:

Examine: [*SELECT FROM*: Identification and authentication policy; procedures addressing identifier management; procedures addressing account management; information system design documentation; information system configuration settings and associated documentation; information system audit records; other relevant documents or records].

Interview: [*SELECT FROM*: Organizational personnel with identifier management responsibilities; organizational personnel with information security responsibilities; system/network administrators; system developers].

Test: [*SELECT FROM*: Automated mechanisms supporting and/or implementing dynamic identifier management].

IA-4(6)	IDENTIFIER MANAGEMENT	*CROSS-ORGANIZATION MANAGEMENT*

ASSESSMENT OBJECTIVE:

Determine if the organization:

IA-4(6)[1]	*defines external organizations with whom to coordinate cross-organization management of identifiers; and*
IA-4(6)[2]	*coordinates with organization-defined external organizations for cross-organization management of identifiers.*

Special Publication 800-53A
Revision 4

Assessing Security and Privacy Controls in Federal Information Systems
and Organizations — *Building Effective Assessment Plans*

POTENTIAL ASSESSMENT METHODS AND OBJECTS:

Examine: [*SELECT FROM:* Identification and authentication policy; procedures addressing identifier management; procedures addressing account management; security plan; other relevant documents or records].

Interview: [*SELECT FROM:* Organizational personnel with identifier management responsibilities; organizational personnel with information security responsibilities].

Test: [*SELECT FROM:* Automated mechanisms supporting and/or implementing identifier management].

IA-4(7)	IDENTIFIER MANAGEMENT | *IN-PERSON REGISTRATION*
	ASSESSMENT OBJECTIVE: *Determine if the organization requires that the registration process to receive an individual identifier be conducted in person before a designated registration authority.*
	POTENTIAL ASSESSMENT METHODS AND OBJECTS: **Examine**: [*SELECT FROM:* Identification and authentication policy; procedures addressing identifier management; procedures addressing account management; information system design documentation; information system configuration settings and associated documentation; information system audit records; other relevant documents or records]. **Interview**: [*SELECT FROM:* Organizational personnel with identifier management responsibilities; organizational personnel with information security responsibilities].

IA-5	AUTHENTICATOR MANAGEMENT	
	ASSESSMENT OBJECTIVE: *Determine if the organization manages information system authenticators by:*	
IA-5(a)	*verifying, as part of the initial authenticator distribution, the identity of:*	
	IA-5(a)[1]	*the individual receiving the authenticator;*
	IA-5(a)[2]	*the group receiving the authenticator;*
	IA-5(a)[3]	*the role receiving the authenticator; and/or*
	IA-5(a)[4]	*the device receiving the authenticator;*
IA-5(b)	*establishing initial authenticator content for authenticators defined by the organization;*	
IA-5(c)	*ensuring that authenticators have sufficient strength of mechanism for their intended use;*	
IA-5(d)	IA-5(d)[1]	*establishing and implementing administrative procedures for initial authenticator distribution;*
	IA-5(d)[2]	*establishing and implementing administrative procedures for lost/compromised or damaged authenticators;*
	IA-5(d)[3]	*establishing and implementing administrative procedures for revoking authenticators;*
IA-5(e)	*changing default content of authenticators prior to information system installation;*	
IA-5(f)	IA-5(f)[1]	*establishing minimum lifetime restrictions for authenticators;*
	IA-5(f)[2]	*establishing maximum lifetime restrictions for authenticators;*
	IA-5(f)[3]	*establishing reuse conditions for authenticators;*

Special Publication 800-53A
Revision 4

Assessing Security and Privacy Controls in Federal Information Systems
and Organizations — *Building Effective Assessment Plans*

	IA-5(g)	IA-5(g)[1]	*defining a time period (by authenticator type) for changing/refreshing authenticators;*
		IA-5(g)[2]	*changing/refreshing authenticators with the organization-defined time period by authenticator type;*
	IA-5(h)		*protecting authenticator content from unauthorized:*
		IA-5(h)[1]	*disclosure;*
		IA-5(h)[2]	*modification;*
	IA-5(i)	IA-5(i)[1]	*requiring individuals to take specific security safeguards to protect authenticators;*
		IA-5(i)[2]	*having devices implement specific security safeguards to protect authenticators; and*
	IA-5(j)		*changing authenticators for group/role accounts when membership to those accounts changes.*

POTENTIAL ASSESSMENT METHODS AND OBJECTS:

Examine: [*SELECT FROM*: Identification and authentication policy; procedures addressing authenticator management; information system design documentation; information system configuration settings and associated documentation; list of information system authenticator types; change control records associated with managing information system authenticators; information system audit records; other relevant documents or records].

Interview: [*SELECT FROM*: Organizational personnel with authenticator management responsibilities; organizational personnel with information security responsibilities; system/network administrators].

Test: [*SELECT FROM*: Automated mechanisms supporting and/or implementing authenticator management capability].

IA-5(1)	**AUTHENTICATOR MANAGEMENT** | *PASSWORD-BASED AUTHENTICATION*		
	ASSESSMENT OBJECTIVE: *Determine if, for password-based authentication:*		
	IA-5(1)(a)	IA-5(1)(a)[1]	*the organization defines requirements for case sensitivity;*
		IA-5(1)(a)[2]	*the organization defines requirements for number of characters;*
		IA-5(1)(a)[3]	*the organization defines requirements for the mix of upper-case letters, lower-case letters, numbers and special characters;*
		IA-5(1)(a)[4]	*the organization defines minimum requirements for each type of character;*
		IA-5(1)(a)[5]	*the information system enforces minimum password complexity of organization-defined requirements for case sensitivity, number of characters, mix of upper-case letters, lower-case letters, numbers, and special characters, including minimum requirements for each type;*
	IA-5(1)(b)	IA-5(1)(b)[1]	*the organization defines a minimum number of changed characters to be enforced when new passwords are created;*
		IA-5(1)(b)[2]	*the information system enforces at least the organization-defined minimum number of characters that must be changed when new passwords are created;*

Special Publication 800-53A
Revision 4

Assessing Security and Privacy Controls in Federal Information Systems
and Organizations — *Building Effective Assessment Plans*

	IA-5(1)(c)		the information system stores and transmits only encrypted representations of passwords;
	IA-5(1)(d)	IA-5(1)(d)[1]	the organization defines numbers for password minimum lifetime restrictions to be enforced for passwords;
		IA-5(1)(d)[2]	the organization defines numbers for password maximum lifetime restrictions to be enforced for passwords;
		IA-5(1)(d)[3]	the information system enforces password minimum lifetime restrictions of organization-defined numbers for lifetime minimum;
		IA-5(1)(d)[4]	the information system enforces password maximum lifetime restrictions of organization-defined numbers for lifetime maximum;
	IA-5(1)(e)	IA-5(1)(e)[1]	the organization defines the number of password generations to be prohibited from password reuse;
		IA-5(1)(e)[2]	the information system prohibits password reuse for the organization-defined number of generations; and
	IA-5(1)(f)		the information system allows the use of a temporary password for system logons with an immediate change to a permanent password.

POTENTIAL ASSESSMENT METHODS AND OBJECTS:

Examine: [*SELECT FROM:* Identification and authentication policy; password policy; procedures addressing authenticator management; security plan; information system design documentation; information system configuration settings and associated documentation; password configurations and associated documentation; other relevant documents or records].

Interview: [*SELECT FROM:* Organizational personnel with authenticator management responsibilities; organizational personnel with information security responsibilities; system/network administrators; system developers].

Test: [*SELECT FROM:* Automated mechanisms supporting and/or implementing password-based authenticator management capability].

IA-5(2)	AUTHENTICATOR MANAGEMENT	*PKI-BASED AUTHENTICATION*	
	ASSESSMENT OBJECTIVE: *Determine if the information system, for PKI-based authentication:*		
	IA-5(2)(a)	IA-5(2)(a)[1]	validates certifications by constructing a certification path to an accepted trust anchor;
		IA-5(2)(a)[2]	validates certifications by verifying a certification path to an accepted trust anchor;
		IA-5(2)(a)[3]	includes checking certificate status information when constructing and verifying the certification path;
	IA-5(2)(b)		enforces authorized access to the corresponding private key;
	IA-5(2)(c)		maps the authenticated identity to the account of the individual or group; and
	IA-5(2)(d)		implements a local cache of revocation data to support path discovery and validation in case of inability to access revocation information via the network.

Special Publication 800-53A
Revision 4

Assessing Security and Privacy Controls in Federal Information Systems
and Organizations — *Building Effective Assessment Plans*

POTENTIAL ASSESSMENT METHODS AND OBJECTS:

Examine: [*SELECT FROM:* Identification and authentication policy; procedures addressing authenticator management; security plan; information system design documentation; information system configuration settings and associated documentation; PKI certification validation records; PKI certification revocation lists; other relevant documents or records].

Interview: [*SELECT FROM:* Organizational personnel with PKI-based, authenticator management responsibilities; organizational personnel with information security responsibilities; system/network administrators; system developers].

Test: [*SELECT FROM:* Automated mechanisms supporting and/or implementing PKI-based, authenticator management capability].

IA-5(3)	AUTHENTICATOR MANAGEMENT | *IN-PERSON OR TRUSTED THIRD-PARTY REGISTRATION*

ASSESSMENT OBJECTIVE:

Determine if the organization:

IA-5(3)[1]	*defines types of and/or specific authenticators to be received in person or by a trusted third party;*
IA-5(3)[2]	*defines the registration authority with oversight of the registration process for receipt of organization-defined types of and/or specific authenticators;*
IA-5(3)[3]	*defines personnel or roles responsible for authorizing organization-defined registration authority;*
IA-5(3)[4]	*defines if the registration process is to be conducted:*

IA-5(3)[4][a]	*in person; or*
IA-5(3)[4][b]	*by a trusted third party; and*

IA-5(3)[5]	*requires that the registration process to receive organization-defined types of and/or specific authenticators be conducted in person or by a trusted third party before organization-defined registration authority with authorization by organization-defined personnel or roles.*

POTENTIAL ASSESSMENT METHODS AND OBJECTS:

Examine: [*SELECT FROM:* Identification and authentication policy; procedures addressing authenticator management; registration process for receiving information system authenticators; list of authenticators requiring in-person registration; list of authenticators requiring trusted third party registration; authenticator registration documentation; other relevant documents or records].

Interview: [*SELECT FROM:* Organizational personnel with authenticator management responsibilities; registration authority; organizational personnel with information security responsibilities].

IA-5(4)	AUTHENTICATOR MANAGEMENT | *AUTOMATED SUPPORT FOR PASSWORD STRENGTH DETERMINATION*

ASSESSMENT OBJECTIVE:

Determine if the organization:

IA-5(4)[1]	*defines requirements to be satisfied by password authenticators; and*
IA-5(4)[2]	*employs automated tools to determine if password authenticators are sufficiently strong to satisfy organization-defined requirements.*

Special Publication 800-53A
Revision 4

Assessing Security and Privacy Controls in Federal Information Systems
and Organizations — *Building Effective Assessment Plans*

	POTENTIAL ASSESSMENT METHODS AND OBJECTS: **Examine**: [*SELECT FROM:* Identification and authentication policy; procedures addressing authenticator management; information system design documentation; information system configuration settings and associated documentation; automated tools for evaluating password authenticators; password strength assessment results; other relevant documents or records]. **Interview**: [*SELECT FROM:* Organizational personnel with authenticator management responsibilities; organizational personnel with information security responsibilities; system/network administrators]. **Test**: [*SELECT FROM:* Automated mechanisms supporting and/or implementing password-based authenticator management capability; automated tools for determining password strength].

IA-5(5)	**AUTHENTICATOR MANAGEMENT** | *CHANGE AUTHENTICATORS PRIOR TO DELIVERY*
	ASSESSMENT OBJECTIVE: *Determine if the organization requires developers/installers of information system components to:*
	<table><tr><td>IA-5(5)[1]</td><td>*provide unique authenticators prior to delivery/installation; or*</td></tr><tr><td>IA-5(5)[2]</td><td>*change default authenticators prior to delivery/installation.*</td></tr></table>
	POTENTIAL ASSESSMENT METHODS AND OBJECTS: **Examine**: [*SELECT FROM:* Identification and authentication policy; system and services acquisition policy; procedures addressing authenticator management; procedures addressing the integration of security requirements into the acquisition process; acquisition documentation; acquisition contracts for information system procurements or services; other relevant documents or records]. **Interview**: [*SELECT FROM:* Organizational personnel with authenticator management responsibilities; organizational personnel with information system security, acquisition, and contracting responsibilities; system developers]. **Test**: [*SELECT FROM:* Automated mechanisms supporting and/or implementing authenticator management capability].

IA-5(6)	**AUTHENTICATOR MANAGEMENT** | *PROTECTION OF AUTHENTICATORS*
	ASSESSMENT OBJECTIVE: *Determine if the organization protects authenticators commensurate with the security category of the information to which use of the authenticator permits access.*
	POTENTIAL ASSESSMENT METHODS AND OBJECTS: **Examine**: [*SELECT FROM:* Identification and authentication policy; procedures addressing authenticator management; security categorization documentation for the information system; security assessments of authenticator protections; risk assessment results; security plan; other relevant documents or records]. **Interview**: [*SELECT FROM:* Organizational personnel with authenticator management responsibilities; organizational personnel implementing and/or maintaining authenticator protections; organizational personnel with information security responsibilities; system/network administrators]. **Test**: [*SELECT FROM:* Automated mechanisms supporting and/or implementing authenticator management capability; automated mechanisms protecting authenticators].

IA-5(7)	**AUTHENTICATOR MANAGEMENT** | *NO EMBEDDED UNENCRYPTED STATIC AUTHENTICATORS*
	ASSESSMENT OBJECTIVE: *Determine if the organization ensures that unencrypted static authenticators are not:*
	<table><tr><td>IA-5(7)[1]</td><td>*embedded in applications;*</td></tr></table>

Special Publication 800-53A
Revision 4

Assessing Security and Privacy Controls in Federal Information Systems
and Organizations — *Building Effective Assessment Plans*

IA-5(7)[2]	*embedded in access scripts; or*
IA-5(7)[3]	*stored on function keys.*

POTENTIAL ASSESSMENT METHODS AND OBJECTS:

Examine: [*SELECT FROM:* Identification and authentication policy; procedures addressing authenticator management; information system design documentation; information system configuration settings and associated documentation; logical access scripts; application code reviews for detecting unencrypted static authenticators; other relevant documents or records].

Interview: [*SELECT FROM:* Organizational personnel with authenticator management responsibilities; organizational personnel with information security responsibilities; system/network administrators; system developers].

Test: [*SELECT FROM:* Automated mechanisms supporting and/or implementing authenticator management capability; automated mechanisms implementing authentication in applications].

IA-5(8)	**AUTHENTICATOR MANAGEMENT** | *MULTIPLE INFORMATION SYSTEM ACCOUNTS*

ASSESSMENT OBJECTIVE:

Determine if the organization:

IA-5(8)[1]	*defines security safeguards to manage the risk of compromise due to individuals having accounts on multiple information systems; and*
IA-5(8)[2]	*implements organization-defined security safeguards to manage the risk of compromise due to individuals having accounts on multiple information systems.*

POTENTIAL ASSESSMENT METHODS AND OBJECTS:

Examine: [*SELECT FROM:* Identification and authentication policy; procedures addressing authenticator management; security plan; list of individuals having accounts on multiple information systems; list of security safeguards intended to manage risk of compromise due to individuals having accounts on multiple information systems; other relevant documents or records].

Interview: [*SELECT FROM:* Organizational personnel with authenticator management responsibilities; organizational personnel with information security responsibilities; system/network administrators].

Test: [*SELECT FROM:* Automated mechanisms supporting and/or implementing safeguards for authenticator management].

IA-5(9)	**AUTHENTICATOR MANAGEMENT** | *CROSS-ORGANIZATIONAL CREDENTIAL MANAGEMENT*

ASSESSMENT OBJECTIVE:

Determine if the organization:

IA-5(9)[1]	*defines external organizations with whom to coordinate cross-organizational management of credentials; and*
IA-5(9)[2]	*coordinates with organization-defined external organizations for cross-organizational management of credentials.*

POTENTIAL ASSESSMENT METHODS AND OBJECTS:

Examine: [*SELECT FROM:* Identification and authentication policy; procedures addressing authenticator management; procedures addressing account management; security plan; information security agreements; other relevant documents or records].

Interview: [*SELECT FROM:* Organizational personnel with authenticator management responsibilities; organizational personnel with information security responsibilities; system/network administrators].

Test: [*SELECT FROM:* Automated mechanisms supporting and/or implementing safeguards for authenticator management].

Special Publication 800-53A
Revision 4

Assessing Security and Privacy Controls in Federal Information Systems
and Organizations — *Building Effective Assessment Plans*

IA-5(10)	AUTHENTICATOR MANAGEMENT | *DYNAMIC CREDENTIAL ASSOCIATION*
	ASSESSMENT OBJECTIVE: *Determine if the information system dynamically provisions identifiers.*
	POTENTIAL ASSESSMENT METHODS AND OBJECTS: **Examine**: [*SELECT FROM:* Identification and authentication policy; procedures addressing identifier management; security plan; information system design documentation; automated mechanisms providing dynamic binding of identifiers and authenticators; information system configuration settings and associated documentation; information system audit records; other relevant documents or records]. **Interview**: [*SELECT FROM:* Organizational personnel with identifier management responsibilities; organizational personnel with information security responsibilities; system/network administrators]. **Test**: [*SELECT FROM:* Automated mechanisms implementing identifier management capability; automated mechanisms implementing dynamic provisioning of identifiers].

IA-5(11)	AUTHENTICATOR MANAGEMENT | *HARDWARE TOKEN-BASED AUTHENTICATION*
	ASSESSMENT OBJECTIVE: *Determine if, for hardware token-based authentication:*
IA-5(11)[1]	*the organization defines token quality requirements to be satisfied; and*
IA-5(11)[2]	*the information system employs mechanisms that satisfy organization-defined token quality requirements.*
	POTENTIAL ASSESSMENT METHODS AND OBJECTS: **Examine**: [*SELECT FROM:* Identification and authentication policy; procedures addressing authenticator management; security plan; information system design documentation; automated mechanisms employing hardware token-based authentication for the information system; list of token quality requirements; information system configuration settings and associated documentation; information system audit records; other relevant documents or records]. **Interview**: [*SELECT FROM:* Organizational personnel with authenticator management responsibilities; organizational personnel with information security responsibilities; system/network administrators; system developers]. **Test**: [*SELECT FROM:* Automated mechanisms supporting and/or implementing hardware token-based authenticator management capability].

IA-5(12)	AUTHENTICATOR MANAGEMENT | *BIOMETRIC AUTHENTICATION*
	ASSESSMENT OBJECTIVE: *Determine if, for biometric-based authentication:*
IA-5(12)[1]	*the organization defines biometric quality requirements to be satisfied; and*
IA-5(12)[2]	*the information system employs mechanisms that satisfy organization-defined biometric quality requirements.*
	POTENTIAL ASSESSMENT METHODS AND OBJECTS: **Examine**: [*SELECT FROM:* Identification and authentication policy; procedures addressing authenticator management; security plan; information system design documentation; automated mechanisms employing biometric-based authentication for the information system; list of biometric quality requirements; information system configuration settings and associated documentation; information system audit records; other relevant documents or records]. **Interview**: [*SELECT FROM:* Organizational personnel with authenticator management responsibilities; organizational personnel with information security responsibilities; system/network administrators; system developers]. **Test**: [*SELECT FROM:* Automated mechanisms supporting and/or implementing biometric-based authenticator management capability].

Special Publication 800-53A
Revision 4

Assessing Security and Privacy Controls in Federal Information Systems
and Organizations — *Building Effective Assessment Plans*

IA-5(13)	AUTHENTICATOR MANAGEMENT	*EXPIRATION OF CACHED AUTHENTICATORS*

	ASSESSMENT OBJECTIVE:
	Determine if:

IA-5(13)[1]	*the organization defines the time period after which the information system is to prohibit the use of cached authenticators; and*
IA-5(13)[2]	*the information system prohibits the use of cached authenticators after the organization-defined time period.*

POTENTIAL ASSESSMENT METHODS AND OBJECTS:

Examine: [*SELECT FROM:* Identification and authentication policy; procedures addressing authenticator management; security plan; information system design documentation; information system configuration settings and associated documentation; information system audit records; other relevant documents or records].

Interview: [*SELECT FROM:* Organizational personnel with authenticator management responsibilities; organizational personnel with information security responsibilities; system/network administrators; system developers].

Test: [*SELECT FROM:* Automated mechanisms supporting and/or implementing authenticator management capability].

IA-5(14)	AUTHENTICATOR MANAGEMENT	*MANAGING CONTENT OF PKI TRUST STORES*

	ASSESSMENT OBJECTIVE:
	Determine if the organization, for PKI-based authentication, employs a deliberate organization-wide methodology for managing the content of PKI trust stores installed across all platforms including:

IA-5(14)[1]	*networks;*
IA-5(14)[2]	*operating systems;*
IA-5(14)[3]	*browsers; and*
IA-5(14)[4]	*applications.*

POTENTIAL ASSESSMENT METHODS AND OBJECTS:

Examine: [*SELECT FROM:* Identification and authentication policy; procedures addressing authenticator management; security plan; organizational methodology for managing content of PKI trust stores across installed all platforms; information system design documentation; information system configuration settings and associated documentation; enterprise security architecture documentation; enterprise architecture documentation; other relevant documents or records].

Interview: [*SELECT FROM:* Organizational personnel with authenticator management responsibilities; organizational personnel with information security responsibilities; system/network administrators; system developers].

Test: [*SELECT FROM:* Automated mechanisms supporting and/or implementing PKI-based authenticator management capability; automated mechanisms supporting and/or implementing the PKI trust store capability].

IA-5(15)	AUTHENTICATOR MANAGEMENT	*FICAM-APPROVED PRODUCTS AND SERVICES*

	ASSESSMENT OBJECTIVE:
	Determine if the organization uses only FICAM-approved path discovery and validation products and services.

Special Publication 800-53A
Revision 4

Assessing Security and Privacy Controls in Federal Information Systems
and Organizations — *Building Effective Assessment Plans*

POTENTIAL ASSESSMENT METHODS AND OBJECTS:

Examine: [*SELECT FROM:* Identification and authentication policy; procedures addressing identifier management; security plan; information system design documentation; automated mechanisms providing dynamic binding of identifiers and authenticators; information system configuration settings and associated documentation; information system audit records; other relevant documents or records].

Interview: [*SELECT FROM:* Organizational personnel with identification and authentication management responsibilities; organizational personnel with information security responsibilities; system/network administrators].

Test: [*SELECT FROM:* Automated mechanisms supporting and/or implementing account management capability; automated mechanisms supporting and/or implementing identification and authentication management capability for the information system].

IA-6	AUTHENTICATOR FEEDBACK

ASSESSMENT OBJECTIVE:

Determine if the information system obscures feedback of authentication information during the authentication process to protect the information from possible exploitation/use by unauthorized individuals.

POTENTIAL ASSESSMENT METHODS AND OBJECTS:

Examine: [*SELECT FROM:* Identification and authentication policy; procedures addressing authenticator feedback; information system design documentation; information system configuration settings and associated documentation; information system audit records; other relevant documents or records].

Interview: [*SELECT FROM:* Organizational personnel with information security responsibilities; system/network administrators; system developers].

Test: [*SELECT FROM:* Automated mechanisms supporting and/or implementing the obscuring of feedback of authentication information during authentication].

IA-7	CRYPTOGRAPHIC MODULE AUTHENTICATION

ASSESSMENT OBJECTIVE:

Determine if the information system implements mechanisms for authentication to a cryptographic module that meet the requirements of applicable federal laws, Executive Orders, directives, policies, regulations, standards, and guidance for such authentication.

POTENTIAL ASSESSMENT METHODS AND OBJECTS:

Examine: [*SELECT FROM:* Identification and authentication policy; procedures addressing cryptographic module authentication; information system design documentation; information system configuration settings and associated documentation; information system audit records; other relevant documents or records].

Interview: [*SELECT FROM:* Organizational personnel with responsibility for cryptographic module authentication; organizational personnel with information security responsibilities; system/network administrators; system developers].

Test: [*SELECT FROM:* Automated mechanisms supporting and/or implementing cryptographic module authentication].

IA-8	IDENTIFICATION AND AUTHENTICATION (NON-ORGANIZATIONAL USERS)

ASSESSMENT OBJECTIVE:

Determine if the information system uniquely identifies and authenticates non-organizational users (or processes acting on behalf of non-organizational users).

Special Publication 800-53A
Revision 4

Assessing Security and Privacy Controls in Federal Information Systems
and Organizations — *Building Effective Assessment Plans*

POTENTIAL ASSESSMENT METHODS AND OBJECTS:

Examine: [*SELECT FROM:* Identification and authentication policy; procedures addressing user identification and authentication; information system design documentation; information system configuration settings and associated documentation; information system audit records; list of information system accounts; other relevant documents or records].

Interview: [*SELECT FROM:* Organizational personnel with information system operations responsibilities; organizational personnel with information security responsibilities; system/network administrators; organizational personnel with account management responsibilities].

Test: [*SELECT FROM:* Automated mechanisms supporting and/or implementing identification and authentication capability].

IA-8(1)	**IDENTIFICATION AND AUTHENTICATION** | *ACCEPTANCE OF PIV CREDENTIALS FROM OTHER AGENCIES*

ASSESSMENT OBJECTIVE:

Determine if the information system:

IA-8(1)[1]	*accepts Personal Identity Verification (PIV) credentials from other agencies; and*
IA-8(1)[2]	*electronically verifies Personal Identity Verification (PIV) credentials from other agencies.*

POTENTIAL ASSESSMENT METHODS AND OBJECTS:

Examine: [*SELECT FROM:* Identification and authentication policy; procedures addressing user identification and authentication; information system design documentation; information system configuration settings and associated documentation; information system audit records; PIV verification records; evidence of PIV credentials; PIV credential authorizations; other relevant documents or records].

Interview: [*SELECT FROM:* Organizational personnel with information system operations responsibilities; organizational personnel with information security responsibilities; system/network administrators; system developers; organizational personnel with account management responsibilities].

Test: [*SELECT FROM:* Automated mechanisms supporting and/or implementing identification and authentication capability; automated mechanisms that accept and verify PIV credentials].

IA-8(2)	**IDENTIFICATION AND AUTHENTICATION** | *ACCEPTANCE OF THIRD-PARTY CREDENTIALS*

ASSESSMENT OBJECTIVE:

Determine if the information system accepts only FICAM-approved third-party credentials.

POTENTIAL ASSESSMENT METHODS AND OBJECTS:

Examine: [*SELECT FROM:* Identification and authentication policy; procedures addressing user identification and authentication; information system design documentation; information system configuration settings and associated documentation; information system audit records; list of FICAM-approved, third-party credentialing products, components, or services procured and implemented by organization; third-party credential verification records; evidence of FICAM-approved third-party credentials; third-party credential authorizations; other relevant documents or records].

Interview: [*SELECT FROM:* Organizational personnel with information system operations responsibilities; organizational personnel with information security responsibilities; system/network administrators; system developers; organizational personnel with account management responsibilities].

Test: [*SELECT FROM:* Automated mechanisms supporting and/or implementing identification and authentication capability; automated mechanisms that accept FICAM-approved credentials].

Special Publication 800-53A
Revision 4

Assessing Security and Privacy Controls in Federal Information Systems
and Organizations — *Building Effective Assessment Plans*

IA-8(3)	IDENTIFICATION AND AUTHENTICATION | *USE OF FICAM-APPROVED PRODUCTS*
	ASSESSMENT OBJECTIVE: *Determine if the organization:*
	IA-8(3)[1] *defines information systems in which only FICAM-approved information system components are to be employed to accept third-party credentials; and*
	IA-8(3)[2] *employs only FICAM-approved information system components in organization-defined information systems to accept third-party credentials.*
	POTENTIAL ASSESSMENT METHODS AND OBJECTS: **Examine**: [*SELECT FROM:* Identification and authentication policy; system and services acquisition policy; procedures addressing user identification and authentication; procedures addressing the integration of security requirements into the acquisition process; information system design documentation; information system configuration settings and associated documentation; information system audit records; third-party credential validations; third-party credential authorizations; third-party credential records; list of FICAM-approved information system components procured and implemented by organization; acquisition documentation; acquisition contracts for information system procurements or services; other relevant documents or records]. **Interview**: [*SELECT FROM:* Organizational personnel with information system operations responsibilities; system/network administrators; organizational personnel with account management responsibilities; organizational personnel with information system security, acquisition, and contracting responsibilities]. **Test**: [*SELECT FROM:* Automated mechanisms supporting and/or implementing identification and authentication capability].

IA-8(4)	IDENTIFICATION AND AUTHENTICATION | *USE OF FICAM-ISSUED PROFILES*
	ASSESSMENT OBJECTIVE: *Determine if the information system conforms to FICAM-issued profiles.*
	POTENTIAL ASSESSMENT METHODS AND OBJECTS: **Examine**: [*SELECT FROM:* Identification and authentication policy; system and services acquisition policy; procedures addressing user identification and authentication; procedures addressing the integration of security requirements into the acquisition process; information system design documentation; information system configuration settings and associated documentation; information system audit records; list of FICAM-issued profiles and associated, approved protocols; acquisition documentation; acquisition contracts for information system procurements or services; other relevant documents or records]. **Interview**: [*SELECT FROM:* Organizational personnel with information system operations responsibilities; organizational personnel with information security responsibilities; system/network administrators; system developers; organizational personnel with account management responsibilities]. **Test**: [*SELECT FROM:* Automated mechanisms supporting and/or implementing identification and authentication capability; automated mechanisms supporting and/or implementing conformance with FICAM-issued profiles].

IA-8(5)	IDENTIFICATION AND AUTHENTICATION | *ACCEPTANCE OF PIV-I CREDENTIALS*
	ASSESSMENT OBJECTIVE: *Determine if the information system:*
	IA-8(5)[1] *accepts Personal Identity Verification-I (PIV-I) credentials; and*
	IA-8(5)[2] *electronically verifies Personal Identity Verification-I (PIV-I) credentials.*

POTENTIAL ASSESSMENT METHODS AND OBJECTS:

Examine: [*SELECT FROM:* Identification and authentication policy; procedures addressing user identification and authentication; information system design documentation; information system configuration settings and associated documentation; information system audit records; PIV-I verification records; evidence of PIV-I credentials; PIV-I credential authorizations; other relevant documents or records].

Interview: [*SELECT FROM:* Organizational personnel with information system operations responsibilities; organizational personnel with information security responsibilities; system/network administrators; system developers; organizational personnel with account management responsibilities].

Test: [*SELECT FROM:* Automated mechanisms supporting and/or implementing identification and authentication capability; automated mechanisms that accept and verify PIV-I credentials].

IA-9	SERVICE IDENTIFICATION AND AUTHENTICATION

ASSESSMENT OBJECTIVE:

Determine if the organization:

IA-9[1]	*defines information system services to be identified and authenticated using security safeguards;*
IA-9[2]	*defines security safeguards to be used to identify and authenticate organization-defined information system services; and*
IA-9[3]	*identifies and authenticates organization-defined information system services using organization-defined security safeguards.*

POTENTIAL ASSESSMENT METHODS AND OBJECTS:

Examine: [*SELECT FROM:* Identification and authentication policy; procedures addressing service identification and authentication; security plan; information system design documentation; security safeguards used to identify and authenticate information system services; information system configuration settings and associated documentation; information system audit records; other relevant documents or records].

Interview: [*SELECT FROM:* Organizational personnel with information system operations responsibilities; organizational personnel with information security responsibilities; system/network administrators; system developers; organizational personnel with identification and authentication responsibilities].

Test: [*SELECT FROM:* Security safeguards implementing service identification and authentication capability].

IA-9(1)	SERVICE IDENTIFICATION AND AUTHENTICATION | *INFORMATION EXCHANGE*

ASSESSMENT OBJECTIVE:

Determine if the organization ensures that service providers:

IA-9(1)[1]	*receive identification and authentication information;*
IA-9(1)[2]	*validate identification and authentication information; and*
IA-9(1)[3]	*transmit identification and authentication information.*

Special Publication 800-53A
Revision 4

Assessing Security and Privacy Controls in Federal Information Systems
and Organizations — *Building Effective Assessment Plans*

POTENTIAL ASSESSMENT METHODS AND OBJECTS:

Examine: [*SELECT FROM:* Identification and authentication policy; procedures addressing service identification and authentication; security plan; information system design documentation; information system configuration settings and associated documentation; information system audit records; other relevant documents or records].

Interview: [*SELECT FROM:* Organizational personnel with identification and authentication responsibilities; organizational personnel with information security responsibilities; system/network administrators; service providers].

Test: [*SELECT FROM:* Automated mechanisms implementing service identification and authentication capabilities].

IA-9(2)	SERVICE IDENTIFICATION AND AUTHENTICATION	*TRANSMISSION OF DECISIONS*

ASSESSMENT OBJECTIVE:

Determine if the organization:

IA-9(2)[1]	*defines services for which identification and authentication decisions transmitted between such services are to be consistent with organizational policies; and*
IA-9(2)[2]	*ensures that identification and authentication decisions are transmitted between organization-defined services consistent with organizational policies.*

POTENTIAL ASSESSMENT METHODS AND OBJECTS:

Examine: [*SELECT FROM:* Identification and authentication policy; procedures addressing service identification and authentication; security plan; information system design documentation; information system configuration settings and associated documentation; information system audit records; transmission records; transmission verification records; rules for identification and authentication transmission decisions between organizational services; other relevant documents or records].

Interview: [*SELECT FROM:* Organizational personnel with identification and authentication responsibilities; organizational personnel with information security responsibilities; system/network administrators].

Test: [*SELECT FROM:* Automated mechanisms implementing service identification and authentication capabilities].

IA-10	ADAPTIVE IDENTIFICATION AND AUTHENTICATION

ASSESSMENT OBJECTIVE:

Determine if the organization:

IA-10[1]	*defines specific circumstances or situations that require individuals accessing the information system to employ supplemental authentication techniques or mechanisms;*
IA-10[2]	*defines supplemental authentication techniques or mechanisms to be employed when accessing the information system under specific organization-defined circumstances or situations; and*
IA-10[3]	*requires that individuals accessing the information system employ organization-defined supplemental authentication techniques or mechanisms under specific organization-defined circumstances or situations.*

Special Publication 800-53A
Revision 4

Assessing Security and Privacy Controls in Federal Information Systems
and Organizations — *Building Effective Assessment Plans*

	POTENTIAL ASSESSMENT METHODS AND OBJECTS: **Examine**: [*SELECT FROM:* Identification and authentication policy; procedures addressing adaptive/ supplemental identification and authentication techniques or mechanisms; security plan; information system design documentation; information system configuration settings and associated documentation; supplemental identification and authentication techniques or mechanisms; information system audit records; other relevant documents or records]. **Interview**: [*SELECT FROM:* Organizational personnel with information system operations responsibilities; organizational personnel with information security responsibilities; system/network administrators; system developers; organizational personnel with identification and authentication responsibilities]. **Test**: [*SELECT FROM:* Automated mechanisms supporting and/or implementing identification and authentication capability].

IA-11	**RE-AUTHENTICATION**
	ASSESSMENT OBJECTIVE: *Determine if the organization:*

IA-11[1]	*defines circumstances or situations requiring re-authentication;*
IA-11[2]	*requires users to re-authenticate when organization-defined circumstances or situations require re-authentication; and*
IA-11[3]	*requires devices to re-authenticate when organization-defined circumstances or situations require re-authentication.*

	POTENTIAL ASSESSMENT METHODS AND OBJECTS: **Examine**: [*SELECT FROM:* Identification and authentication policy; procedures addressing user and device re-authentication; security plan; information system design documentation; information system configuration settings and associated documentation; list of circumstances or situations requiring re-authentication; information system audit records; other relevant documents or records]. **Interview**: [*SELECT FROM:* Organizational personnel with information system operations responsibilities; organizational personnel with information security responsibilities; system/network administrators; system developers; organizational personnel with identification and authentication responsibilities]. **Test**: [*SELECT FROM:* Automated mechanisms supporting and/or implementing identification and authentication capability].

Special Publication 800-53A
Revision 4

Assessing Security and Privacy Controls in Federal Information Systems
and Organizations — *Building Effective Assessment Plans*

FAMILY: INCIDENT RESPONSE

IR-1	INCIDENT RESPONSE POLICY AND PROCEDURES			
	ASSESSMENT OBJECTIVE: *Determine if the organization:*			
	IR-1(a)(1)	IR-1(a)(1)[1]	*develops and documents an incident response policy that addresses:*	
			IR-1(a)(1)[1][a]	*purpose;*
			IR-1(a)(1)[1][b]	*scope;*
			IR-1(a)(1)[1][c]	*roles;*
			IR-1(a)(1)[1][d]	*responsibilities;*
			IR-1(a)(1)[1][e]	*management commitment;*
			IR-1(a)(1)[1][f]	*coordination among organizational entities;*
			IR-1(a)(1)[1][g]	*compliance;*
		IR-1(a)(1)[2]	*defines personnel or roles to whom the incident response policy is to be disseminated;*	
		IR-1(a)(1)[3]	*disseminates the incident response policy to organization-defined personnel or roles;*	
	IR-1(a)(2)	IR-1(a)(2)[1]	*develops and documents procedures to facilitate the implementation of the incident response policy and associated incident response controls;*	
		IR-1(a)(2)[2]	*defines personnel or roles to whom the procedures are to be disseminated;*	
		IR-1(a)(2)[3]	*disseminates the procedures to organization-defined personnel or roles;*	
	IR-1(b)(1)	IR-1(b)(1)[1]	*defines the frequency to review and update the current incident response policy;*	
		IR-1(b)(1)[2]	*reviews and updates the current incident response policy with the organization-defined frequency;*	
	IR-1(b)(2)	IR-1(b)(2)[1]	*defines the frequency to review and update the current incident response procedures; and*	
		IR-1(b)(2)[2]	*reviews and updates the current incident response procedures with the organization-defined frequency.*	
	POTENTIAL ASSESSMENT METHODS AND OBJECTS: **Examine:** [*SELECT FROM:* Incident response policy and procedures; other relevant documents or records]. **Interview:** [*SELECT FROM:* Organizational personnel with incident response responsibilities; organizational personnel with information security responsibilities].			

Special Publication 800-53A
Revision 4

Assessing Security and Privacy Controls in Federal Information Systems
and Organizations — *Building Effective Assessment Plans*

IR-2	INCIDENT RESPONSE TRAINING		
	ASSESSMENT OBJECTIVE: *Determine if the organization:*		
	IR-2(a)	IR-2(a)[1]	*defines a time period within which incident response training is to be provided to information system users assuming an incident response role or responsibility;*
		IR-2(a)[2]	*provides incident response training to information system users consistent with assigned roles and responsibilities within the organization-defined time period of assuming an incident response role or responsibility;*
	IR-2(b)	*provides incident response training to information system users consistent with assigned roles and responsibilities when required by information system changes;*	
	IR-2(c)	IR-2(c)[1]	*defines the frequency to provide refresher incident response training to information system users consistent with assigned roles or responsibilities; and*
		IR-2(c)[2]	*after the initial incident response training, provides refresher incident response training to information system users consistent with assigned roles and responsibilities in accordance with the organization-defined frequency to provide refresher training.*
	POTENTIAL ASSESSMENT METHODS AND OBJECTS: **Examine**: [SELECT FROM: Incident response policy; procedures addressing incident response training; incident response training curriculum; incident response training materials; security plan; incident response plan; security plan; incident response training records; other relevant documents or records]. **Interview**: [SELECT FROM: Organizational personnel with incident response training and operational responsibilities; organizational personnel with information security responsibilities].		

IR-2(1)	INCIDENT RESPONSE TRAINING | *SIMULATED EVENTS*
	ASSESSMENT OBJECTIVE: *Determine if the organization incorporates simulated events into incident response training to facilitate effective response by personnel in crisis situations.*
	POTENTIAL ASSESSMENT METHODS AND OBJECTS: **Examine**: [SELECT FROM: Incident response policy; procedures addressing incident response training; incident response training curriculum; incident response training materials; incident response plan; security plan; other relevant documents or records]. **Interview**: [SELECT FROM: Organizational personnel with incident response training and operational responsibilities; organizational personnel with information security responsibilities]. **Test**: [SELECT FROM: Automated mechanisms that support and/or implement simulated events for incident response training].

IR-2(2)	INCIDENT RESPONSE TRAINING | *AUTOMATED TRAINING ENVIRONMENTS*
	ASSESSMENT OBJECTIVE: *Determine if the organization employs automated mechanisms to provide a more thorough and realistic incident response training environment.*

Special Publication 800-53A
Revision 4

Assessing Security and Privacy Controls in Federal Information Systems
and Organizations — *Building Effective Assessment Plans*

POTENTIAL ASSESSMENT METHODS AND OBJECTS:

Examine: [*SELECT FROM:* Incident response policy; procedures addressing incident response training; incident response training curriculum; incident response training materials; automated mechanisms supporting incident response training; incident response plan; security plan; other relevant documents or records].

Interview: [*SELECT FROM:* Organizational personnel with incident response training and operational responsibilities; organizational personnel with information security responsibilities].

Test: [*SELECT FROM:* Automated mechanisms that provide a thorough and realistic incident response training environment].

IR-3	INCIDENT RESPONSE TESTING

ASSESSMENT OBJECTIVE:

Determine if the organization:

IR-3[1]	*defines incident response tests to test the incident response capability for the information system;*
IR-3[2]	*defines the frequency to test the incident response capability for the information system; and*
IR-3[3]	*tests the incident response capability for the information system with the organization-defined frequency, using organization-defined tests to determine the incident response effectiveness and documents the results.*

POTENTIAL ASSESSMENT METHODS AND OBJECTS:

Examine: [*SELECT FROM:* Incident response policy; contingency planning policy; procedures addressing incident response testing; procedures addressing contingency plan testing; incident response testing material; incident response test results; incident response test plan; incident response plan; contingency plan; security plan; other relevant documents or records].

Interview: [*SELECT FROM:* Organizational personnel with incident response testing responsibilities; organizational personnel with information security responsibilities].

IR-3(1)	INCIDENT RESPONSE TESTING | *AUTOMATED TESTING*

ASSESSMENT OBJECTIVE:

Determine if the organization employs automated mechanisms to more thoroughly and effectively test the incident response capability.

POTENTIAL ASSESSMENT METHODS AND OBJECTS:

Examine: [*SELECT FROM:* Incident response policy; contingency planning policy; procedures addressing incident response testing; procedures addressing contingency plan testing; incident response testing documentation; incident response test results; incident response test plan; incident response plan; contingency plan; security plan; automated mechanisms supporting incident response tests; other relevant documents or records].

Interview: [*SELECT FROM:* Organizational personnel with incident response testing responsibilities; organizational personnel with information security responsibilities].

Test: [*SELECT FROM:* Automated mechanisms that more thoroughly and effectively test the incident response capability].

IR-3(2)	INCIDENT RESPONSE TESTING | *COORDINATION WITH RELATED PLANS*

ASSESSMENT OBJECTIVE:

Determine if the organization coordinates incident response testing with organizational elements responsible for related plans.

Special Publication 800-53A
Revision 4

Assessing Security and Privacy Controls in Federal Information Systems
and Organizations — *Building Effective Assessment Plans*

POTENTIAL ASSESSMENT METHODS AND OBJECTS:

Examine: [*SELECT FROM:* Incident response policy; contingency planning policy; procedures addressing incident response testing; incident response testing documentation; incident response plan; business continuity plans; contingency plans; disaster recovery plans; continuity of operations plans; crisis communications plans; critical infrastructure plans; occupant emergency plans; security plan; other relevant documents or records].

Interview: [*SELECT FROM:* Organizational personnel with incident response testing responsibilities; organizational personnel with responsibilities for testing organizational plans related to incident response testing; organizational personnel with information security responsibilities].

IR-4	INCIDENT HANDLING		
	ASSESSMENT OBJECTIVE: *Determine if the organization:*		
	IR-4(a)	*implements an incident handling capability for security incidents that includes:*	
		IR-4(a)[1]	*preparation;*
		IR-4(a)[2]	*detection and analysis;*
		IR-4(a)[3]	*containment;*
		IR-4(a)[4]	*eradication;*
		IR-4(a)[5]	*recovery;*
	IR-4(b)	*coordinates incident handling activities with contingency planning activities;*	
	IR-4(c)	IR-4(c)[1]	*incorporates lessons learned from ongoing incident handling activities into:*
			IR-4(c)[1][a] *incident response procedures;*
			IR-4(c)[1][b] *training;*
			IR-4(c)[1][c] *testing/exercises;*
		IR-4(c)[2]	*implements the resulting changes accordingly to:*
			IR-4(c)[2][a] *incident response procedures;*
			IR-4(c)[2][b] *training; and*
			IR-4(c)[2][c] *testing/exercises.*

POTENTIAL ASSESSMENT METHODS AND OBJECTS:

Examine: [*SELECT FROM:* Incident response policy; contingency planning policy; procedures addressing incident handling; incident response plan; contingency plan; security plan; other relevant documents or records].

Interview: [*SELECT FROM:* Organizational personnel with incident handling responsibilities; organizational personnel with contingency planning responsibilities; organizational personnel with information security responsibilities].

Test: [*SELECT FROM:* Incident handling capability for the organization].

IR-4(1)	INCIDENT HANDLING	*AUTOMATED INCIDENT HANDLING PROCESSES*
	ASSESSMENT OBJECTIVE: *Determine if the organization employs automated mechanisms to support the incident handling process.*

Special Publication 800-53A
Revision 4

Assessing Security and Privacy Controls in Federal Information Systems
and Organizations — *Building Effective Assessment Plans*

POTENTIAL ASSESSMENT METHODS AND OBJECTS:

Examine: [*SELECT FROM:* Incident response policy; procedures addressing incident handling; automated mechanisms supporting incident handling; information system design documentation; information system configuration settings and associated documentation; information system audit records; incident response plan; security plan; other relevant documents or records].

Interview: [*SELECT FROM:* Organizational personnel with incident handling responsibilities; organizational personnel with information security responsibilities].

Test: [*SELECT FROM:* Automated mechanisms that support and/or implement the incident handling process].

IR-4(2)	INCIDENT HANDLING	*DYNAMIC RECONFIGURATION*

ASSESSMENT OBJECTIVE:

Determine if the organization:

IR-4(2)[1]	*defines information system components to be dynamically reconfigured as part of the incident response capability; and*
IR-4(2)[2]	*includes dynamic reconfiguration of organization-defined information system components as part of the incident response capability.*

POTENTIAL ASSESSMENT METHODS AND OBJECTS:

Examine: [*SELECT FROM:* Incident response policy; procedures addressing incident handling; automated mechanisms supporting incident handling; list of system components to be dynamically reconfigured as part of incident response capability; information system design documentation; information system configuration settings and associated documentation; information system audit records; incident response plan; security plan; other relevant documents or records].

Interview: [*SELECT FROM:* Organizational personnel with incident handling responsibilities; organizational personnel with information security responsibilities].

Test: [*SELECT FROM:* Automated mechanisms that support and/or implement dynamic reconfiguration of components as part of incident response].

IR-4(3)	INCIDENT HANDLING	*CONTINUITY OF OPERATIONS*

ASSESSMENT OBJECTIVE:

Determine if the organization:

IR-4(3)[1]	*defines classes of incidents requiring an organization-defined action to be taken;*
IR-4(3)[2]	*defines actions to be taken in response to organization-defined classes of incidents; and*
IR-4(3)[3]	*identifies organization-defined classes of incidents and organization-defined actions to take in response to classes of incidents to ensure continuation of organizational missions and business functions.*

POTENTIAL ASSESSMENT METHODS AND OBJECTS:

Examine: [*SELECT FROM:* Incident response policy; procedures addressing incident handling; incident response plan; security plan; list of classes of incidents; list of appropriate incident response actions; other relevant documents or records].

Interview: [*SELECT FROM:* Organizational personnel with incident handling responsibilities; organizational personnel with information security responsibilities].

Test: [*SELECT FROM:* Automated mechanisms that support and/or implement continuity of operations].

Special Publication 800-53A
Revision 4

Assessing Security and Privacy Controls in Federal Information Systems
and Organizations — *Building Effective Assessment Plans*

IR-4(4)	INCIDENT HANDLING | *INFORMATION CORRELATION*
	ASSESSMENT OBJECTIVE: *Determine if the organization correlates incident information and individual incident responses to achieve an organization-wide perspective on incident awareness and response.*
	POTENTIAL ASSESSMENT METHODS AND OBJECTS: **Examine**: [*SELECT FROM:* Incident response policy; procedures addressing incident handling; incident response plan; security plan; automated mechanisms supporting incident and event correlation; information system design documentation; information system configuration settings and associated documentation; incident management correlation logs; event management correlation logs; security information and event management logs; incident management correlation reports; event management correlation reports; security information and event management reports; audit records; other relevant documents or records]. **Interview**: [*SELECT FROM:* Organizational personnel with incident handling responsibilities; organizational personnel with information security responsibilities; organizational personnel with whom incident information and individual incident responses are to be correlated]. **Test**: [*SELECT FROM:* Organizational processes for correlating incident information and individual incident responses; automated mechanisms that support and or implement correlation of incident response information with individual incident responses].

IR-4(5)	INCIDENT HANDLING | *AUTOMATIC DISABLING OF INFORMATION SYSTEM.*
	ASSESSMENT OBJECTIVE: *Determine if the organization:*
IR-4(5)[1]	*defines security violations that, if detected, initiate a configurable capability to automatically disable the information system; and*
IR-4(5)[2]	*implements a configurable capability to automatically disable the information system if any of the organization-defined security violations are detected.*
	POTENTIAL ASSESSMENT METHODS AND OBJECTS: **Examine**: [*SELECT FROM:* Incident response policy; procedures addressing incident handling; automated mechanisms supporting incident handling; information system design documentation; information system configuration settings and associated documentation; incident response plan; security plan; other relevant documents or records]. **Interview**: [*SELECT FROM:* Organizational personnel with incident handling responsibilities; organizational personnel with information security responsibilities; system developers]. **Test**: [*SELECT FROM:* Incident handling capability for the organization; automated mechanisms supporting and/or implementing automatic disabling of the information system].

IR-4(6)	INCIDENT HANDLING | *INSIDER THREATS – SPECIFIC CAPABILITIES*
	ASSESSMENT OBJECTIVE: *Determine if the organization implements incident handling capability for insider threats.*
	POTENTIAL ASSESSMENT METHODS AND OBJECTS: **Examine**: [*SELECT FROM:* Incident response policy; procedures addressing incident handling; automated mechanisms supporting incident handling; information system design documentation; information system configuration settings and associated documentation; incident response plan; security plan; audit records; other relevant documents or records]. **Interview**: [*SELECT FROM:* Organizational personnel with incident handling responsibilities; organizational personnel with information security responsibilities]. **Test**: [*SELECT FROM:* Incident handling capability for the organization].

Special Publication 800-53A
Revision 4

Assessing Security and Privacy Controls in Federal Information Systems
and Organizations — *Building Effective Assessment Plans*

IR-4(7)	INCIDENT HANDLING	*INSIDER THREATS – INTRA-ORGANIZATION COORDINATION*
	ASSESSMENT OBJECTIVE: *Determine if the organization:*	
	IR-4(7)[1]	*defines components or elements of the organization with whom the incident handling capability for insider threats is to be coordinated; and*
	IR-4(7)[2]	*coordinates incident handling capability for insider threats across organization-defined components or elements of the organization.*
	POTENTIAL ASSESSMENT METHODS AND OBJECTS: **Examine**: [*SELECT FROM:* Incident response policy; procedures addressing incident handling; incident response plan; security plan; other relevant documents or records]. **Interview**: [*SELECT FROM:* Organizational personnel with incident handling responsibilities; organizational personnel with information security responsibilities; organizational personnel/elements with whom incident handling capability is to be coordinated]. **Test**: [*SELECT FROM:* Organizational processes for coordinating incident handling].	

IR-4(8)	INCIDENT HANDLING	*CORRELATION WITH EXTERNAL ORGANIZATIONS*
	ASSESSMENT OBJECTIVE: *Determine if the organization:*	
	IR-4(8)[1]	*defines external organizations with whom organizational incident information is to be coordinated;*
	IR-4(8)[2]	*defines incident information to be correlated and shared with organization-defined external organizations; and*
	IR-4(8)[3]	*the organization coordinates with organization-defined external organizations to correlate and share organization-defined information to achieve a cross-organization perspective on incident awareness and more effective incident responses.*
	POTENTIAL ASSESSMENT METHODS AND OBJECTS: **Examine**: [*SELECT FROM:* Incident response policy; procedures addressing incident handling; list of external organizations; records of incident handling coordination with external organizations; incident response plan; security plan; other relevant documents or records]. **Interview**: [*SELECT FROM:* Organizational personnel with incident handling responsibilities; organizational personnel with information security responsibilities; personnel from external organizations with whom incident response information is to be coordinated/shared/correlated]. **Test**: [*SELECT FROM:* Organizational processes for coordinating incident handling information with external organizations].	

IR-4(9)	INCIDENT HANDLING	*DYNAMIC RESPONSE CAPABILITY*
	ASSESSMENT OBJECTIVE: *Determine if the organization:*	
	IR-4(9)[1]	*defines dynamic response capabilities to be employed to effectively respond to security incidents; and*
	IR-4(9)[2]	*employs organization-defined dynamic response capabilities to effectively respond to security incidents.*

Special Publication 800-53A
Revision 4

Assessing Security and Privacy Controls in Federal Information Systems
and Organizations — *Building Effective Assessment Plans*

POTENTIAL ASSESSMENT METHODS AND OBJECTS:

Examine: [*SELECT FROM:* Incident response policy; procedures addressing incident handling; automated mechanisms supporting dynamic response capabilities; information system design documentation; information system configuration settings and associated documentation; incident response plan; security plan; audit records; other relevant documents or records].

Interview: [*SELECT FROM:* Organizational personnel with incident handling responsibilities; organizational personnel with information security responsibilities].

Test: [*SELECT FROM:* Organizational processes for dynamic response capability; automated mechanisms supporting and/or implementing the dynamic response capability for the organization].

IR-4(10)	INCIDENT HANDLING | *SUPPLY CHAIN COORDINATION*

ASSESSMENT OBJECTIVE:

Determine if the organization coordinates incident handling activities involving supply chain events with other organizations involved in the supply chain.

POTENTIAL ASSESSMENT METHODS AND OBJECTS:

Examine: [*SELECT FROM:* Incident response policy; procedures addressing supply chain coordination; acquisition contracts; service-level agreements; incident response plan; security plan; incident response plans of other organization involved in supply chain activities; other relevant documents or records].

Interview: [*SELECT FROM:* Organizational personnel with incident handling responsibilities; organizational personnel with information security responsibilities; organizational personnel with supply chain responsibilities].

IR-5	INCIDENT MONITORING

ASSESSMENT OBJECTIVE:

Determine if the organization:

IR-5[1]	*tracks information system security incidents; and*
IR-5[2]	*documents information system security incidents.*

POTENTIAL ASSESSMENT METHODS AND OBJECTS:

Examine: [*SELECT FROM:* Incident response policy; procedures addressing incident monitoring; incident response records and documentation; incident response plan; security plan; other relevant documents or records].

Interview: [*SELECT FROM:* Organizational personnel with incident monitoring responsibilities; organizational personnel with information security responsibilities].

Test: [*SELECT FROM:* Incident monitoring capability for the organization; automated mechanisms supporting and/or implementing tracking and documenting of system security incidents].

IR-5(1)	INCIDENT MONITORING | *AUTOMATED TRACKING / DATA COLLECTION / ANALYSIS*

ASSESSMENT OBJECTIVE:

Determine if the organization employs automated mechanisms to assist in:

IR-5(1)[1]	*the tracking of security incidents;*
IR-5(1)[2]	*the collection of incident information; and*
IR-5(1)[3]	*the analysis of incident information.*

Special Publication 800-53A
Revision 4

Assessing Security and Privacy Controls in Federal Information Systems
and Organizations — *Building Effective Assessment Plans*

	POTENTIAL ASSESSMENT METHODS AND OBJECTS:
	Examine: [*SELECT FROM:* Incident response policy; procedures addressing incident monitoring; automated mechanisms supporting incident monitoring; information system design documentation; information system configuration settings and associated documentation; incident response plan; security plan; audit records; other relevant documents or records].
	Interview: [*SELECT FROM:* Organizational personnel with incident monitoring responsibilities; organizational personnel with information security responsibilities].
	Test: [*SELECT FROM:* Automated mechanisms assisting in tracking of security incidents and in the collection and analysis of incident information].

IR-6	INCIDENT REPORTING		
	ASSESSMENT OBJECTIVE:		
	Determine if the organization:		
	IR-6(a)	IR-6(a)[1]	*defines the time period within which personnel report suspected security incidents to the organizational incident response capability;*
		IR-6(a)[2]	*requires personnel to report suspected security incidents to the organizational incident response capability within the organization-defined time period;*
	IR-6(b)	IR-6(b)[1]	*defines authorities to whom security incident information is to be reported; and*
		IR-6(b)[2]	*reports security incident information to organization-defined authorities.*
	POTENTIAL ASSESSMENT METHODS AND OBJECTS:		
	Examine: [*SELECT FROM:* Incident response policy; procedures addressing incident reporting; incident reporting records and documentation; incident response plan; security plan; other relevant documents or records].		
	Interview: [*SELECT FROM:* Organizational personnel with incident reporting responsibilities; organizational personnel with information security responsibilities; personnel who have/should have reported incidents; personnel (authorities) to whom incident information is to be reported].		
	Test: [*SELECT FROM:* Organizational processes for incident reporting; automated mechanisms supporting and/or implementing incident reporting].		

IR-6(1)	INCIDENT REPORTING | *AUTOMATED REPORTING*
	ASSESSMENT OBJECTIVE:
	Determine if the organization employs automated mechanisms to assist in the reporting of security incidents.
	POTENTIAL ASSESSMENT METHODS AND OBJECTS:
	Examine: [*SELECT FROM:* Incident response policy; procedures addressing incident reporting; automated mechanisms supporting incident reporting; information system design documentation; information system configuration settings and associated documentation; incident response plan; security plan; other relevant documents or records].
	Interview: [*SELECT FROM:* Organizational personnel with incident reporting responsibilities; organizational personnel with information security responsibilities].
	Test: [*SELECT FROM:* Organizational processes for incident reporting; automated mechanisms supporting and/or implementing reporting of security incidents].

Special Publication 800-53A
Revision 4

Assessing Security and Privacy Controls in Federal Information Systems
and Organizations — *Building Effective Assessment Plans*

IR-6(2)	INCIDENT REPORTING | *VULNERABILITIES RELATED TO INCIDENTS*
	ASSESSMENT OBJECTIVE:
	Determine if the organization:
	IR-6(2)[1] *defines personnel or roles to whom information system vulnerabilities associated with reported security incidents are to be reported; and*
	IR-6(2)[2] *reports information system vulnerabilities associated with reported security incidents to organization-defined personnel or roles.*
	POTENTIAL ASSESSMENT METHODS AND OBJECTS:
	Examine: [*SELECT FROM*: Incident response policy; procedures addressing incident reporting; incident response plan; security plan; security incident reports and associated information system vulnerabilities; other relevant documents or records].
	Interview: [*SELECT FROM*: Organizational personnel with incident reporting responsibilities; organizational personnel with information security responsibilities; system/network administrators; personnel to whom vulnerabilities associated with security incidents are to be reported].
	Test: [*SELECT FROM*: Organizational processes for incident reporting; automated mechanisms supporting and/or implementing reporting of vulnerabilities associated with security incidents].

IR-6(3)	INCIDENT REPORTING | *COORDINATION WITH SUPPLY CHAIN*
	ASSESSMENT OBJECTIVE:
	Determine if the organization provides security incident information to other organizations involved in the supply chain for information systems or information system components related to the incident.
	POTENTIAL ASSESSMENT METHODS AND OBJECTS:
	Examine: [*SELECT FROM*: Incident response policy; procedures addressing supply chain coordination; acquisition contracts; service-level agreements; incident response plan; security plan; plans of other organization involved in supply chain activities; other relevant documents or records].
	Interview: [*SELECT FROM*: Organizational personnel with incident reporting responsibilities; organizational personnel with information security responsibilities; organizational personnel with supply chain responsibilities].
	Test: [*SELECT FROM*: Organizational processes for incident reporting; automated mechanisms supporting and/or implementing reporting of incident information involved in the supply chain].

IR-7	INCIDENT RESPONSE ASSISTANCE
	ASSESSMENT OBJECTIVE:
	Determine if the organization provides an incident response support resource:
	IR-7[1] *that is integral to the organizational incident response capability; and*
	IR-7[2] *that offers advice and assistance to users of the information system for the handling and reporting of security incidents.*
	POTENTIAL ASSESSMENT METHODS AND OBJECTS:
	Examine: [*SELECT FROM*: Incident response policy; procedures addressing incident response assistance; incident response plan; security plan; other relevant documents or records].
	Interview: [*SELECT FROM*: Organizational personnel with incident response assistance and support responsibilities; organizational personnel with access to incident response support and assistance capability; organizational personnel with information security responsibilities].
	Test: [*SELECT FROM*: Organizational processes for incident response assistance; automated mechanisms supporting and/or implementing incident response assistance].

Special Publication 800-53A
Revision 4

Assessing Security and Privacy Controls in Federal Information Systems
and Organizations — *Building Effective Assessment Plans*

IR-7(1)	INCIDENT RESPONSE ASSISTANCE | *AUTOMATION SUPPORT FOR AVAILABILITY OF INFORMATION / SUPPORT*
	ASSESSMENT OBJECTIVE: *Determine if the organization employs automated mechanisms to increase the availability of incident response-related information and support.*
	POTENTIAL ASSESSMENT METHODS AND OBJECTS: **Examine**: [*SELECT FROM:* Incident response policy; procedures addressing incident response assistance; automated mechanisms supporting incident response support and assistance; information system design documentation; information system configuration settings and associated documentation; incident response plan; security plan; other relevant documents or records]. **Interview**: [*SELECT FROM:* Organizational personnel with incident response support and assistance responsibilities; organizational personnel with access to incident response support and assistance capability; organizational personnel with information security responsibilities]. **Test**: [*SELECT FROM:* Organizational processes for incident response assistance; automated mechanisms supporting and/or implementing an increase in the availability of incident response information and support].

IR-7(2)	INCIDENT RESPONSE ASSISTANCE | *COORDINATION WITH EXTERNAL PROVIDERS*	
	ASSESSMENT OBJECTIVE: *Determine if the organization:*	
	IR-7(2)(a)	*establishes a direct, cooperative relationship between its incident response capability and external providers of information system protection capability; and*
	IR-7(2)(b)	*identifies organizational incident response team members to the external providers.*
	POTENTIAL ASSESSMENT METHODS AND OBJECTS: **Examine**: [*SELECT FROM:* Incident response policy; procedures addressing incident response assistance; incident response plan; security plan; other relevant documents or records]. **Interview**: [*SELECT FROM:* Organizational personnel with incident response support and assistance responsibilities; external providers of information system protection capability; organizational personnel with information security responsibilities].	

IR-8	INCIDENT RESPONSE PLAN			
	ASSESSMENT OBJECTIVE: *Determine if the organization:*			
	IR-8(a)	*develops an incident response plan that:*		
		IR-8(a)(1)	*provides the organization with a roadmap for implementing its incident response capability;*	
		IR-8(a)(2)	*describes the structure and organization of the incident response capability;*	
		IR-8(a)(3)	*provides a high-level approach for how the incident response capability fits into the overall organization;*	
		IR-8(a)(4)	*meets the unique requirements of the organization, which relate to:*	
			IR-8(a)(4)[1]	*mission;*
			IR-8(a)(4)[2]	*size;*

Special Publication 800-53A
Revision 4

Assessing Security and Privacy Controls in Federal Information Systems
and Organizations — *Building Effective Assessment Plans*

		IR-8(a)(4)[3]		*structure;*
		IR-8(a)(4)[4]		*functions;*
	IR-8(a)(5)			*defines reportable incidents;*
	IR-8(a)(6)			*provides metrics for measuring the incident response capability within the organization;*
	IR-8(a)(7)			*defines the resources and management support needed to effectively maintain and mature an incident response capability;*
	IR-8(a)(8)	IR-8(a)(8)[1]		*defines personnel or roles to review and approve the incident response plan;*
		IR-8(a)(8)[2]		*is reviewed and approved by organization-defined personnel or roles;*
IR-8(b)	IR-8(b)[1]	IR-8(b)[1][a]		*defines incident response personnel (identified by name and/or by role) to whom copies of the incident response plan are to be distributed;*
		IR-8(b)[1][b]		*defines organizational elements to whom copies of the incident response plan are to be distributed;*
	IR-8(b)[2]			*distributes copies of the incident response plan to organization-defined incident response personnel (identified by name and/or by role) and organizational elements;*
IR-8(c)	IR-8(c)[1]			*defines the frequency to review the incident response plan;*
	IR-8(c)[2]			*reviews the incident response plan with the organization-defined frequency;*
IR-8(d)	*updates the incident response plan to address system/organizational changes or problems encountered during plan:*			
	IR-8(d)[1]			*implementation;*
	IR-8(d)[2]			*execution; or*
	IR-8(d)[3]			*testing;*
IR-8(e)	IR-8(e)[1]	IR-8(e)[1][a]		*defines incident response personnel (identified by name and/or by role) to whom incident response plan changes are to be communicated;*
		IR-8(e)[1][b]		*defines organizational elements to whom incident response plan changes are to be communicated;*
	IR-8(e)[2]			*communicates incident response plan changes to organization-defined incident response personnel (identified by name and/or by role) and organizational elements; and*
IR-8(f)	*protects the incident response plan from unauthorized disclosure and modification.*			

POTENTIAL ASSESSMENT METHODS AND OBJECTS:

Examine: [*SELECT FROM:* Incident response policy; procedures addressing incident response planning; incident response plan; records of incident response plan reviews and approvals; other relevant documents or records].

Interview: [*SELECT FROM:* Organizational personnel with incident response planning responsibilities; organizational personnel with information security responsibilities].

Test: [*SELECT FROM:* Organizational incident response plan and related organizational processes].

Special Publication 800-53A
Revision 4

Assessing Security and Privacy Controls in Federal Information Systems
and Organizations — *Building Effective Assessment Plans*

IR-9	INFORMATION SPILLAGE RESPONSE	
	ASSESSMENT OBJECTIVE: *Determine if the organization:*	
	IR-9(a)	*responds to information spills by identifying the specific information causing the information system contamination;*
	IR-9(b) IR-9(b)[1]	*defines personnel to be alerted of the information spillage;*
	IR-9(b)[2]	*identifies a method of communication not associated with the information spill to use to alert organization-defined personnel of the spill;*
	IR-9(b)[3]	*responds to information spills by alerting organization-defined personnel of the information spill using a method of communication not associated with the spill;*
	IR-9(c)	*responds to information spills by isolating the contaminated information system;*
	IR-9(d)	*responds to information spills by eradicating the information from the contaminated information system;*
	IR-9(e)	*responds to information spills by identifying other information systems that may have been subsequently contaminated;*
	IR-9(f) IR-9(f)[1]	*defines other actions to be performed in response to information spills; and*
	IR-9(f)[2]	*responds to information spills by performing other organization-defined actions.*

POTENTIAL ASSESSMENT METHODS AND OBJECTS:

Examine: [*SELECT FROM:* Incident response policy; procedures addressing information spillage; incident response plan; records of information spillage alerts/notifications, list of personnel who should receive alerts of information spillage; list of actions to be performed regarding information spillage; other relevant documents or records].

Interview: [*SELECT FROM:* Organizational personnel with incident response responsibilities; organizational personnel with information security responsibilities].

Test: [*SELECT FROM:* Organizational processes for information spillage response; automated mechanisms supporting and/or implementing information spillage response actions and related communications].

IR-9(1)	INFORMATION SPILLAGE RESPONSE | *RESPONSIBLE PERSONNEL*	
	ASSESSMENT OBJECTIVE: *Determine if the organization:*	
	IR-9(1)[1]	*defines personnel with responsibility for responding to information spills; and*
	IR-9(1)[2]	*assigns organization-defined personnel with responsibility for responding to information spills.*

POTENTIAL ASSESSMENT METHODS AND OBJECTS:

Examine: [*SELECT FROM:* Incident response policy; procedures addressing information spillage; incident response plan; list of personnel responsible for responding to information spillage; other relevant documents or records].

Interview: [*SELECT FROM:* Organizational personnel with incident response responsibilities; organizational personnel with information security responsibilities].

Special Publication 800-53A
Revision 4

Assessing Security and Privacy Controls in Federal Information Systems
and Organizations — *Building Effective Assessment Plans*

IR-9(2)	INFORMATION SPILLAGE RESPONSE | *TRAINING*
	ASSESSMENT OBJECTIVE: *Determine if the organization:*
	IR-9(2)[1] *defines the frequency to provide information spillage response training; and*
	IR-9(2)[2] *provides information spillage response training with the organization-defined frequency.*
	POTENTIAL ASSESSMENT METHODS AND OBJECTS: **Examine**: [*SELECT FROM:* Incident response policy; procedures addressing information spillage response training; information spillage response training curriculum; information spillage response training materials; incident response plan; information spillage response training records; other relevant documents or records]. **Interview**: [*SELECT FROM:* Organizational personnel with incident response training responsibilities; organizational personnel with information security responsibilities].

IR-9(3)	INFORMATION SPILLAGE RESPONSE | *POST-SPILL OPERATIONS*
	ASSESSMENT OBJECTIVE: *Determine if the organization:*
	IR-9(3)[1] *defines procedures that ensure organizational personnel impacted by information spills can continue to carry out assigned tasks while contaminated systems are undergoing corrective actions; and*
	IR-9(3)[2] *implements organization-defined procedures to ensure that organizational personnel impacted by information spills can continue to carry out assigned tasks while contaminated systems are undergoing corrective actions.*
	POTENTIAL ASSESSMENT METHODS AND OBJECTS: **Examine**: [*SELECT FROM:* Incident response policy; procedures addressing incident handling; procedures addressing information spillage; incident response plan; other relevant documents or records]. **Interview**: [*SELECT FROM:* Organizational personnel with incident response responsibilities; organizational personnel with information security responsibilities]. **Test**: [*SELECT FROM:* Organizational processes for post-spill operations].

IR-9(4)	INFORMATION SPILLAGE RESPONSE | *EXPOSURE TO UNAUTHORIZED PERSONNEL*
	ASSESSMENT OBJECTIVE: *Determine if the organization:*
	IR-9(4)[1] *defines security safeguards to be employed for personnel exposed to information not within assigned access authorizations; and*
	IR-9(4)[2] *employs organization-defined security safeguards for personnel exposed to information not within assigned access authorizations.*
	POTENTIAL ASSESSMENT METHODS AND OBJECTS: **Examine**: [*SELECT FROM:* Incident response policy; procedures addressing incident handling; procedures addressing information spillage; incident response plan; security safeguards regarding information spillage/exposure to unauthorized personnel; other relevant documents or records]. **Interview**: [*SELECT FROM:* Organizational personnel with incident response responsibilities; organizational personnel with information security responsibilities]. **Test**: [*SELECT FROM:* Organizational processes for dealing with information exposed to unauthorized personnel; automated mechanisms supporting and/or implementing safeguards for personnel exposed to information not within assigned access authorizations].

Special Publication 800-53A
Revision 4

Assessing Security and Privacy Controls in Federal Information Systems
and Organizations — *Building Effective Assessment Plans*

IR-10	INTEGRATED INFORMATION SECURITY ANALYSIS TEAM
	ASSESSMENT OBJECTIVE: *Determine if the organization establishes an integrated team of forensic/malicious code analyst, tool developers, and real-time operations personnel.*
	POTENTIAL ASSESSMENT METHODS AND OBJECTS: **Examine**: [*SELECT FROM:* Incident response policy; procedures addressing incident response planning and security analysis team integration; incident response plan; other relevant documents or records]. **Interview**: [*SELECT FROM:* Organizational personnel with incident response and information security analysis responsibilities; organizational personnel with information security responsibilities; organizational personnel participating on integrated security analysis teams].

Special Publication 800-53A
Revision 4

Assessing Security and Privacy Controls in Federal Information Systems
and Organizations — *Building Effective Assessment Plans*

FAMILY: MAINTENANCE

MA-1	SYSTEM MAINTENANCE POLICY AND PROCEDURES		
	ASSESSMENT OBJECTIVE: *Determine if the organization:*		
	MA-1(a)(1)	**MA-1(a)(1)[1]**	*develops and documents a system maintenance policy that addresses:*
		MA-1(a)(1)[1][a]	*purpose;*
		MA-1(a)(1)[1][b]	*scope;*
		MA-1(a)(1)[1][c]	*roles;*
		MA-1(a)(1)[1][d]	*responsibilities;*
		MA-1(a)(1)[1][e]	*management commitment;*
		MA-1(a)(1)[1][f]	*coordination among organizational entities;*
		MA-1(a)(1)[1][g]	*compliance;*
		MA-1(a)(1)[2]	*defines personnel or roles to whom the system maintenance policy is to be disseminated;*
		MA-1(a)(1)[3]	*disseminates the system maintenance policy to organization-defined personnel or roles;*
	MA-1(a)(2)	**MA-1(a)(2)[1]**	*develops and documents procedures to facilitate the implementation of the maintenance policy and associated system maintenance controls;*
		MA-1(a)(2)[2]	*defines personnel or roles to whom the procedures are to be disseminated;*
		MA-1(a)(2)[3]	*disseminates the procedures to organization-defined personnel or roles;*
	MA-1(b)(1)	**MA-1(b)(1)[1]**	*defines the frequency to review and update the current system maintenance policy;*
		MA-1(b)(1)[2]	*reviews and updates the current system maintenance policy with the organization-defined frequency;*
	MA-1(b)(2)	**MA-1(b)(2)[1]**	*defines the frequency to review and update the current system maintenance procedures; and*
		MA-1(b)(2)[2]	*reviews and updates the current system maintenance procedures with the organization-defined frequency.*
	POTENTIAL ASSESSMENT METHODS AND OBJECTS: **Examine**: [*SELECT FROM:* Maintenance policy and procedures; other relevant documents or records]. **Interview**: [*SELECT FROM:* Organizational personnel with maintenance responsibilities; organizational personnel with information security responsibilities].		

Special Publication 800-53A
Revision 4

Assessing Security and Privacy Controls in Federal Information Systems
and Organizations — *Building Effective Assessment Plans*

MA-2	CONTROLLED MAINTENANCE		
	ASSESSMENT OBJECTIVE: *Determine if the organization:*		
	MA-2(a)	**MA-2(a)[1]**	*schedules maintenance and repairs on information system components in accordance with:*
		MA-2(a)[1][a]	*manufacturer or vendor specifications; and/or*
		MA-2(a)[1][b]	*organizational requirements;*
		MA-2(a)[2]	*performs maintenance and repairs on information system components in accordance with:*
		MA-2(a)[2][a]	*manufacturer or vendor specifications; and/or*
		MA-2(a)[2][b]	*organizational requirements;*
		MA-2(a)[3]	*documents maintenance and repairs on information system components in accordance with:*
		MA-2(a)[3][a]	*manufacturer or vendor specifications; and/or*
		MA-2(a)[3][b]	*organizational requirements;*
		MA-2(a)[4]	*reviews records of maintenance and repairs on information system components in accordance with:*
		MA-2(a)[4][a]	*manufacturer or vendor specifications; and/or*
		MA-2(a)[4][b]	*organizational requirements;*
	MA-2(b)	**MA-2(b)[1]**	*approves all maintenance activities, whether performed on site or remotely and whether the equipment is serviced on site or removed to another location;*
		MA-2(b)[2]	*monitors all maintenance activities, whether performed on site or remotely and whether the equipment is serviced on site or removed to another location;*
	MA-2(c)	**MA-2(c)[1]**	*defines personnel or roles required to explicitly approve the removal of the information system or system components from organizational facilities for off-site maintenance or repairs;*
		MA-2(c)[2]	*requires that organization-defined personnel or roles explicitly approve the removal of the information system or system components from organizational facilities for off-site maintenance or repairs;*
	MA-2(d)	*sanitizes equipment to remove all information from associated media prior to removal from organizational facilities for off-site maintenance or repairs;*	
	MA-2(e)	*checks all potentially impacted security controls to verify that the controls are still functioning properly following maintenance or repair actions;*	
	MA-2(f)	**MA-2(f)[1]**	*defines maintenance-related information to be included in organizational maintenance records; and*
		MA-2(f)[2]	*includes organization-defined maintenance-related information in organizational maintenance records.*

Special Publication 800-53A
Revision 4

Assessing Security and Privacy Controls in Federal Information Systems
and Organizations — *Building Effective Assessment Plans*

POTENTIAL ASSESSMENT METHODS AND OBJECTS:

Examine: [*SELECT FROM:* Information system maintenance policy; procedures addressing controlled information system maintenance; maintenance records; manufacturer/vendor maintenance specifications; equipment sanitization records; media sanitization records; other relevant documents or records].

Interview: [*SELECT FROM:* Organizational personnel with information system maintenance responsibilities; organizational personnel with information security responsibilities; organizational personnel responsible for media sanitization; system/network administrators].

Test: [*SELECT FROM:* Organizational processes for scheduling, performing, documenting, reviewing, approving, and monitoring maintenance and repairs for the information system; organizational processes for sanitizing information system components; automated mechanisms supporting and/or implementing controlled maintenance; automated mechanisms implementing sanitization of information system components].

MA-2(1)	CONTROLLED MAINTENANCE | *RECORD CONTENT*
	[Withdrawn: Incorporated into MA-2].

MA-2(2)	CONTROLLED MAINTENANCE | *AUTOMATED MAINTENANCE ACTIVITIES*

ASSESSMENT OBJECTIVE:
Determine if the organization:

MA-2(2)(a)	*employs automated mechanisms to:*	
	MA-2(2)(a)[1]	*schedule maintenance and repairs;*
	MA-2(2)(a)[2]	*conduct maintenance and repairs;*
	MA-2(2)(a)[3]	*document maintenance and repairs;*
MA-2(2)(b)	*produces up-to-date, accurate, and complete records of all maintenance and repair actions:*	
	MA-2(2)(b)[1]	*requested;*
	MA-2(2)(b)[2]	*scheduled;*
	MA-2(2)(b)[3]	*in process; and*
	MA-2(2)(b)[4]	*completed.*

POTENTIAL ASSESSMENT METHODS AND OBJECTS:

Examine: [*SELECT FROM:* Information system maintenance policy; procedures addressing controlled information system maintenance; automated mechanisms supporting information system maintenance activities; information system configuration settings and associated documentation; maintenance records; other relevant documents or records].

Interview: [*SELECT FROM:* Organizational personnel with information system maintenance responsibilities; organizational personnel with information security responsibilities; system/network administrators].

Test: [*SELECT FROM:* Automated mechanisms supporting and/or implementing controlled maintenance; automated mechanisms supporting and/or implementing production of records of maintenance and repair actions].

MA-3	MAINTENANCE TOOLS

ASSESSMENT OBJECTIVE:
Determine if the organization:

MA-3[1]	*approves information system maintenance tools;*

Special Publication 800-53A
Revision 4

Assessing Security and Privacy Controls in Federal Information Systems
and Organizations — *Building Effective Assessment Plans*

MA-3[2]	*controls information system maintenance tools; and*
MA-3[3]	*monitors information system maintenance tools.*

POTENTIAL ASSESSMENT METHODS AND OBJECTS:

Examine: [*SELECT FROM:* Information system maintenance policy; procedures addressing information system maintenance tools; information system maintenance tools and associated documentation; maintenance records; other relevant documents or records].

Interview: [*SELECT FROM:* Organizational personnel with information system maintenance responsibilities; organizational personnel with information security responsibilities].

Test: [*SELECT FROM:* Organizational processes for approving, controlling, and monitoring maintenance tools; automated mechanisms supporting and/or implementing approval, control, and/or monitoring of maintenance tools].

MA-3(1)	MAINTENANCE TOOLS | *INSPECT TOOLS*

ASSESSMENT OBJECTIVE:

Determine if the organization inspects the maintenance tools carried into a facility by maintenance personnel for improper or unauthorized modifications.

POTENTIAL ASSESSMENT METHODS AND OBJECTS:

Examine: [*SELECT FROM:* Information system maintenance policy; procedures addressing information system maintenance tools; information system maintenance tools and associated documentation; maintenance tool inspection records; maintenance records; other relevant documents or records].

Interview: [*SELECT FROM:* Organizational personnel with information system maintenance responsibilities; organizational personnel with information security responsibilities].

Test: [*SELECT FROM:* Organizational processes for inspecting maintenance tools; automated mechanisms supporting and/or implementing inspection of maintenance tools].

MA-3(2)	MAINTENANCE TOOLS | *INSPECT MEDIA*

ASSESSMENT OBJECTIVE:

Determine if the organization checks media containing diagnostic and test programs for malicious code before the media are used in the information system.

POTENTIAL ASSESSMENT METHODS AND OBJECTS:

Examine: [*SELECT FROM:* Information system maintenance policy; procedures addressing information system maintenance tools; information system maintenance tools and associated documentation; maintenance records; other relevant documents or records].

Interview: [*SELECT FROM:* Organizational personnel with information system maintenance responsibilities; organizational personnel with information security responsibilities].

Test: [*SELECT FROM:* Organizational process for inspecting media for malicious code; automated mechanisms supporting and/or implementing inspection of media used for maintenance].

MA-3(3)	MAINTENANCE TOOLS | *PREVENT UNAUTHORIZED REMOVAL*

ASSESSMENT OBJECTIVE:

Determine if the organization prevents the unauthorized removal of maintenance equipment containing organizational information by:

MA-3(3)(a)	*verifying that there is no organizational information contained on the equipment;*
MA-3(3)(b)	*sanitizing or destroying the equipment;*
MA-3(3)(c)	*retaining the equipment within the facility; or*

Special Publication 800-53A
Revision 4

Assessing Security and Privacy Controls in Federal Information Systems
and Organizations — *Building Effective Assessment Plans*

	MA-3(3)(d)	MA-3(3)(d)[1]	*defining personnel or roles that can grant an exemption from explicitly authorizing removal of the equipment from the facility; and*
		MA-3(3)(d)[2]	*obtaining an exemption from organization-defined personnel or roles explicitly authorizing removal of the equipment from the facility.*

POTENTIAL ASSESSMENT METHODS AND OBJECTS:

Examine: [*SELECT FROM*: Information system maintenance policy; procedures addressing information system maintenance tools; information system maintenance tools and associated documentation; maintenance records; equipment sanitization records; media sanitization records; exemptions for equipment removal; other relevant documents or records].

Interview: [*SELECT FROM*: Organizational personnel with information system maintenance responsibilities; organizational personnel with information security responsibilities; organizational personnel responsible for media sanitization].

Test: [*SELECT FROM*: Organizational process for preventing unauthorized removal of information; automated mechanisms supporting media sanitization or destruction of equipment; automated mechanisms supporting verification of media sanitization].

MA-3(4)	**MAINTENANCE TOOLS	*RESTRICTED TOOL USE***

ASSESSMENT OBJECTIVE:

Determine if the organization restricts the use of maintenance tools to authorized personnel only.

POTENTIAL ASSESSMENT METHODS AND OBJECTS:

Examine: [*SELECT FROM*: Information system maintenance policy; procedures addressing information system maintenance tools; information system maintenance tools and associated documentation; list of personnel authorized to use maintenance tools; maintenance tool usage records; maintenance records; other relevant documents or records].

Interview: [*SELECT FROM*: Organizational personnel with information system maintenance responsibilities; organizational personnel with information security responsibilities].

Test: [*SELECT FROM*: Organizational process for restricting use of maintenance tools; automated mechanisms supporting and/or implementing restricted use of maintenance tools].

MA-4	**NONLOCAL MAINTENANCE**

ASSESSMENT OBJECTIVE:

Determine if the organization:

MA-4(a)	MA-4(a)[1]	*approves nonlocal maintenance and diagnostic activities;*
	MA-4(a)[2]	*monitors nonlocal maintenance and diagnostic activities;*
MA-4(b)	*allows the use of nonlocal maintenance and diagnostic tools only:*	
	MA-4(b)[1]	*as consistent with organizational policy;*
	MA-4(b)[2]	*as documented in the security plan for the information system;*
MA-4(c)	*employs strong authenticators in the establishment of nonlocal maintenance and diagnostic sessions;*	
MA-4(d)	*maintains records for nonlocal maintenance and diagnostic activities;*	
MA-4(e)	MA-4(e)[1]	*terminates sessions when nonlocal maintenance or diagnostics is completed; and*

Special Publication 800-53A
Revision 4

Assessing Security and Privacy Controls in Federal Information Systems
and Organizations — *Building Effective Assessment Plans*

		MA-4(e)[2]	*terminates network connections when nonlocal maintenance or diagnostics is completed.*

POTENTIAL ASSESSMENT METHODS AND OBJECTS:

Examine: [*SELECT FROM*: Information system maintenance policy; procedures addressing nonlocal information system maintenance; security plan; information system design documentation; information system configuration settings and associated documentation; maintenance records; diagnostic records; other relevant documents or records].

Interview: [*SELECT FROM*: Organizational personnel with information system maintenance responsibilities; organizational personnel with information security responsibilities; system/network administrators].

Test: [*SELECT FROM*: Organizational processes for managing nonlocal maintenance; automated mechanisms implementing, supporting, and/or managing nonlocal maintenance; automated mechanisms for strong authentication of nonlocal maintenance diagnostic sessions; automated mechanisms for terminating nonlocal maintenance sessions and network connections].

MA-4(1)	NONLOCAL MAINTENANCE	*AUDITING AND REVIEW*

ASSESSMENT OBJECTIVE:

Determine if the organization:

MA-4(1)(a)	MA-4(1)(a)[1]	*defines audit events to audit nonlocal maintenance and diagnostic sessions;*
	MA-4(1)(a)[2]	*audits organization-defined audit events for non-local maintenance and diagnostic sessions; and*

MA-4(1)(b)	*reviews records of the maintenance and diagnostic sessions.*

POTENTIAL ASSESSMENT METHODS AND OBJECTS:

Examine: [*SELECT FROM*: Information system maintenance policy; procedures addressing nonlocal information system maintenance; list of audit events; information system configuration settings and associated documentation; maintenance records; diagnostic records; audit records; reviews of maintenance and diagnostic session records; other relevant documents or records].

Interview: [*SELECT FROM*: Organizational personnel with information system maintenance responsibilities; organizational personnel with information security responsibilities; organizational personnel with audit and review responsibilities; system/network administrators].

Test: [*SELECT FROM*: Organizational processes for audit and review of nonlocal maintenance; automated mechanisms supporting and/or implementing audit and review of nonlocal maintenance].

MA-4(2)	NONLOCAL MAINTENANCE	*DOCUMENT NONLOCAL MAINTENANCE*

ASSESSMENT OBJECTIVE:

Determine if the organization documents in the security plan for the information system:

MA-4(2)[1]	*the policies for the establishment and use of nonlocal maintenance and diagnostic connections; and*
MA-4(2)[2]	*the procedures for the establishment and use of nonlocal maintenance and diagnostic connections.*

POTENTIAL ASSESSMENT METHODS AND OBJECTS:

Examine: [*SELECT FROM*: Information system maintenance policy; procedures addressing non-local information system maintenance; security plan; maintenance records; diagnostic records; audit records; other relevant documents or records].

Interview: [*SELECT FROM*: Organizational personnel with information system maintenance responsibilities; organizational personnel with information security responsibilities].

Special Publication 800-53A
Revision 4

Assessing Security and Privacy Controls in Federal Information Systems
and Organizations — *Building Effective Assessment Plans*

MA-4(3)	NONLOCAL MAINTENANCE | *COMPARABLE SECURITY / SANITIZATION*		
	ASSESSMENT OBJECTIVE: *Determine if the organization:*		
	MA-4(3)(a)	*requires that nonlocal maintenance and diagnostic services be performed from an information system that implements a security capability comparable to the capability implemented on the system being serviced; or*	
	MA-4(3)(b)	MA-4(3)(b)[1]	*removes the component to be serviced from the information system;*
		MA-4(3)(b)[2]	*sanitizes the component (with regard to organizational information) prior to nonlocal maintenance or diagnostic services and/or before removal from organizational facilities; and*
		MA-4(3)(b)[3]	*inspects and sanitizes the component (with regard to potentially malicious software) after service is performed on the component and before reconnecting the component to the information system.*
	POTENTIAL ASSESSMENT METHODS AND OBJECTS: **Examine**: [*SELECT FROM:* Information system maintenance policy; procedures addressing nonlocal information system maintenance; service provider contracts and/or service-level agreements; maintenance records; inspection records; audit records; equipment sanitization records; media sanitization records; other relevant documents or records]. **Interview**: [*SELECT FROM:* Organizational personnel with information system maintenance responsibilities; information system maintenance provider; organizational personnel with information security responsibilities; organizational personnel responsible for media sanitization; system/network administrators]. **Test**: [*SELECT FROM:* Organizational processes for comparable security and sanitization for nonlocal maintenance; organizational processes for removal, sanitization, and inspection of components serviced via nonlocal maintenance; automated mechanisms supporting and/or implementing component sanitization and inspection].		

MA-4(4)	NONLOCAL MAINTENANCE | *AUTHENTICATION / SEPARATION OF MAINTENANCE SESSIONS*		
	ASSESSMENT OBJECTIVE: *Determine if the organization protects nonlocal maintenance sessions by:*		
	MA-4(4)(a)	MA-4(4)(a)[1]	*defining replay resistant authenticators to be employed to protect nonlocal maintenance sessions;*
		MA-4(4)(a)[2]	*employing organization-defined authenticators that are replay resistant;*
	MA-4(4)(b)	*separating the maintenance sessions from other network sessions with the information system by either:*	
		MA-4(4)(b)(1)	*physically separated communications paths; or*
		MA-4(4)(b)(2)	*logically separated communications paths based upon encryption.*

Special Publication 800-53A
Revision 4

Assessing Security and Privacy Controls in Federal Information Systems
and Organizations — *Building Effective Assessment Plans*

	POTENTIAL ASSESSMENT METHODS AND OBJECTS: **Examine**: [*SELECT FROM:* Information system maintenance policy; procedures addressing nonlocal information system maintenance; information system design documentation; information system configuration settings and associated documentation; maintenance records; audit records; other relevant documents or records]. **Interview**: [*SELECT FROM:* Organizational personnel with information system maintenance responsibilities; network engineers; organizational personnel with information security responsibilities; system/network administrators]. **Test**: [*SELECT FROM:* Organizational processes for protecting nonlocal maintenance sessions; automated mechanisms implementing replay resistant authenticators; automated mechanisms implementing logically separated/encrypted communications paths].

MA-4(5)	NONLOCAL MAINTENANCE | *APPROVALS AND NOTIFICATIONS*		
	ASSESSMENT OBJECTIVE: *Determine if the organization:*		
	MA-4(5)(a)	**MA-4(5)(a)[1]**	*defines personnel or roles required to approve each nonlocal maintenance session;*
		MA-4(5)(a)[2]	*requires the approval of each nonlocal maintenance session by organization-defined personnel or roles;*
	MA-4(5)(b)	**MA-4(5)(b)[1]**	*defines personnel or roles to be notified of the date and time of planned nonlocal maintenance; and*
		MA-4(5)(b)[2]	*notifies organization-defined personnel roles of the date and time of planned nonlocal maintenance.*
	POTENTIAL ASSESSMENT METHODS AND OBJECTS: **Examine**: [*SELECT FROM:* Information system maintenance policy; procedures addressing non-local information system maintenance; security plan; notifications supporting nonlocal maintenance sessions; maintenance records; audit records; other relevant documents or records]. **Interview**: [*SELECT FROM:* Organizational personnel with information system maintenance responsibilities; organizational personnel with notification responsibilities; organizational personnel with approval responsibilities; organizational personnel with information security responsibilities]. **Test**: [*SELECT FROM:* Organizational processes for approving and notifying personnel regarding nonlocal maintenance; automated mechanisms supporting notification and approval of nonlocal maintenance].		

MA-4(6)	NONLOCAL MAINTENANCE | *CRYPTOGRAPHIC PROTECTION*
	ASSESSMENT OBJECTIVE: *Determine if the information system implements cryptographic mechanisms to protect the integrity and confidentiality of nonlocal maintenance and diagnostic communications.*
	POTENTIAL ASSESSMENT METHODS AND OBJECTS: **Examine**: [*SELECT FROM:* Information system maintenance policy; procedures addressing non-local information system maintenance; information system design documentation; information system configuration settings and associated documentation; cryptographic mechanisms protecting nonlocal maintenance activities; maintenance records; diagnostic records; audit records; other relevant documents or records]. **Interview**: [*SELECT FROM:* Organizational personnel with information system maintenance responsibilities; network engineers; organizational personnel with information security responsibilities; system/network administrators]. **Test**: [*SELECT FROM:* Cryptographic mechanisms protecting nonlocal maintenance and diagnostic communications].

Special Publication 800-53A
Revision 4

Assessing Security and Privacy Controls in Federal Information Systems
and Organizations — *Building Effective Assessment Plans*

MA-4(7)	NONLOCAL MAINTENANCE | *REMOTE DISCONNECT VERIFICATION*
	ASSESSMENT OBJECTIVE: *Determine if the information system implements remote disconnect verification at the termination of nonlocal maintenance and diagnostic sessions.*
	POTENTIAL ASSESSMENT METHODS AND OBJECTS: **Examine**: [*SELECT FROM:* Information system maintenance policy; procedures addressing non-local information system maintenance; information system design documentation; information system configuration settings and associated documentation; cryptographic mechanisms protecting nonlocal maintenance activities; maintenance records; diagnostic records; audit records; other relevant documents or records]. **Interview**: [*SELECT FROM:* Organizational personnel with information system maintenance responsibilities; network engineers; organizational personnel with information security responsibilities; system/network administrators]. **Test**: [*SELECT FROM:* Automated mechanisms implementing remote disconnect verifications of terminated nonlocal maintenance and diagnostic sessions].

MA-5	MAINTENANCE PERSONNEL	
	ASSESSMENT OBJECTIVE: *Determine if the organization:*	
MA-5(a)	**MA-5(a)[1]**	*establishes a process for maintenance personnel authorization;*
	MA-5(a)[2]	*maintains a list of authorized maintenance organizations or personnel;*
MA-5(b)	*ensures that non-escorted personnel performing maintenance on the information system have required access authorizations; and*	
MA-5(c)	*designates organizational personnel with required access authorizations and technical competence to supervise the maintenance activities of personnel who do not possess the required access authorizations.*	
	POTENTIAL ASSESSMENT METHODS AND OBJECTS: **Examine**: [*SELECT FROM:* Information system maintenance policy; procedures addressing maintenance personnel; service provider contracts; service-level agreements; list of authorized personnel; maintenance records; access control records; other relevant documents or records]. **Interview**: [*SELECT FROM:* Organizational personnel with information system maintenance responsibilities; organizational personnel with information security responsibilities]. **Test**: [*SELECT FROM:* Organizational processes for authorizing and managing maintenance personnel; automated mechanisms supporting and/or implementing authorization of maintenance personnel].	

MA-5(1)	MAINTENANCE PERSONNEL	*INDIVIDUALS WITHOUT APPROPRIATE ACCESS*	
	ASSESSMENT OBJECTIVE: *Determine if the organization:*	
MA-5(1)(a)	*implements procedures for the use of maintenance personnel that lack appropriate security clearances or are not U.S. citizens, that include the following requirements:*	
	MA-5(1)(a)(1)	*maintenance personnel who do not have needed access authorizations, clearances, or formal access approvals are escorted and supervised during the performance of maintenance and diagnostic activities on the information system by approved organizational personnel who:*

Special Publication 800-53A
Revision 4

Assessing Security and Privacy Controls in Federal Information Systems
and Organizations — *Building Effective Assessment Plans*

			MA-5(1)(a)(1)[1]	*are fully cleared;*
			MA-5(1)(a)(1)[2]	*have appropriate access authorizations;*
			MA-5(1)(a)(1)[3]	*are technically qualified;*
		MA-5(1)(a)(2)	*prior to initiating maintenance or diagnostic activities by personnel who do not have needed access authorizations, clearances, or formal access approvals:*	
			MA-5(1)(a)(2)[1]	*all volatile information storage components within the information system are sanitized; and*
			MA-5(1)(a)(2)[2]	*all nonvolatile storage media are removed; or*
			MA-5(1)(a)(2)[3]	*all nonvolatile storage media are physically disconnected from the system and secured; and*
	MA-5(1)(b)	*develops and implements alternative security safeguards in the event an information system component cannot be sanitized, removed, or disconnected from the system.*		

POTENTIAL ASSESSMENT METHODS AND OBJECTS:

Examine: [*SELECT FROM:* Information system maintenance policy; procedures addressing maintenance personnel; information system media protection policy; physical and environmental protection policy; security plan; list of maintenance personnel requiring escort/supervision; maintenance records; access control records; other relevant documents or records].

Interview: [*SELECT FROM:* Organizational personnel with information system maintenance responsibilities; organizational personnel with personnel security responsibilities; organizational personnel with physical access control responsibilities; organizational personnel with information security responsibilities; organizational personnel responsible for media sanitization; system/network administrators].

Test: [*SELECT FROM:* Organizational processes for managing maintenance personnel without appropriate access; automated mechanisms supporting and/or implementing alternative security safeguards; automated mechanisms supporting and/or implementing information storage component sanitization].

MA-5(2)	MAINTENANCE PERSONNEL | *SECURITY CLEARANCES FOR CLASSIFIED SYSTEMS*
	ASSESSMENT OBJECTIVE: *Determine if the organization ensures that personnel performing maintenance and diagnostic activities on an information system processing, storing, or transmitting classified information possess:*

MA-5(2)[1]	*security clearances for at least the highest classification level on the system;*
MA-5(2)[2]	*security clearances for all compartments of information on the system;*
MA-5(2)[3]	*formal access approvals for at least the highest classification level on the system; and*
MA-5(2)[4]	*formal access approvals for all compartments of information on the system.*

Special Publication 800-53A
Revision 4

Assessing Security and Privacy Controls in Federal Information Systems
and Organizations — *Building Effective Assessment Plans*

POTENTIAL ASSESSMENT METHODS AND OBJECTS:

Examine: [*SELECT FROM:* Information system maintenance policy; procedures addressing maintenance personnel; personnel records; maintenance records; access control records; access credentials; access authorizations; other relevant documents or records].

Interview: [*SELECT FROM:* Organizational personnel with information system maintenance responsibilities; organizational personnel with personnel security responsibilities; organizational personnel with physical access control responsibilities; organizational personnel with information security responsibilities].

Test: [*SELECT FROM:* Organizational processes for managing security clearances for maintenance personnel].

MA-5(3)	MAINTENANCE PERSONNEL | *CITIZENSHIP REQUIREMENTS FOR CLASSIFIED SYSTEMS*

ASSESSMENT OBJECTIVE:

Determine if the organization ensures that personnel performing maintenance and diagnostic activities on an information system processing, storing, or transmitting classified information are U.S. citizens.

POTENTIAL ASSESSMENT METHODS AND OBJECTS:

Examine: [*SELECT FROM:* Information system maintenance policy; procedures addressing maintenance personnel; personnel records; maintenance records; access control records; access credentials; access authorizations; other relevant documents or records].

Interview: [*SELECT FROM:* Organizational personnel with information system maintenance responsibilities; organizational personnel with personnel security responsibilities; organizational personnel with information security responsibilities].

MA-5(4)	MAINTENANCE PERSONNEL | *FOREIGN NATIONALS*

ASSESSMENT OBJECTIVE:

Determine if the organization ensures that:

MA-5(4)(a)	*cleared foreign nationals (i.e., foreign nationals with appropriate security clearances) are used to conduct maintenance and diagnostic activities on classified information systems only when the systems are:*	
	MA-5(4)(a)[1]	*jointly owned and operated by the United States and foreign allied governments; or*
	MA-5(4)(a)[2]	*owned and operated solely by foreign allied governments; and*
MA-5(4)(b)	*approvals, consents, and detailed operational conditions regarding the use of foreign nationals to conduct maintenance and diagnostic activities on classified information systems are fully documented within Memoranda of Agreements.*	

POTENTIAL ASSESSMENT METHODS AND OBJECTS:

Examine: [*SELECT FROM:* Information system maintenance policy; procedures addressing maintenance personnel; information system media protection policy; access control policy and procedures; physical and environmental protection policy and procedures; memorandum of agreement; maintenance records; access control records; access credentials; access authorizations; other relevant documents or records].

Interview: [*SELECT FROM:* Organizational personnel with information system maintenance responsibilities, organizational personnel with personnel security responsibilities; organizational personnel managing memoranda of agreements; organizational personnel with information security responsibilities].

Test: [*SELECT FROM:* Organizational processes for managing foreign national maintenance personnel].

Special Publication 800-53A
Revision 4

Assessing Security and Privacy Controls in Federal Information Systems
and Organizations — *Building Effective Assessment Plans*

MA-5(5)	MAINTENANCE PERSONNEL | *NONSYSTEM-RELATED MAINTENANCE*
	ASSESSMENT OBJECTIVE: *Determine if the organization ensures that non-escorted personnel performing maintenance activities not directly associated with the information system but in the physical proximity of the system, have required access authorizations.* **POTENTIAL ASSESSMENT METHODS AND OBJECTS:** **Examine**: [*SELECT FROM:* Information system maintenance policy; procedures addressing maintenance personnel; information system media protection policy; access control policy and procedures; physical and environmental protection policy and procedures; maintenance records; access control records; access authorizations; other relevant documents or records]. **Interview**: [*SELECT FROM:* Organizational personnel with information system maintenance responsibilities; organizational personnel with personnel security responsibilities; organizational personnel with physical access control responsibilities; organizational personnel with information security responsibilities].

MA-6	TIMELY MAINTENANCE	
	ASSESSMENT OBJECTIVE: *Determine if the organization:*	
	MA-6[1]	*defines information system components for which maintenance support and/or spare parts are to be obtained;*
	MA-6[2]	*defines the time period within which maintenance support and/or spare parts are to be obtained after a failure;*
	MA-6[3]	**MA-6[3][a]** *obtains maintenance support for organization-defined information system components within the organization-defined time period of failure; and/or*
		MA-6[3][b] *obtains spare parts for organization-defined information system components within the organization-defined time period of failure.*
	POTENTIAL ASSESSMENT METHODS AND OBJECTS: **Examine**: [*SELECT FROM:* Information system maintenance policy; procedures addressing information system maintenance; service provider contracts; service-level agreements; inventory and availability of spare parts; security plan; other relevant documents or records]. **Interview**: [*SELECT FROM:* Organizational personnel with information system maintenance responsibilities; organizational personnel with acquisition responsibilities; organizational personnel with information security responsibilities; system/network administrators]. **Test**: [*SELECT FROM:* Organizational processes for ensuring timely maintenance].	

MA-6(1)	TIMELY MAINTENANCE | *PREVENTIVE MAINTENANCE*
	ASSESSMENT OBJECTIVE: *Determine if the organization:*
	MA-6(1)[1] *defines information system components on which preventive maintenance is to be performed;*
	MA-6(1)[2] *defines time intervals within which preventive maintenance is to be performed on organization-defined information system components; and*
	MA-6(1)[3] *performs preventive maintenance on organization-defined information system components at organization-defined time intervals.*

Special Publication 800-53A
Revision 4

Assessing Security and Privacy Controls in Federal Information Systems
and Organizations — *Building Effective Assessment Plans*

<table>
<tr><td></td><td>

POTENTIAL ASSESSMENT METHODS AND OBJECTS:

Examine: [*SELECT FROM:* Information system maintenance policy; procedures addressing information system maintenance; service provider contracts; service-level agreements; security plan; maintenance records; list of system components requiring preventive maintenance; other relevant documents or records].

Interview: [*SELECT FROM:* Organizational personnel with information system maintenance responsibilities; organizational personnel with information security responsibilities; system/network administrators].

Test: [*SELECT FROM:* Organizational processes for preventive maintenance; automated mechanisms supporting and/or implementing preventive maintenance].

</td></tr>
</table>

<table>
<tr><td>**MA-6(2)**</td><td colspan="2">**TIMELY MAINTENANCE | *PREDICTIVE MAINTENANCE***</td></tr>
<tr><td rowspan="9"></td><td colspan="2">

ASSESSMENT OBJECTIVE:

Determine if the organization:

</td></tr>
<tr><td>**MA-6(2)[1]**</td><td>*defines information system components on which predictive maintenance is to be performed;*</td></tr>
<tr><td>**MA-6(2)[2]**</td><td>*defines time intervals within which predictive maintenance is to be performed on organization-defined information system components; and*</td></tr>
<tr><td>**MA-6(2)[3]**</td><td>*performs predictive maintenance on organization-defined information system components at organization-defined time intervals.*</td></tr>
<tr><td colspan="2">

POTENTIAL ASSESSMENT METHODS AND OBJECTS:

Examine: [*SELECT FROM:* Information system maintenance policy; procedures addressing information system maintenance; service provider contracts; service-level agreements; security plan; maintenance records; list of system components requiring predictive maintenance; other relevant documents or records].

Interview: [*SELECT FROM:* Organizational personnel with information system maintenance responsibilities; organizational personnel with information security responsibilities; system/network administrators].

Test: [*SELECT FROM:* Organizational processes for predictive maintenance; automated mechanisms supporting and/or implementing predictive maintenance].

</td></tr>
</table>

<table>
<tr><td>**MA-6(3)**</td><td>**TIMELY MAINTENANCE | *AUTOMATED SUPPORT FOR PREDICTIVE MAINTENANCE***</td></tr>
<tr><td rowspan="2"></td><td>

ASSESSMENT OBJECTIVE:

Determine if the organization employs automated mechanisms to transfer predictive maintenance data to a computerized maintenance management system.

</td></tr>
<tr><td>

POTENTIAL ASSESSMENT METHODS AND OBJECTS:

Examine: [*SELECT FROM:* Information system maintenance policy; procedures addressing information system maintenance; service provider contracts; service-level agreements; security plan; maintenance records; list of system components requiring predictive maintenance; other relevant documents or records].

Interview: [*SELECT FROM:* Organizational personnel with information system maintenance responsibilities; organizational personnel with information security responsibilities; system/network administrators].

Test: [*SELECT FROM:* Automated mechanisms implementing the transfer of predictive maintenance data to a computerized maintenance management system; operations of the computer maintenance management system].

</td></tr>
</table>

Special Publication 800-53A
Revision 4

Assessing Security and Privacy Controls in Federal Information Systems
and Organizations — *Building Effective Assessment Plans*

FAMILY: MEDIA PROTECTION

MP-1	MEDIA PROTECTION POLICY AND PROCEDURES			
	ASSESSMENT OBJECTIVE: *Determine if the organization:*			
	MP-1(a)(1)	MP-1(a)(1)[1]	*develops and documents a media protection policy that addresses:*	
			MP-1(a)(1)[1][a]	*purpose;*
			MP-1(a)(1)[1][b]	*scope;*
			MP-1(a)(1)[1][c]	*roles;*
			MP-1(a)(1)[1][d]	*responsibilities;*
			MP-1(a)(1)[1][e]	*management commitment;*
			MP-1(a)(1)[1][f]	*coordination among organizational entities;*
			MP-1(a)(1)[1][g]	*compliance;*
		MP-1(a)(1)[2]	*defines personnel or roles to whom the media protection policy is to be disseminated;*	
		MP-1(a)(1)[3]	*disseminates the media protection policy to organization-defined personnel or roles;*	
	MP-1(a)(2)	MP-1(a)(2)[1]	*develops and documents procedures to facilitate the implementation of the media protection policy and associated media protection controls;*	
		MP-1(a)(2)[2]	*defines personnel or roles to whom the procedures are to be disseminated;*	
		MP-1(a)(2)[3]	*disseminates the procedures to organization-defined personnel or roles;*	
	MP-1(b)(1)	MP-1(b)(1)[1]	*defines the frequency to review and update the current media protection policy;*	
		MP-1(b)(1)[2]	*reviews and updates the current media protection policy with the organization-defined frequency;*	
	MP-1(b)(2)	MP-1(b)(2)[1]	*defines the frequency to review and update the current media protection procedures; and*	
		MP-1(b)(2)[2]	*reviews and updates the current media protection procedures with the organization-defined frequency.*	
	POTENTIAL ASSESSMENT METHODS AND OBJECTS: **Examine**: [*SELECT FROM:* Media protection policy and procedures; other relevant documents or records]. **Interview**: [*SELECT FROM:* Organizational personnel with media protection responsibilities; organizational personnel with information security responsibilities].			

Special Publication 800-53A
Revision 4

Assessing Security and Privacy Controls in Federal Information Systems
and Organizations — *Building Effective Assessment Plans*

MP-2	MEDIA ACCESS
	ASSESSMENT OBJECTIVE: *Determine if the organization:*

	MP-2[1]	*defines types of digital and/or non-digital media requiring restricted access;*
	MP-2[2]	*defines personnel or roles authorized to access organization-defined types of digital and/or non-digital media; and*
	MP-2[3]	*restricts access to organization-defined types of digital and/or non-digital media to organization-defined personnel or roles.*

POTENTIAL ASSESSMENT METHODS AND OBJECTS:

Examine: [*SELECT FROM:* Information system media protection policy; procedures addressing media access restrictions; access control policy and procedures; physical and environmental protection policy and procedures; media storage facilities; access control records; other relevant documents or records].

Interview: [*SELECT FROM:* Organizational personnel with information system media protection responsibilities; organizational personnel with information security responsibilities; system/network administrators].

Test: [*SELECT FROM:* Organizational processes for restricting information media; automated mechanisms supporting and/or implementing media access restrictions].

MP-2(1)	MEDIA ACCESS | *AUTOMATED RESTRICTED ACCESS*
[Withdrawn: Incorporated into MP-4(2)].	

MP-2(2)	MEDIA ACCESS | *CRYPTOGRAPHIC PROTECTION*
[Withdrawn: Incorporated into SC-28(1)].	

MP-3	MEDIA MARKING
	ASSESSMENT OBJECTIVE: *Determine if the organization:*

	MP-3(a)	*marks information system media indicating the:*
		MP-3(a)[1]	*distribution limitations of the information;*
		MP-3(a)[2]	*handling caveats of the information;*
		MP-3(a)[3]	*applicable security markings (if any) of the information;*
	MP-3(b)	MP-3(b)[1]	*defines types of information system media to be exempted from marking as long as the media remain in designated controlled areas;*
		MP-3(b)[2]	*defines controlled areas where organization-defined types of information system media exempt from marking are to be retained; and*
		MP-3(b)[3]	*exempts organization-defined types of information system media from marking as long as the media remain within organization-defined controlled areas.*

Special Publication 800-53A
Revision 4

Assessing Security and Privacy Controls in Federal Information Systems
and Organizations — *Building Effective Assessment Plans*

POTENTIAL ASSESSMENT METHODS AND OBJECTS:

Examine: [*SELECT FROM*: Information system media protection policy; procedures addressing media marking; physical and environmental protection policy and procedures; security plan; list of information system media marking security attributes; designated controlled areas; other relevant documents or records].

Interview: [*SELECT FROM*: Organizational personnel with information system media protection and marking responsibilities; organizational personnel with information security responsibilities].

Test: [*SELECT FROM*: Organizational processes for marking information media; automated mechanisms supporting and/or implementing media marking].

MP-4	MEDIA STORAGE		
	ASSESSMENT OBJECTIVE: *Determine if the organization:*		
	MP-4(a)	**MP-4(a)[1]**	*defines types of digital and/or non-digital media to be physically controlled and securely stored within designated controlled areas;*
		MP-4(a)[2]	*defines controlled areas designated to physically control and securely store organization-defined types of digital and/or non-digital media;*
		MP-4(a)[3]	*physically controls organization-defined types of digital and/or non-digital media within organization-defined controlled areas;*
		MP-4(a)[4]	*securely stores organization-defined types of digital and/or non-digital media within organization-defined controlled areas; and*
	MP-4(b)	*protects information system media until the media are destroyed or sanitized using approved equipment, techniques, and procedures.*	
	POTENTIAL ASSESSMENT METHODS AND OBJECTS: **Examine**: [*SELECT FROM*: Information system media protection policy; procedures addressing media storage; physical and environmental protection policy and procedures; access control policy and procedures; security plan; information system media; designated controlled areas; other relevant documents or records]. **Interview**: [*SELECT FROM*: Organizational personnel with information system media protection and storage responsibilities; organizational personnel with information security responsibilities]. **Test**: [*SELECT FROM*: Organizational processes for storing information media; automated mechanisms supporting and/or implementing secure media storage/media protection].		

MP-4(1)	MEDIA STORAGE | *CRYPTOGRAPHIC PROTECTION*
[Withdrawn: Incorporated into SC-28(1)].	

MP-4(2)	MEDIA STORAGE | *AUTOMATED RESTRICTED ACCESS*	
	ASSESSMENT OBJECTIVE: *Determine if the organization employs automated mechanisms to:*	
	MP-4(2)[1]	*restrict access to media storage areas;*
	MP-4(2)[2]	*audit access attempts; and*
	MP-4(2)[3]	*audit access granted.*

Special Publication 800-53A
Revision 4

Assessing Security and Privacy Controls in Federal Information Systems
and Organizations — *Building Effective Assessment Plans*

POTENTIAL ASSESSMENT METHODS AND OBJECTS:

Examine: [*SELECT FROM*: Information system media protection policy; procedures addressing media storage; access control policy and procedures; physical and environmental protection policy and procedures; information system design documentation; information system configuration settings and associated documentation; media storage facilities; access control devices; access control records; audit records; other relevant documents or records].

Interview: [*SELECT FROM*: Organizational personnel with information system media protection and storage responsibilities; organizational personnel with information security responsibilities; system/network administrators].

Test: [*SELECT FROM*: Automated mechanisms restricting access to media storage areas; automated mechanisms auditing access attempts and access granted to media storage areas].

MP-5	MEDIA TRANSPORT	
	ASSESSMENT OBJECTIVE: *Determine if the organization:*	
	MP-5(a)	**MP-5(a)[1]**	*defines types of information system media to be protected and controlled during transport outside of controlled areas;*
		MP-5(a)[2]	*defines security safeguards to protect and control organization-defined information system media during transport outside of controlled areas;*
		MP-5(a)[3]	*protects and controls organization-defined information system media during transport outside of controlled areas using organization-defined security safeguards;*
	MP-5(b)	*maintains accountability for information system media during transport outside of controlled areas;*	
	MP-5(c)	*documents activities associated with the transport of information system media; and*	
	MP-5(d)	*restricts the activities associated with transport of information system media to authorized personnel.*	

POTENTIAL ASSESSMENT METHODS AND OBJECTS:

Examine: [*SELECT FROM*: Information system media protection policy; procedures addressing media storage; physical and environmental protection policy and procedures; access control policy and procedures; security plan; information system media; designated controlled areas; other relevant documents or records].

Interview: [*SELECT FROM*: Organizational personnel with information system media protection and storage responsibilities; organizational personnel with information security responsibilities; system/network administrators].

Test: [*SELECT FROM*: Organizational processes for storing information media; automated mechanisms supporting and/or implementing media storage/media protection].

MP-5(1)	MEDIA TRANSPORT	*PROTECTION OUTSIDE OF CONTROLLED AREAS*
[Withdrawn: Incorporated into MP-5].	

MP-5(2)	MEDIA TRANSPORT	*DOCUMENTATION OF ACTIVITIES*
[Withdrawn: Incorporated into MP-5].	

Special Publication 800-53A
Revision 4

Assessing Security and Privacy Controls in Federal Information Systems
and Organizations — *Building Effective Assessment Plans*

MP-5(3)	MEDIA TRANSPORT	*CUSTODIANS*

	ASSESSMENT OBJECTIVE:
	Determine if the organization employs an identified custodian during transport of information system media outside of controlled areas.

	POTENTIAL ASSESSMENT METHODS AND OBJECTS:
	Examine: [*SELECT FROM:* Information system media protection policy; procedures addressing media transport; physical and environmental protection policy and procedures; information system media transport records; audit records; other relevant documents or records].
	Interview: [*SELECT FROM:* Organizational personnel with information system media transport responsibilities; organizational personnel with information security responsibilities].

MP-5(4)	MEDIA TRANSPORT	*CRYPTOGRAPHIC PROTECTION*

	ASSESSMENT OBJECTIVE:
	Determine if the organization employs cryptographic mechanisms to protect the confidentiality and integrity of information stored on digital media during transport outside of controlled areas.

	POTENTIAL ASSESSMENT METHODS AND OBJECTS:
	Examine: [*SELECT FROM:* Information system media protection policy; procedures addressing media transport; information system design documentation; information system configuration settings and associated documentation; information system media transport records; audit records; other relevant documents or records].
	Interview: [*SELECT FROM:* Organizational personnel with information system media transport responsibilities; organizational personnel with information security responsibilities].
	Test: [*SELECT FROM:* Cryptographic mechanisms protecting information on digital media during transportation outside controlled areas].

MP-6	MEDIA SANITIZATION		

	ASSESSMENT OBJECTIVE:		
	Determine if the organization:		
MP-6(a)	MP-6(a)[1]	*defines information system media to be sanitized prior to:*	
		MP-6(a)[1][a]	*disposal;*
		MP-6(a)[1][b]	*release out of organizational control; or*
		MP-6(a)[1][c]	*release for reuse;*
	MP-6(a)[2]	*defines sanitization techniques or procedures to be used for sanitizing organization-defined information system media prior to:*	
		MP-6(a)[2][a]	*disposal;*
		MP-6(a)[2][b]	*release out of organizational control; or*
		MP-6(a)[2][c]	*release for reuse;*
	MP-6(a)[3]	*sanitizes organization-defined information system media prior to disposal, release out of organizational control, or release for reuse using organization-defined sanitization techniques or procedures in accordance with applicable federal and organizational standards and policies; and*	

Special Publication 800-53A
Revision 4

Assessing Security and Privacy Controls in Federal Information Systems
and Organizations — *Building Effective Assessment Plans*

MP-6(b)	*employs sanitization mechanisms with strength and integrity commensurate with the security category or classification of the information.*

POTENTIAL ASSESSMENT METHODS AND OBJECTS:

Examine: [*SELECT FROM:* Information system media protection policy; procedures addressing media sanitization and disposal; applicable federal standards and policies addressing media sanitization; media sanitization records; audit records; information system design documentation; information system configuration settings and associated documentation; other relevant documents or records].

Interview: [*SELECT FROM:* Organizational personnel with media sanitization responsibilities; organizational personnel with information security responsibilities; system/network administrators].

Test: [*SELECT FROM:* Organizational processes for media sanitization; automated mechanisms supporting and/or implementing media sanitization].

MP-6(1)	**MEDIA SANITIZATION** | *REVIEW / APPROVE / TRACK / DOCUMENT / VERIFY*

ASSESSMENT OBJECTIVE:

Determine if the organization:

MP-6(1)[1]	*reviews media sanitization and disposal actions;*
MP-6(1)[2]	*approves media sanitization and disposal actions;*
MP-6(1)[3]	*tracks media sanitization and disposal actions;*
MP-6(1)[4]	*documents media sanitization and disposal actions; and*
MP-6(1)[5]	*verifies media sanitization and disposal actions.*

POTENTIAL ASSESSMENT METHODS AND OBJECTS:

Examine: [*SELECT FROM:* Information system media protection policy; procedures addressing media sanitization and disposal; media sanitization and disposal records; review records for media sanitization and disposal actions; approvals for media sanitization and disposal actions; tracking records; verification records; audit records; other relevant documents or records].

Interview: [*SELECT FROM:* Organizational personnel with information system media sanitization and disposal responsibilities; organizational personnel with information security responsibilities; system/network administrators].

Test: [*SELECT FROM:* Organizational processes for media sanitization; automated mechanisms supporting and/or implementing media sanitization].

MP-6(2)	**MEDIA SANITIZATION** | *EQUIPMENT TESTING*

ASSESSMENT OBJECTIVE:

Determine if the organization:

MP-6(2)[1]	*defines the frequency for testing sanitization equipment and procedures to verify that the intended sanitization is being achieved; and*
MP-6(2)[2]	*tests sanitization equipment and procedures with the organization-defined frequency to verify that the intended sanitization is being achieved.*

Special Publication 800-53A
Revision 4

Assessing Security and Privacy Controls in Federal Information Systems
and Organizations — *Building Effective Assessment Plans*

POTENTIAL ASSESSMENT METHODS AND OBJECTS:

Examine: [*SELECT FROM:* Information system media protection policy; procedures addressing media sanitization and disposal; procedures addressing testing of media sanitization equipment; results of media sanitization equipment and procedures testing; audit records; other relevant documents or records].

Interview: [*SELECT FROM:* Organizational personnel with information system media sanitization responsibilities; organizational personnel with information security responsibilities].

Test: [*SELECT FROM:* Organizational processes for media sanitization; automated mechanisms supporting and/or implementing media sanitization].

MP-6(3)	MEDIA SANITIZATION | *NONDESTRUCTIVE TECHNIQUES*

ASSESSMENT OBJECTIVE:

Determine if the organization:

MP-6(3)[1]	*defines circumstances requiring sanitization of portable storage devices; and*
MP-6(3)[2]	*applies nondestructive sanitization techniques to portable storage devices prior to connecting such devices to the information system under organization-defined circumstances requiring sanitization of portable storage devices.*

POTENTIAL ASSESSMENT METHODS AND OBJECTS:

Examine: [*SELECT FROM:* Information system media protection policy; procedures addressing media sanitization and disposal; list of circumstances requiring sanitization of portable storage devices; media sanitization records; audit records; other relevant documents or records].

Interview: [*SELECT FROM:* Organizational personnel with information system media sanitization responsibilities; organizational personnel with information security responsibilities].

Test: [*SELECT FROM:* Organizational processes for media sanitization of portable storage devices; automated mechanisms supporting and/or implementing media sanitization].

MP-6(4)	MEDIA SANITIZATION | *CONTROLLED UNCLASSIFIED INFORMATION*
[Withdrawn: Incorporated into MP-6].	

MP-6(5)	MEDIA SANITIZATION | *CLASSIFIED INFORMATION*
[Withdrawn: Incorporated into MP-6].	

MP-6(6)	MEDIA SANITIZATION | *•MEDIA DESTRUCTION*
[Withdrawn: Incorporated into MP-6].	

MP-6(7)	MEDIA SANITIZATION | *DUAL AUTHORIZATION*

ASSESSMENT OBJECTIVE:

Determine if the organization:

MP-6(7)[1]	*defines information system media requiring dual authorization to be enforced for sanitization of such media; and*
MP-6(7)[2]	*enforces dual authorization for the sanitization of organization-defined information system media.*

Special Publication 800-53A
Revision 4

Assessing Security and Privacy Controls in Federal Information Systems
and Organizations — *Building Effective Assessment Plans*

	POTENTIAL ASSESSMENT METHODS AND OBJECTS: **Examine**: [*SELECT FROM:* Information system media protection policy; procedures addressing media sanitization and disposal; list of information system media requiring dual authorization for sanitization; authorization records; media sanitization records; audit records; other relevant documents or records]. **Interview**: [*SELECT FROM:* Organizational personnel with information system media sanitization responsibilities; organizational personnel with information security responsibilities; system/network administrators]. **Test**: [*SELECT FROM:* Organizational processes requiring dual authorization for media sanitization; automated mechanisms supporting and/or implementing media sanitization; automated mechanisms supporting and/or implementing dual authorization].

MP-6(8)	MEDIA SANITIZATION | *REMOTE PURGING / WIPING OF INFORMATION*
	ASSESSMENT OBJECTIVE: *Determine if the organization:*

MP-6(8)[1]	*defines information systems, system components, or devices to purge/wipe either remotely or under specific organizational conditions;*	
MP-6(8)[2]	*defines conditions under which information is to be purged/wiped from organization-defined information systems, system components, or devices; and*	
MP-6(8)[3]	*provides the capability to purge/wipe information from organization-defined information systems, system components, or devices either:*	
	MP-6(8)[3][a]	*remotely; or*
	MP-6(8)[3][b]	*under organization-defined conditions.*

POTENTIAL ASSESSMENT METHODS AND OBJECTS: **Examine**: [*SELECT FROM:* Information system media protection policy; procedures addressing media sanitization and disposal; information system design documentation; information system configuration settings and associated documentation; media sanitization records; audit records; other relevant documents or records]. **Interview**: [*SELECT FROM:* Organizational personnel with information system media sanitization responsibilities; organizational personnel with information security responsibilities; system/network administrators]. **Test**: [*SELECT FROM:* Organizational processes for purging/wiping media; automated mechanisms supporting and/or implementing purge/wipe capabilities].	

MP-7	MEDIA USE •
	ASSESSMENT OBJECTIVE: *Determine if the organization:*

MP-7[1]	*defines types of information system media to be:*	
	MP-7[1][a]	*restricted on information systems or system components; or*
	MP-7[1][b]	*prohibited from use on information systems or system components;*
MP-7[2]	*defines information systems or system components on which the use of organization-defined types of information system media is to be one of the following:*	
	MP-7[2][a]	*restricted; or*
	MP-7[2][b]	*prohibited;*

Special Publication 800-53A
Revision 4

Assessing Security and Privacy Controls in Federal Information Systems
and Organizations — *Building Effective Assessment Plans*

MP-7[3]	*defines security safeguards to be employed to restrict or prohibit the use of organization-defined types of information system media on organization-defined information systems or system components; and*
MP-7[4]	*restricts or prohibits the use of organization-defined information system media on organization-defined information systems or system components using organization-defined security safeguards.*

POTENTIAL ASSESSMENT METHODS AND OBJECTS:

Examine: [*SELECT FROM:* Information system media protection policy; system use policy; procedures addressing media usage restrictions; security plan; rules of behavior; information system design documentation; information system configuration settings and associated documentation; audit records; other relevant documents or records].

Interview: [*SELECT FROM:* Organizational personnel with information system media use responsibilities; organizational personnel with information security responsibilities; system/network administrators].

Test: [*SELECT FROM:* Organizational processes for media use; automated mechanisms restricting or prohibiting use of information system media on information systems or system components].

MP-7(1)	MEDIA USE	*PROHIBIT USE WITHOUT OWNER*

ASSESSMENT OBJECTIVE:

Determine if the organization prohibits the use of portable storage devices in organizational information systems when such devices have no identifiable owner.

POTENTIAL ASSESSMENT METHODS AND OBJECTS:

Examine: [*SELECT FROM:* Information system media protection policy; system use policy; procedures addressing media usage restrictions; security plan; rules of behavior; information system design documentation; information system configuration settings and associated documentation; audit records; other relevant documents or records].

Interview: [*SELECT FROM:* Organizational personnel with information system media use responsibilities; organizational personnel with information security responsibilities; system/network administrators].

Test: [*SELECT FROM:* Organizational processes for media use; automated mechanisms prohibiting use of media on information systems or system components].

MP-7(2)	MEDIA USE	*PROHIBIT USE OF SANITIZATION-RESISTANT MEDIA*

ASSESSMENT OBJECTIVE:

Determine if the organization prohibits the use of sanitization-resistant media in organizational information systems.

POTENTIAL ASSESSMENT METHODS AND OBJECTS:

Examine: [*SELECT FROM:* Information system media protection policy, system use policy; procedures addressing media usage restrictions; rules of behavior; audit records; other relevant documents or records].

Interview: [*SELECT FROM:* Organizational personnel with information system media use responsibilities; organizational personnel with information security responsibilities; system/network administrators].

Test: [*SELECT FROM:* Organizational processes for media use; automated mechanisms prohibiting use of media on information systems or system components].

MP-8	MEDIA DOWNGRADING

ASSESSMENT OBJECTIVE:

Determine if the organization:

Special Publication 800-53A
Revision 4

Assessing Security and Privacy Controls in Federal Information Systems
and Organizations — *Building Effective Assessment Plans*

	MP-8(a)	MP-8(a)[1]	*defines the information system media downgrading process;*
		MP-8(a)[2]	*defines the strength and integrity with which media downgrading mechanisms are to be employed;*
		MP-8(a)[3]	*establishes an organization-defined information system media downgrading process that includes employing downgrading mechanisms with organization-defined strength and integrity;*
	MP-8(b)	*ensures that the information system media downgrading process is commensurate with the:*	
		MP-8(b)[1]	*security category and/or classification level of the information to be removed;*
		MP-8(b)[2]	*access authorizations of the potential recipients of the downgraded information;*
	MP-8(c)	*identifies/defines information system media requiring downgrading; and*	
	MP-8(d)	*downgrades the identified information system media using the established process.*	

POTENTIAL ASSESSMENT METHODS AND OBJECTS:

Examine: [*SELECT FROM:* Information system media protection policy; procedures addressing media downgrading; system categorization documentation; list of media requiring downgrading; records of media downgrading; audit records; other relevant documents or records].

Interview: [*SELECT FROM:* Organizational personnel with information system media downgrading responsibilities; organizational personnel with information security responsibilities; system/network administrators].

Test: [*SELECT FROM:* Organizational processes for media downgrading; automated mechanisms supporting and/or implementing media downgrading].

MP-8(1)	MEDIA DOWNGRADING | *DOCUMENTATION OF PROCESS*
	ASSESSMENT OBJECTIVE: *Determine if the organization documents information system media downgrading actions.*
	POTENTIAL ASSESSMENT METHODS AND OBJECTS: **Examine**: [*SELECT FROM:* Information system media protection policy; procedures addressing media downgrading; list of media requiring downgrading; records of media downgrading; audit records; other relevant documents or records]. **Interview**: [*SELECT FROM:* Organizational personnel with information system media downgrading responsibilities; organizational personnel with information security responsibilities]. **Test**: [*SELECT FROM:* Organizational processes for media downgrading; automated mechanisms supporting and/or implementing media downgrading].

MP-8(2)	MEDIA DOWNGRADING | *EQUIPMENT TESTING*		
	ASSESSMENT OBJECTIVE: *Determine if the organization:*		
	MP-8(2)[1]	MP-8(2)[1][a]	*defines tests to be employed for downgrading equipment;*
		MP-8(2)[1][b]	*defines procedures to verify correct performance;*
	MP-8(2)[2]	*defines the frequency for employing tests of downgrading equipment and procedures to verify correct performance; and*	

Special Publication 800-53A
Revision 4

Assessing Security and Privacy Controls in Federal Information Systems
and Organizations — *Building Effective Assessment Plans*

MP-8(2)[3]	*employs organization-defined tests of downgrading equipment and procedures to verify correct performance with the organization-defined frequency.*

POTENTIAL ASSESSMENT METHODS AND OBJECTS:

Examine: [*SELECT FROM:* Information system media protection policy; procedures addressing media downgrading; procedures addressing testing of media downgrading equipment; results of downgrading equipment and procedures testing; audit records: other relevant documents or records].

Interview: [*SELECT FROM:* Organizational personnel with information system media downgrading responsibilities; organizational personnel with information security responsibilities].

Test: [*SELECT FROM:* Organizational processes for media downgrading; automated mechanisms supporting and/or implementing media downgrading; automated mechanisms supporting and/or implementing tests for downgrading equipment].

MP-8(3)	MEDIA DOWNGRADING | *CONTROLLED UNCLASSIFIED INFORMATION*

ASSESSMENT OBJECTIVE:

Determine if the organization:

MP-8(3)[1]	*defines Controlled Unclassified Information (CUI) contained on information system media that requires downgrading prior to public release; and*
MP-8(3)[2]	*downgrades information system media containing organization-defined CUI prior to public release in accordance with applicable federal and organizational standards and policies.*

POTENTIAL ASSESSMENT METHODS AND OBJECTS:

Examine: [*SELECT FROM:* Information system media protection policy; access authorization policy; procedures addressing downgrading of media containing CUI; applicable federal and organizational standards and policies regarding protection of CUI; media downgrading records; other relevant documents or records].

Interview: [*SELECT FROM:* Organizational personnel with information system media downgrading responsibilities; organizational personnel with information security responsibilities].

Test: [*SELECT FROM:* Organizational processes for media downgrading; automated mechanisms supporting and/or implementing media downgrading].

MP-8(4)	MEDIA DOWNGRADING | *CLASSIFIED INFORMATION*

ASSESSMENT OBJECTIVE:

Determine if the organization downgrades information system media containing classified information prior to release to individuals without required access authorizations in accordance with NSA standards and policies.

POTENTIAL ASSESSMENT METHODS AND OBJECTS:

Examine: [*SELECT FROM:* Information system media protection policy; access authorization policy; procedures addressing downgrading of media containing classified information; procedures addressing handling of classified information; NSA standards and policies regarding protection of classified information; media downgrading records; other relevant documents or records].

Interview: [*SELECT FROM:* Organizational personnel with information system media downgrading responsibilities; organizational personnel with information security responsibilities].

Test: [*SELECT FROM:* Organizational processes for media downgrading; automated mechanisms supporting and/or implementing media downgrading].

Special Publication 800-53A
Revision 4

Assessing Security and Privacy Controls in Federal Information Systems
and Organizations — *Building Effective Assessment Plans*

FAMILY: PHYSICAL AND ENVIRONMENTAL PROTECTION

PE-1	PHYSICAL AND ENVIRONMENTAL PROTECTION POLICY AND PROCEDURES		
	ASSESSMENT OBJECTIVE: *Determine if the organization:*		
	PE-1(a)(1)	PE-1(a)(1)[1]	*develops and documents a physical and environmental protection policy that addresses:*
		PE-1(a)(1)[1][a]	*purpose;*
		PE-1(a)(1)[1][b]	*scope;*
		PE-1(a)(1)[1][c]	*roles;*
		PE-1(a)(1)[1][d]	*responsibilities;*
		PE-1(a)(1)[1][e]	*management commitment;*
		PE-1(a)(1)[1][f]	*coordination among organizational entities;*
		PE-1(a)(1)[1][g]	*compliance;*
		PE-1(a)(1)[2]	*defines personnel or roles to whom the physical and environmental protection policy is to be disseminated;*
		PE-1(a)(1)[3]	*disseminates the physical and environmental protection policy to organization-defined personnel or roles;*
	PE-1(a)(2)	PE-1(a)(2)[1]	*develops and documents procedures to facilitate the implementation of the physical and environmental protection policy and associated physical and environmental protection controls;*
		PE-1(a)(2)[2]	*defines personnel or roles to whom the procedures are to be disseminated;*
		PE-1(a)(2)[3]	*disseminates the procedures to organization-defined personnel or roles;*
	PE-1(b)(1)	PE-1(b)(1)[1]	*defines the frequency to review and update the current physical and environmental protection policy;*
		PE-1(b)(1)[2]	*reviews and updates the current physical and environmental protection policy with the organization-defined frequency;*
	PE-1(b)(2)	PE-1(b)(2)[1]	*defines the frequency to review and update the current physical and environmental protection procedures; and*
		PE-1(b)(2)[2]	*reviews and updates the current physical and environmental protection procedures with the organization-defined frequency.*
	POTENTIAL ASSESSMENT METHODS AND OBJECTS: **Examine:** [*SELECT FROM:* Physical and environmental protection policy and procedures; other relevant documents or records]. **Interview:** [*SELECT FROM:* Organizational personnel with physical and environmental protection responsibilities; organizational personnel with information security responsibilities].		

Special Publication 800-53A
Revision 4

Assessing Security and Privacy Controls in Federal Information Systems
and Organizations — *Building Effective Assessment Plans*

PE-2	PHYSICAL ACCESS AUTHORIZATIONS	
	ASSESSMENT OBJECTIVE: *Determine if the organization:*	
	PE-2(a)	**PE-2(a)[1]** *develops a list of individuals with authorized access to the facility where the information system resides;*
		PE-2(a)[2] *approves a list of individuals with authorized access to the facility where the information system resides;*
		PE-2(a)[3] *maintains a list of individuals with authorized access to the facility where the information system resides;*
	PE-2(b)	*issues authorization credentials for facility access;*
	PE-2(c)	**PE-2(c)[1]** *defines the frequency to review the access list detailing authorized facility access by individuals;*
		PE-2(c)[2] *reviews the access list detailing authorized facility access by individuals with the organization-defined frequency; and*
	PE-2(d)	*removes individuals from the facility access list when access is no longer required.*
	POTENTIAL ASSESSMENT METHODS AND OBJECTS: **Examine**: [*SELECT FROM:* Physical and environmental protection policy; procedures addressing physical access authorizations; security plan; authorized personnel access list; authorization credentials; physical access list reviews; physical access termination records and associated documentation; other relevant documents or records]. **Interview**: [*SELECT FROM:* Organizational personnel with physical access authorization responsibilities; organizational personnel with physical access to information system facility; organizational personnel with information security responsibilities]. **Test**: [*SELECT FROM:* Organizational processes for physical access authorizations; automated mechanisms supporting and/or implementing physical access authorizations].	

PE-2(1)	PHYSICAL ACCESS AUTHORIZATIONS	*ACCESS BY POSITION / ROLE*
	ASSESSMENT OBJECTIVE: *Determine if the organization authorizes physical access to the facility where the information system resides based on position or role.*	
	POTENTIAL ASSESSMENT METHODS AND OBJECTS: **Examine**: [*SELECT FROM:* Physical and environmental protection policy; procedures addressing physical access authorizations; physical access control logs or records; list of positions/roles and corresponding physical access authorizations; information system entry and exit points; other relevant documents or records]. **Interview**: [*SELECT FROM:* Organizational personnel with physical access authorization responsibilities; organizational personnel with physical access to information system facility; organizational personnel with information security responsibilities]. **Test**: [*SELECT FROM:* Organizational processes for physical access authorizations; automated mechanisms supporting and/or implementing physical access authorizations].	

PE-2(2)	PHYSICAL ACCESS AUTHORIZATIONS	*TWO FORMS OF IDENTIFICATION*
	ASSESSMENT OBJECTIVE: *Determine if the organization:*	

Special Publication 800-53A
Revision 4

Assessing Security and Privacy Controls in Federal Information Systems
and Organizations — *Building Effective Assessment Plans*

PE-2(2)[1]	*defines a list of acceptable forms of identification for visitor access to the facility where the information system resides; and*
PE-2(2)[2]	*requires two forms of identification from the organization-defined list of acceptable forms of identification for visitor access to the facility where the information system resides.*

POTENTIAL ASSESSMENT METHODS AND OBJECTS:

Examine: [*SELECT FROM:* Physical and environmental protection policy; procedures addressing physical access authorizations; list of acceptable forms of identification for visitor access to the facility where information system resides; access authorization forms; access credentials; physical access control logs or records; other relevant documents or records].

Interview: [*SELECT FROM:* Organizational personnel with physical access authorization responsibilities; organizational personnel with physical access to information system facility; organizational personnel with information security responsibilities].

Test: [*SELECT FROM:* Organizational processes for physical access authorizations; automated mechanisms supporting and/or implementing physical access authorizations].

PE-2(3)	PHYSICAL ACCESS AUTHORIZATIONS | *RESTRICT UNESCORTED ACCESS*

ASSESSMENT OBJECTIVE:

Determine if the organization:

PE-2(3)[1]		*defines credentials to be employed to restrict unescorted access to the facility where the information system resides to authorized personnel;*
PE-2(3)[2]		*restricts unescorted access to the facility where the information system resides to personnel with one or more of the following:*
	PE-2(3)[2][a]	*security clearances for all information contained within the system;*
	PE-2(3)[2][b]	*formal access authorizations for all information contained within the system;*
	PE-2(3)[2][c]	*need for access to all information contained within the system; and/or*
	PE-2(3)[2][d]	*organization-defined credentials.*

POTENTIAL ASSESSMENT METHODS AND OBJECTS:

Examine: [*SELECT FROM:* Physical and environmental protection policy; procedures addressing physical access authorizations; authorized personnel access list; security clearances; access authorizations; access credentials; physical access control logs or records; other relevant documents or records].

Interview: [*SELECT FROM:* Organizational personnel with physical access authorization responsibilities; organizational personnel with physical access to information system facility; organizational personnel with information security responsibilities].

Test: [*SELECT FROM:* Organizational processes for physical access authorizations; automated mechanisms supporting and/or implementing physical access authorizations].

PE-3	PHYSICAL ACCESS CONTROL

ASSESSMENT OBJECTIVE:

Determine if the organization:

PE-3(a)	**PE-3(a)[1]**	*defines entry/exit points to the facility where the information system resides;*

Special Publication 800-53A
Revision 4

Assessing Security and Privacy Controls in Federal Information Systems
and Organizations — *Building Effective Assessment Plans*

		PE-3(a)[2]	*enforces physical access authorizations at organization-defined entry/exit points to the facility where the information system resides by:*			
			PE-3(a)[2](1)	*verifying individual access authorizations before granting access to the facility;*		
			PE-3(a)[2](2)	PE-3(a)[2](2)[a]	*defining physical access control systems/devices to be employed to control ingress/egress to the facility where the information system resides;*	
				PE-3(a)[2](2)[b]	*using one or more of the following ways to control ingress/egress to the facility:*	
					PE-3(a)[2](2)[b][1]	*organization-defined physical access control systems/devices; and/or*
					PE-3(a)[2](2)[b][2]	*guards;*
	PE-3(b)	PE-3(b)[1]	*defines entry/exit points for which physical access audit logs are to be maintained;*			
		PE-3(b)[2]	*maintains physical access audit logs for organization-defined entry/exit points;*			
	PE-3(c)	PE-3(c)[1]	*defines security safeguards to be employed to control access to areas within the facility officially designated as publicly accessible;*			
		PE-3(c)[2]	*provides organization-defined security safeguards to control access to areas within the facility officially designated as publicly accessible;*			
	PE-3(d)	PE-3(d)[1]	*defines circumstances requiring visitor:*			
			PE-3(d)[1][a]	*escorts;*		
			PE-3(d)[1][b]	*monitoring;*		
		PE-3(d)[2]	*in accordance with organization-defined circumstances requiring visitor escorts and monitoring:*			
			PE-3(d)[2][a]	*escorts visitors;*		
			PE-3(d)[2][b]	*monitors visitor activities;*		
	PE-3(e)	PE-3(e)[1]	*secures keys;*			
		PE-3(e)[2]	*secures combinations;*			
		PE-3(e)[3]	*secures other physical access devices;*			
	PE-3(f)	PE-3(f)[1]	*defines physical access devices to be inventoried;*			
		PE-3(f)[2]	*defines the frequency to inventory organization-defined physical access devices;*			

Special Publication 800-53A
Revision 4

Assessing Security and Privacy Controls in Federal Information Systems
and Organizations — *Building Effective Assessment Plans*

		PE-3(f)[3]	*inventories the organization-defined physical access devices with the organization-defined frequency;*
	PE-3(g)	PE-3(g)[1]	*defines the frequency to change combinations and keys; and*
		PE-3(g)[2]	*changes combinations and keys with the organization-defined frequency and/or when:*
		PE-3(g)[2][a]	*keys are lost;*
		PE-3(g)[2][b]	*combinations are compromised;*
		PE-3(g)[2][c]	*individuals are transferred or terminated.*

POTENTIAL ASSESSMENT METHODS AND OBJECTS:

Examine: [*SELECT FROM:* Physical and environmental protection policy; procedures addressing physical access control; security plan; physical access control logs or records; inventory records of physical access control devices; information system entry and exit points; records of key and lock combination changes; storage locations for physical access control devices; physical access control devices; list of security safeguards controlling access to designated publicly accessible areas within facility; other relevant documents or records].

Interview: [*SELECT FROM:* Organizational personnel with physical access control responsibilities; organizational personnel with information security responsibilities].

Test: [*SELECT FROM:* Organizational processes for physical access control; automated mechanisms supporting and/or implementing physical access control; physical access control devices].

PE-3(1)	PHYSICAL ACCESS CONTROL | *INFORMATION SYSTEM ACCESS*

ASSESSMENT OBJECTIVE:

Determine if the organization:

PE-3(1)[1]	*defines physical spaces containing one or more components of the information system; and*
PE-3(1)[2]	*enforces physical access authorizations to the information system in addition to the physical access controls for the facility at organization-defined physical spaces containing one or more components of the information system.*

POTENTIAL ASSESSMENT METHODS AND OBJECTS:

Examine: [*SELECT FROM:* Physical and environmental protection policy; procedures addressing physical access control; physical access control logs or records; physical access control devices; access authorizations; access credentials; information system entry and exit points; list of areas within the facility containing concentrations of information system components or information system components requiring additional physical protection; other relevant documents or records].

Interview: [*SELECT FROM:* Organizational personnel with physical access authorization responsibilities; organizational personnel with information security responsibilities].

Test: [*SELECT FROM:* Organizational processes for physical access control to the information system/components; automated mechanisms supporting and/or implementing physical access control for facility areas containing information system components].

PE-3(2)	PHYSICAL ACCESS CONTROL | *FACILITY/INFORMATION SYSTEM BOUNDARIES*

ASSESSMENT OBJECTIVE:

Determine if the organization:

PE-3(2)[1]	*defines the frequency to perform security checks at the physical boundary of the facility or information system for:*
PE-3(2)[1][a]	*unauthorized exfiltration of information; or*

Special Publication 800-53A
Revision 4

Assessing Security and Privacy Controls in Federal Information Systems
and Organizations — *Building Effective Assessment Plans*

	PE-3(2)[1][b]	*removal of information system components; and*
PE-3(2)[2]		*performs security checks with the organization-defined frequency at the physical boundary of the facility or information system for:*
	PE-3(2)[2][a]	*unauthorized exfiltration of information; or*
	PE-3(2)[2][b]	*removal of information system components.*

POTENTIAL ASSESSMENT METHODS AND OBJECTS:

Examine: [*SELECT FROM:* Physical and environmental protection policy; procedures addressing physical access control; physical access control logs or records; records of security checks; security audit reports; security inspection reports; facility layout documentation; information system entry and exit points; other relevant documents or records].

Interview: [*SELECT FROM:* Organizational personnel with physical access control responsibilities; organizational personnel with information security responsibilities].

Test: [*SELECT FROM:* Organizational processes for physical access control to the facility and/or information system; automated mechanisms supporting and/or implementing physical access control for the facility or information system; automated mechanisms supporting and/or implementing security checks for unauthorized exfiltration of information].

PE-3(3)	PHYSICAL ACCESS CONTROL	*CONTINUOUS GUARDS / ALARMS / MONITORING*

ASSESSMENT OBJECTIVE:

Determine if the organization employs one or more of the following to monitor every physical access point to the facility where the information system resides 24 hours per day, 7 days per week:

PE-3(3)[1]	*guards; and/or*
PE-3(3)[2]	*alarms.*

POTENTIAL ASSESSMENT METHODS AND OBJECTS:

Examine: [*SELECT FROM:* Physical and environmental protection policy; procedures addressing physical access control; physical access control logs or records; physical access control devices; facility surveillance records; facility layout documentation; information system entry and exit points; other relevant documents or records].

Interview: [*SELECT FROM:* Organizational personnel with physical access control responsibilities; organizational personnel with information security responsibilities].

Test: [*SELECT FROM:* Organizational processes for physical access control to the facility where the information system resides; automated mechanisms supporting and/or implementing physical access control for the facility where the information system resides].

PE-3(4)	PHYSICAL ACCESS CONTROL	*LOCKABLE CASINGS*

ASSESSMENT OBJECTIVE:

Determine if the organization:

PE-3(4)[1]	*defines information system components to be protected from unauthorized physical access using lockable physical casings; and*
PE-3(4)[2]	*uses lockable physical casings to protect organization-defined information system components from unauthorized physical access.*

Special Publication 800-53A
Revision 4

Assessing Security and Privacy Controls in Federal Information Systems
and Organizations — *Building Effective Assessment Plans*

POTENTIAL ASSESSMENT METHODS AND OBJECTS:

Examine: [*SELECT FROM:* Physical and environmental protection policy; procedures addressing physical access control; security plan; list of information system components requiring protection through lockable physical casings; lockable physical casings; other relevant documents or records].

Interview: [*SELECT FROM:* Organizational personnel with physical access control responsibilities; organizational personnel with information security responsibilities].

Test: [*SELECT FROM:* Lockable physical casings].

PE-3(5)	PHYSICAL ACCESS CONTROL | *TAMPER PROTECTION*

ASSESSMENT OBJECTIVE:

Determine if the organization:

PE-3(5)[1]	*defines security safeguards to be employed to detect and/or prevent physical tampering or alteration of organization-defined hardware components within the information system;*
PE-3(5)[2]	*defines hardware components within the information system for which security safeguards are to be employed to detect and/or prevent physical tampering or alteration of such components;*
PE-3(5)[3]	*employs organization-defined security safeguards to do one or more of the following:*

	PE-3(5)[3][a]	*detect physical tampering or alteration of organization-defined hardware components within the information system; and/or*
	PE-3(5)[3][b]	*prevent physical tampering or alteration of organization-defined hardware components within the information system.*

POTENTIAL ASSESSMENT METHODS AND OBJECTS:

Examine: [*SELECT FROM:* Physical and environmental protection policy; procedures addressing physical access control; list of security safeguards to detect/prevent physical tampering or alteration of information system hardware components; other relevant documents or records].

Interview: [*SELECT FROM:* Organizational personnel with physical access control responsibilities; organizational personnel with information security responsibilities].

Test: [*SELECT FROM:* Organizational processes to detect/prevent physical tampering or alteration of information system hardware components; automated mechanisms/security safeguards supporting and/or implementing detection/prevention of physical tampering/alternation of information system hardware components].

PE-3(6)	PHYSICAL ACCESS CONTROL | *FACILITY PENETRATION TESTING*

ASSESSMENT OBJECTIVE:

Determine if the organization:

PE-3(6)[1]	*defines the frequency of unannounced attempts to be included in a penetration testing process to bypass or circumvent security controls associated with physical access points to the facility; and*
PE-3(6)[2]	*employs a penetration testing process with the organization-defined frequency that includes unannounced attempts to bypass or circumvent security controls associated with physical access points to the facility.*

Special Publication 800-53A
Revision 4

Assessing Security and Privacy Controls in Federal Information Systems
and Organizations — *Building Effective Assessment Plans*

POTENTIAL ASSESSMENT METHODS AND OBJECTS:

Examine: [*SELECT FROM:* Physical and environmental protection policy; procedures addressing physical access control; procedures addressing penetration testing; rules of engagement and associated documentation; penetration test results; security plan; other relevant documents or records].

Interview: [*SELECT FROM:* Organizational personnel with physical access control responsibilities; organizational personnel with information security responsibilities].

Test: [*SELECT FROM:* Organizational processes for facility penetration testing; automated mechanisms supporting and/or implementing facility penetration testing].

PE-4	ACCESS CONTROL FOR TRANSMISSION MEDIUM

ASSESSMENT OBJECTIVE:

Determine if the organization:

PE-4[1]	*defines information system distribution and transmission lines requiring physical access controls;*
PE-4[2]	*defines security safeguards to be employed to control physical access to organization-defined information system distribution and transmission lines within organizational facilities; and*
PE-4[3]	*controls physical access to organization-defined information system distribution and transmission lines within organizational facilities using organization-defined security safeguards.*

POTENTIAL ASSESSMENT METHODS AND OBJECTS:

Examine: [*SELECT FROM:* Physical and environmental protection policy; procedures addressing access control for transmission medium; information system design documentation; facility communications and wiring diagrams; list of physical security safeguards applied to information system distribution and transmission lines; other relevant documents or records].

Interview: [*SELECT FROM:* Organizational personnel with physical access control responsibilities; organizational personnel with information security responsibilities].

Test: [*SELECT FROM:* Organizational processes for access control to distribution and transmission lines; automated mechanisms/security safeguards supporting and/or implementing access control to distribution and transmission lines].

PE-5	ACCESS CONTROL FOR OUTPUT DEVICES

ASSESSMENT OBJECTIVE:

Determine if the organization controls physical access to information system output devices to prevent unauthorized individuals from obtaining the output.

POTENTIAL ASSESSMENT METHODS AND OBJECTS:

Examine: [*SELECT FROM:* Physical and environmental protection policy; procedures addressing access control for display medium; facility layout of information system components; actual displays from information system components; other relevant documents or records].

Interview: [*SELECT FROM:* Organizational personnel with physical access control responsibilities; organizational personnel with information security responsibilities].

Test: [*SELECT FROM:* Organizational processes for access control to output devices; automated mechanisms supporting and/or implementing access control to output devices].

PE-5(1)	ACCESS CONTROL FOR OUTPUT DEVICES | *ACCESS TO OUTPUT BY AUTHORIZED INDIVIDUALS*

ASSESSMENT OBJECTIVE:

Determine if the organization:

Special Publication 800-53A
Revision 4

Assessing Security and Privacy Controls in Federal Information Systems
and Organizations — *Building Effective Assessment Plans*

	PE-5(1)(a)	PE-5(1)(a)[1]	*defines output devices whose output requires physical access controls;*
		PE-5(1)(a)[2]	*controls physical access to output from organization-defined output devices; and*
	PE-5(1)(b)		*ensures that only authorized individuals receive output from the device.*

POTENTIAL ASSESSMENT METHODS AND OBJECTS:

Examine: [*SELECT FROM:* Physical and environmental protection policy; procedures addressing physical access control; list of output devices and associated outputs requiring physical access controls; physical access control logs or records for areas containing output devices and related outputs; other relevant documents or records].

Interview: [*SELECT FROM:* Organizational personnel with physical access control responsibilities; organizational personnel with information security responsibilities].

Test: [*SELECT FROM:* Organizational processes for access control to output devices; automated mechanisms supporting and/or implementing access control to output devices].

PE-5(2)	ACCESS CONTROL FOR OUTPUT DEVICES	*ACCESS TO OUTPUT BY INDIVIDUAL IDENTITY*

ASSESSMENT OBJECTIVE:

Determine if:

	PE-5(2)(a)	PE-5(2)(a)[1]	*the organization defines output devices whose output requires physical access controls;*
		PE-5(2)(a)[2]	*the information system controls physical access to output from organization-defined output devices; and*
	PE-5(2)(b)		*the information system links individual identity to receipt of the output from the device.*

POTENTIAL ASSESSMENT METHODS AND OBJECTS:

Examine: [*SELECT FROM:* Physical and environmental protection policy; procedures addressing physical access control; information system design documentation; information system configuration settings and associated documentation; list of output devices and associated outputs requiring physical access controls; physical access control logs or records for areas containing output devices and related outputs; information system audit records; other relevant documents or records].

Interview: [*SELECT FROM:* Organizational personnel with physical access control responsibilities; organizational personnel with information security responsibilities; system/network administrators; system developers].

Test: [*SELECT FROM:* Organizational processes for access control to output devices; automated mechanisms supporting and/or implementing access control to output devices].

PE-5(3)	ACCESS CONTROL FOR OUTPUT DEVICES	*MARKING OUTPUT DEVICES*

ASSESSMENT OBJECTIVE:

Determine if the organization:

	PE-5(3)[1]	*defines information system output devices to be marked with appropriate security marking of the information permitted to be output from such devices; and*
	PE-5(3)[2]	*marks organization-defined information system output devices indicating the appropriate security marking of the information permitted to be output from the device.*

Special Publication 800-53A
Revision 4

Assessing Security and Privacy Controls in Federal Information Systems
and Organizations — *Building Effective Assessment Plans*

	POTENTIAL ASSESSMENT METHODS AND OBJECTS: **Examine**: [*SELECT FROM*: Physical and environmental protection policy; procedures addressing physical access control; security markings for information types permitted as output from information system output devices; other relevant documents or records]. **Interview**: [*SELECT FROM*: Organizational personnel with physical access control responsibilities; organizational personnel with information security responsibilities]. **Test**: [*SELECT FROM*: Organizational processes for marking output devices].

PE-6	MONITORING PHYSICAL ACCESS	
	ASSESSMENT OBJECTIVE: *Determine if the organization:*	
	PE-6(a)	*monitors physical access to the facility where the information system resides to detect and respond to physical security incidents;*
	PE-6(b)	**PE-6(b)[1]** — *defines the frequency to review physical access logs;*
		PE-6(b)[2] — *defines events or potential indication of events requiring physical access logs to be reviewed;*
		PE-6(b)[3] — *reviews physical access logs with the organization-defined frequency and upon occurrence of organization-defined events or potential indications of events; and*
	PE-6(c)	*coordinates results of reviews and investigations with the organizational incident response capability.*
	POTENTIAL ASSESSMENT METHODS AND OBJECTS: **Examine**: [*SELECT FROM*: Physical and environmental protection policy; procedures addressing physical access monitoring; security plan; physical access logs or records; physical access monitoring records; physical access log reviews; other relevant documents or records]. **Interview**: [*SELECT FROM*: Organizational personnel with physical access monitoring responsibilities; organizational personnel with incident response responsibilities; organizational personnel with information security responsibilities]. **Test**: [*SELECT FROM*: Organizational processes for monitoring physical access; automated mechanisms supporting and/or implementing physical access monitoring; automated mechanisms supporting and/or implementing reviewing of physical access logs].	

PE-6(1)	MONITORING PHYSICAL ACCESS | *INTRUSION ALARMS / SURVEILLANCE EQUIPMENT*
	ASSESSMENT OBJECTIVE: *Determine if the organization monitors physical intrusion alarms and surveillance equipment.*
	POTENTIAL ASSESSMENT METHODS AND OBJECTS: **Examine**: [*SELECT FROM*: Physical and environmental protection policy; procedures addressing physical access monitoring; security plan; physical access logs or records; physical access monitoring records; physical access log reviews; other relevant documents or records]. **Interview**: [*SELECT FROM*: Organizational personnel with physical access monitoring responsibilities; organizational personnel with incident response responsibilities; organizational personnel with information security responsibilities]. **Test**: [*SELECT FROM*: Organizational processes for monitoring physical intrusion alarms and surveillance equipment; automated mechanisms supporting and/or implementing physical access monitoring; automated mechanisms supporting and/or implementing physical intrusion alarms and surveillance equipment].

Special Publication 800-53A
Revision 4

Assessing Security and Privacy Controls in Federal Information Systems
and Organizations — *Building Effective Assessment Plans*

PE-6(2)	MONITORING PHYSICAL ACCESS | *AUTOMATED INTRUSION RECOGNITION / RESPONSES*
	ASSESSMENT OBJECTIVE: *Determine if the organization:*

	PE-6(2)[1]	*defines classes/types of intrusions to be recognized by automated mechanisms;*
	PE-6(2)[2]	*defines response actions to be initiated by automated mechanisms when organization-defined classes/types of intrusions are recognized; and*
	PE-6(2)[3]	*employs automated mechanisms to recognize organization-defined classes/types of intrusions and initiate organization-defined response actions.*

POTENTIAL ASSESSMENT METHODS AND OBJECTS:

Examine: [*SELECT FROM:* Physical and environmental protection policy; procedures addressing physical access monitoring; information system design documentation; information system configuration settings and associated documentation; information system audit records; list of response actions to be initiated when specific classes/types of intrusions are recognized; other relevant documents or records].

Interview: [*SELECT FROM:* Organizational personnel with physical access monitoring responsibilities; organizational personnel with information security responsibilities].

Test: [*SELECT FROM:* Organizational processes for monitoring physical access; automated mechanisms supporting and/or implementing physical access monitoring; automated mechanisms supporting and/or implementing recognition of classes/types of intrusions and initiation of a response].

PE-6(3)	MONITORING PHYSICAL ACCESS | *VIDEO SURVEILLANCE*
	ASSESSMENT OBJECTIVE: *Determine if the organization:*

	PE-6(3)[1]		*defines operational areas where video surveillance is to be employed;*
	PE-6(3)[2]		*defines a time period to retain video recordings of organization-defined operational areas;*
	PE-6(3)[3]	PE-6(3)[3][a]	*employs video surveillance of organization-defined operational areas; and*
		PE-6(3)[3][b]	*retains video recordings for the organization-defined time period.*

POTENTIAL ASSESSMENT METHODS AND OBJECTS:

Examine: [*SELECT FROM:* Physical and environmental protection policy; procedures addressing physical access monitoring; video surveillance equipment used to monitor operational areas; video recordings of operational areas where video surveillance is employed; video surveillance equipment logs or records; other relevant documents or records].

Interview: [*SELECT FROM:* Organizational personnel with physical access monitoring responsibilities; organizational personnel with information security responsibilities].

Test: [*SELECT FROM:* Organizational processes for monitoring physical access; automated mechanisms supporting and/or implementing physical access monitoring; automated mechanisms supporting and/or implementing video surveillance].

PE-6(4)	MONITORING PHYSICAL ACCESS | *MONITORING PHYSICAL ACCESS TO INFORMATION SYSTEMS*
	ASSESSMENT OBJECTIVE: *Determine if the organization:*

	PE-6(4)[1]	*defines physical spaces containing one or more components of the information system; and*

Special Publication 800-53A
Revision 4

Assessing Security and Privacy Controls in Federal Information Systems
and Organizations — *Building Effective Assessment Plans*

	PE-6(4)[2]	*monitors physical access to the information system in addition to the physical access monitoring of the facility at organization-defined physical spaces containing one or more components of the information system.*

POTENTIAL ASSESSMENT METHODS AND OBJECTS:

Examine: [*SELECT FROM:* Physical and environmental protection policy; procedures addressing physical access monitoring; physical access control logs or records; physical access control devices; access authorizations; access credentials; list of areas within the facility containing concentrations of information system components or information system components requiring additional physical access monitoring; other relevant documents or records].

Interview: [*SELECT FROM:* Organizational personnel with physical access monitoring responsibilities; organizational personnel with information security responsibilities].

Test: [*SELECT FROM:* Organizational processes for monitoring physical access to the information system; automated mechanisms supporting and/or implementing physical access monitoring for facility areas containing information system components].

PE-7	VISITOR CONTROL
[Withdrawn: Incorporated into PE-2 and PE-3].	

PE-8	VISITOR ACCESS RECORDS

ASSESSMENT OBJECTIVE:

Determine if the organization:

PE-8(a)	PE-8(a)[1]	*defines the time period to maintain visitor access records to the facility where the information system resides;*
	PE-8(a)[2]	*maintains visitor access records to the facility where the information system resides for the organization-defined time period;*
PE-8(b)	PE-8(b)[1]	*defines the frequency to review visitor access records; and*
	PE-8(b)[2]	*reviews visitor access records with the organization-defined frequency.*

POTENTIAL ASSESSMENT METHODS AND OBJECTS:

Examine: [*SELECT FROM:* Physical and environmental protection policy; procedures addressing visitor access records; security plan; visitor access control logs or records; visitor access record or log reviews; other relevant documents or records].

Interview: [*SELECT FROM:* Organizational personnel with visitor access records responsibilities; organizational personnel with information security responsibilities].

Test: [*SELECT FROM:* Organizational processes for maintaining and reviewing visitor access records; automated mechanisms supporting and/or implementing maintenance and review of visitor access records].

PE-8(1)	VISITOR ACCESS RECORDS	*AUTOMATED RECORDS MAINTENANCE / REVIEW*

ASSESSMENT OBJECTIVE:

Determine if the organization employs automated mechanisms to facilitate the maintenance and review of visitor access records.

Special Publication 800-53A
Revision 4

Assessing Security and Privacy Controls in Federal Information Systems
and Organizations — *Building Effective Assessment Plans*

POTENTIAL ASSESSMENT METHODS AND OBJECTS:

Examine: [*SELECT FROM:* Physical and environmental protection policy; procedures addressing visitor access records; automated mechanisms supporting management of visitor access records; visitor access control logs or records; other relevant documents or records].

Interview: [*SELECT FROM:* Organizational personnel with visitor access records responsibilities; organizational personnel with information security responsibilities].

Test: [*SELECT FROM:* Organizational processes for maintaining and reviewing visitor access records; automated mechanisms supporting and/or implementing maintenance and review of visitor access records].

PE-8(2)	VISITOR ACCESS RECORDS | *PHYSICAL ACCESS RECORDS*
	[Withdrawn: Incorporated into PE-2].

PE-9	POWER EQUIPMENT AND CABLING

ASSESSMENT OBJECTIVE:

Determine if the organization protects power equipment and power cabling for the information system from damage and destruction.

POTENTIAL ASSESSMENT METHODS AND OBJECTS:

Examine: [*SELECT FROM:* Physical and environmental protection policy; procedures addressing power equipment/cabling protection; facilities housing power equipment/cabling; other relevant documents or records].

Interview: [*SELECT FROM:* Organizational personnel with responsibility for protecting power equipment/cabling; organizational personnel with information security responsibilities].

Test: [*SELECT FROM:* Automated mechanisms supporting and/or implementing protection of power equipment/cabling].

PE-9(1)	POWER EQUIPMENT AND CABLING | *REDUNDANT CABLING*

ASSESSMENT OBJECTIVE:
Determine if the organization:

PE-9(1)[1]	*defines the distance by which redundant power cabling paths are to be physically separated; and*
PE-9(1)[2]	*employs redundant power cabling paths that are physically separated by organization-defined distance.*

POTENTIAL ASSESSMENT METHODS AND OBJECTS:

Examine: [*SELECT FROM:* Physical and environmental protection policy; procedures addressing power equipment/cabling protection; facilities housing power equipment/cabling; other relevant documents or records].

Interview: [*SELECT FROM:* Organizational personnel with responsibility for protecting power equipment/cabling; organizational personnel with information security responsibilities].

Test: [*SELECT FROM:* Automated mechanisms supporting and/or implementing protection of power equipment/cabling].

PE-9(2)	POWER EQUIPMENT AND CABLING | *AUTOMATIC VOLTAGE CONTROLS*

ASSESSMENT OBJECTIVE:
Determine if the organization:

PE-9(2)[1]	*defines critical information system components that require automatic voltage controls; and*

Special Publication 800-53A
Revision 4

Assessing Security and Privacy Controls in Federal Information Systems
and Organizations — *Building Effective Assessment Plans*

	PE-9(2)[2]	*employs automatic voltage controls for organization-defined critical information system components.*
	POTENTIAL ASSESSMENT METHODS AND OBJECTS: **Examine**: [*SELECT FROM:* Physical and environmental protection policy; procedures addressing voltage control; security plan; list of critical information system components requiring automatic voltage controls; automatic voltage control mechanisms and associated configurations; other relevant documents or records]. **Interview**: [*SELECT FROM:* Organizational personnel with responsibility for environmental protection of information system components; organizational personnel with information security responsibilities]. **Test**: [*SELECT FROM:* Automated mechanisms supporting and/or implementing automatic voltage controls].	

PE-10	**EMERGENCY SHUTOFF**		
	ASSESSMENT OBJECTIVE: *Determine if the organization:*		
	PE-10(a)	*provides the capability of shutting off power to the information system or individual system components in emergency situations;*	
	PE-10(b)	PE-10(b)[1]	*defines the location of emergency shutoff switches or devices by information system or system component;*
		PE-10(b)[2]	*places emergency shutoff switches or devices in the organization-defined location by information system or system component to facilitate safe and easy access for personnel; and*
	PE-10(c)	*protects emergency power shutoff capability from unauthorized activation.*	
	POTENTIAL ASSESSMENT METHODS AND OBJECTS: **Examine**: [*SELECT FROM:* Physical and environmental protection policy; procedures addressing power source emergency shutoff; security plan; emergency shutoff controls or switches; locations housing emergency shutoff switches and devices; security safeguards protecting emergency power shutoff capability from unauthorized activation; other relevant documents or records]. **Interview**: [*SELECT FROM:* Organizational personnel with responsibility for emergency power shutoff capability (both implementing and using the capability); organizational personnel with information security responsibilities]. **Test**: [*SELECT FROM:* Automated mechanisms supporting and/or implementing emergency power shutoff].		

PE-10(1)	**EMERGENCY SHUTOFF** | *ACCIDENTAL / UNAUTHORIZED ACTIVATION*
[Withdrawn: Incorporated into PE-10].	

PE-11	**EMERGENCY POWER**	
	ASSESSMENT OBJECTIVE: *Determine if the organization provides a short-term uninterruptible power supply to facilitate one or more of the following in the event of a primary power source loss:*	
	PE-11[1]	*an orderly shutdown of the information system; and/or*
	PE-11[2]	*transition of the information system to long-term alternate power.*

Special Publication 800-53A
Revision 4

Assessing Security and Privacy Controls in Federal Information Systems
and Organizations — *Building Effective Assessment Plans*

POTENTIAL ASSESSMENT METHODS AND OBJECTS:

Examine: [*SELECT FROM:* Physical and environmental protection policy; procedures addressing emergency power; uninterruptible power supply; uninterruptible power supply documentation; uninterruptible power supply test records; other relevant documents or records].

Interview: [*SELECT FROM:* Organizational personnel with responsibility for emergency power and/or planning; organizational personnel with information security responsibilities].

Test: [*SELECT FROM:* Automated mechanisms supporting and/or implementing uninterruptible power supply; the uninterruptable power supply].

PE-11(1)	EMERGENCY POWER | *LONG-TERM ALTERNATE POWER SUPPLY – MINIMAL OPERATIONAL CAPABILITY*

ASSESSMENT OBJECTIVE:

Determine if the organization provides a long-term alternate power supply for the information system that is capable of maintaining minimally required operational capability in the event of an extended loss of the primary power source.

POTENTIAL ASSESSMENT METHODS AND OBJECTS:

Examine: [*SELECT FROM:* Physical and environmental protection policy; procedures addressing emergency power; alternate power supply; alternate power supply documentation; alternate power supply test records; other relevant documents or records].

Interview: [*SELECT FROM:* Organizational personnel with responsibility for emergency power and/or planning; organizational personnel with information security responsibilities].

Test: [*SELECT FROM:* Automated mechanisms supporting and/or implementing alternate power supply; the alternate power supply].

PE-11(2)	EMERGENCY POWER | *LONG-TERM ALTERNATE POWER SUPPLY – SELF-CONTAINED*

ASSESSMENT OBJECTIVE:

Determine if the organization provides a long-term alternate power supply for the information system that is:

PE-11(2)(a)	*self-contained;*	
PE-11(2)(b)	*not reliant on external power generation;*	
PE-11(2)(c)	*capable of maintaining one of the following in the event of an extended loss of the primary power source:*	
	PE-11(2)(c)[1]	*minimally required operational capability; or*
	PE-11(2)(c)[2]	*full operational capability.*

POTENTIAL ASSESSMENT METHODS AND OBJECTS:

Examine: [*SELECT FROM:* Physical and environmental protection policy; procedures addressing emergency power; alternate power supply; alternate power supply documentation; alternate power supply test records; other relevant documents or records].

Interview: [*SELECT FROM:* Organizational personnel with responsibility for emergency power and/or planning; organizational personnel with information security responsibilities].

Test: [*SELECT FROM:* Automated mechanisms supporting and/or implementing alternate power supply; the alternate power supply].

PE-12	EMERGENCY LIGHTING

ASSESSMENT OBJECTIVE:

Determine if the organization employs and maintains automatic emergency lighting for the information system that:

Special Publication 800-53A
Revision 4

Assessing Security and Privacy Controls in Federal Information Systems
and Organizations — *Building Effective Assessment Plans*

PE-12[1]	*activates in the event of a power outage or disruption; and*
PE-12[2]	*covers emergency exits and evacuation routes within the facility.*

POTENTIAL ASSESSMENT METHODS AND OBJECTS:

Examine: [*SELECT FROM:* Physical and environmental protection policy; procedures addressing emergency lighting; emergency lighting documentation; emergency lighting test records; emergency exits and evacuation routes; other relevant documents or records].

Interview: [*SELECT FROM:* Organizational personnel with responsibility for emergency lighting and/or planning; organizational personnel with information security responsibilities].

Test: [*SELECT FROM:* Automated mechanisms supporting and/or implementing emergency lighting capability].

PE-12(1)	**EMERGENCY LIGHTING**	*ESSENTIAL MISSIONS / BUSINESS FUNCTIONS*

ASSESSMENT OBJECTIVE:

Determine if the organization provides emergency lighting for all areas within the facility supporting essential missions and business functions.

POTENTIAL ASSESSMENT METHODS AND OBJECTS:

Examine: [*SELECT FROM:* Physical and environmental protection policy; procedures addressing emergency lighting; emergency lighting documentation; emergency lighting test records; emergency exits and evacuation routes; areas/locations within facility supporting essential missions and business functions; other relevant documents or records].

Interview: [*SELECT FROM:* Organizational personnel with responsibility for emergency lighting and/or planning; organizational personnel with information security responsibilities].

Test: [*SELECT FROM:* Automated mechanisms supporting and/or implementing emergency lighting capability].

PE-13	**FIRE PROTECTION**

ASSESSMENT OBJECTIVE:

Determine if the organization:

PE-13[1]	*employs fire suppression and detection devices/systems for the information system that are supported by an independent energy source; and*
PE-13[2]	*maintains fire suppression and detection devices/systems for the information system that are supported by an independent energy source.*

POTENTIAL ASSESSMENT METHODS AND OBJECTS:

Examine: [*SELECT FROM:* Physical and environmental protection policy; procedures addressing fire protection; fire suppression and detection devices/systems; fire suppression and detection devices/systems documentation; test records of fire suppression and detection devices/systems; other relevant documents or records].

Interview: [*SELECT FROM:* Organizational personnel with responsibilities for fire detection and suppression devices/systems; organizational personnel with information security responsibilities].

Test: [*SELECT FROM:* Automated mechanisms supporting and/or implementing fire suppression/detection devices/systems].

PE-13(1)	**FIRE PROTECTION**	*DETECTION DEVICES / SYSTEMS*

ASSESSMENT OBJECTIVE:
Determine if the organization:

PE-13(1)[1]	*defines personnel or roles to be notified in the event of a fire;*

Special Publication 800-53A
Revision 4

Assessing Security and Privacy Controls in Federal Information Systems
and Organizations — *Building Effective Assessment Plans*

PE-13(1)[2]	*defines emergency responders to be notified in the event of a fire;*
PE-13(1)[3]	*employs fire detection devices/systems for the information system that, in the event of a fire,:*

	PE-13(1)[3][a]	*activate automatically;*
	PE-13(1)[3][b]	*notify organization-defined personnel or roles; and*
	PE-13(1)[3][c]	*notify organization-defined emergency responders.*

POTENTIAL ASSESSMENT METHODS AND OBJECTS:

Examine: [*SELECT FROM:* Physical and environmental protection policy; procedures addressing fire protection; facility housing the information system; alarm service-level agreements; test records of fire suppression and detection devices/systems; fire suppression and detection devices/systems documentation; alerts/notifications of fire events; other relevant documents or records].

Interview: [*SELECT FROM:* Organizational personnel with responsibilities for fire detection and suppression devices/systems; organizational personnel with responsibilities for notifying appropriate personnel, roles, and emergency responders of fires; organizational personnel with information security responsibilities].

Test: [*SELECT FROM:* Automated mechanisms supporting and/or implementing fire detection devices/systems; activation of fire detection devices/systems (simulated); automated notifications].

PE-13(2)	FIRE PROTECTION	*SUPPRESSION DEVICES / SYSTEMS*

ASSESSMENT OBJECTIVE:

Determine if the organization:

PE-13(2)[1]	*defines personnel or roles to be provided automatic notification of any activation of fire suppression devices/systems for the information system;*
PE-13(2)[2]	*defines emergency responders to be provided automatic notification of any activation of fire suppression devices/systems for the information system;*
PE-13(2)[3]	*employs fire suppression devices/systems for the information system that provide automatic notification of any activation to:*

	PE-13(2)[3][a]	*organization-defined personnel or roles; and*
	PE-13(2)[3][b]	*organization-defined emergency responders.*

POTENTIAL ASSESSMENT METHODS AND OBJECTS:

Examine: [*SELECT FROM:* Physical and environmental protection policy; procedures addressing fire protection; fire suppression and detection devices/systems documentation; facility housing the information system; alarm service-level agreements; test records of fire suppression and detection devices/systems; other relevant documents or records].

Interview: [*SELECT FROM:* Organizational personnel with responsibilities for fire detection and suppression devices/systems; organizational personnel with responsibilities for providing automatic notifications of any activation of fire suppression devices/systems to appropriate personnel, roles, and emergency responders; organizational personnel with information security responsibilities].

Test: [*SELECT FROM:* Automated mechanisms supporting and/or implementing fire suppression devices/systems; activation of fire suppression devices/systems (simulated); automated notifications].

PE-13(3)	FIRE PROTECTION	*AUTOMATIC FIRE SUPPRESSION*

ASSESSMENT OBJECTIVE:

Determine if the organization employs an automatic fire suppression capability for the information system when the facility is not staffed on a continuous basis.

Special Publication 800-53A
Revision 4

Assessing Security and Privacy Controls in Federal Information Systems
and Organizations — *Building Effective Assessment Plans*

POTENTIAL ASSESSMENT METHODS AND OBJECTS:

Examine: [*SELECT FROM:* Physical and environmental protection policy; procedures addressing fire protection; fire suppression and detection devices/systems documentation; facility housing the information system; alarm service-level agreements; test records of fire suppression and detection devices/systems; other relevant documents or records].

Interview: [*SELECT FROM:* Organizational personnel with responsibilities for fire detection and suppression devices/systems; organizational personnel with responsibilities for providing automatic notifications of any activation of fire suppression devices/systems to appropriate personnel, roles, and emergency responders; organizational personnel with information security responsibilities].

Test: [*SELECT FROM:* Automated mechanisms supporting and/or implementing fire suppression devices/systems; activation of fire suppression devices/systems (simulated)].

PE-13(4)	FIRE PROTECTION | *INSPECTIONS*	
	ASSESSMENT OBJECTIVE: *Determine if the organization:*	
	PE-13(4)[1]	*defines the frequency of inspections to be conducted on the facility by authorized and qualified inspectors;*
	PE-13(4)[2]	*ensures that the facility undergoes inspections by authorized and qualified inspectors with the organization-defined frequency;*
	PE-13(4)[3]	*defines a time period to resolve deficiencies identified when the facility undergoes such inspections; and*
	PE-13(4)[4]	*resolves identified deficiencies within the organization-defined time period.*

POTENTIAL ASSESSMENT METHODS AND OBJECTS:

Examine: [*SELECT FROM:* Physical and environmental protection policy; procedures addressing fire protection; security plan; facility housing the information system; inspection plans; inspection results; inspect reports; test records of fire suppression and detection devices/systems; other relevant documents or records].

Interview: [*SELECT FROM:* Organizational personnel with responsibilities for planning, approving, and executing fire inspections; organizational personnel with information security responsibilities].

PE-14	TEMPERATURE AND HUMIDITY CONTROLS		
	ASSESSMENT OBJECTIVE: *Determine if the organization:*		
	PE-14(a)	PE-14(a)[1]	*defines acceptable temperature levels to be maintained within the facility where the information system resides;*
		PE-14(a)[2]	*defines acceptable humidity levels to be maintained within the facility where the information system resides;*
		PE-14(a)[3]	*maintains temperature levels within the facility where the information system resides at the organization-defined levels;*
		PE-14(a)[4]	*maintains humidity levels within the facility where the information system resides at the organization-defined levels;*
	PE-14(b)	PE-14(b)[1]	*defines the frequency to monitor temperature levels;*
		PE-14(b)[2]	*defines the frequency to monitor humidity levels;*
		PE-14(b)[3]	*monitors temperature levels with the organization-defined frequency; and*

Special Publication 800-53A
Revision 4

Assessing Security and Privacy Controls in Federal Information Systems
and Organizations — *Building Effective Assessment Plans*

	PE-14(b)[4]	*monitors humidity levels with the organization-defined frequency.*

POTENTIAL ASSESSMENT METHODS AND OBJECTS:

Examine: [*SELECT FROM:* Physical and environmental protection policy; procedures addressing temperature and humidity control; security plan; temperature and humidity controls; facility housing the information system; temperature and humidity controls documentation; temperature and humidity records; other relevant documents or records].

Interview: [*SELECT FROM:* Organizational personnel with responsibilities for information system environmental controls; organizational personnel with information security responsibilities].

Test: [*SELECT FROM:* Automated mechanisms supporting and/or implementing maintenance and monitoring of temperature and humidity levels].

PE-14(1)	TEMPERATURE AND HUMIDITY CONTROLS	*AUTOMATIC CONTROLS*

ASSESSMENT OBJECTIVE:

Determine if the organization:

PE-14(1)[1]	*employs automatic temperature controls in the facility to prevent fluctuations potentially harmful to the information system; and*
PE-14(1)[2]	*employs automatic humidity controls in the facility to prevent fluctuations potentially harmful to the information system.*

POTENTIAL ASSESSMENT METHODS AND OBJECTS:

Examine: [*SELECT FROM:* Physical and environmental protection policy; procedures addressing temperature and humidity controls; facility housing the information system; automated mechanisms for temperature and humidity; temperature and humidity controls; temperature and humidity documentation; other relevant documents or records].

Interview: [*SELECT FROM:* Organizational personnel with responsibilities for information system environmental controls; organizational personnel with information security responsibilities].

Test: [*SELECT FROM:* Automated mechanisms supporting and/or implementing temperature and humidity levels].

PE-14(2)	TEMPERATURE AND HUMIDITY CONTROLS	*MONITORING WITH ALARMS / NOTIFICATIONS*

ASSESSMENT OBJECTIVE:

Determine if the organization:

PE-14(2)[1]	*employs temperature monitoring that provides an alarm of changes potentially harmful to personnel or equipment; and/or*
PE-14(2)[2]	*employs temperature monitoring that provides notification of changes potentially harmful to personnel or equipment;*
PE-14(2)[3]	*employs humidity monitoring that provides an alarm of changes potentially harmful to personnel or equipment; and/or*
PE-14(2)[4]	*employs humidity monitoring that provides notification of changes potentially harmful to personnel or equipment.*

POTENTIAL ASSESSMENT METHODS AND OBJECTS:

Examine: [*SELECT FROM:* Physical and environmental protection policy; procedures addressing temperature and humidity monitoring; facility housing the information system; logs or records of temperature and humidity monitoring; records of changes to temperature and humidity levels that generate alarms or notifications; other relevant documents or records].

Interview: [*SELECT FROM:* Organizational personnel with responsibilities for information system environmental controls; organizational personnel with information security responsibilities].

Test: [*SELECT FROM:* Automated mechanisms supporting and/or implementing temperature and humidity monitoring].

Special Publication 800-53A
Revision 4

Assessing Security and Privacy Controls in Federal Information Systems
and Organizations — *Building Effective Assessment Plans*

PE-15	WATER DAMAGE PROTECTION
	ASSESSMENT OBJECTIVE: *Determine if the organization protects the information system from damage resulting from water leakage by providing master shutoff or isolation valves that are:*
	PE-15[1] | *accessible;*
	PE-15[2] | *working properly; and*
	PE-15[3] | *known to key personnel.*
	POTENTIAL ASSESSMENT METHODS AND OBJECTS: **Examine**: [*SELECT FROM:* Physical and environmental protection policy; procedures addressing water damage protection; facility housing the information system; master shutoff valves; list of key personnel with knowledge of location and activation procedures for master shutoff valves for the plumbing system; master shutoff valve documentation; other relevant documents or records]. **Interview**: [*SELECT FROM:* Organizational personnel with responsibilities for information system environmental controls; organizational personnel with information security responsibilities]. **Test**: [*SELECT FROM:* Master water-shutoff valves; organizational process for activating master water-shutoff].

PE-15(1)	WATER DAMAGE PROTECTION | *AUTOMATION SUPPORT*
	ASSESSMENT OBJECTIVE: *Determine if the organization:*
	PE-15(1)[1] | *defines personnel or roles to be alerted when the presence of water is detected in the vicinity of the information system;*
	PE-15(1)[2] | *employs automated mechanisms to detect the presence of water in the vicinity of the information system; and*
	PE-15(1)[3] | *alerts organization-defined personnel or roles when the presence of water is detected in the vicinity of the information system.*
	POTENTIAL ASSESSMENT METHODS AND OBJECTS: **Examine**: [*SELECT FROM:* Physical and environmental protection policy; procedures addressing water damage protection; facility housing the information system; automated mechanisms for water shutoff valves; automated mechanisms detecting presence of water in vicinity of information system; alerts/notifications of water detection in information system facility; other relevant documents or records]. **Interview**: [*SELECT FROM:* Organizational personnel with responsibilities for information system environmental controls; organizational personnel with information security responsibilities]. **Test**: [*SELECT FROM:* Automated mechanisms supporting and/or implementing water detection capability and alerts for the information system].

PE-16	DELIVERY AND REMOVAL
	ASSESSMENT OBJECTIVE: *Determine if the organization:*
	PE-16[1] | *defines types of information system components to be authorized, monitored, and controlled as such components are entering and exiting the facility;*
	PE-16[2] | *authorizes organization-defined information system components entering the facility;*

Special Publication 800-53A
Revision 4

Assessing Security and Privacy Controls in Federal Information Systems
and Organizations — *Building Effective Assessment Plans*

PE-16[3]	*monitors organization-defined information system components entering the facility;*	
PE-16[4]	*controls organization-defined information system components entering the facility;*	
PE-16[5]	*authorizes organization-defined information system components exiting the facility;*	
PE-16[6]	*monitors organization-defined information system components exiting the facility;*	
PE-16[7]	*controls organization-defined information system components exiting the facility;*	
PE-16[8]	*maintains records of information system components entering the facility; and*	
PE-16[9]	*maintains records of information system components exiting the facility.*	

POTENTIAL ASSESSMENT METHODS AND OBJECTS:

Examine: [*SELECT FROM:* Physical and environmental protection policy; procedures addressing delivery and removal of information system components from the facility; security plan; facility housing the information system; records of items entering and exiting the facility; other relevant documents or records].

Interview: [*SELECT FROM:* Organizational personnel with responsibilities for controlling information system components entering and exiting the facility; organizational personnel with information security responsibilities].

Test: [*SELECT FROM:* Organizational process for authorizing, monitoring, and controlling information system-related items entering and exiting the facility; automated mechanisms supporting and/or implementing authorizing, monitoring, and controlling information system-related items entering and exiting the facility].

PE-17	ALTERNATE WORK SITE		
	ASSESSMENT OBJECTIVE: *Determine if the organization:*		
	PE-17(a)	**PE-17(a)[1]**	*defines security controls to be employed at alternate work sites;*
		PE-17(a)[2]	*employs organization-defined security controls at alternate work sites;*
	PE-17(b)	*assesses, as feasible, the effectiveness of security controls at alternate work sites; and*	
	PE-17(c)	*provides a means for employees to communicate with information security personnel in case of security incidents or problems.*	

POTENTIAL ASSESSMENT METHODS AND OBJECTS:

Examine: [*SELECT FROM:* Physical and environmental protection policy; procedures addressing alternate work sites for organizational personnel; security plan; list of security controls required for alternate work sites; assessments of security controls at alternate work sites; other relevant documents or records].

Interview: [*SELECT FROM:* Organizational personnel approving use of alternate work sites; organizational personnel using alternate work sites; organizational personnel assessing controls at alternate work sites; organizational personnel with information security responsibilities].

Test: [*SELECT FROM:* Organizational processes for security at alternate work sites; automated mechanisms supporting alternate work sites; security controls employed at alternate work sites; means of communications between personnel at alternate work sites and security personnel].

Special Publication 800-53A
Revision 4

Assessing Security and Privacy Controls in Federal Information Systems
and Organizations — *Building Effective Assessment Plans*

PE-18	LOCATION OF INFORMATION SYSTEM COMPONENTS
	ASSESSMENT OBJECTIVE: *Determine if the organization:*

	PE-18[1]	*defines physical hazards that could result in potential damage to information system components within the facility;*
	PE-18[2]	*defines environmental hazards that could result in potential damage to information system components within the facility;*
	PE-18[3]	*positions information system components within the facility to minimize potential damage from organization-defined physical and environmental hazards; and*
	PE-18[4]	*positions information system components within the facility to minimize the opportunity for unauthorized access.*

	POTENTIAL ASSESSMENT METHODS AND OBJECTS: **Examine**: [*SELECT FROM:* Physical and environmental protection policy; procedures addressing positioning of information system components; documentation providing the location and position of information system components within the facility; locations housing information system components within the facility; list of physical and environmental hazards with potential to damage information system components within the facility; other relevant documents or records]. **Interview**: [*SELECT FROM:* Organizational personnel with responsibilities for positioning information system components; organizational personnel with information security responsibilities]. **Test**: [*SELECT FROM:* Organizational processes for positioning information system components].

PE-18(1)	LOCATION OF INFORMATION SYSTEM COMPONENTS | *FACILITY SITE*
	ASSESSMENT OBJECTIVE: *Determine if the organization:*

	PE-18(1)[1]	*plans the location or site of the facility where the information system resides with regard to physical hazards;*
	PE-18(1)[2]	*plans the location or site of the facility where the information system resides with regard to environmental hazards;*
	PE-18(1)[3]	*for existing facilities, considers the physical hazards in its risk mitigation strategy; and*
	PE-18(1)[4]	*for existing facilities, considers the environmental hazards in its risk mitigation strategy.*

	POTENTIAL ASSESSMENT METHODS AND OBJECTS: **Examine**: [*SELECT FROM:* Physical and environmental protection policy; physical site planning documents; organizational assessment of risk, contingency plan; risk mitigation strategy documentation; other relevant documents or records]. **Interview**: [*SELECT FROM:* Organizational personnel with site selection responsibilities for the facility housing the information system; organizational personnel with risk mitigation responsibilities; organizational personnel with information security responsibilities]. **Test**: [*SELECT FROM:* Organizational processes for site planning].

PE-19	INFORMATION LEAKAGE
	ASSESSMENT OBJECTIVE: *Determine if the organization protects the information system from information leakage due to electromagnetic signals emanations.*

Special Publication 800-53A
Revision 4

Assessing Security and Privacy Controls in Federal Information Systems
and Organizations — *Building Effective Assessment Plans*

POTENTIAL ASSESSMENT METHODS AND OBJECTS:

Examine: [*SELECT FROM:* Physical and environmental protection policy; procedures addressing information leakage due to electromagnetic signals emanations; mechanisms protecting the information system against electronic signals emanation; facility housing the information system; records from electromagnetic signals emanation tests; other relevant documents or records].

Interview: [*SELECT FROM:* Organizational personnel with responsibilities for information system environmental controls; organizational personnel with information security responsibilities].

Test: [*SELECT FROM:* Automated mechanisms supporting and/or implementing protection from information leakage due to electromagnetic signals emanations].

PE-19(1)	INFORMATION LEAKAGE	*NATIONAL EMISSIONS / TEMPEST POLICIES AND PROCEDURES*

ASSESSMENT OBJECTIVE:

Determine if the organization ensures that the following are protected in accordance with national emissions and TEMPEST policies and procedures based on the security category or classification of the information:

PE-19(1)[1]	*information system components;*
PE-19(1)[2]	*associated data communications; and*
PE-19(1)[3]	*networks.*

POTENTIAL ASSESSMENT METHODS AND OBJECTS:

Examine: [*SELECT FROM:* Physical and environmental protection policy; procedures addressing information leakage that comply with national emissions and TEMPEST policies and procedures; information system component design documentation; information system configuration settings and associated documentation other relevant documents or records].

Interview: [*SELECT FROM:* Organizational personnel with responsibilities for information system environmental controls; organizational personnel with information security responsibilities].

Test: [*SELECT FROM:* Information system components for compliance with national emissions and TEMPEST policies and procedures].

PE-20	ASSET MONITORING AND TRACKING	

ASSESSMENT OBJECTIVE:

Determine if the organization:

PE-20(a)	PE-20(a)[1]	*defines assets whose location and movement are to be tracked and monitored;*
	PE-20(a)[2]	*defines asset location technologies to be employed to track and monitor the location and movement of organization-defined assets;*
	PE-20(a)[3]	*defines controlled areas within which to track and monitor organization-defined assets;*
	PE-20(a)[4]	*employs organization-defined asset location technologies to track and monitor the location and movement of organization-defined assets within organization-defined controlled areas; and*
PE-20(b)	*ensures that asset location technologies are employed in accordance with applicable federal laws, Executive Orders, directives, regulations, policies, standards and guidance.*	

Special Publication 800-53A
Revision 4

Assessing Security and Privacy Controls in Federal Information Systems
and Organizations — *Building Effective Assessment Plans*

POTENTIAL ASSESSMENT METHODS AND OBJECTS:

Examine: [*SELECT FROM:* Physical and environmental protection policy; procedures addressing asset monitoring and tracking; asset location technologies and associated configuration documentation; list of organizational assets requiring tracking and monitoring; asset monitoring and tracking records; other relevant documents or records].

Interview: [*SELECT FROM:* Organizational personnel with asset monitoring and tracking responsibilities; organizational personnel with information security responsibilities].

Test: [*SELECT FROM:* Organizational processes for tracking and monitoring assets; automated mechanisms supporting and/or implementing tracking and monitoring of assets].

Special Publication 800-53A
Revision 4

Assessing Security and Privacy Controls in Federal Information Systems
and Organizations — *Building Effective Assessment Plans*

FAMILY: PLANNING

PL-1	SECURITY PLANNING POLICY AND PROCEDURES			
	ASSESSMENT OBJECTIVE: *Determine if the organization:*			
	PL-1(a)(1)	PL-1(a)(1)[1]	*develops and documents a planning policy that addresses:*	
			PL-1(a)(1)[1][a]	*purpose;*
			PL-1(a)(1)[1][b]	*scope;*
			PL-1(a)(1)[1][c]	*roles;*
			PL-1(a)(1)[1][d]	*responsibilities;*
			PL-1(a)(1)[1][e]	*management commitment;*
			PL-1(a)(1)[1][f]	*coordination among organizational entities;*
			PL-1(a)(1)[1][g]	*compliance;*
		PL-1(a)(1)[2]	*defines personnel or roles to whom the planning policy is to be disseminated;*	
		PL-1(a)(1)[3]	*disseminates the planning policy to organization-defined personnel or roles;*	
	PL-1(a)(2)	PL-1(a)(2)[1]	*develops and documents procedures to facilitate the implementation of the planning policy and associated planning controls;*	
		PL-1(a)(2)[2]	*defines personnel or roles to whom the procedures are to be disseminated;*	
		PL-1(a)(2)[3]	*disseminates the procedures to organization-defined personnel or roles;*	
	PL-1(b)(1)	PL-1(b)(1)[1]	*defines the frequency to review and update the current planning policy;*	
		PL-1(b)(1)[2]	*reviews and updates the current planning policy with the organization-defined frequency;*	
	PL-1(b)(2)	PL-1(b)(2)[1]	*defines the frequency to review and update the current planning procedures; and*	
		PL-1(b)(2)[2]	*reviews and updates the current planning procedures with the organization-defined frequency.*	
	POTENTIAL ASSESSMENT METHODS AND OBJECTS: **Examine:** [*SELECT FROM:* Planning policy and procedures; other relevant documents or records]. **Interview:** [*SELECT FROM:* Organizational personnel with planning responsibilities; organizational personnel with information security responsibilities].			

Special Publication 800-53A
Revision 4

Assessing Security and Privacy Controls in Federal Information Systems
and Organizations — *Building Effective Assessment Plans*

PL-2	SYSTEM SECURITY PLAN	
	ASSESSMENT OBJECTIVE: *Determine if the organization:*	
	PL-2(a)	*develops a security plan for the information system that:*
		PL-2(a)(1) *is consistent with the organization's enterprise architecture;*
		PL-2(a)(2) *explicitly defines the authorization boundary for the system;*
		PL-2(a)(3) *describes the operational context of the information system in terms of missions and business processes;*
		PL-2(a)(4) *provides the security categorization of the information system including supporting rationale;*
		PL-2(a)(5) *describes the operational environment for the information system and relationships with or connections to other information systems;*
		PL-2(a)(6) *provides an overview of the security requirements for the system;*
		PL-2(a)(7) *identifies any relevant overlays, if applicable;*
		PL-2(a)(8) *describes the security controls in place or planned for meeting those requirements including a rationale for the tailoring and supplemental decisions;*
		PL-2(a)(9) *is reviewed and approved by the authorizing official or designated representative prior to plan implementation;*
	PL-2(b)	PL-2(b)[1] *defines personnel or roles to whom copies of the security plan are to be distributed and subsequent changes to the plan are to be communicated;*
		PL-2(b)[2] *distributes copies of the security plan and communicates subsequent changes to the plan to organization-defined personnel or roles;*
	PL-2(c)	PL-2(c)[1] *defines the frequency to review the security plan for the information system;*
		PL-2(c)[2] *reviews the security plan for the information system with the organization-defined frequency;*
	PL-2(d)	*updates the plan to address:*
		PL-2(d)[1] *changes to the information system/environment of operation;*
		PL-2(d)[2] *problems identified during plan implementation;*
		PL-2(d)[3] *problems identified during security control assessments;*
	PL-2(e)	*protects the security plan from unauthorized:*
		PL-2(e)[1] *disclosure; and*
		PL-2(e)[2] *modification.*

Special Publication 800-53A
Revision 4

Assessing Security and Privacy Controls in Federal Information Systems
and Organizations — *Building Effective Assessment Plans*

<table>
<tr><td colspan="2">

POTENTIAL ASSESSMENT METHODS AND OBJECTS:

Examine: [*SELECT FROM:* Security planning policy; procedures addressing security plan development and implementation; procedures addressing security plan reviews and updates; enterprise architecture documentation; security plan for the information system; records of security plan reviews and updates; other relevant documents or records].

Interview: [*SELECT FROM:* Organizational personnel with security planning and plan implementation responsibilities; organizational personnel with information security responsibilities].

Test: [*SELECT FROM:* Organizational processes for security plan development/review/update/approval; automated mechanisms supporting the information system security plan].

</td></tr>
</table>

PL-2(1)	SYSTEM SECURITY PLAN | *CONCEPT OF OPERATIONS*
[Withdrawn: Incorporated into PL-7].	

PL-2(2)	SYSTEM SECURITY PLAN | *FUNCTIONAL ARCHITECTURE*
[Withdrawn: Incorporated into PL-8].	

PL-2(3)	SYSTEM SECURITY PLAN | *PLAN / COORDINATE WITH OTHER ORGANIZATIONAL ENTITIES*
ASSESSMENT OBJECTIVE: *Determine if the organization:*	
PL-2(3)[1]	*defines individuals or groups with whom security-related activities affecting the information system are to be planned and coordinated before conducting such activities in order to reduce the impact on other organizational entities; and*
PL-2(3)[2]	*plans and coordinates security-related activities affecting the information system with organization-defined individuals or groups before conducting such activities in order to reduce the impact on other organizational entities.*

POTENTIAL ASSESSMENT METHODS AND OBJECTS:

Examine: [*SELECT FROM:* Security planning policy; access control policy; contingency planning policy; procedures addressing security-related activity planning for the information system; security plan for the information system; contingency plan for the information system; information system design documentation; other relevant documents or records].

Interview: [*SELECT FROM:* Organizational personnel with security planning and plan implementation responsibilities; organizational individuals or groups with whom security-related activities are to be planned and coordinated; organizational personnel with information security responsibilities].

PL-3	SYSTEM SECURITY PLAN UPDATE
[Withdrawn: Incorporated into PL-2].	

PL-4	RULES OF BEHAVIOR	
ASSESSMENT OBJECTIVE: *Determine if the organization:*		
PL-4(a)	**PL-4(a)[1]**	*establishes, for individuals requiring access to the information system, the rules that describe their responsibilities and expected behavior with regard to information and information system usage;*

Special Publication 800-53A
Revision 4

Assessing Security and Privacy Controls in Federal Information Systems
and Organizations — *Building Effective Assessment Plans*

		PL-4(a)[2]	*makes readily available to individuals requiring access to the information system, the rules that describe their responsibilities and expected behavior with regard to information and information system usage;*
	PL-4(b)		*receives a signed acknowledgement from such individuals, indicating that they have read, understand, and agree to abide by the rules of behavior, before authorizing access to information and the information system;*
	PL-4(c)	PL-4(c)[1]	*defines the frequency to review and update the rules of behavior;*
		PL-4(c)[2]	*reviews and updates the rules of behavior with the organization-defined frequency; and*
	PL-4(d)		*requires individuals who have signed a previous version of the rules of behavior to read and resign when the rules of behavior are revised/updated.*

POTENTIAL ASSESSMENT METHODS AND OBJECTS:

Examine: [*SELECT FROM:* Security planning policy; procedures addressing rules of behavior for information system users; rules of behavior; signed acknowledgements; records for rules of behavior reviews and updates; other relevant documents or records].

Interview: [*SELECT FROM:* Organizational personnel with responsibility for establishing, reviewing, and updating rules of behavior; organizational personnel who are authorized users of the information system and have signed and resigned rules of behavior; organizational personnel with information security responsibilities].

Test: [*SELECT FROM:* Organizational processes for establishing, reviewing, disseminating, and updating rules of behavior; automated mechanisms supporting and/or implementing the establishment, review, dissemination, and update of rules of behavior].

PL-4(1)	**RULES OF BEHAVIOR** | *SOCIAL MEDIA AND NETWORKING RESTRICTIONS*
	ASSESSMENT OBJECTIVE:

Determine if the organization includes the following in the rules of behavior:

	PL-4(1)[1]	*explicit restrictions on the use of social media/networking sites; and*
	PL-4(1)[2]	*posting organizational information on public websites.*

POTENTIAL ASSESSMENT METHODS AND OBJECTS:

Examine: [*SELECT FROM:* Security planning policy; procedures addressing rules of behavior for information system users; rules of behavior; other relevant documents or records].

Interview: [*SELECT FROM:* Organizational personnel with responsibility for establishing, reviewing, and updating rules of behavior; organizational personnel who are authorized users of the information system and have signed rules of behavior; organizational personnel with information security responsibilities].

Test: [*SELECT FROM:* Organizational processes for establishing rules of behavior; automated mechanisms supporting and/or implementing the establishment of rules of behavior].

PL-5	**PRIVACY IMPACT ASSESSMENT**
[Withdrawn: Incorporated into Appendix J, AR-2].	

PL-6	**SECURITY-RELATED ACTIVITY PLANNING**
[Withdrawn: Incorporated into PL-2].	

Special Publication 800-53A
Revision 4

Assessing Security and Privacy Controls in Federal Information Systems
and Organizations — *Building Effective Assessment Plans*

PL-7	SECURITY CONCEPT OF OPERATIONS	
	ASSESSMENT OBJECTIVE: *Determine if the organization:*	
	PL-7(a)	*develops a security Concept of Operations (CONOPS) for the information system containing at a minimum, how the organization intends to operate the system from the perspective of information security;*
	PL-7(b)	**PL-7(b)[1]** *defines the frequency to review and update the security CONOPS; and*
		PL-7(b)[2] *reviews and updates the security CONOPS with the organization-defined frequency.*
	POTENTIAL ASSESSMENT METHODS AND OBJECTS: **Examine**: [*SELECT FROM:* Security planning policy; procedures addressing security CONOPS development; procedures addressing security CONOPS reviews and updates; security CONOPS for the information system; security plan for the information system; records of security CONOPS reviews and updates; other relevant documents or records]. **Interview**: [*SELECT FROM:* Organizational personnel with security planning and plan implementation responsibilities; organizational personnel with information security responsibilities]. **Test**: [*SELECT FROM:* Organizational processes for developing, reviewing, and updating the security CONOPS; automated mechanisms supporting and/or implementing the development, review, and update of the security CONOPS].	

PL-8	INFORMATION SECURITY ARCHITECTURE	
	ASSESSMENT OBJECTIVE: *Determine if the organization:*	
	PL-8(a)	*develops an information security architecture for the information system that describes:*
		PL-8(a)(1) *the overall philosophy, requirements, and approach to be taken with regard to protecting the confidentiality, integrity, and availability of organizational information;*
		PL-8(a)(2) *how the information security architecture is integrated into and supports the enterprise architecture;*
		PL-8(a)(3) *any information security assumptions about, and dependencies on, external services;*
	PL-8(b)	**PL-8(b)[1]** *defines the frequency to review and update the information security architecture;*
		PL-8(b)[2] *reviews and updates the information security architecture with the organization-defined frequency to reflect updates in the enterprise architecture;*
	PL-8(c)	*ensures that planned information security architecture changes are reflected in:*
		PL-8(c)[1] *the security plan;*
		PL-8(c)[2] *the security Concept of Operations (CONOPS); and*
		PL-8(c)[3] *the organizational procurements/acquisitions.*

Special Publication 800-53A
Revision 4

Assessing Security and Privacy Controls in Federal Information Systems
and Organizations — *Building Effective Assessment Plans*

POTENTIAL ASSESSMENT METHODS AND OBJECTS:

Examine: [*SELECT FROM:* Security planning policy; procedures addressing information security architecture development; procedures addressing information security architecture reviews and updates; enterprise architecture documentation; information security architecture documentation; security plan for the information system; security CONOPS for the information system; records of information security architecture reviews and updates; other relevant documents or records].

Interview: [*SELECT FROM:* Organizational personnel with security planning and plan implementation responsibilities; organizational personnel with information security architecture development responsibilities; organizational personnel with information security responsibilities].

Test: [*SELECT FROM:* Organizational processes for developing, reviewing, and updating the information security architecture; automated mechanisms supporting and/or implementing the development, review, and update of the information security architecture].

PL-8(1)	INFORMATION SECURITY ARCHITECTURE | *DEFENSE-IN-DEPTH*		
	ASSESSMENT OBJECTIVE: *Determine if the organization:*		
	PL-8(1)(a)	**PL-8(1)(a)[1]**	*defines security safeguards to be allocated to locations and architectural layers within the design of its security architecture;*
		PL-8(1)(a)[2]	*defines locations and architectural layers of its security architecture in which organization-defined security safeguards are to be allocated;*
		PL-8(1)(a)[3]	*designs its security architecture using a defense-in-depth approach that allocates organization-defined security safeguards to organization-defined locations and architectural layers; and*
	PL-8(1)(b)	*designs its security architecture using a defense-in-depth approach that ensures the allocated organization-defined security safeguards operate in a coordinated and mutually reinforcing manner.*	

POTENTIAL ASSESSMENT METHODS AND OBJECTS:

Examine: [*SELECT FROM:* Security planning policy; procedures addressing information security architecture development; enterprise architecture documentation; information security architecture documentation; security plan for the information system; security CONOPS for the information system; other relevant documents or records].

Interview: [*SELECT FROM:* Organizational personnel with security planning and plan implementation responsibilities; organizational personnel with information security architecture development responsibilities; organizational personnel with information security responsibilities].

Test: [*SELECT FROM:* Organizational processes for designing the information security architecture; automated mechanisms supporting and/or implementing the design of the information security architecture].

PL-8(2)	INFORMATION SECURITY ARCHITECTURE | *SUPPLIER DIVERSITY*	
	ASSESSMENT OBJECTIVE: *Determine if the organization:*	
	PL-8(2)[1]	*defines security safeguards to be allocated to locations and architectural layers within the design of its security architecture;*
	PL-8(2)[2]	*defines locations and architectural layers of its security architecture in which organization-defined security safeguards are to be allocated; and*

Special Publication 800-53A
Revision 4

Assessing Security and Privacy Controls in Federal Information Systems
and Organizations — *Building Effective Assessment Plans*

	PL-8(2)[3]	*requires that organization-defined security safeguards allocated to organization-defined locations and architectural layers are obtained from different suppliers.*

POTENTIAL ASSESSMENT METHODS AND OBJECTS:

Examine: [*SELECT FROM:* Security planning policy; procedures addressing information security architecture development; enterprise architecture documentation; information security architecture documentation; security plan for the information system; security CONOPS for the information system; other relevant documents or records].

Interview: [*SELECT FROM:* Organizational personnel with security planning and plan implementation responsibilities; organizational personnel with information security architecture development responsibilities; organizational personnel with acquisition responsibilities; organizational personnel with information security responsibilities].

Test: [*SELECT FROM:* Organizational processes for obtaining information security safeguards from different suppliers].

PL-9	**CENTRAL MANAGEMENT**

ASSESSMENT OBJECTIVE:

Determine if the organization:

PL-9[1]	*defines security controls and related processes to be centrally managed; and*
PL-9[2]	*centrally manages organization-defined security controls and related processes.*

POTENTIAL ASSESSMENT METHODS AND OBJECTS:

Examine: [*SELECT FROM:* Security planning policy; procedures addressing security plan development and implementation; security plan for the information system; other relevant documents or records].

Interview: [*SELECT FROM:* Organizational personnel with security planning and plan implementation responsibilities; organizational personnel with responsibilities for planning/implementing central management of security controls and related processes; organizational personnel with information security responsibilities].

Test: [*SELECT FROM:* Organizational processes for central management of security controls and related processes; automated mechanisms supporting and/or implementing central management of security controls and related processes].

Special Publication 800-53A
Revision 4

Assessing Security and Privacy Controls in Federal Information Systems
and Organizations — *Building Effective Assessment Plans*

FAMILY: PROGRAM MANAGEMENT

PM-1	INFORMATION SECURITY PROGRAM PLAN			
	ASSESSMENT OBJECTIVE: *Determine if the organization:*			
	PM-1(a)	*develops and disseminates an organization-wide information security program plan that:*		
		PM-1(a)(1)	PM-1(a)(1)[1]	*provides an overview of the requirements for the security program;*
			PM-1(a)(1)[2]	*provides a description of the:*
				PM-1(a)(1)[2][a]	*security program management controls in place or planned for meeting those requirements;*
				PM-1(a)(1)[2][b]	*common controls in place or planned for meeting those requirements;*
		PM-1(a)(2)	*includes the identification and assignment of:*	
			PM-1(a)(2)[1]	*roles;*
			PM-1(a)(2)[2]	*responsibilities;*
			PM-1(a)(2)[3]	*management commitment;*
			PM-1(a)(2)[4]	*coordination among organizational entities;*
			PM-1(a)(2)[5]	*compliance;*
		PM-1(a)(3)	*reflects coordination among organizational entities responsible for the different aspects of information security (i.e., technical, physical, personnel, cyber-physical);*	
		PM-1(a)(4)	*is approved by a senior official with responsibility and accountability for the risk being incurred to organizational operations, organizational assets, individuals, other organizations, and the Nation;*	
	PM-1(b)	PM-1(b)[1]	*defines the frequency to review the security program plan for the information system;*	
		PM-1(b)[2]	*reviews the organization-wide information security program plan with the organization-defined frequency;*	
	PM-1(c)	*updates the plan to address organizational:*		
		PM-1(c)[1]	*changes identified during plan implementation;*	
		PM-1(c)[2]	*changes identified during security control assessments;*	
		PM-1(c)[3]	*problems identified during plan implementation;*	
		PM-1(c)[4]	*problems identified during security control assessments;*	
	PM-1(d)	*protects the information security program plan from unauthorized:*		
		PM-1(d)[1]	*disclosure; and*	
		PM-1(d)[2]	*modification.*	

Special Publication 800-53A
Revision 4

Assessing Security and Privacy Controls in Federal Information Systems
and Organizations — *Building Effective Assessment Plans*

POTENTIAL ASSESSMENT METHODS AND OBJECTS:

Examine: [*SELECT FROM:* Information security program plan; procedures addressing program plan development and implementation; procedures addressing program plan reviews and updates; procedures addressing coordination of the program plan with relevant entities; procedures for program plan approvals; records of program plan reviews and updates; other relevant documents or records].

Interview: [*SELECT FROM:* Organizational personnel with information security program planning and plan implementation responsibilities; organizational personnel with information security responsibilities].

Test: [*SELECT FROM:* Organizational processes for information security program plan development/review/update/approval; automated mechanisms supporting and/or implementing the information security program plan].

PM-2	SENIOR INFORMATION SECURITY OFFICER

ASSESSMENT OBJECTIVE:

Determine if the organization appoints a senior information security officer with the mission and resources to:

PM-2[1]	*coordinate an organization-wide information security program;*
PM-2[2]	*develop an organization-wide information security program;*
PM-2[3]	*implement an organization-wide information security program; and*
PM-2[4]	*maintain an organization-wide information security program.*

POTENTIAL ASSESSMENT METHODS AND OBJECTS:

Examine: [*SELECT FROM:* Information security program plan; procedures addressing program plan development and implementation; procedures addressing program plan reviews and updates; procedures addressing coordination of the program plan with relevant entities; other relevant documents or records].

Interview: [*SELECT FROM:* Organizational personnel with information security program planning and plan implementation responsibilities; senior information security officer; organizational personnel with information security responsibilities].

PM-3	INFORMATION SECURITY RESOURCES	

ASSESSMENT OBJECTIVE:

Determine if the organization:

PM-3(a)	PM-3(a)[1]	*ensures that all capital planning and investment requests include the resources needed to implement the information security program plan;*
	PM-3(a)[2]	*documents all exceptions to the requirement;*
PM-3(b)	*employs a business case/Exhibit 300/Exhibit 53 to record the resources required; and*	
PM-3(c)	*ensures that information security resources are available for expenditure as planned.*	

Special Publication 800-53A
Revision 4

Assessing Security and Privacy Controls in Federal Information Systems
and Organizations — *Building Effective Assessment Plans*

POTENTIAL ASSESSMENT METHODS AND OBJECTS:

Examine: [*SELECT FROM:* Information security program plan; Exhibits 300; Exhibits 53; business cases for capital planning and investment; procedures for capital planning and investment; documentation of exceptions to capital planning requirements; other relevant documents or records].

Interview: [*SELECT FROM:* Organizational personnel with information security program planning responsibilities; organizational personnel responsible for capital planning and investment; organizational personnel with information security responsibilities].

Test: [*SELECT FROM:* Organizational processes for capital planning and investment; organizational processes for business case/Exhibit 300/Exhibit 53 development; automated mechanisms supporting the capital planning and investment process].

PM-4	PLAN OF ACTION AND MILESTONES PROCESS		
	ASSESSMENT OBJECTIVE: *Determine if the organization:*		
	PM-4(a)	*implements a process for ensuring that plans of action and milestones for the security program and associated organizational information systems:*	
		PM-4(a)(1)	PM-4(a)(1)[1]	*are developed;*
			PM-4(a)(1)[2]	*are maintained;*
		PM-4(a)(2)	*document the remedial information security actions to adequately respond to risk to organizational operations and assets, individuals, other organizations, and the Nation;*
		PM-4(a)(3)	*are reported in accordance with OMB FISMA reporting requirements;*
	PM-4(b)	*reviews plans of action and milestones for consistency with:*	
		PM-4(b)[1]	*the organizational risk management strategy; and*
		PM-4(b)[2]	*organization-wide priorities for risk response actions.*

POTENTIAL ASSESSMENT METHODS AND OBJECTS:

Examine: [*SELECT FROM:* Information security program plan; plans of action and milestones; procedures addressing plans of action and milestones development and maintenance; procedures addressing plans of action and milestones reporting; procedures for review of plans of action and milestones for consistency with risk management strategy and risk response priorities; results of risk assessments associated with plans of action and milestones; OMB FISMA reporting requirements; other relevant documents or records].

Interview: [*SELECT FROM:* Organizational personnel with responsibility for developing, maintaining, reviewing, and reporting plans of action and milestones; organizational personnel with information security responsibilities].

Test: [*SELECT FROM:* Organizational processes for plan of action and milestones development, review, maintenance, reporting; automated mechanisms supporting plans of action and milestones].

PM-5	INFORMATION SYSTEM INVENTORY	
	ASSESSMENT OBJECTIVE: *Determine if the organization:*	
	PM-5[1]	*develops an inventory of its information systems; and*
	PM-5[2]	*maintains the inventory of its information systems.*

Special Publication 800-53A
Revision 4

Assessing Security and Privacy Controls in Federal Information Systems
and Organizations — *Building Effective Assessment Plans*

POTENTIAL ASSESSMENT METHODS AND OBJECTS:

Examine: [*SELECT FROM:* Information security program plan; information system inventory; procedures addressing information system inventory development and maintenance; OMB FISMA reporting guidance; other relevant documents or records].

Interview: [*SELECT FROM:* Organizational personnel with information security program planning and plan implementation responsibilities; organizational personnel responsible for developing and maintaining the information system inventory; organizational personnel with information security responsibilities].

Test: [*SELECT FROM:* Organizational processes for information system inventory development and maintenance; automated mechanisms supporting the information system inventory].

PM-6	INFORMATION SECURITY MEASURES OF PERFORMANCE

ASSESSMENT OBJECTIVE:

Determine if the organization:

PM-6[1]	*develops information security measures of performance;*
PM-6[2]	*monitors information security measures of performance; and*
PM-6[3]	*reports information security measures of performance.*

POTENTIAL ASSESSMENT METHODS AND OBJECTS:

Examine: [*SELECT FROM:* Information security program plan; information security measures of performance; procedures addressing development, monitoring, and reporting of information security measures of performance; other relevant documents or records].

Interview: [*SELECT FROM:* Organizational personnel with information security program planning and plan implementation responsibilities; organizational personnel responsible for developing, monitoring, and reporting information security measures of performance; organizational personnel with information security responsibilities].

Test: [*SELECT FROM:* Organizational processes for developing, monitoring, and reporting information security measures of performance; automated mechanisms supporting the development, monitoring, and reporting of information security measures of performance].

PM-7	ENTERPRISE ARCHITECTURE

ASSESSMENT OBJECTIVE:

Determine if the organization develops an enterprise architecture with consideration for:

PM-7[1]	*information security; and*
PM-7[2]	*the resulting risk to organizational operations, organizational assets, individuals, other organizations, and the Nation.*

POTENTIAL ASSESSMENT METHODS AND OBJECTS:

Examine: [*SELECT FROM:* Information security program plan; enterprise architecture documentation; procedures addressing enterprise architecture development; results of risk assessment of enterprise architecture; other relevant documents or records].

Interview: [*SELECT FROM:* Organizational personnel with information security program planning and plan implementation responsibilities; organizational personnel responsible for developing enterprise architecture; organizational personnel responsible for risk assessment of enterprise architecture; organizational personnel with information security responsibilities].

Test: [*SELECT FROM:* Organizational processes for enterprise architecture development; automated mechanisms supporting the enterprise architecture and its development].

Special Publication 800-53A
Revision 4

Assessing Security and Privacy Controls in Federal Information Systems
and Organizations — *Building Effective Assessment Plans*

PM-8	CRITICAL INFRASTRUCTURE PLAN

ASSESSMENT OBJECTIVE:

Determine if the organization addresses information security issues in the:

PM-8[1]	*development of a critical infrastructure and key resources protection plan;*
PM-8[2]	*documentation of a critical infrastructure and key resources protection plan; and*
PM-8[3]	*updating of the critical infrastructure and key resources protection plan.*

POTENTIAL ASSESSMENT METHODS AND OBJECTS:

Examine: [*SELECT FROM:* Information security program plan; critical infrastructure and key resources protection plan; procedures addressing development, documentation, and updating of the critical infrastructure and key resources protection plan; HSPD 7; National Infrastructure Protection Plan; other relevant documents or records].

Interview: [*SELECT FROM:* Organizational personnel with information security program planning and plan implementation responsibilities; organizational personnel responsible for developing, documenting, and updating the critical infrastructure and key resources protection plan; organizational personnel with information security responsibilities].

Test: [*SELECT FROM:* Organizational processes for developing, documenting, and updating the critical infrastructure and key resources protection plan; automated mechanisms supporting the development, documentation, and updating of the critical infrastructure and key resources protection plan].

PM-9	RISK MANAGEMENT STRATEGY

ASSESSMENT OBJECTIVE:

Determine if the organization:

PM-9(a)	*develops a comprehensive strategy to manage risk to organizational operations and assets, individuals, other organizations, and the Nation associated with the operation and use of information systems;*
PM-9(b)	*implements the risk management strategy consistently across the organization;*

PM-9(c)	PM-9(c)[1]	*defines the frequency to review and update the risk management strategy;*	
	PM-9(c)[2]	*reviews and updates the risk management strategy to address organizational changes:*	
		PM-9(c)[2][a]	*with the organization-defined frequency; or*
		PM-9(c)[2][b]	*as required.*

POTENTIAL ASSESSMENT METHODS AND OBJECTS:

Examine: [*SELECT FROM:* Information security program plan; risk management strategy; procedures addressing development, implementation, review, and update of the risk management strategy; risk assessment results relevant to the risk management strategy; other relevant documents or records].

Interview: [*SELECT FROM:* Organizational personnel with information security program planning and plan implementation responsibilities; organizational personnel responsible for development, implementation, review, and update of the risk management strategy; organizational personnel with information security responsibilities].

Test: [*SELECT FROM:* Organizational processes for development, implementation, review, and update of the risk management strategy; automated mechanisms supporting the development, implementation, review, and update of the risk management strategy].

Special Publication 800-53A
Revision 4

Assessing Security and Privacy Controls in Federal Information Systems
and Organizations — *Building Effective Assessment Plans*

PM-10	SECURITY AUTHORIZATION PROCESS
	ASSESSMENT OBJECTIVE: *Determine if the organization:*
	PM-10(a) *manages (i.e., documents, tracks, and reports) the security state of organizational information systems and the environments in which those systems operate through security authorization processes;*
	PM-10(b) *designates individuals to fulfill specific roles and responsibilities within the organizational risk management process; and*
	PM-10(c) *fully integrates the security authorization processes into an organization-wide risk management program.*
	POTENTIAL ASSESSMENT METHODS AND OBJECTS:
	Examine: [*SELECT FROM:* Information security program plan; procedures addressing management (i.e., documentation, tracking, and reporting) of the security authorization process; security authorization documents; lists or other documentation about security authorization process roles and responsibilities; risk assessment results relevant to the security authorization process and the organization-wide risk management program; organizational risk management strategy; other relevant documents or records].
	Interview: [*SELECT FROM:* Organizational personnel with information security program planning and plan implementation responsibilities; organizational personnel responsible for management of the security authorization process; authorizing officials; system owners, senior information security officer; organizational personnel with information security responsibilities].
	Test: [*SELECT FROM:* Organizational processes for security authorization; automated mechanisms supporting the security authorization process].

PM-11	MISSION/BUSINESS PROCESS DEFINITION	
	ASSESSMENT OBJECTIVE: *Determine if the organization:*	
	PM-11(a) *defines mission/business processes with consideration for information security and the resulting risk to organizational operations, organizational assets, individuals, other organizations, and the Nation;*	
	PM-11(b)	**PM-11(b)[1]** *determines information protection needs arising from the defined mission/business process; and*
		PM-11(b)[2] *revises the processes as necessary until achievable protection needs are obtained.*
	POTENTIAL ASSESSMENT METHODS AND OBJECTS:	
	Examine: [*SELECT FROM:* Information security program plan; risk management strategy; procedures for determining mission/business protection needs; risk assessment results relevant to determination of mission/business protection needs; other relevant documents or records].	
	Interview: [*SELECT FROM:* Organizational personnel with information security program planning and plan implementation responsibilities; organizational personnel responsible for mission/business processes; organizational personnel responsible for determining information protection needs for mission/business processes; organizational personnel with information security responsibilities].	
	Test: [*SELECT FROM:* Organizational processes for defining mission/business processes and their information protection needs].	

Special Publication 800-53A
Revision 4

Assessing Security and Privacy Controls in Federal Information Systems
and Organizations — *Building Effective Assessment Plans*

PM-12	INSIDER THREAT PROGRAM
	ASSESSMENT OBJECTIVE:
	Determine if the organization implements an insider threat program that includes a cross-discipline insider threat incident handling team.
	POTENTIAL ASSESSMENT METHODS AND OBJECTS:
	Examine: [*SELECT FROM:* Information security program plan; insider threat program documentation; procedures for the insider threat program; risk assessment results relevant to insider threats; list or other documentation on the cross-discipline insider threat incident handling team; other relevant documents or records].
	Interview: [*SELECT FROM:* Organizational personnel with information security program planning and plan implementation responsibilities; organizational personnel responsible for the insider threat program; members of the cross-discipline insider threat incident handling team; organizational personnel with information security responsibilities].
	Test: [*SELECT FROM:* Organizational processes for implementing the insider threat program and the cross-discipline insider threat incident handling team; automated mechanisms supporting and/or implementing the insider threat program and the cross-discipline insider threat incident handling team].

PM-13	INFORMATION SECURITY WORKFORCE
	ASSESSMENT OBJECTIVE:
	Determine if the organization establishes an information security workforce development and improvement program.
	POTENTIAL ASSESSMENT METHODS AND OBJECTS:
	Examine: [*SELECT FROM:* Information security program plan; information security workforce development and improvement program documentation; procedures for the information security workforce development and improvement program; other relevant documents or records].
	Interview: [*SELECT FROM:* Organizational personnel with information security program planning and plan implementation responsibilities; organizational personnel responsible for the information security workforce development and improvement program; organizational personnel with information security responsibilities].
	Test: [*SELECT FROM:* Organizational processes for implementing information security workforce development and improvement program; automated mechanisms supporting and/or implementing the information security workforce development and improvement program].

PM-14	TESTING, TRAINING, AND MONITORING			
	ASSESSMENT OBJECTIVE:			
	Determine if the organization:			
	PM-14(a)	*implements a process for ensuring that organizational plans for conducting security testing, training, and monitoring activities associated with organizational information systems:*		
		PM-14(a)(1)	**PM-14(a)(1)[1]**	*are developed;*
			PM-14(a)(1)[2]	*are maintained;*
		PM-14(a)(2)	*continue to be executed in a timely manner;*	
	PM-14(b)	*reviews testing, training, and monitoring plans for consistency with:*		
		PM-14(b)[1]	*the organizational risk management strategy; and*	
		PM-14(b)[2]	*organization-wide priorities for risk response actions.*	

Special Publication 800-53A
Revision 4

Assessing Security and Privacy Controls in Federal Information Systems
and Organizations — *Building Effective Assessment Plans*

POTENTIAL ASSESSMENT METHODS AND OBJECTS:

Examine: [*SELECT FROM:* Information security program plan; plans for conducting security testing, training, and monitoring activities; organizational procedures addressing development and maintenance of plans for conducting security testing, training, and monitoring activities; risk management strategy; procedures for review of plans for conducting security testing, training, and monitoring activities for consistency with risk management strategy and risk response priorities; results of risk assessments associated with conducting security testing, training, and monitoring activities; evidence that plans for conducting security testing, training, and monitoring activities are executed in a timely manner; other relevant documents or records].

Interview: [*SELECT FROM:* Organizational personnel with responsibility for developing and maintaining plans for conducting security testing, training, and monitoring activities; organizational personnel with information security responsibilities].

Test: [*SELECT FROM:* Organizational processes for development and maintenance of plans for conducting security testing, training, and monitoring activities; automated mechanisms supporting development and maintenance of plans for conducting security testing, training, and monitoring activities].

PM-15	CONTACTS WITH SECURITY GROUPS AND ASSOCIATIONS

ASSESSMENT OBJECTIVE:

Determine if the organization establishes and institutionalizes contact with selected groups and associations with the security community to:

PM-15(a)	*facilitate ongoing security education and training for organizational personnel;*
PM-15(b)	*maintain currency with recommended security practices, techniques, and technologies; and*
PM-15(c)	*share current security-related information including threats, vulnerabilities, and incidents.*

POTENTIAL ASSESSMENT METHODS AND OBJECTS:

Examine: [*SELECT FROM:* Information security program plan; risk management strategy; procedures for contacts with security groups and associations; evidence of established and institutionalized contact with security groups and associations; lists or other documentation about contact with and/or membership in security groups and associations; other relevant documents or records].

Interview: [*SELECT FROM:* Organizational personnel with information security program planning and plan implementation responsibilities; organizational personnel responsible for establishing and institutionalizing contact with security groups and associations; organizational personnel with information security responsibilities; personnel from selected groups and associations with which the organization has established and institutionalized contact].

Test: [*SELECT FROM:* Organizational processes for establishing and institutionalizing contact with security groups and associations; automated mechanisms supporting contacts with security groups and associations].

PM-16	THREAT AWARENESS PROGRAM

ASSESSMENT OBJECTIVE:

Determine if the organization implements a threat awareness program that includes a cross-organization information-sharing capability.

Special Publication 800-53A
Revision 4

Assessing Security and Privacy Controls in Federal Information Systems
and Organizations — *Building Effective Assessment Plans*

POTENTIAL ASSESSMENT METHODS AND OBJECTS:

Examine: [*SELECT FROM:* Information security program plan; threat awareness program documentation; procedures for the threat awareness program; risk assessment results relevant to threat awareness; list or other documentation on the cross-organization information-sharing capability; other relevant documents or records].

Interview: [*SELECT FROM:* Organizational personnel with information security program planning and plan implementation responsibilities; organizational personnel responsible for the threat awareness program; organizational personnel with responsibility for the cross-organization information-sharing capability; organizational personnel with information security responsibilities; personnel with whom threat awareness information is shared by the organization].

Test: [*SELECT FROM:* Organizational processes for implementing the threat awareness program; Organizational processes for implementing the cross-organization information-sharing capability; automated mechanisms supporting and/or implementing the threat awareness program; automated mechanisms supporting and/or implementing the cross-organization information-sharing capability].

Special Publication 800-53A
Revision 4

Assessing Security and Privacy Controls in Federal Information Systems
and Organizations — *Building Effective Assessment Plans*

FAMILY: PERSONNEL SECURITY

PS-1	PERSONNEL SECURITY POLICY AND PROCEDURES			
	ASSESSMENT OBJECTIVE: *Determine if the organization:*			
	PS-1(a)(1)	**PS-1(a)(1)[1]**	*develops and documents an personnel security policy that addresses:*	
			PS-1(a)(1)[1][a]	*purpose;*
			PS-1(a)(1)[1][b]	*scope;*
			PS-1(a)(1)[1][c]	*roles;*
			PS-1(a)(1)[1][d]	*responsibilities;*
			PS-1(a)(1)[1][e]	*management commitment;*
			PS-1(a)(1)[1][f]	*coordination among organizational entities;*
			PS-1(a)(1)[1][g]	*compliance;*
		PS-1(a)(1)[2]	*defines personnel or roles to whom the personnel security policy is to be disseminated;*	
		PS-1(a)(1)[3]	*disseminates the personnel security policy to organization-defined personnel or roles;*	
	PS-1(a)(2)	**PS-1(a)(2)[1]**	*develops and documents procedures to facilitate the implementation of the personnel security policy and associated personnel security controls;*	
		PS-1(a)(2)[2]	*defines personnel or roles to whom the procedures are to be disseminated;*	
		PS-1(a)(2)[3]	*disseminates the procedures to organization-defined personnel or roles;*	
	PS-1(b)(1)	**PS-1(b)(1)[1]**	*defines the frequency to review and update the current personnel security policy;*	
		PS-1(b)(1)[2]	*reviews and updates the current personnel security policy with the organization-defined frequency;*	
	PS-1(b)(2)	**PS-1(b)(2)[1]**	*defines the frequency to review and update the current personnel security procedures; and*	
		PS-1(b)(2)[2]	*reviews and updates the current personnel security procedures with the organization-defined frequency.*	
	POTENTIAL ASSESSMENT METHODS AND OBJECTS: **Examine**: [*SELECT FROM:* Personnel security policy and procedures; other relevant documents or records]. **Interview**: [*SELECT FROM:* Organizational personnel with access control responsibilities; organizational personnel with information security responsibilities].			

Special Publication 800-53A
Revision 4

Assessing Security and Privacy Controls in Federal Information Systems
and Organizations — *Building Effective Assessment Plans*

PS-2	POSITION RISK DESIGNATION	
	ASSESSMENT OBJECTIVE: *Determine if the organization:*	
	PS-2(a)	*assigns a risk designation to all organizational positions;*
	PS-2(b)	*establishes screening criteria for individuals filling those positions;*
	PS-2(c) **PS-2(c)[1]**	*defines the frequency to review and update position risk designations; and*
	PS-2(c)[2]	*reviews and updates position risk designations with the organization-defined frequency.*
	POTENTIAL ASSESSMENT METHODS AND OBJECTS: **Examine**: [*SELECT FROM:* Personnel security policy; procedures addressing position categorization; appropriate codes of federal regulations; list of risk designations for organizational positions; security plan; records of position risk designation reviews and updates; other relevant documents or records]. **Interview**: [*SELECT FROM:* Organizational personnel with personnel security responsibilities; organizational personnel with information security responsibilities]. **Test**: [*SELECT FROM:* Organizational processes for assigning, reviewing, and updating position risk designations; organizational processes for establishing screening criteria].	

PS-3	PERSONNEL SCREENING	
	ASSESSMENT OBJECTIVE: *Determine if the organization:*	
	PS-3(a)	*screens individuals prior to authorizing access to the information system;*
	PS-3(b) **PS-3(b)[1]**	*defines conditions requiring re-screening;*
	PS-3(b)[2]	*defines the frequency of re-screening where it is so indicated; and*
	PS-3(b)[3]	*re-screens individuals in accordance with organization-defined conditions requiring re-screening and, where re-screening is so indicated, with the organization-defined frequency of such re-screening.*
	POTENTIAL ASSESSMENT METHODS AND OBJECTS: **Examine**: [*SELECT FROM:* Personnel security policy; procedures addressing personnel screening; records of screened personnel; security plan; other relevant documents or records]. **Interview**: [*SELECT FROM:* Organizational personnel with personnel security responsibilities; organizational personnel with information security responsibilities]. **Test**: [*SELECT FROM:* Organizational processes for personnel screening].	

PS-3(1)	PERSONNEL SCREENING	*CLASSIFIED INFORMATION*	
	ASSESSMENT OBJECTIVE: *Determine if the organization:*	
	PS-3(1)[1]	*ensures that individuals accessing an information system processing, storing, or transmitting classified information are cleared to the highest classification level of the information to which they have access on the system; and*

Special Publication 800-53A
Revision 4

Assessing Security and Privacy Controls in Federal Information Systems
and Organizations — *Building Effective Assessment Plans*

PS-3(1)[2]	*ensures that individuals accessing an information system processing, storing, or transmitting classified information are indoctrinated to the highest classification level of the information to which they have access on the system.*

POTENTIAL ASSESSMENT METHODS AND OBJECTS:

Examine: [*SELECT FROM:* Personnel security policy; procedures addressing personnel screening; records of screened personnel; other relevant documents or records].

Interview: [*SELECT FROM:* Organizational personnel with personnel security responsibilities; organizational personnel with information security responsibilities].

Test: [*SELECT FROM:* Organizational processes for clearing and indoctrinating personnel for access to classified information].

PS-3(2)	**PERSONNEL SCREENING**	*FORMAL INDOCTRINATION*

ASSESSMENT OBJECTIVE:

Determine if the organization ensures that individuals accessing an information system processing, storing, or transmitting types of classified information which require formal indoctrination, are formally indoctrinated for all of the relevant types of information to which they have access on the system.

POTENTIAL ASSESSMENT METHODS AND OBJECTS:

Examine: [*SELECT FROM:* Personnel security policy; procedures addressing personnel screening; records of screened personnel; other relevant documents or records].

Interview: [*SELECT FROM:* Organizational personnel with personnel security responsibilities; organizational personnel with information security responsibilities].

Test: [*SELECT FROM:* Organizational processes for formal indoctrination for all relevant types of information to which personnel have access].

PS-3(3)	**PERSONNEL SCREENING**	*INFORMATION WITH SPECIAL PROTECTION MEASURES*

ASSESSMENT OBJECTIVE:

Determine if the organization:

PS-3(3)(a)		*ensures that individuals accessing an information system processing, storing, or transmitting information requiring special protection have valid access authorizations that are demonstrated by assigned official government duties;*
PS-3(3)(b)	PS-3(3)(b)[1]	*defines additional personnel screening criteria to be satisfied for individuals accessing an information system processing, storing, or transmitting information requiring special protection; and*
	PS-3(3)(b)[2]	*ensures that individuals accessing an information system processing, storing, or transmitting information requiring special protection satisfy organization-defined additional personnel screening criteria.*

POTENTIAL ASSESSMENT METHODS AND OBJECTS:

Examine: [*SELECT FROM:* Personnel security policy; access control policy, procedures addressing personnel screening; records of screened personnel; screening criteria; records of access authorizations; other relevant documents or records].

Interview: [*SELECT FROM:* Organizational personnel with personnel security responsibilities; organizational personnel with information security responsibilities].

Test: [*SELECT FROM:* Organizational processes for ensuring valid access authorizations for information requiring special protection; organizational process for additional personnel screening for information requiring special protection].

Special Publication 800-53A
Revision 4

Assessing Security and Privacy Controls in Federal Information Systems
and Organizations — *Building Effective Assessment Plans*

PS-4	PERSONNEL TERMINATION	
	ASSESSMENT OBJECTIVE: *Determine if the organization, upon termination of individual employment,:*	
	PS-4(a)	**PS-4(a)[1]**	*defines a time period within which to disable information system access;*
		PS-4(a)[2]	*disables information system access within the organization-defined time period;*
	PS-4(b)	*terminates/revokes any authenticators/credentials associated with the individual;*	
	PS-4(c)	**PS-4(c)[1]**	*defines information security topics to be discussed when conducting exit interviews;*
		PS-4(c)[2]	*conducts exit interviews that include a discussion of organization-defined information security topics;*
	PS-4(d)	*retrieves all security-related organizational information system-related property;*	
	PS-4(e)	*retains access to organizational information and information systems formerly controlled by the terminated individual;*	
	PS-4(f)	**PS-4(f)[1]**	*defines personnel or roles to be notified of the termination;*
		PS-4(f)[2]	*defines the time period within which to notify organization-defined personnel or roles; and*
		PS-4(f)[3]	*notifies organization-defined personnel or roles within the organization-defined time period.*
	POTENTIAL ASSESSMENT METHODS AND OBJECTS: **Examine**: [*SELECT FROM:* Personnel security policy; procedures addressing personnel termination; records of personnel termination actions; list of information system accounts; records of terminated or revoked authenticators/credentials; records of exit interviews; other relevant documents or records]. **Interview**: [*SELECT FROM:* Organizational personnel with personnel security responsibilities; organizational personnel with account management responsibilities; system/network administrators; organizational personnel with information security responsibilities]. **Test**: [*SELECT FROM:* Organizational processes for personnel termination; automated mechanisms supporting and/or implementing personnel termination notifications; automated mechanisms for disabling information system access/revoking authenticators].	

PS-4(1)	PERSONNEL TERMINATION | *POST-EMPLOYMENT REQUIREMENTS*	
	ASSESSMENT OBJECTIVE: *Determine if the organization:*	
	PS-4(1)(a)	*notifies terminated individuals of applicable, legally binding, post-employment requirements for the protection of organizational information; and*
	PS-4(1)(b)	*requires terminated individuals to sign an acknowledgement of post-employment requirements as part of the organizational termination process.*

Special Publication 800-53A
Revision 4

Assessing Security and Privacy Controls in Federal Information Systems
and Organizations — *Building Effective Assessment Plans*

POTENTIAL ASSESSMENT METHODS AND OBJECTS:

Examine: [*SELECT FROM*: Personnel security policy; procedures addressing personnel termination; signed post-employment acknowledgement forms; list of applicable, legally binding post-employment requirements; other relevant documents or records].

Interview: [*SELECT FROM*: Organizational personnel with personnel security responsibilities; organizational personnel with information security responsibilities].

Test: [*SELECT FROM*: Organizational processes for post-employment requirements].

PS-4(2)	PERSONNEL TERMINATION | *AUTOMATED NOTIFICATION*

ASSESSMENT OBJECTIVE:

Determine if the organization:

PS-4(2)[1]	*defines personnel or roles to be notified upon termination of an individual; and*
PS-4(2)[2]	*employs automated mechanisms to notify organization-defined personnel or roles upon termination of an individual.*

POTENTIAL ASSESSMENT METHODS AND OBJECTS:

Examine: [*SELECT FROM*: Personnel security policy; procedures addressing personnel termination; information system design documentation; information system configuration settings and associated documentation; records of personnel termination actions; automated notifications of employee terminations; other relevant documents or records].

Interview: [*SELECT FROM*: Organizational personnel with personnel security responsibilities; organizational personnel with information security responsibilities].

Test: [*SELECT FROM*: Organizational processes for personnel termination; automated mechanisms supporting and/or implementing personnel termination notifications].

PS-5	PERSONNEL TRANSFER

ASSESSMENT OBJECTIVE:

Determine if the organization:

PS-5(a)		*when individuals are reassigned or transferred to other positions within the organization, reviews and confirms ongoing operational need for current:*
	PS-5(a)[1]	*logical access authorizations to information systems;*
	PS-5(a)[2]	*physical access authorizations to information systems and facilities;*
PS-5(b)	PS-5(b)[1]	*defines transfer or reassignment actions to be initiated following transfer or reassignment;*
	PS-5(b)[2]	*defines the time period within which transfer or reassignment actions must occur following transfer or reassignment;*
	PS-5(b)[3]	*initiates organization-defined transfer or reassignment actions within the organization-defined time period following transfer or reassignment;*
PS-5(c)		*modifies access authorization as needed to correspond with any changes in operational need due to reassignment or transfer;*
PS-5(d)	PS-5(d)[1]	*defines personnel or roles to be notified when individuals are reassigned or transferred to other positions within the organization;*
	PS-5(d)[2]	*defines the time period within which to notify organization-defined personnel or roles when individuals are reassigned or transferred to other positions within the organization; and*

Special Publication 800-53A
Revision 4

Assessing Security and Privacy Controls in Federal Information Systems
and Organizations — *Building Effective Assessment Plans*

		PS-5(d)[3]	*notifies organization-defined personnel or roles within the organization-defined time period when individuals are reassigned or transferred to other positions within the organization.*

POTENTIAL ASSESSMENT METHODS AND OBJECTS:

Examine: [*SELECT FROM:* Personnel security policy; procedures addressing personnel transfer; security plan; records of personnel transfer actions; list of information system and facility access authorizations; other relevant documents or records].

Interview: [*SELECT FROM:* Organizational personnel with personnel security responsibilities organizational personnel with account management responsibilities; system/network administrators; organizational personnel with information security responsibilities].

Test: [*SELECT FROM:* Organizational processes for personnel transfer; automated mechanisms supporting and/or implementing personnel transfer notifications; automated mechanisms for disabling information system access/revoking authenticators].

PS-6	ACCESS AGREEMENTS

ASSESSMENT OBJECTIVE:

Determine if the organization:

PS-6(a)		*develops and documents access agreements for organizational information systems;*
PS-6(b)	PS-6(b)[1]	*defines the frequency to review and update the access agreements;*
	PS-6(b)[2]	*reviews and updates the access agreements with the organization-defined frequency;*
PS-6(c)	PS-6(c)(1)	*ensures that individuals requiring access to organizational information and information systems sign appropriate access agreements prior to being granted access;*

		PS-6(c)(2)	PS-6(c)(2)[1]	*defines the frequency to re-sign access agreements to maintain access to organizational information systems when access agreements have been updated;*
			PS-6(c)(2)[2]	*ensures that individuals requiring access to organizational information and information systems re-sign access agreements to maintain access to organizational information systems when access agreements have been updated or with the organization-defined frequency.*

POTENTIAL ASSESSMENT METHODS AND OBJECTS:

Examine: [*SELECT FROM:* Personnel security policy; procedures addressing access agreements for organizational information and information systems; security plan; access agreements; records of access agreement reviews and updates; other relevant documents or records].

Interview: [*SELECT FROM:* Organizational personnel with personnel security responsibilities; organizational personnel who have signed/resigned access agreements; organizational personnel with information security responsibilities].

Test: [*SELECT FROM:* Organizational processes for access agreements; automated mechanisms supporting access agreements].

PS-6(1)	ACCESS AGREEMENTS	*INFORMATION REQUIRING SPECIAL PROTECTION*

[Withdrawn: Incorporated into PS-3].

Special Publication 800-53A
Revision 4

Assessing Security and Privacy Controls in Federal Information Systems
and Organizations — *Building Effective Assessment Plans*

PS-6(2)	ACCESS AGREEMENTS | *CLASSIFIED INFORMATION REQUIRING SPECIAL PROTECTION*
	ASSESSMENT OBJECTIVE: *Determine if the organization ensures that access to classified information requiring special protection is granted only to individuals who:*

	PS-6(2)(a)	*have a valid access authorization that is demonstrated by assigned official government duties;*
	PS-6(2)(b)	*satisfy associated personnel security criteria; and*
	PS-6(2)(c)	*have read, understood, and signed a nondisclosure agreement.*

	POTENTIAL ASSESSMENT METHODS AND OBJECTS: **Examine**: [*SELECT FROM:* Personnel security policy; procedures addressing access agreements for organizational information and information systems; access agreements; access authorizations; personnel security criteria; signed nondisclosure agreements; other relevant documents or records]. **Interview**: [*SELECT FROM:* Organizational personnel with personnel security responsibilities; organizational personnel who have signed nondisclosure agreements; organizational personnel with information security responsibilities]. **Test**: [*SELECT FROM:* Organizational processes for access to classified information requiring special protection].

PS-6(3)	ACCESS AGREEMENTS | *POST-EMPLOYMENT REQUIREMENTS*
	ASSESSMENT OBJECTIVE: *Determine if the organization:*

	PS-6(3)(a)	*notifies individuals of applicable, legally binding post-employment requirements for protection of organizational information; and*
	PS-6(3)(b)	*requires individuals to sign an acknowledgement of these requirements, if applicable, as part of granting initial access to covered information.*

	POTENTIAL ASSESSMENT METHODS AND OBJECTS: **Examine**: [*SELECT FROM:* Personnel security policy; procedures addressing access agreements for organizational information and information systems; signed post-employment acknowledgement forms; access agreements; list of applicable, legally binding post-employment requirements; other relevant documents or records]. **Interview**: [*SELECT FROM:* Organizational personnel with personnel security responsibilities; organizational personnel who have signed access agreements that include post-employment requirements; organizational personnel with information security responsibilities]. **Test**: [*SELECT FROM:* Organizational processes for post-employment requirements; automated mechanisms supporting notifications and individual acknowledgements of post-employment requirements].

PS-7	THIRD-PARTY PERSONNEL SECURITY
	ASSESSMENT OBJECTIVE: *Determine if the organization:*

	PS-7(a)	*establishes personnel security requirements, including security roles and responsibilities, for third-party providers;*
	PS-7(b)	*requires third-party providers to comply with personnel security policies and procedures established by the organization;*
	PS-7(c)	*documents personnel security requirements;*

Special Publication 800-53A
Revision 4

Assessing Security and Privacy Controls in Federal Information Systems
and Organizations — *Building Effective Assessment Plans*

	PS-7(d)	PS-7(d)[1]	*defines personnel or roles to be notified of any personnel transfers or terminations of third-party personnel who possess organizational credentials and/or badges, or who have information system privileges;*
		PS-7(d)[2]	*defines the time period within which third-party providers are required to notify organization-defined personnel or roles of any personnel transfers or terminations of third-party personnel who possess organizational credentials and/or badges, or who have information system privileges;*
		PS-7(d)[3]	*requires third-party providers to notify organization-defined personnel or roles within the organization-defined time period of any personnel transfers or terminations of third-party personnel who possess organizational credentials and/or badges, or who have information system privileges; and*
	PS-7(e)	*monitors provider compliance.*	

POTENTIAL ASSESSMENT METHODS AND OBJECTS:

Examine: [*SELECT FROM:* Personnel security policy; procedures addressing third-party personnel security; list of personnel security requirements; acquisition documents; service-level agreements; compliance monitoring process; other relevant documents or records].

Interview: [*SELECT FROM:* Organizational personnel with personnel security responsibilities; third-party providers; system/network administrators; organizational personnel with account management responsibilities; organizational personnel with information security responsibilities].

Test: [*SELECT FROM:* Organizational processes for managing and monitoring third-party personnel security; automated mechanisms supporting and/or implementing monitoring of provider compliance].

PS-8	**PERSONNEL SANCTIONS**

ASSESSMENT OBJECTIVE:

Determine if the organization:

	PS-8(a)	*employs a formal sanctions process for individuals failing to comply with established information security policies and procedures;*	
	PS-8(b)	PS-8(b)[1]	*defines personnel or roles to be notified when a formal employee sanctions process is initiated;*
		PS-8(b)[2]	*defines the time period within which organization-defined personnel or roles must be notified when a formal employee sanctions process is initiated; and*
		PS-8(b)[3]	*notifies organization-defined personnel or roles within the organization-defined time period when a formal employee sanctions process is initiated, identifying the individual sanctioned and the reason for the sanction.*

POTENTIAL ASSESSMENT METHODS AND OBJECTS:

Examine: [*SELECT FROM:* Personnel security policy; procedures addressing personnel sanctions; rules of behavior; records of formal sanctions; other relevant documents or records].

Interview: [*SELECT FROM:* Organizational personnel with personnel security responsibilities; organizational personnel with information security responsibilities].

Test: [*SELECT FROM:* Organizational processes for managing personnel sanctions; automated mechanisms supporting and/or implementing notifications].

Special Publication 800-53A
Revision 4

Assessing Security and Privacy Controls in Federal Information Systems
and Organizations — *Building Effective Assessment Plans*

FAMILY: RISK ASSESSMENT

RA-1	RISK ASSESSMENT POLICY AND PROCEDURES			
	ASSESSMENT OBJECTIVE: *Determine if the organization:*			
	RA-1(a)(1)	RA-1(a)(1)[1]	*develops and documents a risk assessment policy that addresses:*	
			RA-1(a)(1)[1][a]	*purpose;*
			RA-1(a)(1)[1][b]	*scope;*
			RA-1(a)(1)[1][c]	*roles;*
			RA-1(a)(1)[1][d]	*responsibilities;*
			RA-1(a)(1)[1][e]	*management commitment;*
			RA-1(a)(1)[1][f]	*coordination among organizational entities;*
			RA-1(a)(1)[1][g]	*compliance;*
		RA-1(a)(1)[2]	*defines personnel or roles to whom the risk assessment policy is to be disseminated;*	
		RA-1(a)(1)[3]	*disseminates the risk assessment policy to organization-defined personnel or roles;*	
	RA-1(a)(2)	RA-1(a)(2)[1]	*develops and documents procedures to facilitate the implementation of the risk assessment policy and associated risk assessment controls;*	
		RA-1(a)(2)[2]	*defines personnel or roles to whom the procedures are to be disseminated;*	
		RA-1(a)(2)[3]	*disseminates the procedures to organization-defined personnel or roles;*	
	RA-1(b)(1)	RA-1(b)(1)[1]	*defines the frequency to review and update the current risk assessment policy;*	
		RA-1(b)(1)[2]	*reviews and updates the current risk assessment policy with the organization-defined frequency;*	
	RA-1(b)(2)	RA-1(b)(2)[1]	*defines the frequency to review and update the current risk assessment procedures; and*	
		RA-1(b)(2)[2]	*reviews and updates the current risk assessment procedures with the organization-defined frequency.*	
	POTENTIAL ASSESSMENT METHODS AND OBJECTS: **Examine:** [*SELECT FROM:* risk assessment policy and procedures; other relevant documents or records]. **Interview:** [*SELECT FROM:* Organizational personnel with risk assessment responsibilities; organizational personnel with information security responsibilities].				

Special Publication 800-53A
Revision 4

Assessing Security and Privacy Controls in Federal Information Systems
and Organizations — *Building Effective Assessment Plans*

RA-2	SECURITY CATEGORIZATION	
	ASSESSMENT OBJECTIVE: *Determine if the organization:*	
	RA-2(a)	*categorizes information and the information system in accordance with applicable federal laws, Executive Orders, directives, policies, regulations, standards, and guidance;*
	RA-2(b)	*documents the security categorization results (including supporting rationale) in the security plan for the information system; and*
	RA-2(c)	*ensures the authorizing official or authorizing official designated representative reviews and approves the security categorization decision.*
	POTENTIAL ASSESSMENT METHODS AND OBJECTS: **Examine:** [*SELECT FROM:* Risk assessment policy; security planning policy and procedures; procedures addressing security categorization of organizational information and information systems; security plan; security categorization documentation; other relevant documents or records]. **Interview:** [*SELECT FROM:* Organizational personnel with security categorization and risk assessment responsibilities; organizational personnel with information security responsibilities]. **Test:** [*SELECT FROM:* Organizational processes for security categorization].	

RA-3	RISK ASSESSMENT		
	ASSESSMENT OBJECTIVE: *Determine if the organization:*		
	RA-3(a)	*conducts an assessment of risk, including the likelihood and magnitude of harm, from the unauthorized access, use, disclosure, disruption, modification, or destruction of:*	
		RA-3(a)[1]	*the information system;*
		RA-3(a)[2]	*the information the system processes, stores, or transmits;*
	RA-3(b)	**RA-3(b)[1]**	*defines a document in which risk assessment results are to be documented (if not documented in the security plan or risk assessment report);*
		RA-3(b)[2]	*documents risk assessment results in one of the following:*
		RA-3(b)[2][a]	*the security plan;*
		RA-3(b)[2][b]	*the risk assessment report; or*
		RA-3(b)[2][c]	*the organization-defined document;*
	RA-3(c)	**RA-3(c)[1]**	*defines the frequency to review risk assessment results;*
		RA-3(c)[2]	*reviews risk assessment results with the organization-defined frequency;*
	RA-3(d)	**RA-3(d)[1]**	*defines personnel or roles to whom risk assessment results are to be disseminated;*
		RA-3(d)[2]	*disseminates risk assessment results to organization-defined personnel or roles;*
	RA-3(e)	**RA-3(e)[1]**	*defines the frequency to update the risk assessment;*
		RA-3(e)[2]	*updates the risk assessment:*

Special Publication 800-53A
Revision 4

Assessing Security and Privacy Controls in Federal Information Systems
and Organizations — *Building Effective Assessment Plans*

			RA-3(e)[2][a]	*with the organization-defined frequency;*
			RA-3(e)[2][b]	*whenever there are significant changes to the information system or environment of operation (including the identification of new threats and vulnerabilities); and*
			RA-3(e)[2][c]	*whenever there are other conditions that may impact the security state of the system.*

POTENTIAL ASSESSMENT METHODS AND OBJECTS:

Examine: [*SELECT FROM:* Risk assessment policy; security planning policy and procedures; procedures addressing organizational assessments of risk; security plan; risk assessment; risk assessment results; risk assessment reviews; risk assessment updates; other relevant documents or records].

Interview: [*SELECT FROM:* Organizational personnel with risk assessment responsibilities; organizational personnel with information security responsibilities].

Test: [*SELECT FROM:* Organizational processes for risk assessment; automated mechanisms supporting and/or for conducting, documenting, reviewing, disseminating, and updating the risk assessment].

RA-4	RISK ASSESSMENT UPDATE
[Withdrawn: Incorporated into RA-3].	

RA-5	VULNERABILITY SCANNING			
	ASSESSMENT OBJECTIVE: *Determine if the organization:*			
	RA-5(a)	RA-5(a)[1]	RA-5(a)[1][a]	*defines the frequency for conducting vulnerability scans on the information system and hosted applications; and/or*
			RA-5(a)[1][b]	*defines the process for conducting random vulnerability scans on the information system and hosted applications;*
		RA-5(a)[2]	*in accordance with the organization-defined frequency and/or organization-defined process for conducting random scans, scans for vulnerabilities in:*	
			RA-5(a)[2][a]	*the information system;*
			RA-5(a)[2][b]	*hosted applications;*
		RA-5(a)[3]	*when new vulnerabilities potentially affecting the system/applications are identified and reported, scans for vulnerabilities in:*	
			RA-5(a)[3][a]	*the information system;*
			RA-5(a)[3][b]	*hosted applications;*
	RA-5(b)	*employs vulnerability scanning tools and techniques that facilitate interoperability among tools and automate parts of the vulnerability management process by using standards for:*		
		RA-5(b)(1)	RA-5(b)(1)[1]	*enumerating platforms;*
			RA-5(b)(1)[2]	*enumerating software flaws;*

Special Publication 800-53A
Revision 4

Assessing Security and Privacy Controls in Federal Information Systems
and Organizations — *Building Effective Assessment Plans*

		RA-5(b)(1)[3]	*enumerating improper configurations;*
	RA-5(b)(2)	RA-5(b)(2)[1]	*formatting checklists;*
		RA-5(b)(2)[2]	*formatting test procedures;*
	RA-5(b)(3)	*measuring vulnerability impact;*	
RA-5(c)	RA-5(c)[1]	*analyzes vulnerability scan reports;*	
	RA-5(c)[2]	*analyzes results from security control assessments;*	
RA-5(d)	RA-5(d)[1]	*defines response times to remediate legitimate vulnerabilities in accordance with an organizational assessment of risk;*	
	RA-5(d)[2]	*remediates legitimate vulnerabilities within the organization-defined response times in accordance with an organizational assessment of risk;*	
RA-5(e)	RA-5(e)[1]	*defines personnel or roles with whom information obtained from the vulnerability scanning process and security control assessments is to be shared;*	
	RA-5(e)[2]	*shares information obtained from the vulnerability scanning process with organization-defined personnel or roles to help eliminate similar vulnerabilities in other information systems (i.e., systemic weaknesses or deficiencies); and*	
	RA-5(e)[3]	*shares information obtained from security control assessments with organization-defined personnel or roles to help eliminate similar vulnerabilities in other information systems (i.e., systemic weaknesses or deficiencies).*	

POTENTIAL ASSESSMENT METHODS AND OBJECTS:

Examine: [*SELECT FROM:* Risk assessment policy; procedures addressing vulnerability scanning; risk assessment; security plan; security assessment report; vulnerability scanning tools and associated configuration documentation; vulnerability scanning results; patch and vulnerability management records; other relevant documents or records].

Interview: [*SELECT FROM:* Organizational personnel with risk assessment, security control assessment and vulnerability scanning responsibilities; organizational personnel with vulnerability scan analysis responsibilities; organizational personnel with vulnerability remediation responsibilities; organizational personnel with information security responsibilities; system/network administrators].

Test: [*SELECT FROM:* Organizational processes for vulnerability scanning, analysis, remediation, and information sharing; automated mechanisms supporting and/or implementing vulnerability scanning, analysis, remediation, and information sharing].

RA-5(1)	VULNERABILITY SCANNING | *UPDATE TOOL CAPABILITY*
	ASSESSMENT OBJECTIVE: *Determine if the organization employs vulnerability scanning tools that include the capability to readily update the information system vulnerabilities to be scanned.* **POTENTIAL ASSESSMENT METHODS AND OBJECTS:** **Examine:** [*SELECT FROM:* Procedures addressing vulnerability scanning; security plan; security assessment report; vulnerability scanning tools and associated configuration documentation; vulnerability scanning results; patch and vulnerability management records; other relevant documents or records]. **Interview:** [*SELECT FROM:* Organizational personnel with vulnerability scanning responsibilities; organizational personnel with information security responsibilities]. **Test:** [*SELECT FROM:* Organizational processes for vulnerability scanning; automated mechanisms/tools supporting and/or implementing vulnerability scanning].

Special Publication 800-53A
Revision 4

Assessing Security and Privacy Controls in Federal Information Systems
and Organizations — *Building Effective Assessment Plans*

RA-5(2)	VULNERABILITY SCANNING	*UPDATE BY FREQUENCY / PRIOR TO NEW SCAN / WHEN IDENTIFIED*	
	ASSESSMENT OBJECTIVE: *Determine if the organization:*		
	RA-5(2)[1]	*defines the frequency to update the information system vulnerabilities scanned;*	
	RA-5(2)[2]	*updates the information system vulnerabilities scanned one or more of the following:*	
		RA-5(2)[2][a]	*with the organization-defined frequency;*
		RA-5(2)[2][b]	*prior to a new scan; and/or*
		RA-5(2)[2][c]	*when new vulnerabilities are identified and reported.*
	POTENTIAL ASSESSMENT METHODS AND OBJECTS: **Examine**: [*SELECT FROM:* Procedures addressing vulnerability scanning; security plan; security assessment report; vulnerability scanning tools and associated configuration documentation; vulnerability scanning results; patch and vulnerability management records; other relevant documents or records]. **Interview**: [*SELECT FROM:* Organizational personnel with vulnerability scanning responsibilities; organizational personnel with vulnerability scan analysis responsibilities; organizational personnel with information security responsibilities; system/network administrators]. **Test**: [*SELECT FROM:* Organizational processes for vulnerability scanning; automated mechanisms/tools supporting and/or implementing vulnerability scanning].		

RA-5(3)	VULNERABILITY SCANNING	*BREADTH / DEPTH OF COVERAGE*
	ASSESSMENT OBJECTIVE: *Determine if the organization employs vulnerability scanning procedures that can identify:*	
	RA-5(3)[1]	*the breadth of coverage (i.e., information system components scanned); and*
	RA-5(3)[2]	*the depth of coverage (i.e., vulnerabilities checked).*
	POTENTIAL ASSESSMENT METHODS AND OBJECTS: **Examine**: [*SELECT FROM:* Procedures addressing vulnerability scanning; security plan; security assessment report; vulnerability scanning tools and associated configuration documentation; vulnerability scanning results; patch and vulnerability management records; other relevant documents or records]. **Interview**: [*SELECT FROM:* Organizational personnel with vulnerability scanning responsibilities; organizational personnel with vulnerability scan analysis responsibilities; organizational personnel with information security responsibilities]. **Test**: [*SELECT FROM:* Organizational processes for vulnerability scanning; automated mechanisms/tools supporting and/or implementing vulnerability scanning].	

RA-5(4)	VULNERABILITY SCANNING	*DISCOVERABLE INFORMATION*
	ASSESSMENT OBJECTIVE: *Determine if the organization:*	
	RA-5(4)[1]	*defines corrective actions to be taken if information about the information system is discoverable by adversaries;*
	RA-5(4)[2]	*determines what information about the information system is discoverable by adversaries; and*
	RA-5(4)[3]	*subsequently takes organization-defined corrective actions.*

Special Publication 800-53A
Revision 4

Assessing Security and Privacy Controls in Federal Information Systems
and Organizations — *Building Effective Assessment Plans*

POTENTIAL ASSESSMENT METHODS AND OBJECTS:

Examine: [*SELECT FROM*: Procedures addressing vulnerability scanning; security assessment report; penetration test results; vulnerability scanning results; risk assessment report; records of corrective actions taken; incident response records; audit records; other relevant documents or records].

Interview: [*SELECT FROM*: Organizational personnel with vulnerability scanning and/or penetration testing responsibilities; organizational personnel with vulnerability scan analysis responsibilities; organizational personnel responsible for risk response; organizational personnel responsible for incident management and response; organizational personnel with information security responsibilities].

Test: [*SELECT FROM*: Organizational processes for vulnerability scanning; organizational processes for risk response; organizational processes for incident management and response; automated mechanisms/tools supporting and/or implementing vulnerability scanning; automated mechanisms supporting and/or implementing risk response; automated mechanisms supporting and/or implementing incident management and response].

RA-5(5)	VULNERABILITY SCANNING | *PRIVILEGED ACCESS*

ASSESSMENT OBJECTIVE:

Determine if:

RA-5(5)[1]	*the organization defines information system components to which privileged access is authorized for selected vulnerability scanning activities;*
RA-5(5)[2]	*the organization defines vulnerability scanning activities selected for privileged access authorization to organization-defined information system components; and*
RA-5(5)[3]	*the information system implements privileged access authorization to organization-defined information system components for selected organization-defined vulnerability scanning activities.*

POTENTIAL ASSESSMENT METHODS AND OBJECTS:

Examine: [*SELECT FROM*: Risk assessment policy; procedures addressing vulnerability scanning; security plan; information system design documentation; information system configuration settings and associated documentation; list of information system components for vulnerability scanning; personnel access authorization list; authorization credentials; access authorization records; other relevant documents or records].

Interview: [*SELECT FROM*: Organizational personnel with vulnerability scanning responsibilities; system/network administrators; organizational personnel responsible for access control to the information system; organizational personnel responsible for configuration management of the information system; system developers; organizational personnel with information security responsibilities].

Test: [*SELECT FROM*: Organizational processes for vulnerability scanning; organizational processes for access control; automated mechanisms supporting and/or implementing access control; automated mechanisms/tools supporting and/or implementing vulnerability scanning].

RA-5(6)	VULNERABILITY SCANNING | *AUTOMATED TREND ANALYSES*

ASSESSMENT OBJECTIVE:

Determine if the organization employs automated mechanisms to compare the results of vulnerability scans over time to determine trends in information system vulnerabilities.

Special Publication 800-53A
Revision 4

Assessing Security and Privacy Controls in Federal Information Systems
and Organizations — *Building Effective Assessment Plans*

POTENTIAL ASSESSMENT METHODS AND OBJECTS:

Examine: [*SELECT FROM:* Risk assessment policy; procedures addressing vulnerability scanning; information system design documentation; vulnerability scanning tools and techniques documentation; vulnerability scanning results; other relevant documents or records].

Interview: [*SELECT FROM:* Organizational personnel with vulnerability scanning responsibilities; organizational personnel with vulnerability scan analysis responsibilities; organizational personnel with information security responsibilities].

Test: [*SELECT FROM:* Organizational processes for vulnerability scanning; automated mechanisms/tools supporting and/or implementing vulnerability scanning; automated mechanisms supporting and/or implementing trend analysis of vulnerability scan results].

RA-5(7)	VULNERABILITY SCANNING | *AUTOMATED DETECTION AND NOTIFICATION OF UNAUTHORIZED COMPONENTS*

[Withdrawn: Incorporated into CM-8].

RA-5(8)	VULNERABILITY SCANNING | *REVIEW HISTORIC AUDIT LOGS*

ASSESSMENT OBJECTIVE:

Determine if the organization reviews historic audit logs to determine if a vulnerability identified in the information system has been previously exploited.

POTENTIAL ASSESSMENT METHODS AND OBJECTS:

Examine: [*SELECT FROM:* Risk assessment policy; procedures addressing vulnerability scanning; audit logs; records of audit log reviews; vulnerability scanning results; patch and vulnerability management records; other relevant documents or records].

Interview: [*SELECT FROM:* Organizational personnel with vulnerability scanning responsibilities; organizational personnel with vulnerability scan analysis responsibilities; ; organizational personnel with audit record review responsibilities; system/network administrators; organizational personnel with information security responsibilities].

Test: [*SELECT FROM:* Organizational processes for vulnerability scanning; organizational process for audit record review and response; automated mechanisms/tools supporting and/or implementing vulnerability scanning; automated mechanisms supporting and/or implementing audit record review].

RA-5(9)	VULNERABILITY SCANNING | *PENETRATION TESTING AND ANALYSES*

[Withdrawn: Incorporated into CA-8].

RA-5(10)	VULNERABILITY SCANNING | *CORRELATE SCANNING INFORMATION*

ASSESSMENT OBJECTIVE:

Determine if the organization correlates the output from vulnerability scanning tools to determine the presence of multi-vulnerability/multi-hop attack vectors.

POTENTIAL ASSESSMENT METHODS AND OBJECTS:

Examine: [*SELECT FROM:* Risk assessment policy; procedures addressing vulnerability scanning; risk assessment; security plan; vulnerability scanning tools and techniques documentation; vulnerability scanning results; vulnerability management records; audit records; event/vulnerability correlation logs; other relevant documents or records].

Interview: [*SELECT FROM:* Organizational personnel with vulnerability scanning responsibilities; organizational personnel with vulnerability scan analysis responsibilities; organizational personnel with information security responsibilities].

Test: [*SELECT FROM:* Organizational processes for vulnerability scanning; automated mechanisms/tools supporting and/or implementing vulnerability scanning; automated mechanisms implementing correlation of vulnerability scan results].

Special Publication 800-53A
Revision 4

Assessing Security and Privacy Controls in Federal Information Systems
and Organizations — *Building Effective Assessment Plans*

RA-6	TECHNICAL SURVEILLANCE COUNTERMEASURES SURVEY	
	ASSESSMENT OBJECTIVE: *Determine if the organization:*	
	RA-6[1]	*defines locations to employ technical surveillance countermeasure surveys;*
	RA-6[2]	*defines a frequency to employ technical surveillance countermeasure surveys;*
	RA-6[3]	*defines events or indicators which, if they occur, trigger a technical surveillance countermeasures survey;*
	RA-6[4]	*employs a technical surveillance countermeasures survey at organization-defined locations one or more of the following:*
		RA-6[4][a] *with the organization-defined frequency; and/or*
		RA-6[4][b] *when organization-defined events or indicators occur.*
	POTENTIAL ASSESSMENT METHODS AND OBJECTS: **Examine**: [*SELECT FROM:* Risk assessment policy; procedures addressing technical surveillance countermeasures surveys; security plan; audit records/event logs; other relevant documents or records]. **Interview**: [*SELECT FROM:* Organizational personnel with technical surveillance countermeasures surveys responsibilities; system/network administrators; organizational personnel with information security responsibilities]. **Test**: [*SELECT FROM:* Organizational processes for technical surveillance countermeasures surveys; automated mechanisms/tools supporting and/or implementing technical surveillance countermeasures surveys].	

Special Publication 800-53A
Revision 4

Assessing Security and Privacy Controls in Federal Information Systems
and Organizations — *Building Effective Assessment Plans*

FAMILY: SYSTEM AND SERVICES ACQUISITION

SA-1	SYSTEM AND SERVICES ACQUISITION POLICY AND PROCEDURES		
	ASSESSMENT OBJECTIVE: *Determine if the organization:*		
	SA-1(a)(1)	SA-1(a)(1)[1]	*develops and documents a system and services acquisition policy that addresses:*
		SA-1(a)(1)[1][a]	*purpose;*
		SA-1(a)(1)[1][b]	*scope;*
		SA-1(a)(1)[1][c]	*roles;*
		SA-1(a)(1)[1][d]	*responsibilities;*
		SA-1(a)(1)[1][e]	*management commitment;*
		SA-1(a)(1)[1][f]	*coordination among organizational entities;*
		SA-1(a)(1)[1][g]	*compliance;*
		SA-1(a)(1)[2]	*defines personnel or roles to whom the system and services acquisition policy is to be disseminated;*
		SA-1(a)(1)[3]	*disseminates the system and services acquisition policy to organization-defined personnel or roles;*
	SA-1(a)(2)	SA-1(a)(2)[1]	*develops and documents procedures to facilitate the implementation of the system and services acquisition policy and associated system and services acquisition controls;*
		SA-1(a)(2)[2]	*defines personnel or roles to whom the procedures are to be disseminated;*
		SA-1(a)(2)[3]	*disseminates the procedures to organization-defined personnel or roles;*
	SA-1(b)(1)	SA-1(b)(1)[1]	*defines the frequency to review and update the current system and services acquisition policy;*
		SA-1(b)(1)[2]	*reviews and updates the current system and services acquisition policy with the organization-defined frequency;*
	SA-1(b)(2)	SA-1(b)(2)[1]	*defines the frequency to review and update the current system and services acquisition procedures; and*
		SA-1(b)(2)[2]	*reviews and updates the current system and services acquisition procedures with the organization-defined frequency.*
	POTENTIAL ASSESSMENT METHODS AND OBJECTS: **Examine**: [*SELECT FROM:* System and services acquisition policy and procedures; other relevant documents or records]. **Interview**: [*SELECT FROM:* Organizational personnel with system and services acquisition responsibilities; organizational personnel with information security responsibilities].		

Special Publication 800-53A
Revision 4

Assessing Security and Privacy Controls in Federal Information Systems
and Organizations — *Building Effective Assessment Plans*

SA-2	ALLOCATION OF RESOURCES	
	ASSESSMENT OBJECTIVE: *Determine if the organization:*	
	SA-2(a)	*determines information security requirements for the information system or information system service in mission/business process planning;*
	SA-2(b)	*to protect the information system or information system service as part of its capital planning and investment control process:*
	SA-2(b)[1]	*determines the resources required;*
	SA-2(b)[2]	*documents the resources required;*
	SA-2(b)[3]	*allocates the resources required; and*
	SA-2(c)	*establishes a discrete line item for information security in organizational programming and budgeting documentation.*
	POTENTIAL ASSESSMENT METHODS AND OBJECTS: **Examine**: [*SELECT FROM:* System and services acquisition policy; procedures addressing the allocation of resources to information security requirements; procedures addressing capital planning and investment control; organizational programming and budgeting documentation; other relevant documents or records]. **Interview**: [*SELECT FROM:* Organizational personnel with capital planning, investment control, organizational programming and budgeting responsibilities; organizational personnel responsible for determining information security requirements for information systems/services; organizational personnel with information security responsibilities]. **Test**: [*SELECT FROM:* Organizational processes for determining information security requirements; organizational processes for capital planning, programming, and budgeting; automated mechanisms supporting and/or implementing organizational capital planning, programming, and budgeting].	

SA-3	SYSTEM DEVELOPMENT LIFE CYCLE		
	ASSESSMENT OBJECTIVE: *Determine if the organization:*		
	SA-3(a)	**SA-3(a)[1]**	*defines a system development life cycle that incorporates information security considerations to be used to manage the information system;*
		SA-3(a)[2]	*manages the information system using the organization-defined system development life cycle;*
	SA-3(b)	*defines and documents information security roles and responsibilities throughout the system development life cycle;*	
	SA-3(c)	*identifies individuals having information security roles and responsibilities; and*	
	SA-3(d)	*integrates the organizational information security risk management process into system development life cycle activities.*	

Special Publication 800-53A
Revision 4

Assessing Security and Privacy Controls in Federal Information Systems
and Organizations — *Building Effective Assessment Plans*

<table>
<tr><td colspan="3">

POTENTIAL ASSESSMENT METHODS AND OBJECTS:

Examine: [*SELECT FROM*: System and services acquisition policy; procedures addressing the integration of information security into the system development life cycle process; information system development life cycle documentation; information security risk management strategy/program documentation; other relevant documents or records].

Interview: [*SELECT FROM*: Organizational personnel with information security and system life cycle development responsibilities; organizational personnel with information security risk management responsibilities; organizational personnel with information security responsibilities].

Test: [*SELECT FROM*: Organizational processes for defining and documenting the SDLC; organizational processes for identifying SDLC roles and responsibilities; organizational process for integrating information security risk management into the SDLC; automated mechanisms supporting and/or implementing the SDLC].

</td></tr>
</table>

SA-4	**ACQUISITION PROCESS**	

ASSESSMENT OBJECTIVE:

Determine if the organization includes the following requirements, descriptions, and criteria, explicitly or by reference, in the acquisition contracts for the information system, system component, or information system service in accordance with applicable federal laws, Executive Orders, directives, policies, regulations, standards, guidelines, and organizational mission/business needs:

SA-4(a)	*security functional requirements;*	
SA-4(b)	*security strength requirements;*	
SA-4(c)	*security assurance requirements;*	
SA-4(d)	*security-related documentation requirements;*	
SA-4(e)	*requirements for protecting security-related documentation;*	
SA-4(f)	*description of:*	
	SA-4(f)[1]	*the information system development environment;*
	SA-4(f)[2]	*the environment in which the system is intended to operate; and*
SA-4(g)	*acceptance criteria.*	

POTENTIAL ASSESSMENT METHODS AND OBJECTS:

Examine: [*SELECT FROM*: System and services acquisition policy; procedures addressing the integration of information security requirements, descriptions, and criteria into the acquisition process; acquisition contracts for the information system, system component, or information system service; information system design documentation; other relevant documents or records].

Interview: [*SELECT FROM*: Organizational personnel with acquisition/contracting responsibilities; organizational personnel with responsibility for determining information system security functional, strength, and assurance requirements; system/network administrators; organizational personnel with information security responsibilities].

Test: [*SELECT FROM*: Organizational processes for determining information system security functional, strength, and assurance requirements; organizational processes for developing acquisition contracts; automated mechanisms supporting and/or implementing acquisitions and inclusion of security requirements in contracts].

SA-4(1)	**ACQUISITION PROCESS	*FUNCTIONAL PROPERTIES OF SECURITY CONTROLS***

ASSESSMENT OBJECTIVE:

Determine if the organization requires the developer of the information system, system component, or information system service to provide a description of the functional properties of the security controls to be employed.

Special Publication 800-53A
Revision 4

Assessing Security and Privacy Controls in Federal Information Systems
and Organizations — *Building Effective Assessment Plans*

POTENTIAL ASSESSMENT METHODS AND OBJECTS:

Examine: [*SELECT FROM:* System and services acquisition policy; procedures addressing the integration of information security requirements, descriptions, and criteria into the acquisition process; solicitation documents; acquisition documentation; acquisition contracts for the information system, system component, or information system services; other relevant documents or records].

Interview: [*SELECT FROM:* Organizational personnel with acquisition/contracting responsibilities; organizational personnel with responsibility for determining information system security functional requirements; information system developer or service provider; organizational personnel with information security responsibilities].

Test: [*SELECT FROM:* Organizational processes for determining information system security functional, requirements; organizational processes for developing acquisition contracts; automated mechanisms supporting and/or implementing acquisitions and inclusion of security requirements in contracts].

SA-4(2)	ACQUISITION PROCESS | *DESIGN / IMPLEMENTATION INFORMATION FOR SECURITY CONTROLS*

ASSESSMENT OBJECTIVE:

Determine if the organization:

SA-4(2)[1]	*defines level of detail that the developer is required to provide in design and implementation information for the security controls to be employed in the information system, system component, or information system service;*
SA-4(2)[2]	*defines design/implementation information that the developer is to provide for the security controls to be employed (if selected);*
SA-4(2)[3]	*requires the developer of the information system, system component, or information system service to provide design and implementation information for the security controls to be employed that includes, at the organization-defined level of detail, one or more of the following:*

	SA-4(2)[3][a]	*security-relevant external system interfaces;*
	SA-4(2)[3][b]	*high-level design;*
	SA-4(2)[3][c]	*low-level design;*
	SA-4(2)[3][d]	*source code;*
	SA-4(2)[3][e]	*hardware schematics; and/or*
	SA-4(2)[3][f]	*organization-defined design/implementation information.*

POTENTIAL ASSESSMENT METHODS AND OBJECTS:

Examine: [*SELECT FROM:* System and services acquisition policy; procedures addressing the integration of information security requirements, descriptions, and criteria into the acquisition process; solicitation documents; acquisition documentation; acquisition contracts for the information system, system components, or information system services; design and implementation information for security controls employed in the information system, system component, or information system service; other relevant documents or records].

Interview: [*SELECT FROM:* Organizational personnel with acquisition/contracting responsibilities; organizational personnel with responsibility for determining information system security requirements; information system developer or service provider; organizational personnel with information security responsibilities].

Test: [*SELECT FROM:* Organizational processes for determining level of detail for system design and security controls; organizational processes for developing acquisition contracts; automated mechanisms supporting and/or implementing development of system design details].

Special Publication 800-53A
Revision 4

Assessing Security and Privacy Controls in Federal Information Systems
and Organizations — *Building Effective Assessment Plans*

SA-4(3)	ACQUISITION PROCESS | *DEVELOPMENT METHODS / TECHNIQUES / PRACTICES*	
	ASSESSMENT OBJECTIVE: *Determine if the organization:*	
	SA-4(3)[1]	*defines state-of-the-practice system/security engineering methods to be included in the system development life cycle employed by the developer of the information system, system component, or information system service;*
	SA-4(3)[2]	*defines software development methods to be included in the system development life cycle employed by the developer of the information system, system component, or information system service;*
	SA-4(3)[3]	*defines testing/evaluation/validation techniques to be included in the system development life cycle employed by the developer of the information system, system component, or information system service;*
	SA-4(3)[4]	*defines quality control processes to be included in the system development life cycle employed by the developer of the information system, system component, or information system service;*
	SA-4(3)[5]	*requires the developer of the information system, system component, or information system service to demonstrate the use of a system development life cycle that includes:*

		SA-4(3)[5][a]	*organization-defined state-of-the-practice system/security engineering methods;*
		SA-4(3)[5][b]	*organization-defined software development methods;*
		SA-4(3)[5][c]	*organization-defined testing/evaluation/validation techniques; and*
		SA-4(3)[5][d]	*organization-defined quality control processes.*

POTENTIAL ASSESSMENT METHODS AND OBJECTS:

Examine: [*SELECT FROM:* System and services acquisition policy; procedures addressing the integration of information security requirements, descriptions, and criteria into the acquisition process; solicitation documents; acquisition documentation; acquisition contracts for the information system, system component, or information system service; list of system/security engineering methods to be included in developer's system development life cycle process; list of software development methods to be included in developer's system development life cycle process; list of testing/evaluation/validation techniques to be included in developer's system development life cycle process; list of quality control processes to be included in developer's system development life cycle process; other relevant documents or records].

Interview: [*SELECT FROM:* Organizational personnel with acquisition/contracting responsibilities; organizational personnel with responsibility for determining information system security requirements; organizational personnel with information security and system life cycle responsibilities; information system developer or service provider].

Test: [*SELECT FROM:* Organizational processes for development methods, techniques, and processes].

SA-4(4)	ACQUISITION PROCESS | *ASSIGNMENT OF COMPONENTS TO SYSTEMS*
[Withdrawn: Incorporated into CM-8(9)].	

SA-4(5)	ACQUISITION PROCESS | *SYSTEM / COMPONENT / SERVICE CONFIGURATIONS*
	ASSESSMENT OBJECTIVE: *Determine if the organization:*

Special Publication 800-53A
Revision 4

Assessing Security and Privacy Controls in Federal Information Systems
and Organizations — *Building Effective Assessment Plans*

	SA-4(5)(a)	SA-4(5)(a)[1]	*defines security configurations to be implemented by the developer of the information system, system component, or information system service;*
		SA-4(5)(a)[2]	*requires the developer of the information system, system component, or information system service to deliver the system, component, or service with organization-defined security configurations implemented; and*
	SA-4(5)(b)		*requires the developer of the information system, system component, or information system service to use the configurations as the default for any subsequent system, component, or service reinstallation or upgrade.*

POTENTIAL ASSESSMENT METHODS AND OBJECTS:

Examine: [*SELECT FROM:* System and services acquisition policy; procedures addressing the integration of information security requirements, descriptions, and criteria into the acquisition process; solicitation documents; acquisition documentation; acquisition contracts for the information system, system component, or information system service; security configurations to be implemented by developer of the information system, system component, or information system service; service-level agreements; other relevant documents or records].

Interview: [*SELECT FROM:* Organizational personnel with acquisition/contracting responsibilities; organizational personnel with responsibility for determining information system security requirements; information system developer or service provider; organizational personnel with information security responsibilities].

Test: [*SELECT FROM:* Automated mechanisms used to verify that the configuration of the information system, component, or service, as delivered, is as specified].

SA-4(6)	ACQUISITION PROCESS | *USE OF INFORMATION ASSURANCE PRODUCTS*

ASSESSMENT OBJECTIVE:

Determine if the organization:

	SA-4(6)(a)	*employs only government off-the-shelf (GOTS) or commercial off-the-shelf (COTS) information assurance (IA) and IA-enabled information technology products that compose an NSA-approved solution to protect classified information when the networks used to transmit the information are at a lower classification level than the information being transmitted; and*
	SA-4(6)(b)	*ensures that these products have been evaluated and/or validated by the NSA or in accordance with NSA-approved procedures.*

POTENTIAL ASSESSMENT METHODS AND OBJECTS:

Examine: [*SELECT FROM:* System and services acquisition policy; procedures addressing the integration of information security requirements, descriptions, and criteria into the acquisition process; solicitation documents; acquisition documentation; acquisition contracts for the information system, system component, or information system service; security configurations to be implemented by developer of the information system, system component, or information system service; service-level agreements; other relevant documents or records].

Interview: [*SELECT FROM:* Organizational personnel with acquisition/contracting responsibilities; organizational personnel with responsibility for determining information system security requirements; organizational personnel responsible for ensuring information assurance products are NSA-approved and are evaluated and/or validated products in accordance with NSA-approved procedures; organizational personnel with information security responsibilities].

Test: [*SELECT FROM:* Organizational processes for selecting and employing evaluated and/or validated information assurance products and services that compose an NSA-approved solution to protect classified information].

Special Publication 800-53A
Revision 4

Assessing Security and Privacy Controls in Federal Information Systems
and Organizations — *Building Effective Assessment Plans*

SA-4(7)	ACQUISITION PROCESS	*NIAP-APPROVED PROTECTION PROFILES*	

	ASSESSMENT OBJECTIVE:	
	Determine if the organization:	
	SA-4(7)(a)	*limits the use of commercially-provided information assurance (IA) and IA-enabled information technology products to those products that have been successfully evaluated against a National Information Assurance partnership (NIAP)-approved Protection Profile for a specific technology type, if such a profile exists; and*
	SA-4(7)(b)	*requires, if no NIAP-approved Protection Profile exists for a specific technology type but a commercially provided information technology product relies on cryptographic functionality to enforce its security policy, that the cryptographic module is FIPS-validated.*

POTENTIAL ASSESSMENT METHODS AND OBJECTS:

Examine: [*SELECT FROM:* System and services acquisition policy; procedures addressing the integration of information security requirements, descriptions, and criteria into the acquisition process; solicitation documents; acquisition documentation; acquisition contracts for the information system, system component, or information system service; NAIP-approved protection profiles; FIPS-validation information for cryptographic functionality; other relevant documents or records].

Interview: [*SELECT FROM:* Organizational personnel with acquisition/contracting responsibilities; organizational personnel with responsibility for determining information system security requirements; organizational personnel responsible for ensuring information assurance products are have been evaluated against a NIAP-approved protection profile or for ensuring products relying on cryptographic functionality are FIPS-validated; organizational personnel with information security responsibilities].

Test: [*SELECT FROM:* Organizational processes for selecting and employing products/services evaluated against a NIAP-approved protection profile or FIPS-validated products].

SA-4(8)	ACQUISITION PROCESS	*CONTINUOUS MONITORING PLAN*	

	ASSESSMENT OBJECTIVE:	
	Determine if the organization:	
	SA-4(8)[1]	*defines the level of detail the developer of the information system, system component, or information system service is required to provide when producing a plan for the continuous monitoring of security control effectiveness; and*
	SA-4(8)[2]	*requires the developer of the information system, system component, or information system service to produce a plan for the continuous monitoring of security control effectiveness that contains the organization-defined level of detail.*

POTENTIAL ASSESSMENT METHODS AND OBJECTS:

Examine: [*SELECT FROM:* System and services acquisition policy; procedures addressing developer continuous monitoring plans; procedures addressing the integration of information security requirements, descriptions, and criteria into the acquisition process; developer continuous monitoring plans; security assessment plans; acquisition contracts for the information system, system component, or information system service; acquisition documentation; solicitation documentation; service-level agreements; other relevant documents or records].

Interview: [*SELECT FROM:* Organizational personnel with acquisition/contracting responsibilities; organizational personnel with responsibility for determining information system security requirements; information system developers; organizational personnel with information security responsibilities].

Test: [*SELECT FROM:* Vendor processes for continuous monitoring; automated mechanisms supporting and/or implementing developer continuous monitoring].

Special Publication 800-53A
Revision 4

Assessing Security and Privacy Controls in Federal Information Systems
and Organizations — *Building Effective Assessment Plans*

SA-4(9)	**ACQUISITION PROCESS** | *FUNCTIONS / PORTS / PROTOCOLS / SERVICES IN USE*
	ASSESSMENT OBJECTIVE: *Determine if the organization requires the developer of the information system, system component, or information system service to identify early in the system development life cycle:*

	SA-4(9)[1]	*the functions intended for organizational use;*
	SA-4(9)[2]	*the ports intended for organizational use;*
	SA-4(9)[3]	*the protocols intended for organizational use; and*
	SA-4(9)[4]	*the services intended for organizational use.*

	POTENTIAL ASSESSMENT METHODS AND OBJECTS:
	Examine: [*SELECT FROM:* System and services acquisition policy; procedures addressing the integration of information security requirements, descriptions, and criteria into the acquisition process; information system design documentation; information system documentation including functions, ports, protocols, and services intended for organizational use; acquisition contracts for information systems or services; acquisition documentation; solicitation documentation; service-level agreements; organizational security requirements, descriptions, and criteria for developers of information systems, system components, and information system services; other relevant documents or records].
	Interview: [*SELECT FROM:* Organizational personnel with acquisition/contracting responsibilities; organizational personnel with responsibility for determining information system security requirements; system/network administrators; organizational personnel operating, using, and/or maintaining the information system; information system developers; organizational personnel with information security responsibilities].

SA-4(10)	**ACQUISITION PROCESS** | *USE OF APPROVED PIV PRODUCTS*
	ASSESSMENT OBJECTIVE: *Determine if the organization employs only information technology products on the FIPS 201-approved products list for Personal Identity Verification (PIV) capability implemented within organizational information systems.*
	POTENTIAL ASSESSMENT METHODS AND OBJECTS:
	Examine: [*SELECT FROM:* System and services acquisition policy; procedures addressing the integration of information security requirements, descriptions, and criteria into the acquisition process; solicitation documentation; acquisition documentation; acquisition contracts for the information system, system component, or information system service; service-level agreements; other relevant documents or records].
	Interview: [*SELECT FROM:* Organizational personnel with acquisition/contracting responsibilities; organizational personnel with responsibility for determining information system security requirements; organizational personnel with responsibility for ensuring only FIPS 201-approved products are implemented; organizational personnel with information security responsibilities].
	Test: [*SELECT FROM:* Organizational processes for selecting and employing FIPS 201-approved products].

SA-5	**INFORMATION SYSTEM DOCUMENTATION**
	ASSESSMENT OBJECTIVE: *Determine if the organization:*

	SA-5(a)	*obtains administrator documentation for the information system, system component, or information system service that describes:*

Special Publication 800-53A
Revision 4

Assessing Security and Privacy Controls in Federal Information Systems
and Organizations — *Building Effective Assessment Plans*

		SA-5(a)(1)	SA-5(a)(1)[1]	*secure configuration of the system, system component, or service;*
			SA-5(a)(1)[2]	*secure installation of the system, system component, or service;*
			SA-5(a)(1)[3]	*secure operation of the system, system component, or service;*
		SA-5(a)(2)	SA-5(a)(2)[1]	*effective use of the security features/mechanisms;*
			SA-5(a)(2)[2]	*effective maintenance of the security features/mechanisms;*
		SA-5(a)(3)		*known vulnerabilities regarding configuration and use of administrative (i.e., privileged) functions;*
	SA-5(b)	*obtains user documentation for the information system, system component, or information system service that describes:*		
		SA-5(b)(1)	SA-5(b)(1)[1]	*user-accessible security functions/mechanisms;*
			SA-5(b)(1)[2]	*how to effectively use those functions/mechanisms;*
		SA-5(b)(2)		*methods for user interaction, which enables individuals to use the system, component, or service in a more secure manner;*
		SA-5(b)(3)		*user responsibilities in maintaining the security of the system, component, or service;*
	SA-5(c)	SA-5(c)[1]		*defines actions to be taken after documented attempts to obtain information system, system component, or information system service documentation when such documentation is either unavailable or nonexistent;*
		SA-5(c)[2]		*documents attempts to obtain information system, system component, or information system service documentation when such documentation is either unavailable or nonexistent;*
		SA-5(c)[3]		*takes organization-defined actions in response;*
	SA-5(d)	*protects documentation as required, in accordance with the risk management strategy;*		
	SA-5(e)	SA-5(e)[1]		*defines personnel or roles to whom documentation is to be distributed; and*
		SA-5(e)[2]		*distributes documentation to organization-defined personnel or roles.*

POTENTIAL ASSESSMENT METHODS AND OBJECTS:

Examine: [*SELECT FROM:* System and services acquisition policy; procedures addressing information system documentation; information system documentation including administrator and user guides; records documenting attempts to obtain unavailable or nonexistent information system documentation; list of actions to be taken in response to documented attempts to obtain information system, system component, or information system service documentation; risk management strategy documentation; other relevant documents or records].

Interview: [*SELECT FROM:* Organizational personnel with acquisition/contracting responsibilities; organizational personnel with responsibility for determining information system security requirements; system administrators; organizational personnel operating, using, and/or maintaining the information system; information system developers; organizational personnel with information security responsibilities].

Test: [*SELECT FROM:* Organizational processes for obtaining, protecting, and distributing information system administrator and user documentation].

Special Publication 800-53A
Revision 4

Assessing Security and Privacy Controls in Federal Information Systems
and Organizations — *Building Effective Assessment Plans*

SA-5(1)	INFORMATION SYSTEM DOCUMENTATION | *FUNCTIONAL PROPERTIES OF SECURITY CONTROLS*
[Withdrawn: Incorporated into SA-4(1)].	

SA-5(2)	INFORMATION SYSTEM DOCUMENTATION | *SECURITY-RELEVANT EXTERNAL SYSTEM INTERFACES*
[Withdrawn: Incorporated into SA-4(2)].	

SA-5(3)	INFORMATION SYSTEM DOCUMENTATION | *HIGH-LEVEL DESIGN*
[Withdrawn: Incorporated into SA-4(2)].	

SA-5(4)	INFORMATION SYSTEM DOCUMENTATION | *LOW-LEVEL DESIGN*
[Withdrawn: Incorporated into SA-4(2)].	

SA-5(5)	INFORMATION SYSTEM DOCUMENTATION | *SOURCE CODE*
[Withdrawn: Incorporated into SA-4(2)].	

SA-6	SOFTWARE USAGE RESTRICTIONS
[Withdrawn: Incorporated into CM-10 and SI-7].	

SA-7	USER- INSTALLED SOFTWARE
[Withdrawn: Incorporated into CM-11 and SI-7].	

SA-8	SECURITY ENGINEERING PRINCIPLES	
	ASSESSMENT OBJECTIVE: *Determine if the organization applies information system security engineering principles in:*	
	SA-8[1]	*the specification of the information system;*
	SA-8[2]	*the design of the information system;*
	SA-8[3]	*the development of the information system;*
	SA-8[4]	*the implementation of the information system; and*
	SA-8[5]	*the modification of the information system.*

Special Publication 800-53A
Revision 4

Assessing Security and Privacy Controls in Federal Information Systems
and Organizations — *Building Effective Assessment Plans*

POTENTIAL ASSESSMENT METHODS AND OBJECTS:

Examine: [*SELECT FROM:* System and services acquisition policy; procedures addressing security engineering principles used in the specification, design, development, implementation, and modification of the information system; information system design documentation; information security requirements and specifications for the information system; other relevant documents or records].

Interview: [*SELECT FROM:* Organizational personnel with acquisition/contracting responsibilities; organizational personnel with responsibility for determining information system security requirements; organizational personnel with information system specification, design, development, implementation, and modification responsibilities; information system developers; organizational personnel with information security responsibilities].

Test: [*SELECT FROM:* Organizational processes for applying security engineering principles in information system specification, design, development, implementation, and modification; automated mechanisms supporting the application of security engineering principles in information system specification, design, development, implementation, and modification].

SA-9	EXTERNAL INFORMATION SYSTEM SERVICES	

ASSESSMENT OBJECTIVE:

Determine if the organization:

SA-9(a)	SA-9(a)[1]	*defines security controls to be employed by providers of external information system services;*
	SA-9(a)[2]	*requires that providers of external information system services comply with organizational information security requirements;*
	SA-9(a)[3]	*requires that providers of external information system services employ organization-defined security controls in accordance with applicable federal laws, Executive Orders, directives, policies, regulations, standards, and guidance;*
SA-9(b)	SA-9(b)[1]	*defines and documents government oversight with regard to external information system services;*
	SA-9(b)[2]	*defines and documents user roles and responsibilities with regard to external information system services;*
SA-9(c)	SA-9(c)[1]	*defines processes, methods, and techniques to be employed to monitor security control compliance by external service providers; and*
	SA-9(c)[2]	*employs organization-defined processes, methods, and techniques to monitor security control compliance by external service providers on an ongoing basis.*

POTENTIAL ASSESSMENT METHODS AND OBJECTS:

Examine: [*SELECT FROM:* System and services acquisition policy; procedures addressing external information system services; procedures addressing methods and techniques for monitoring security control compliance by external service providers of information system services; acquisition contracts, service-level agreements; organizational security requirements and security specifications for external provider services; security control assessment evidence from external providers of information system services; other relevant documents or records].

Interview: [*SELECT FROM:* Organizational personnel with system and services acquisition responsibilities; external providers of information system services; organizational personnel with information security responsibilities].

Test: [*SELECT FROM:* Organizational processes for monitoring security control compliance by external service providers on an ongoing basis; automated mechanisms for monitoring security control compliance by external service providers on an ongoing basis].

Special Publication 800-53A
Revision 4

Assessing Security and Privacy Controls in Federal Information Systems
and Organizations — *Building Effective Assessment Plans*

SA-9(1)	EXTERNAL INFORMATION SYSTEM SERVICES | *RISK ASSESSMENTS / ORGANIZATIONAL APPROVALS*		
	ASSESSMENT OBJECTIVE: *Determine if the organization:*		
	SA-9(1)(a)	*conducts an organizational assessment of risk prior to the acquisition or outsourcing of dedicated information security services;*	
	SA-9(1)(b)	**SA-9(1)(b)[1]**	*defines personnel or roles designated to approve the acquisition or outsourcing of dedicated information security services; and*
		SA-9(1)(b)[2]	*ensures that the acquisition or outsourcing of dedicated information security services is approved by organization-defined personnel or roles.*
	POTENTIAL ASSESSMENT METHODS AND OBJECTS: **Examine**: [*SELECT FROM:* System and services acquisition policy; procedures addressing external information system services; acquisition documentation; acquisition contracts for the information system, system component, or information system service; risk assessment reports; approval records for acquisition or outsourcing of dedicated information security services; other relevant documents or records]. **Interview**: [*SELECT FROM:* Organizational personnel with system and services acquisition responsibilities; organizational personnel with information system security responsibilities; external providers of information system services; organizational personnel with information security responsibilities]. **Test**: [*SELECT FROM:* Organizational processes for conducting a risk assessment prior to acquiring or outsourcing dedicated information security services; organizational processes for approving the outsourcing of dedicated information security services; automated mechanisms supporting and/or implementing risk assessment; automated mechanisms supporting and/or implementing approval processes].		

SA-9(2)	EXTERNAL INFORMATION SYSTEM SERVICES | *IDENTIFICATION OF FUNCTIONS / PORTS / PROTOCOLS / SERVICES*		
	ASSESSMENT OBJECTIVE: *Determine if the organization:*		
	SA-9(2)[1]	*defines external information system services for which providers of such services are to identify the functions, ports, protocols, and other services required for the use of such services;*	
	SA-9(2)[2]	*requires providers of organization-defined external information system services to identify:*	
		SA-9(2)[2][a]	*the functions required for the use of such services;*
		SA-9(2)[2][b]	*the ports required for the use of such services;*
		SA-9(2)[2][c]	*the protocols required for the use of such services; and*
		SA-9(2)[2][d]	*the other services required for the use of such services.*

Special Publication 800-53A
Revision 4

Assessing Security and Privacy Controls in Federal Information Systems
and Organizations — *Building Effective Assessment Plans*

POTENTIAL ASSESSMENT METHODS AND OBJECTS:

Examine: [*SELECT FROM:* System and services acquisition policy; procedures addressing external information system services; acquisition contracts for the information system, system component, or information system service; acquisition documentation; solicitation documentation, service-level agreements; organizational security requirements and security specifications for external service providers; list of required functions, ports, protocols, and other services; other relevant documents or records].

Interview: [*SELECT FROM:* Organizational personnel with system and services acquisition responsibilities; organizational personnel with information security responsibilities; system/network administrators; external providers of information system services].

SA-9(3)	EXTERNAL INFORMATION SYSTEM SERVICES | *ESTABLISH / MAINTAIN TRUST RELATIONSHIP WITH PROVIDERS*

ASSESSMENT OBJECTIVE:

Determine if the organization:

SA-9(3)[1]	*defines requirements, properties, factors, or conditions defining acceptable trust relationships;*	
SA-9(3)[2]	*based on organization-defined requirements, properties, factors, or conditions defining acceptable trust relationships:*	
	SA-9(3)[2][a]	*establishes trust relationships with external service providers;*
	SA-9(3)[2][b]	*documents trust relationships with external service providers; and*
	SA-9(3)[2][c]	*maintains trust relationships with external service providers.*

POTENTIAL ASSESSMENT METHODS AND OBJECTS:

Examine: [*SELECT FROM:* System and services acquisition policy; procedures addressing external information system services; acquisition contracts for the information system, system component, or information system service; acquisition documentation; solicitation documentation; service-level agreements; organizational security requirements, properties, factors, or conditions defining acceptable trust relationships; documentation of trust relationships with external service providers; other relevant documents or records].

Interview: [*SELECT FROM:* Organizational personnel with system and services acquisition responsibilities; organizational personnel with information security responsibilities; external providers of information system services].

SA-9(4)	EXTERNAL INFORMATION SYSTEM SERVICES | *CONSISTENT INTERESTS OF CONSUMERS AND PROVIDERS*

ASSESSMENT OBJECTIVE:

Determine if the organization:

SA-9(4)[1]	*defines external service providers whose interests are to be consistent with and reflect organizational interests;*
SA-9(4)[2]	*defines security safeguards to be employed to ensure that the interests of organization-defined external service providers are consistent with and reflect organizational interests; and*
SA-9(4)[3]	*employs organization-defined security safeguards to ensure that the interests of organization-defined external service providers are consistent with and reflect organizational interests.*

Special Publication 800-53A
Revision 4

Assessing Security and Privacy Controls in Federal Information Systems
and Organizations — *Building Effective Assessment Plans*

POTENTIAL ASSESSMENT METHODS AND OBJECTS:

Examine: [*SELECT FROM:* System and services acquisition policy; procedures addressing external information system services; acquisition contracts for the information system, system component, or information system service; solicitation documentation; acquisition documentation; service-level agreements; organizational security requirements/safeguards for external service providers; personnel security policies for external service providers; assessments performed on external service providers; other relevant documents or records].

Interview: [*SELECT FROM:* Organizational personnel with system and services acquisition responsibilities; organizational personnel with information security responsibilities; external providers of information system services].

Test: [*SELECT FROM:* Organizational processes for defining and employing safeguards to ensure consistent interests with external service providers; automated mechanisms supporting and/or implementing safeguards to ensure consistent interests with external service providers].

SA-9(5)	EXTERNAL INFORMATION SYSTEM SERVICES | *PROCESSING, STORAGE, AND SERVICE LOCATION*	

ASSESSMENT OBJECTIVE:

Determine if the organization:

SA-9(5)[1]	*defines locations where organization-defined information processing, information/data, and/or information system services are to be restricted;*	
SA-9(5)[2]	*defines requirements or conditions to restrict the location of information processing, information/data, and/or information system services;*	
SA-9(5)[3]	*restricts the location of one or more of the following to organization-defined locations based on organization-defined requirements or conditions:*	
	SA-9(5)[3][a]	*information processing;*
	SA-9(5)[3][b]	*information/data; and/or*
	SA-9(5)[3][c]	*information services.*

POTENTIAL ASSESSMENT METHODS AND OBJECTS:

Examine: [*SELECT FROM:* System and services acquisition policy; procedures addressing external information system services; acquisition contracts for the information system, system component, or information system service; solicitation documentation; acquisition documentation; service-level agreements; restricted locations for information processing; information/data and/or information system services; information processing, information/data, and/or information system services to be maintained in restricted locations; organizational security requirements or conditions for external providers; other relevant documents or records].

Interview: [*SELECT FROM:* Organizational personnel with system and services acquisition responsibilities; organizational personnel with information security responsibilities; external providers of information system services].

Test: [*SELECT FROM:* Organizational processes for defining requirements to restrict locations of information processing, information/data, or information services; organizational processes for ensuring the location is restricted in accordance with requirements or conditions].

SA-10	DEVELOPER CONFIGURATION MANAGEMENT	

ASSESSMENT OBJECTIVE:

Determine if the organization:

SA-10(a)	*requires the developer of the information system, system component, or information system service to perform configuration management during one or more of the following:*	
	SA-10(a)[1]	*system, component, or service design;*

Special Publication 800-53A
Revision 4

Assessing Security and Privacy Controls in Federal Information Systems
and Organizations — *Building Effective Assessment Plans*

		SA-10(a)[2]	*system, component, or service development;*	
		SA-10(a)[3]	*system, component, or service implementation; and/or*	
		SA-10(a)[4]	*system, component, or service operation;*	
	SA-10(b)	SA-10(b)[1]	*defines configuration items to be placed under configuration management;*	
		SA-10(b)[2]	*requires the developer of the information system, system component, or information system service to:*	
			SA-10(b)[2][a]	*document the integrity of changes to organization-defined items under configuration management;*
			SA-10(b)[2][b]	*manage the integrity of changes to organization-defined items under configuration management;*
			SA-10(b)[2][c]	*control the integrity of changes to organization-defined items under configuration management;*
	SA-10(c)	*requires the developer of the information system, system component, or information system service to implement only organization-approved changes to the system, component, or service;*		
	SA-10(d)	*requires the developer of the information system, system component, or information system service to document:*		
		SA-10(d)[1]	*approved changes to the system, component, or service;*	
		SA-10(d)[2]	*the potential security impacts of such changes;*	
	SA-10(e)	SA-10(e)[1]	*defines personnel to whom findings, resulting from security flaws and flaw resolution tracked within the system, component, or service, are to be reported;*	
		SA-10(e)[2]	*requires the developer of the information system, system component, or information system service to:*	
			SA-10(e)[2][a]	*track security flaws within the system, component, or service;*
			SA-10(e)[2][b]	*track security flaw resolution within the system, component, or service; and*
			SA-10(e)[2][c]	*report findings to organization-defined personnel.*

POTENTIAL ASSESSMENT METHODS AND OBJECTS:

Examine: [*SELECT FROM:* System and services acquisition policy; procedures addressing system developer configuration management; solicitation documentation; acquisition documentation; service-level agreements; acquisition contracts for the information system, system component, or information system service; system developer configuration management plan; security flaw and flaw resolution tracking records; system change authorization records; change control records; configuration management records; other relevant documents or records].

Interview: [*SELECT FROM:* Organizational personnel with system and services acquisition responsibilities; organizational personnel with information security responsibilities; organizational personnel with configuration management responsibilities; system developers].

Test: [*SELECT FROM:* Organizational processes for monitoring developer configuration management; automated mechanisms supporting and/or implementing the monitoring of developer configuration management].

Special Publication 800-53A
Revision 4

Assessing Security and Privacy Controls in Federal Information Systems
and Organizations — *Building Effective Assessment Plans*

SA-10(1)	DEVELOPER CONFIGURATION MANAGEMENT	*SOFTWARE / FIRMWARE INTEGRITY VERIFICATION*

ASSESSMENT OBJECTIVE:

Determine if the organization requires the developer of the information system, system component, or information system service to enable integrity verification of software and firmware components.

POTENTIAL ASSESSMENT METHODS AND OBJECTS:

Examine: [*SELECT FROM:* System and services acquisition policy; procedures addressing system developer configuration management; solicitation documentation; acquisition documentation; service-level agreements; acquisition contracts for the information system; system component, or information system service; system developer configuration management plan; software and firmware integrity verification records; system change authorization records; change control records; configuration management records; other relevant documents or records].

Interview: [*SELECT FROM:* Organizational personnel with system and services acquisition responsibilities; organizational personnel with information security responsibilities; organizational personnel with configuration management responsibilities; system developers].

Test: [*SELECT FROM:* Organizational processes for monitoring developer configuration management; automated mechanisms supporting and/or implementing the monitoring of developer configuration management].

SA-10(2)	DEVELOPER CONFIGURATION MANAGEMENT	*ALTERNATIVE CONFIGURATION MANAGEMENT PROCESSES*

ASSESSMENT OBJECTIVE:

Determine if the organization provides an alternative configuration management process with organizational personnel in the absence of a dedicated developer configuration management team.

POTENTIAL ASSESSMENT METHODS AND OBJECTS:

Examine: [*SELECT FROM:* System and services acquisition policy; procedures addressing system developer configuration management; procedures addressing configuration management; solicitation documentation; acquisition documentation; service-level agreements; acquisition contracts for the information system; system component, or information system service; system developer configuration management plan; other relevant documents or records].

Interview: [*SELECT FROM:* Organizational personnel with system and services acquisition responsibilities; organizational personnel with information security responsibilities; organizational personnel with configuration management responsibilities; system developers].

Test: [*SELECT FROM:* Organizational processes for monitoring developer configuration management; automated mechanisms supporting and/or implementing the monitoring of developer configuration management].

SA-10(3)	DEVELOPER CONFIGURATION MANAGEMENT	*HARDWARE INTEGRITY VERIFICATION*

ASSESSMENT OBJECTIVE:

Determine if the organization requires the developer of the information system, system component, or information system service to enable integrity verification of hardware components.

Special Publication 800-53A
Revision 4

Assessing Security and Privacy Controls in Federal Information Systems
and Organizations — *Building Effective Assessment Plans*

<table>
<tr><td>

POTENTIAL ASSESSMENT METHODS AND OBJECTS:

Examine: [*SELECT FROM*: System and services acquisition policy; procedures addressing system developer configuration management; solicitation documentation; acquisition documentation; service-level agreements; acquisition contracts for the information system, system component, or information system service; system developer configuration management plan; hardware integrity verification records; other relevant documents or records].

Interview: [*SELECT FROM*: Organizational personnel with system and services acquisition responsibilities; organizational personnel with information security responsibilities; organizational personnel with configuration management responsibilities; system developers].

Test: [*SELECT FROM*: Organizational processes for monitoring developer configuration management; automated mechanisms supporting and/or implementing the monitoring of developer configuration management].

</td></tr>
</table>

SA-10(4)	DEVELOPER CONFIGURATION MANAGEMENT	*TRUSTED GENERATION*

ASSESSMENT OBJECTIVE:

Determine if the organization requires the developer of the information system, system component, or information system service to employ tools for comparing newly generated versions of:

SA-10(4)[1]	*security-relevant hardware descriptions with previous versions; and*
SA-10(4)[2]	*software/firmware source and object code with previous versions.*

POTENTIAL ASSESSMENT METHODS AND OBJECTS:

Examine: [*SELECT FROM*: System and services acquisition policy; procedures addressing system developer configuration management; solicitation documentation; acquisition documentation; service-level agreements; acquisition contracts for the information system, system component, or information system service; system developer configuration management plan; change control records; configuration management records; configuration control audit records; other relevant documents or records].

Interview: [*SELECT FROM*: Organizational personnel with system and services acquisition responsibilities; organizational personnel with information security responsibilities; organizational personnel with configuration management responsibilities; system developers].

Test: [*SELECT FROM*: Organizational processes for monitoring developer configuration management; automated mechanisms supporting and/or implementing the monitoring of developer configuration management].

SA-10(5)	DEVELOPER CONFIGURATION MANAGEMENT	*MAPPING INTEGRITY FOR VERSION CONTROL*

ASSESSMENT OBJECTIVE:

Determine if the organization requires the developer of the information system, system component, or information system service to maintain the integrity of the mapping between the master build data (hardware drawings and software/firmware code) describing the current version of security-relevant hardware, software, and firmware and the on-site master copy of the data for the current version.

Special Publication 800-53A
Revision 4

Assessing Security and Privacy Controls in Federal Information Systems
and Organizations — *Building Effective Assessment Plans*

POTENTIAL ASSESSMENT METHODS AND OBJECTS:

Examine: [*SELECT FROM:* System and services acquisition policy; procedures addressing system developer configuration management; solicitation documentation; acquisition documentation; service-level agreements; acquisition contracts for the information system, system component, or information system service; system developer configuration management plan; change control records; configuration management records; version control change/update records; integrity verification records between master copies of security-relevant hardware, software, and firmware (including designs and source code); other relevant documents or records].

Interview: [*SELECT FROM:* Organizational personnel with system and services acquisition responsibilities; organizational personnel with information security responsibilities; organizational personnel with configuration management responsibilities; system developers].

Test: [*SELECT FROM:* Organizational processes for monitoring developer configuration management; automated mechanisms supporting and/or implementing the monitoring of developer configuration management].

SA-10(6)	DEVELOPER CONFIGURATION MANAGEMENT | *TRUSTED DISTRIBUTION*

ASSESSMENT OBJECTIVE:

Determine if the organization requires the developer of the information system, system component, or information system service to execute procedures for ensuring that security-relevant hardware, software, and firmware updates distributed to the organization are exactly as specified by the master copies.

POTENTIAL ASSESSMENT METHODS AND OBJECTS:

Examine: [*SELECT FROM:* System and services acquisition policy; procedures addressing system developer configuration management; solicitation documentation; acquisition documentation; service-level agreements; acquisition contracts for the information system; system component, or information system service; system developer configuration management plan; change control records; configuration management records; other relevant documents or records].

Interview: [*SELECT FROM:* Organizational personnel with system and services acquisition responsibilities; organizational personnel with information security responsibilities; organizational personnel with configuration management responsibilities; system developers].

Test: [*SELECT FROM:* Organizational processes for monitoring developer configuration management; automated mechanisms supporting and/or implementing the monitoring of developer configuration management].

SA-11	DEVELOPER SECURITY TESTING AND EVALUATION	

ASSESSMENT OBJECTIVE:
Determine if the organization:

SA-11(a)		*requires the developer of the information system, system component, or information system service to create and implement a security plan;*
SA-11(b)	SA-11(b)[1]	*defines the depth of testing/evaluation to be performed by the developer of the information system, system component, or information system service;*
	SA-11(b)[2]	*defines the coverage of testing/evaluation to be performed by the developer of the information system, system component, or information system service;*
	SA-11(b)[3]	*requires the developer of the information system, system component, or information system service to perform one or more of the following testing/evaluation at the organization-defined depth and coverage:*
	SA-11(b)[3][a]	*unit testing/evaluation;*

Special Publication 800-53A
Revision 4

Assessing Security and Privacy Controls in Federal Information Systems
and Organizations — *Building Effective Assessment Plans*

		SA-11(b)[3][b]	*integration testing/evaluation;*
		SA-11(b)[3][c]	*system testing/evaluation; and/or*
		SA-11(b)[3][d]	*regression testing/evaluation;*
	SA-11(c)	*requires the developer of the information system, system component, or information system service to produce evidence of:*	
		SA-11(c)[1]	*the execution of the security assessment plan;*
		SA-11(c)[2]	*the results of the security testing/evaluation;*
	SA-11(d)	*requires the developer of the information system, system component, or information system service to implement a verifiable flaw remediation process; and*	
	SA-11(e)	*requires the developer of the information system, system component, or information system service to correct flaws identified during security testing/evaluation.*	

POTENTIAL ASSESSMENT METHODS AND OBJECTS:

Examine: [*SELECT FROM:* System and services acquisition policy; procedures addressing system developer security testing; procedures addressing flaw remediation; solicitation documentation; acquisition documentation; service-level agreements; acquisition contracts for the information system, system component, or information system service; system developer security test plans; records of developer security testing results for the information system, system component, or information system service; security flaw and remediation tracking records; other relevant documents or records].

Interview: [*SELECT FROM:* Organizational personnel with system and services acquisition responsibilities; organizational personnel with information security responsibilities; organizational personnel with developer security testing responsibilities; system developers].

Test: [*SELECT FROM:* Organizational processes for monitoring developer security testing and evaluation; automated mechanisms supporting and/or implementing the monitoring of developer security testing and evaluation].

SA-11(1)	DEVELOPER SECURITY TESTING AND EVALUATION | *STATIC CODE ANALYSIS*
	ASSESSMENT OBJECTIVE: *Determine if the organization requires the developer of the information system, system component, or information system service to employ static code analysis tools to identify common flaws and document the results of the analysis.* **POTENTIAL ASSESSMENT METHODS AND OBJECTS:** **Examine**: [*SELECT FROM:* System and services acquisition policy; procedures addressing system developer security testing; procedures addressing flaw remediation; solicitation documentation; acquisition documentation; service-level agreements; acquisition contracts for the information system, system component, or information system service; system developer security test plans; system developer security testing results; security flaw and remediation tracking records; other relevant documents or records]. **Interview**: [*SELECT FROM:* Organizational personnel with system and services acquisition responsibilities; organizational personnel with information security responsibilities; organizational personnel with developer security testing responsibilities; organizational personnel with configuration management responsibilities; system developers]. **Test**: [*SELECT FROM:* Organizational processes for monitoring developer security testing and evaluation; automated mechanisms supporting and/or implementing the monitoring of developer security testing and evaluation; static code analysis tools].

Special Publication 800-53A
Revision 4

Assessing Security and Privacy Controls in Federal Information Systems
and Organizations — *Building Effective Assessment Plans*

SA-11(2)	DEVELOPER SECURITY TESTING AND EVALUATION	*THREAT AND VULNERABILITY ANALYSES*	
	ASSESSMENT OBJECTIVE: *Determine if the organization requires the developer of the information system, system component, or information system service to perform:*		
	SA-11(2)[1]	*threat analyses of the as-built, system component, or service;*	
	SA-11(2)[2]	*vulnerability analyses of the as-built, system component, or service; and*	
	SA-11(2)[3]	*subsequent testing/evaluation of the as-built, system component, or service.*	
	POTENTIAL ASSESSMENT METHODS AND OBJECTS: **Examine**: [*SELECT FROM:* System and services acquisition policy; procedures addressing system developer security testing; solicitation documentation; acquisition documentation; service-level agreements; acquisition contracts for the information system, system component, or information system service; system developer security test plans; records of developer security testing results for the information system, system component, or information system service; vulnerability scanning results; information system risk assessment reports; threat and vulnerability analysis reports; other relevant documents or records]. **Interview**: [*SELECT FROM:* Organizational personnel with system and services acquisition responsibilities; organizational personnel with information security responsibilities; organizational personnel with developer security testing responsibilities; system developers]. **Test**: [*SELECT FROM:* Organizational processes for monitoring developer security testing and evaluation; automated mechanisms supporting and/or implementing the monitoring of developer security testing and evaluation].		

SA-11(3)	DEVELOPER SECURITY TESTING AND EVALUATION	*INDEPENDENT VERIFICATION OF ASSESSMENT PLANS / EVIDENCE*		
	ASSESSMENT OBJECTIVE: *Determine if the organization:*			
	SA-11(3)(a)	SA-11(3)(a)[1]	*defines independence criteria that an independent agent is required to satisfy;*	
		SA-11(3)(a)[2]	*requires an independent agent satisfying organization-defined independence criteria to verify:*	
			SA-11(3)(a)[2][a]	*the correct implementation of the developer security assessment plan;*
			SA-11(3)(a)[2][b]	*the evidence produced during security testing/evaluation;*
	SA-11(3)(b)	*ensures that the independent agent is either:*		
		SA-11(3)(b)[1]	*provided with sufficient information to complete the verification process; or*	
		SA-11(3)(b)[2]	*granted the authority to obtain such information.*	

Special Publication 800-53A
Revision 4

Assessing Security and Privacy Controls in Federal Information Systems
and Organizations — *Building Effective Assessment Plans*

POTENTIAL ASSESSMENT METHODS AND OBJECTS:

Examine: [*SELECT FROM:* System and services acquisition policy; procedures addressing system developer security testing; solicitation documentation; acquisition documentation; service-level agreements; acquisition contracts for the information system, system component, or information system service; independent verification and validation reports; security test and evaluation plans; security test and evaluation results for the information system, system component, or information system service; other relevant documents or records].

Interview: [*SELECT FROM:* Organizational personnel with system and services acquisition responsibilities; organizational personnel with information security responsibilities; organizational personnel with developer security testing responsibilities; system developers; independent verification agent].

Test: [*SELECT FROM:* Organizational processes for monitoring developer security testing and evaluation; automated mechanisms supporting and/or implementing the monitoring of developer security testing and evaluation].

SA-11(4)	DEVELOPER SECURITY TESTING AND EVALUATION	*MANUAL CODE REVIEWS*

ASSESSMENT OBJECTIVE:

Determine if the organization:

SA-11(4)[1]	*defines specific code for which the developer of the information system, system component, or information system service is required to perform a manual code review;*
SA-11(4)[2]	*defines processes, procedures, and/or techniques to be used when the developer performs a manual code review of organization-defined specific code; and*
SA-11(4)[3]	*requires the developer of the information system, system component, or information system service to perform a manual code review of organization-defined specific code using organization-defined processes, procedures, and/or techniques.*

POTENTIAL ASSESSMENT METHODS AND OBJECTS:

Examine: [*SELECT FROM:* System and services acquisition policy; procedures addressing system developer security testing; processes, procedures, and/or techniques for performing manual code reviews; solicitation documentation; acquisition documentation; service-level agreements; acquisition contracts for the information system, system component, or information system service; system developer security testing and evaluation plans; system developer security testing and evaluation results; list of code requiring manual reviews; records of manual code reviews; other relevant documents or records].

Interview: [*SELECT FROM:* Organizational personnel with system and services acquisition responsibilities; organizational personnel with information security responsibilities; organizational personnel with developer security testing responsibilities; system developers; independent verification agent].

Test: [*SELECT FROM:* Organizational processes for monitoring developer security testing and evaluation; automated mechanisms supporting and/or implementing the monitoring of developer security testing and evaluation].

SA-11(5)	DEVELOPER SECURITY TESTING AND EVALUATION	*PENETRATION TESTING / ANALYSIS*

ASSESSMENT OBJECTIVE:

Determine if the organization:

SA-11(5)[1]	*defines for the developer of the information system, system component, or information system service:*	
	SA-11(5)[1][a]	*the breadth of penetration testing to be performed by the developer;*

Special Publication 800-53A
Revision 4

Assessing Security and Privacy Controls in Federal Information Systems
and Organizations — *Building Effective Assessment Plans*

	SA-11(5)[1][b]	*the depth of penetration testing to be performed by the developer;*
	SA-11(5)[2]	*defines constraints under which the developer is to perform penetration testing; and*
	SA-11(5)[3]	*requires the developer of the information system, system component, or information system service to perform penetration testing at organization-defined breadth/depth and with organization-defined constraints.*

POTENTIAL ASSESSMENT METHODS AND OBJECTS:

Examine: [*SELECT FROM:* System and services acquisition policy; procedures addressing system developer security testing; solicitation documentation; acquisition documentation; service-level agreements; acquisition contracts for the information system, system component, or information system service; system developer penetration testing and evaluation plans; system developer penetration testing and evaluation results; other relevant documents or records].

Interview: [*SELECT FROM:* Organizational personnel with system and services acquisition responsibilities; organizational personnel with information security responsibilities; organizational personnel with developer security testing responsibilities; system developers; independent verification agent].

Test: [*SELECT FROM:* Organizational processes for monitoring developer security testing and evaluation; automated mechanisms supporting and/or implementing the monitoring of developer security testing and evaluation].

SA-11(6)	DEVELOPER SECURITY TESTING AND EVALUATION | *ATTACK SURFACE REVIEWS*

ASSESSMENT OBJECTIVE:

Determine if the organization requires the developer of the information system, system component, or information system service to perform attack surface reviews.

POTENTIAL ASSESSMENT METHODS AND OBJECTS:

Examine: [*SELECT FROM:* System and services acquisition policy; procedures addressing system developer security testing; solicitation documentation; acquisition documentation; service-level agreements; acquisition contracts for the information system, system component, or information system service; system developer security testing and evaluation plans; system developer security testing and evaluation results; records of attack surface reviews; other relevant documents or records].

Interview: [*SELECT FROM:* Organizational personnel with system and services acquisition responsibilities; organizational personnel with information security responsibilities; organizational personnel with developer security testing responsibilities; organizational personnel with configuration management responsibilities; system developers].

Test: [*SELECT FROM:* Organizational processes for monitoring developer security testing and evaluation; automated mechanisms supporting and/or implementing the monitoring of developer security testing and evaluation].

SA-11(7)	DEVELOPER SECURITY TESTING AND EVALUATION | *VERIFY SCOPE OF TESTING / EVALUATION*

ASSESSMENT OBJECTIVE:

Determine if the organization:

	SA-11(7)[1]	*defines the depth of testing/evaluation to ensure the scope of security/testing evaluation provides complete coverage of required security controls; and*
	SA-11(7)[2]	*requires the developer of the information system, system component, or information system service to verify that the scope of security testing/evaluation provides complete coverage of required security controls at the organization-defined depth of testing/evaluation.*

Special Publication 800-53A
Revision 4

Assessing Security and Privacy Controls in Federal Information Systems
and Organizations — *Building Effective Assessment Plans*

POTENTIAL ASSESSMENT METHODS AND OBJECTS:

Examine: [*SELECT FROM:* System and services acquisition policy; procedures addressing system developer security testing; solicitation documentation; acquisition documentation; service-level agreements; acquisition contracts for the information system, system component, or information system service; system developer security testing and evaluation plans; system developer security testing and evaluation results; other relevant documents or records].

Interview: [*SELECT FROM:* Organizational personnel with system and services acquisition responsibilities; organizational personnel with information security responsibilities; organizational personnel with developer security testing responsibilities; system developers; independent verification agent].

Test: [*SELECT FROM:* Organizational processes for monitoring developer security testing and evaluation; automated mechanisms supporting and/or implementing the monitoring of developer security testing and evaluation].

SA-11(8)	DEVELOPER SECURITY TESTING AND EVALUATION | *DYNAMIC CODE ANALYSIS*

ASSESSMENT OBJECTIVE:

Determine if the organization requires the developer of the information system, system component, or information system service to employ dynamic code analysis tools to identify common flaws and document the results of the analysis.

POTENTIAL ASSESSMENT METHODS AND OBJECTS:

Examine: [*SELECT FROM:* System and services acquisition policy; procedures addressing system developer security testing; procedures addressing flaw remediation; solicitation documentation; acquisition documentation; service-level agreements; acquisition contracts for the information system, system component, or information system service; system developer security test and evaluation plans; security test and evaluation results; security flaw and remediation tracking reports; other relevant documents or records].

Interview: [*SELECT FROM:* Organizational personnel with system and services acquisition responsibilities; organizational personnel with information security responsibilities; organizational personnel with developer security testing responsibilities; organizational personnel with configuration management responsibilities; system developers].

Test: [*SELECT FROM:* Organizational processes for monitoring developer security testing and evaluation; automated mechanisms supporting and/or implementing the monitoring of developer security testing and evaluation].

SA-12	SUPPLY CHAIN PROTECTION

ASSESSMENT OBJECTIVE:
Determine if the organization:

SA-12[1]	*defines security safeguards to be employed to protect against supply chain threats to the information system, system component, or information system service; and*
SA-12[2]	*protects against supply chain threats to the information system, system component, or information system service by employing organization-defined security safeguards as part of a comprehensive, defense-in-breadth information security strategy.*

Special Publication 800-53A
Revision 4

Assessing Security and Privacy Controls in Federal Information Systems
and Organizations — *Building Effective Assessment Plans*

	POTENTIAL ASSESSMENT METHODS AND OBJECTS:
	Examine: [*SELECT FROM:* System and services acquisition policy; procedures addressing supply chain protection; procedures addressing the integration of information security requirements into the acquisition process; solicitation documentation; acquisition documentation; service-level agreements; acquisition contracts for the information system, system component, or information system service; list of supply chain threats; list of security safeguards to be taken against supply chain threats; system development life cycle documentation; other relevant documents or records].
	Interview: [*SELECT FROM:* Organizational personnel with system and services acquisition responsibilities; organizational personnel with information security responsibilities; organizational personnel with supply chain protection responsibilities].
	Test: [*SELECT FROM:* Organizational processes for defining safeguards for and protecting against supply chain threats; automated mechanisms supporting and/or implementing safeguards for supply chain threats].

SA-12(1)	SUPPLY CHAIN PROTECTION | *ACQUISITION STRATEGIES / TOOLS / METHODS*		
	ASSESSMENT OBJECTIVE: *Determine if the organization:*		
	SA-12(1)[1]	*defines the following to be employed for the purchase of the information system, system component, or information system service from suppliers:*	
		SA-12(1)[1][a]	*tailored acquisition strategies;*
		SA-12(1)[1][b]	*contract tools;*
		SA-12(1)[1][c]	*procurement methods; and*
	SA-12(1)[2]	*employs organization-defined tailored acquisition strategies, contract tools, and procurement methods for the purchase of the information system, system component, or information system service from suppliers.*	
	POTENTIAL ASSESSMENT METHODS AND OBJECTS:		
	Examine: [*SELECT FROM:* System and services acquisition policy; procedures addressing supply chain protection; procedures addressing the integration of information security requirements into the acquisition process; procedures addressing the integration of acquisition strategies, contract tools, and procure methods into the acquisition process; solicitation documentation; acquisition documentation; service-level agreements; acquisition contracts for information systems or services; purchase orders/requisitions for the information system; system component; or information system service from suppliers; other relevant documents or records].		
	Interview: [*SELECT FROM:* Organizational personnel with system and services acquisition responsibilities; organizational personnel with information security responsibilities; organizational personnel with supply chain protection responsibilities].		
	Test: [*SELECT FROM:* Organizational processes for defining and employing tailored acquisition strategies, contract tools, and procurement methods; automated mechanisms supporting and/or implementing the definition and employment of tailored acquisition strategies, contract tools, and procurement methods].		

SA-12(2)	SUPPLY CHAIN PROTECTION | *SUPPLIER REVIEWS*
	ASSESSMENT OBJECTIVE: *Determine if the organization conducts a supplier review prior to entering into a contractual agreement to acquire the information system, system component, or information system service.*

Special Publication 800-53A
Revision 4

Assessing Security and Privacy Controls in Federal Information Systems
and Organizations — *Building Effective Assessment Plans*

POTENTIAL ASSESSMENT METHODS AND OBJECTS:

Examine: [*SELECT FROM:* System and services acquisition policy; procedures addressing supply chain protection; procedures addressing the integration of information security requirements into the acquisition process; records of supplier due diligence reviews; other relevant documents or records].

Interview: [*SELECT FROM:* Organizational personnel with system and services acquisition responsibilities; organizational personnel with information security responsibilities; organizational personnel with supply chain protection responsibilities].

Test: [*SELECT FROM:* Organizational processes for conducting supplier reviews; automated mechanisms supporting and/or implementing supplier reviews].

SA-12(3)	SUPPLY CHAIN PROTECTION | *TRUSTED SHIPPING AND WAREHOUSING*

[Withdrawn: Incorporated into SA-12(1)].

SA-12(4)	SUPPLY CHAIN PROTECTION | *DIVERSITY OF SUPPLIERS*

[Withdrawn: Incorporated into SA-12(13)].

SA-12(5)	SUPPLY CHAIN PROTECTION | *LIMITATION OF HARM*

ASSESSMENT OBJECTIVE:

Determine if the organization:

SA-12(5)[1]	*defines security safeguards to be employed to limit harm from potential adversaries identifying and targeting the organizational supply chain; and*
SA-12(5)[2]	*employs organization-defined security safeguards to limit harm from potential adversaries identifying and targeting the organizational supply chain.*

POTENTIAL ASSESSMENT METHODS AND OBJECTS:

Examine: [*SELECT FROM:* System and services acquisition policy; configuration management policy; procedures addressing supply chain protection; procedures addressing the integration of information security requirements into the acquisition process; procedures addressing the baseline configuration of the information system; configuration management plan; information system design documentation; information system architecture and associated configuration documentation; solicitation documentation; acquisition documentation; acquisition contracts for the information system, system component, or information system service; list of security safeguards to be taken to protect organizational supply chain against potential supply chain threats; other relevant documents or records].

Interview: [*SELECT FROM:* Organizational personnel with system and services acquisition responsibilities; organizational personnel with information security responsibilities; organizational personnel with supply chain protection responsibilities].

Test: [*SELECT FROM:* Organizational processes for defining and employing safeguards to limit harm from adversaries of the organizational supply chain; automated mechanisms supporting and/or implementing the definition and employment of safeguards to protect the organizational supply chain].

SA-12(6)	SUPPLY CHAIN PROTECTION | *MINIMIZING PROCUREMENT TIME*

[Withdrawn: Incorporated into SA-12(1)].

Special Publication 800-53A
Revision 4

Assessing Security and Privacy Controls in Federal Information Systems
and Organizations — *Building Effective Assessment Plans*

SA-12(7)	SUPPLY CHAIN PROTECTION | *ASSESSMENTS PRIOR TO SELECTION / ACCEPTANCE / UPDATE*
	ASSESSMENT OBJECTIVE: *Determine if the organization conducts an assessment of the information system, system component, or information system service prior to:*

	SA-12(7)[1]	*selection;*
	SA-12(7)[2]	*acceptance; or*
	SA-12(7)[3]	*update.*

POTENTIAL ASSESSMENT METHODS AND OBJECTS:

Examine: [*SELECT FROM*: System and services acquisition policy; procedures addressing supply chain protection; procedures addressing the integration of information security requirements into the acquisition process; security test and evaluation results; vulnerability assessment results; penetration testing results; organizational risk assessment results; other relevant documents or records].

Interview: [*SELECT FROM*: Organizational personnel with system and services acquisition responsibilities; organizational personnel with information security responsibilities; organizational personnel with supply chain protection responsibilities].

Test: [*SELECT FROM*: Organizational processes for conducting assessments prior to selection, acceptance, or update; automated mechanisms supporting and/or implementing the conducting of assessments prior to selection, acceptance, or update].

SA-12(8)	SUPPLY CHAIN PROTECTION | *USE OF ALL-SOURCE INTELLIGENCE*
	ASSESSMENT OBJECTIVE: *Determine if the organization uses all-source intelligence analysis of:*

	SA-12(8)[1]	*suppliers of the information system, system component, or information system service; and*
	SA-12(8)[2]	*potential suppliers of the information system, system component, or information system service.*

POTENTIAL ASSESSMENT METHODS AND OBJECTS:

Examine: [*SELECT FROM*: System and services acquisition policy; procedures addressing supply chain protection; solicitation documentation; acquisition documentation; acquisition contracts for the information system, system component, or information system service; records of all-source intelligence analyses; other relevant documents or records].

Interview: [*SELECT FROM*: Organizational personnel with system and services acquisition responsibilities; organizational personnel with information security responsibilities; organizational personnel with supply chain protection responsibilities].

Test: [*SELECT FROM*: Organizational processes for use of an all-source analysis of suppliers and potential suppliers; automated mechanisms supporting and/or implementing the use of all-source analysis of suppliers and potential suppliers].

SA-12(9)	SUPPLY CHAIN PROTECTION | *OPERATIONS SECURITY*
	ASSESSMENT OBJECTIVE: *Determine if the organization:*

	SA-12(9)[1]	*defines Operations Security (OPSEC) safeguards to be employed in accordance with classification guides to protect supply chain-related information for the information system, system component, or information system service; and*

Special Publication 800-53A
Revision 4

Assessing Security and Privacy Controls in Federal Information Systems
and Organizations — *Building Effective Assessment Plans*

	SA-12(9)[2]	*employs organization-defined OPSEC safeguards in accordance with classification guides to protect supply chain-related information for the information system, system component, or information system service.*

POTENTIAL ASSESSMENT METHODS AND OBJECTS:

Examine: [*SELECT FROM*: System and services acquisition policy; procedures addressing supply chain protection; solicitation documentation; acquisition documentation; acquisition contracts for the information system, system component, or information system service; records of all-source intelligence analyses; other relevant documents or records].

Interview: [*SELECT FROM*: Organizational personnel with system and services acquisition responsibilities; organizational personnel with information security responsibilities; organizational personnel with supply chain protection responsibilities].

Test: [*SELECT FROM*: Organizational processes for defining and employing OPSEC safeguards; automated mechanisms supporting and/or implementing the definition and employment of OPSEC safeguards].

SA-12(10)	**SUPPLY CHAIN PROTECTION** | *VALIDATE AS GENUINE AND NOT ALTERED*

ASSESSMENT OBJECTIVE:

Determine if the organization:

	SA-12(10)[1]	*defines security safeguards to be employed to validate that the information system or system component received is genuine and has not been altered; and*
	SA-12(10)[2]	*employs organization-defined security safeguards to validate that the information system or system components received is genuine and has not been altered.*

POTENTIAL ASSESSMENT METHODS AND OBJECTS:

Examine: [*SELECT FROM*: System and services acquisition policy; procedures addressing supply chain protection; procedures address the integration of information security requirements into the acquisition process; solicitation documentation; acquisition documentation; service-level agreements; acquisition contracts for the information system, system component, or information system service; evidentiary documentation (including applicable configurations) indicating the information system, system component, or information system service are genuine and have not been altered; other relevant documents or records].

Interview: [*SELECT FROM*: Organizational personnel with system and services acquisition responsibilities; organizational personnel with information security responsibilities; organizational personnel with supply chain protection responsibilities].

Test: [*SELECT FROM*: Organizational processes for defining and employing validation safeguards; automated mechanisms supporting and/or implementing the definition and employment of validation safeguards].

SA-12(11)	**SUPPLY CHAIN PROTECTION** | *PENETRATION TESTING / ANALYSIS OF ELEMENTS, PROCESSES, AND ACTORS*

ASSESSMENT OBJECTIVE:

Determine if the organization:

	SA-12(11)[1]	*defines supply chain:*	
		SA-12(11)[1][a]	*elements to be analyzed and/or tested;*
		SA-12(11)[1][b]	*processes to be analyzed and/or tested;*
		SA-12(11)[1][c]	*actors to be analyzed and/or tested;*

Special Publication 800-53A
Revision 4

Assessing Security and Privacy Controls in Federal Information Systems
and Organizations — *Building Effective Assessment Plans*

	SA-12(11)[2]	*employs one or more of the following to analyze and/or test organization-defined supply chain elements, processes, and actors associated with the information system, system component, or information system service:*
	SA-12(11)[2][a]	*organizational analysis;*
	SA-12(11)[2][b]	*independent third party analysis;*
	SA-12(11)[2][c]	*organizational penetration testing; and/or*
	SA-12(11)[2][d]	*independent third-party penetration testing.*

POTENTIAL ASSESSMENT METHODS AND OBJECTS:

Examine: [*SELECT FROM*: System and services acquisition policy; procedures addressing supply chain protection; evidence of organizational analysis, independent third-party analysis, organizational penetration testing, and/or independent third-party penetration testing; list of supply chain elements, processes, and actors (associated with the information system, system component, or information system service) subject to analysis and/or testing; other relevant documents or records].

Interview: [*SELECT FROM*: Organizational personnel with system and services acquisition responsibilities; organizational personnel with information security responsibilities; organizational personnel with supply chain protection responsibilities; organizational personnel with responsibilities for analyzing and/or testing supply chain elements, processes, and actors].

Test: [*SELECT FROM*: Organizational processes for defining and employing methods of analysis/testing of supply chain elements, processes, and actors; automated mechanisms supporting and/or implementing the analysis/testing of supply chain elements, processes, and actors].

SA-12(12)	**SUPPLY CHAIN PROTECTION**	*INTER-ORGANIZATIONAL AGREEMENTS*

ASSESSMENT OBJECTIVE:

Determine if the organization establishes, with entities involved in the supply chain for the information system, system component, or information system service,:

	SA-12(12)[1]	*inter-organizational agreements; and*
	SA-12(12)[2]	*inter-organizational procedures.*

POTENTIAL ASSESSMENT METHODS AND OBJECTS:

Examine: [*SELECT FROM*: System and services acquisition policy; procedures addressing supply chain protection; acquisition documentation; service-level agreements; acquisition contracts for the information system, system component, or information system service; inter-organizational agreements and procedures; other relevant documents or records].

Interview: [*SELECT FROM*: Organizational personnel with system and services acquisition responsibilities; organizational personnel with information security responsibilities; organizational personnel with supply chain protection responsibilities].

Test: [*SELECT FROM*: Organizational processes for establishing inter-organizational agreements and procedures with supply chain entities].

SA-12(13)	**SUPPLY CHAIN PROTECTION**	*CRITICAL INFORMATION SYSTEM COMPONENTS*

ASSESSMENT OBJECTIVE:

Determine if the organization:

	SA-12(13)[1]	*defines critical information system components for which security safeguards are to be employed to ensure an adequate supply of such components;*
	SA-12(13)[2]	*defines security safeguards to be employed to ensure an adequate supply of organization-defined critical information components; and*

Special Publication 800-53A
Revision 4

Assessing Security and Privacy Controls in Federal Information Systems
and Organizations — *Building Effective Assessment Plans*

	SA-12(13)[3]	*employs organization-defined security safeguards to ensure an adequate supply of organization-defined critical information system components.*

POTENTIAL ASSESSMENT METHODS AND OBJECTS:

Examine: [*SELECT FROM*: System and services acquisition policy; procedures addressing supply chain protection; physical inventory of critical information system components; inventory records of critical information system components; list of security safeguards ensuring adequate supply of critical information system components; other relevant documents or records].

Interview: [*SELECT FROM*: Organizational personnel with system and services acquisition responsibilities; organizational personnel with information security responsibilities; organizational personnel with supply chain protection responsibilities].

Test: [*SELECT FROM:* Organizational processes for defining and employing security safeguards to ensure an adequate supply of critical information system components; automated mechanisms supporting and/or implementing the security safeguards that ensure an adequate supply of critical information system components].

SA-12(14)	**SUPPLY CHAIN PROTECTION**	*IDENTITY AND TRACEABILITY*

ASSESSMENT OBJECTIVE:

Determine if the organization:

	SA-12(14)[1]	*defines the following for the establishment and retention of unique identification:*	
		SA-12(14)[1][a]	*supply chain elements;*
		SA-12(14)[1][b]	*supply chain processes;*
		SA-12(14)[1][c]	*supply chain actors; and*
	SA-12(14)[2]	*establishes and retains unique identification of organization-defined supply chain elements, processes, and actors for the information system, system component, or information system service.*	

POTENTIAL ASSESSMENT METHODS AND OBJECTS:

Examine: [*SELECT FROM:* System and services acquisition policy; procedures addressing supply chain protection; procedures addressing the integration of information security requirements into the acquisition process; list of supply chain elements, processes, and actors (associated with the information system, system component, or information system service) requiring implementation of unique identification processes, procedures, tools, mechanisms, equipment, techniques and/or configurations; other relevant documents or records].

Interview: [*SELECT FROM:* Organizational personnel with system and services acquisition responsibilities; organizational personnel with information security responsibilities; organizational personnel with supply chain protection responsibilities; organizational personnel with responsibilities for establishing and retaining unique identification of supply chain elements, processes, and actors].

Test: [*SELECT FROM:* Organizational processes for defining, establishing, and retaining unique identification for supply chain elements, processes, and actors; automated mechanisms supporting and/or implementing the definition, establishment, and retention of unique identification for supply chain elements, processes, and actors].

SA-12(15)	**SUPPLY CHAIN PROTECTION**	*PROCESSES TO ADDRESS WEAKNESSES OR DEFICIENCIES*

ASSESSMENT OBJECTIVE:

Determine if the organization establishes a process to address weaknesses or deficiencies in supply chain elements identified during independent or organizational assessments of such elements.

Special Publication 800-53A
Revision 4

Assessing Security and Privacy Controls in Federal Information Systems
and Organizations — *Building Effective Assessment Plans*

POTENTIAL ASSESSMENT METHODS AND OBJECTS:

Examine: [*SELECT FROM:* System and services acquisition policy; procedures addressing supply chain protection; procedures addressing weaknesses or deficiencies in supply chain elements; results of independent or organizational assessments of supply chain controls and processes; acquisition contracts, service-level agreements; other relevant documents or records].

Interview: [*SELECT FROM:* Organizational personnel with system and services acquisition responsibilities; organizational personnel with information security responsibilities; organizational personnel with supply chain protection responsibilities].

Test: [*SELECT FROM:* Organizational processes for addressing weaknesses or deficiencies in supply chain elements; automated mechanisms supporting and/or implementing the addressing of weaknesses or deficiencies in supply chain elements].

SA-13	TRUSTWORTHINESS	

ASSESSMENT OBJECTIVE:

Determine if the organization:

SA-13(a)	SA-13(a)[1]	*defines information system, system component, or information system service for which the trustworthiness required is to be described;*
	SA-13(a)[2]	*describes the trustworthiness required in organization-defined information system, information system component, or information system service supporting its critical mission/business functions;*
SA-13(b)	SA-13(b)[1]	*defines an assurance overlay to be implemented to achieve such trustworthiness; and*
	SA-13(b)[2]	*organization implements the organization-defined assurance overlay to achieve such trustworthiness.*

POTENTIAL ASSESSMENT METHODS AND OBJECTS:

Examine: [*SELECT FROM:* System and services acquisition policy; procedures addressing trustworthiness requirements for the information system, system component, or information system service; security plan; information system design documentation; information system configuration settings and associated documentation; security categorization documentation/results; security authorization package for the information system, system component, or information system service; other relevant documents or records].

Interview: [*SELECT FROM:* Organizational personnel with system and services acquisition responsibilities; organizational personnel with information security responsibilities; authorizing official].

SA-14	CRITICALITY ANALYSIS	

ASSESSMENT OBJECTIVE:

Determine if the organization:

SA-14[1]	*defines information systems, information system components, or information system services requiring a criticality analysis to identify critical information system components and functions;*
SA-14[2]	*defines decision points in the system development life cycle when a criticality analysis is to be performed for organization-defined information systems, information system components, or information system services; and*
SA-14[3]	*identifies critical information system components and functions by performing a criticality analysis for organization-defined information systems, information system components, or information system services at organization-defined decisions points in the system development life cycle.*

Special Publication 800-53A
Revision 4

Assessing Security and Privacy Controls in Federal Information Systems
and Organizations — *Building Effective Assessment Plans*

POTENTIAL ASSESSMENT METHODS AND OBJECTS:

Examine: [*SELECT FROM:* System and services acquisition policy; procedures addressing criticality analysis requirements for information systems, security plan; contingency plan; list of information systems, information system components, or information system services requiring criticality analyses; list of critical information system components and functions identified by criticality analyses; criticality analysis documentation; business impact analysis documentation; system development life cycle documentation; other relevant documents or records].

Interview: [*SELECT FROM:* Organizational personnel with system and services acquisition responsibilities; organizational personnel with information security responsibilities; organizational personnel with responsibilities for performing criticality analysis for the information system].

SA-14(1)	CRITICALITY ANALYSIS | *CRITICAL COMPONENTS WITH NO VIABLE ALTERNATIVE SOURCING*

[Withdrawn: Incorporated into SA-20].

SA-15	DEVELOPMENT PROCESS, STANDARDS, AND TOOLS		

ASSESSMENT OBJECTIVE:

Determine if the organization:

SA-15(a)	*requires the developer of the information system, system component, or information system service to follow a documented development process that:*		
	SA-15(a)(1)	*explicitly addresses security requirements;*	
	SA-15(a)(2)	*identifies the standards and tools used in the development process;*	
	SA-15(a)(3)	SA-15(a)(3)[1]	*documents the specific tool options used in the development process;*
		SA-15(a)(3)[2]	*documents the specific tool configurations used in the development process;*
	SA-15(a)(4)	SA-15(a)(4)[1]	*documents changes to the process and/or tools used in the development;*
		SA-15(a)(4)[2]	*manages changes to the process and/or tools used in the development;*
		SA-15(a)(4)[3]	*ensures the integrity of changes to the process and/or tools used in the development;*
SA-15(b)	SA-15(b)[1]	*defines a frequency to review the development process, standards, tools, and tool options/configurations;*	
	SA-15(b)[2]	*defines security requirements to be satisfied by the process, standards, tools, and tool option/configurations selected and employed; and*	
	SA-15(b)[3]	SA-15(b)[3][a]	*reviews the development process with the organization-defined frequency to determine if the process selected and employed can satisfy organization-defined security requirements;*
		SA-15(b)[3][b]	*reviews the development standards with the organization-defined frequency to determine if the standards selected and employed can satisfy organization-defined security requirements;*

Special Publication 800-53A
Revision 4

Assessing Security and Privacy Controls in Federal Information Systems
and Organizations — *Building Effective Assessment Plans*

				SA-15(b)[3][c]	*reviews the development tools with the organization-defined frequency to determine if the tools selected and employed can satisfy organization-defined security requirements; and*
				SA-15(b)[3][d]	*reviews the development tool options/configurations with the organization-defined frequency to determine if the tool options/configurations selected and employed can satisfy organization-defined security requirements.*

POTENTIAL ASSESSMENT METHODS AND OBJECTS:

Examine: [*SELECT FROM*: System and services acquisition policy; procedures addressing development process, standards, and tools; procedures addressing the integration of security requirements during the development process; solicitation documentation; acquisition documentation; service-level agreements; acquisition contracts for the information system, system component, or information system service; system developer documentation listing tool options/configuration guides, configuration management records; change control records; configuration control records; documented reviews of development process, standards, tools, and tool options/configurations; other relevant documents or records].

Interview: [*SELECT FROM*: Organizational personnel with system and services acquisition responsibilities; organizational personnel with information security responsibilities; system developer].

SA-15(1)	DEVELOPMENT PROCESS, STANDARDS, AND TOOLS	*QUALITY METRICS*		

ASSESSMENT OBJECTIVE:

Determine if the organization:

	SA-15(1)(a)	*requires the developer of the information system, system component, or information system service to define quality metrics at the beginning of the development process;*	
	SA-15(1)(b)	SA-15(1)(b)[1]	*defines a frequency to provide evidence of meeting the quality metrics;*
		SA-15(1)(b)[2]	*defines program review milestones to provide evidence of meeting the quality metrics;*
		SA-15(1)(b)[3]	*requires the developer of the information system, system component, or information system service to provide evidence of meeting the quality metrics one or more of the following:*
		SA-15(1)(b)[3][a]	*with the organization-defined frequency;*
		SA-15(1)(b)[3][b]	*in accordance with the organization-defined program review milestones; and/or*
		SA-15(1)(b)[3][c]	*upon delivery of the information system, system component, or information system service.*

POTENTIAL ASSESSMENT METHODS AND OBJECTS:

Examine: [*SELECT FROM*: System and services acquisition policy; procedures addressing development process, standards, and tools; procedures addressing the integration of security requirements into the acquisition process; solicitation documentation; acquisition documentation; service-level agreements; acquisition contracts for the information system, system component, or information system service; list of quality metrics; documentation evidence of meeting quality metrics; other relevant documents or records].

Interview: [*SELECT FROM*: Organizational personnel with system and services acquisition responsibilities; organizational personnel with information security responsibilities; system developer].

Special Publication 800-53A
Revision 4

Assessing Security and Privacy Controls in Federal Information Systems
and Organizations — *Building Effective Assessment Plans*

SA-15(2)	DEVELOPMENT PROCESS, STANDARDS, AND TOOLS | *SECURITY TRACKING TOOLS*
	ASSESSMENT OBJECTIVE: *Determine if the organization requires the developer of the information system, system component, or information system service to select and employ a security tracking tool for use during the development process.*
	POTENTIAL ASSESSMENT METHODS AND OBJECTS: **Examine:** [*SELECT FROM:* System and services acquisition policy; procedures addressing development process, standards, and tools; procedures addressing the integration of security requirements into the acquisition process; solicitation documentation; acquisition documentation; service-level agreements; acquisition contracts for the information system, system component, or information system service; list of quality metrics; documentation evidence of meeting quality metrics; other relevant documents or records]. **Interview:** [*SELECT FROM:* Organizational personnel with system and services acquisition responsibilities; organizational personnel with information security responsibilities; system developer].

SA-15(3)	DEVELOPMENT PROCESS, STANDARDS, AND TOOLS | *CRITICALITY ANALYSIS*
	ASSESSMENT OBJECTIVE: *Determine if the organization:*
SA-15(3)[1]	*defines the breadth of criticality analysis to be performed by the developer of the information system, system component, or information system service;*
SA-15(3)[2]	*defines the depth of criticality analysis to be performed by the developer of the information system, system component, or information system service;*
SA-15(3)[3]	*defines decision points in the system development life cycle when a criticality analysis is to be performed for the information system, system component, or information system service; and*
SA-15(3)[4]	*requires the developer of the information system, system component, or information system service to perform a criticality analysis at the organization-defined breadth/depth and at organization-defined decision points in the system development life cycle.*
	POTENTIAL ASSESSMENT METHODS AND OBJECTS: **Examine:** [*SELECT FROM:* System and services acquisition policy; procedures addressing development process, standards, and tools; procedures addressing criticality analysis requirements for the information system, system component, or information system service; solicitation documentation; acquisition documentation; service-level agreements; acquisition contracts for the information system, system component, or information system service; criticality analysis documentation; business impact analysis documentation; software development life cycle documentation; other relevant documents or records]. **Interview:** [*SELECT FROM:* Organizational personnel with system and services acquisition responsibilities; organizational personnel with information security responsibilities; organizational personnel responsibility for performing criticality analysis; system developer]. **Test:** [*SELECT FROM:* Organizational processes for performing criticality analysis; automated mechanisms supporting and/or implementing criticality analysis].

SA-15(4)	DEVELOPMENT PROCESS, STANDARDS, AND TOOLS | *THREAT MODELING / VULNERABILITY ANALYSIS*
	ASSESSMENT OBJECTIVE: *Determine if the organization:*
SA-15(4)[1]	*defines the breadth of threat modeling and vulnerability analysis to be performed by developers for the information system;*

Special Publication 800-53A
Revision 4

Assessing Security and Privacy Controls in Federal Information Systems
and Organizations — *Building Effective Assessment Plans*

SA-15(4)[2]	*defines the depth of threat modeling and vulnerability analysis to be performed by developers for the information system;*	
SA-15(4)[3]	*defines information concerning impact, environment of operations, known or assumed threats, and acceptable risk levels to be used in threat modeling and vulnerability analysis;*	
SA-15(4)[4]	*defines tools and methods to be employed in threat modeling and vulnerability analysis;*	
SA-15(4)[5]	*defines acceptance criteria for evidence produced from threat modeling and vulnerability analysis;*	
SA-15(4)[6]	*requires that developers perform threat modeling and a vulnerability analysis for the information system at the organization-defined breadth/depth that:*	
	SA-15(4)[6](a)	*uses organization-defined information concerning impact, environment of operations, known or assumed threats, and acceptable risk levels;*
	SA-15(4)[6](b)	*employs organization-defined tools and methods; and*
	SA-15(4)[6](c)	*produces evidence that meets organization-defined acceptance criteria.*

POTENTIAL ASSESSMENT METHODS AND OBJECTS:

Examine: [*SELECT FROM*: System and services acquisition policy; procedures addressing development process, standards, and tools; solicitation documentation; acquisition documentation; service-level agreements; acquisition contracts for the information system, system component, or information system service; threat modeling documentation; vulnerability analysis results; organizational risk assessments; acceptance criteria for evidence produced from threat modeling and vulnerability analysis; other relevant documents or records].

Interview: [*SELECT FROM*: Organizational personnel with system and services acquisition responsibilities; organizational personnel with information security responsibilities; system developer].

Test: [*SELECT FROM*: Organizational processes for performing development threat modeling and vulnerability analysis; automated mechanisms supporting and/or implementing development threat modeling and vulnerability analysis].

SA-15(5)	DEVELOPMENT PROCESS, STANDARDS, AND TOOLS | *ATTACK SURFACE REDUCTION*
	ASSESSMENT OBJECTIVE: *Determine if the organization:*

	SA-15(5)[1]	*defines thresholds to which attack surfaces are to be reduced; and*
	SA-15(5)[2]	*requires the developer of the information system, system component, or information system service to reduce attack surfaces to organization-defined thresholds.*

POTENTIAL ASSESSMENT METHODS AND OBJECTS:

Examine: [*SELECT FROM*: System and services acquisition policy; procedures addressing development process, standards, and tools; procedures addressing attack surface reduction; solicitation documentation; acquisition documentation; service-level agreements; acquisition contracts for the information system, or information system service; information system design documentation; network diagram; information system configuration settings and associated documentation establishing/enforcing organization-defined thresholds for reducing attack surfaces; list of restricted ports, protocols, functions and services; other relevant documents or records].

Interview: [*SELECT FROM*: Organizational personnel with system and services acquisition responsibilities; organizational personnel with information security responsibilities; organizational personnel responsibility for attack surface reduction thresholds; system developer].

Test: [*SELECT FROM*: Organizational processes for defining attack surface reduction thresholds].

Special Publication 800-53A
Revision 4

Assessing Security and Privacy Controls in Federal Information Systems
and Organizations — *Building Effective Assessment Plans*

SA-15(6)	DEVELOPMENT PROCESS, STANDARDS, AND TOOLS	*CONTINUOUS IMPROVEMENT*

	ASSESSMENT OBJECTIVE: *Determine if the organization requires the developer of the information system, system component, or information system service to implement an explicit process to continuously improve the development process.*
	POTENTIAL ASSESSMENT METHODS AND OBJECTS: **Examine**: [*SELECT FROM:* System and services acquisition policy; procedures addressing development process, standards, and tools; solicitation documentation; acquisition documentation; service-level agreements; acquisition contracts for the information system, system component, or information system service; quality goals and metrics for improving system development process; security assessments and/or quality control reviews of system development process; plans of action and milestones for improving system development process; other relevant documents or records]. **Interview**: [*SELECT FROM:* Organizational personnel with system and services acquisition responsibilities; organizational personnel with information security responsibilities; system developer].

SA-15(7)	DEVELOPMENT PROCESS, STANDARDS, AND TOOLS	*AUTOMATED VULNERABILITY ANALYSIS*

	ASSESSMENT OBJECTIVE: *Determine if the organization:*		
	SA-15(7)(a)	SA-15(7)(a)[1]	*defines tools to be used to perform automated vulnerability analysis of the information system, system component, or information system service;*
		SA-15(7)(a)[2]	*requires the developer of the information system, system component, or information system service to perform an automated vulnerability analysis using organization-defined tools;*
	SA-15(7)(b)	*requires the developer of the information system, system component, or information system service to determine the exploitation potential for discovered vulnerabilities;*	
	SA-15(7)(c)	*requires the developer of the information system, system component, or information system service to determine potential risk mitigations for delivered vulnerabilities;*	
	SA-15(7)(d)	SA-15(7)(d)[1]	*defines personnel or roles to whom the output of the tools and results of the analysis are to be delivered; and*
		SA-15(7)(d)[2]	*requires the developer of the information system, system component, or information system service to deliver the outputs of the tools and results of the analysis to organization-defined personnel or roles.*

Special Publication 800-53A
Revision 4

Assessing Security and Privacy Controls in Federal Information Systems
and Organizations — *Building Effective Assessment Plans*

	POTENTIAL ASSESSMENT METHODS AND OBJECTS: **Examine**: [*SELECT FROM*: System and services acquisition policy; procedures addressing development process, standards, and tools; solicitation documentation; acquisition documentation; service-level agreements; acquisition contracts for the information system, system component, or information system service; vulnerability analysis tools and associated documentation; risk assessment reports; vulnerability analysis results; vulnerability mitigation reports; risk mitigation strategy documentation; other relevant documents or records]. **Interview**: [*SELECT FROM*: Organizational personnel with system and services acquisition responsibilities; organizational personnel with information security responsibilities; system developer; organizational personnel performing automated vulnerability analysis on the information system]. **Test**: [*SELECT FROM*: Organizational processes for vulnerability analysis of information systems, system components, or information system services under development; automated mechanisms supporting and/or implementing vulnerability analysis of information systems, system components, or information system services under development].

SA-15(8)	DEVELOPMENT PROCESS, STANDARDS, AND TOOLS | *REUSE OF THREAT / VULNERABILITY INFORMATION*
	ASSESSMENT OBJECTIVE: *Determine if the organization requires the developer of the information system, system component, or information system service to use threat modeling and vulnerability analyses from similar systems, components, or services to inform the current development process.*
	POTENTIAL ASSESSMENT METHODS AND OBJECTS: **Examine**: [*SELECT FROM*: System and services acquisition policy; procedures addressing development process, standards, and tools; solicitation documentation; acquisition documentation; service-level agreements; acquisition contracts for the information system, system component, or information system service; threat modeling and vulnerability analyses from similar information systems, system components, or information system service; other relevant documents or records]. **Interview**: [*SELECT FROM*: Organizational personnel with system and services acquisition responsibilities; organizational personnel with information security responsibilities; system developer].

SA-15(9)	DEVELOPMENT PROCESS, STANDARDS, AND TOOLS | *USE OF LIVE DATA*
	ASSESSMENT OBJECTIVE: *Determine if the organization, for the information system, system component, or information system service:*
SA-15(9)[1]	*approves the use of live data in development and test environments;*
SA-15(9)[2]	*documents the use of live data in development and test environments; and*
SA-15(9)[3]	*controls the use of live data in development and test environments.*
	POTENTIAL ASSESSMENT METHODS AND OBJECTS: **Examine**: [*SELECT FROM*: System and services acquisition policy; procedures addressing development process, standards, and tools; solicitation documentation; acquisition documentation; service-level agreements; acquisition contracts for the information system, system component, or information system service; information system design documentation; information system configuration settings and associated documentation; documentation authorizing use of live data in development and test environments; other relevant documents or records]. **Interview**: [*SELECT FROM*: Organizational personnel with system and services acquisition responsibilities; organizational personnel with information security responsibilities; system developer]. **Test**: [*SELECT FROM*: Organizational processes for approving, documenting, and controlling the use of live data in development and test environments; automated mechanisms supporting and/or implementing the approval, documentation, and control of the use of live data in development and test environments].

Special Publication 800-53A
Revision 4

Assessing Security and Privacy Controls in Federal Information Systems
and Organizations — *Building Effective Assessment Plans*

SA-15(10)	DEVELOPMENT PROCESS, STANDARDS, AND TOOLS | *INCIDENT RESPONSE PLAN*
	ASSESSMENT OBJECTIVE: *Determine if the organization requires the developer of the information system, system component, or information system service to provide an incident response plan.*
	POTENTIAL ASSESSMENT METHODS AND OBJECTS: **Examine**: [*SELECT FROM*: System and services acquisition policy; procedures addressing development process, standards, and tools; solicitation documentation; acquisition documentation; service-level agreements; acquisition contracts for the information system, or services; acquisition documentation; solicitation documentation; service-level agreements; developer incident response plan; other relevant documents or records]. **Interview**: [*SELECT FROM:* Organizational personnel with system and services acquisition responsibilities; organizational personnel with information security responsibilities; system developer].

SA-15(11)	DEVELOPMENT PROCESS, STANDARDS, AND TOOLS | *ARCHIVE INFORMATION SYSTEM / COMPONENT*
	ASSESSMENT OBJECTIVE: *Determine if the organization requires the developer of the information system or system component to archive the system or component to be released or delivered together with the corresponding evidence supporting the final security review.*
	POTENTIAL ASSESSMENT METHODS AND OBJECTS: **Examine**: [*SELECT FROM*: System and services acquisition policy; procedures addressing development process, standards, and tools; solicitation documentation; acquisition documentation; service-level agreements; acquisition contracts for the information system, or services; acquisition documentation; solicitation documentation; service-level agreements; developer incident response plan; other relevant documents or records]. **Interview**: [*SELECT FROM:* Organizational personnel with system and services acquisition responsibilities; organizational personnel with information security responsibilities; system developer].

SA-16	DEVELOPER-PROVIDED TRAINING	
	ASSESSMENT OBJECTIVE: *Determine if the organization:*	
	SA-16[1]	*defines training to be provided by the developer of the information system, system component, or information system service; and*
	SA-16[2]	*requires the developer of the information system, system component, or information system service to provide organization-defined training on the correct use and operation of the implemented security functions, controls, and/or mechanisms.*
	POTENTIAL ASSESSMENT METHODS AND OBJECTS: **Examine**: [*SELECT FROM*: System and services acquisition policy; procedures addressing developer-provided training; solicitation documentation; acquisition documentation; service-level agreements; acquisition contracts for the information system, system component, or information system service; developer-provided training materials; training records; other relevant documents or records]. **Interview**: [*SELECT FROM:* Organizational personnel with system and services acquisition responsibilities; organizational personnel with information system security responsibilities; system developer; organizational or third-party developers with training responsibilities for the information system, system component, or information system service].	

Special Publication 800-53A
Revision 4

Assessing Security and Privacy Controls in Federal Information Systems
and Organizations — *Building Effective Assessment Plans*

SA-17	DEVELOPER SECURITY ARCHITECTURE AND DESIGN

ASSESSMENT OBJECTIVE:

Determine if the organization requires the developer of the information system, system component, or information system service to produce a design specification and security architecture that:

SA-17(a)	*is consistent with and supportive of the organization's security architecture which is established within and is an integrated part of the organization's enterprise architecture;*

SA-17(b)	*accurately and completely describes:*	
	SA-17(b)[1]	*the required security functionality;*
	SA-17(b)[2]	*the allocation of security controls among physical and logical components; and*

SA-17(c)	*expresses how individual security functions, mechanisms, and services work together to provide required security capabilities and a unified approach to protection.*

POTENTIAL ASSESSMENT METHODS AND OBJECTS:

Examine: [*SELECT FROM*: System and services acquisition policy; enterprise architecture policy; procedures addressing developer security architecture and design specification for the information system; solicitation documentation; acquisition documentation; service-level agreements; acquisition contracts for the information system, system component, or information system service; design specification and security architecture documentation for the system; information system design documentation; information system configuration settings and associated documentation; other relevant documents or records].

Interview: [*SELECT FROM*: Organizational personnel with system and services acquisition responsibilities; organizational personnel with information security responsibilities; system developer; organizational personnel with security architecture and design responsibilities].

SA-17(1)	DEVELOPER SECURITY ARCHITECTURE AND DESIGN	*FORMAL POLICY MODEL*

ASSESSMENT OBJECTIVE:

Determine if the organization:

SA-17(1)(a)	SA-17(1)(a)[1]	*defines elements of the organizational security policy to be enforced under a formal policy model produced by the developer as an integral part of the development process for the information system, system component, or information system service;*
	SA-17(1)(a)[2]	*requires the developer of the information system, system component, or information system service to produce, as an integral part of the development process, a formal policy model describing the organization-defined elements of organizational security policy to be enforced; and*

SA-17(1)(b)	*requires the developer of the information system, system component, or information system service to prove that the formal policy model is internally consistent and sufficient to enforce the defined elements of the organizational security policy when implemented.*

Special Publication 800-53A
Revision 4

Assessing Security and Privacy Controls in Federal Information Systems
and Organizations — *Building Effective Assessment Plans*

POTENTIAL ASSESSMENT METHODS AND OBJECTS:

Examine: [*SELECT FROM:* System and services acquisition policy; enterprise architecture policy; procedures addressing developer security architecture and design specification for the information system; solicitation documentation; acquisition documentation; service-level agreements; acquisition contracts for the information system, system component, or information system service; design specification and security architecture documentation for the system; information system design documentation; information system configuration settings and associated documentation; other relevant documents or records].

Interview: [*SELECT FROM:* Organizational personnel with system and services acquisition responsibilities; organizational personnel with information security responsibilities; system developer; organizational personnel with security architecture and design responsibilities].

SA-17(2)	DEVELOPER SECURITY ARCHITECTURE AND DESIGN | *SECURITY-RELEVANT COMPONENTS*

ASSESSMENT OBJECTIVE:

Determine if the organization requires the developer of the information system, system component, or information system service to:

SA-17(2)(a)	SA-17(2)(a)[1]	*define security-relevant hardware;*
	SA-17(2)(a)[2]	*define security-relevant software;*
	SA-17(2)(a)[3]	*define security-relevant firmware; and*
SA-17(2)(b)	*provide a rationale that the definition for security-relevant hardware, software, and firmware components is complete.*	

POTENTIAL ASSESSMENT METHODS AND OBJECTS:

Examine: [*SELECT FROM:* System and services acquisition policy; enterprise architecture policy; procedures addressing developer security architecture and design specification for the information system; solicitation documentation; acquisition documentation; service-level agreements; acquisition contracts for the information system, system component, or information system service; list of security-relevant hardware, software, and firmware components; documented rationale of completeness regarding definitions provided for security-relevant hardware, software, and firmware; other relevant documents or records].

Interview: [*SELECT FROM:* Organizational personnel with system and services acquisition responsibilities; organizational personnel with information security responsibilities; system developers; organizational personnel with security architecture and design responsibilities].

SA-17(3)	DEVELOPER SECURITY ARCHITECTURE AND DESIGN | *FORMAL CORRESPONDENCE*

ASSESSMENT OBJECTIVE:

Determine if the organization requires the developer of the information system, system component, or information system service to:

SA-17(3)(a)	*produce, as an integral part of the development process, a formal top-level specification that specifies the interfaces to security-relevant hardware, software, and firmware in terms of:*	
	SA-17(3)(a)[1]	*exceptions;*
	SA-17(3)(a)[2]	*error messages;*
	SA-17(3)(a)[3]	*effects;*
SA-17(3)(b)	*show via proof to the extent feasible with additional informal demonstration as necessary, that the formal top-level specification is consistent with the formal policy model;*	

Special Publication 800-53A
Revision 4

Assessing Security and Privacy Controls in Federal Information Systems
and Organizations — *Building Effective Assessment Plans*

	SA-17(3)(c)	*show via informal demonstration, that the formal top-level specification completely covers the interfaces to security-relevant hardware, software, and firmware;*
	SA-17(3)(d)	*show that the formal top-level specification is an accurate description of the implemented security-relevant hardware, software, and firmware; and*
	SA-17(3)(e)	*describe the security-relevant hardware, software, and firmware mechanisms not addressed in the formal top-level specification but strictly internal to the security-relevant hardware, software, and firmware.*

POTENTIAL ASSESSMENT METHODS AND OBJECTS:

Examine: [*SELECT FROM*: System and services acquisition policy; enterprise architecture policy; formal policy model; procedures addressing developer security architecture and design specification for the information system; solicitation documentation; acquisition documentation; service-level agreements; acquisition contracts for the information system, system component, or information system service; formal top-level specification documentation; information system security architecture and design documentation; information system design documentation; information system configuration settings and associated documentation; documentation describing security-relevant hardware, software and firmware mechanisms not addressed in the formal top-level specification documentation; other relevant documents or records].

Interview: [*SELECT FROM*: Organizational personnel with system and services acquisition responsibilities; organizational personnel with information security responsibilities; system developer; organizational personnel with security architecture and design responsibilities].

SA-17(4)	DEVELOPER SECURITY ARCHITECTURE AND DESIGN | *INFORMAL CORRESPONDENCE*	
	ASSESSMENT OBJECTIVE: *Determine if the organization requires the developer of the information system, system component, or information system service to:*	
	SA-17(4)(a)	*produce, as an integral part of the development process, an informal descriptive top-level specification that specifies the interfaces to security-relevant hardware, software, and firmware in terms of:*
		SA-17(4)(a)[1] *exceptions;*
		SA-17(4)(a)[2] *error messages;*
		SA-17(4)(a)[3] *effects;*
	SA-17(4)(b)	*show via informal demonstration and/or convincing argument with formal methods as feasible that the descriptive top-level specification is consistent with the formal policy model;*
	SA-17(4)(c)	*show via informal demonstration, that the descriptive top-level specification completely covers the interfaces to security-relevant hardware, software, and firmware;*
	SA-17(4)(d)	*show that the descriptive top-level specification is an accurate description of the interfaces to the security-relevant hardware, software, and firmware; and*
	SA-17(4)(e)	*describe the security-relevant hardware, software, and firmware mechanisms not addressed in the descriptive top-level specification but strictly internal to the security-relevant hardware, software, and firmware.*

Special Publication 800-53A
Revision 4

Assessing Security and Privacy Controls in Federal Information Systems
and Organizations — *Building Effective Assessment Plans*

	POTENTIAL ASSESSMENT METHODS AND OBJECTS: **Examine:** [*SELECT FROM*: System and services acquisition policy; enterprise architecture policy; formal policy model; procedures addressing developer security architecture and design specification for the information system; solicitation documentation; acquisition documentation; service-level agreements; acquisition contracts for the information system, system component, or information system service; informal descriptive top-level specification documentation; information system security architecture and design documentation; information system design documentation; information system configuration settings and associated documentation; documentation describing security-relevant hardware, software and firmware mechanisms not addressed in the informal descriptive top-level specification documentation; other relevant documents or records]. **Interview:** [*SELECT FROM:* Organizational personnel with system and services acquisition responsibilities; organizational personnel with information security responsibilities; system developer; organizational personnel with security architecture and design responsibilities].

SA-17(5)	DEVELOPER SECURITY ARCHITECTURE AND DESIGN | *CONCEPTUALLY SIMPLE DESIGN*
	ASSESSMENT OBJECTIVE: *Determine if the organization requires the developer of the information system, system component, or information system service to:*

	SA-17(5)(a)	*design and structure the security-relevant hardware, software, and firmware to use a complete, conceptually simple protection mechanism with precisely defined semantics; and*
	SA-17(5)(b)	*internally structure the security-relevant hardware, software, and firmware with specific regard for this mechanism.*

	POTENTIAL ASSESSMENT METHODS AND OBJECTS: **Examine:** [*SELECT FROM*: System and services acquisition policy; enterprise architecture policy; procedures addressing developer security architecture and design specification for the information system; solicitation documentation; acquisition documentation; service-level agreements; acquisition contracts for the information system, system component, or information system service; information system design documentation; information system security architecture documentation; information system configuration settings and associated documentation; developer documentation describing design and structure of security-relevant hardware, software, and firmware components; other relevant documents or records]. **Interview:** [*SELECT FROM:* Organizational personnel with system and services acquisition responsibilities; organizational personnel with information security responsibilities; system developer; organizational personnel with security architecture and design responsibilities].

SA-17(6)	DEVELOPER SECURITY ARCHITECTURE AND DESIGN | *STRUCTURE FOR TESTING*
	ASSESSMENT OBJECTIVE: *Determine if the organization requires the developer of the information system, system component, or information system service to structure security-relevant hardware, software, and firmware to facilitate testing.*

Special Publication 800-53A
Revision 4

Assessing Security and Privacy Controls in Federal Information Systems
and Organizations — *Building Effective Assessment Plans*

POTENTIAL ASSESSMENT METHODS AND OBJECTS:

Examine: [*SELECT FROM*: System and services acquisition policy; enterprise architecture policy; procedures addressing developer security architecture and design specification for the information system; solicitation documentation; acquisition documentation; service-level agreements; acquisition contracts for the information system, system component, or information system service; information system design documentation; information system security architecture documentation; information system configuration settings and associated documentation; developer documentation describing design and structure of security-relevant hardware, software, and firmware components to facilitate testing; other relevant documents or records].

Interview: [*SELECT FROM:* Organizational personnel with system and services acquisition responsibilities; organizational personnel with information security responsibilities; system developer; organizational personnel with security architecture and design responsibilities].

SA-17(7)	DEVELOPER SECURITY ARCHITECTURE AND DESIGN	*STRUCTURE FOR LEAST PRIVILEGE*

ASSESSMENT OBJECTIVE:

Determine if the organization requires the developer of the information system, system component, or information system service to structure security-relevant hardware, software, and firmware to facilitate controlling access with least privilege.

POTENTIAL ASSESSMENT METHODS AND OBJECTS:

Examine: [*SELECT FROM*: System and services acquisition policy; enterprise architecture policy; procedures addressing developer security architecture and design specification for the information system; solicitation documentation; acquisition documentation; service-level agreements; acquisition contracts for the information system, system component, or information system service; information system design documentation; information system security architecture documentation; information system configuration settings and associated documentation; developer documentation describing design and structure of security-relevant hardware, software, and firmware components to facilitate controlling access with least privilege; other relevant documents or records].

Interview: [*SELECT FROM:* Organizational personnel with system and services acquisition responsibilities; organizational personnel with information security responsibilities; system developer; organizational personnel with security architecture and design responsibilities].

SA-18	TAMPER RESISTANCE AND DETECTION

ASSESSMENT OBJECTIVE:

Determine if the organization implements a tamper protection program for the information system, system component, or information system service.

POTENTIAL ASSESSMENT METHODS AND OBJECTS:

Examine: [*SELECT FROM*: System and services acquisition policy; procedures addressing tamper resistance and detection; tamper protection program documentation; tamper protection tools and techniques documentation; tamper resistance and detection tools and techniques documentation; other relevant documents or records].

Interview: [*SELECT FROM:* Organizational personnel with system and services acquisition responsibilities; organizational personnel with information security responsibilities; organizational personnel with responsibility for the tamper protection program].

Test: [*SELECT FROM:* Organizational processes for implementation of the tamper protection program; automated mechanisms supporting and/or implementing the tamper protection program].

SA-18(1)	TAMPER RESISTANCE AND DETECTION	*MULTIPLE PHASES OF SDLC*

ASSESSMENT OBJECTIVE:

Determine if the organization employs anti-tamper technologies and techniques during multiple phases in the system development life cycle including:

Special Publication 800-53A
Revision 4

Assessing Security and Privacy Controls in Federal Information Systems
and Organizations — *Building Effective Assessment Plans*

SA-18(1)[1]	*design;*
SA-18(1)[2]	*development;*
SA-18(1)[3]	*integration;*
SA-18(1)[4]	*operations; and*
SA-18(1)[5]	*maintenance.*

POTENTIAL ASSESSMENT METHODS AND OBJECTS:

Examine: [*SELECT FROM*: System and services acquisition policy; procedures addressing tamper resistance and detection; tamper protection program documentation; tamper protection tools and techniques documentation; tamper resistance and detection tools (technologies) and techniques documentation; system development life cycle documentation; other relevant documents or records].

Interview: [*SELECT FROM*: Organizational personnel with system and services acquisition responsibilities; organizational personnel with information security responsibilities; organizational personnel with responsibility for the tamper protection program; organizational personnel with SDLC responsibilities].

Test: [*SELECT FROM*: Organizational processes for employing anti-tamper technologies; automated mechanisms supporting and/or implementing anti-tamper technologies].

SA-18(2)	**TAMPER RESISTANCE AND DETECTION** | *INSPECTION OF INFORMATION SYSTEMS, COMPONENTS, OR DEVICES*

ASSESSMENT OBJECTIVE:

Determine if the organization:

SA-18(2)[1]	*defines information systems, system components, or devices to be inspected to detect tampering;*	
SA-18(2)[2]	*defines the frequency to inspect organization-defined information systems, system components, or devices to detect tampering;*	
SA-18(2)[3]	*defines indications of need for inspection of organization-defined information systems, system components, or devices to detect tampering;*	
SA-18(2)[4]	*inspects organization-defined information systems, system components, or devices to detect tampering, selecting one or more of the following:*	
	SA-18(2)[4][a]	*at random;*
	SA-18(2)[4][b]	*with the organization-defined frequency; and/or*
	SA-18(2)[4][c]	*upon organization-defined indications of need for inspection.*

POTENTIAL ASSESSMENT METHODS AND OBJECTS:

Examine: [*SELECT FROM*: System and services acquisition policy; procedures addressing tamper resistance and detection; records of random inspections; inspection reports/results; assessment reports/results; other relevant documents or records].

Interview: [*SELECT FROM*: Organizational personnel with system and services acquisition responsibilities; organizational personnel with information security responsibilities; organizational personnel with responsibility for the tamper protection program].

Test: [*SELECT FROM*: Organizational processes for inspecting information systems, system components, or devices to detect tampering; automated mechanisms supporting and/or implementing tampering detection].

Special Publication 800-53A
Revision 4

Assessing Security and Privacy Controls in Federal Information Systems
and Organizations — *Building Effective Assessment Plans*

SA-19	COMPONENT AUTHENTICITY

ASSESSMENT OBJECTIVE:

Determine if the organization:

SA-19(a)		*develops and implements anti-counterfeit policy and procedures that include the means to detect and prevent counterfeit components from entering the information system;*
SA-19(b)	SA-19(b)[1]	*defines external reporting organizations to whom counterfeit information system components are to be reported;*
	SA-19(b)[2]	*defines personnel or roles to whom counterfeit information system components are to be reported;*
	SA-19(b)[3]	*reports counterfeit information system components to one or more of the following:*

		SA-19(b)[3][a]	*the source of counterfeit component;*
		SA-19(b)[3][b]	*the organization-defined external reporting organizations; and/or*
		SA-19(b)[3][c]	*the organization-defined personnel or roles.*

POTENTIAL ASSESSMENT METHODS AND OBJECTS:

Examine: [*SELECT FROM*: System and services acquisition policy; anti-counterfeit policy and procedures; media disposal policy; media protection policy; incident response policy; training materials addressing counterfeit information system components; training records on detection and prevention of counterfeit components from entering the information system; reports notifying developers/manufacturers/vendors/ contractors and/or external reporting organizations of counterfeit information system components; other relevant documents or records].

Interview: [*SELECT FROM*: Organizational personnel with system and services acquisition responsibilities; organizational personnel with information security responsibilities; organizational personnel with responsibility for anti-counterfeit policy, procedures, and reporting].

Test: [*SELECT FROM*: Organizational processes for anti-counterfeit detection, prevention, and reporting; automated mechanisms supporting and/or implementing anti-counterfeit detection, prevention, and reporting].

SA-19(1)	COMPONENT AUTHENTICITY | *ANTI-COUNTERFEIT TRAINING*

ASSESSMENT OBJECTIVE:

Determine if the organization:

SA-19(1)[1]	*defines personnel or roles to be trained to detect counterfeit information system components (including hardware, software, and firmware); and*
SA-19(1)[2]	*trains organization-defined personnel or roles to detect counterfeit information system components (including hardware, software, and firmware).*

POTENTIAL ASSESSMENT METHODS AND OBJECTS:

Examine: [*SELECT FROM*: System and services acquisition policy; anti-counterfeit policy and procedures; media disposal policy; media protection policy; incident response policy; training materials addressing counterfeit information system components; training records on detection of counterfeit information system components; other relevant documents or records].

Interview: [*SELECT FROM*: Organizational personnel with system and services acquisition responsibilities; organizational personnel with information security responsibilities; organizational personnel with responsibility for anti-counterfeit policy, procedures, and training].

Test: [*SELECT FROM*: Organizational processes for anti-counterfeit training].

Special Publication 800-53A
Revision 4

Assessing Security and Privacy Controls in Federal Information Systems
and Organizations — *Building Effective Assessment Plans*

SA-19(2)	COMPONENT AUTHENTICITY	*CONFIGURATION CONTROL FOR COMPONENT SERVICE / REPAIR*
	ASSESSMENT OBJECTIVE: *Determine if the organization:*	
	SA-19(2)[1]	*defines information system components requiring configuration control to be maintained when awaiting service/repair;*
	SA-19(2)[2]	*defines information system components requiring configuration control to be maintained when awaiting return to service; and*
	SA-19(2)[3]	*maintains configuration control over organization-defined information system components awaiting service/repairs and serviced/repaired components awaiting return to service.*
	POTENTIAL ASSESSMENT METHODS AND OBJECTS: **Examine**: [*SELECT FROM*: System and services acquisition policy; anti-counterfeit policy and procedures; media protection policy; configuration management plan; information system design documentation; information system configuration settings and associated documentation; configuration control records for components awaiting service/repair; configuration control records for serviced/repaired components awaiting return to service; information system maintenance records; information system audit records; inventory management records; other relevant documents or records]. **Interview**: [*SELECT FROM*: Organizational personnel with system and services acquisition responsibilities; organizational personnel with information security responsibilities; organizational personnel with responsibility for anti-counterfeit policy and procedures; organizational personnel with responsibility for configuration management]. **Test**: [*SELECT FROM*: Organizational processes for configuration management; automated mechanisms supporting and/or implementing configuration management].	

SA-19(3)	COMPONENT AUTHENTICITY	*COMPONENT DISPOSAL*
	ASSESSMENT OBJECTIVE: *Determine if the organization:*	
	SA-19(3)[1]	*defines techniques and methods to dispose of information system components; and*
	SA-19(3)[2]	*disposes of information system components using organization-defined techniques and methods.*
	POTENTIAL ASSESSMENT METHODS AND OBJECTS: **Examine**: [*SELECT FROM*: System and services acquisition policy; anti-counterfeit policy and procedures; media disposal policy; media protection policy; disposal records for information system components; documentation of disposal techniques and methods employed for information system components; other relevant documents or records]. **Interview**: [*SELECT FROM*: Organizational personnel with system and services acquisition responsibilities; organizational personnel with information security responsibilities; organizational personnel with responsibility for anti-counterfeit policy and procedures; organizational personnel with responsibility for disposal of information system components]. **Test**: [*SELECT FROM*: Organizational techniques and methods for information system component disposal; automated mechanisms supporting and/or implementing system component disposal].	

SA-19(4)	COMPONENT AUTHENTICITY	*ANTI-COUNTERFEIT SCANNING*
	ASSESSMENT OBJECTIVE: *Determine if the organization:*	

Special Publication 800-53A
Revision 4

Assessing Security and Privacy Controls in Federal Information Systems
and Organizations — *Building Effective Assessment Plans*

SA-19(4)[1]	*defines a frequency to scan for counterfeit information system components; and*
SA-19(4)[2]	*scans for counterfeit information system components with the organization-defined frequency.*

POTENTIAL ASSESSMENT METHODS AND OBJECTS:

Examine: [*SELECT FROM*: System and services acquisition policy; anti-counterfeit policy and procedures; information system design documentation; information system configuration settings and associated documentation; scanning tools and associated documentation; scanning results; other relevant documents or records].

Interview: [*SELECT FROM*: Organizational personnel with system and services acquisition responsibilities; organizational personnel with information security responsibilities; organizational personnel with responsibility for anti-counterfeit policy and procedures; organizational personnel with responsibility for anti-counterfeit scanning].

Test: [*SELECT FROM*: Organizational processes for anti-counterfeit scanning; automated mechanisms supporting and/or implementing anti-counterfeit scanning].

SA-20	**CUSTOMIZED DEVELOPMENT OF CRITICAL COMPONENTS**

ASSESSMENT OBJECTIVE:

Determine if the organization:

SA-20[1]	*defines critical information system components to be re-implemented or custom developed; and*
SA-20[2]	*re-implements or custom develops organization-defined information system components.*

POTENTIAL ASSESSMENT METHODS AND OBJECTS:

Examine: [*SELECT FROM*: System and services acquisition policy; procedures addressing customized development of critical information system components; information system design documentation; information system configuration settings and associated documentation; system development life cycle documentation addressing custom development of critical information system components; configuration management records; information system audit records; other relevant documents or records].

Interview: [*SELECT FROM*: Organizational personnel with system and services acquisition responsibilities; organizational personnel with information security responsibilities; organizational personnel with responsibility re-implementation or customized development of critical information system components].

Test: [*SELECT FROM*: Organizational processes for re-implementing or customized development of critical information system components; automated mechanisms supporting and/or implementing re-implementation or customized development of critical information system components].

SA-21	**DEVELOPER SCREENING**

ASSESSMENT OBJECTIVE:

Determine if the organization:

SA-21[1]	*defines the information system, system component, or information system service for which the developer is to be screened;*
SA-21[2]	*defines official government duties to be used to determine appropriate access authorizations for the developer;*
SA-21[3]	*defines additional personnel screening criteria to be satisfied by the developer;*

Special Publication 800-53A
Revision 4

Assessing Security and Privacy Controls in Federal Information Systems
and Organizations — *Building Effective Assessment Plans*

	SA-21[4]	SA-21[4][a]	*requires that the developer of organization-defined information system, system component, or information system service have appropriate access authorizations as determined by assigned organization-defined official government duties; and*
		SA-21[4][b]	*requires that the developer of organization-defined information system, system component, or information system service satisfy organization-defined additional personnel screening criteria.*

POTENTIAL ASSESSMENT METHODS AND OBJECTS:

Examine: [*SELECT FROM*: System and services acquisition policy; personnel security policy and procedures; procedures addressing personnel screening; information system design documentation; information system configuration settings and associated documentation; list of appropriate access authorizations required by developers of the information system; personnel screening criteria and associated documentation; other relevant documents or records].

Interview: [*SELECT FROM*: Organizational personnel with system and services acquisition responsibilities; organizational personnel with information security responsibilities; organizational personnel with responsibility for developer screening].

Test: [*SELECT FROM:* Organizational processes for developer screening; automated mechanisms supporting developer screening].

SA-21(1)	DEVELOPER SCREENING	*VALIDATION OF SCREENING*

ASSESSMENT OBJECTIVE:

Determine if the organization:

	SA-21(1)[1]	*defines actions to be taken by the developer of the information system, system component, or information system service to ensure that the required access authorizations and screening criteria are satisfied; and*
	SA-21(1)[2]	*requires the developer of the information system, system component, or information system service take organization-defined actions to ensure that the required access authorizations and screening criteria are satisfied.*

POTENTIAL ASSESSMENT METHODS AND OBJECTS:

Examine: [*SELECT FROM*: System and services acquisition policy; personnel security policy and procedures; procedures addressing personnel screening; information system design documentation; information system configuration settings and associated documentation; list of appropriate access authorizations required by developers of the information system; personnel screening criteria and associated documentation; list of actions ensuring required access authorizations and screening criteria are satisfied; other relevant documents or records].

Interview: [*SELECT FROM*: Organizational personnel with system and services acquisition responsibilities; organizational personnel with information security responsibilities; organizational personnel with responsibility for developer screening; system developer].

Test: [*SELECT FROM*: Organizational processes for developer screening; automated mechanisms supporting developer screening].

SA-22	UNSUPPORTED SYSTEM COMPONENTS	

ASSESSMENT OBJECTIVE:

Determine if the organization:

	SA-22(a)		*replaces information system components when support for the components is no longer available from the developer, vendor, or manufacturer;*
	SA-22(b)	SA-22(b)[1]	*provides justification for the continued use of unsupported system components required to satisfy mission/business needs; and*

Special Publication 800-53A
Revision 4

Assessing Security and Privacy Controls in Federal Information Systems
and Organizations — *Building Effective Assessment Plans*

		SA-22(b)[2]	*documents approval for the continued use of unsupported system components required to satisfy mission/business needs.*

POTENTIAL ASSESSMENT METHODS AND OBJECTS:

Examine: [*SELECT FROM:* System and services acquisition policy; procedures addressing replacement or continued use of unsupported information system components; documented evidence of replacing unsupported information system components; documented approvals (including justification) for continued use of unsupported information system components; other relevant documents or records].

Interview: [*SELECT FROM:* Organizational personnel with system and services acquisition responsibilities; organizational personnel with information security responsibilities; organizational personnel with responsibility system development life cycle; organizational personnel responsible for configuration management].

Test: [*SELECT FROM:* Organizational processes for replacing unsupported system components; automated mechanisms supporting and/or implementing replacement of unsupported system components].

SA-22(1)	UNSUPPORTED SYSTEM COMPONENTS	*ALTERNATIVE SOURCES FOR CONTINUED SUPPORT*

ASSESSMENT OBJECTIVE:
Determine if the organization:

SA-22(1)[1]	*defines support from external providers to be provided for unsupported information system components;*

SA-22(1)[2]	*provides and/or obtains support for unsupported information system components from one or more of the following:*

	SA-22(1)[2][a]	*in-house support; and/or*
	SA-22(1)[2][b]	*organization-defined support from external providers.*

POTENTIAL ASSESSMENT METHODS AND OBJECTS:

Examine: [*SELECT FROM:* System and services acquisition policy; procedures addressing support for unsupported information system components; solicitation documentation; acquisition documentation; acquisition contracts; service-level agreements; other relevant documents or records].

Interview: [*SELECT FROM:* Organizational personnel with system and services acquisition responsibilities; organizational personnel with information security responsibilities; organizational personnel with responsibility system development life cycle; organizational personnel or third-party external providers supporting information system components no longer supported by original developers, vendors, or manufacturers].

Test: [*SELECT FROM:* Organizational processes for supporting system components no longer supported by original developers, vendors, or manufacturers; automated mechanisms providing support for system components no longer supported by original developers, vendors, or manufacturers].

Special Publication 800-53A
Revision 4

Assessing Security and Privacy Controls in Federal Information Systems
and Organizations — *Building Effective Assessment Plans*

FAMILY: SYSTEM AND COMMUNICATIONS PROTECTION

SC-1	SYSTEM AND COMMUNICATIONS PROTECTION POLICY AND PROCEDURES		
	ASSESSMENT OBJECTIVE: *Determine if the organization:*		
	SC-1(a)(1)	SC-1(a)(1)[1]	*develops and documents a system and communications protection policy that addresses:*
			SC-1(a)(1)[1][a]	*purpose;*
			SC-1(a)(1)[1][b]	*scope;*
			SC-1(a)(1)[1][c]	*roles;*
			SC-1(a)(1)[1][d]	*responsibilities;*
			SC-1(a)(1)[1][e]	*management commitment;*
			SC-1(a)(1)[1][f]	*coordination among organizational entities;*
			SC-1(a)(1)[1][g]	*compliance;*
		SC-1(a)(1)[2]	*defines personnel or roles to whom the system and communications protection policy is to be disseminated;*
		SC-1(a)(1)[3]	*disseminates the system and communications protection policy to organization-defined personnel or roles;*
	SC-1(a)(2)	SC-1(a)(2)[1]	*develops and documents procedures to facilitate the implementation of the system and communications protection policy and associated system and communications protection controls;*
		SC-1(a)(2)[2]	*defines personnel or roles to whom the procedures are to be disseminated;*
		SC-1(a)(2)[3]	*disseminates the procedures to organization-defined personnel or roles;*
	SC-1(b)(1)	SC-1(b)(1)[1]	*defines the frequency to review and update the current system and communications protection policy;*
		SC-1(b)(1)[2]	*reviews and updates the current system and communications protection policy with the organization-defined frequency;*
	SC-1(b)(2)	SC-1(b)(2)[1]	*defines the frequency to review and update the current system and communications protection procedures; and*
		SC-1(b)(2)[2]	*reviews and updates the current system and communications protection procedures with the organization-defined frequency.*
	POTENTIAL ASSESSMENT METHODS AND OBJECTS: **Examine:** [*SELECT FROM:* System and communications protection policy and procedures; other relevant documents or records]. **Interview:** [*SELECT FROM:* Organizational personnel with system and communications protection responsibilities; organizational personnel with information security responsibilities].		

Special Publication 800-53A
Revision 4

Assessing Security and Privacy Controls in Federal Information Systems
and Organizations — *Building Effective Assessment Plans*

SC-2	APPLICATION PARTITIONING
	ASSESSMENT OBJECTIVE: *Determine if the information system separates user functionality (including user interface services) from information system management functionality.*
	POTENTIAL ASSESSMENT METHODS AND OBJECTS: **Examine**: [*SELECT FROM:* System and communications protection policy; procedures addressing application partitioning; information system design documentation; information system configuration settings and associated documentation; information system audit records; other relevant documents or records]. **Interview**: [*SELECT FROM:* System/network administrators; organizational personnel with information security responsibilities; system developer]. **Test**: [*SELECT FROM:* Separation of user functionality from information system management functionality].

SC-2(1)	APPLICATION PARTITIONING | *INTERFACES FOR NON-PRIVILEGED USERS*
	ASSESSMENT OBJECTIVE: *Determine if the information system prevents the presentation of information system management-related functionality at an interface for non-privileged users.*
	POTENTIAL ASSESSMENT METHODS AND OBJECTS: **Examine**: [*SELECT FROM:* System and communications protection policy; procedures addressing application partitioning; information system design documentation; information system configuration settings and associated documentation; information system audit records; other relevant documents or records]. **Interview**: [*SELECT FROM:* System/network administrators; organizational personnel with information security responsibilities; non-privileged users of the information system; system developer]. **Test**: [*SELECT FROM:* Separation of user functionality from information system management functionality].

SC-3	SECURITY FUNCTION ISOLATION
	ASSESSMENT OBJECTIVE: *Determine if the information system isolates security functions from nonsecurity functions.*
	POTENTIAL ASSESSMENT METHODS AND OBJECTS: **Examine**: [*SELECT FROM:* System and communications protection policy; procedures addressing security function isolation; list of security functions to be isolated from nonsecurity functions; information system design documentation; information system configuration settings and associated documentation; information system audit records; other relevant documents or records]. **Interview**: [*SELECT FROM:* System/network administrators; organizational personnel with information security responsibilities; system developer]. **Test**: [*SELECT FROM:* Separation of security functions from nonsecurity functions within the information system].

SC-3(1)	SECURITY FUNCTION ISOLATION | *HARDWARE SEPARATION*
	ASSESSMENT OBJECTIVE: *Determine if the information system utilizes underlying hardware separation mechanisms to implement security function isolation.*

Special Publication 800-53A
Revision 4

Assessing Security and Privacy Controls in Federal Information Systems
and Organizations — *Building Effective Assessment Plans*

	POTENTIAL ASSESSMENT METHODS AND OBJECTS: **Examine**: [*SELECT FROM:* System and communications protection policy; procedures addressing security function isolation; information system design documentation; hardware separation mechanisms; information system configuration settings and associated documentation; information system audit records; other relevant documents or records]. **Interview**: [*SELECT FROM:* System/network administrators; organizational personnel with information security responsibilities; system developer]. **Test**: [*SELECT FROM:* Separation of security functions from nonsecurity functions within the information system].

SC-3(2)	SECURITY FUNCTION ISOLATION | *ACCESS/FLOW CONTROL FUNCTIONS*
	ASSESSMENT OBJECTIVE: *Determine if the information system isolates security functions enforcing:*
SC-3(2)[1]	*access control from nonsecurity functions;*
SC-3(2)[2]	*information flow control from nonsecurity functions;*
SC-3(2)[3]	*access control from other security functions; and*
SC-3(2)[4]	*information flow control from other security functions.*
	POTENTIAL ASSESSMENT METHODS AND OBJECTS: **Examine**: [*SELECT FROM:* System and communications protection policy; procedures addressing security function isolation; list of critical security functions; information system design documentation; information system configuration settings and associated documentation; information system audit records; other relevant documents or records]. **Interview**: [*SELECT FROM:* System/network administrators; organizational personnel with information security responsibilities; system developer]. **Test**: [*SELECT FROM:* Isolation of security functions enforcing access and information flow control].

SC-3(3)	SECURITY FUNCTION ISOLATION | *MINIMIZE NONSECURITY FUNCTIONALITY*
	ASSESSMENT OBJECTIVE: *Determine if the organization implements an information system isolation boundary to minimize the number of nonsecurity functions included within the boundary containing security functions.*
	POTENTIAL ASSESSMENT METHODS AND OBJECTS: **Examine**: [*SELECT FROM:* System and communications protection policy; procedures addressing security function isolation; information system design documentation; information system configuration settings and associated documentation; information system audit records; other relevant documents or records]. **Interview**: [*SELECT FROM:* System/network administrators; organizational personnel with information security responsibilities]. **Test**: [*SELECT FROM:* Automated mechanisms supporting and/or implementing an isolation boundary].

SC-3(4)	SECURITY FUNCTION ISOLATION | *MODULE COUPLING AND COHESIVENESS*
	ASSESSMENT OBJECTIVE: *Determine if the organization implements security functions as largely independent modules that:*
SC-3(4)[1]	*maximize internal cohesiveness within modules; and*
SC-3(4)[2]	*minimize coupling between modules.*

Special Publication 800-53A
Revision 4

Assessing Security and Privacy Controls in Federal Information Systems
and Organizations — *Building Effective Assessment Plans*

POTENTIAL ASSESSMENT METHODS AND OBJECTS:

Examine: [*SELECT FROM:* System and communications protection policy; procedures addressing security function isolation; information system design documentation; information system configuration settings and associated documentation; information system audit records; other relevant documents or records].

Interview: [*SELECT FROM:* System/network administrators; organizational personnel with information security responsibilities].

Test: [*SELECT FROM:* Organizational processes for maximizing internal cohesiveness within modules and minimizing coupling between modules; automated mechanisms supporting and/or implementing security functions as independent modules].

SC-3(5)	SECURITY FUNCTION ISOLATION | *LAYERED STRUCTURES*

ASSESSMENT OBJECTIVE:

Determine if the organization implements security functions as a layered structure:

SC-3(5)[1]	*minimizing interactions between layers of the design; and*
SC-3(5)[2]	*avoiding any dependence by lower layers on the functionality or correctness of higher layers.*

POTENTIAL ASSESSMENT METHODS AND OBJECTS:

Examine: [*SELECT FROM:* System and communications protection policy; procedures addressing security function isolation; information system design documentation; information system configuration settings and associated documentation; information system audit records; other relevant documents or records].

Interview: [*SELECT FROM:* System/network administrators; organizational personnel with information security responsibilities].

Test: [*SELECT FROM:* Organizational processes for implementing security functions as a layered structure that minimizes interactions between layers and avoids dependence by lower layers on functionality/correctness of higher layers; automated mechanisms supporting and/or implementing security functions as a layered structure].

SC-4	INFORMATION IN SHARED RESOURCES

ASSESSMENT OBJECTIVE:

Determine if the information system prevents unauthorized and unintended information transfer via shared system resources.

POTENTIAL ASSESSMENT METHODS AND OBJECTS:

Examine: [*SELECT FROM:* System and communications protection policy; procedures addressing information protection in shared system resources; information system design documentation; information system configuration settings and associated documentation; information system audit records; other relevant documents or records].

Interview: [*SELECT FROM:* System/network administrators; organizational personnel with information security responsibilities; system developer].

Test: [*SELECT FROM:* Automated mechanisms preventing unauthorized and unintended transfer of information via shared system resources].

SC-4(1)	INFORMATION IN SHARED RESOURCES | *SECURITY LEVELS*

[Withdrawn: Incorporated into SC-4].

SC-4(2)	INFORMATION IN SHARED RESOURCES | *PERIODS PROCESSING*

ASSESSMENT OBJECTIVE:

Determine if:

Special Publication 800-53A
Revision 4

Assessing Security and Privacy Controls in Federal Information Systems
and Organizations — *Building Effective Assessment Plans*

	SC-4(2)[1]	*the organization defines procedures to be employed to ensure unauthorized information transfer via shared resources is prevented when system processing explicitly switches between different information classification levels or security categories; and*
	SC-4(2)[2]	*the information system prevents unauthorized information transfer via shared resources in accordance with organization-defined procedures when system processing explicitly switches between different information classification levels or security categories.*

POTENTIAL ASSESSMENT METHODS AND OBJECTS:

Examine: [*SELECT FROM:* System and communications protection policy; procedures addressing information protection in shared system resources; information system design documentation; information system configuration settings and associated documentation; information system audit records; other relevant documents or records].

Interview: [*SELECT FROM:* System/network administrators; organizational personnel with information security responsibilities; system developer].

Test: [*SELECT FROM:* Automated mechanisms preventing unauthorized transfer of information via shared system resources].

SC-5	**DENIAL OF SERVICE PROTECTION**	
	ASSESSMENT OBJECTIVE: *Determine if:*	
	SC-5[1]	*the organization defines types of denial of service attacks or reference to source of such information for the information system to protect against or limit the effects;*
	SC-5[2]	*the organization defines security safeguards to be employed by the information system to protect against or limit the effects of organization-defined types of denial of service attacks; and*
	SC-5[3]	*the information system protects against or limits the effects of the organization-defined denial or service attacks (or reference to source for such information) by employing organization-defined security safeguards.*

POTENTIAL ASSESSMENT METHODS AND OBJECTS:

Examine: [*SELECT FROM:* System and communications protection policy; procedures addressing denial of service protection; information system design documentation; security plan; list of denial of services attacks requiring employment of security safeguards to protect against or limit effects of such attacks; list of security safeguards protecting against or limiting the effects of denial of service attacks; information system configuration settings and associated documentation; information system audit records; other relevant documents or records].

Interview: [*SELECT FROM:* System/network administrators; organizational personnel with information security responsibilities; organizational personnel with incident response responsibilities; system developer].

Test: [*SELECT FROM:* Automated mechanisms protecting against or limiting the effects of denial of service attacks].

SC-5(1)	**DENIAL OF SERVICE PROTECTION** | *RESTRICT INTERNAL USERS*	
	ASSESSMENT OBJECTIVE: *Determine if:*	
	SC-5(1)[1]	*the organization defines denial of service attacks for which the information system is required to restrict the ability of individuals to launch such attacks against other information systems; and*

Special Publication 800-53A
Revision 4

Assessing Security and Privacy Controls in Federal Information Systems
and Organizations — *Building Effective Assessment Plans*

SC-5(1)[2]	*the information system restricts the ability of individuals to launch organization-defined denial of service attacks against other information systems.*

POTENTIAL ASSESSMENT METHODS AND OBJECTS:

Examine: [*SELECT FROM*: System and communications protection policy; procedures addressing denial of service protection; information system design documentation; security plan; list of denial of service attacks launched by individuals against information systems; information system configuration settings and associated documentation; information system audit records; other relevant documents or records].

Interview: [*SELECT FROM*: System/network administrators; organizational personnel with information security responsibilities; organizational personnel with incident response responsibilities; system developer].

Test: [*SELECT FROM*: Automated mechanisms restricting the ability to launch denial of service attacks against other information systems].

SC-5(2)	DENIAL OF SERVICE PROTECTION	*EXCESS CAPACITY / BANDWIDTH / REDUNDANCY*

ASSESSMENT OBJECTIVE:

Determine if the information system, to limit the effects of information flooding denial of service attacks, manages:

SC-5(2)[1]	*excess capacity;*
SC-5(2)[2]	*bandwidth; or*
SC-5(2)[3]	*other redundancy.*

POTENTIAL ASSESSMENT METHODS AND OBJECTS:

Examine: [*SELECT FROM*: System and communications protection policy; procedures addressing denial of service protection; information system design documentation; information system configuration settings and associated documentation; information system audit records; other relevant documents or records].

Interview: [*SELECT FROM*: System/network administrators; organizational personnel with information security responsibilities; organizational personnel with incident response responsibilities; system developer].

Test: [*SELECT FROM*: Automated mechanisms implementing management of information system bandwidth, capacity, and redundancy to limit the effects of information flooding denial of service attacks].

SC-5(3)	DENIAL OF SERVICE PROTECTION	*DETECTION / MONITORING*

ASSESSMENT OBJECTIVE:

Determine if the organization:

SC-5(3)(a)	SC-5(3)(a)[1]	*defines monitoring tools to be employed to detect indicators of denial of service attacks against the information system;*
	SC-5(3)(a)[2]	*employs organization-defined monitoring tools to detect indicators of denial of service attacks against the information system;*
SC-5(3)(b)	SC-5(3)(b)[1]	*defines information system resources to be monitored to determine if sufficient resources exist to prevent effective denial of service attacks; and*
	SC-5(3)(b)[2]	*monitors organization-defined information system resources to determine if sufficient resources exist to prevent effective denial of service attacks.*

Special Publication 800-53A
Revision 4

Assessing Security and Privacy Controls in Federal Information Systems
and Organizations — *Building Effective Assessment Plans*

	POTENTIAL ASSESSMENT METHODS AND OBJECTS: **Examine**: [*SELECT FROM:* System and communications protection policy; procedures addressing denial of service protection; information system design documentation; information system monitoring tools and techniques documentation; information system configuration settings and associated documentation; information system audit records; other relevant documents or records]. **Interview**: [*SELECT FROM:* System/network administrators; organizational personnel with information security responsibilities; organizational personnel with detection and monitoring responsibilities]. **Test**: [*SELECT FROM:* Automated mechanisms/tools implementing information system monitoring for denial of service attacks].

SC-6	**RESOURCE AVAILABILITY**		
	ASSESSMENT OBJECTIVE: *Determine if:*		
	SC-6[1]	*the organization defines resources to be allocated to protect the availability of resources;*	
	SC-6[2]	*the organization defines security safeguards to be employed to protect the availability of resources;*	
	SC-6[3]	*the information system protects the availability of resources by allocating organization-defined resources by one or more of the following:*	
		SC-6[3][a]	*priority;*
		SC-6[3][b]	*quota; and/or*
		SC-6[3][c]	*organization-defined safeguards.*
	POTENTIAL ASSESSMENT METHODS AND OBJECTS: **Examine**: [*SELECT FROM:* System and communications protection policy; procedures addressing prioritization of information system resources; information system design documentation; information system configuration settings and associated documentation; information system audit records; other relevant documents or records]. **Interview**: [*SELECT FROM:* System/network administrators; organizational personnel with information security responsibilities; system developer]. **Test**: [*SELECT FROM:* Automated mechanisms supporting and/or implementing resource allocation capability; safeguards employed to protect availability of resources].		

SC-7	**BOUNDARY PROTECTION**		
	ASSESSMENT OBJECTIVE: *Determine if the information system:*		
	SC-7(a)	**SC-7(a)[1]**	*monitors communications at the external boundary of the information system;*
		SC-7(a)[2]	*monitors communications at key internal boundaries within the system;*
		SC-7(a)[3]	*controls communications at the external boundary of the information system;*
		SC-7(a)[4]	*controls communications at key internal boundaries within the system;*
	SC-7(b)	*implements subnetworks for publicly accessible system components that are either:*	

Special Publication 800-53A
Revision 4

Assessing Security and Privacy Controls in Federal Information Systems
and Organizations — *Building Effective Assessment Plans*

	SC-7(b)[1]	*physically separated from internal organizational networks; and/or*
	SC-7(b)[2]	*logically separated from internal organizational networks; and*
SC-7(c)	*connects to external networks or information systems only through managed interfaces consisting of boundary protection devices arranged in accordance with an organizational security architecture.*	

POTENTIAL ASSESSMENT METHODS AND OBJECTS:

Examine: [*SELECT FROM:* System and communications protection policy; procedures addressing boundary protection; list of key internal boundaries of the information system; information system design documentation; boundary protection hardware and software; information system configuration settings and associated documentation; enterprise security architecture documentation; information system audit records; other relevant documents or records].

Interview: [*SELECT FROM:* System/network administrators; organizational personnel with information security responsibilities; system developer; organizational personnel with boundary protection responsibilities].

Test: [*SELECT FROM:* Automated mechanisms implementing boundary protection capability].

SC-7(1)	**BOUNDARY PROTECTION** | *PHYSICALLY SEPARATED SUBNETWORKS*
[Withdrawn: Incorporated into SC-7].	

SC-7(2)	**BOUNDARY PROTECTION** | *PUBLIC ACCESS*
[Withdrawn: Incorporated into SC-7].	

SC-7(3)	**BOUNDARY PROTECTION** | *ACCESS POINTS*

ASSESSMENT OBJECTIVE:

Determine if the organization limits the number of external network connections to the information system.

POTENTIAL ASSESSMENT METHODS AND OBJECTS:

Examine: [*SELECT FROM:* System and communications protection policy; procedures addressing boundary protection; information system design documentation; boundary protection hardware and software; information system architecture and configuration documentation; information system configuration settings and associated documentation; communications and network traffic monitoring logs; information system audit records; other relevant documents or records].

Interview: [*SELECT FROM:* System/network administrators; organizational personnel with information security responsibilities; organizational personnel with boundary protection responsibilities].

Test: [*SELECT FROM:* Automated mechanisms implementing boundary protection capability; automated mechanisms limiting the number of external network connections to the information system].

SC-7(4)	**BOUNDARY PROTECTION** | *EXTERNAL TELECOMMUNICATIONS SERVICES*	
ASSESSMENT OBJECTIVE:		
Determine if the organization:		
	SC-7(4)(a)	*implements a managed interface for each external telecommunication service;*
	SC-7(4)(b)	*establishes a traffic flow policy for each managed interface;*
	SC-7(4)(c)	*protects the confidentiality and integrity of the information being transmitted across each interface;*
	SC-7(4)(d)	*documents each exception to the traffic flow policy with:*

Special Publication 800-53A
Revision 4

Assessing Security and Privacy Controls in Federal Information Systems
and Organizations — *Building Effective Assessment Plans*

		SC-7(4)(d)[1]	*a supporting mission/business need;*
		SC-7(4)(d)[2]	*duration of that need;*
	SC-7(4)(e)	SC-7(4)(e)[1]	*defines a frequency to review exceptions to traffic flow policy;*
		SC-7(4)(e)[2]	*reviews exceptions to the traffic flow policy with the organization-defined frequency; and*
		SC-7(4)(e)[3]	*removes traffic flow policy exceptions that are no longer supported by an explicit mission/business need*

POTENTIAL ASSESSMENT METHODS AND OBJECTS:

Examine: [*SELECT FROM:* System and communications protection policy; traffic flow policy; information flow control policy; procedures addressing boundary protection; information system security architecture; information system design documentation; boundary protection hardware and software; information system architecture and configuration documentation; information system configuration settings and associated documentation; records of traffic flow policy exceptions; information system audit records; other relevant documents or records].

Interview: [*SELECT FROM:* System/network administrators; organizational personnel with information security responsibilities; organizational personnel with boundary protection responsibilities].

Test: [*SELECT FROM:* Organizational processes for documenting and reviewing exceptions to the traffic flow policy; organizational processes for removing exceptions to the traffic flow policy; automated mechanisms implementing boundary protection capability; managed interfaces implementing traffic flow policy].

SC-7(5)	BOUNDARY PROTECTION | *DENY BY DEFAULT / ALLOW BY EXCEPTION*

ASSESSMENT OBJECTIVE:

Determine if the information system, at managed interfaces:

SC-7(5)[1]	*denies network traffic by default; and*
SC-7(5)[2]	*allows network traffic by exception.*

POTENTIAL ASSESSMENT METHODS AND OBJECTS:

Examine: [*SELECT FROM:* System and communications protection policy; procedures addressing boundary protection; information system design documentation; information system configuration settings and associated documentation; information system audit records; other relevant documents or records].

Interview: [*SELECT FROM:* System/network administrators; organizational personnel with information security responsibilities; system developer; organizational personnel with boundary protection responsibilities].

Test: [*SELECT FROM:* Automated mechanisms implementing traffic management at managed interfaces].

SC-7(6)	BOUNDARY PROTECTION | *RESPONSE TO RECOGNIZED FAILURES*

[Withdrawn: Incorporated into SC-7(18)].

SC-7(7)	BOUNDARY PROTECTION | *PREVENT SPLIT TUNNELING FOR REMOTE DEVICES*

ASSESSMENT OBJECTIVE:

Determine if the information system, in conjunction with a remote device, prevents the device from simultaneously establishing non-remote connections with the system and communicating via some other connection to resources in external networks.

Special Publication 800-53A
Revision 4

Assessing Security and Privacy Controls in Federal Information Systems
and Organizations — *Building Effective Assessment Plans*

	POTENTIAL ASSESSMENT METHODS AND OBJECTS: **Examine**: [*SELECT FROM:* System and communications protection policy; procedures addressing boundary protection; information system design documentation; information system hardware and software; information system architecture; information system configuration settings and associated documentation; information system audit records; other relevant documents or records]. **Interview**: [*SELECT FROM:* System/network administrators; organizational personnel with information security responsibilities; system developer; organizational personnel with boundary protection responsibilities]. **Test**: [*SELECT FROM:* Automated mechanisms implementing boundary protection capability; automated mechanisms supporting/restricting non-remote connections].

SC-7(8)	**BOUNDARY PROTECTION** | *ROUTE TRAFFIC TO AUTHENTICATED PROXY SERVERS*
	ASSESSMENT OBJECTIVE: *Determine if:*
	SC-7(8)[1] *the organization defines internal communications traffic to be routed to external networks;*
	SC-7(8)[2] *the organization defines external networks to which organization-defined internal communications traffic is to be routed; and*
	SC-7(8)[3] *the information system routes organization-defined internal communications traffic to organization-defined external networks through authenticated proxy servers at managed interfaces.*
	POTENTIAL ASSESSMENT METHODS AND OBJECTS: **Examine**: [*SELECT FROM:* System and communications protection policy; procedures addressing boundary protection; information system design documentation; information system hardware and software; information system architecture; information system configuration settings and associated documentation; information system audit records; other relevant documents or records]. **Interview**: [*SELECT FROM:* System/network administrators; organizational personnel with information security responsibilities; system developer; organizational personnel with boundary protection responsibilities]. **Test**: [*SELECT FROM:* Automated mechanisms implementing traffic management through authenticated proxy servers at managed interfaces].

SC-7(9)	**BOUNDARY PROTECTION** | *RESTRICT THREATENING OUTGOING COMMUNICATIONS TRAFFIC*	
	ASSESSMENT OBJECTIVE: *Determine if the information system:*	
SC-7(9)(a)	**SC-7(9)(a)[1]**	*detects outgoing communications traffic posing a threat to external information systems; and*
	SC-7(9)(a)[2]	*denies outgoing communications traffic posing a threat to external information systems; and*
SC-7(9)(b)	*audits the identity of internal users associated with denied communications.*	

Special Publication 800-53A
Revision 4

Assessing Security and Privacy Controls in Federal Information Systems
and Organizations — *Building Effective Assessment Plans*

POTENTIAL ASSESSMENT METHODS AND OBJECTS:

Examine: [*SELECT FROM:* System and communications protection policy; procedures addressing boundary protection; information system design documentation; information system hardware and software; information system architecture; information system configuration settings and associated documentation; information system audit records; other relevant documents or records].

Interview: [*SELECT FROM:* System/network administrators; organizational personnel with information security responsibilities; system developer; organizational personnel with boundary protection responsibilities].

Test: [*SELECT FROM:* Automated mechanisms implementing boundary protection capability; automated mechanisms implementing detection and denial of threatening outgoing communications traffic; automated mechanisms implementing auditing of outgoing communications traffic].

SC-7(10)	BOUNDARY PROTECTION | *PREVENT UNAUTHORIZED EXFILTRATION*

ASSESSMENT OBJECTIVE:

Determine if the organization prevents the unauthorized exfiltration of information across managed interfaces.

POTENTIAL ASSESSMENT METHODS AND OBJECTS:

Examine: [*SELECT FROM:* System and communications protection policy; procedures addressing boundary protection; information system design documentation; information system configuration settings and associated documentation; information system audit records; other relevant documents or records].

Interview: [*SELECT FROM:* System/network administrators; organizational personnel with information security responsibilities; organizational personnel with boundary protection responsibilities].

Test: [*SELECT FROM:* Automated mechanisms implementing boundary protection capability; preventing unauthorized exfiltration of information across managed interfaces].

SC-7(11)	BOUNDARY PROTECTION | *RESTRICT INCOMING COMMUNICATIONS TRAFFIC*

ASSESSMENT OBJECTIVE:
Determine if:

SC-7(11)[1]	*the organization defines internal communications traffic to be routed to external networks;*
SC-7(11)[2]	*the organization defines authorized destinations only to which that incoming communications from organization-defined authorized sources may be routed; and*
SC-7(11)[3]	*the information system only allows incoming communications from organization-defined authorized sources to be routed to organization-defined authorized destinations.*

POTENTIAL ASSESSMENT METHODS AND OBJECTS:

Examine: [*SELECT FROM:* System and communications protection policy; procedures addressing boundary protection; information system design documentation; information system configuration settings and associated documentation; information system audit records; other relevant documents or records].

Interview: [*SELECT FROM:* System/network administrators; organizational personnel with information security responsibilities; system developer; organizational personnel with boundary protection responsibilities].

Test: [*SELECT FROM:* Automated mechanisms implementing boundary protection capabilities with respect to source/destination address pairs].

Special Publication 800-53A
Revision 4

Assessing Security and Privacy Controls in Federal Information Systems
and Organizations — *Building Effective Assessment Plans*

SC-7(12)	BOUNDARY PROTECTION | *HOST-BASED PROTECTION*
	ASSESSMENT OBJECTIVE: *Determine if the organization:*

	SC-7(12)[1]	*defines host-based boundary protection mechanisms;*
	SC-7(12)[2]	*defines information system components where organization-defined host-based boundary protection mechanisms are to be implemented; and*
	SC-7(12)[3]	*implements organization-defined host-based boundary protection mechanisms at organization-defined information system components.*

POTENTIAL ASSESSMENT METHODS AND OBJECTS:

Examine: [*SELECT FROM:* System and communications protection policy; procedures addressing boundary protection; information system design documentation; boundary protection hardware and software; information system configuration settings and associated documentation; information system audit records; other relevant documents or records].

Interview: [*SELECT FROM:* System/network administrators; organizational personnel with information security responsibilities; organizational personnel with boundary protection responsibilities; information system users].

Test: [*SELECT FROM:* Automated mechanisms implementing host-based boundary protection capabilities].

SC-7(13)	BOUNDARY PROTECTION | *ISOLATION OF SECURITY TOOLS / MECHANISMS / SUPPORT COMPONENTS*
	ASSESSMENT OBJECTIVE: *Determine if the organization:*

	SC-7(13)[1]	*defines information security tools, mechanisms, and support components to be isolated from other internal information system components; and*
	SC-7(13)[2]	*isolates organization-defined information security tools, mechanisms, and support components from other internal information system components by implementing physically separate subnetworks with managed interfaces to other components of the system.*

POTENTIAL ASSESSMENT METHODS AND OBJECTS:

Examine: [*SELECT FROM:* System and communications protection policy; procedures addressing boundary protection; information system design documentation; information system hardware and software; information system architecture; information system configuration settings and associated documentation; list of security tools and support components to be isolated from other internal information system components; information system audit records; other relevant documents or records].

Interview: [*SELECT FROM:* System/network administrators; organizational personnel with information security responsibilities; organizational personnel with boundary protection responsibilities].

Test: [*SELECT FROM:* Automated mechanisms supporting and/or implementing isolation of information security tools, mechanisms, and support components].

SC-7(14)	BOUNDARY PROTECTION | *PROTECTS AGAINST UNAUTHORIZED PHYSICAL CONNECTIONS*
	ASSESSMENT OBJECTIVE: *Determine if the organization:*

	SC-7(14)[1]	*defines managed interfaces to be protected against unauthorized physical connections; and*
	SC-7(14)[2]	*protects against unauthorized physical connections at organization-defined managed interfaces.*

Special Publication 800-53A
Revision 4

Assessing Security and Privacy Controls in Federal Information Systems
and Organizations — *Building Effective Assessment Plans*

	POTENTIAL ASSESSMENT METHODS AND OBJECTS: **Examine**: [*SELECT FROM:* System and communications protection policy; procedures addressing boundary protection; information system design documentation; information system hardware and software; information system architecture; information system configuration settings and associated documentation; facility communications and wiring diagram; other relevant documents or records]. **Interview**: [*SELECT FROM:* System/network administrators; organizational personnel with information security responsibilities; organizational personnel with boundary protection responsibilities]. **Test**: [*SELECT FROM:* Automated mechanisms supporting and/or implementing protection against unauthorized physical connections].

SC-7(15)	**BOUNDARY PROTECTION** | *ROUTE PRIVILEGED NETWORK ACCESSES*
	ASSESSMENT OBJECTIVE: *Determine if the information system routes all networked, privileged accesses through a dedicated, managed interface for the purposes of:*

SC-7(15)[1]	*access control; and*
SC-7(15)[2]	*auditing.*

	POTENTIAL ASSESSMENT METHODS AND OBJECTS: **Examine**: [*SELECT FROM:* System and communications protection policy; procedures addressing boundary protection; information system design documentation; information system hardware and software; information system architecture; information system configuration settings and associated documentation; audit logs; other relevant documents or records]. **Interview**: [*SELECT FROM:* System/network administrators; organizational personnel with information security responsibilities; system developer; organizational personnel with boundary protection responsibilities]. **Test**: [*SELECT FROM:* Automated mechanisms supporting and/or implementing the routing of networked, privileged access through dedicated managed interfaces].

SC-7(16)	**BOUNDARY PROTECTION** | *PREVENT DISCOVERY OF COMPONENTS / DEVICES*
	ASSESSMENT OBJECTIVE: *Determine if the information system prevents discovery of specific system components composing a managed interface.*
	POTENTIAL ASSESSMENT METHODS AND OBJECTS: **Examine**: [*SELECT FROM:* System and communications protection policy; procedures addressing boundary protection; information system design documentation; information system hardware and software; information system architecture; information system configuration settings and associated documentation; information system audit records; other relevant documents or records]. **Interview**: [*SELECT FROM:* System/network administrators; organizational personnel with information security responsibilities; system developer; organizational personnel with boundary protection responsibilities]. **Test**: [*SELECT FROM:* Automated mechanisms supporting and/or implementing the prevention of discovery of system components at managed interfaces].

SC-7(17)	**BOUNDARY PROTECTION** | *AUTOMATED ENFORCEMENT OF PROTOCOL FORMATS*
	ASSESSMENT OBJECTIVE: *Determine if the information system enforces adherence to protocol formats.*

Special Publication 800-53A
Revision 4

Assessing Security and Privacy Controls in Federal Information Systems
and Organizations — *Building Effective Assessment Plans*

POTENTIAL ASSESSMENT METHODS AND OBJECTS:

Examine: [*SELECT FROM:* System and communications protection policy; procedures addressing boundary protection; information system design documentation; information system architecture; information system configuration settings and associated documentation; information system audit records; other relevant documents or records].

Interview: [*SELECT FROM:* System/network administrators; organizational personnel with information security responsibilities; system developer; organizational personnel with boundary protection responsibilities].

Test: [*SELECT FROM:* Automated mechanisms supporting and/or implementing enforcement of adherence to protocol formats].

SC-7(18)	BOUNDARY PROTECTION | *FAIL SECURE*

ASSESSMENT OBJECTIVE:

Determine if the information system fails securely in the event of an operational failure of a boundary protection device.

POTENTIAL ASSESSMENT METHODS AND OBJECTS:

Examine: [*SELECT FROM:* System and communications protection policy; procedures addressing boundary protection; information system design documentation; information system architecture; information system configuration settings and associated documentation; information system audit records; other relevant documents or records].

Interview: [*SELECT FROM:* System/network administrators; organizational personnel with information security responsibilities; system developer; organizational personnel with boundary protection responsibilities].

Test: [*SELECT FROM:* Automated mechanisms supporting and/or implementing secure failure].

SC-7(19)	BOUNDARY PROTECTION | *BLOCKS COMMUNICATION FROM NON-ORGANIZATIONALLY CONFIGURED HOSTS*

ASSESSMENT OBJECTIVE:

Determine if the organization:

SC-7(19)[1]	*defines communication clients that are independently configured by end users and external service providers; and*

SC-7(19)[2]	*blocks, between organization-defined communication clients that are independently configured by end users and external service providers,:*

	SC-7(19)[2][a]	*inbound communications traffic; and*
	SC-7(19)[2][b]	*outbound communications traffic.*

POTENTIAL ASSESSMENT METHODS AND OBJECTS:

Examine: [*SELECT FROM:* System and communications protection policy; procedures addressing boundary protection; information system design documentation; information system hardware and software; information system architecture; information system configuration settings and associated documentation; list of communication clients independently configured by end users and external service providers; information system audit records; other relevant documents or records].

Interview: [*SELECT FROM:* System/network administrators; organizational personnel with information security responsibilities; organizational personnel with boundary protection responsibilities].

Test: [*SELECT FROM:* Automated mechanisms supporting and/or implementing the blocking of inbound and outbound communications traffic between communication clients independently configured by end users and external service providers].

Special Publication 800-53A
Revision 4

Assessing Security and Privacy Controls in Federal Information Systems
and Organizations — *Building Effective Assessment Plans*

SC-7(20)	BOUNDARY PROTECTION | *DYNAMIC ISOLATION / SEGREGATION*
	ASSESSMENT OBJECTIVE: *Determine if:*
	SC-7(20)[1] — *the organization defines information system components to be dynamically isolated/segregated from other components of the system; and*
	SC-7(20)[2] — *the information system provides the capability to dynamically isolate/segregate organization-defined information system components from other components of the system.*
	POTENTIAL ASSESSMENT METHODS AND OBJECTS: **Examine**: [*SELECT FROM:* System and communications protection policy; procedures addressing boundary protection; information system design documentation; information system hardware and software; information system architecture; information system configuration settings and associated documentation; list of information system components to be dynamically isolated/segregated from other components of the system; information system audit records; other relevant documents or records]. **Interview**: [*SELECT FROM:* System/network administrators; organizational personnel with information security responsibilities; system developer; organizational personnel with boundary protection responsibilities]. **Test**: [*SELECT FROM:* Automated mechanisms supporting and/or implementing the capability to dynamically isolate/segregate information system components].

SC-7(21)	BOUNDARY PROTECTION | *ISOLATION OF INFORMATION SYSTEM COMPONENTS*
	ASSESSMENT OBJECTIVE: *Determine if the organization:*
	SC-7(21)[1] — *defines information system components to be separated by boundary protection mechanisms;*
	SC-7(21)[2] — *defines missions and/or business functions to be supported by organization-defined information system components separated by boundary protection mechanisms; and*
	SC-7(21)[3] — *employs boundary protection mechanisms to separate organization-defined information system components supporting organization-defined missions and/or business functions.*
	POTENTIAL ASSESSMENT METHODS AND OBJECTS: **Examine**: [*SELECT FROM:* System and communications protection policy; procedures addressing boundary protection; information system design documentation; information system hardware and software; enterprise architecture documentation; information system architecture; information system configuration settings and associated documentation; information system audit records; other relevant documents or records]. **Interview**: [*SELECT FROM:* System/network administrators; organizational personnel with information security responsibilities; organizational personnel with boundary protection responsibilities]. **Test**: [*SELECT FROM:* Automated mechanisms supporting and/or implementing the capability to separate information system components supporting organizational missions and/or business functions].

SC-7(22)	BOUNDARY PROTECTION | *SEPARATE SUBNETS FOR CONNECTING TO DIFFERENT SECURITY DOMAINS*
	ASSESSMENT OBJECTIVE: *Determine if the information system implements separate network addresses (i.e., different subnets) to connect to systems in different security domains.*

Special Publication 800-53A
Revision 4

Assessing Security and Privacy Controls in Federal Information Systems
and Organizations — *Building Effective Assessment Plans*

POTENTIAL ASSESSMENT METHODS AND OBJECTS:

Examine: [*SELECT FROM*: System and communications protection policy; procedures addressing boundary protection; information system design documentation; information system hardware and software; information system architecture; information system configuration settings and associated documentation; information system audit records; other relevant documents or records].

Interview: [*SELECT FROM*: System/network administrators; organizational personnel with information security responsibilities; system developer; organizational personnel with boundary protection responsibilities].

Test: [*SELECT FROM*: Automated mechanisms supporting and/or implementing separate network addresses/different subnets].

SC-7(23)	BOUNDARY PROTECTION | *DISABLE SENDER FEEDBACK ON PROTOCOL VALIDATION FAILURE*

ASSESSMENT OBJECTIVE:

Determine if the information system disables feedback to senders on protocol format validation failure.

POTENTIAL ASSESSMENT METHODS AND OBJECTS:

Examine: [*SELECT FROM*: System and communications protection policy; procedures addressing boundary protection; information system design documentation; information system hardware and software; information system architecture; information system configuration settings and associated documentation; information system audit records; other relevant documents or records].

Interview: [*SELECT FROM*: System/network administrators; organizational personnel with information security responsibilities; system developer; organizational personnel with boundary protection responsibilities].

Test: [*SELECT FROM*: Automated mechanisms supporting and/or implementing the disabling of feedback to senders on protocol format validation failure].

SC-8	TRANSMISSION CONFIDENTIALITY AND INTEGRITY

ASSESSMENT OBJECTIVE:

Determine if the information system protects one or more of the following:

SC-8[1]	*confidentiality of transmitted information; and/or*
SC-8[2]	*integrity of transmitted information.*

POTENTIAL ASSESSMENT METHODS AND OBJECTS:

Examine: [*SELECT FROM*: System and communications protection policy; procedures addressing transmission confidentiality and integrity; information system design documentation; information system configuration settings and associated documentation; information system audit records; other relevant documents or records].

Interview: [*SELECT FROM*: System/network administrators; organizational personnel with information security responsibilities; system developer].

Test: [*SELECT FROM*: Automated mechanisms supporting and/or implementing transmission confidentiality and/or integrity].

SC-8(1)	TRANSMISSION CONFIDENTIALITY AND INTEGRITY | *CRYPTOGRAPHIC OR ALTERNATE PHYSICAL PROTECTION*

ASSESSMENT OBJECTIVE:

Determine if:

SC-8(1)[1]	*the organization defines physical safeguards to be implemented to protect information during transmission when cryptographic mechanisms are not implemented; and*

Special Publication 800-53A
Revision 4

Assessing Security and Privacy Controls in Federal Information Systems
and Organizations — *Building Effective Assessment Plans*

	SC-8(1)[2]	*the information system implements cryptographic mechanisms to do one or more of the following during transmission unless otherwise protected by organization-defined alternative physical safeguards:*
	SC-8(1)[2][a]	*prevent unauthorized disclosure of information; and/or*
	SC-8(1)[2][b]	*detect changes to information.*

POTENTIAL ASSESSMENT METHODS AND OBJECTS:

Examine: [*SELECT FROM:* System and communications protection policy; procedures addressing transmission confidentiality and integrity; information system design documentation; information system configuration settings and associated documentation; information system audit records; other relevant documents or records].

Interview: [*SELECT FROM:* System/network administrators; organizational personnel with information security responsibilities; system developer].

Test: [*SELECT FROM:* Cryptographic mechanisms supporting and/or implementing transmission confidentiality and/or integrity; automated mechanisms supporting and/or implementing alternative physical safeguards; organizational processes for defining and implementing alternative physical safeguards].

SC-8(2)	**TRANSMISSION CONFIDENTIALITY AND INTEGRITY	*PRE / POST TRANSMISSION HANDLING***

ASSESSMENT OBJECTIVE:

Determine if the information system maintains one or more of the following:

SC-8(2)[1]	*confidentiality of information during preparation for transmission;*
SC-8(2)[2]	*confidentiality of information during reception; and/or*
SC-8(2)[3]	*integrity of information during preparation for transmission;*
SC-8(2)[4]	*integrity of information during reception.*

POTENTIAL ASSESSMENT METHODS AND OBJECTS:

Examine: [*SELECT FROM:* System and communications protection policy; procedures addressing transmission confidentiality and integrity; information system design documentation; information system configuration settings and associated documentation; information system audit records; other relevant documents or records].

Interview: [*SELECT FROM:* System/network administrators; organizational personnel with information security responsibilities; system developer].

Test: [*SELECT FROM:* Automated mechanisms supporting and/or implementing transmission confidentiality and/or integrity].

SC-8(3)	**TRANSMISSION CONFIDENTIALITY AND INTEGRITY	*CRYPTOGRAPHIC PROTECTION FOR MESSAGE EXTERNALS***

ASSESSMENT OBJECTIVE:

Determine if:

SC-8(3)[1]	*the organization defines alternative physical safeguards to be implemented to protect message externals; and*
SC-8(3)[2]	*the information system implements cryptographic mechanisms to protect message externals unless otherwise protected by organization-defined alternative physical safeguards.*

Special Publication 800-53A
Revision 4

Assessing Security and Privacy Controls in Federal Information Systems
and Organizations — *Building Effective Assessment Plans*

POTENTIAL ASSESSMENT METHODS AND OBJECTS:

Examine: [*SELECT FROM:* System and communications protection policy; procedures addressing transmission confidentiality and integrity; information system design documentation; information system configuration settings and associated documentation; information system audit records; other relevant documents or records].

Interview: [*SELECT FROM:* System/network administrators; organizational personnel with information security responsibilities; system developer].

Test: [*SELECT FROM:* Cryptographic mechanisms supporting and/or implementing transmission confidentiality and/or integrity for message externals; automated mechanisms supporting and/or implementing alternative physical safeguards; organizational processes for defining and implementing alternative physical safeguards].

SC-8(4)	TRANSMISSION CONFIDENTIALITY AND INTEGRITY | *CONCEAL / RANDOMIZE COMMUNICATIONS*

ASSESSMENT OBJECTIVE:

Determine if:

SC-8(4)[1]	*the organization defines alternative physical safeguards to be implemented to protect against unauthorized disclosure of communication patterns;*
SC-8(4)[2]	*the information system, unless otherwise protected by organization-defined alternative physical safeguards, implements cryptographic mechanisms to:*

	SC-8(4)[2][a]	*conceal communication patterns; or*
	SC-8(4)[2][b]	*randomize communication patterns.*

POTENTIAL ASSESSMENT METHODS AND OBJECTS:

Examine: [*SELECT FROM:* System and communications protection policy; procedures addressing transmission confidentiality and integrity; information system design documentation; information system configuration settings and associated documentation; information system audit records; other relevant documents or records].

Interview: [*SELECT FROM:* System/network administrators; organizational personnel with information security responsibilities; system developer].

Test: [*SELECT FROM:* Cryptographic mechanisms supporting and/or implementing concealment or randomization of communications patterns; automated mechanisms supporting and/or implementing alternative physical safeguards; organizational processes for defining and implementing alternative physical safeguards].

SC-9	TRANSMISSION CONFIDENTIALITY

[Withdrawn: Incorporated into SC-8].

SC-10	NETWORK DISCONNECT

ASSESSMENT OBJECTIVE:

Determine if:

SC-10[1]	*the organization defines a time period of inactivity after which the information system terminates a network connection associated with a communications session; and*
SC-10[2]	*the information system terminates the network connection associated with a communication session at the end of the session or after the organization-defined time period of inactivity.*

Special Publication 800-53A
Revision 4

Assessing Security and Privacy Controls in Federal Information Systems
and Organizations — *Building Effective Assessment Plans*

	POTENTIAL ASSESSMENT METHODS AND OBJECTS: **Examine**: [*SELECT FROM:* System and communications protection policy; procedures addressing network disconnect; information system design documentation; security plan; information system configuration settings and associated documentation; information system audit records; other relevant documents or records]. **Interview**: [*SELECT FROM:* System/network administrators; organizational personnel with information security responsibilities; system developer]. **Test**: [*SELECT FROM:* Automated mechanisms supporting and/or implementing network disconnect capability].

SC-11	**TRUSTED PATH**
	ASSESSMENT OBJECTIVE: *Determine if:*
	SC-11[1] — *the organization defines security functions of the information system;*
	SC-11[2] — *the organization-defined security functions include at a minimum, information system authentication and re-authentication; and*
	SC-11[3] — *the information system establishes a trusted communications path between the user and the organization-defined security functions of the system.*
	POTENTIAL ASSESSMENT METHODS AND OBJECTS: **Examine**: [*SELECT FROM:* System and communications protection policy; procedures addressing trusted communications paths; security plan; information system design documentation; information system configuration settings and associated documentation; assessment results from independent, testing organizations; information system audit records; other relevant documents or records]. **Interview**: [*SELECT FROM:* System/network administrators; organizational personnel with information security responsibilities; system developer]. **Test**: [*SELECT FROM:* Automated mechanisms supporting and/or implementing trusted communications paths].

SC-11(1)	**TRUSTED PATH** | *LOGICAL ISOLATION*
	ASSESSMENT OBJECTIVE: *Determine if the information system provides a trusted communications path that is:*
	SC-11(1)[1] — *logically isolated; and*
	SC-11(1)[2] — *distinguishable from other paths.*
	POTENTIAL ASSESSMENT METHODS AND OBJECTS: **Examine**: [*SELECT FROM:* System and communications protection policy; procedures addressing trusted communications paths; security plan; information system design documentation; information system configuration settings and associated documentation; assessment results from independent, testing organizations; information system audit records; other relevant documents or records]. **Interview**: [*SELECT FROM:* System/network administrators; organizational personnel with information security responsibilities; system developer]. **Test**: [*SELECT FROM:* Automated mechanisms supporting and/or implementing trusted communications paths].

SC-12	**CRYPTOGRAPHIC KEY ESTABLISHMENT AND MANAGEMENT**
	ASSESSMENT OBJECTIVE: *Determine if the organization:*

Special Publication 800-53A
Revision 4

Assessing Security and Privacy Controls in Federal Information Systems
and Organizations — *Building Effective Assessment Plans*

SC-12[1]	*defines requirements for cryptographic key:*	
	SC-12[1][a]	*generation;*
	SC-12[1][b]	*distribution;*
	SC-12[1][c]	*storage;*
	SC-12[1][d]	*access;*
	SC-12[1][e]	*destruction; and*
SC-12[2]	*establishes and manages cryptographic keys for required cryptography employed within the information system in accordance with organization-defined requirements for key generation, distribution, storage, access, and destruction.*	

POTENTIAL ASSESSMENT METHODS AND OBJECTS:

Examine: [*SELECT FROM*: System and communications protection policy; procedures addressing cryptographic key establishment and management; information system design documentation; cryptographic mechanisms; information system configuration settings and associated documentation; information system audit records; other relevant documents or records].

Interview: [*SELECT FROM*: System/network administrators; organizational personnel with information security responsibilities; organizational personnel with responsibilities for cryptographic key establishment and/or management].

Test: [*SELECT FROM*: Automated mechanisms supporting and/or implementing cryptographic key establishment and management].

SC-12(1)	**CRYPTOGRAPHIC KEY ESTABLISHMENT AND MANAGEMENT	*AVAILABILITY***

ASSESSMENT OBJECTIVE:

Determine if the organization maintains availability of information in the event of the loss of cryptographic keys by users.

POTENTIAL ASSESSMENT METHODS AND OBJECTS:

Examine: [*SELECT FROM*: System and communications protection policy; procedures addressing cryptographic key establishment, management, and recovery; information system design documentation; information system configuration settings and associated documentation; information system audit records; other relevant documents or records].

Interview: [*SELECT FROM*: System/network administrators; organizational personnel with information security responsibilities; organizational personnel with responsibilities for cryptographic key establishment or management].

Test: [*SELECT FROM*: Automated mechanisms supporting and/or implementing cryptographic key establishment and management].

SC-12(2)	**CRYPTOGRAPHIC KEY ESTABLISHMENT AND MANAGEMENT	*SYMMETRIC KEYS***	

ASSESSMENT OBJECTIVE:

Determine if the organization produces, controls, and distributes symmetric cryptographic keys using one of the following:

SC-12(2)[1]	*NIST FIPS-compliant key management technology and processes; or*
SC-12(2)[2]	*NSA-approved key management technology and processes.*

Revision 4Special Publication 800-53A
Special Publication 800-53A
Revision 4

Assessing Security and Privacy Controls in Federal Information Systems
and Organizations — *Building Effective Assessment Plans*

	POTENTIAL ASSESSMENT METHODS AND OBJECTS: **Examine**: [*SELECT FROM:* System and communications protection policy; procedures addressing cryptographic key establishment and management; information system design documentation; information system configuration settings and associated documentation; information system audit records; list of FIPS validated cryptographic products; list of NSA-approved cryptographic products; other relevant documents or records]. **Interview**: [*SELECT FROM:* System/network administrators; organizational personnel with information security responsibilities; system developer; organizational personnel with responsibilities for cryptographic key establishment or management]. **Test**: [*SELECT FROM:* Automated mechanisms supporting and/or implementing symmetric cryptographic key establishment and management].

SC-12(3)	CRYPTOGRAPHIC KEY ESTABLISHMENT AND MANAGEMENT | *ASYMMETRIC KEYS*
	ASSESSMENT OBJECTIVE: *Determine if the organization produces, controls, and distributes asymmetric cryptographic keys using one of the following:*

SC-12(3)[1]	*NSA-approved key management technology and processes;*
SC-12(3)[2]	*approved PKI Class 3 certificates or prepositioned keying material; or*
SC-12(3)[3]	*approved PKI Class 3 or Class 4 certificates and hardware security tokens that protect the user's private key.*

	POTENTIAL ASSESSMENT METHODS AND OBJECTS: **Examine**: [*SELECT FROM:* System and communications protection policy; procedures addressing cryptographic key establishment and management; information system design documentation; information system configuration settings and associated documentation; information system audit records; list of NSA-approved cryptographic products; list of approved PKI Class 3 and Class 4 certificates; other relevant documents or records]. **Interview**: [*SELECT FROM:* System/network administrators; organizational personnel with information security responsibilities; system developer; organizational personnel with responsibilities for cryptographic key establishment or management; organizational personnel with responsibilities for PKI certificates]. **Test**: [*SELECT FROM:* Automated mechanisms supporting and/or implementing asymmetric cryptographic key establishment and management].

SC-12(4)	CRYPTOGRAPHIC KEY ESTABLISHMENT AND MANAGEMENT | *PKI CERTIFICATES*
[Withdrawn: Incorporated into SC-12].	

SC-12(5)	CRYPTOGRAPHIC KEY ESTABLISHMENT AND MANAGEMENT | *PKI CERTIFICATES / HARDWARE TOKENS*
[Withdrawn: Incorporated into SC-12].	

SC-13	CRYPTOGRAPHIC PROTECTION
	ASSESSMENT OBJECTIVE: *Determine if:*

SC-13[1]	*the organization defines cryptographic uses; and*
SC-13[2]	*the organization defines the type of cryptography required for each use; and*

Special Publication 800-53A
Revision 4

Assessing Security and Privacy Controls in Federal Information Systems
and Organizations — *Building Effective Assessment Plans*

SC-13[3]	*the information system implements the organization-defined cryptographic uses and type of cryptography required for each use in accordance with applicable federal laws, Executive Orders, directives, policies, regulations, and standards.*

POTENTIAL ASSESSMENT METHODS AND OBJECTS:

Examine: [*SELECT FROM:* System and communications protection policy; procedures addressing cryptographic protection; information system design documentation; information system configuration settings and associated documentation; cryptographic module validation certificates; list of FIPS validated cryptographic modules; information system audit records; other relevant documents or records].

Interview: [*SELECT FROM:* System/network administrators; organizational personnel with information security responsibilities; system developer; organizational personnel with responsibilities for cryptographic protection].

Test: [*SELECT FROM:* Automated mechanisms supporting and/or implementing cryptographic protection].

SC-13(1)	**CRYPTOGRAPHIC PROTECTION**	*FIPS-VALIDATED CRYPTOGRAPHY*

[Withdrawn: Incorporated into SC-13].

SC-13(2)	**CRYPTOGRAPHIC PROTECTION**	*NSA-APPROVED CRYPTOGRAPHY*

[Withdrawn: Incorporated into SC-13].

SC-13(3)	**CRYPTOGRAPHIC PROTECTION**	*INDIVIDUALS WITHOUT FORMAL ACCESS APPROVALS*

[Withdrawn: Incorporated into SC-13].

SC-13(4)	**CRYPTOGRAPHIC PROTECTION**	*DIGITAL SIGNATURES*

[Withdrawn: Incorporated into SC-13].

SC-14	**PUBLIC ACCESS PROTECTIONS**

[Withdrawn: Capability provided by AC-2, AC-3, AC-5, AC-6, SI-3, SI-4, SI-5, SI-7, SI-10].

SC-15	**COLLABORATIVE COMPUTING DEVICES**		

ASSESSMENT OBJECTIVE:
Determine if:

SC-15(a)	SC-15(a)[1]	*the organization defines exceptions where remote activation of collaborative computing devices is to be allowed;*
	SC-15(a)[2]	*the information system prohibits remote activation of collaborative computing devices, except for organization-defined exceptions where remote activation is to be allowed; and*
SC-15(b)		*the information system provides an explicit indication of use to users physically present at the devices.*

Special Publication 800-53A
Revision 4

Assessing Security and Privacy Controls in Federal Information Systems
and Organizations — *Building Effective Assessment Plans*

POTENTIAL ASSESSMENT METHODS AND OBJECTS:

Examine: [*SELECT FROM:* System and communications protection policy; procedures addressing collaborative computing; access control policy and procedures; information system design documentation; information system configuration settings and associated documentation; information system audit records; other relevant documents or records].

Interview: [*SELECT FROM:* System/network administrators; organizational personnel with information security responsibilities; system developer; organizational personnel with responsibilities for managing collaborative computing devices].

Test: [*SELECT FROM:* Automated mechanisms supporting and/or implementing management of remote activation of collaborative computing devices; automated mechanisms providing an indication of use of collaborative computing devices].

SC-15(1)	COLLABORATIVE COMPUTING DEVICES	*PHYSICAL DISCONNECT*

ASSESSMENT OBJECTIVE:

Determine if the information system provides physical disconnect of collaborative computing devices in a manner that supports ease of use.

POTENTIAL ASSESSMENT METHODS AND OBJECTS:

Examine: [*SELECT FROM:* System and communications protection policy; procedures addressing collaborative computing; access control policy and procedures; information system design documentation; information system configuration settings and associated documentation; information system audit records; other relevant documents or records].

Interview: [*SELECT FROM:* System/network administrators; organizational personnel with information security responsibilities; system developer; organizational personnel with responsibilities for managing collaborative computing devices].

Test: [*SELECT FROM:* Automated mechanisms supporting and/or implementing physical disconnect of collaborative computing devices].

SC-15(2)	COLLABORATIVE COMPUTING DEVICES	*BLOCKING INBOUND / OUTBOUND COMMUNICATIONS TRAFFIC*

[Withdrawn: Incorporated into SC-7].

SC-15(3)	COLLABORATIVE COMPUTING DEVICES	*DISABLING / REMOVAL IN SECURE WORK AREAS*

ASSESSMENT OBJECTIVE:

Determine if the organization:

SC-15(3)[1]	*defines information systems or information system components from which collaborative computing devices are to be disabled or removed;*
SC-15(3)[2]	*defines secure work areas where collaborative computing devices are to be disabled or removed from information systems or information system components placed in such work areas; and*
SC-15(3)[3]	*disables or removes collaborative computing devices from organization-defined information systems or information system components in organization-defined secure work areas.*

Special Publication 800-53A
Revision 4

Assessing Security and Privacy Controls in Federal Information Systems
and Organizations — *Building Effective Assessment Plans*

POTENTIAL ASSESSMENT METHODS AND OBJECTS:

Examine: [*SELECT FROM:* System and communications protection policy; procedures addressing collaborative computing; access control policy and procedures; information system design documentation; information system configuration settings and associated documentation; information system audit records; list of secure work areas; information systems or information system components in secured work areas where collaborative computing devices are to be disabled or removed; other relevant documents or records].

Interview: [*SELECT FROM:* System/network administrators; organizational personnel with information security responsibilities; organizational personnel with responsibilities for managing collaborative computing devices].

Test: [*SELECT FROM:* Automated mechanisms supporting and/or implementing the capability to disable collaborative computing devices].

SC-15(4)	COLLABORATIVE COMPUTING DEVICES | *EXPLICITLY INDICATE CURRENT PARTICIPANTS*

ASSESSMENT OBJECTIVE:

Determine if:

SC-15(4)[1]	*the organization defines online meetings and teleconferences for which an explicit indication of current participants is to be provided; and*
SC-15(4)[2]	*the information system provides an explicit indication of current participants in organization-defined meetings and teleconferences.*

POTENTIAL ASSESSMENT METHODS AND OBJECTS:

Examine: [*SELECT FROM:* System and communications protection policy; procedures addressing collaborative computing; access control policy and procedures; information system design documentation; information system configuration settings and associated documentation; information system audit records; list of types of meetings and teleconferences requiring explicit indication of current participants; other relevant documents or records].

Interview: [*SELECT FROM:* System/network administrators; organizational personnel with information security responsibilities; organizational personnel with responsibilities for managing collaborative computing devices].

Test: [*SELECT FROM:* Automated mechanisms supporting and/or implementing the capability to indicate participants on collaborative computing devices].

SC-16	TRANSMISSION OF SECURITY ATTRIBUTES

ASSESSMENT OBJECTIVE:

Determine if:

SC-16[1]	*the organization defines security attributes to be associated with information exchanged:*	
	SC-16[1][a]	*between information systems;*
	SC-16[1][b]	*between system components;*
SC-16[2]	*the information system associates organization-defined security attributes with information exchanged:*	
	SC-16[2][a]	*between information systems; and*
	SC-16[2][b]	*between system components.*

Special Publication 800-53A
Revision 4

Assessing Security and Privacy Controls in Federal Information Systems
and Organizations — *Building Effective Assessment Plans*

POTENTIAL ASSESSMENT METHODS AND OBJECTS:

Examine: [*SELECT FROM:* System and communications protection policy; procedures addressing transmission of security attributes; access control policy and procedures; information system design documentation; information system configuration settings and associated documentation; information system audit records; other relevant documents or records].

Interview: [*SELECT FROM:* System/network administrators; organizational personnel with information security responsibilities].

Test: [*SELECT FROM:* Automated mechanisms supporting and/or implementing transmission of security attributes between information systems].

SC-16(1)	TRANSMISSION OF SECURITY ATTRIBUTES | *INTEGRITY VALIDATION*
	ASSESSMENT OBJECTIVE: *Determine if the information system validates the integrity of transmitted security attributes.* **POTENTIAL ASSESSMENT METHODS AND OBJECTS:** **Examine**: [*SELECT FROM:* System and communications protection policy; procedures addressing transmission of security attributes; access control policy and procedures; information system design documentation; information system configuration settings and associated documentation; information system audit records; other relevant documents or records]. **Interview**: [*SELECT FROM:* System/network administrators; organizational personnel with information security responsibilities]. **Test**: [*SELECT FROM:* Automated mechanisms supporting and/or implementing validation of the integrity of transmitted security attributes].

SC-17	PUBLIC KEY INFRASTRUCTURE CERTIFICATES	
	ASSESSMENT OBJECTIVE: *Determine if the organization:*	
SC-17[1]	*defines a certificate policy for issuing public key certificates;*	
SC-17[2]	*issues public key certificates:*	
	SC-17[2][a]	*under an organization-defined certificate policy: or*
	SC-17[2][b]	*obtains public key certificates from an approved service provider.*

POTENTIAL ASSESSMENT METHODS AND OBJECTS:

Examine: [*SELECT FROM:* System and communications protection policy; procedures addressing public key infrastructure certificates; public key certificate policy or policies; public key issuing process; other relevant documents or records].

Interview: [*SELECT FROM:* System/network administrators; organizational personnel with information security responsibilities; organizational personnel with responsibilities for issuing public key certificates; service providers].

Test: [*SELECT FROM:* Automated mechanisms supporting and/or implementing the management of public key infrastructure certificates].

SC-18	MOBILE CODE	
	ASSESSMENT OBJECTIVE: *Determine if the organization:*	
SC-18(a)	*defines acceptable and unacceptable mobile code and mobile code technologies;*	
SC-18(b)	SC-18(b)[1]	*establishes usage restrictions for acceptable mobile code and mobile code technologies;*

Special Publication 800-53A
Revision 4

Assessing Security and Privacy Controls in Federal Information Systems
and Organizations — *Building Effective Assessment Plans*

		SC-18(b)[2]	*establishes implementation guidance for acceptable mobile code and mobile code technologies;*
	SC-18(c)	SC-18(c)[1]	*authorizes the use of mobile code within the information system;*
		SC-18(c)[2]	*monitors the use of mobile code within the information system; and*
		SC-18(c)[3]	*controls the use of mobile code within the information system.*

POTENTIAL ASSESSMENT METHODS AND OBJECTS:

Examine: [*SELECT FROM:* System and communications protection policy; procedures addressing mobile code; mobile code usage restrictions, mobile code implementation policy and procedures; list of acceptable mobile code and mobile code technologies; list of unacceptable mobile code and mobile technologies; authorization records; information system monitoring records; information system audit records; other relevant documents or records].

Interview: [*SELECT FROM:* System/network administrators; organizational personnel with information security responsibilities; organizational personnel with responsibilities for managing mobile code].

Test: [*SELECT FROM:* Organizational process for controlling, authorizing, monitoring, and restricting mobile code; automated mechanisms supporting and/or implementing the management of mobile code; automated mechanisms supporting and/or implementing the monitoring of mobile code].

SC-18(1)	MOBILE CODE	*IDENTIFY UNACCEPTABLE CODE / TAKE CORRECTION ACTIONS*

ASSESSMENT OBJECTIVE:

Determine if:

SC-18(1)[1]	*the organization defines unacceptable mobile code to be identified by the information system;*	
SC-18(1)[2]	*the organization defines correctives actions to be taken when the information system identifies organization-defined unacceptable mobile code;*	
SC-18(1)[3]	*the information system:*	
	SC-18(1)[3][a]	*identifies organization-defined unacceptable mobile code; and*
	SC-18(1)[3][b]	*takes organization-defined corrective actions.*

POTENTIAL ASSESSMENT METHODS AND OBJECTS:

Examine: [*SELECT FROM:* System and communications protection policy; procedures addressing mobile code; mobile code usage restrictions, mobile code implementation policy and procedures; information system design documentation; information system configuration settings and associated documentation; list of unacceptable mobile code; list of corrective actions to be taken when unacceptable mobile code is identified; information system monitoring records; information system audit records; other relevant documents or records].

Interview: [*SELECT FROM:* System/network administrators; organizational personnel with information security responsibilities; system developer; organizational personnel with responsibilities for managing mobile code].

Test: [*SELECT FROM:* Automated mechanisms supporting and/or implementing mobile code detection, inspection, and corrective capability].

SC-18(2)	MOBILE CODE	*ACQUISITION / DEVELOPMENT / USE*

ASSESSMENT OBJECTIVE:

Determine if the organization:

SC-18(2)[1]	*defines requirements for:*	
	SC-18(2)[1][a]	*the acquisition of mobile code;*
	SC-18(2)[1][b]	*the development of mobile code;*

Special Publication 800-53A
Revision 4

Assessing Security and Privacy Controls in Federal Information Systems
and Organizations — *Building Effective Assessment Plans*

SC-18(2)[1][c]	*the use of mobile code; and*
SC-18(2)[2]	*ensures that the acquisition, development, and use of mobile code to be deployed in the information system meets organization-defined mobile code requirements.*

POTENTIAL ASSESSMENT METHODS AND OBJECTS:

Examine: [*SELECT FROM:* System and communications protection policy; procedures addressing mobile code; mobile code requirements; mobile code usage restrictions, mobile code implementation policy and procedures; acquisition documentation; acquisition contracts for information system, system component, or information system service; system development life cycle documentation; other relevant documents or records].

Interview: [*SELECT FROM:* System/network administrators; organizational personnel with information security responsibilities; organizational personnel with responsibilities for managing mobile code; organizational personnel with acquisition and contracting responsibilities].

Test: [*SELECT FROM:* Organizational processes for the acquisition, development, and use of mobile code].

SC-18(3)	MOBILE CODE | *PREVENT DOWNLOADING / EXECUTION*

ASSESSMENT OBJECTIVE:

Determine if:

SC-18(3)[1]	*the organization defines unacceptable mobile code to be prevented from downloading and execution;*	
SC-18(3)[2]	*the information system prevents the:*	
	SC-18(3)[2][a]	*download of organization-defined unacceptable mobile code; and*
	SC-18(3)[2][b]	*execution of organization-defined unacceptable mobile code.*

POTENTIAL ASSESSMENT METHODS AND OBJECTS:

Examine: [*SELECT FROM:* System and communications protection policy; procedures addressing mobile code; mobile code usage restrictions, mobile code implementation policy and procedures; information system design documentation; information system configuration settings and associated documentation; information system audit records; other relevant documents or records].

Interview: [*SELECT FROM:* System/network administrators; organizational personnel with information security responsibilities; system developer; organizational personnel with responsibilities for managing mobile code].

Test: [*SELECT FROM:* Automated mechanisms preventing download and execution of unacceptable mobile code].

SC-18(4)	MOBILE CODE | *PREVENT AUTOMATIC EXECUTION*

ASSESSMENT OBJECTIVE:

Determine if:

SC-18(4)[1]	*the organization defines software applications in which the automatic execution of mobile code is to be prohibited;*
SC-18(4)[2]	*the organization defines actions to be enforced by the information system prior to executing mobile code;*
SC-18(4)[3]	*the information system prevents the automatic execution of mobile code in the organization-defined software applications; and*
SC-18(4)[4]	*the information system enforces organization-defined actions prior to executing the code.*

Special Publication 800-53A
Revision 4

Assessing Security and Privacy Controls in Federal Information Systems
and Organizations — *Building Effective Assessment Plans*

POTENTIAL ASSESSMENT METHODS AND OBJECTS:

Examine: [*SELECT FROM:* System and communications protection policy; procedures addressing mobile code; mobile code usage restrictions; mobile code implementation policy and procedures; information system design documentation; information system configuration settings and associated documentation; list of software applications for which automatic execution of mobile code must be prohibited; list of actions required before execution of mobile code; other relevant documents or records].

Interview: [*SELECT FROM:* System/network administrators; organizational personnel with information security responsibilities; system developer; organizational personnel with responsibilities for managing mobile code].

Test: [*SELECT FROM:* Automated mechanisms preventing automatic execution of unacceptable mobile code; automated mechanisms enforcing actions to be taken prior to the execution of the mobile code].

SC-18(5)	MOBILE CODE | *ALLOW EXECUTION ONLY IN CONFINED ENVIRONMENTS*

ASSESSMENT OBJECTIVE:

Determine if the organization allows execution of permitted mobile code only in confined virtual machine environments.

POTENTIAL ASSESSMENT METHODS AND OBJECTS:

Examine: [*SELECT FROM:* System and communications protection policy; procedures addressing mobile code; mobile code usage allowances; mobile code usage restrictions; information system design documentation; information system configuration settings and associated documentation; list of confined virtual machine environments for which execution of organizationally-acceptable mobile code is allowed; information system audit records; other relevant documents or records].

Interview: [*SELECT FROM:* System/network administrators; organizational personnel with information security responsibilities; system developer; organizational personnel with responsibilities for managing mobile code].

Test: [*SELECT FROM:* Automated mechanisms allowing execution of permitted mobile code in confined virtual machine environments].

SC-19	VOICE OVER INTERNET PROTOCOL	

ASSESSMENT OBJECTIVE:

Determine if the organization:

SC-19(a)	SC-19(a)[1]	*establishes usage restrictions for Voice over Internet Protocol (VoIP) technologies based on the potential to cause damage to the information system if used maliciously;*
	SC-19(a)[2]	*establishes implementation guidance for Voice over Internet Protocol (VoIP) technologies based on the potential to cause damage to the information system if used maliciously;*
SC-19(b)	SC-19(b)[1]	*authorizes the use of VoIP within the information system;*
	SC-19(b)[2]	*monitors the use of VoIP within the information system; and*
	SC-19(b)[3]	*controls the use of VoIP within the information system.*

Special Publication 800-53A
Revision 4

Assessing Security and Privacy Controls in Federal Information Systems
and Organizations — *Building Effective Assessment Plans*

	POTENTIAL ASSESSMENT METHODS AND OBJECTS: **Examine**: [*SELECT FROM:* System and communications protection policy; procedures addressing VoIP; VoIP usage restrictions; VoIP implementation guidance; information system design documentation; information system configuration settings and associated documentation; information system monitoring records; information system audit records; other relevant documents or records]. **Interview**: [*SELECT FROM:* System/network administrators; organizational personnel with information security responsibilities; organizational personnel with responsibilities for managing VoIP]. **Test**: [*SELECT FROM:* Organizational process for authorizing, monitoring, and controlling VoIP; automated mechanisms supporting and/or implementing authorizing, monitoring, and controlling VoIP].

SC-20	SECURE NAME / ADDRESS RESOLUTION SERVICE (AUTHORITATIVE SOURCE)
	ASSESSMENT OBJECTIVE: *Determine if the information system:*

	SC-20(a)	*provides additional data origin and integrity verification artifacts along with the authoritative name resolution data the system returns in response to external name/address resolution queries;*
	SC-20(b)	*provides the means to, when operating as part of a distributed, hierarchical namespace:*
	SC-20(b)[1]	*indicate the security status of child zones; and*
	SC-20(b)[2]	*enable verification of a chain of trust among parent and child domains (if the child supports secure resolution services).*

	POTENTIAL ASSESSMENT METHODS AND OBJECTS: **Examine**: [*SELECT FROM:* System and communications protection policy; procedures addressing secure name/address resolution service (authoritative source); information system design documentation; information system configuration settings and associated documentation; other relevant documents or records]. **Interview**: [*SELECT FROM:* System/network administrators; organizational personnel with information security responsibilities; organizational personnel with responsibilities for managing DNS]. **Test**: [*SELECT FROM:* Automated mechanisms supporting and/or implementing secure name/address resolution service].

SC-20(1)	SECURE NAME / ADDRESS RESOLUTION SERVICE (AUTHORITATIVE SOURCE) | *CHILD SUBSPACES*
[Withdrawn: Incorporated into SC-20].	

SC-20(2)	SECURE NAME/ADDRESS RESOLUTION SERVICE (AUTHORITATIVE SOURCE) | *DATA ORIGIN / DATA INTEGRITY*
	ASSESSMENT OBJECTIVE: *Determine if the information system provides data origin and integrity protection artifacts for internal name/address resolution queries.*
	POTENTIAL ASSESSMENT METHODS AND OBJECTS: **Examine**: [*SELECT FROM:* System and communications protection policy; procedures addressing secure name/address resolution service (authoritative source); information system design documentation; information system configuration settings and associated documentation; information system audit records; other relevant documents or records]. **Interview**: [*SELECT FROM:* System/network administrators; organizational personnel with information security responsibilities; organizational personnel with responsibilities for managing DNS]. **Test**: [*SELECT FROM:* Automated mechanisms supporting and/or implementing data origin and integrity protection for internal name/address resolution service queries].

Special Publication 800-53A
Revision 4

Assessing Security and Privacy Controls in Federal Information Systems
and Organizations — *Building Effective Assessment Plans*

SC-21	SECURE NAME / ADDRESS RESOLUTION SERVICE (RECURSIVE OR CACHING RESOLVER)
	ASSESSMENT OBJECTIVE: *Determine if the information system:*
	SC-21[1]	*requests data origin authentication on the name/address resolution responses the system receives from authoritative sources;*
	SC-21[2]	*requests data integrity verification on the name/address resolution responses the system receives from authoritative sources;*
	SC-21[3]	*performs data origin authentication on the name/address resolution responses the system receives from authoritative sources; and*
	SC-21[4]	*performs data integrity verification on the name/address resolution responses the system receives from authoritative sources.*
	POTENTIAL ASSESSMENT METHODS AND OBJECTS: **Examine**: [*SELECT FROM:* System and communications protection policy; procedures addressing secure name/address resolution service (recursive or caching resolver); information system design documentation; information system configuration settings and associated documentation; information system audit records; other relevant documents or records]. **Interview**: [*SELECT FROM:* System/network administrators; organizational personnel with information security responsibilities; organizational personnel with responsibilities for managing DNS]. **Test**: [*SELECT FROM:* Automated mechanisms supporting and/or implementing data origin authentication and data integrity verification for name/address resolution services].

SC-21(1)	SECURE NAME / ADDRESS RESOLUTION SERVICE (RECURSIVE OR CACHING RESOLVER) | *DATA ORIGIN / INTEGRITY*
[Withdrawn: Incorporated into SC-21].	

SC-22	ARCHITECTURE AND PROVISIONING FOR NAME / ADDRESS RESOLUTION SERVICE
	ASSESSMENT OBJECTIVE: *Determine if the information systems that collectively provide name/address resolution service for an organization:*
	SC-22[1]	*are fault tolerant; and*
	SC-22[2]	*implement internal/external role separation.*
	POTENTIAL ASSESSMENT METHODS AND OBJECTS: **Examine**: [*SELECT FROM:* System and communications protection policy; procedures addressing architecture and provisioning for name/address resolution service; access control policy and procedures; information system design documentation; assessment results from independent, testing organizations; information system configuration settings and associated documentation; information system audit records; other relevant documents or records]. **Interview**: [*SELECT FROM:* System/network administrators; organizational personnel with information security responsibilities; organizational personnel with responsibilities for managing DNS]. **Test**: [*SELECT FROM:* Automated mechanisms supporting and/or implementing name/address resolution service for fault tolerance and role separation].

SC-23	SESSION AUTHENTICITY
	ASSESSMENT OBJECTIVE: *Determine if the information system protects the authenticity of communications sessions.*

Special Publication 800-53A
Revision 4

Assessing Security and Privacy Controls in Federal Information Systems
and Organizations — *Building Effective Assessment Plans*

POTENTIAL ASSESSMENT METHODS AND OBJECTS:

Examine: [*SELECT FROM:* System and communications protection policy; procedures addressing session authenticity; information system design documentation; information system configuration settings and associated documentation; information system audit records; other relevant documents or records].

Interview: [*SELECT FROM:* System/network administrators; organizational personnel with information security responsibilities].

Test: [*SELECT FROM:* Automated mechanisms supporting and/or implementing session authenticity].

SC-23(1)	SESSION AUTHENTICITY | *INVALIDATE SESSION IDENTIFIERS AT LOGOUT*

ASSESSMENT OBJECTIVE:

Determine if the information system invalidates session identifiers upon user logout or other session termination.

POTENTIAL ASSESSMENT METHODS AND OBJECTS:

Examine: [*SELECT FROM:* System and communications protection policy; procedures addressing session authenticity; information system design documentation; information system configuration settings and associated documentation; information system audit records; other relevant documents or records].

Interview: [*SELECT FROM:* System/network administrators; organizational personnel with information security responsibilities].

Test: [*SELECT FROM:* Automated mechanisms supporting and/or implementing session identifier invalidation upon session termination].

SC-23(2)	SESSION AUTHENTICITY | *USER-INITIATED LOGOUTS / MESSAGE DISPLAYS*

[Withdrawn: Incorporated into AC-12(1)].

SC-23(3)	SESSION AUTHENTICITY | *UNIQUE SESSION IDENTIFIERS WITH RANDOMIZATION*

ASSESSMENT OBJECTIVE:
Determine if:

SC-23(3)[1]	*the organization defines randomness requirements for generating a unique session identifier for each session;*
SC-23(3)[2]	*the information system generates a unique session identifier for each session with organization-defined randomness requirements; and*
SC-23(3)[3]	*the information system recognizes only session identifiers that are system-generated.*

POTENTIAL ASSESSMENT METHODS AND OBJECTS:

Examine: [*SELECT FROM:* System and communications protection policy; procedures addressing session authenticity; information system design documentation; information system configuration settings and associated documentation; information system audit records; other relevant documents or records].

Interview: [*SELECT FROM:* System/network administrators; organizational personnel with information security responsibilities].

Test: [*SELECT FROM:* Automated mechanisms supporting and/or implementing generating and monitoring unique session identifiers; automated mechanisms supporting and/or implementing randomness requirements].

SC-23(4)	SESSION AUTHENTICITY | *UNIQUE SESSION IDENTIFIERS WITH RANDOMIZATION*

[Withdrawn: Incorporated into SC-23(3)].

Special Publication 800-53A
Revision 4

Assessing Security and Privacy Controls in Federal Information Systems
and Organizations — *Building Effective Assessment Plans*

SC-23(5)	SESSION AUTHENTICITY | *ALLOWED CERTIFICATE AUTHORITIES*
	ASSESSMENT OBJECTIVE: *Determine if:*

	SC-23(5)[1]	*the organization defines certificate authorities to be allowed for verification of the establishment of protected sessions; and*
	SC-23(5)[2]	*the information system only allows the use of organization-defined certificate authorities for verification of the establishment of protected sessions.*

POTENTIAL ASSESSMENT METHODS AND OBJECTS:

Examine: [*SELECT FROM:* System and communications protection policy; procedures addressing session authenticity; information system design documentation; information system configuration settings and associated documentation; list of certificate authorities allowed for verification of the establishment of protected sessions; information system audit records; other relevant documents or records].

Interview: [*SELECT FROM:* System/network administrators; organizational personnel with information security responsibilities].

Test: [*SELECT FROM:* Automated mechanisms supporting and/or implementing management of certificate authorities].

SC-24	FAIL IN KNOWN STATE
	ASSESSMENT OBJECTIVE: *Determine if:*

	SC-24[1]	*the organization defines a known-state to which the information system is to fail in the event of a system failure;*
	SC-24[2]	*the organization defines types of failures for which the information system is to fail to an organization-defined known-state;*
	SC-24[3]	*the organization defines system state information to be preserved in the event of a system failure;*
	SC-24[4]	*the information system fails to the organization-defined known-state for organization-defined types of failures; and*
	SC-24[5]	*the information system preserves the organization-defined system state information in the event of a system failure.*

POTENTIAL ASSESSMENT METHODS AND OBJECTS:

Examine: [*SELECT FROM:* System and communications protection policy; procedures addressing information system failure to known state; information system design documentation; information system configuration settings and associated documentation; list of failures requiring information system to fail in a known state; state information to be preserved in system failure; information system audit records; other relevant documents or records].

Interview: [*SELECT FROM:* System/network administrators; organizational personnel with information security responsibilities; system developer].

Test: [*SELECT FROM:* Automated mechanisms supporting and/or implementing fail-in-known state capability; automated mechanisms preserving system state information in the event of a system failure].

SC-25	THIN NODES
	ASSESSMENT OBJECTIVE: *Determine if the organization:*

Special Publication 800-53A
Revision 4

Assessing Security and Privacy Controls in Federal Information Systems
and Organizations — *Building Effective Assessment Plans*

	SC-25[1]	*defines information system components to be employed with minimal functionality and information storage; and*
	SC-25[2]	*employs organization-defined information system components with minimal functionality and information storage.*

POTENTIAL ASSESSMENT METHODS AND OBJECTS:

Examine: [*SELECT FROM:* System and communications protection policy; procedures addressing use of thin nodes; information system design documentation; information system configuration settings and associated documentation; information system audit records; other relevant documents or records].

Interview: [*SELECT FROM:* System/network administrators; organizational personnel with information security responsibilities].

Test: [*SELECT FROM:* Automated mechanisms supporting and/or implementing thin nodes].

SC-26	**HONEY POTS**

ASSESSMENT OBJECTIVE:

Determine if the information system includes components specifically designed to be the target of malicious attacks for the purpose of detecting, deflecting, and analyzing such attacks.

POTENTIAL ASSESSMENT METHODS AND OBJECTS:

Examine: [*SELECT FROM:* System and communications protection policy; procedures addressing use of honeypots; information system design documentation; information system configuration settings and associated documentation; information system audit records; other relevant documents or records].

Interview: [*SELECT FROM:* System/network administrators; organizational personnel with information security responsibilities; system developer].

Test: [*SELECT FROM:* Automated mechanisms supporting and/or implementing honey pots].

SC-26(1)	**HONEY POTS** | *DETECTION OF MALICIOUS CODE*

[Withdrawn: Incorporated into SC-35].

SC-27	**PLATFORM-INDEPENDENT APPLICATIONS**

ASSESSMENT OBJECTIVE:

Determine if:

	SC-27[1]	*the organization defines platform-independent applications; and*
	SC-27[2]	*the information system includes organization-defined platform-independent applications.*

POTENTIAL ASSESSMENT METHODS AND OBJECTS:

Examine: [*SELECT FROM:* System and communications protection policy; procedures addressing platform-independent applications; information system design documentation; information system configuration settings and associated documentation; list of platform-independent applications; information system audit records; other relevant documents or records].

Interview: [*SELECT FROM:* System/network administrators; organizational personnel with information security responsibilities; system developer].

Test: [*SELECT FROM:* Automated mechanisms supporting and/or implementing platform-independent applications].

Special Publication 800-53A
Revision 4

Assessing Security and Privacy Controls in Federal Information Systems
and Organizations — *Building Effective Assessment Plans*

SC-28	PROTECTION OF INFORMATION AT REST		
	ASSESSMENT OBJECTIVE: *Determine if:*		
	SC-28[1]	*the organization defines information at rest requiring one or more of the following:*	
		SC-28[1][a]	*confidentiality protection; and/or*
		SC-28[1][b]	*integrity protection;*
	SC-28[2]	*the information system protects:*	
		SC-28[2][a]	*the confidentiality of organization-defined information at rest; and/or*
		SC-28[2][b]	*the integrity of organization-defined information at rest.*
	POTENTIAL ASSESSMENT METHODS AND OBJECTS: **Examine**: [*SELECT FROM:* System and communications protection policy; procedures addressing protection of information at rest; information system design documentation; information system configuration settings and associated documentation; cryptographic mechanisms and associated configuration documentation; list of information at rest requiring confidentiality and integrity protections; other relevant documents or records]. **Interview**: [*SELECT FROM:* System/network administrators; organizational personnel with information security responsibilities; system developer]. **Test**: [*SELECT FROM:* Automated mechanisms supporting and/or implementing confidentiality and integrity protections for information at rest].		

SC-28(1)	PROTECTION OF INFORMATION AT REST | *CRYPTOGRAPHIC PROTECTIONS*	
	ASSESSMENT OBJECTIVE: *Determine if:*	
	SC-28(1)[1]	*the organization defines information requiring cryptographic protection;*
	SC-28(1)[2]	*the organization defines information system components with organization-defined information requiring cryptographic protection; and*
	SC-28(1)[3]	*the information system employs cryptographic mechanisms to prevent unauthorized disclosure and modification of organization-defined information on organization-defined information system components.*
	POTENTIAL ASSESSMENT METHODS AND OBJECTS: **Examine**: [*SELECT FROM:* System and communications protection policy; procedures addressing protection of information at rest; information system design documentation; information system configuration settings and associated documentation; cryptographic mechanisms and associated configuration documentation; information system audit records; other relevant documents or records]. **Interview**: [*SELECT FROM:* System/network administrators; organizational personnel with information security responsibilities; system developer]. **Test**: [*SELECT FROM:* Cryptographic mechanisms implementing confidentiality and integrity protections for information at rest].	

SC-28(2)	PROTECTION OF INFORMATION AT REST | *OFF-LINE STORAGE*
	ASSESSMENT OBJECTIVE: *Determine if the organization:*

Special Publication 800-53A
Revision 4

Assessing Security and Privacy Controls in Federal Information Systems
and Organizations — *Building Effective Assessment Plans*

SC-28(2)[1]	*defines information to be removed from online storage and stored off-line in a secure location; and*
SC-28(2)[2]	*removes organization-defined information from online storage; and*
SC-28(2)[3]	*stores such information off-line in a secure location.*

POTENTIAL ASSESSMENT METHODS AND OBJECTS:

Examine: [*SELECT FROM:* System and communications protection policy; procedures addressing protection of information at rest; information system design documentation; information system configuration settings and associated documentation; cryptographic mechanisms and associated configuration documentation; off-line storage locations for information at rest; information system audit records; other relevant documents or records].

Interview: [*SELECT FROM:* System/network administrators; organizational personnel with information security responsibilities].

Test: [*SELECT FROM:* Automated mechanisms supporting and/or implementing removal of information from online storage; automated mechanisms supporting and/or implementing storage of information off-line].

SC-29	**HETEROGENEITY**

ASSESSMENT OBJECTIVE:

Determine if the organization:

SC-29[1]	*defines information system components requiring a diverse set of information technologies to be employed in the implementation of the information system; and*
SC-29[2]	*employs a diverse set of information technologies for organization-defined information system components in the implementation of the information system.*

POTENTIAL ASSESSMENT METHODS AND OBJECTS:

Examine: [*SELECT FROM:* System and communications protection policy; information system design documentation; information system configuration settings and associated documentation; list of technologies deployed in the information system; acquisition documentation; acquisition contracts for information system components or services; other relevant documents or records].

Interview: [*SELECT FROM:* System/network administrators; organizational personnel with information security responsibilities; organizational personnel with information system acquisition, development, and implementation responsibilities].

Test: [*SELECT FROM:* Automated mechanisms supporting and/or implementing employment of a diverse set of information technologies].

SC-29(1)	**HETEROGENEITY	*VIRTUALIZATION TECHNIQUES***

ASSESSMENT OBJECTIVE:

Determine if the organization:

SC-29(1)[1]	*defines a frequency to change the diversity of operating systems and applications deployed using virtualization techniques; and*
SC-29(1)[2]	*employs virtualization techniques to support the deployment of a diversity of operating systems and applications that are changed with the organization-defined frequency.*

Special Publication 800-53A
Revision 4

Assessing Security and Privacy Controls in Federal Information Systems
and Organizations — *Building Effective Assessment Plans*

POTENTIAL ASSESSMENT METHODS AND OBJECTS:

Examine: [*SELECT FROM:* System and communications protection policy; configuration management policy and procedures; information system design documentation; information system configuration settings and associated documentation; information system architecture; list of operating systems and applications deployed using virtualization techniques; change control records; configuration management records; information system audit records; other relevant documents or records].

Interview: [*SELECT FROM:* System/network administrators; organizational personnel with information security responsibilities; organizational personnel with responsibilities for implementing approved virtualization techniques to the information system].

Test: [*SELECT FROM:* Automated mechanisms supporting and/or implementing employment of a diverse set of information technologies; automated mechanisms supporting and/or implementing virtualization techniques].

SC-30	CONCEALMENT AND MISDIRECTION

ASSESSMENT OBJECTIVE:

Determine if the organization:

SC-30[1]	*defines concealment and misdirection techniques to be employed to confuse and mislead adversaries potentially targeting organizational information systems;*
SC-30[2]	*defines information systems for which organization-defined concealment and misdirection techniques are to be employed;*
SC-30[3]	*defines time periods to employ organization-defined concealment and misdirection techniques for organization-defined information systems; and*
SC-30[4]	*employs organization-defined concealment and misdirection techniques for organization-defined information systems at organization-defined time periods to confuse and mislead adversaries.*

POTENTIAL ASSESSMENT METHODS AND OBJECTS:

Examine: [*SELECT FROM:* System and communications protection policy; procedures addressing concealment and misdirection techniques for the information system; information system design documentation; information system configuration settings and associated documentation; information system architecture; list of concealment and misdirection techniques to be employed for organizational information systems; information system audit records; other relevant documents or records].

Interview: [*SELECT FROM:* System/network administrators; organizational personnel with information security responsibilities; organizational personnel with responsibility for implementing concealment and misdirection techniques for information systems].

Test: [*SELECT FROM:* Automated mechanisms supporting and/or implementing concealment and misdirection techniques].

SC-30(1)	CONCEALMENT AND MISDIRECTION | *VIRTUALIZATION TECHNIQUES*

[Withdrawn: Incorporated into SC-29(1)].

SC-30(2)	CONCEALMENT AND MISDIRECTION | *RANDOMNESS*

ASSESSMENT OBJECTIVE:

Determine if the organization:

SC-30(2)[1]	*defines techniques to be employed to introduce randomness into organizational operations and assets; and*
SC-30(2)[2]	*employs organization-defined techniques to introduce randomness into organizational operations and assets.*

Special Publication 800-53A
Revision 4

Assessing Security and Privacy Controls in Federal Information Systems
and Organizations — *Building Effective Assessment Plans*

POTENTIAL ASSESSMENT METHODS AND OBJECTS:

Examine: [*SELECT FROM:* System and communications protection policy; procedures addressing concealment and misdirection techniques for the information system; information system design documentation; information system configuration settings and associated documentation; information system architecture; list of techniques to be employed to introduce randomness into organizational operations and assets; information system audit records; other relevant documents or records].

Interview: [*SELECT FROM:* System/network administrators; organizational personnel with information security responsibilities; organizational personnel with responsibility for implementing concealment and misdirection techniques for information systems].

Test: [*SELECT FROM:* Automated mechanisms supporting and/or implementing randomness as a concealment and misdirection technique].

SC-30(3)	CONCEALMENT AND MISDIRECTION | *CHANGE PROCESSING / STORAGE LOCATIONS*	
	ASSESSMENT OBJECTIVE: *Determine if the organization:*	
	SC-30(3)[1]	*defines processing and/or storage locations to be changed at time intervals specified by the organization;*
	SC-30(3)[2]	*defines a frequency to change the location of organization-defined processing and/or storage; and*
	SC-30(3)[3]	*changes the location of organization-defined processing and/or storage at one of the following:*
	SC-30(3)[3][a]	*organization-defined time intervals; or*
	SC-30(3)[3][b]	*random time intervals.*

POTENTIAL ASSESSMENT METHODS AND OBJECTS:

Examine: [*SELECT FROM:* System and communications protection policy; configuration management policy and procedures; procedures addressing concealment and misdirection techniques for the information system; list of processing/storage locations to be changed at organizational time intervals; change control records; configuration management records; information system audit records; other relevant documents or records].

Interview: [*SELECT FROM:* System/network administrators; organizational personnel with information security responsibilities; organizational personnel with responsibility for changing processing and/or storage locations].

Test: [*SELECT FROM:* Automated mechanisms supporting and/or implementing changing processing and/or storage locations].

SC-30(4)	CONCEALMENT AND MISDIRECTION | *MISLEADING INFORMATION*	
	ASSESSMENT OBJECTIVE: *Determine if the organization:*	
	SC-30(4)[1]	*defines information system components in which to employ realistic, but misleading information regarding its security state or posture; and*
	SC-30(4)[2]	*employs realistic, but misleading information in organization-defined information system components with regard to its security state or posture.*

Special Publication 800-53A
Revision 4

Assessing Security and Privacy Controls in Federal Information Systems
and Organizations — *Building Effective Assessment Plans*

POTENTIAL ASSESSMENT METHODS AND OBJECTS:

Examine: [*SELECT FROM:* System and communications protection policy; configuration management policy and procedures; procedures addressing concealment and misdirection techniques for the information system; information system design documentation; information system configuration settings and associated documentation; information system audit records; other relevant documents or records].

Interview: [*SELECT FROM:* System/network administrators; organizational personnel with information security responsibilities; organizational personnel with responsibility for defining and employing realistic, but misleading information about the security posture of information system components].

Test: [*SELECT FROM:* Automated mechanisms supporting and/or implementing employment of realistic, but misleading information about the security posture of information system components].

SC-30(5)	CONCEALMENT AND MISDIRECTION | *CONCEALMENT OF SYSTEM COMPONENTS*

ASSESSMENT OBJECTIVE:

Determine if the organization:

SC-30(5)[1]	*defines techniques to be employed to hide or conceal information system components;*
SC-30(5)[2]	*defines information system components to be hidden or concealed using organization-defined techniques; and*
SC-30(5)[3]	*employs organization-defined techniques to hide or conceal organization-defined information system components.*

POTENTIAL ASSESSMENT METHODS AND OBJECTS:

Examine: [*SELECT FROM:* System and communications protection policy; configuration management policy and procedures; procedures addressing concealment and misdirection techniques for the information system; information system design documentation; information system configuration settings and associated documentation; list of techniques employed to hide or conceal information system components; list of information system components to be hidden or concealed; other relevant documents or records].

Interview: [*SELECT FROM:* System/network administrators; organizational personnel with information security responsibilities; organizational personnel with responsibility for concealment of system components].

Test: [*SELECT FROM:* Automated mechanisms supporting and/or implementing techniques for concealment of system components].

SC-31	COVERT CHANNEL ANALYSIS

ASSESSMENT OBJECTIVE:

Determine if the organization:

SC-31(a)	*performs a covert channel analysis to identify those aspects of communications within the information system that are potential avenues for one or more of the following:*	
	SC-31(a)[1]	*covert storage channels; and/or*
	SC-31(a)[2]	*covert timing channels; and*
SC-31(b)	*estimates the maximum bandwidth of those channels.*	

Special Publication 800-53A
Revision 4

Assessing Security and Privacy Controls in Federal Information Systems
and Organizations — *Building Effective Assessment Plans*

POTENTIAL ASSESSMENT METHODS AND OBJECTS:

Examine: [*SELECT FROM:* System and communications protection policy; procedures addressing covert channel analysis; information system design documentation; information system configuration settings and associated documentation; covert channel analysis documentation; information system audit records; other relevant documents or records].

Interview: [*SELECT FROM:* System/network administrators; organizational personnel with information security responsibilities; organizational personnel with covert channel analysis responsibilities; information system developers/integrators].

Test: [*SELECT FROM:* Organizational process for conducting covert channel analysis; automated mechanisms supporting and/or implementing covert channel analysis; automated mechanisms supporting and/or implementing the capability to estimate the bandwidth of covert channels].

SC-31(1)	COVERT CHANNEL ANALYSIS | *TEST COVERT CHANNELS FOR EXPLOITABILITY*

ASSESSMENT OBJECTIVE:

Determine if the organization tests a subset of identified covert channels to determine which channels are exploitable.

POTENTIAL ASSESSMENT METHODS AND OBJECTS:

Examine: [*SELECT FROM:* System and communications protection policy; procedures addressing covert channel analysis; information system design documentation; information system configuration settings and associated documentation; list of covert channels; covert channel analysis documentation; information system audit records; other relevant documents or records].

Interview: [*SELECT FROM:* System/network administrators; organizational personnel with information security responsibilities; organizational personnel with covert channel analysis responsibilities].

Test: [*SELECT FROM:* Organizational process for testing covert channels; automated mechanisms supporting and/or implementing testing of covert channels analysis].

SC-31(2)	COVERT CHANNEL ANALYSIS | *MAXIMUM BANDWIDTH*

ASSESSMENT OBJECTIVE:

Determine if the organization:

SC-31(2)[1]	*defines values to be employed as the maximum bandwidth allowed for identified covert channels; and*	
SC-31(2)[2]	*reduces the maximum bandwidth to organization-defined values for one or more of the following identified:*	
	SC-31(2)[2][a]	*covert storage channels; and/or*
	SC-31(2)[2][b]	*covert timing channels.*

POTENTIAL ASSESSMENT METHODS AND OBJECTS:

Examine: [*SELECT FROM:* System and communications protection policy; procedures addressing covert channel analysis; acquisition contracts for information systems or services; acquisition documentation; information system design documentation; information system configuration settings and associated documentation; covert channel analysis documentation; information system audit records; other relevant documents or records].

Interview: [*SELECT FROM:* System/network administrators; organizational personnel with information security responsibilities; organizational personnel with covert channel analysis responsibilities; information system developers/integrators].

Test: [*SELECT FROM:* Organizational process for conducting covert channel analysis; automated mechanisms supporting and/or implementing covert channel analysis; automated mechanisms supporting and/or implementing the capability to reduce the bandwidth of covert channels].

Special Publication 800-53A
Revision 4

Assessing Security and Privacy Controls in Federal Information Systems
and Organizations — *Building Effective Assessment Plans*

SC-31(3)	COVERT CHANNEL ANALYSIS | *MEASURE BANDWIDTH IN OPERATIONAL ENVIRONMENTS*
	ASSESSMENT OBJECTIVE: *Determine if the organization:*
	SC-31(3)[1] — *defines subset of identified covert channels whose bandwidth is to be measured in the operational environment of the information system; and*
	SC-31(3)[2] — *measures the bandwidth of the organization-defined subset of identified covert channels in the operational environment of the information system.*
	POTENTIAL ASSESSMENT METHODS AND OBJECTS: **Examine**: [*SELECT FROM:* System and communications protection policy; procedures addressing covert channel analysis; information system design documentation; information system configuration settings and associated documentation; covert channel analysis documentation; information system audit records; other relevant documents or records]. **Interview**: [*SELECT FROM:* System/network administrators; organizational personnel with information security responsibilities; organizational personnel with covert channel analysis responsibilities; information system developers/integrators]. **Test**: [*SELECT FROM:* Organizational process for conducting covert channel analysis; automated mechanisms supporting and/or implementing covert channel analysis; automated mechanisms supporting and/or implementing the capability to measure the bandwidth of covert channels].

SC-32	INFORMATION SYSTEM PARTITIONING
	ASSESSMENT OBJECTIVE: *Determine if the organization:*
	SC-32[1] — *defines circumstances for physical separation of information system components into information system partitions;*
	SC-32[2] — *defines information system components to reside in separate physical domains or environments based on organization-defined circumstances for physical separation of components; and*
	SC-32[3] — *partitions the information system into organization-defined information system components residing in separate physical domains or environments based on organization-defined circumstances for physical separation of components.*
	POTENTIAL ASSESSMENT METHODS AND OBJECTS: **Examine**: [*SELECT FROM:* System and communications protection policy; procedures addressing information system partitioning; information system design documentation; information system configuration settings and associated documentation; information system architecture; list of information system physical domains (or environments); information system facility diagrams; information system network diagrams; other relevant documents or records]. **Interview**: [*SELECT FROM:* System/network administrators; organizational personnel with information security responsibilities; organizational personnel installing, configuring, and/or maintaining the information system; information system developers/integrators]. **Test**: [*SELECT FROM:* Automated mechanisms supporting and/or implementing physical separation of information system components].

SC-33	TRANSMISSION PREPARATION INTEGRITY
[Withdrawn: Incorporated into SC-8].	

Special Publication 800-53A
Revision 4

Assessing Security and Privacy Controls in Federal Information Systems
and Organizations — *Building Effective Assessment Plans*

SC-34	NON-MODIFIABLE EXECUTABLE PROGRAMS

ASSESSMENT OBJECTIVE:

Determine if:

SC-34[1]	*the organization defines information system components for which the operating environment and organization-defined applications are to be loaded and executed from hardware-enforced, read-only media;*
SC-34[2]	*the organization defines applications to be loaded and executed from hardware-enforced, read-only media;*
SC-34[3]	*the information system, at organization-defined information system components:*

	SC-34[3](a)	*loads and executes the operating environment from hardware-enforced, read-only media; and*
	SC-34[3](b)	*loads and executes organization-defined applications from hardware-enforced, read-only media.*

POTENTIAL ASSESSMENT METHODS AND OBJECTS:

Examine: [*SELECT FROM:* System and communications protection policy; procedures addressing non-modifiable executable programs; information system design documentation; information system configuration settings and associated documentation; information system architecture; list of operating system components to be loaded from hardware-enforced, read-only media; list of applications to be loaded from hardware-enforced, read-only media; media used to load and execute information system operating environment; media used to load and execute information system applications; information system audit records; other relevant documents or records].

Interview: [*SELECT FROM:* System/network administrators; organizational personnel with information security responsibilities; system developer; organizational personnel installing, configuring, and/or maintaining the information system; information system developers/integrators].

Test: [*SELECT FROM:* Automated mechanisms supporting and/or implementing loading and executing the operating environment from hardware-enforced, read-only media; automated mechanisms supporting and/or implementing loading and executing applications from hardware-enforced, read-only media].

SC-34(1)	NON-MODIFIABLE EXECUTABLE PROGRAMS	*NO WRITABLE STORAGE*

ASSESSMENT OBJECTIVE:

Determine if the organization:

SC-34(1)[1]	*defines information system components to be employed with no writeable storage; and*
SC-34(1)[2]	*employs organization-defined information system components with no writeable storage that is persistent across component restart or power on/off.*

POTENTIAL ASSESSMENT METHODS AND OBJECTS:

Examine: [*SELECT FROM:* System and communications protection policy; procedures addressing non-modifiable executable programs; information system design documentation; information system configuration settings and associated documentation; information system architecture; list of information system components to be employed without writeable storage capability; information system audit records; other relevant documents or records].

Interview: [*SELECT FROM:* System/network administrators; organizational personnel with information security responsibilities; organizational personnel installing, configuring, and/or maintaining the information system; information system developers/integrators].

Test: [*SELECT FROM:* Automated mechanisms supporting and/or implementing employment of components with no writeable storage; automated mechanisms supporting and/or implementing persistent non-writeable storage across component restart and power on/off].

Special Publication 800-53A
Revision 4

Assessing Security and Privacy Controls in Federal Information Systems
and Organizations — *Building Effective Assessment Plans*

SC-34(2)	NON-MODIFIABLE EXECUTABLE PROGRAMS | *INTEGRITY PROTECTION/READ-ONLY MEDIA*	
	ASSESSMENT OBJECTIVE: *Determine if the organization:*	
	SC-34(2)[1]	*protects the integrity of the information prior to storage on read-only media; and*
	SC-34(2)[2]	*controls the media after such information has been recorded onto the media.*
	POTENTIAL ASSESSMENT METHODS AND OBJECTS: **Examine**: [*SELECT FROM:* System and communications protection policy; procedures addressing non-modifiable executable programs; information system design documentation; information system configuration settings and associated documentation; information system architecture; information system audit records; other relevant documents or records]. **Interview**: [*SELECT FROM:* System/network administrators; organizational personnel with information security responsibilities; organizational personnel installing, configuring, and/or maintaining the information system; information system developers/integrators]. **Test**: [*SELECT FROM:* Automated mechanisms supporting and/or implementing capability for protecting information integrity on read-only media prior to storage and after information has been recorded onto the media].	

SC-34(3)	NON-MODIFIABLE EXECUTABLE PROGRAMS | *HARDWARE-BASED PROTECTION*		
	ASSESSMENT OBJECTIVE: *Determine if the organization:*		
	SC-34(3)(a)	SC-34(3)(a)[1]	*defines information system firmware components for which hardware-based, write-protection is to be employed;*
		SC-34(3)(a)[2]	*employs hardware-based, write-protection for organization-defined information system firmware components;*
	SC-34(3)(b)	SC-34(3)(b)[1]	*defines individuals authorized to manually disable hardware write-protect for firmware modifications and re-enable the write-protect prior to returning to operational mode; and*
		SC-34(3)(b)[2]	*implements specific procedures for organization-defined authorized individuals to manually disable hardware write-protect for firmware modifications and re-enable the write-protect prior to returning to operational mode.*
	POTENTIAL ASSESSMENT METHODS AND OBJECTS: **Examine**: [*SELECT FROM:* System and communications protection policy; procedures addressing firmware modifications; information system design documentation; information system configuration settings and associated documentation; information system architecture; information system audit records; other relevant documents or records]. **Interview**: [*SELECT FROM:* System/network administrators; organizational personnel with information security responsibilities; organizational personnel installing, configuring, and/or maintaining the information system; information system developers/integrators]. **Test**: [*SELECT FROM:* Organizational processes for modifying firmware; automated mechanisms supporting and/or implementing hardware-based, write-protection for firmware].		

SC-35	HONEYCLIENTS
	ASSESSMENT OBJECTIVE: *Determine if the information system includes components that proactively seek to identify malicious websites and/or web-based malicious code.*

Special Publication 800-53A
Revision 4

Assessing Security and Privacy Controls in Federal Information Systems
and Organizations — *Building Effective Assessment Plans*

POTENTIAL ASSESSMENT METHODS AND OBJECTS:

Examine: [*SELECT FROM*: System and communications protection policy; procedures addressing honeyclients; information system design documentation; information system configuration settings and associated documentation; information system components deployed to identify malicious websites and/or web-based malicious code; information system audit records; other relevant documents or records].

Interview: [*SELECT FROM*: System/network administrators; organizational personnel with information security responsibilities; system developer; organizational personnel installing, configuring, and/or maintaining the information system; information system developers/integrators].

Test: [*SELECT FROM*: Automated mechanisms supporting and/or implementing honeyclients].

SC-36	DISTRIBUTED PROCESSING AND STORAGE

ASSESSMENT OBJECTIVE:

Determine if the organization:

SC-36[1]	*defines processing and storage to be distributed across multiple physical locations; and*
SC-36[2]	*distributes organization-defined processing and storage across multiple physical locations.*

POTENTIAL ASSESSMENT METHODS AND OBJECTS:

Examine: [*SELECT FROM*: System and communications protection policy; contingency planning policy and procedures; contingency plan; information system design documentation; information system configuration settings and associated documentation; information system architecture; list of information system physical locations (or environments) with distributed processing and storage; information system facility diagrams; processing site agreements; storage site agreements; other relevant documents or records].

Interview: [*SELECT FROM*: System/network administrators; organizational personnel with information security responsibilities; organizational personnel installing, configuring, and/or maintaining the information system; organizational personnel with contingency planning and plan implementation responsibilities; information system developers/integrators].

Test: [*SELECT FROM*: Organizational processes for distributing processing and storage across multiple physical locations; automated mechanisms supporting and/or implementing capability for distributing processing and storage across multiple physical locations].

SC-36(1)	DISTRIBUTED PROCESSING AND STORAGE | *POLLING TECHNIQUES*

ASSESSMENT OBJECTIVE:

Determine if the organization:

SC-36(1)[1]	*defines distributed processing and storage components for which polling techniques are to be employed to identify potential faults, errors, or compromises; and*
SC-36(1)[2]	*employs polling techniques to identify potential faults, errors, or compromises to organization-defined distributed processing and storage components.*

POTENTIAL ASSESSMENT METHODS AND OBJECTS:

Examine: [*SELECT FROM*: System and communications protection policy; information system design documentation; information system configuration settings and associated documentation; information system architecture; list of distributed processing and storage components subject to polling; information system polling techniques and associated documentation or records; information system audit records; other relevant documents or records].

Interview: [*SELECT FROM*: System/network administrators; organizational personnel with information security responsibilities; organizational personnel installing, configuring, and/or maintaining the information system; information system developers/integrators].

Test: [*SELECT FROM*: Automated mechanisms supporting and/or implementing polling techniques].

Special Publication 800-53A
Revision 4

Assessing Security and Privacy Controls in Federal Information Systems
and Organizations — *Building Effective Assessment Plans*

SC-37	OUT-OF-BAND CHANNELS
	ASSESSMENT OBJECTIVE: *Determine if the organization:*

	SC-37[1]	*defines out-of-band channels to be employed for the physical delivery or electronic transmission of information, information system components, or devices to individuals or information systems;*
	SC-37[2]	*defines information, information system components, or devices for which physical delivery or electronic transmission of such information, information system components, or devices to individuals or information systems requires employment of organization-defined out-of-band channels;*
	SC-37[3]	*defines individuals or information systems to which physical delivery or electronic transmission of organization-defined information, information system components, or devices is to be achieved via employment of organization-defined out-of-band channels; and*
	SC-37[4]	*employs organization-defined out-of-band channels for the physical delivery or electronic transmission of organization-defined information, information system components, or devices to organization-defined individuals or information systems.*

POTENTIAL ASSESSMENT METHODS AND OBJECTS:

Examine: [*SELECT FROM:* System and communications protection policy; procedures addressing use of out-of-band channels; access control policy and procedures; identification and authentication policy and procedures; information system design documentation; information system architecture; information system configuration settings and associated documentation; list of out-of-band channels; types of information, information system components, or devices requiring use of out-of-band channels for physical delivery or electronic transmission to authorized individuals or information systems; physical delivery records; electronic transmission records; information system audit records; other relevant documents or records].

Interview: [*SELECT FROM:* System/network administrators; organizational personnel with information security responsibilities; organizational personnel installing, configuring, and/or maintaining the information system; organizational personnel authorizing, installing, configuring, operating, and/or using out-of-band channels; information system developers/integrators].

Test: [*SELECT FROM:* Organizational processes for use of out-of-band channels; automated mechanisms supporting and/or implementing use of out-of-band channels].

SC-37(1)	OUT-OF-BAND CHANNELS | ENSURE DELIVERY / TRANSMISSION
	ASSESSMENT OBJECTIVE: *Determine if the organization:*

	SC-37(1)[1]	*defines security safeguards to be employed to ensure that only designated individuals or information systems receive specific information, information system components, or devices;*
	SC-37(1)[2]	*defines individuals or information systems designated to receive specific information, information system components, or devices;*
	SC-37(1)[3]	*defines information, information system components, or devices that only organization-defined individuals or information systems are designated to receive; and*
	SC-37(1)[4]	*employs organization-defined security safeguards to ensure that only organization-defined individuals or information systems receive the organization-defined information, information system components, or devices.*

Special Publication 800-53A
Revision 4

Assessing Security and Privacy Controls in Federal Information Systems
and Organizations — *Building Effective Assessment Plans*

	POTENTIAL ASSESSMENT METHODS AND OBJECTS: **Examine**: [*SELECT FROM:* System and communications protection policy; procedures addressing use of out-of-band channels; access control policy and procedures; identification and authentication policy and procedures; information system design documentation; information system architecture; information system configuration settings and associated documentation; list of security safeguards to be employed to ensure designated individuals or information systems receive organization-defined information, information system components, or devices; list of security safeguards for delivering designated information, information system components, or devices to designated individuals or information systems; list of information, information system components, or devices to be delivered to designated individuals or information systems; information system audit records; other relevant documents or records]. **Interview**: [*SELECT FROM:* System/network administrators; organizational personnel with information security responsibilities; organizational personnel installing, configuring, and/or maintaining the information system; organizational personnel authorizing, installing, configuring, operating, and/or using out-of-band channels; information system developers/integrators]. **Test**: [*SELECT FROM:* Organizational processes for use of out-of-band channels; automated mechanisms supporting and/or implementing use of out-of-band channels; automated mechanisms supporting/implementing safeguards to ensure delivery of designated information, system components, or devices].

SC-38	**OPERATIONS SECURITY**
	ASSESSMENT OBJECTIVE: *Determine if the organization:*
	SC-38[1] — *defines operations security safeguards to be employed to protect key organizational information throughout the system development life cycle; and*
	SC-38[2] — *employs organization-defined operations security safeguards to protect key organizational information throughout the system development life cycle.*
	POTENTIAL ASSESSMENT METHODS AND OBJECTS: **Examine**: [*SELECT FROM:* System and communications protection policy; procedures addressing operations security; security plan; list of operations security safeguards; security control assessments; risk assessments; threat and vulnerability assessments; plans of action and milestones; system development life cycle documentation; other relevant documents or records]. **Interview**: [*SELECT FROM:* System/network administrators; organizational personnel with information security responsibilities; organizational personnel installing, configuring, and/or maintaining the information system; information system developers/integrators]. **Test**: [*SELECT FROM:* Organizational processes for protecting organizational information throughout the SDLC; automated mechanisms supporting and/or implementing safeguards to protect organizational information throughout the SDLC].

SC-39	**PROCESS ISOLATION**
	ASSESSMENT OBJECTIVE: *Determine if the information system maintains a separate execution domain for each executing process.*
	POTENTIAL ASSESSMENT METHODS AND OBJECTS: **Examine**: [*SELECT FROM:* Information system design documentation; information system architecture; independent verification and validation documentation; testing and evaluation documentation, other relevant documents or records]. **Interview**: [*SELECT FROM:* Information system developers/integrators; information system security architect]. **Test**: [*SELECT FROM:* Automated mechanisms supporting and/or implementing separate execution domains for each executing process].

Special Publication 800-53A
Revision 4

Assessing Security and Privacy Controls in Federal Information Systems
and Organizations — *Building Effective Assessment Plans*

SC-39(1)	PROCESS ISOLATION	*HARDWARE SEPARATION*

	ASSESSMENT OBJECTIVE: *Determine if the information system implements underlying hardware separation mechanisms to facilitate process separation.*
	POTENTIAL ASSESSMENT METHODS AND OBJECTS: **Examine**: [*SELECT FROM:* System and communications protection policy; information system design documentation; information system configuration settings and associated documentation; information system architecture; information system documentation for hardware separation mechanisms; information system documentation from vendors, manufacturers or developers; independent verification and validation documentation; other relevant documents or records]. **Interview**: [*SELECT FROM:* System/network administrators; organizational personnel with information security responsibilities; system developer; organizational personnel installing, configuring, and/or maintaining the information system; information system developers/integrators]. **Test**: [*SELECT FROM:* Information system capability implementing underlying hardware separation mechanisms for process separation].

SC-39(2)	PROCESS ISOLATION	*THREAD ISOLATION*

	ASSESSMENT OBJECTIVE:	
	Determine if the information system:	
	SC-39(2)[1]	*defines multi-threaded processing for which a separate execution domain is to be maintained for each thread in multi-threaded processing; and*
	SC-39(2)[2]	*maintains a separate execution domain for each thread in organization-defined multi-threaded processing.*

	POTENTIAL ASSESSMENT METHODS AND OBJECTS: **Examine**: [*SELECT FROM:* System and communications protection policy; information system design documentation; information system configuration settings and associated documentation; information system architecture; list of information system execution domains for each thread in multi-threaded processing; information system documentation for multi-threaded processing; information system documentation from vendors, manufacturers or developers; independent verification and validation documentation; other relevant documents or records]. **Interview**: [*SELECT FROM:* System/network administrators; organizational personnel with information security responsibilities; system developer; organizational personnel installing, configuring, and/or maintaining the information system; information system developers/integrators]. **Test**: [*SELECT FROM:* Information system capability implementing a separate execution domain for each thread in multi-threaded processing].

SC-40	WIRELESS LINK PROTECTION

	ASSESSMENT OBJECTIVE:		
	Determine if:		
	SC-40[1]	*the organization defines:*	
		SC-40[1][a]	*internal wireless links to be protected from particular types of signal parameter attacks;*
		SC-40[1][b]	*external wireless links to be protected from particular types of signal parameter attacks;*
	SC-40[2]	*the organization defines types of signal parameter attacks or references to sources for such attacks that are based upon exploiting the signal parameters of organization-defined internal and external wireless links; and*	

Special Publication 800-53A
Revision 4

Assessing Security and Privacy Controls in Federal Information Systems
and Organizations — *Building Effective Assessment Plans*

	SC-40[3]	*the information system protects internal and external organization-defined wireless links from organization-defined types of signal parameter attacks or references to sources for such attacks.*
	POTENTIAL ASSESSMENT METHODS AND OBJECTS:	
	Examine: [*SELECT FROM:* System and communications protection policy; access control policy and procedures; procedures addressing wireless link protection; information system design documentation; wireless network diagrams; information system configuration settings and associated documentation; information system architecture; list or internal and external wireless links; list of signal parameter attacks or references to sources for attacks; information system audit records; other relevant documents or records].	
	Interview: [*SELECT FROM:* System/network administrators; organizational personnel with information security responsibilities; system developer; organizational personnel installing, configuring, and/or maintaining the information system; organizational personnel authorizing, installing, configuring and/or maintaining internal and external wireless links].	
	Test: [*SELECT FROM:* Automated mechanisms supporting and/or implementing protection of wireless links].	

SC-40(1)	**WIRELESS LINK PROTECTION | *ELECTROMAGNETIC INTERFERENCE***	
	ASSESSMENT OBJECTIVE: *Determine if:*	
	SC-40(1)[1]	*the organization defines level of protection to be employed against the effects of intentional electromagnetic interference; and*
	SC-40(1)[2]	*the information system employs cryptographic mechanisms that achieve organization-defined level of protection against the effects of intentional electromagnetic interference.*
	POTENTIAL ASSESSMENT METHODS AND OBJECTS:	
	Examine: [*SELECT FROM:* System and communications protection policy; access control policy and procedures; procedures addressing wireless link protection; information system design documentation; wireless network diagrams; information system configuration settings and associated documentation; information system architecture; information system communications hardware and software; security categorization results; information system audit records; other relevant documents or records].	
	Interview: [*SELECT FROM:* System/network administrators; organizational personnel with information security responsibilities; system developer; organizational personnel installing, configuring, and/or maintaining the information system; organizational personnel authorizing, installing, configuring and/or maintaining internal and external wireless links].	
	Test: [*SELECT FROM:* Cryptographic mechanisms enforcing protections against effects of intentional electromagnetic interference].	

SC-40(2)	**WIRELESS LINK PROTECTION | *REDUCE DETECTION POTENTIAL***	
	ASSESSMENT OBJECTIVE: *Determine if:*	
	SC-40(2)[1]	*the organization defines level of reduction to be achieved to reduce the detection potential of wireless links; and*
	SC-40(2)[2]	*the information system implements cryptographic mechanisms to reduce the detection potential of wireless links to organization-defined level of reduction.*

Special Publication 800-53A
Revision 4

Assessing Security and Privacy Controls in Federal Information Systems
and Organizations — *Building Effective Assessment Plans*

POTENTIAL ASSESSMENT METHODS AND OBJECTS:

Examine: [*SELECT FROM*: System and communications protection policy; access control policy and procedures; procedures addressing wireless link protection; information system design documentation; wireless network diagrams; information system configuration settings and associated documentation; information system architecture; information system communications hardware and software; security categorization results; information system audit records; other relevant documents or records].

Interview: [*SELECT FROM*: System/network administrators; organizational personnel with information security responsibilities; system developer; organizational personnel installing, configuring, and/or maintaining the information system; organizational personnel authorizing, installing, configuring and/or maintaining internal and external wireless links].

Test: [*SELECT FROM*: Cryptographic mechanisms enforcing protections to reduce detection of wireless links].

SC-40(3)	WIRELESS LINK PROTECTION | *IMITATIVE OR MANIPULATIVE COMMUNICATIONS DECEPTION*

ASSESSMENT OBJECTIVE:

Determine if the information system implements cryptographic mechanisms to:

SC-40(3)[1]	*identify wireless transmissions that are deliberate attempts to achieve imitative or manipulative communications deception based on signal parameters; and*
SC-40(3)[2]	*reject wireless transmissions that are deliberate attempts to achieve imitative or manipulative communications deception based on signal parameters.*

POTENTIAL ASSESSMENT METHODS AND OBJECTS:

Examine: [*SELECT FROM*: System and communications protection policy; access control policy and procedures; procedures addressing information system design documentation; wireless network diagrams; information system configuration settings and associated documentation; information system architecture; information system communications hardware and software; information system audit records; other relevant documents or records].

Interview: [*SELECT FROM*: System/network administrators; organizational personnel with information security responsibilities; system developer; organizational personnel installing, configuring, and/or maintaining the information system; organizational personnel authorizing, installing, configuring and/or maintaining internal and external wireless links].

Test: [*SELECT FROM*: Cryptographic mechanisms enforcing wireless link protections against imitative or manipulative communications deception].

SC-40(4)	WIRELESS LINK PROTECTION | *SIGNAL PARAMETER IDENTIFICATION*

ASSESSMENT OBJECTIVE:

Determine if:

SC-40(4)[1]	*the organization defines wireless transmitters for which cryptographic mechanisms are to be implemented to prevent identification of such transmitters by using the transmitter signal parameters; and*
SC-40(4)[2]	*the information system implements cryptographic mechanisms to prevent the identification of organization-defined wireless transmitters by using the transmitter signal parameters.*

Special Publication 800-53A
Revision 4

Assessing Security and Privacy Controls in Federal Information Systems
and Organizations — *Building Effective Assessment Plans*

POTENTIAL ASSESSMENT METHODS AND OBJECTS:

Examine: [*SELECT FROM:* System and communications protection policy; access control policy and procedures; procedures addressing information system design documentation; wireless network diagrams; information system configuration settings and associated documentation; information system architecture; information system communications hardware and software; information system audit records; other relevant documents or records].

Interview: [*SELECT FROM:* System/network administrators; organizational personnel with information security responsibilities; system developer; organizational personnel installing, configuring, and/or maintaining the information system; organizational personnel authorizing, installing, configuring and/or maintaining internal and external wireless links].

Test: [*SELECT FROM:* Cryptographic mechanisms preventing the identification of wireless transmitters].

SC-41	PORT AND I/O DEVICE ACCESS

ASSESSMENT OBJECTIVE:

Determine if the organization:

SC-41[1]	*defines connection ports or input/output devices to be physically disabled or removed on information systems or information system components;*
SC-41[2]	*defines information systems or information system components with organization-defined connection ports or input/output devices that are to be physically disabled or removed; and*
SC-41[3]	*physically disables or removes organization-defined connection ports or input/output devices on organization-defined information systems or information system components.*

POTENTIAL ASSESSMENT METHODS AND OBJECTS:

Examine: [*SELECT FROM:* System and communications protection policy; access control policy and procedures; procedures addressing port and input/output device access; information system design documentation; information system configuration settings and associated documentation; information system architecture; information systems or information system components list of connection ports or input/output devices to be physically disabled or removed on information systems or information system components; other relevant documents or records].

Interview: [*SELECT FROM:* System/network administrators; organizational personnel with information security responsibilities; organizational personnel installing, configuring, and/or maintaining the information system].

Test: [*SELECT FROM:* Automated mechanisms supporting and/or implementing disabling of connection ports or input/output devices].

SC-42	SENSOR CAPABILITY AND DATA

ASSESSMENT OBJECTIVE:

Determine if:

SC-42(a)	SC-42(a)[1]	*the organization defines exceptions where remote activation of sensors is to be allowed;*
	SC-42(a)[2]	*the information system prohibits the remote activation of sensors, except for organization-defined exceptions where remote activation of sensors is to be allowed;*
SC-42(b)	SC-42(b)[1]	*the organization defines the class of users to whom an explicit indication of sensor use is to be provided; and*
	SC-42(b)[2]	*the information system provides an explicit indication of sensor use to the organization-defined class of users.*

Special Publication 800-53A
Revision 4

Assessing Security and Privacy Controls in Federal Information Systems
and Organizations — *Building Effective Assessment Plans*

POTENTIAL ASSESSMENT METHODS AND OBJECTS:

Examine: [*SELECT FROM:* System and communications protection policy; procedures addressing sensor capability and data collection; access control policy and procedures; information system design documentation; information system configuration settings and associated documentation; information system audit records; other relevant documents or records].

Interview: [*SELECT FROM:* System/network administrators; organizational personnel with information security responsibilities; system developer; organizational personnel installing, configuring, and/or maintaining the information system; organizational personnel with responsibility for sensor capability].

Test: [*SELECT FROM:* Automated mechanisms implementing access controls for remote activation of information system sensor capabilities; automated mechanisms implementing capability to indicate sensor use].

SC-42(1)	SENSOR CAPABILITY AND DATA | *REPORTING TO AUTHORIZED INDIVIDUALS OR ROLES*
	ASSESSMENT OBJECTIVE: *Determine if the organization:*
	SC-42(1)[1] *defines sensors to be used to collect data or information only reported to authorized individuals or roles; and*
	SC-42(1)[2] *ensures that the information system is configured so that data or information collected by the organization-defined sensors is only reported to authorized individuals or roles.*

POTENTIAL ASSESSMENT METHODS AND OBJECTS:

Examine: [*SELECT FROM:* System and communications protection policy; access control policy and procedures; procedures addressing sensor capability and data collection; information system design documentation; information system configuration settings and associated documentation; information system architecture; information system audit records; other relevant documents or records].

Interview: [*SELECT FROM:* System/network administrators; organizational personnel with information security responsibilities; system developer; organizational personnel installing, configuring, and/or maintaining the information system; organizational personnel with responsibility for sensor capability].

Test: [*SELECT FROM:* Automated mechanisms restricting reporting of sensor information only to those authorized; sensor data collection and reporting capability for the information system].

SC-42(2)	SENSOR CAPABILITY AND DATA | *AUTHORIZED USE*
	ASSESSMENT OBJECTIVE: *Determine if the organization:*
	SC-42(2)[1] *defines measures to be employed so that data or information collected by sensors is only used for authorized purposes;*
	SC-42(2)[2] *defines sensors to be used to collect data or information for authorized purposes only; and*
	SC-42(2)[3] *employs organization-defined measures so that data or information collected by organization-defined sensors is only used for authorized purposes.*

Special Publication 800-53A
Revision 4

Assessing Security and Privacy Controls in Federal Information Systems
and Organizations — *Building Effective Assessment Plans*

POTENTIAL ASSESSMENT METHODS AND OBJECTS:

Examine: [*SELECT FROM:* System and communications protection policy; access control policy and procedures; sensor capability and data collection; information system design documentation; information system configuration settings and associated documentation; information system architecture; list of measures to be employed to ensure data or information collected by sensors is only used for authorized purposes; information system audit records; other relevant documents or records].

Interview: [*SELECT FROM:* System/network administrators; organizational personnel with information security responsibilities; organizational personnel installing, configuring, and/or maintaining the information system; organizational personnel with responsibility for sensor capability].

Test: [*SELECT FROM:* Automated mechanisms supporting and/or implementing measures to ensure sensor information is only used for authorized purposes; sensor information collection capability for the information system].

SC-42(3)	SENSOR CAPABILITY AND DATA	*PROHIBIT USE OF DEVICES*

ASSESSMENT OBJECTIVE:

Determine if the organization:

SC-42(3)[1]	*defines environmental sensing capabilities to be prohibited from use in facilities, areas, or systems;*
SC-42(3)[2]	*defines facilities, areas, or systems where the use of devices possessing organization-defined environmental sensing capabilities is to be prohibited; and*
SC-42(3)[3]	*prohibits the use of devices possessing organization-defined environmental sensing capabilities in organization-defined facilities, areas, or systems.*

POTENTIAL ASSESSMENT METHODS AND OBJECTS:

Examine: [*SELECT FROM:* System and communications protection policy; access control policy and procedures; procedures addressing sensor capability and data collection; information system design documentation; wireless network diagrams; information system configuration settings and associated documentation; information system architecture; facilities, areas, or systems where use of devices possessing environmental sensing capabilities is prohibited; list of devices possessing environmental sensing capabilities; other relevant documents or records].

Interview: [*SELECT FROM:* System/network administrators; organizational personnel with information security responsibilities; organizational personnel installing, configuring, and/or maintaining the information system; organizational personnel with responsibility for sensor capability].

SC-43	USAGE RESTRICTIONS		

ASSESSMENT OBJECTIVE:

Determine if the organization:

SC-43(a)	SC-43(a)[1]	*defines information system components for which usage restrictions and implementation guidance are to be established;*	
	SC-43(a)[2]	*establishes, for organization-defined information system components:*	
		SC-43(a)[2][a]	*usage restrictions based on the potential to cause damage to the information system if used maliciously;*
		SC-43(a)[2][b]	*implementation guidance based on the potential to cause damage to the information system if used maliciously;*

Special Publication 800-53A
Revision 4

Assessing Security and Privacy Controls in Federal Information Systems
and Organizations — *Building Effective Assessment Plans*

	SC-43(b)	SC-43(b)[1]	*authorizes the use of such components within the information system;*
		SC-43(b)[2]	*monitors the use of such components within the information system; and*
		SC-43(b)[3]	*controls the use of such components within the information system.*

POTENTIAL ASSESSMENT METHODS AND OBJECTS:

Examine: [*SELECT FROM:* System and communications protection policy; procedures addressing usage restrictions; usage restrictions; implementation policy and procedures; authorization records; information system monitoring records; information system audit records; other relevant documents or records].

Interview: [*SELECT FROM:* System/network administrators; organizational personnel with information security responsibilities; organizational personnel installing, configuring, and/or maintaining the information system].

Test: [*SELECT FROM:* Organizational processes for authorizing, monitoring, and controlling use of components with usage restrictions; Automated mechanisms supporting and/or implementing authorizing, monitoring, and controlling use of components with usage restrictions].

SC-44	**DETONATION CHAMBERS**	

ASSESSMENT OBJECTIVE:

Determine if the organization:

	SC-44[1]	*defines information system, system component, or location where a detonation chamber capability is to be employed; and*
	SC-44[2]	*employs a detonation chamber capability within organization-defined information system, system component, or location.*

POTENTIAL ASSESSMENT METHODS AND OBJECTS:

Examine: [*SELECT FROM:* System and communications protection policy; procedures addressing detonation chambers; information system design documentation; information system configuration settings and associated documentation; information system audit records; other relevant documents or records].

Interview: [*SELECT FROM:* System/network administrators; organizational personnel with information security responsibilities; organizational personnel installing, configuring, and/or maintaining the information system].

Test: [*SELECT FROM:* Automated mechanisms supporting and/or implementing detonation chamber capability].

Special Publication 800-53A
Revision 4

Assessing Security and Privacy Controls in Federal Information Systems
and Organizations — *Building Effective Assessment Plans*

FAMILY: SYSTEM AND INFORMATION INTEGRITY

SI-1	SYSTEM AND INFORMATION INTEGRITY POLICY AND PROCEDURES		
	ASSESSMENT OBJECTIVE: *Determine if the organization:*		
	SI-1(a)(1)	SI-1(a)(1)[1]	*develops and documents a system and information integrity policy that addresses:*
			SI-1(a)(1)[1][a]	*purpose;*
			SI-1(a)(1)[1][b]	*scope;*
			SI-1(a)(1)[1][c]	*roles;*
			SI-1(a)(1)[1][d]	*responsibilities;*
			SI-1(a)(1)[1][e]	*management commitment;*
			SI-1(a)(1)[1][f]	*coordination among organizational entities;*
			SI-1(a)(1)[1][g]	*compliance;*
		SI-1(a)(1)[2]	*defines personnel or roles to whom the system and information integrity policy is to be disseminated;*
		SI-1(a)(1)[3]	*disseminates the system and information integrity policy to organization-defined personnel or roles;*
	SI-1(a)(2)	SI-1(a)(2)[1]	*develops and documents procedures to facilitate the implementation of the system and information integrity policy and associated system and information integrity controls;*
		SI-1(a)(2)[2]	*defines personnel or roles to whom the procedures are to be disseminated;*
		SI-1(a)(2)[3]	*disseminates the procedures to organization-defined personnel or roles;*
	SI-1(b)(1)	SI-1(b)(1)[1]	*defines the frequency to review and update the current system and information integrity policy;*
		SI-1(b)(1)[2]	*reviews and updates the current system and information integrity policy with the organization-defined frequency;*
	SI-1(b)(2)	SI-1(b)(2)[1]	*defines the frequency to review and update the current system and information integrity procedures; and*
		SI-1(b)(2)[2]	*reviews and updates the current system and information integrity procedures with the organization-defined frequency.*
	POTENTIAL ASSESSMENT METHODS AND OBJECTS: **Examine**: [*SELECT FROM:* System and information integrity policy and procedures; other relevant documents or records]. **Interview**: [*SELECT FROM:* Organizational personnel with system and information integrity responsibilities; organizational personnel with information security responsibilities].		

Special Publication 800-53A
Revision 4

Assessing Security and Privacy Controls in Federal Information Systems
and Organizations — *Building Effective Assessment Plans*

SI-2	FLAW REMEDIATION	
	ASSESSMENT OBJECTIVE: *Determine if the organization:*	
	SI-2(a)	SI-2(a)[1]	*identifies information system flaws;*
		SI-2(a)[2]	*reports information system flaws;*
		SI-2(a)[3]	*corrects information system flaws;*
	SI-2(b)	SI-2(b)[1]	*tests software updates related to flaw remediation for effectiveness and potential side effects before installation;*
		SI-2(b)[2]	*tests firmware updates related to flaw remediation for effectiveness and potential side effects before installation;*
	SI-2(c)	SI-2(c)[1]	*defines the time period within which to install security-relevant software updates after the release of the updates;*
		SI-2(c)[2]	*defines the time period within which to install security-relevant firmware updates after the release of the updates;*
		SI-2(c)[3]	*installs software updates within the organization-defined time period of the release of the updates;*
		SI-2(c)[4]	*installs firmware updates within the organization-defined time period of the release of the updates; and*
	SI-2(d)	*incorporates flaw remediation into the organizational configuration management process.*	
	POTENTIAL ASSESSMENT METHODS AND OBJECTS: **Examine**: [*SELECT FROM:* System and information integrity policy; procedures addressing flaw remediation; procedures addressing configuration management; list of flaws and vulnerabilities potentially affecting the information system; list of recent security flaw remediation actions performed on the information system (e.g., list of installed patches, service packs, hot fixes, and other software updates to correct information system flaws); test results from the installation of software and firmware updates to correct information system flaws; installation/change control records for security-relevant software and firmware updates; other relevant documents or records]. **Interview**: [*SELECT FROM:* System/network administrators; organizational personnel with information security responsibilities; organizational personnel installing, configuring, and/or maintaining the information system; organizational personnel with responsibility for flaw remediation; organizational personnel with configuration management responsibility]. **Test**: [*SELECT FROM:* Organizational processes for identifying, reporting, and correcting information system flaws; organizational process for installing software and firmware updates; automated mechanisms supporting and/or implementing reporting, and correcting information system flaws; automated mechanisms supporting and/or implementing testing software and firmware updates].	

SI-2(1)	FLAW REMEDIATION	*CENTRAL MANAGEMENT*
	ASSESSMENT OBJECTIVE: *Determine if the organization centrally manages the flaw remediation process.*

Special Publication 800-53A
Revision 4

Assessing Security and Privacy Controls in Federal Information Systems
and Organizations — *Building Effective Assessment Plans*

POTENTIAL ASSESSMENT METHODS AND OBJECTS:

Examine: [*SELECT FROM:* System and information integrity policy; procedures addressing flaw remediation; automated mechanisms supporting centralized management of flaw remediation; information system design documentation; information system configuration settings and associated documentation; information system audit records; other relevant documents or records].

Interview: [*SELECT FROM:* System/network administrators; organizational personnel with information security responsibilities; organizational personnel installing, configuring, and/or maintaining the information system; organizational personnel with responsibility for flaw remediation].

Test: [*SELECT FROM:* Organizational processes for central management of the flaw remediation process; automated mechanisms supporting and/or implementing central management of the flaw remediation process].

SI-2(2)	FLAW REMEDIATION | *AUTOMATED FLAW REMEDIATION STATUS*

ASSESSMENT OBJECTIVE:

Determine if the organization:

SI-2(2)[1]	*defines a frequency to employ automated mechanisms to determine the state of information system components with regard to flaw remediation; and*
SI-2(2)[2]	*employs automated mechanisms with the organization-defined frequency to determine the state of information system components with regard to flaw remediation.*

POTENTIAL ASSESSMENT METHODS AND OBJECTS:

Examine: [*SELECT FROM:* System and information integrity policy; procedures addressing flaw remediation; automated mechanisms supporting centralized management of flaw remediation; information system design documentation; information system configuration settings and associated documentation; information system audit records; other relevant documents or records].

Interview: [*SELECT FROM:* System/network administrators; organizational personnel with information security responsibilities; organizational personnel installing, configuring, and/or maintaining the information system; organizational personnel with responsibility for flaw remediation].

Test: [*SELECT FROM:* Automated mechanisms used to determine the state of information system components with regard to flaw remediation].

SI-2(3)	FLAW REMEDIATION | *TIME TO REMEDIATE FLAWS / BENCHMARKS FOR CORRECTION ACTIONS*

ASSESSMENT OBJECTIVE:

Determine if the organization:

SI-2(3)(a)		*measures the time between flaw identification and flaw remediation;*
SI-2(3)(b)	SI-2(3)(b)[1]	*defines benchmarks for taking corrective actions; and*
	SI-2(3)(b)[2]	*establishes organization-defined benchmarks for taking corrective actions.*

POTENTIAL ASSESSMENT METHODS AND OBJECTS:

Examine: [*SELECT FROM:* System and information integrity policy; procedures addressing flaw remediation; information system design documentation; information system configuration settings and associated documentation; list of benchmarks for taking corrective action on flaws identified; records providing time stamps of flaw identification and subsequent flaw remediation activities; other relevant documents or records].

Interview: [*SELECT FROM:* System/network administrators; organizational personnel with information security responsibilities; organizational personnel installing, configuring, and/or maintaining the information system; organizational personnel with responsibility for flaw remediation].

Test: [*SELECT FROM:* Organizational processes for identifying, reporting, and correcting information system flaws; automated mechanisms used to measure the time between flaw identification and flaw remediation].

SI-2(4)	FLAW REMEDIATION | *AUTOMATED PATCH MANAGEMENT TOOLS*
[Withdrawn: Incorporated into SI-2].	

SI-2(5)	FLAW REMEDIATION | *AUTOMATIC SOFTWARE / FIRMWARE UPDATES*

ASSESSMENT OBJECTIVE:

Determine if the organization:

SI-2(5)[1]	SI-2(5)[1][a]	*defines information system components requiring security-relevant software updates to be automatically installed;*
	SI-2(5)[1][b]	*defines information system components requiring security-relevant firmware updates to be automatically installed;*
SI-2(5)[2]	SI-2(5)[2][a]	*defines security-relevant software updates to be automatically installed to organization-defined information system components;*
	SI-2(5)[2][b]	*defines security-relevant firmware updates to be automatically installed to organization-defined information system components;*
SI-2(5)[3]	SI-2(5)[3][a]	*installs organization-defined security-relevant software updates automatically to organization-defined information system components; and*
	SI-2(5)[3][b]	*installs organization-defined security-relevant firmware updates automatically to organization-defined information system components.*

POTENTIAL ASSESSMENT METHODS AND OBJECTS:

Examine: [*SELECT FROM:* System and information integrity policy; procedures addressing flaw remediation; automated mechanisms supporting flaw remediation and automatic software/firmware updates; information system design documentation; information system configuration settings and associated documentation; records of recent security-relevant software and firmware updates automatically installed to information system components; information system audit records; other relevant documents or records].

Interview: [*SELECT FROM:* System/network administrators; organizational personnel with information security responsibilities; organizational personnel installing, configuring, and/or maintaining the information system; organizational personnel with responsibility for flaw remediation].

Test: [*SELECT FROM:* Automated mechanisms implementing automatic software/firmware updates].

SI-2(6)	FLAW REMEDIATION | *REMOVAL OF PREVIOUS VERSIONS OF SOFTWARE / FIRMWARE*

ASSESSMENT OBJECTIVE:

Determine if the organization:

Special Publication 800-53A
Revision 4

Assessing Security and Privacy Controls in Federal Information Systems
and Organizations — *Building Effective Assessment Plans*

	SI-2(6)[1]	SI-2(6)[1][a]	*defines software components to be removed after updated versions have been installed;*
		SI-2(6)[1][b]	*defines firmware components to be removed after updated versions have been installed;*
	SI-2(6)[2]	SI-2(6)[2][a]	*removes organization-defined software components after updated versions have been installed; and*
		SI-2(6)[2][b]	*removes organization-defined firmware components after updated versions have been installed.*

POTENTIAL ASSESSMENT METHODS AND OBJECTS:

Examine: [*SELECT FROM:* System and information integrity policy; procedures addressing flaw remediation; automated mechanisms supporting flaw remediation; information system design documentation; information system configuration settings and associated documentation; records of software and firmware component removals after updated versions are installed; information system audit records; other relevant documents or records].

Interview: [*SELECT FROM:* System/network administrators; organizational personnel with information security responsibilities; organizational personnel installing, configuring, and/or maintaining the information system; organizational personnel with responsibility for flaw remediation].

Test: [*SELECT FROM:* Automated mechanisms supporting and/or implementing removal of previous versions of software/firmware].

SI-3	**MALICIOUS CODE PROTECTION**				
	ASSESSMENT OBJECTIVE: *Determine if the organization:*				
	SI-3(a)	*employs malicious code protection mechanisms to detect and eradicate malicious code at information system:*			
		SI-3(a)[1]	*entry points;*		
		SI-3(a)[2]	*exit points;*		
	SI-3(b)	*updates malicious code protection mechanisms whenever new releases are available in accordance with organizational configuration management policy and procedures (as identified in CM-1);*			
	SI-3(c)	SI-3(c)[1]	*defines a frequency for malicious code protection mechanisms to perform periodic scans of the information system;*		
		SI-3(c)[2]	*defines action to be initiated by malicious protection mechanisms in response to malicious code detection;*		
		SI-3(c)[3]	SI-3(c)[3](1)	*configures malicious code protection mechanisms to:*	
				SI-3(c)[3](1)[a]	*perform periodic scans of the information system with the organization-defined frequency;*
				SI-3(c)[3](1)[b]	*perform real-time scans of files from external sources at endpoint and/or network entry/exit points as the files are downloaded, opened, or executed in accordance with organizational security policy;*
			SI-3(c)[3](2)	*configures malicious code protection mechanisms to do one or more of the following:*	

Special Publication 800-53A
Revision 4

Assessing Security and Privacy Controls in Federal Information Systems
and Organizations — *Building Effective Assessment Plans*

				SI-3(c)[3](2)[a]	*block malicious code in response to malicious code detection;*
				SI-3(c)[3](2)[b]	*quarantine malicious code in response to malicious code detection;*
				SI-3(c)[3](2)[c]	*send alert to administrator in response to malicious code detection; and/or*
				SI-3(c)[3](2)[d]	*initiate organization-defined action in response to malicious code detection;*
	SI-3(d)	SI-3(d)[1]			*addresses the receipt of false positives during malicious code detection and eradication; and*
		SI-3(d)[2]			*addresses the resulting potential impact on the availability of the information system.*

POTENTIAL ASSESSMENT METHODS AND OBJECTS:

Examine: [*SELECT FROM:* System and information integrity policy; configuration management policy and procedures; procedures addressing malicious code protection; malicious code protection mechanisms; records of malicious code protection updates; information system design documentation; information system configuration settings and associated documentation; scan results from malicious code protection mechanisms; record of actions initiated by malicious code protection mechanisms in response to malicious code detection; information system audit records; other relevant documents or records].

Interview: [*SELECT FROM:* System/network administrators; organizational personnel with information security responsibilities; organizational personnel installing, configuring, and/or maintaining the information system; organizational personnel with responsibility for malicious code protection; organizational personnel with configuration management responsibility].

Test: [*SELECT FROM:* Organizational processes for employing, updating, and configuring malicious code protection mechanisms; organizational process for addressing false positives and resulting potential impact; automated mechanisms supporting and/or implementing employing, updating, and configuring malicious code protection mechanisms; automated mechanisms supporting and/or implementing malicious code scanning and subsequent actions].

SI-3(1)	MALICIOUS CODE PROTECTION	*CENTRAL MANAGEMENT*
	ASSESSMENT OBJECTIVE: *Determine if the organization centrally manages malicious code protection mechanisms.* **POTENTIAL ASSESSMENT METHODS AND OBJECTS:** **Examine**: [*SELECT FROM:* System and information integrity policy; procedures addressing malicious code protection; automated mechanisms supporting centralized management of malicious code protection mechanisms; information system design documentation; information system configuration settings and associated documentation; information system audit records; other relevant documents or records]. **Interview**: [*SELECT FROM:* System/network administrators; organizational personnel with information security responsibilities; organizational personnel installing, configuring, and/or maintaining the information system; organizational personnel with responsibility for malicious code protection]. **Test**: [*SELECT FROM:* Organizational processes for central management of malicious code protection mechanisms; automated mechanisms supporting and/or implementing central management of malicious code protection mechanisms].

SI-3(2)	MALICIOUS CODE PROTECTION	*AUTOMATIC UPDATES*
	ASSESSMENT OBJECTIVE: *Determine if the information system automatically updates malicious code protection mechanisms.*

Special Publication 800-53A
Revision 4

Assessing Security and Privacy Controls in Federal Information Systems
and Organizations — *Building Effective Assessment Plans*

POTENTIAL ASSESSMENT METHODS AND OBJECTS:

Examine: [*SELECT FROM:* System and information integrity policy; procedures addressing malicious code protection; automated mechanisms supporting centralized management of malicious code protection mechanisms; information system design documentation; information system configuration settings and associated documentation; information system audit records; other relevant documents or records].

Interview: [*SELECT FROM:* System/network administrators; organizational personnel with information security responsibilities; system developers; organizational personnel installing, configuring, and/or maintaining the information system; organizational personnel with responsibility for malicious code protection].

Test: [*SELECT FROM:* Automated mechanisms supporting and/or implementing automatic updates to malicious code protection capability].

SI-3(3)	MALICIOUS CODE PROTECTION	*NON-PRIVILEGED USERS*

[Withdrawn: Incorporated into AC-6(10)].

SI-3(4)	MALICIOUS CODE PROTECTION	*UPDATES ONLY BY PRIVILEGED USERS*

ASSESSMENT OBJECTIVE:

Determine if the information system updates malicious code protection mechanisms only when directed by a privileged user.

POTENTIAL ASSESSMENT METHODS AND OBJECTS:

Examine: [*SELECT FROM:* System and information integrity policy; procedures addressing malicious code protection; information system design documentation; malicious code protection mechanisms; records of malicious code protection updates; information system configuration settings and associated documentation; information system audit records; other relevant documents or records].

Interview: [*SELECT FROM:* System/network administrators; organizational personnel with information security responsibilities; system developers; organizational personnel installing, configuring, and/or maintaining the information system; organizational personnel with responsibility for malicious code protection].

Test: [*SELECT FROM:* Automated mechanisms supporting and/or implementing malicious code protection capability].

SI-3(5)	MALICIOUS CODE PROTECTION	*PORTABLE STORAGE DEVICES*

[Withdrawn: Incorporated into MP-7].

SI-3(6)	MALICIOUS CODE PROTECTION	*TESTING / VERIFICATION*

ASSESSMENT OBJECTIVE:
Determine if the organization:

SI-3(6)(a)	SI-3(6)(a)[1]	*defines a frequency to test malicious code protection mechanisms;*
	SI-3(6)(a)[2]	*tests malicious code protection mechanisms with the organization-defined frequency by introducing a known benign, non-spreading test case into the information system;*
SI-3(6)(b)	SI-3(6)(b)[1]	*verifies that detection of the test case occurs; and*
	SI-3(6)(b)[2]	*verifies that associated incident reporting occurs.*

Special Publication 800-53A
Revision 4

Assessing Security and Privacy Controls in Federal Information Systems
and Organizations — *Building Effective Assessment Plans*

POTENTIAL ASSESSMENT METHODS AND OBJECTS:

Examine: [*SELECT FROM:* System and information integrity policy; procedures addressing malicious code protection; information system design documentation; information system configuration settings and associated documentation; test cases; records providing evidence of test cases executed on malicious code protection mechanisms; information system audit records; other relevant documents or records].

Interview: [*SELECT FROM:* System/network administrators; organizational personnel with information security responsibilities; organizational personnel installing, configuring, and/or maintaining the information system; organizational personnel with responsibility for malicious code protection].

Test: [*SELECT FROM:* Automated mechanisms supporting and/or implementing testing and verification of malicious code protection capability].

SI-3(7)	**MALICIOUS CODE PROTECTION** | *NONSIGNATURE-BASED DETECTION*

ASSESSMENT OBJECTIVE:

Determine if the information system implements non signature-based malicious code detection mechanisms.

POTENTIAL ASSESSMENT METHODS AND OBJECTS:

Examine: [*SELECT FROM:* System and information integrity policy; procedures addressing malicious code protection; information system design documentation; malicious code protection mechanisms; records of malicious code protection updates; information system configuration settings and associated documentation; information system audit records; other relevant documents or records].

Interview: [*SELECT FROM:* System/network administrators; organizational personnel with information security responsibilities; system developers; organizational personnel installing, configuring, and/or maintaining the information system; organizational personnel with responsibility for malicious code protection].

Test: [*SELECT FROM:* Automated mechanisms supporting and/or implementing nonsignature-based malicious code protection capability].

SI-3(8)	**MALICIOUS CODE PROTECTION** | *DETECT UNAUTHORIZED COMMANDS*

ASSESSMENT OBJECTIVE:
Determine if:

SI-3(8)[1]	*the organization defines unauthorized operating system commands to be detected by the information system;*
SI-3(8)[2]	*the organization defines information system hardware components for which organization-defined unauthorized operating system commands are to be detected through the kernel application programming interface;*
SI-3(8)[3]	*the information system detects organization-defined unauthorized operating system commands through the kernel application programming interface at organization-defined information system hardware components, and does one or more of the following:*

	SI-3(8)[3][a]	*issues a warning;*
	SI-3(8)[3][b]	*audits the command execution; and/or*
	SI-3(8)[3][c]	*prevents the execution of the command.*

Special Publication 800-53A
Revision 4

Assessing Security and Privacy Controls in Federal Information Systems
and Organizations — *Building Effective Assessment Plans*

	POTENTIAL ASSESSMENT METHODS AND OBJECTS: **Examine**: [*SELECT FROM:* System and information integrity policy; procedures addressing malicious code protection; information system design documentation; malicious code protection mechanisms; warning messages sent upon detection of unauthorized operating system command execution; information system configuration settings and associated documentation; information system audit records; other relevant documents or records]. **Interview**: [*SELECT FROM:* System/network administrators; organizational personnel with information security responsibilities; system developers; organizational personnel installing, configuring, and/or maintaining the information system; organizational personnel with responsibility for malicious code protection]. **Test**: [*SELECT FROM:* Automated mechanisms supporting and/or implementing malicious code protection capability; automated mechanisms supporting and/or implementing detection of unauthorized operating system commands through the kernel application programming interface].

SI-3(9)	**MALICIOUS CODE PROTECTION** | *AUTHENTICATE REMOTE COMMANDS*
	ASSESSMENT OBJECTIVE: *Determine if:*

	SI-3(9)[1]	*the organization defines security safeguards to be implemented by the information system to authenticate organization-defined remote commands;*
	SI-3(9)[2]	*the organization defines remote commands to be authenticated by organization-defined security safeguards; and*
	SI-3(9)[3]	*the information system implements organization-defined security safeguards to authenticate organization-defined remote commands.*

	POTENTIAL ASSESSMENT METHODS AND OBJECTS: **Examine**: [*SELECT FROM:* System and information integrity policy; procedures addressing malicious code protection; information system design documentation; malicious code protection mechanisms; warning messages sent upon detection of unauthorized operating system command execution; information system configuration settings and associated documentation; information system audit records; other relevant documents or records]. **Interview**: [*SELECT FROM:* System/network administrators; organizational personnel with information security responsibilities; system developers; organizational personnel installing, configuring, and/or maintaining the information system; organizational personnel with responsibility for malicious code protection]. **Test**: [*SELECT FROM:* Automated mechanisms supporting and/or implementing malicious code protection capability; automated mechanisms implementing authentication of remote commands; automated mechanisms supporting and/or implementing security safeguards to authenticate remote commands].

SI-3(10)	**MALICIOUS CODE PROTECTION** | *MALICIOUS CODE ANALYSIS*
	ASSESSMENT OBJECTIVE: *Determine if the organization:*

SI-3(10)(a)	SI-3(10)(a)[1]	*defines tools and techniques to be employed to analyze the characteristics and behavior of malicious code;*
	SI-3(10)(a)[2]	*employs organization-defined tools and techniques to analyze the characteristics and behavior of malicious code; and*
SI-3(10)(b)		*incorporates the results from malicious code analysis into incident response and flaw remediate processes.*

Special Publication 800-53A
Revision 4

Assessing Security and Privacy Controls in Federal Information Systems
and Organizations — *Building Effective Assessment Plans*

POTENTIAL ASSESSMENT METHODS AND OBJECTS:

Examine: [*SELECT FROM:* System and information integrity policy; procedures addressing malicious code protection; procedures addressing incident response; procedures addressing flaw remediation; information system design documentation; malicious code protection mechanisms, tools, and techniques; information system configuration settings and associated documentation; results from malicious code analyses; records of flaw remediation events resulting from malicious code analyses; information system audit records; other relevant documents or records].

Interview: [*SELECT FROM:* System/network administrators; organizational personnel with information security responsibilities; organizational personnel installing, configuring, and/or maintaining the information system; organizational personnel with responsibility for malicious code protection; organizational personnel responsible for flaw remediation; organizational personnel responsible for incident response/management].

Test: [*SELECT FROM:* Organizational process for incident response; organizational process for flaw remediation; automated mechanisms supporting and/or implementing malicious code protection capability; tools and techniques for analysis of malicious code characteristics and behavior].

SI-4	INFORMATION SYSTEM MONITORING			
	ASSESSMENT OBJECTIVE: *Determine if the organization:*			
	SI-4(a)	SI-4(a)(1)	SI-4(a)(1)[1]	*defines monitoring objectives to detect attacks and indicators of potential attacks on the information system;*
			SI-4(a)(1)[2]	*monitors the information system to detect, in accordance with organization-defined monitoring objectives,:*
			SI-4(a)(1)[2][a]	*attacks;*
			SI-4(a)(1)[2][b]	*indicators of potential attacks;*
		SI-4(a)(2)	*monitors the information system to detect unauthorized:*	
			SI-4(a)(2)[1]	*local connections;*
			SI-4(a)(2)[2]	*network connections;*
			SI-4(a)(2)[3]	*remote connections;*
	SI-4(b)	SI-4(b)(1)	*defines techniques and methods to identify unauthorized use of the information system;*	
		SI-4(b)(2)	*identifies unauthorized use of the information system through organization-defined techniques and methods;*	
	SI-4(c)	*deploys monitoring devices:*		
		SI-4(c)[1]	*strategically within the information system to collect organization-determined essential information;*	
		SI-4(c)[2]	*at ad hoc locations within the system to track specific types of transactions of interest to the organization;*	
	SI-4(d)	*protects information obtained from intrusion-monitoring tools from unauthorized:*		
		SI-4(d)[1]	*access;*	
		SI-4(d)[2]	*modification;*	
		SI-4(d)[3]	*deletion;*	

Special Publication 800-53A
Revision 4

Assessing Security and Privacy Controls in Federal Information Systems
and Organizations — *Building Effective Assessment Plans*

	SI-4(e)	*heightens the level of information system monitoring activity whenever there is an indication of increased risk to organizational operations and assets, individuals, other organizations, or the Nation based on law enforcement information, intelligence information, or other credible sources of information;*	
	SI-4(f)	*obtains legal opinion with regard to information system monitoring activities in accordance with applicable federal laws, Executive Orders, directives, policies, or regulations;*	
	SI-4(g)	SI-4(g)[1]	*defines personnel or roles to whom information system monitoring information is to be provided;*
		SI-4(g)[2]	*defines information system monitoring information to be provided to organization-defined personnel or roles;*
		SI-4(g)[3]	*defines a frequency to provide organization-defined information system monitoring to organization-defined personnel or roles;*
		SI-4(g)[4]	*provides organization-defined information system monitoring information to organization-defined personnel or roles one or more of the following:*
		SI-4(g)[4][a]	*as needed; and/or*
		SI-4(g)[4][b]	*with the organization-defined frequency.*

POTENTIAL ASSESSMENT METHODS AND OBJECTS:

Examine: [*SELECT FROM:* Continuous monitoring strategy; system and information integrity policy; procedures addressing information system monitoring tools and techniques; facility diagram/layout; information system design documentation; information system monitoring tools and techniques documentation; locations within information system where monitoring devices are deployed; information system configuration settings and associated documentation; other relevant documents or records].

Interview: [*SELECT FROM:* System/network administrators; organizational personnel with information security responsibilities; organizational personnel installing, configuring, and/or maintaining the information system; organizational personnel with responsibility monitoring the information system].

Test: [*SELECT FROM:* Organizational processes for information system monitoring; automated mechanisms supporting and/or implementing information system monitoring capability].

SI-4(1)	INFORMATION SYSTEM MONITORING	*SYSTEM-WIDE INTRUSION DETECTION SYSTEM*	
	ASSESSMENT OBJECTIVE: *Determine if the organization:*		
	SI-4(1)[1]	*connects individual intrusion detection tools into an information system-wide intrusion detection system; and*	
	SI-4(1)[2]	*configures individual intrusion detection tools into an information system-wide intrusion detection system.*	

Special Publication 800-53A
Revision 4

Assessing Security and Privacy Controls in Federal Information Systems
and Organizations — *Building Effective Assessment Plans*

<table>
<tr><td colspan="2">

POTENTIAL ASSESSMENT METHODS AND OBJECTS:

Examine: [*SELECT FROM:* System and information integrity policy; procedures addressing information system monitoring tools and techniques; information system design documentation; information system monitoring tools and techniques documentation; information system configuration settings and associated documentation; information system audit records; other relevant documents or records].

Interview: [*SELECT FROM:* System/network administrators; organizational personnel with information security responsibilities; organizational personnel installing, configuring, and/or maintaining the information system; organizational personnel with responsibility for monitoring the information system; organizational personnel with responsibility for the intrusion detection system].

Test: [*SELECT FROM:* Organizational processes for intrusion detection/information system monitoring; automated mechanisms supporting and/or implementing intrusion detection capability].
</td></tr>
</table>

SI-4(2)	**INFORMATION SYSTEM MONITORING** | *AUTOMATED TOOLS FOR REAL-TIME ANALYSIS*
	ASSESSMENT OBJECTIVE: *Determine if the organization employs automated tools to support near real-time analysis of events.*
	POTENTIAL ASSESSMENT METHODS AND OBJECTS: **Examine**: [*SELECT FROM:* System and information integrity policy; procedures addressing information system monitoring tools and techniques; information system design documentation; information system monitoring tools and techniques documentation; information system configuration settings and associated documentation; information system audit records; other relevant documents or records]. **Interview**: [*SELECT FROM:* System/network administrators; organizational personnel with information security responsibilities; organizational personnel installing, configuring, and/or maintaining the information system; organizational personnel with responsibility for monitoring the information system; organizational personnel with responsibility for incident response/management]. **Test**: [*SELECT FROM:* Organizational processes for near real-time analysis of events; organizational processes for information system monitoring; automated mechanisms supporting and/or implementing information system monitoring; automated mechanisms/tools supporting and/or implementing analysis of events].

SI-4(3)	**INFORMATION SYSTEM MONITORING** | *AUTOMATED TOOL INTEGRATION*	
	ASSESSMENT OBJECTIVE: *Determine if the organization, for rapid response to attacks by enabling reconfiguration of intrusion detection tools in support of attack isolation and elimination, employs automated tools to integrate intrusion detection tools into:*	
	SI-4(3)[1]	*access control mechanisms; and*
	SI-4(3)[2]	*flow control mechanisms.*

Special Publication 800-53A
Revision 4

Assessing Security and Privacy Controls in Federal Information Systems
and Organizations — *Building Effective Assessment Plans*

	POTENTIAL ASSESSMENT METHODS AND OBJECTS:
	Examine: [*SELECT FROM*: System and information integrity policy; access control policy and procedures; procedures addressing information system monitoring tools and techniques; information system design documentation; information system monitoring tools and techniques documentation; information system configuration settings and associated documentation; information system audit records; other relevant documents or records].
	Interview: [*SELECT FROM*: System/network administrators; organizational personnel with information security responsibilities; organizational personnel installing, configuring, and/or maintaining the information system; organizational personnel with responsibility for monitoring the information system; organizational personnel with responsibility for the intrusion detection system].
	Test: [*SELECT FROM*: Organizational processes for intrusion detection/information system monitoring; automated mechanisms supporting and/or implementing intrusion detection/information system monitoring capability; automated mechanisms/tools supporting and/or implementing access/flow control capability; automated mechanisms/tools supporting and/or implementing integration of intrusion detection tools into access/flow control mechanisms].

SI-4(4)	INFORMATION SYSTEM MONITORING | *INBOUND AND OUTBOUND COMMUNICATIONS TRAFFIC*	
	ASSESSMENT OBJECTIVE: *Determine if the organization:*	
	SI-4(4)[1]	*defines a frequency to monitor:*
	SI-4(4)[1][a]	*inbound communications traffic for unusual or unauthorized activities or conditions;*
	SI-4(4)[1][b]	*outbound communications traffic for unusual or unauthorized activities or conditions;*
	SI-4(4)[2]	*monitors, with the organization-defined frequency:*
	SI-4(4)[2][a]	*inbound communications traffic for unusual or unauthorized activities or conditions; and*
	SI-4(4)[2][b]	*outbound communications traffic for unusual or unauthorized activities or conditions.*
	POTENTIAL ASSESSMENT METHODS AND OBJECTS:	
	Examine: [*SELECT FROM*: System and information integrity policy; procedures addressing information system monitoring tools and techniques; information system design documentation; information system monitoring tools and techniques documentation; information system configuration settings and associated documentation; information system protocols; information system audit records; other relevant documents or records].	
	Interview: [*SELECT FROM*: System/network administrators; organizational personnel with information security responsibilities; organizational personnel installing, configuring, and/or maintaining the information system; organizational personnel with responsibility for monitoring the information system; organizational personnel with responsibility for the intrusion detection system].	
	Test: [*SELECT FROM*: Organizational processes for intrusion detection/information system monitoring; automated mechanisms supporting and/or implementing intrusion detection capability/information system monitoring; automated mechanisms supporting and/or implementing monitoring of inbound/outbound communications traffic].	

SI-4(5)	INFORMATION SYSTEM MONITORING | *SYSTEM-GENERATED ALERTS*	
	ASSESSMENT OBJECTIVE: *Determine if:*	
	SI-4(5)[1]	*the organization defines compromise indicators for the information system;*

SI-4(5)[2]	*the organization defines personnel or roles to be alerted when indications of compromise or potential compromise occur; and*
SI-4(5)[3]	*the information system alerts organization-defined personnel or roles when organization-defined compromise indicators occur.*

POTENTIAL ASSESSMENT METHODS AND OBJECTS:

Examine: [*SELECT FROM:* System and information integrity policy; procedures addressing information system monitoring tools and techniques; information system monitoring tools and techniques documentation; information system configuration settings and associated documentation; alerts/notifications generated based on compromise indicators; information system audit records; other relevant documents or records].

Interview: [*SELECT FROM:* System/network administrators; organizational personnel with information security responsibilities; system developers;; organizational personnel installing, configuring, and/or maintaining the information system; organizational personnel with responsibility for monitoring the information system; organizational personnel with responsibility for the intrusion detection system].

Test: [*SELECT FROM:* Organizational processes for intrusion detection/information system monitoring; automated mechanisms supporting and/or implementing intrusion detection/information system monitoring capability; automated mechanisms supporting and/or implementing alerts for compromise indicators].

SI-4(6)	**INFORMATION SYSTEM MONITORING** | *RESTRICT NON-PRIVILEGED USERS*

[Withdrawn: Incorporated into AC-6(10)].

SI-4(7)	**INFORMATION SYSTEM MONITORING** | *AUTOMATED RESPONSE TO SUSPICIOUS EVENTS*

ASSESSMENT OBJECTIVE:
Determine if:

SI-4(7)[1]	*the organization defines incident response personnel (identified by name and/or by role) to be notified of detected suspicious events;*
SI-4(7)[2]	*the organization defines least-disruptive actions to be taken by the information system to terminate suspicious events;*
SI-4(7)[3]	*the information system notifies organization-defined incident response personnel of detected suspicious events; and*
SI-4(7)[4]	*the information system takes organization-defined least-disruptive actions to terminate suspicious events.*

POTENTIAL ASSESSMENT METHODS AND OBJECTS:

Examine: [*SELECT FROM:* System and information integrity policy; procedures addressing information system monitoring tools and techniques; information system design documentation; information system monitoring tools and techniques documentation; information system configuration settings and associated documentation; alerts/notifications generated based on detected suspicious events; records of actions taken to terminate suspicious events; information system audit records; other relevant documents or records].

Interview: [*SELECT FROM:* System/network administrators; organizational personnel with information security responsibilities; system developers; organizational personnel installing, configuring, and/or maintaining the information system; organizational personnel with responsibility for monitoring the information system; organizational personnel with responsibility for the intrusion detection system].

Test: [*SELECT FROM:* Organizational processes for intrusion detection/information system monitoring; automated mechanisms supporting and/or implementing intrusion detection/information system monitoring capability; automated mechanisms supporting and/or implementing notifications to incident response personnel; automated mechanisms supporting and/or implementing actions to terminate suspicious events].

Special Publication 800-53A
Revision 4

Assessing Security and Privacy Controls in Federal Information Systems
and Organizations — *Building Effective Assessment Plans*

SI-4(8)	INFORMATION SYSTEM MONITORING | *PROTECTION OF MONITORING INFORMATION*
	[Withdrawn: Incorporated into SI-4].

SI-4(9)	INFORMATION SYSTEM MONITORING | *TESTING OF MONITORING TOOLS*
	ASSESSMENT OBJECTIVE: *Determine if the organization:*

SI-4(9)[1]	*defines a frequency to test intrusion-monitoring tools; and*
SI-4(9)[2]	*tests intrusion-monitoring tools with the organization-defined frequency.*

POTENTIAL ASSESSMENT METHODS AND OBJECTS:

Examine: [*SELECT FROM:* System and information integrity policy; procedures addressing testing of information system monitoring tools and techniques; documentation providing evidence of testing intrusion-monitoring tools; other relevant documents or records].

Interview: [*SELECT FROM:* System/network administrators; organizational personnel with information security responsibilities; organizational personnel installing, configuring, and/or maintaining the information system; organizational personnel with responsibility for monitoring the information system; organizational personnel with responsibility for the intrusion detection system].

Test: [*SELECT FROM:* Organizational processes for intrusion detection/information system monitoring; automated mechanisms supporting and/or implementing intrusion detection/information system monitoring capability; automated mechanisms supporting and/or implementing testing of intrusion-monitoring tools].

SI-4(10)	INFORMATION SYSTEM MONITORING | *VISIBILITY OF ENCRYPTED COMMUNICATIONS*
	ASSESSMENT OBJECTIVE: *Determine if the organization:*

SI-4(10)[1]	*defines encrypted communications traffic required to be visible to information system monitoring tools;*
SI-4(10)[2]	*defines information system monitoring tools to be provided access to organization-defined encrypted communications traffic; and*
SI-4(10)[3]	*makes provisions so that organization-defined encrypted communications traffic is visible to organization-defined information system monitoring tools.*

POTENTIAL ASSESSMENT METHODS AND OBJECTS:

Examine: [*SELECT FROM:* System and information integrity policy; procedures addressing information system monitoring tools and techniques; information system design documentation; information system monitoring tools and techniques documentation; information system configuration settings and associated documentation; information system protocols; other relevant documents or records].

Interview: [*SELECT FROM:* System/network administrators; organizational personnel with information security responsibilities; organizational personnel installing, configuring, and/or maintaining the information system; organizational personnel with responsibility for monitoring the information system; organizational personnel with responsibility for the intrusion detection system].

Test: [*SELECT FROM:* Organizational processes for intrusion detection/information system monitoring; automated mechanisms supporting and/or implementing intrusion detection/information system monitoring capability; automated mechanisms supporting and/or implementing visibility of encrypted communications traffic to monitoring tools].

Special Publication 800-53A
Revision 4

Assessing Security and Privacy Controls in Federal Information Systems
and Organizations — *Building Effective Assessment Plans*

SI-4(11)	INFORMATION SYSTEM MONITORING	*ANALYZE COMMUNICATIONS TRAFFIC ANOMALIES*

ASSESSMENT OBJECTIVE:

Determine if the organization:

SI-4(11)[1]	*defines interior points within the system (e.g., subnetworks, subsystems) where communications traffic is to be analyzed;*	
SI-4(11)[2]	*analyzes outbound communications traffic to discover anomalies at:*	
	SI-4(11)[2][a]	*the external boundary of the information system; and*
	SI-4(11)[2][b]	*selected organization-defined interior points within the system.*

POTENTIAL ASSESSMENT METHODS AND OBJECTS:

Examine: [*SELECT FROM:* System and information integrity policy; procedures addressing information system monitoring tools and techniques; information system design documentation; network diagram; information system monitoring tools and techniques documentation; information system configuration settings and associated documentation; information system monitoring logs or records; information system audit records; other relevant documents or records].

Interview: [*SELECT FROM:* System/network administrators; organizational personnel with information security responsibilities; organizational personnel installing, configuring, and/or maintaining the information system; organizational personnel with responsibility for monitoring the information system; organizational personnel with responsibility for the intrusion detection system].

Test: [*SELECT FROM:* Organizational processes for intrusion detection/information system monitoring; automated mechanisms supporting and/or implementing intrusion detection/information system monitoring capability; automated mechanisms supporting and/or implementing analysis of communications traffic].

SI-4(12)	INFORMATION SYSTEM MONITORING	*AUTOMATED ALERTS*

ASSESSMENT OBJECTIVE:

Determine if the organization:

SI-4(12)[1]	*defines activities that trigger alerts to security personnel based on inappropriate or unusual activities with security implications; and*
SI-4(12)[2]	*employs automated mechanisms to alert security personnel of organization-defined activities that trigger alerts based on inappropriate or unusual activities with security implications.*

POTENTIAL ASSESSMENT METHODS AND OBJECTS:

Examine: [*SELECT FROM:* System and information integrity policy; procedures addressing information system monitoring tools and techniques; information system design documentation; information system monitoring tools and techniques documentation; information system configuration settings and associated documentation; list of inappropriate or unusual activities (with security implications) that trigger alerts; alerts/notifications provided to security personnel; information system monitoring logs or records; information system audit records; other relevant documents or records].

Interview: [*SELECT FROM:* System/network administrators; organizational personnel with information security responsibilities; system developers; organizational personnel installing, configuring, and/or maintaining the information system; organizational personnel with responsibility for monitoring the information system; organizational personnel with responsibility for the intrusion detection system].

Test: [*SELECT FROM:* Organizational processes for intrusion detection/information system monitoring; automated mechanisms supporting and/or implementing intrusion detection/information system monitoring capability; automated mechanisms supporting and/or implementing automated alerts to security personnel].

Special Publication 800-53A
Revision 4

Assessing Security and Privacy Controls in Federal Information Systems
and Organizations — *Building Effective Assessment Plans*

SI-4(13)	INFORMATION SYSTEM MONITORING | *ANALYZE TRAFFIC/EVENT PATTERNS*
	ASSESSMENT OBJECTIVE: *Determine if the organization:*
	SI-4(13)(a) — *analyzes communications traffic/event patterns for the information system;*
	SI-4(13)(b) — *develops profiles representing common traffic patterns and/or events;*
	SI-4(13)(c) — *uses the traffic/event profiles in tuning system-monitoring devices to reduce the number of false positives and false negatives.*
	POTENTIAL ASSESSMENT METHODS AND OBJECTS: **Examine**: [*SELECT FROM:* System and information integrity policy; procedures addressing information system monitoring tools and techniques; information system design documentation; information system monitoring tools and techniques documentation; information system configuration settings and associated documentation; list of profiles representing common traffic patterns and/or events; information system protocols documentation; list of acceptable thresholds for false positives and false negatives; other relevant documents or records]. **Interview**: [*SELECT FROM:* System/network administrators; organizational personnel with information security responsibilities; organizational personnel installing, configuring, and/or maintaining the information system; organizational personnel with responsibility for monitoring the information system; organizational personnel with responsibility for the intrusion detection system]. **Test**: [*SELECT FROM:* Organizational processes for intrusion detection/information system monitoring; automated mechanisms supporting and/or implementing intrusion detection/information system monitoring capability; automated mechanisms supporting and/or implementing analysis of communications traffic/event patterns].

SI-4(14)	INFORMATION SYSTEM MONITORING | *WIRELESS INTRUSION DETECTION*
	ASSESSMENT OBJECTIVE: *Determine if the organization employs a wireless intrusion detection system to:*
	SI-4(14)[1] — *identify rogue wireless devices;*
	SI-4(14)[2] — *detect attack attempts to the information system; and*
	SI-4(14)[3] — *detect potential compromises/breaches to the information system.*
	POTENTIAL ASSESSMENT METHODS AND OBJECTS: **Examine**: [*SELECT FROM:* System and information integrity policy; procedures addressing information system monitoring tools and techniques; information system design documentation; information system monitoring tools and techniques documentation; information system configuration settings and associated documentation; information system protocols; information system audit records; other relevant documents or records]. **Interview**: [*SELECT FROM:* System/network administrators; organizational personnel with information security responsibilities; organizational personnel installing, configuring, and/or maintaining the information system; organizational personnel with responsibility for monitoring the information system; organizational personnel with responsibility for the intrusion detection system]. **Test**: [*SELECT FROM:* Organizational processes for intrusion detection; automated mechanisms supporting and/or implementing wireless intrusion detection capability].

SI-4(15)	INFORMATION SYSTEM MONITORING | *WIRELESS TO WIRELINE COMMUNICATIONS*
	ASSESSMENT OBJECTIVE: *Determine if the organization employs an intrusion detection system to monitor wireless communications traffic as the traffic passes from wireless to wireline networks.*

Special Publication 800-53A
Revision 4

Assessing Security and Privacy Controls in Federal Information Systems
and Organizations — *Building Effective Assessment Plans*

POTENTIAL ASSESSMENT METHODS AND OBJECTS:

Examine: [*SELECT FROM:* System and information integrity policy; procedures addressing information system monitoring tools and techniques; information system design documentation; information system monitoring tools and techniques documentation; information system configuration settings and associated documentation; information system protocols documentation; information system audit records; other relevant documents or records].

Interview: [*SELECT FROM:* System/network administrators; organizational personnel with information security responsibilities; organizational personnel installing, configuring, and/or maintaining the information system; organizational personnel with responsibility for monitoring the information system; organizational personnel with responsibility for the intrusion detection system].

Test: [*SELECT FROM:* Organizational processes for intrusion detection/information system monitoring; automated mechanisms supporting and/or implementing intrusion detection/information system monitoring capability; automated mechanisms supporting and/or implementing wireless intrusion detection capability].

SI-4(16)	INFORMATION SYSTEM MONITORING | *CORRELATE MONITORING INFORMATION*
	ASSESSMENT OBJECTIVE: *Determine if the organization correlates information from monitoring tools employed throughout the information system.*
	POTENTIAL ASSESSMENT METHODS AND OBJECTS: **Examine**: [*SELECT FROM:* System and information integrity policy; procedures addressing information system monitoring tools and techniques; information system design documentation; information system monitoring tools and techniques documentation; information system configuration settings and associated documentation; event correlation logs or records; information system audit records; other relevant documents or records]. **Interview**: [*SELECT FROM:* System/network administrators; organizational personnel with information security responsibilities; organizational personnel installing, configuring, and/or maintaining the information system; organizational personnel with responsibility for monitoring the information system; organizational personnel with responsibility for the intrusion detection system]. **Test**: [*SELECT FROM:* Organizational processes for intrusion detection/information system monitoring; automated mechanisms supporting and/or implementing intrusion detection/information system monitoring capability; automated mechanisms supporting and/or implementing correlation of information from monitoring tools].

SI-4(17)	INFORMATION SYSTEM MONITORING | *INTEGRATED SITUATIONAL AWARENESS*
	ASSESSMENT OBJECTIVE: *Determine if the organization, to achieve integrated, organization-wide situational awareness, correlates information from monitoring:*
	SI-4(17)[1] — *physical activities;*
	SI-4(17)[2] — *cyber activities; and*
	SI-4(17)[3] — *supply chain activities.*

Special Publication 800-53A
Revision 4

Assessing Security and Privacy Controls in Federal Information Systems
and Organizations — *Building Effective Assessment Plans*

POTENTIAL ASSESSMENT METHODS AND OBJECTS:

Examine: [*SELECT FROM:* System and information integrity policy; procedures addressing information system monitoring tools and techniques; information system design documentation; information system monitoring tools and techniques documentation; information system configuration settings and associated documentation; event correlation logs or records resulting from physical, cyber, and supply chain activities; information system audit records; other relevant documents or records].

Interview: [*SELECT FROM:* System/network administrators; organizational personnel with information security responsibilities; organizational personnel installing, configuring, and/or maintaining the information system; organizational personnel with responsibility for monitoring the information system; organizational personnel with responsibility for the intrusion detection system].

Test: [*SELECT FROM:* Organizational processes for intrusion detection/information system monitoring; automated mechanisms supporting and/or implementing intrusion detection/system monitoring capability; automated mechanisms supporting and/or implementing correlation of information from monitoring tools].

SI-4(18)	INFORMATION SYSTEM MONITORING | *ANALYZE TRAFFIC / COVERT EXFILTRATION*

ASSESSMENT OBJECTIVE:

Determine if the organization:

SI-4(18)[1]	*defines interior points within the system (e.g., subsystems, subnetworks) where communications traffic is to be analyzed;*	
SI-4(18)[2]	*to detect covert exfiltration of information, analyzes outbound communications traffic at:*	
	SI-4(18)[2][a]	*the external boundary of the information system (i.e., system perimeter); and*
	SI-4(18)[2][b]	*organization-defined interior points within the system.*

POTENTIAL ASSESSMENT METHODS AND OBJECTS:

Examine: [*SELECT FROM:* System and information integrity policy; procedures addressing information system monitoring tools and techniques; information system design documentation; network diagram; information system monitoring tools and techniques documentation; information system configuration settings and associated documentation; information system monitoring logs or records; information system audit records; other relevant documents or records].

Interview: [*SELECT FROM:* System/network administrators; organizational personnel with information security responsibilities; organizational personnel installing, configuring, and/or maintaining the information system; organizational personnel with responsibility for monitoring the information system; organizational personnel with responsibility for the intrusion detection system].

Test: [*SELECT FROM:* Organizational processes for intrusion detection/information system monitoring; automated mechanisms supporting and/or implementing intrusion detection/system monitoring capability; automated mechanisms supporting and/or implementing analysis of outbound communications traffic].

SI-4(19)	INFORMATION SYSTEM MONITORING | *INDIVIDUALS POSING GREATER RISK*

ASSESSMENT OBJECTIVE:

Determine if the organization:

SI-4(19)[1]	*defines sources that identify individuals who pose an increased level of risk;*
SI-4(19)[2]	*defines additional monitoring to be implemented on individuals who have been identified by organization-defined sources as posing an increased level of risk; and*

Special Publication 800-53A
Revision 4

Assessing Security and Privacy Controls in Federal Information Systems
and Organizations — *Building Effective Assessment Plans*

SI-4(19)[3]	*implements organization-defined additional monitoring of individuals who have been identified by organization-defined sources as posing an increased level of risk.*

POTENTIAL ASSESSMENT METHODS AND OBJECTS:

Examine: [*SELECT FROM:* System and information integrity policy; procedures addressing information system monitoring; information system design documentation; list of individuals who have been identified as posing an increased level of risk; information system monitoring tools and techniques documentation; information system configuration settings and associated documentation; information system audit records; other relevant documents or records].

Interview: [*SELECT FROM:* System/network administrators; organizational personnel with information security responsibilities; organizational personnel installing, configuring, and/or maintaining the information system; organizational personnel with responsibility for monitoring the information system].

Test: [*SELECT FROM:* Organizational processes for information system monitoring; automated mechanisms supporting and/or implementing system monitoring capability].

SI-4(20)	INFORMATION SYSTEM MONITORING | *PRIVILEGED USERS*

ASSESSMENT OBJECTIVE:

Determine if the organization:

SI-4(20)[1]	*defines additional monitoring to be implemented on privileged users; and*
SI-4(20)[2]	*implements organization-defined additional monitoring of privileged users;*

POTENTIAL ASSESSMENT METHODS AND OBJECTS:

Examine: [*SELECT FROM:* System and information integrity policy; procedures addressing information system monitoring tools and techniques; information system design documentation; list of privileged users; information system monitoring tools and techniques documentation; information system configuration settings and associated documentation; information system monitoring logs or records; information system audit records; other relevant documents or records].

Interview: [*SELECT FROM:* System/network administrators; organizational personnel with information security responsibilities; organizational personnel installing, configuring, and/or maintaining the information system; organizational personnel with responsibility for monitoring the information system].

Test: [*SELECT FROM:* Organizational processes for information system monitoring; automated mechanisms supporting and/or implementing system monitoring capability].

SI-4(21)	INFORMATION SYSTEM MONITORING | *PROBATIONARY PERIODS*

ASSESSMENT OBJECTIVE:

Determine if the organization:

SI-4(21)[1]	*defines additional monitoring to be implemented on individuals during probationary periods;*
SI-4(21)[2]	*defines probationary period during which organization-defined additional monitoring of individuals is to be performed; and*
SI-4(21)[3]	*implements organization-defined additional monitoring of individuals during organization-defined probationary period.*

Special Publication 800-53A
Revision 4

Assessing Security and Privacy Controls in Federal Information Systems
and Organizations — *Building Effective Assessment Plans*

POTENTIAL ASSESSMENT METHODS AND OBJECTS:

Examine: [*SELECT FROM:* System and information integrity policy; procedures addressing information system monitoring; information system design documentation; information system monitoring tools and techniques documentation; information system configuration settings and associated documentation; information system monitoring logs or records; information system audit records; other relevant documents or records].

Interview: [*SELECT FROM:* System/network administrators; organizational personnel with information security responsibilities; organizational personnel installing, configuring, and/or maintaining the information system; organizational personnel with responsibility for monitoring the information system].

Test: [*SELECT FROM:* Organizational processes for information system monitoring; automated mechanisms supporting and/or implementing system monitoring capability].

SI-4(22)	INFORMATION SYSTEM MONITORING | *UNAUTHORIZED NETWORK SERVICES*

ASSESSMENT OBJECTIVE:
Determine if:

SI-4(22)[1]	*the organization defines authorization or approval processes for network services;*
SI-4(22)[2]	*the organization defines personnel or roles to be alerted upon detection of network services that have not been authorized or approved by organization-defined authorization or approval processes;*
SI-4(22)[3]	*the information system detects network services that have not been authorized or approved by organization-defined authorization or approval processes and does one or more of the following:*

	SI-4(22)[3][a]	*audits; and/or*
	SI-4(22)[3][b]	*alerts organization-defined personnel or roles.*

POTENTIAL ASSESSMENT METHODS AND OBJECTS:

Examine: [*SELECT FROM:* System and information integrity policy; procedures addressing information system monitoring tools and techniques; information system design documentation; information system monitoring tools and techniques documentation; information system configuration settings and associated documentation; documented authorization/approval of network services; notifications or alerts of unauthorized network services; information system monitoring logs or records; information system audit records; other relevant documents or records].

Interview: [*SELECT FROM:* System/network administrators; organizational personnel with information security responsibilities; system developer; organizational personnel installing, configuring, and/or maintaining the information system; organizational personnel with responsibility for monitoring the information system].

Test: [*SELECT FROM:* Organizational processes for information system monitoring; automated mechanisms supporting and/or implementing system monitoring capability; automated mechanisms for auditing network services; automated mechanisms for providing alerts].

SI-4(23)	INFORMATION SYSTEM MONITORING | *HOST-BASED DEVICES*

ASSESSMENT OBJECTIVE:
Determine if the organization:

SI-4(23)[1]	*defines host-based monitoring mechanisms to be implemented;*
SI-4(23)[2]	*defines information system components where organization-defined host-based monitoring is to be implemented; and*

Special Publication 800-53A
Revision 4

Assessing Security and Privacy Controls in Federal Information Systems
and Organizations — *Building Effective Assessment Plans*

SI-4(23)[3]	*implements organization-defined host-based monitoring mechanisms at organization-defined information system components.*

POTENTIAL ASSESSMENT METHODS AND OBJECTS:

Examine: [*SELECT FROM:* System and information integrity policy; procedures addressing information system monitoring tools and techniques; information system design documentation; host-based monitoring mechanisms; information system monitoring tools and techniques documentation; information system configuration settings and associated documentation; list of information system components requiring host-based monitoring; information system monitoring logs or records; information system audit records; other relevant documents or records].

Interview: [*SELECT FROM:* System/network administrators; organizational personnel with information security responsibilities; organizational personnel installing, configuring, and/or maintaining the information system; organizational personnel with responsibility for monitoring information system hosts].

Test: [*SELECT FROM:* Organizational processes for information system monitoring; automated mechanisms supporting and/or implementing host-based monitoring capability].

SI-4(24)	**INFORMATION SYSTEM MONITORING**	*INDICATORS OF COMPROMISE*

ASSESSMENT OBJECTIVE:

Determine if the information system:

SI-4(24)[1]	*discovers indicators of compromise;*
SI-4(24)[2]	*collects indicators of compromise;*
SI-4(24)[3]	*distributes indicators of compromise; and*
SI-4(24)[4]	*uses indicators of compromise.*

POTENTIAL ASSESSMENT METHODS AND OBJECTS:

Examine: [*SELECT FROM:* System and information integrity policy; procedures addressing information system monitoring; information system design documentation; information system monitoring tools and techniques documentation; information system configuration settings and associated documentation; information system monitoring logs or records; information system audit records; other relevant documents or records].

Interview: [*SELECT FROM:* System/network administrators; organizational personnel with information security responsibilities; system developer; organizational personnel installing, configuring, and/or maintaining the information system; organizational personnel with responsibility for monitoring information system hosts].

Test: [*SELECT FROM:* Organizational processes for information system monitoring; organizational processes for discovery, collection, distribution, and use of indicators of compromise; automated mechanisms supporting and/or implementing system monitoring capability; automated mechanisms supporting and/or implementing the discovery, collection, distribution, and use of indicators of compromise].

SI-5	**SECURITY ALERTS, ADVISORIES, AND DIRECTIVES**	

ASSESSMENT OBJECTIVE:

Determine if the organization:

SI-5(a)	SI-5(a)[1]	*defines external organizations from whom information system security alerts, advisories and directives are to be received;*
	SI-5(a)[2]	*receives information system security alerts, advisories, and directives from organization-defined external organizations on an ongoing basis;*
SI-5(b)	*generates internal security alerts, advisories, and directives as deemed necessary;*	

Special Publication 800-53A
Revision 4

Assessing Security and Privacy Controls in Federal Information Systems
and Organizations — *Building Effective Assessment Plans*

	SI-5(c)	SI-5(c)[1]	*defines personnel or roles to whom security alerts, advisories, and directives are to be provided;*	
		SI-5(c)[2]	*defines elements within the organization to whom security alerts, advisories, and directives are to be provided;*	
		SI-5(c)[3]	*defines external organizations to whom security alerts, advisories, and directives are to be provided;*	
		SI-5(c)[4]	*disseminates security alerts, advisories, and directives to one or more of the following:*	
			SI-5(c)[4][a]	*organization-defined personnel or roles;*
			SI-5(c)[4][b]	*organization-defined elements within the organization; and/or*
			SI-5(c)[4][c]	*organization-defined external organizations; and*
	SI-5(d)	SI-5(d)[1]	*implements security directives in accordance with established time frames; or*	
		SI-5(d)[2]	*notifies the issuing organization of the degree of noncompliance.*	

POTENTIAL ASSESSMENT METHODS AND OBJECTS:

Examine: [*SELECT FROM:* System and information integrity policy; procedures addressing security alerts, advisories, and directives; records of security alerts and advisories; other relevant documents or records].

Interview: [*SELECT FROM:* Organizational personnel with security alert and advisory responsibilities; organizational personnel implementing, operating, maintaining, and using the information system; organizational personnel, organizational elements, and/or external organizations to whom alerts, advisories, and directives are to be disseminated; system/network administrators; organizational personnel with information security responsibilities].

Test: [*SELECT FROM:* Organizational processes for defining, receiving, generating, disseminating, and complying with security alerts, advisories, and directives; automated mechanisms supporting and/or implementing definition, receipt, generation, and dissemination of security alerts, advisories, and directives; automated mechanisms supporting and/or implementing security directives].

SI-5(1)	SECURITY ALERTS, ADVISORIES, AND DIRECTIVES | *AUTOMATED ALERTS AND ADVISORIES*

ASSESSMENT OBJECTIVE:

Determine if the organization employs automated mechanisms to make security alert and advisory information available throughout the organization.

POTENTIAL ASSESSMENT METHODS AND OBJECTS:

Examine: [*SELECT FROM:* System and information integrity policy; procedures addressing security alerts, advisories, and directives; information system design documentation; information system configuration settings and associated documentation; automated mechanisms supporting the distribution of security alert and advisory information; records of security alerts and advisories; information system audit records; other relevant documents or records].

Interview: [*SELECT FROM:* Organizational personnel with security alert and advisory responsibilities; organizational personnel implementing, operating, maintaining, and using the information system; organizational personnel, organizational elements, and/or external organizations to whom alerts and advisories are to be disseminated; system/network administrators; organizational personnel with information security responsibilities].

Test: [*SELECT FROM:* Organizational processes for defining, receiving, generating, and disseminating security alerts and advisories; automated mechanisms supporting and/or implementing dissemination of security alerts and advisories].

Special Publication 800-53A
Revision 4

Assessing Security and Privacy Controls in Federal Information Systems
and Organizations — *Building Effective Assessment Plans*

SI-6	SECURITY FUNCTION VERIFICATION		
	ASSESSMENT OBJECTIVE: *Determine if:*		
	SI-6(a)	SI-6(a)[1]	*the organization defines security functions to be verified for correct operation;*
		SI-6(a)[2]	*the information system verifies the correct operation of organization-defined security functions;*
	SI-6(b)	SI-6(b)[1]	*the organization defines system transitional states requiring verification of organization-defined security functions;*
		SI-6(b)[2]	*the organization defines a frequency to verify the correct operation of organization-defined security functions;*
		SI-6(b)[3]	*the information system performs this verification one or more of the following:*
		SI-6(b)[3][a]	*at organization-defined system transitional states;*
		SI-6(b)[3][b]	*upon command by user with appropriate privilege; and/or*
		SI-6(b)[3][c]	*with the organization-defined frequency;*
	SI-6(c)	SI-6(c)[1]	*the organization defines personnel or roles to be notified of failed security verification tests;*
		SI-6(c)[2]	*the information system notifies organization-defined personnel or roles of failed security verification tests;*
	SI-6(d)	SI-6(d)[1]	*the organization defines alternative action(s) to be performed when anomalies are discovered;*
		SI-6(d)[2]	*the information system performs one or more of the following actions when anomalies are discovered:*
		SI-6(d)[2][a]	*shuts the information system down;*
		SI-6(d)[2][b]	*restarts the information system; and/or*
		SI-6(d)[2][c]	*performs organization-defined alternative action(s).*
	POTENTIAL ASSESSMENT METHODS AND OBJECTS: **Examine**: [*SELECT FROM*: System and information integrity policy; procedures addressing security function verification; information system design documentation; information system configuration settings and associated documentation; alerts/notifications of failed security verification tests; list of system transition states requiring security functionality verification; information system audit records; other relevant documents or records]. **Interview**: [*SELECT FROM*: Organizational personnel with security function verification responsibilities; organizational personnel implementing, operating, and maintaining the information system; system/network administrators; organizational personnel with information security responsibilities; system developer]. **Test**: [*SELECT FROM*: Organizational processes for security function verification; automated mechanisms supporting and/or implementing security function verification capability].		

SI-6(1)	SECURITY FUNCTION VERIFICATION	*NOTIFICATION OF FAILED SECURITY TESTS*
[Withdrawn: Incorporated into SI-6].		

Special Publication 800-53A
Revision 4

Assessing Security and Privacy Controls in Federal Information Systems
and Organizations — *Building Effective Assessment Plans*

SI-6(2)	SECURITY FUNCTION VERIFICATION	*AUTOMATION SUPPORT FOR DISTRIBUTED TESTING*

	ASSESSMENT OBJECTIVE: *Determine if the information system implements automated mechanisms to support the management of distributed security testing.*
	POTENTIAL ASSESSMENT METHODS AND OBJECTS: **Examine**: [*SELECT FROM:* System and information integrity policy; procedures addressing security function verification; information system design documentation; information system configuration settings and associated documentation; information system audit records; other relevant documents or records]. **Interview**: [*SELECT FROM:* Organizational personnel with security function verification responsibilities; organizational personnel implementing, operating, and maintaining the information system; system/network administrators; organizational personnel with information security responsibilities]. **Test**: [*SELECT FROM:* Organizational processes for security function verification; automated mechanisms supporting and/or implementing the management of distributed security testing].

SI-6(3)	SECURITY FUNCTION VERIFICATION	*REPORT VERIFICATION RESULTS*

	ASSESSMENT OBJECTIVE: *Determine if the organization:*	
	SI-6(3)[1]	*defines personnel or roles designated to receive the results of security function verification; and*
	SI-6(3)[2]	*reports the results of security function verification to organization-defined personnel or roles.*
	POTENTIAL ASSESSMENT METHODS AND OBJECTS: **Examine**: [*SELECT FROM:* System and information integrity policy; procedures addressing security function verification; information system design documentation; information system configuration settings and associated documentation; records of security function verification results; information system audit records; other relevant documents or records]. **Interview**: [*SELECT FROM:* Organizational personnel with security function verification responsibilities; organizational personnel with information security responsibilities]. **Test**: [*SELECT FROM:* Organizational processes for reporting security function verification results; automated mechanisms supporting and/or implementing the reporting of security function verification results].	

SI-7	SOFTWARE, FIRMWARE, AND INFORMATION INTEGRITY	

	ASSESSMENT OBJECTIVE: *Determine if the organization:*		
	SI-7[1]	SI-7[1][a]	*defines software requiring integrity verification tools to be employed to detect unauthorized changes;*
		SI-7[1][b]	*defines firmware requiring integrity verification tools to be employed to detect unauthorized changes;*
		SI-7[1][c]	*defines information requiring integrity verification tools to be employed to detect unauthorized changes;*
	SI-7[2]	*employs integrity verification tools to detect unauthorized changes to organization-defined:*	
		SI-7[2][a]	*software;*

Special Publication 800-53A
Revision 4

Assessing Security and Privacy Controls in Federal Information Systems
and Organizations — *Building Effective Assessment Plans*

		SI-7[2][b]	*firmware; and*
		SI-7[2][c]	*information.*

POTENTIAL ASSESSMENT METHODS AND OBJECTS:

Examine: [*SELECT FROM:* System and information integrity policy; procedures addressing software, firmware, and information integrity; information system design documentation; information system configuration settings and associated documentation; integrity verification tools and associated documentation; records generated/triggered from integrity verification tools regarding unauthorized software, firmware, and information changes; information system audit records; other relevant documents or records].

Interview: [*SELECT FROM:* Organizational personnel with responsibility for software, firmware, and/or information integrity; organizational personnel with information security responsibilities; system/network administrators].

Test: [*SELECT FROM:* Software, firmware, and information integrity verification tools].

SI-7(1)	**SOFTWARE, FIRMWARE, AND INFORMATION INTEGRITY	*INTEGRITY CHECKS***	
	ASSESSMENT OBJECTIVE: *Determine if:*	
	SI-7(1)[1]	*the organization defines:*
		SI-7(1)[1][a]	*software requiring integrity checks to be performed;*
		SI-7(1)[1][b]	*firmware requiring integrity checks to be performed;*
		SI-7(1)[1][c]	*information requiring integrity checks to be performed;*
	SI-7(1)[2]	*the organization defines transitional states or security-relevant events requiring integrity checks of organization-defined:*
		SI-7(1)[2][a]	*software;*
		SI-7(1)[2][b]	*firmware;*
		SI-7(1)[2][c]	*information;*
	SI-7(1)[3]	*the organization defines a frequency with which to perform an integrity check of organization-defined:*
		SI-7(1)[3][a]	*software;*
		SI-7(1)[3][b]	*firmware;*
		SI-7(1)[3][c]	*information;*
	SI-7(1)[4]	*the information system performs an integrity check of organization-defined software, firmware, and information one or more of the following:*
		SI-7(1)[4][a]	*at startup;*
		SI-7(1)[4][b]	*at organization-defined transitional states or security-relevant events; and/or*
		SI-7(1)[4][c]	*with the organization-defined frequency.*

Special Publication 800-53A
Revision 4

Assessing Security and Privacy Controls in Federal Information Systems
and Organizations — *Building Effective Assessment Plans*

POTENTIAL ASSESSMENT METHODS AND OBJECTS:

Examine: [*SELECT FROM:* System and information integrity policy; procedures addressing software, firmware, and information integrity; information system design documentation; information system configuration settings and associated documentation; integrity verification tools and associated documentation; records of integrity scans; other relevant documents or records].

Interview: [*SELECT FROM:* Organizational personnel with responsibility for software, firmware, and/or information integrity; organizational personnel with information security responsibilities; system/network administrators; system developer].

Test: [*SELECT FROM:* Software, firmware, and information integrity verification tools].

SI-7(2)	SOFTWARE, FIRMWARE, AND INFORMATION INTEGRITY | *AUTOMATED NOTIFICATIONS OF INTEGRITY VIOLATIONS*

ASSESSMENT OBJECTIVE:

Determine if the organization:

SI-7(2)[1]	*defines personnel or roles to whom notification is to be provided upon discovering discrepancies during integrity verification; and*
SI-7(2)[2]	*employs automated tools that provide notification to organization-defined personnel or roles upon discovering discrepancies during integrity verification.*

POTENTIAL ASSESSMENT METHODS AND OBJECTS:

Examine: [*SELECT FROM:* System and information integrity policy; procedures addressing software, firmware, and information integrity; information system design documentation; information system configuration settings and associated documentation; integrity verification tools and associated documentation; records of integrity scans; automated tools supporting alerts and notifications for integrity discrepancies; alerts/notifications provided upon discovering discrepancies during integrity verifications; information system audit records; other relevant documents or records].

Interview: [*SELECT FROM:* Organizational personnel with responsibility for software, firmware, and/or information integrity; organizational personnel with information security responsibilities].

Test: [*SELECT FROM:* Software, firmware, and information integrity verification tools; automated mechanisms providing integrity discrepancy notifications].

SI-7(3)	SOFTWARE, FIRMWARE, AND INFORMATION INTEGRITY | *CENTRALLY-MANAGED INTEGRITY TOOLS*

ASSESSMENT OBJECTIVE:

Determine if the organization employs centrally managed integrity verification tools.

POTENTIAL ASSESSMENT METHODS AND OBJECTS:

Examine: [*SELECT FROM:* System and information integrity policy; procedures addressing software, firmware, and information integrity; information system design documentation; information system configuration settings and associated documentation; integrity verification tools and associated documentation; records of integrity scans; other relevant documents or records].

Interview: [*SELECT FROM:* Organizational personnel with responsibility for central management of integrity verification tools; organizational personnel with information security responsibilities].

Test: [*SELECT FROM:* Automated mechanisms supporting and/or implementing central management of integrity verification tools].

SI-7(4)	SECURITY FUNCTION VERIFICATION | *TAMPER-EVIDENT PACKAGING*
[Withdrawn: Incorporated into SA-12].	

Special Publication 800-53A
Revision 4

Assessing Security and Privacy Controls in Federal Information Systems
and Organizations — *Building Effective Assessment Plans*

SI-7(5)	SOFTWARE, FIRMWARE, AND INFORMATION INTEGRITY | *AUTOMATED RESPONSE TO INTEGRITY VIOLATIONS*
	ASSESSMENT OBJECTIVE: *Determine if:*
	SI-7(5)[1] | *the organization defines security safeguards to be implemented when integrity violations are discovered;*
	SI-7(5)[2] | *the information system automatically performs one or more of the following actions when integrity violations are discovered:*
	SI-7(5)[2][a] | *shuts the information system down;*
	SI-7(5)[2][b] | *restarts the information system; and/or*
	SI-7(5)[2][c] | *implements the organization-defined security safeguards.*
	POTENTIAL ASSESSMENT METHODS AND OBJECTS: **Examine**: [*SELECT FROM*: System and information integrity policy; procedures addressing software, firmware, and information integrity; information system design documentation; information system configuration settings and associated documentation; integrity verification tools and associated documentation; records of integrity scans; records of integrity checks and responses to integrity violations; information audit records; other relevant documents or records]. **Interview**: [*SELECT FROM*: Organizational personnel with responsibility for software, firmware, and/or information integrity; organizational personnel with information security responsibilities; system/network administrators; system developer]. **Test**: [*SELECT FROM*: Software, firmware, and information integrity verification tools; automated mechanisms providing an automated response to integrity violations; automated mechanisms supporting and/or implementing security safeguards to be implemented when integrity violations are discovered].

SI-7(6)	SOFTWARE, FIRMWARE, AND INFORMATION INTEGRITY | *CRYPTOGRAPHIC PROTECTION*
	ASSESSMENT OBJECTIVE: *Determine if the information system employs cryptographic mechanism to detect unauthorized changes to:*
	SI-7(6)[1] | *software;*
	SI-7(6)[2] | *firmware; and*
	SI-7(6)[3] | *information.*
	POTENTIAL ASSESSMENT METHODS AND OBJECTS: **Examine**: [*SELECT FROM*: System and information integrity policy; procedures addressing software, firmware, and information integrity; information system design documentation; information system configuration settings and associated documentation; cryptographic mechanisms and associated documentation; records of detected unauthorized changes to software, firmware, and information; information system audit records; other relevant documents or records]. **Interview**: [*SELECT FROM*: Organizational personnel with responsibility for software, firmware, and/or information integrity; organizational personnel with information security responsibilities; system/network administrators; system developer]. **Test**: [*SELECT FROM*: Software, firmware, and information integrity verification tools; cryptographic mechanisms implementing software, firmware, and information integrity].

Special Publication 800-53A
Revision 4

Assessing Security and Privacy Controls in Federal Information Systems
and Organizations — *Building Effective Assessment Plans*

SI-7(7)	**SOFTWARE, FIRMWARE, AND INFORMATION INTEGRITY** | *INTEGRATION OF DETECTION AND RESPONSE*		
	ASSESSMENT OBJECTIVE: *Determine if the organization:*		
	SI-7(7)[1]	*defines unauthorized security-relevant changes to the information system; and*	
	SI-7(7)[2]	*incorporates the detection of unauthorized organization-defined security-relevant changes to the information system into the organizational incident response capability.*	
	POTENTIAL ASSESSMENT METHODS AND OBJECTS: **Examine**: [*SELECT FROM:* System and information integrity policy; procedures addressing software, firmware, and information integrity; procedures addressing incident response; information system design documentation; information system configuration settings and associated documentation; incident response records; information audit records; other relevant documents or records]. **Interview**: [*SELECT FROM:* Organizational personnel with responsibility for software, firmware, and/or information integrity; organizational personnel with information security responsibilities; organizational personnel with incident response responsibilities]. **Test**: [*SELECT FROM:* Organizational processes for incorporating detection of unauthorized security-relevant changes into the incident response capability; software, firmware, and information integrity verification tools; automated mechanisms supporting and/or implementing incorporation of detection of unauthorized security-relevant changes into the incident response capability].		

SI-7(8)	**SOFTWARE, FIRMWARE, AND INFORMATION INTEGRITY** | *AUDITING CAPABILITY FOR SIGNIFICANT EVENTS*			
	ASSESSMENT OBJECTIVE: *Determine if:*			
	SI-7(8)[1]	*the organization defines personnel or roles to be alerted upon detection of a potential integrity violation;*		
	SI-7(8)[2]	*the organization defines other actions to be taken upon detection of a potential integrity violation;*		
	SI-7(8)[3]	**SI-7(8)[3][a]**	*the information system, upon detection of a potential integrity violation, provides the capability to audit the event;*	
		SI-7(8)[3][b]	*the information system, upon detection of a potential integrity violation, initiates one or more of the following actions:*	
			SI-7(8)[3][b][1]	*generates an audit record;*
			SI-7(8)[3][b][2]	*alerts current user;*
			SI-7(8)[3][b][3]	*alerts organization-defined personnel or roles; and/or*
			SI-7(8)[3][b][4]	*organization-defined other actions.*

POTENTIAL ASSESSMENT METHODS AND OBJECTS:

Examine: [*SELECT FROM:* System and information integrity policy; procedures addressing software, firmware, and information integrity; information system design documentation; information system configuration settings and associated documentation; integrity verification tools and associated documentation; records of integrity scans; incident response records, list of security-relevant changes to the information system; automated tools supporting alerts and notifications if unauthorized security changes are detected; information system audit records; other relevant documents or records].

Interview: [*SELECT FROM:* Organizational personnel with responsibility for software, firmware, and/or information integrity; organizational personnel with information security responsibilities; system/network administrators; system developer].

Test: [*SELECT FROM:* Software, firmware, and information integrity verification tools; automated mechanisms supporting and/or implementing the capability to audit potential integrity violations; automated mechanisms supporting and/or implementing alerts about potential integrity violations].

SI-7(9)	SOFTWARE, FIRMWARE, AND INFORMATION INTEGRITY | *VERIFY BOOT PROCESS*

ASSESSMENT OBJECTIVE:

Determine if:

SI-7(9)[1]	*the organization defines devices requiring integrity verification of the boot process; and*
SI-7(9)[2]	*the information system verifies the integrity of the boot process of organization-defined devices.*

POTENTIAL ASSESSMENT METHODS AND OBJECTS:

Examine: [*SELECT FROM:* System and information integrity policy; procedures addressing software, firmware, and information integrity; information system design documentation; information system configuration settings and associated documentation; integrity verification tools and associated documentation; documentation; records of integrity verification scans; information system audit records; other relevant documents or records].

Interview: [*SELECT FROM:* Organizational personnel with responsibility for software, firmware, and/or information integrity; organizational personnel with information security responsibilities; system developer].

Test: [*SELECT FROM:* Software, firmware, and information integrity verification tools; automated mechanisms supporting and/or implementing integrity verification of the boot process].

SI-7(10)	SOFTWARE, FIRMWARE, AND INFORMATION INTEGRITY | *PROTECTION OF BOOT SOFTWARE*

ASSESSMENT OBJECTIVE:

Determine if:

SI-7(10)[1]	*the organization defines security safeguards to be implemented to protect the integrity of boot firmware in devices;*
SI-7(10)[2]	*the organization defines devices requiring organization-defined security safeguards to be implemented to protect the integrity of boot firmware; and*
SI-7(10)[3]	*the information system implements organization-defined security safeguards to protect the integrity of boot firmware in organization-defined devices.*

Special Publication 800-53A
Revision 4

Assessing Security and Privacy Controls in Federal Information Systems
and Organizations — *Building Effective Assessment Plans*

	POTENTIAL ASSESSMENT METHODS AND OBJECTS: **Examine**: [*SELECT FROM*: System and information integrity policy; procedures addressing software, firmware, and information integrity; information system design documentation; information system configuration settings and associated documentation; integrity verification tools and associated documentation; records of integrity verification scans; information system audit records; other relevant documents or records]. **Interview**: [*SELECT FROM*: Organizational personnel with responsibility for software, firmware, and/or information integrity; organizational personnel with information security responsibilities; system/network administrators; system developer]. **Test**: [*SELECT FROM*: Software, firmware, and information integrity verification tools; automated mechanisms supporting and/or implementing protection of the integrity of boot firmware; safeguards implementing protection of the integrity of boot firmware].

SI-7(11)	**SOFTWARE, FIRMWARE, AND INFORMATION INTEGRITY** | *CONFINED ENVIRONMENTS WITH LIMITED PRIVILEGES*
	ASSESSMENT OBJECTIVE: *Determine if the organization:*
	SI-7(11)[1] *defines user-installed software to be executed in a confined physical or virtual machine environment with limited privileges; and*
	SI-7(11)[2] *requires that organization-defined user-installed software execute in a confined physical or virtual machine environment with limited privileges.*
	POTENTIAL ASSESSMENT METHODS AND OBJECTS: **Examine**: [*SELECT FROM*: System and information integrity policy; procedures addressing software, firmware, and information integrity; information system design documentation; information system configuration settings and associated documentation; information system audit records; other relevant documents or records]. **Interview**: [*SELECT FROM*: Organizational personnel with responsibility for software, firmware, and/or information integrity; organizational personnel with information security responsibilities]. **Test**: [*SELECT FROM*: Software, firmware, and information integrity verification tools; automated mechanisms supporting and/or implementing execution of software in a confined environment (physical and/or virtual); automated mechanisms supporting and/or implementing limited privileges in the confined environment].

SI-7(12)	**SOFTWARE, FIRMWARE, AND INFORMATION INTEGRITY** | *INTEGRITY VERIFICATION*
	ASSESSMENT OBJECTIVE: *Determine if the organization:*
	SI-7(12)[1] *defines user-installed software requiring integrity verification prior to execution; and*
	SI-7(12)[2] *requires that the integrity of organization-defined user-installed software be verified prior to execution.*
	POTENTIAL ASSESSMENT METHODS AND OBJECTS: **Examine**: [*SELECT FROM*: System and information integrity policy; procedures addressing software, firmware, and information integrity; information system design documentation; information system configuration settings and associated documentation; integrity verification records; information system audit records; other relevant documents or records]. **Interview**: [*SELECT FROM*: Organizational personnel with responsibility for software, firmware, and/or information integrity; organizational personnel with information security responsibilities]. **Test**: [*SELECT FROM*: Software, firmware, and information integrity verification tools; automated mechanisms supporting and/or implementing verification of the integrity of user-installed software prior to execution].

Special Publication 800-53A
Revision 4

Assessing Security and Privacy Controls in Federal Information Systems
and Organizations — *Building Effective Assessment Plans*

SI-7(13)	SOFTWARE, FIRMWARE, AND INFORMATION INTEGRITY | *CODE EXECUTION IN PROTECTED ENVIRONMENTS*	
	ASSESSMENT OBJECTIVE: *Determine if the organization:*	
	SI-7(13)[1]	*allows execution of binary or machine-executable code obtained from sources with limited or no warranty;*
	SI-7(13)[2]	*allows execution of binary or machine-executable code without the provision of source code only in confined physical or virtual machines;*
	SI-7(13)[3]	*defines personnel or roles required to provide explicit approval to allow execution of binary or machine-executable code; and*
	SI-7(13)[4]	*allows execution of binary or machine-executable code with the explicit approval of organization-defined personnel or roles.*
	POTENTIAL ASSESSMENT METHODS AND OBJECTS: **Examine**: [*SELECT FROM:* System and information integrity policy; procedures addressing software, firmware, and information integrity; information system design documentation; information system configuration settings and associated documentation; approval records for execution of binary and machine-executable code; information system audit records; other relevant documents or records]. **Interview**: [*SELECT FROM:* Organizational personnel with responsibility for software, firmware, and/or information integrity; organizational personnel with information security responsibilities; system/network administrators; system developer]. **Test**: [*SELECT FROM:* Software, firmware, and information integrity verification tools; automated mechanisms supporting and/or implementing approvals for execution of binary or machine-executable code].	

SI-7(14)	SOFTWARE, FIRMWARE, AND INFORMATION INTEGRITY | *BINARY OR MACHINE EXECUTABLE CODE*		
	ASSESSMENT OBJECTIVE: *Determine if the organization:*		
	SI-7(14)(a)	SI-7(14)(a)[1]	*prohibits the use of binary or machine-executable code from sources with limited or no warranty;*
		SI-7(14)(a)[2]	*prohibits the use of binary or machine-executable code without the provision of source code;*
	SI-7(14)(b)	SI-7(14)(b)[1]	*provides exceptions to the source code requirement only for compelling mission/operational requirements; and*
		SI-7(14)(b)[2]	*provides exceptions to the source code requirement only with the approval of the authorizing official.*
	POTENTIAL ASSESSMENT METHODS AND OBJECTS: **Examine**: [*SELECT FROM:* System and information integrity policy; procedures addressing software, firmware, and information integrity; information system design documentation; information system configuration settings and associated documentation; approval records for execution of binary and machine-executable code; information system audit records; other relevant documents or records]. **Interview**: [*SELECT FROM:* Organizational personnel with responsibility for software, firmware, and/or information integrity; organizational personnel with information security responsibilities; authorizing official; system/network administrators; system developer]. **Test**: [*SELECT FROM:* Automated mechanisms supporting and/or implementing prohibition of the execution of binary or machine-executable code].		

Special Publication 800-53A
Revision 4

Assessing Security and Privacy Controls in Federal Information Systems
and Organizations — *Building Effective Assessment Plans*

SI-7(15)	SOFTWARE, FIRMWARE, AND INFORMATION INTEGRITY | *CODE AUTHENTICATION*		
	ASSESSMENT OBJECTIVE: *Determine if:*		
	SI-7(15)[1]	SI-7(15)[1][a]	*the organization defines software components to be authenticated by cryptographic mechanisms prior to installation;*
		SI-7(15)[1][b]	*the organization defines firmware components to be authenticated by cryptographic mechanisms prior to installation;*
	SI-7(15)[2]	SI-7(15)[2][a]	*the information system implements cryptographic mechanisms to authenticate organization-defined software components prior to installation; and*
		SI-7(15)[2][b]	*the information system implements cryptographic mechanisms to authenticate organization-defined firmware components prior to installation.*
	POTENTIAL ASSESSMENT METHODS AND OBJECTS: **Examine**: [*SELECT FROM:* System and information integrity policy; procedures addressing software, firmware, and information integrity; information system design documentation; information system configuration settings and associated documentation; cryptographic mechanisms and associated documentation; information system audit records; other relevant documents or records]. **Interview**: [*SELECT FROM:* Organizational personnel with responsibility for software, firmware, and/or information integrity; organizational personnel with information security responsibilities; system/network administrators; system developer]. **Test**: [*SELECT FROM:* Cryptographic mechanisms authenticating software/firmware prior to installation].		

SI-7(16)	SOFTWARE, FIRMWARE, AND INFORMATION INTEGRITY | *TIME LIMIT ON PROCESS EXECUTION WITHOUT SUPERVISION*	
	ASSESSMENT OBJECTIVE: *Determine if the organization:*	
	SI-7(16)[1]	*defines a time period as the maximum period allowed for processes to execute without supervision; and*
	SI-7(16)[2]	*does not allow processes to execute without supervision for more than the organization-defined time period.*
	POTENTIAL ASSESSMENT METHODS AND OBJECTS: **Examine**: [*SELECT FROM:* System and information integrity policy; procedures addressing software and information integrity; information system design documentation; information system configuration settings and associated documentation; information system audit records; other relevant documents or records]. **Interview**: [*SELECT FROM:* Organizational personnel with responsibility for software, firmware, and/or information integrity; organizational personnel with information security responsibilities; system/network administrators; system developer]. **Test**: [*SELECT FROM:* Software, firmware, and information integrity verification tools; automated mechanisms supporting and/or implementing time limits on process execution without supervision].	

Special Publication 800-53A
Revision 4

Assessing Security and Privacy Controls in Federal Information Systems
and Organizations — *Building Effective Assessment Plans*

SI-8	SPAM PROTECTION	
	ASSESSMENT OBJECTIVE: *Determine if the organization:*	
	SI-8(a)	*employs spam protection mechanisms:*
		SI-8(a)[1] *at information system entry points to detect unsolicited messages;*
		SI-8(a)[2] *at information system entry points to take action on unsolicited messages;*
		SI-8(a)[3] *at information system exit points to detect unsolicited messages;*
		SI-8(a)[4] *at information system exit points to take action on unsolicited messages; and*
	SI-8(b)	*updates spam protection mechanisms when new releases are available in accordance with organizational configuration management policy and procedures.*
	POTENTIAL ASSESSMENT METHODS AND OBJECTS: **Examine**: [*SELECT FROM:* System and information integrity policy; configuration management policy and procedures (CM-1); procedures addressing spam protection; spam protection mechanisms; records of spam protection updates; information system design documentation; information system configuration settings and associated documentation; information system audit records; other relevant documents or records]. **Interview**: [*SELECT FROM:* Organizational personnel with responsibility for spam protection; organizational personnel with information security responsibilities; system/network administrators; system developer]. **Test**: [*SELECT FROM:* Organizational processes for implementing spam protection; automated mechanisms supporting and/or implementing spam protection].	

SI-8(1)	SPAM PROTECTION	*CENTRAL MANAGEMENT*
	ASSESSMENT OBJECTIVE: *Determine if the organization centrally manages spam protection mechanisms.*	
	POTENTIAL ASSESSMENT METHODS AND OBJECTS: **Examine**: [*SELECT FROM:* System and information integrity policy; procedures addressing spam protection; spam protection mechanisms; information system design documentation; information system configuration settings and associated documentation; information system audit records; other relevant documents or records]. **Interview**: [*SELECT FROM:* Organizational personnel with responsibility for spam protection; organizational personnel with information security responsibilities; system/network administrators]. **Test**: [*SELECT FROM:* Organizational processes for central management of spam protection; automated mechanisms supporting and/or implementing central management of spam protection].	

SI-8(2)	SPAM PROTECTION	*AUTOMATIC UPDATES*
	ASSESSMENT OBJECTIVE: *Determine if the information system automatically updates spam protection mechanisms.*	

Special Publication 800-53A
Revision 4

Assessing Security and Privacy Controls in Federal Information Systems
and Organizations — *Building Effective Assessment Plans*

POTENTIAL ASSESSMENT METHODS AND OBJECTS:

Examine: [*SELECT FROM:* System and information integrity policy; procedures addressing spam protection; spam protection mechanisms; records of spam protection updates; information system design documentation; information system configuration settings and associated documentation; information system audit records; other relevant documents or records].

Interview: [*SELECT FROM:* Organizational personnel with responsibility for spam protection; organizational personnel with information security responsibilities; system/network administrators; system developer].

Test: [*SELECT FROM:* Organizational processes for spam protection; automated mechanisms supporting and/or implementing automatic updates to spam protection mechanisms].

SI-8(3)	SPAM PROTECTION | *CONTINUOUS LEARNING CAPABILITY*

ASSESSMENT OBJECTIVE:

Determine if the information system implements spam protection mechanisms with a learning capability to more effectively identify legitimate communications traffic.

POTENTIAL ASSESSMENT METHODS AND OBJECTS:

Examine: [*SELECT FROM:* System and information integrity policy; procedures addressing spam protection; spam protection mechanisms; information system design documentation; information system configuration settings and associated documentation; information system audit records; other relevant documents or records].

Interview: [*SELECT FROM:* Organizational personnel with responsibility for spam protection; organizational personnel with information security responsibilities; system/network administrators; system developer].

Test: [*SELECT FROM:* Organizational processes for spam protection; automated mechanisms supporting and/or implementing spam protection mechanisms with a learning capability].

SI-9	INFORMATION INPUT RESTRICTIONS

[Withdrawn: Incorporated into AC-2, AC-3, AC-5, AC-6].

SI-10	INFORMATION INPUT VALIDATION

ASSESSMENT OBJECTIVE:
Determine if:

SI-10[1]	*the organization defines information inputs requiring validity checks; and*
SI-10[2]	*the information system checks the validity of organization-defined information inputs.*

POTENTIAL ASSESSMENT METHODS AND OBJECTS:

Examine: [*SELECT FROM:* System and information integrity policy; access control policy and procedures; separation of duties policy and procedures; procedures addressing information input validation; documentation for automated tools and applications to verify validity of information; list of information inputs requiring validity checks; information system design documentation; information system configuration settings and associated documentation; information system audit records; other relevant documents or records].

Interview: [*SELECT FROM:* Organizational personnel with responsibility for information input validation; organizational personnel with information security responsibilities; system/network administrators; system developer].

Test: [*SELECT FROM:* Automated mechanisms supporting and/or implementing validity checks on information inputs].

Special Publication 800-53A
Revision 4

Assessing Security and Privacy Controls in Federal Information Systems
and Organizations — *Building Effective Assessment Plans*

SI-10(1)	INFORMATION INPUT VALIDATION | *MANUAL OVERRIDE CAPABILITY*		
	ASSESSMENT OBJECTIVE: *Determine if:*		
	SI-10(1)(a)	SI-10(1)(a)[1]	*the organization defines information inputs for which the information system provides a manual override capability for input validation;*
		SI-10(1)(a)[2]	*the information system provides a manual override capability for input validation of organization-defined inputs;*
	SI-10(1)(b)	SI-10(1)(b)[1]	*the organization defines authorized individuals who can use the manual override capability;*
		SI-10(1)(b)[2]	*the information system restricts the use of manual override capability to organization-defined authorized individuals; and*
	SI-10(1)(c)	*the information system audits the use of the manual override capability.*	
	POTENTIAL ASSESSMENT METHODS AND OBJECTS: **Examine**: [*SELECT FROM:* System and information integrity policy; access control policy and procedures; separation of duties policy and procedures; procedures addressing information input validation; information system design documentation; information system configuration settings and associated documentation; information system audit records; other relevant documents or records]. **Interview**: [*SELECT FROM:* Organizational personnel with responsibility for information input validation; organizational personnel with information security responsibilities; system/network administrators; system developer]. **Test**: [*SELECT FROM:* Organizational processes for use of manual override capability; automated mechanisms supporting and/or implementing manual override capability for input validation; automated mechanisms supporting and/or implementing auditing of the use of manual override capability].		

SI-10(2)	INFORMATION INPUT VALIDATION | *REVIEW / RESOLUTION OF ERRORS*	
	ASSESSMENT OBJECTIVE: *Determine if the organization:*	
	SI-10(2)[1]	*defines a time period within which input validation errors are to be reviewed and resolved; and*
	SI-10(2)[2]	*ensures that input validation errors are reviewed and resolved within the organization-defined time period.*
	POTENTIAL ASSESSMENT METHODS AND OBJECTS: **Examine**: [*SELECT FROM:* System and information integrity policy; access control policy and procedures; separation of duties policy and procedures; procedures addressing information input validation; information system design documentation; information system configuration settings and associated documentation; review records of information input validation errors and resulting resolutions; information input validation error logs or records; information system audit records; other relevant documents or records]. **Interview**: [*SELECT FROM:* Organizational personnel with responsibility for information input validation; organizational personnel with information security responsibilities; system/network administrators]. **Test**: [*SELECT FROM:* Organizational processes for review and resolution of input validation errors; automated mechanisms supporting and/or implementing review and resolution of input validation errors].	

Special Publication 800-53A
Revision 4

Assessing Security and Privacy Controls in Federal Information Systems
and Organizations — *Building Effective Assessment Plans*

SI-10(3)	**INFORMATION INPUT VALIDATION** | *PREDICTABLE BEHAVIOR*
	ASSESSMENT OBJECTIVE: *Determine if the information system behaves in a predictable and documented manner that reflects organizational and system objectives when invalid inputs are received.*
	POTENTIAL ASSESSMENT METHODS AND OBJECTS: **Examine**: [*SELECT FROM:* System and information integrity policy; procedures addressing information input validation; information system design documentation; information system configuration settings and associated documentation; information system audit records; other relevant documents or records]. **Interview**: [*SELECT FROM:* Organizational personnel with responsibility for information input validation; organizational personnel with information security responsibilities; system/network administrators; system developer]. **Test**: [*SELECT FROM:* Automated mechanisms supporting and/or implementing predictable behavior when invalid inputs are received].

SI-10(4)	**INFORMATION INPUT VALIDATION** | *REVIEW / TIMING INTERACTIONS*
	ASSESSMENT OBJECTIVE: *Determine if the organization accounts for timing interactions among information system components in determining appropriate responses for invalid inputs.*
	POTENTIAL ASSESSMENT METHODS AND OBJECTS: **Examine**: [*SELECT FROM:* System and information integrity policy; procedures addressing information input validation; information system design documentation; information system configuration settings and associated documentation; information system audit records; other relevant documents or records]. **Interview**: [*SELECT FROM:* Organizational personnel with responsibility for information input validation; organizational personnel with information security responsibilities; system/network administrators; system developer]. **Test**: [*SELECT FROM:* Organizational processes for determining appropriate responses to invalid inputs; automated mechanisms supporting and/or implementing responses to invalid inputs].

SI-10(5)	**INFORMATION INPUT VALIDATION** | *RESTRICT INPUTS TO TRUSTED SOURCES AND APPROVED FORMATS*		
	ASSESSMENT OBJECTIVE: *Determine if the organization:*		
	SI-10(5)[1]	*defines trusted sources to which the use of information inputs is to be restricted;*	
	SI-10(5)[2]	*defines formats to which the use of information inputs is to be restricted;*	
	SI-10(5)[3]	*restricts the use of information inputs to:*	
		SI-10(5)[3][a]	*organization-defined trust sources; and/or*
		SI-10(5)[3][b]	*organization-defined formats.*

Special Publication 800-53A
Revision 4

Assessing Security and Privacy Controls in Federal Information Systems
and Organizations — *Building Effective Assessment Plans*

POTENTIAL ASSESSMENT METHODS AND OBJECTS:

Examine: [*SELECT FROM*: System and information integrity policy; procedures addressing information input validation; information system design documentation; information system configuration settings and associated documentation; list of trusted sources for information inputs; list of acceptable formats for input restrictions; information system audit records; other relevant documents or records].

Interview: [*SELECT FROM*: Organizational personnel with responsibility for information input validation; organizational personnel with information security responsibilities; system/network administrators; system developer].

Test: [*SELECT FROM*: Organizational processes for restricting information inputs; automated mechanisms supporting and/or implementing restriction of information inputs].

SI-11	ERROR HANDLING

ASSESSMENT OBJECTIVE:

Determine if:

SI-11(a)		*the information system generates error messages that provide information necessary for corrective actions without revealing information that could be exploited by adversaries;*
SI-11(b)	SI-11(b)[1]	*the organization defines personnel or roles to whom error messages are to be revealed; and*
	SI-11(b)[2]	*the information system reveals error messages only to organization-defined personnel or roles.*

POTENTIAL ASSESSMENT METHODS AND OBJECTS:

Examine: [*SELECT FROM*: System and information integrity policy; procedures addressing information system error handling; information system design documentation; information system configuration settings and associated documentation; documentation providing structure/content of error messages; information system audit records; other relevant documents or records].

Interview: [*SELECT FROM*: Organizational personnel with responsibility for information input validation; organizational personnel with information security responsibilities; system/network administrators; system developer].

Test: [*SELECT FROM*: Organizational processes for error handling; automated mechanisms supporting and/or implementing error handling; automated mechanisms supporting and/or implementing management of error messages].

SI-12	INFORMATION HANDLING AND RETENTION

ASSESSMENT OBJECTIVE:

Determine if the organization, in accordance with applicable federal laws, Executive Orders, directives, policies, regulations, standards, and operational requirements:

SI-12[1]	*handles information within the information system;*
SI-12[2]	*handles output from the information system;*
SI-12[3]	*retains information within the information system; and*
SI-12[4]	*retains output from the information system.*

Special Publication 800-53A
Revision 4

Assessing Security and Privacy Controls in Federal Information Systems
and Organizations — *Building Effective Assessment Plans*

POTENTIAL ASSESSMENT METHODS AND OBJECTS:

Examine: [*SELECT FROM:* System and information integrity policy; federal laws, Executive Orders, directives, policies, regulations, standards, and operational requirements applicable to information handling and retention; media protection policy and procedures; procedures addressing information system output handling and retention; information retention records, other relevant documents or records].

Interview: [*SELECT FROM:* Organizational personnel with responsibility for information handling and retention; organizational personnel with information security responsibilities/network administrators].

Test: [*SELECT FROM:* Organizational processes for information handling and retention; automated mechanisms supporting and/or implementing information handling and retention].

SI-13	PREDICTABLE FAILURE PREVENTION	
	ASSESSMENT OBJECTIVE: *Determine if the organization:*	
SI-13(a)	SI-13(a)[1]	*defines information system components for which mean time to failure (MTTF) should be determined;*
	SI-13(a)[2]	*determines MTTF for organization-defined information system components in specific environments of operation;*
SI-13(b)	SI-13(b)[1]	*defines MTTF substitution criteria to be used as a means to exchange active and standby components;*
	SI-13(b)[2]	*provides substitute information system components at organization-defined MTTF substitution criteria; and*
	SI-13(b)[3]	*provides a means to exchange active and standby components at organization-defined MTTF substitution criteria.*

POTENTIAL ASSESSMENT METHODS AND OBJECTS:

Examine: [*SELECT FROM:* System and information integrity policy; procedures addressing predictable failure prevention; information system design documentation; information system configuration settings and associated documentation; list of MTTF substitution criteria; information system audit records; other relevant documents or records].

Interview: [*SELECT FROM:* Organizational personnel with responsibility for MTTF determinations and activities; organizational personnel with information security responsibilities; system/network administrators; organizational personnel with contingency planning responsibilities].

Test: [*SELECT FROM:* Organizational processes for managing MTTF].

SI-13(1)	PREDICTABLE FAILURE PREVENTION | *TRANSFERRING COMPONENT RESPONSIBILITIES*	
	ASSESSMENT OBJECTIVE: *Determine if the organization:*	
	SI-13(1)[1]	*defines maximum fraction or percentage of mean time to failure within which to transfer the responsibilities of an information system component that is out of service to a substitute component; and*
	SI-13(1)[2]	*takes the information system component out of service by transferring component responsibilities to substitute components no later than organization-defined fraction or percentage of mean time to failure.*

Special Publication 800-53A
Revision 4

Assessing Security and Privacy Controls in Federal Information Systems
and Organizations — *Building Effective Assessment Plans*

POTENTIAL ASSESSMENT METHODS AND OBJECTS:

Examine: [*SELECT FROM:* System and information integrity policy; procedures addressing predictable failure prevention; information system design documentation; information system configuration settings and associated documentation; information system audit records; other relevant documents or records].

Interview: [*SELECT FROM:* Organizational personnel with responsibility for MTTF activities; organizational personnel with information security responsibilities; system/network administrators; organizational personnel with contingency planning responsibilities].

Test: [*SELECT FROM:* Organizational processes for managing MTTF; automated mechanisms supporting and/or implementing transfer of component responsibilities to substitute components].

SI-13(2)	PREDICTABLE FAILURE PREVENTION	*TIME LIMIT ON PROCESS EXECUTION WITHOUT SUPERVISION*

[Withdrawn: Incorporated into SI-7(16)].

SI-13(3)	PREDICTABLE FAILURE PREVENTION	*MANUAL TRANSFER BETWEEN COMPONENTS*

ASSESSMENT OBJECTIVE:

Determine if the organization:

SI-13(3)[1]	*defines the minimum frequency with which the organization manually initiates a transfer between active and standby information system components if the mean time to failure exceeds the organization-defined time period;*
SI-13(3)[2]	*defines the time period that the mean time to failure must exceed before the organization manually initiates a transfer between active and standby information system components; and*
SI-13(3)[3]	*manually initiates transfers between active and standby information system components at the organization-defined frequency if the mean time to failure exceeds the organization-defined time period.*

POTENTIAL ASSESSMENT METHODS AND OBJECTS:

Examine: [*SELECT FROM:* System and information integrity policy; procedures addressing predictable failure prevention; information system design documentation; information system configuration settings and associated documentation; information system audit records; other relevant documents or records].

Interview: [*SELECT FROM:* Organizational personnel with responsibility for MTTF activities; organizational personnel with information security responsibilities; system/network administrators; organizational personnel with contingency planning responsibilities].

Test: [*SELECT FROM:* Organizational processes for managing MTTF and conducting the manual transfer between active and standby components].

SI-13(4)	PREDICTABLE FAILURE PREVENTION	STANDBY COMPONENT INSTALLATION / NOTIFICATION

ASSESSMENT OBJECTIVE:

Determine if the organization:

SI-13(4)(a)	SI-13(4)(a)[1]	*defines a time period for standby information system components to be successfully and transparently installed when information system component failures are detected;*
	SI-13(4)(a)[2]	*ensures that the standby components are successfully and transparently installed within the organization-defined time period;*

Special Publication 800-53A
Revision 4

Assessing Security and Privacy Controls in Federal Information Systems
and Organizations — *Building Effective Assessment Plans*

SI-13(4)(b)	SI-13(4)(b)[1]	*defines an alarm to be activated when information system component failures are detected;*	
	SI-13(4)(b)[2]	*if information system component failures are detected, does one or more of the following:*	
		SI-13(4)(b)[2][a]	*activates the organization-defined alarm; and/or*
		SI-13(4)(b)[2][b]	*automatically shuts down the information system.*

POTENTIAL ASSESSMENT METHODS AND OBJECTS:

Examine: [*SELECT FROM:* System and information integrity policy; procedures addressing predictable failure prevention; information system design documentation; information system configuration settings and associated documentation; list of actions to be taken once information system component failure is detected; information system audit records; other relevant documents or records].

Interview: [*SELECT FROM:* Organizational personnel with responsibility for MTTF activities; organizational personnel with information security responsibilities; system/network administrators; organizational personnel with contingency planning responsibilities].

Test: [*SELECT FROM:* Organizational processes for managing MTTF; automated mechanisms supporting and/or implementing transparent installation of standby components; automated mechanisms supporting and/or implementing alarms or system shutdown if component failures are detected].

SI-13(5)	**PREDICTABLE FAILURE PREVENTION	*FAILOVER CAPABILITY***	
	ASSESSMENT OBJECTIVE: *Determine if the organization:*	
	SI-13(5)[1]	*defines failover capability to be provided for the information system;*
	SI-13(5)[2]	*provides one of the following organization-defined failover capabilities for the information system:*
	SI-13(5)[2][a]	*real-time failover capability; and/or*
	SI-13(5)[2][b]	*near real-time failover capability.*

POTENTIAL ASSESSMENT METHODS AND OBJECTS:

Examine: [*SELECT FROM:* System and information integrity policy; procedures addressing predictable failure prevention; information system design documentation; information system configuration settings and associated documentation; documentation describing failover capability provided for the information system; information system audit records; other relevant documents or records].

Interview: [*SELECT FROM:* Organizational personnel with responsibility for failover capability; organizational personnel with information security responsibilities; system/network administrators; organizational personnel with contingency planning responsibilities].

Test: [*SELECT FROM:* Organizational processes for managing failover capability; automated mechanisms supporting and/or implementing failover capability].

SI-14	**NON-PERSISTENCE**	
	ASSESSMENT OBJECTIVE: *Determine if the organization:*	
	SI-14[1]	*defines non-persistent information system components and services to be implemented;*

Special Publication 800-53A
Revision 4

Assessing Security and Privacy Controls in Federal Information Systems
and Organizations — *Building Effective Assessment Plans*

	SI-14[2]	SI-14[2][a]	*defines a frequency to terminate non-persistent organization-defined components and services that are initiated in a known state;*
		SI-14[2][b]	*implements non-persistent organization-defined information system components and services that are initiated in a known state and terminated one or more of the following:*
		SI-14[2][b][1]	*upon end of session of use; and/or*
		SI-14[2][b][2]	*periodically at the organization-defined frequency.*

POTENTIAL ASSESSMENT METHODS AND OBJECTS:

Examine: [*SELECT FROM:* System and information integrity policy; procedures addressing non-persistence for information system components; information system design documentation; information system configuration settings and associated documentation; information system audit records; other relevant documents or records].

Interview: [*SELECT FROM:* Organizational personnel with responsibility for non-persistence; organizational personnel with information security responsibilities; system/network administrators; system developer].

Test: [*SELECT FROM:* Automated mechanisms supporting and/or implementing initiation and termination of non-persistent components].

SI-14(1)	**NON-PERSISTENCE** | *REFRESH FROM TRUSTED SOURCES*

ASSESSMENT OBJECTIVE:

Determine if the organization:

SI-14(1)[1]	*defines trusted sources from which software and data employed during information system component and service refreshes are to be obtained; and*
SI-14(1)[2]	*ensures that software and data employed during information system component and service refreshes are obtained from organization-defined trusted sources.*

POTENTIAL ASSESSMENT METHODS AND OBJECTS:

Examine: [*SELECT FROM:* System and information integrity policy; procedures addressing non-persistence for information system components; information system design documentation; information system configuration settings and associated documentation; information system audit records; other relevant documents or records].

Interview: [*SELECT FROM:* Organizational personnel with responsibility for obtaining component and service refreshes from trusted sources; organizational personnel with information security responsibilities].

Test: [*SELECT FROM:* Organizational processes for defining and obtaining component and service refreshes from trusted sources; automated mechanisms supporting and/or implementing component and service refreshes].

SI-15	**INFORMATION OUTPUT FILTERING**

ASSESSMENT OBJECTIVE:

Determine if:

SI-15[1]	*the organization defines software programs and/or applications whose information output requires validation to ensure that the information is consistent with the expected content; and*
SI-15[2]	*the information system validates information output from organization-defined software programs and/or applications to ensure that the information is consistent with the expected content.*

Special Publication 800-53A
Revision 4

Assessing Security and Privacy Controls in Federal Information Systems
and Organizations — *Building Effective Assessment Plans*

POTENTIAL ASSESSMENT METHODS AND OBJECTS:

Examine: [*SELECT FROM*: System and information integrity policy; procedures addressing information output filtering; information system design documentation; information system configuration settings and associated documentation; information system audit records; other relevant documents or records].

Interview: [*SELECT FROM*: Organizational personnel with responsibility for validating information output; organizational personnel with information security responsibilities; system/network administrators; system developer].

Test: [*SELECT FROM*: Organizational processes for validating information output; automated mechanisms supporting and/or implementing information output validation].

SI-16	MEMORY PROTECTION

ASSESSMENT OBJECTIVE:

Determine if:

SI-16[1]	*the organization defines security safeguards to be implemented to protect information system memory from unauthorized code execution; and*
SI-16[2]	*the information system implements organization-defined security safeguards to protect its memory from unauthorized code execution.*

POTENTIAL ASSESSMENT METHODS AND OBJECTS:

Examine: [*SELECT FROM*: System and information integrity policy; procedures addressing memory protection for the information system; information system design documentation; information system configuration settings and associated documentation; list of security safeguards protecting information system memory from unauthorized code execution; information system audit records; other relevant documents or records].

Interview: [*SELECT FROM*: Organizational personnel with responsibility for memory protection; organizational personnel with information security responsibilities; system/network administrators; system developer].

Test: [*SELECT FROM*: Automated mechanisms supporting and/or implementing safeguards to protect information system memory from unauthorized code execution].

SI-17	FAIL-SAFE PROCEDURES

ASSESSMENT OBJECTIVE:

Determine if:

SI-17[1]	*the organization defines fail-safe procedures to be implemented when organization-defined failure conditions occur;*
SI-17[2]	*the organization defines failure conditions resulting in organization-defined fail-safe procedures being implemented when such conditions occur; and*
SI-17[3]	*the information system implements organization-defined fail-safe procedures when organization-defined failure conditions occur.*

POTENTIAL ASSESSMENT METHODS AND OBJECTS:

Examine: [*SELECT FROM*: System and information integrity policy; procedures addressing memory protection for the information system; information system design documentation; information system configuration settings and associated documentation; list of security safeguards protecting information system memory from unauthorized code execution; information system audit records; other relevant documents or records].

Interview: [*SELECT FROM*: Organizational personnel with responsibility for fail-safe procedures; organizational personnel with information security responsibilities; system/network administrators; system developer].

Test: [*SELECT FROM*: Organizational fail-safe procedures; automated mechanisms supporting and/or implementing fail-safe procedures].

Special Publication 800-53A
Revision 4

Assessing Security and Privacy Controls in Federal Information Systems
and Organizations — *Building Effective Assessment Plans*

ASSESSMENT REPORTS
DOCUMENTING THE FINDINGS FROM SECURITY AND PRIVACY CONTROL ASSESSMENTS

T he primary purpose of the *security* and *privacy assessment reports* is to convey the results of the security and privacy control assessments to appropriate organizational officials. The security assessment report is included in the security authorization package along with the security plan (including an updated risk assessment) and the plan of action and milestones to provide authorizing officials with the information necessary to make risk-based decisions on whether to place an information system into operation or continue its operation. Organizations may choose to include similar privacy-related artifacts in the authorization package to convey essential information to authorizing officials. All issues associated with compliance to privacy-related legislation, directives, regulations, or policies are coordinated with the Senior Agency Official for Privacy (SAOP)/Chief Privacy Officer.[49] As the assessment and authorization process becomes more dynamic in nature, relying to a greater degree on the continuous monitoring aspects of the process as an integrated and tightly coupled part of the system development life cycle, the ability to update the security and privacy assessment reports frequently becomes a critical aspect of information security and privacy programs.

It is important to emphasize the relationship, described in Special Publication 800-37, among the three key documents in the authorization package (i.e., the security plan, the security assessment report, and the plan of action and milestones). It is these documents that provide the most reliable indication of the overall security state of the information system and the ability of the system to protect to the degree necessary, the organization's operations and assets, individuals, other organizations, and the Nation. Updates to these key documents are provided on an ongoing basis in accordance with the continuous monitoring program established by the organization. Updates to similar privacy-related documents occur at a frequency and format determined by the SAOP in coordination with authorizing officials.

The security and privacy assessment reports provide a disciplined and structured approach for documenting the findings of the assessor and the recommendations for correcting any weaknesses or deficiencies in the security and privacy controls.[50] This appendix provides a template for reporting the results from security and privacy control assessments. Organizations are not restricted to the specific template format; however, it is anticipated that the overall report of an assessment will include similar information to that detailed in the template for each security and privacy control assessed, preceded by a summary providing the list of all security and privacy controls assessed and the overall status of each control.

---

[49] In accordance with Office of Management and Budget (OMB) policy, an assessment of compliance with applicable Appendix J privacy controls must be conducted by the Senior Agency Official for Privacy (SAOP) or the SAOP's designated representative. SAOP approval is required as a *precondition* for the issuance of an authorization to operate. Organizations have the flexibility to determine the appropriate process for SAOP approval.

[50] While the rationale for each determination made is a part of the formal *Security* and *Privacy Assessment Reports*, the complete set of records produced as a part of the assessment is likely not included in the report. However, organizations retain the portion of these records necessary for maintaining an audit trail of assessment evidence, facilitating reuse of evidence and promoting repeatability of assessor actions.

Special Publication 800-53A
Revision 4

Assessing Security and Privacy Controls in Federal Information Systems
and Organizations — *Building Effective Assessment Plans*

Key Elements for Assessment Reporting

The following elements are included in security and privacy assessment reports:[51]

- Information system name;

- Security categorization;

- Site(s) assessed and assessment date(s);

- Assessor's name/identification;

- Previous assessment results (if reused);

- Security/privacy control or control enhancement designator;

- Selected assessment methods and objects;

- Depth and coverage attributes values;

- Assessment finding summary (indicating satisfied or other than satisfied);

- Assessor comments (weaknesses or deficiencies noted); and

- Assessor recommendations (priorities, remediation, corrective actions, or improvements).

The Assessment Findings

Each determination statement executed by an assessor results in one of the following findings: (i) satisfied (S); or (ii) other than satisfied (O). Consider the following example for security control CP-2(3). The assessor executes the assessment procedure for CP-2(3) and produces the following findings:

CP-3	CONTINGENCY TRAINING	
	ASSESSMENT OBJECTIVE: *Determine if the organization provides contingency training to information system users consistent with assigned roles and responsibilities:*	
	CP-3(a)	CP-3(a)[1]	*within the organization-defined time period of assuming a contingency role or responsibility;* **(S)**
		CP-3(a)[2]	*defines a time period within which contingency training is to be provided to information system users assuming a contingency role or responsibility;* **(S)**
	CP-3(b)	*when required by information system changes;* **(O)**
	CP-3(c)	CP-3(c)[1]	*thereafter, in accordance with the organization-defined frequency;* **(S)**
		CP-3(c)[2]	*defines the frequency for contingency training.* **(S)**
	Comments and Recommendations: CP-3(b) is marked as *other than satisfied* because assessors could not find evidence that the organization provided contingency training to information system users consistent with their assigned roles and responsibilities when there were significant changes to the system.	

---

[51] Information available in other key organizational documents (e.g., security or privacy plans, risk assessments, plans of action and milestones, or security or privacy assessment plans) need not be duplicated in the security and privacy assessment reports.

Special Publication 800-53A
Revision 4

Assessing Security and Privacy Controls in Federal Information Systems
and Organizations — *Building Effective Assessment Plans*

During an actual security and privacy control assessment, the assessment findings, comments, and recommendations are documented on appropriate organization-defined reporting forms. Organizations are encouraged to develop standard templates for reporting that contain the key elements for assessment reporting described above. Whenever possible, automation is used to make assessment data collection and reporting cost-effective, timely, and efficient.

Special Publication 800-53A
Revision 4

Assessing Security and Privacy Controls in Federal Information Systems
and Organizations — *Building Effective Assessment Plans*

ASSESSMENT CASES
WORKED EXAMPLES OF ASSESSOR ACTIONS DERIVED FROM ASSESSMENT PROCEDURES

DISCONTINUANCE OF ASSESSMENT CASE PROJECT

NIST initiated the *Assessment Case Development Project* in October 2007 in a joint partnership with the Departments of Justice, Energy, Transportation, and the Intelligence Community. The interagency task force developed a full suite of assessment cases based on the assessment procedures in Special Publication 800-53A, Revision 1. There will be no further development of assessment cases effective with the publication of Special Publication 800-53A, Revision 4. All previously developed assessment cases will continue to be available and can be downloaded from the NIST website at http://csrc.nist.gov/sec-cert. The material contained in Appendix H, including the exemplary templates for developing assessment cases will also continue to be available in the archived versions of Special Publication 800-53A, Revision 1.

Special Publication 800-53A
Revision 4

Assessing Security and Privacy Controls in Federal Information Systems
and Organizations — *Building Effective Assessment Plans*

APPENDIX I

ONGOING ASSESSMENT AND AUTOMATION
USING AUTOMATED TECHNIQUES TO ACHIEVE MORE EFFICIENT ASSESSMENTS

Ongoing security assessment is the continuous evaluation of the effectiveness of security control implementation.[52] It is an essential subset of *Information Security Continuous Monitoring (ISCM)* activities.[53] Ongoing assessment encompasses ISCM Steps 3 and 4 and is initiated as part of ISCM Step 3, *Implement*, when the collection of security-related information begins in accordance with the organization-defined frequencies. Ongoing assessment continues as the security-related information generated as part of ISCM Step 3 is correlated, analyzed, and reported to senior leaders as part of ISCM Step 4. As noted in Special Publication 800-137, security-related information is generated, correlated, analyzed, and reported using automated tools to the extent that it is possible and practical to do so. When it is not possible and practical to use automated tools, security-related information is generated, correlated, analyzed, and reported using manual or procedural methods. In this way, senior leaders are provided with the security-related information necessary to make credible, risk-based decisions regarding information security risk to the mission/business.[54]

Automating assessments is a fundamental element in helping organizations manage information security risks. Evolving threats create a challenge for organizations that design, implement, and operate complex information systems that contain many hardware, firmware, and software components. The ability to assess all implemented security controls as frequently as needed using manual or procedural methods has become impractical for most organizations due to the size, complexity, and scope of their information technology infrastructures.

One strategy to increase the number of security controls for which assessment/monitoring can be automated depends on defining a *desired state specification* and expressing the desired state in a form that can be compared automatically with the actual state. The desired state is a defined value or *specification* to which the actual state value can be compared. Mismatches of the two values indicate a defect is present in the effectiveness of one or more security controls. For example, an organizational policy may state that user accounts will be locked after three unsuccessful logon attempts. The desired state specification would be that applicable devices are configured to lock accounts after three unsuccessful logon attempts. If, during automated assessment, the security-related information collected indicates a specific device is configured such that accounts are locked only after *five* unsuccessful logon attempts, a mismatch between the desired state (three attempts allowed before lockout) and the actual state (five attempts allowed before lockout) is identified. This mismatch may reflect a problem with the effectiveness of Special Publication 800-53 security controls AC-7, Unsuccessful Logon Attempts, AC-2, Account Management, and CM-2, Baseline Configuration. When such a strategy is employed, security-related information generated from ISCM activities is equivalent to security control assessment results.

---

[52] The concepts and techniques employed by organizations for the ongoing assessment of security controls can also be effectively employed for the ongoing assessment of privacy controls.

[53] Special Publication 800-137 provides guidance on *Information Security Continuous Monitoring*.

[54] Continuous monitoring can be applied effectively to privacy controls consistent with the concepts, techniques, and principles described in Special Publication 800-137. Senior Agency Officials for Privacy (SAOPs)/Chief Privacy Officers (CPOs) provide guidance on the ongoing monitoring of privacy controls.

Special Publication 800-53A
Revision 4

Assessing Security and Privacy Controls in Federal Information Systems
and Organizations — *Building Effective Assessment Plans*

In order to effectively automate security control assessments using the desired state specification strategy, it is important to meet the following prerequisites:

- Automated actual state/behavior specifications are defined;

- Data-based desired state specifications (comparable to the actual state) are defined; and

- A method to compute/identify defects (differences between desired and actual state/behavior) is defined.

When the prerequisites are met, the assessment system can automatically compute where differences between desired state and actual state (defects) occur and use that information to create security assessment reports and deliver those reports to designated personnel via a security management console (dashboard).

When automated tools are used to conduct assessments, the *test* assessment method is used.[55] The organization determines and documents: (i) the specific capabilities[56] or security controls that are being assessed by the automated tool; (ii) the frequency with which the tool will assess the capabilities or controls; and (iii) the analysis and reporting requirements for the capabilities or controls.

To help automate ongoing assessment, NIST and the Department of Homeland Security (DHS) have collaborated on the development of a process that leverages the *test* assessment method and ensuring the process is consistent with the Risk Management Framework as described in Special Publication 800-37 and the ISCM guidance in Special Publication 800-137. The automation of the test method for security assessments is facilitated in the form of a new service from DHS known as the Continuous Diagnostics and Mitigation (CDM) program.

The transition from manual to automated assessments requires time to implement the data collection system to support automated assessments and a security management console to present assessment results. It also requires time and effort to modify and update the assessment process. More information on automation support for ongoing assessments and how the DHS CDM program facilitates ongoing assessment is provided in Draft NIST Interagency Report 8011, *Automation Support for Ongoing Assessment* (projected for publication in FY2015).

---

[55] If greater depth and coverage are needed to provide additional assurance, the automated test method may be supplemented by use of manual/procedural assessment methods (i.e., interview, examine, or manual test).

[56] If a security capability is defined, a mapping of all individual controls that support the capability is documented. If organizations define multiple capabilities, a many-to-many relationship between security controls and capabilities is to be expected. See Section 3.5 for additional information regarding security capability assessments.

Special Publication 800-53A
Revision 4

Assessing Security and Privacy Controls in Federal Information Systems
and Organizations — *Building Effective Assessment Plans*

APPENDIX J

PRIVACY ASSESSMENT PROCEDURES

OBJECTIVES, METHODS, AND OBJECTS FOR ASSESSING PRIVACY CONTROLS

FUTURE HOME OF PRIVACY CONTROL ASSESSMENT PROCEDURES

NIST, in cooperation and collaboration with the Best Practices Subcommittee of the Chief Information Officer (CIO) Council Privacy Committee, has initiated an interagency effort to develop assessment procedures for the privacy controls contained in Special Publication 800-53, Appendix J. The format for the privacy assessment procedures will be similar to the security assessment procedure format in Appendix F. The assessment procedures and supplemental material to be included in this appendix will undergo an extensive public review in the same manner that the privacy controls in Special Publication 800-53 were vetted prior to be included in the final publication. Organizations should consult their senior agency officials for privacy/chief privacy officers for guidance on assessing the privacy controls in Special Publication 800-53, Appendix J, until such time when the assessment procedures for Appendix J are completed.

CyberSecurity Standards Library™

Click on a title to obtain a printed copy of these standards at Amazon.com

CyberSecurity Standards Library™

NIST SP 800-65	Integrating IT Security into the Capital Planning and Investment Control Process
NIST SP 800-66	Implementing the Health Insurance Portability and Accountability Act (HIPAA) Security Rule
NIST SP 800-67 R2	Recommendation for Triple Data Encryption Algorithm (TDEA) Block Cipher - Draft
NIST SP 800-68 R1	Guide to Securing Microsoft Windows XP Systems for IT Professionals: A NIST Security Configuration Checklist
NIST SP 800-69	Guidance for Securing Microsoft Windows XP Home Edition: A NIST Security Configuration Checklist
NIST SP 800-70 R4	National Checklist Program for IT Products
NIST SP 800-72	Guidelines on PDA Forensics
NIST SP 800-73-4	Interfaces for Personal Identity Verification
NIST SP 800-76-2	Biometric Specifications for Personal Identity Verification
NIST SP 800-77	Guide to IPsec VPNs
NIST SP 800-78-4	Cryptographic Algorithms and Key Sizes for Personal Identity Verification
NIST SP 800-79-2	Authorization of Personal Identity Verification Card Issuers (PCI) and Derived PIV Credential Issuers (DPCI)
NIST SP 800-81-2	Secure Domain Name System (DNS) Deployment Guide
NIST SP 800-82 R2	Guide to Industrial Control Systems (ICS) Security
NIST SP 800-83	Guide to Malware Incident Prevention and Handling for Desktops and Laptops
NIST SP 800-84	Guide to Test, Training, and Exercise Programs for IT Plans and Capabilities
NIST SP 800-85A-4	PIV Card Application and Middleware Interface Test Guidelines
NIST SP 800-85B-4	PIV Data Model Test Guidelines - Draft
NIST SP 800-86	Guide to Integrating Forensic Techniques into Incident Response
NIST SP 800-87 R1	Codes for Identification of Federal and Federally-Assisted Organizations
NIST SP 800-88 R1	Guidelines for Media Sanitization
NIST SP 800-89	Recommendation for Obtaining Assurances for Digital Signature Applications
NIST SP 800-90A R1	Random Number Generation Using Deterministic Random Bit Generators
NIST SP 800-90B	Recommendation for the Entropy Sources Used for Random Bit Generation
NIST SP 800-90C	Recommendation for Random Bit Generator (RBG) Constructions - 2nd Draft
NIST SP 800-92	Guide to Computer Security Log Management
NIST SP 800-94	Guide to Intrusion Detection and Prevention Systems (IDPS)
NIST SP 800-95	Guide to Secure Web Services
NIST SP 800-97	Establishing Wireless Robust Security Networks: A Guide to IEEE 802.11i
NIST SP 800-98	Guidelines for Securing Radio Frequency Identification (RFID) Systems
NIST SP 800-100	Information Security Handbook: A Guide for Managers
NIST SP 800-101 R1	Guidelines on Mobile Device Forensics
NIST SP 800-102	Recommendation for Digital Signature Timeliness
NIST SP 800-106	Randomized Hashing for Digital Signatures
NIST SP 800-107 R1	Recommendation for Applications Using Approved Hash Algorithms
NIST SP 800-108	Recommendation for Key Derivation Using Pseudorandom Functions
NIST SP 800-111	Guide to Storage Encryption Technologies for End User Devices
NIST SP 800-113	Guide to SSL VPNs
NIST SP 800-114 R1	User's Guide to Telework and Bring Your Own Device (BYOD) Security
NIST SP 800-115	Technical Guide to Information Security Testing and Assessment
NIST SP 800-116	A Recommendation for the Use of PIV Credentials in PACS - Draft
NIST SP 800-117 V1.2	Guide to Adopting and Using the Security Content Automation Protocol (SCAP) - Draft
NIST SP 800-119	Guidelines for the Secure Deployment of IPv6
NIST SP 800-120	Recommendation for EAP Methods Used in Wireless Network Access Authentication
NIST SP 800-121 R2	Guide to Bluetooth Security
NIST SP 800-122	Guide to Protecting the Confidentiality of Personally Identifiable Information
NIST SP 800-123	Guide to General Server Security
NIST SP 800-124 R1	Managing the Security of Mobile Devices in the Enterprise
NIST SP 800-125 (A & B)	Secure Virtual Network Configuration for Virtual Machine (VM) Protection
NIST SP 800-126 R3	Technical Specification for the Security Content Automation Protocol (SCAP)
NIST SP 800-126A	SCAP 1.3 Component Specification 3 Version Updates
NIST SP 800-127	Guide to Securing WiMAX Wireless Communications
NIST SP 800-128	Guide for Security-Focused Configuration Management of Information Systems
NIST SP 800-130	A Framework for Designing Cryptographic Key Management Systems
NIST SP 800-131A R1	Transitions: Recommendation for Transitioning the Use of Cryptographic Algorithms and Key Lengths
NIST SP 800-132	Recommendation for Password-Based Key Derivation - Part 1: Storage Applications
NIST SP 800-133	Recommendation for Cryptographic Key Generation
NIST SP 800-135 R1	Recommendation for Existing Application-Specific Key Derivation Functions
NIST SP 800-137	Information Security Continuous Monitoring (ISCM)
NIST SP 800-142	Practical Combinatorial Testing
NIST SP 800-144	Guidelines on Security and Privacy in Public Cloud Computing
NIST SP 800-145	The NIST Definition of Cloud Computing
NIST SP 800-146	Cloud Computing Synopsis and Recommendations
NIST SP 800-147	BIOS Protection Guidelines & BIOS Integrity Measurement Guidelines
NIST SP 800-147B	BIOS Protection Guidelines for Servers
NIST SP 800-150	Guide to Cyber Threat Information Sharing
NIST SP 800-152	A Profile for U.S. Federal Cryptographic Key Management Systems
NIST SP 800-153	Guidelines for Securing Wireless Local Area Networks (WLANs)
NIST SP 800-154	Guide to Data-Centric System Threat Modeling

Click on a title to obtain a printed copy of these standards at Amazon.com

CyberSecurity Standards Library™

NIST SP 800-155	BIOS Integrity Measurement Guidelines
NIST SP 800-156	Representation of PIV Chain-of-Trust for Import and Export
NIST SP 800-157	Guidelines for Derived Personal Identity Verification (PIV) Credentials
NIST SP 800-160	Systems Security Engineering
NIST SP 800-161	Supply Chain Risk Management Practices for Federal Information Systems and Organizations
NIST SP 800-162	Guide to Attribute Based Access Control (ABAC) Definition and Considerations
NIST SP 800-163	Vetting the Security of Mobile Applications
NIST SP 800-164	Guidelines on Hardware- Rooted Security in Mobile Devices Draft
NIST SP 800-166	Derived PIV Application and Data Model Test Guidelines
NIST SP 800-167	Guide to Application Whitelisting
NIST SP 800-168	Approximate Matching: Definition and Terminology
NIST SP 800-171 R1	Protecting Controlled Unclassified Information in Nonfederal Systems
NIST SP 800-175 (A & B)	Guideline for Using Cryptographic Standards in the Federal Government
NIST SP 800-177 R1	Trustworthy Email
NIST SP 800-178	Comparison of Attribute Based Access Control (ABAC) Standards for Data Service Applications
NIST SP 800-179	Guide to Securing Apple OS X 10.10 Systems for IT Professional
NIST SP 800-180	NIST Definition of Microservices, Application Containers and System Virtual Machines
NIST SP 800-181	National Initiative for Cybersecurity Education (NICE) Cybersecurity Workforce Framework
NIST SP 800-183	Networks of 'Things'
NIST SP 800-184	Guide for Cybersecurity Event Recovery
NIST SP 800-185	SHA-3 Derived Functions: cSHAKE, KMAC, TupleHash and ParallelHash
NIST SP 800-187	Guide to LTE Security - Draft
NIST SP 800-188	De-Identifying Government Datasets - (2nd Draft)
NIST SP 800-190	Application Container Security Guide
NIST SP 800-191	The NIST Definition of Fog Computing
NIST SP 800-192	Verification and Test Methods for Access Control Policies/Models
NIST SP 800-193	Platform Firmware Resiliency Guidelines
NIST SP 1800-1	Securing Electronic Health Records on Mobile Devices
NIST SP 1800-2	Identity and Access Management for Electric Utilities 1800-2a & 1800-2b
NIST SP 1800-2	Identity and Access Management for Electric Utilities 1800-2c
NIST SP 1800-3	Attribute Based Access Control NIST 1800-3a & 3b
NIST SP 1800-3	Attribute Based Access Control NIST 1800-3c Chapters 1 - 6
NIST SP 1800-3	Attribute Based Access Control NIST1800-3c Chapters 7 - 10
NIST SP 1800-4a & 4b	Mobile Device Security: Cloud and Hybrid Builds
NIST SP 1800-4c	Mobile Device Security: Cloud and Hybrid Builds
NIST SP 1800-5	IT Asset Management: Financial Services
NIST SP 1800-6	Domain Name Systems-Based Electronic Mail Security
NIST SP 1800-7	Situational Awareness for Electric Utilities
NIST SP 1800-8	Securing Wireless Infusion Pumps
NIST SP 1800-9a & 9b	Access Rights Management for the Financial Services Sector
NIST SP 1800-9c	Access Rights Management for the Financial Services Sector - How To Guide
NIST SP 1800-11a & 11b	Data Integrity Recovering from Ransomware and Other Destructive Events
NIST SP 1800-11c	Data Integrity Recovering from Ransomware and Other Destructive Events - How To Guide
NIST SP 1800-12	Derived Personal Identity Verification (PIV) Credentials
NISTIR 7100	PDA Forensic Tools: An Overview and Analysis
NISTIR 7188	Specification for the Extensible Configuration Checklist Description Format (XCCDF)
NISTIR 7200	Proximity Beacons and Mobile Device Authentication: An Overview and Implementation
NISTIR 7206	Smart Cards and Mobile Device Authentication: An Overview and Implementation
NISTIR 7250	Cell Phone Forensic Tools: An Overview and Analysis
NISTIR 7275 V1.1	Specification for the Extensible Configuration Checklist Description Format (XCCDF)
NISTIR 7275 R4 V1.2	Specification for the Extensible Configuration Checklist Description Format (XCCDF)
NISTIR 7284	Personal Identity Verification Card Management Report
NISTIR 7290	Fingerprint Identification and Mobile Handheld Devices: An Overview and Implementation
NISTIR 7298 R2	Glossary of Key Information Security Terms
NISTIR 7316	Assessment of Access Control Systems
NISTIR 7337	Personal Identity Verification Demonstration Summary
NISTIR 7358	Program Review for Information Security Management Assistance (PRISMA)
NISTIR 7359	Information Security Guide for Government Executives
NISTIR 7387	Cell Phone Forensic Tools: An Overview and Analysis Update
NISTIR 7435	The Common Vulnerability Scoring System (CVSS) and Its Applicability to Federal Agency Systems
NISTIR 7452	Secure Biometric Match-on-Card Feasibility Report
NISTIR 7497	Security Architecture Design Process for Health Information Exchanges (HIEs)
NISTIR 7502	The Common Configuration Scoring System (CCSS): Metrics for Software Security Configuration Vulnerabilities
NISTIR 7511 R4 V1.2	Security Content Automation Protocol (SCAP) Version 1.2 Validation Program Test Requirements
NISTIR 7516	Forensic Filtering of Cell Phone Protocols
NISTIR 7539	Symmetric Key Injection onto Smart Cards
NISTIR 7551	A Threat Analysis on UOCAVA Voting Systems
NISTIR 7559	Forensics Web Services (FWS)
NISTIR 7564	Directions in Security Metrics Research
NISTIR 7581	System and Network Security Acronyms and Abbreviations

Click on a title to obtain a printed copy of these standards at Amazon.com

CyberSecurity Standards Library™

NISTIR 7601	Framework for Emergency Response Officials (ERO)
NISTIR 7611	Use of ISO/IEC 24727
NISTIR 7617	Mobile Forensic Reference Materials: A Methodology and Reification
NISTIR 7621 R1	Small Business Information Security: The Fundamentals
NISTIR 7622	Notional Supply Chain Risk Management Practices for Federal Information Systems
NISTIR 7628 R1 Vol 1	Guidelines for Smart Grid Cybersecurity - Architecture, and High-Level Requirements
NISTIR 7628 R1 Vol 2	Guidelines for Smart Grid Cybersecurity - Privacy and the Smart Grid
NISTIR 7628 R1 Vol 3	Guidelines for Smart Grid Cybersecurity - Supportive Analyses and References
NISTIR 7658	Guide to SIMfill Use and Development
NISTIR 7676	Maintaining and Using Key History on Personal Identity Verification (PIV) Cards
NISTIR 7682	Information System Security Best Practices for UOCAVA-Supporting Systems
NISTIR 7692 V2	Specification for the Open Checklist Interactive Language (OCIL)
NISTIR 7693	Specification for Asset Identification 1.1
NISTIR 7694	Specification for the Asset Reporting Format 1.1
NISTIR 7696 V2.3	Common Platform Enumeration: Name Matching Specification
NISTIR 7697 V2.3	Common Platform Enumeration: Dictionary Specification
NISTIR 7698 V2.3	Common Platform Enumeration: Applicability Language Specification
NISTIR 7711	Security Best Practices for the Electronic Transmission of Election Materials for UOCAVA Voters
NISTIR 7756	CAESARS Framework Extension: An Enterprise Continuous Monitoring Technical Refer
NISTIR 7764	Status Report on the Second Round of the SHA-3 Cryptographic Hash Algorithm Competition
NISTIR 7770	Security Considerations for Remote Electronic UOCAVA Voting
NISTIR 7771 V2	Conformance Test Architecture for Biometric Data Interchange Formats - Beta
NISTIR 7773	An Application of Combinatorial Methods to Conformance Testing for Document Object Model Events
NISTIR 7788	Security Risk Analysis of Enterprise Networks Using Probabilistic Attack Graphs
NISTIR 7791	Conformance Test Architecture and Test Suite for ANSI/NIST-ITL 1-2007
NISTIR 7799	Continuous Monitoring Reference Model, Workflow, and Specifications - Draft
NISTIR 7800	Applying the Continuous Monitoring Technical Reference Model to the Asset, Configuration, and Vulnerability Management Domains - Draft
NISTIR 7823	Advanced Metering Infrastructure Smart Meter Upgradeability Test Framework
NISTIR 7874	Guidelines for Access Control System Evaluation Metrics
NISTIR 7904	Trusted Geolocation in the Cloud: Proof of Concept Implementation
NISTIR 7924	Reference Certificate Policy
NISTIR 7987	Policy Machine: Features, Architecture, and Specification
NISTIR 8006	NIST Cloud Computing Forensic Science Challenges
NISTIR 8011 Vol 1	Automation Support for Security Control Assessments
NISTIR 8011 Vol 2	Automation Support for Security Control Assessments
NISTIR 8040	Measuring the Usability and Security of Permuted Passwords on Mobile Platforms
NISTIR 8053	De-Identification of Personal Information
NISTIR 8054	NSTIC Pilots: Catalyzing the Identity Ecosystem
NISTIR 8055	Derived Personal Identity Verification (PIV) Credentials (DPC) Proof of Concept Research
NISTIR 8060	Guidelines for the Creation of Interoperable Software Identification (SWID) Tags
NISTIR 8062	Introduction to Privacy Engineering and Risk Management in Federal Systems
NISTIR 8074 Vol 1 & Vol 2	Strategic U.S. Government Engagement in International Standardization to Achieve U.S. Objectives for Cybersecurity
NISTIR 8080	Usability and Security Considerations for Public Safety Mobile Authentication
NISTIR 8089	An Industrial Control System Cybersecurity Performance Testbed
NISTIR 8112	Attribute Metadata - Draft
NISTIR 8135	Identifying and Categorizing Data Types for Public Safety Mobile Applications
NISTIR 8138	Vulnerability Description Ontology (VDO)
NISTIR 8144	Assessing Threats to Mobile Devices & Infrastructure
NISTIR 8151	Dramatically Reducing Software Vulnerabilities
NISTIR 8170	The Cybersecurity Framework
NISTIR 8176	Security Assurance Requirements for Linux Application Container Deployments
NISTIR 8179	Criticality Analysis Process Model
NISTIR 8183	Cybersecurity Framework Manufacturing Profile
NISTIR 8192	Enhancing Resilience of the Internet and Communications Ecosystem
Whitepaper	Cybersecurity Framework Manufacturing Profile
Whitepaper	NIST Framework for Improving Critical Infrastructure Cybersecurity
Whitepaper	Challenging Security Requirements for US Government Cloud Computing Adoption
FIPS PUBS 140-2	Security Requirements for Cryptographic Modules
FIPS PUBS 140-2 Annex A	Approved Security Functions
FIPS PUBS 140-2 Annex B	Approved Protection Profiles
FIPS PUBS 140-2 Annex C	Approved Random Number Generators
FIPS PUBS 140-2 Annex D	Approved Key Establishment Techniques
FIPS PUBS 180-4	Secure Hash Standard (SHS)
FIPS PUBS 186-4	Digital Signature Standard (DSS)
FIPS PUBS 197	Advanced Encryption Standard (AES)
FIPS PUBS 198-1	The Keyed-Hash Message Authentication Code (HMAC)
FIPS PUBS 199	Standards for Security Categorization of Federal Information and Information Systems
FIPS PUBS 200	Minimum Security Requirements for Federal Information and Information Systems

Click on a title to obtain a printed copy of these standards at Amazon.com

CyberSecurity Standards Library™

FIPS PUBS 201-2   Personal Identity Verification (PIV) of Federal Employees and Contractors
FIPS PUBS 202   SHA-3 Standard: Permutation-Based Hash and Extendable-Output Functions

DHS Study   DHS Study on Mobile Device Security

OMB A-130 / FISMA OMB A-130/Federal Information Security Modernization Act

DoD
UFC 3-430-11   Boiler Control Systems
UFC 4-010-06   Cybersecurity of Facility-Related Control Systems
FC 4-141-05N   Navy and Marine Corps Industrial Control Systems Monitoring Stations
MIL-HDBK-232A   RED/BLACK Engineering-Installation Guidelines
MIL-HDBK 1195   Radio Frequency Shielded Enclosures
TM 5-601   Supervisory Control and Data Acquisition (SCADA) Systems for C4ISR Facilities
ESTCP   Facility-Related Control Systems Cybersecurity Guideline
ESTCP   Facility-Related Control Systems Ver 4.0
DoD   Self-Assessing Security Vulnerabilities & Risks of Industrial Controls
DoD   Program Manager's Guidebook for Integrating the Cybersecurity Risk Management Framework (RMF) into the System Acquisition Lifecycle
DoD   Advanced Cyber Industrial Control System Tactics, Techniques, and Procedures (ACI TTP)

NERC
NERC CIP 002-5.1 Cyber Security — BES Cyber System Categorization
NERC CIP 003-6   Cyber Security — Security Management Controls
NERC CIP 003-7(i) Cyber Security — Security Management Controls
NERC CIP 004-6   Cyber Security — Personnel & Training
NERC CIP 005-5   Cyber Security — Electronic Security Perimeter(s)
NERC CIP 006-6   Cyber Security — Physical Security of BES Cyber Systems
NERC CIP 007-6   Cyber Security — Systems Security Management
NERC CIP 008-5   Cyber Security — Incident Reporting and Response Planning
NERC CIP 009-6   Cyber Security — Recovery Plans for BES Cyber Systems
NERC CIP 010-2   Cyber Security — Configuration Change Management and Vulnerability
NERC CIP 011-2   Cyber Security — Information Protection
NERC CIP 014-2   Physical Security

www.ingramcontent.com/pod-product-compliance
Lightning Source LLC
Chambersburg PA
CBHW081454050326
40690CB00015B/2798